Series 65

Uniform Investment Adviser Law Exam

License Exam Manual

3rd Edition

SERIES 65 UNIFORM INVESTMENT ADVISER LAW EXAM,
3RD EDITION
©2007 DF Institute, Inc. All rights reserved.

Published by DF Institute, Inc.

Printed in the United States of America.

ISBN: 1-4277-6093-4

PPN: 3665-0215

07	08	10	9	8	7	6	5	4	3	2	1
J	F	M	A	M	J	J	A	<u>S</u>	O	N	D

Contents

Series 65 Introduction   xi

U N I T   1   **Federal Securities Regulations 1**

The Securities Act of 1933   3
Definitions

Exempted Securities Under The Securities Act of 1933   5
Exemptions under the Securities Act of 1933 Versus Uniform Securities Act

Exempted Transactions Under The Securities Act of 1933   8

Registration of Securities   8
Prospectus ■ Red Herring Prospectus ■ Period Between Filing Date and Effective Date of Registration Statement ■ Liabilities Under the Securities Act of 1933 ■ Stop Orders

SEC Regulation D (Private Placement Exemption)   12
SEC Rule 144 (Sale of Restricted and Control Securities)

The Securities Exchange Act of 1934   14
The Securities and Exchange Commission (SEC) ■ Definitions ■ Registration Under the Securities Exchange Act of 1934 ■ Insider Transactions Under the Securities Exchange Act of 1934 ■ Schedule D Filings ■ Section 13(f) Filings ■ Schedule G Filings ■ Section 16 Filings ■ Credit Requirements (Margin) ■ Market Manipulation

Insider Trading and Securities Fraud Enforcement Act of 1988 (ITSFEA)   24

Financial Responsibility Rules Under the Securities Exchange Act of 1934   25

Securities Acts Amendments of 1975   26

Investment Company Act of 1940   27
Types of Investment Companies ■ Subclassification of Investment Companies ■ Registration of Investment Companies ■ Ineligibility of Certain Affiliated Persons and Underwriters ■ Rule 12b-1 ■ Prohibited Activities of Investment Companies ■ Changes in Investment Policy ■ Sale of Redeemable Securities ■ Periodic and Other Reports ■ Destruction and Falsification of Reports and Records

Money Laundering   35
Currency Transaction Reports (CTRs)

Unit Test   37

Answers and Rationales   41

Quick Quiz Answers   43

UNIT 2   State Regulation Under the Uniform Securities Act (USA) 45

Scope of the Act 47
State Securities Laws (Blue-Sky Laws) ■
The USA Is Model State Securities
Legislation

**Definition of Person in Securities
Law 48**
Exclusion from Definitions and Exemption
From Registration

**Persons Subject to State
Registration 50**
Broker/Dealer ■ Agent ■ Investment
Adviser

General Registration Procedures 61
Submit Application ■ Provide Consent
to Service of Process ■ Pay Initial and
Renewal Filing Fees ■ Effectiveness of
Registration

**What is a Security Under the
Uniform Securities Act? 63**
List of Securities Under the Uniform
Securities Act ■ Nonexempt Security ■
Issuer ■ Initial or Primary Offering

**Registration of Securities under the
Uniform Securities Act 67**
National Securities Markets Improvement
Act of 1996 (NSMIA) ■ Categories of
Federal Covered Securities

**Methods of State Registration of
Securities 69**
Notification (Filing) ■ Registration
by Coordination ■ Registration by
Qualification

Exemptions from Registration 74
Exempt Securities ■ Exempt Transactions

**State Securities Registration
Procedures 79**
Filing the Registration Statement

Antifraud Provisions of the USA 81
Fraudulent and Prohibited Practices in
the Sale of Securities ■ Other Prohibited
Practices when Engaged in the Sale of
Securities

**Jurisdiction and Powers of the State
Administrator 92**
Sale or Sell and Offer or Offer to Sell

Jurisdiction of the Administrator 93
Publishing and Broadcast Exceptions to
Jurisdiction

**Powers of the Administrator within
Its Jurisdiction 96**
Make, Amend, or Rescind Rules and
Orders ■ Conduct Investigations and
Issue Subpoenas ■ Issue Cease and
Desist Orders ■ Deny, Suspend, Cancel,
or Revoke Registrations ■ Nonpunitive
Terminations of Registration

**Penalties for Violations of the
Uniform Securities Act 101**
Civil Liabilities ■ Criminal Penalties ■
Judicial Review of Orders (Appeal)

Unit Test 105

Answers and Rationales 113

Quick Quiz Answers 119

UNIT 3   Federal and State Regulation of Investment Advisers and Their Representatives   123

Investment Advisers Act of 1940   125
Definitions

Who Are Investment Advisers?   126
SEC Release IA-1092 ■ Exclusions from Definition of Investment Adviser Under Federal Law ■ Exclusions from the Definition of Investment Adviser Under State Law

Registration Requirements Under the Investment Advisers Act of 1940   131
Exemption from the Registration Requirements Under Federal Law

Federal Covered Advisers   132
Exemptions from the Registration Requirements under The Uniform Securities Act ■ Registration Requirements under Federal Law ■ Cancellation of Registration ■ Investment Counsel

Registration as an Investment Adviser Under the USA   139
Investment Adviser Representative

Books and Records Required by Federal and State Law   143

Books and Records Required by Advisers Act of 1940   143
Time Period for Maintenance of Records ■ Brochure Rule ■ Exemptions from the Brochure Rule ■ Wrap Fee Programs

Rules on Custody of Funds and Securities   149

Fiduciary Responsibilities of Investment Advisers   155
Disclosure And Consent ■ Hedge Clauses ■ Advertising ■ Investment Advisory Contracts

Agency Cross Transactions   164

Cash Referral Fees   165

Fraudulent and Prohibited Practices When Providing Investment Advice   166

Compliance Programs   171

Enforcement   173

Unit Test   174

Answers and Rationales   180

Quick Quiz Answers   184

UNIT 4   Equity and Debt Securities   189

Equity Securities   191
Common Stock ■ Benefits of Owning
Stock ■ Risks of Owning Stock ■
Preferred Stock ■ Foreign Investments:
American Depositary Receipts (ADRs) ■
Risks of Investing in Foreign Markets

**Real Estate Investment Trusts
(REITs)   202**

Rights and Warrants   203
Rights ■ Warrants

**Fixed-Income or Debt
Securities   204**

Debt Securities ■ Safety of Principal—
Government Securities ■ Repayment of
Principal

Money Market   220
Mortgage-Backed Securities

Unit Test   223

Answers and Rationales   225

Quick Quiz Answers   226

UNIT 5   Other Securities Products   227

**Investment Company
Securities   229**
Types of Investment Companies ■
Characteristics of Mutual Funds ■
Investment Objectives ■ Comparing
Mutual Funds ■ Suitability

Annuities   246
Types of Annuity Contracts ■ Purchasing
Annuities ■ Receiving Distributions from
Annuities ■ Taxation of Annuities

**Direct Participation Programs
(DPPs)   255**
Analysis and Evaluation of Direct
Participation Programs

Derivative Securities—Options   260
Calls and Puts ■ Option Transactions ■
Options Strategies ■ Hedging with
Options

Unit Test   270

Answers and Rationales   273

Quick Quiz Answers   275

UNIT 6   Trading Securities   277

**Markets and Market
Participants   279**
Securities Markets ■ The Role of Broker/
Dealers ■ Bids, Offers, and Quotes ■
Types of Orders

Unit Test   286

Answers and Rationales   287

Quick Quiz Answers   288

U N I T 7 **Retirement Plans 289**

Individual Retirement Arrangements (IRAs) 291
Traditional IRAs ▪ Roth IRAs ▪ Catch-Up Contributions for Older IRA Owners ▪ Coverdell Education Savings Accounts ▪ Characteristics of IRAs ▪ Section 529 Plans

Keogh (HR-10) Plans 302

403(b) Plans (Tax-Exempt Organizations) 304

Corporate-Sponsored Retirement Plans 307
Employee Retirement Income Security Act of 1974 (ERISA)

Summary of Distribution Rules from Both Qualified Plans and IRAs 315
Lifetime Distributions

Nonqualified Corporate Retirement Plans 316
Taxation ▪ Types of Plans

Unit Test 319

Answers and Rationales 321

Quick Quiz Answers 323

U N I T 8 **Customer Accounts 325**

Opening Customer Accounts 327
New Accounts ▪ Opening Cash and Margin Accounts

Types of Accounts 331
Individual Accounts ▪ Joint Accounts ▪ Partnership Accounts ▪ Corporate Accounts ▪ Wrap Accounts ▪ Fiduciary and Custodial Accounts ▪ Discretionary Accounts

Unit Test 344

Answers and Rationales 346

Quick Quiz Answers 347

U N I T 9 **Clients, Risks, Strategies, Portfolios, and Taxation 349**

Types of Clients 351
Business Accounts ▪ Client Personal Profile ▪ Financial Goals/Objectives

Portfolio Management Styles and Strategies 364
Asset Allocation ▪ Active and Passive Management ▪ Funding Techniques

Taxation 370
Corporate Taxes ▪ Individual Income Taxes ▪ Capital Gains and Losses ▪ Estate and Gift Taxes

Unit Test 378

Answers and Rationales 380

Quick Quiz Answers 382

U N I T   1 0   Economics and Analysis   383

Basic Economics   385
Major Schools of Economics ■ Important Terms and Concepts in Economics

Interest Rates and Yield Curves   388
Interest Rates

Economic Indicators   390

Investment Analysis   394
Fundamental Investment Analysis ■ The Tools of Fundamental Analysis: Financial Statements ■ Capital Structure ■ Income Statement ■ Valuation Ratios

Technical Investment Analysis   409
Overbought ■ Oversold ■ Consolidation ■ Trendlines ■ Head and Shoulders ■ Support and Resistance ■ Breakout ■ Moving Averages ■ Indexes and Averages ■ Standard & Poor's 500 ■ New York Stock Exchange (NYSE) Index ■ Dow Jones Industrial Average ■ NASDAQ Composite Index ■ Technical Market Theories ■ Other Market Theories

Quantitative Evaluation Measurements   416

Time Value of Money   416
Present Value ■ Future Value ■ Rule of 72 ■ Investment Return Measurements ■ Bond Yields ■ Total Return ■ Holding Period Return ■ Annualized Return ■ After-Tax Return/Yield ■ Inflation-Adjusted Return (Real Return) ■ Expected Return ■ Net Present Value (NPV) ■ Internal Rate of Return (IRR)

Risk Measurements   424
Correlation and Correlation Coefficient ■ Standard Deviation ■ Beta versus Standard Deviation ■ Sharpe Ratio ■ Duration ■ Monte Carlo Simulations

Sources of Investment Risks   429
Market Risk ■ Business Risk (Unsystematic Risk) ■ Interest Rate Risk ■ Inflation Risk ■ Regulatory Risk (Legislative Risk) ■ Liquidity Risk ■ Opportunity Cost ■ Portfolios ■ Optimal Portfolio

Unit Test   434

Answers and Rationales   437

Quick Quiz Answers   439

Glossary   441

Appendix A   469

Appendix B   471

Appendix C   477

Appendix D   481

Index   513

HotSheets   519

Federal Securities Regulations HotSheet   519

State Regulation under the Uniform Securities Act (USA) HotSheet   523

Definition and Responsibilities of Investment Advisers HotSheet   529

Equity and Debt Securities HotSheet   533

Other Securities Products HotSheet   537

Trading Securities HotSheet   543

Retirement Plans HotSheet   545

Customer Accounts HotSheet   549

Clients, Risks, Strategies, Portfolios, and Taxation HotSheet   551

Economics and Analysis HotSheet   555

Series 65 Introduction

INTRODUCTION

Thank you for choosing this exam preparation system for your educational needs and welcome to the Series 65 License Exam Manual. This manual has applied adult learning principles to give you the tools you'll need to pass your exam on the first attempt.

Some of these special features include:

- exam-focused questions and content to maximize exam preparation;

- an interactive design that integrates content with questions to increase retention; and

- integrated Drill & Practice exam preparation tools to sharpen test-taking skills.

Why Do I Need to Pass the Series 65 Exam?

Most states require investment adviser representatives to pass a qualification exam. To be registered to give investment advice in those states that require Series 65 qualification, you must pass the Series 65 exam.

Are There Any Prerequisites?

Although there are no prerequisites for the Series 65, some states require you to pass the Series 7, which is a corequisite exam that must be completed in addition to the Series 65 before an individual can apply to register with a state. You may take either exam first but must complete both satisfactorily.

What Is the Series 65 Exam Like?

The Series 65 is a 3-hour, 130-question exam prepared by the North American Securities Administrators Association (NASAA) and administered by NASD. It is offered as a computer-based exam at Prometric testing centers around the country.

What Score Must I Achieve to Pass?

You need a score of at least 68.5% on the Series 65 exam to pass and become eligible for registration as a **Registered Investment Adviser Representative**.

What Topics Will I See on the Exam?

The questions you will see on the Series 65 exam do not appear in any particular order. The computer is programmed to select a new, random set of questions for each exam taker according to the preset topic weighting of the exam. Each Series 65 candidate will see the same number of questions on each topic but will see a different mix of questions. The Series 65 exam is divided into 4 critical function areas.

	Number of Questions	Percentage of Exam
1. Economics and Analysis	20	15
2. Investment Vehicles	26	20
3. Investment Recommendations and Strategies	39	30
4. Ethics and Legal Guidelines	45	35

When you complete your exam, you will receive a printout that identifies your performance in each area.

PREPARING FOR THE EXAM

How Is the License Exam Manual Organized?

The License Exam Manual consists of Units and Unit Tests. In addition to the regular text, each Unit has some unique features designed to help you with quick understanding of the material. When an additional point will be valuable to your comprehension, special notes are embedded in the text. Examples of these are included below.

TAKE NOTE   These highlight special or unusual information and amplify important points.

TEST TOPIC ALERT   Each Test Topic Alert! highlights content that is likely to appear on the exam.

EXAMPLE   These give practical examples and numerical instances of the material just covered and convert theory into practice.

You will also see Quick Quizzes, which will help ensure that you understand and retain the material covered in that particular section. Quick Quizzes are a quick interactive review of what you just read.

Answers and rationales for the Quick Quizzes can be found at the end of each Unit.

In addition, HotSheets for each Unit summarize the key points in bullet-point format. For your convenience and use as review notes, these HotSheets are located at the end of the book on perforated pages.

The book is made up of Units organized to explain the material that NASAA has outlined for the exam.

If your study packet includes a Drill & Practice CD-ROM, this CD contains a large bank of questions that are similar in style and content to those you will encounter on the exam. You may use it to generate tests by a specific topic or create exams that are similar in difficulty and proportionate mixture to the exam.

If you prefer to complete written tests, the Practice Final Tests will provide similar practice. The questions on the print tests are included in the CD. Devote a significant amount of your study time to the completion of practice questions and review of rationales on the CD and/or the Practice Final Tests.

Your study packet may also include Mastery Exams.

These are designed to closely simulate the true exam center experience in degree of difficulty and topic coverage and are an exceptional indicator of future actual exam score as well as areas of strength and weakness. When you have completed these exams, you will receive a detailed breakdown by topic of performance. This diagnostic breakdown will alert you to precisely where you need to concentrate further exam practice.

What Topics Are Covered in the Course?

The License Exam Manual consists of 10 Units, each devoted to a particular area of study that you will need to know to pass the Series 65. Each Unit is divided into study sections devoted to more specific areas with which you need to become familiar.

The Series 65 License Exam Manual addresses the following topics.

Unit	Topics	Approximate No. of Questions
1	Federal Securities Regulations	8
2	State Regulation Under the Uniform Securities Act (USA)	25
3	Federal Regulation of Investment Advisers and Their Representatives	12
4	Equity and Debt Securities	12
5	Other Securities Products	14
6	Trading Securities	4
7	Retirement Plans	6
8	Customer Accounts	6
9	Clients, Risks, Strategies, Portfolios, and Taxation	23
10	Economics and Analysis	20

How Much Time Should I Spend Studying?

Plan to spend approximately 45–75 hours reading the material and carefully answering the questions. Spread your study time over the 4–5 weeks before the date on which you are scheduled to take the Series 65 exam. Your actual time may vary depending on your reading rate, comprehension, professional background, and study environment.

What Is the Best Way to Structure My Study Time?

The following schedule is suggested to help you obtain maximum retention from your study efforts. Remember, this is a guideline only, because each individual may require more or less time to complete the steps included.

Step 1: Read a Unit and complete the Unit Test. Review rationales for all questions whether you got them right or wrong (2–3 hours per Unit).

Step 2: On the Drill & Practice CD-ROM, create and complete a test for each topic included under that Unit heading. For best results, select the maximum number of questions within each topic. Carefully review all rationales. Do an additional test on any topic on which you score under 60%. After completion of all topic tests, create a 50-question test comprising all Unit topics. Repeat this 50-question test until you score at least 70% (5–10 hours).

TAKE NOTE

Do not be overly concerned with your score on the first attempt at any of these tests. Instead, take the opportunity to learn from your mistakes and increase your knowledge.

Step 3: When you have finished all of the Units and their Unit Tests on the Drill & Practice CD-ROM, then complete at least 5 of the 130-question exams. Complete as many as necessary to achieve a score of at least 80–90%. Create and complete additional topic tests as necessary to correct problem areas (10–20 hours).

Step 4: Each Mastery Exam mirrors the actual test in number of questions and subject matter coverage. Questions included in Mastery Exams are unique from all other question bank products, so you will see only new questions. Like the actual exam, you will not see the answer key and rationale, but the detailed diagnostic breakdown will provide you with clear guidance on areas where further study is required (2–3 hours per Exam).

Do I Need to Take All of the Practice Final Tests?

The Practice Final Tests assess the knowledge you need to answer the questions on the exam. By completing the Practice Final Tests and checking your answers against the rationales, you should be able to pinpoint areas of difficulty. Review any questions you miss, paying particular attention to the rationales. If any subjects still seem troublesome, go back and review the section(s) covering those topics.

How Well Can I Expect to Do?

The exams prepared by NASAA are not easy. You must display considerable understanding and knowledge of the topics presented in this course to pass the exam and qualify for registration.

If you study diligently, complete all sections of the course, and consistently score at least 85% on the tests, you should be well prepared to pass the exam. However, it is important for you to realize that merely knowing the answers to our questions will not enable you to pass unless you understand the essence of the information behind the question.

SUCCESSFUL TEST-TAKING TIPS

Passing the exam depends not only on how well you learn the subject matter but also on how well you take exams. You can develop your test-taking skills—and improve your score—by learning the following test-taking techniques:

■ Read the full question

■ Avoid jumping to conclusions—watch for hedge clauses

■ Interpret the unfamiliar question

■ Look for key words and phrases

■ Identify the intent of the question

■ Memorize key points

■ Use a calculator

■ Avoid changing answers

■ Pace yourself

Each of these pointers is explained below, including examples that show how to use them to improve your performance on the exam.

Read the Full Question

You cannot expect to answer a question correctly if you do not know what it is asking. If you see a question that seems familiar and easy, you might anticipate the answer, mark it, and move on before you finish reading it. This is a serious mistake. Be sure to read the full question before answering it—questions are often written to trap people who assume too much.

Avoid Jumping to Conclusions—Watch for Hedge Clauses

The questions on NASAA exams are often embellished with deceptive distractors as choices. To avoid being misled by seemingly obvious answers, make it a practice to read each question and each answer twice before selecting your choice. Doing so will provide you with a much better chance of doing well on the exam.

Watch out for hedge clauses embedded in the question. (Examples of hedge clauses include the terms *if, not, all, none,* and *except.*) In the case of *if* statements, the question can be answered correctly only by taking into account the qualifier. If you ignore the qualifier, you will not answer correctly.

Qualifiers are sometimes combined in a question. Some that you will frequently see together are *all* with *except* and *none* with *except.* In general, when a question starts with *all* or *none* and ends with *except,* you are looking for an answer that is opposite to what the question appears to be asking.

Interpret the Unfamiliar Question

Do not be surprised if some questions on the exam seem unfamiliar at first. If you have studied your material, you will have the information to answer all of the questions correctly. The challenge may be a matter of understanding what the question is asking.

Very often, questions present information indirectly. You may have to interpret the meaning of certain elements before you can answer the question. Be aware that the exam will approach a concept from different angles.

Look for Key Words and Phrases

Look for words that are tip-offs to the situation presented. For example, if you see the word *prospectus* in the question, you know the question is about a new issue. Sometimes a question will even supply you with the answer if you can recognize the key words it contains. Few questions provide blatant clues, but many do offer key words that can guide you to selecting the correct answer if you pay attention. Be sure to read all instructional phrases carefully.

Take time to identify the key words to answer this type of question correctly.

Identify the Intent of the Question

Many questions on NASAA exams supply so much information that you lose track of what is being asked. This is often the case in story problems. Learn to separate the story from the question.

Take the time to identify what the question is asking. Of course, your ability to do so assumes you have studied sufficiently. There is no method for correctly answering questions if you don't know the material.

Memorize Key Points

Reasoning and logic will help you answer many questions, but you will have to memorize a good deal of information. The HotSheets summarize some of the most important key points for memorization.

Use a Calculator

For the most part, NASAA exams will not require the use of a calculator. Most of the questions are written so that any math required is simple. However, if you have become accustomed to using a calculator for math, you will be provided with one by the testing center staff.

Avoid Changing Answers

If you are unsure of an answer, your first hunch is the one most likely to be correct. Do not change answers on the exam without good reason. In general, change an answer only if you:

■ discover that you did not read the question correctly; or

■ find new or additional helpful information in another question.

Pace Yourself

Some people will finish the exam early and some do not have time to finish all of the questions. Watch the time carefully (your time remaining will be displayed on your computer screen) and pace yourself throughout the exam.

Do not waste time by dwelling on a question if you simply do not know the answer. Make the best guess you can, mark the question for *Record for Review*, and return to the question if time allows. Make sure that you have time to read all of the questions so that you can record the answers you do know.

THE EXAM

How Do I Enroll in the Exam?

To obtain an admission ticket to a NASAA exam, your firm must file an application form and processing fees with NASD. To take the exam, you should make an appointment with a Prometric Testing Center as far in advance as possible of the date on which you would like to take the exam.

You may schedule your appointment at Prometric, 24 hours a day, 7 days a week, on the secure Prometric Website at **www.prometric.com**. You may also use this site to reschedule or cancel your exam, locate a test center, and get a printed confirmation of your appointment. To speak with a Prometric representative by phone, please contact the Prometric Contact Center at 1-800-578-6273.

What Should I Take to the Exam?

Take one form of personal identification with your signature and photograph as issued by a government agency. You cannot take reference materials or anything else into the testing area. Calculators are available upon request. Scratch paper and pencils will be provided by the testing center, although you cannot take them with you when you leave.

Additional Trial Questions

During your exam, you may see extra trial questions. These are potential exam-bank questions being tested during the course of the exam. These questions are not included in your final score and you will be given extra time to answer them.

Exam Results and Reports

At the end of the exam, your score will be displayed, indicating whether you passed. The next business day after your exam, your results will be mailed to your firm and to the self-regulatory organization and state securities commission specified on your application.

1

Federal Securities Regulations

This Unit discusses federal laws that govern the issuance of corporate securities to the public and the regulation of exchanges on which they trade. The major federal legislation addressed are the Securities Act of 1933, the Securities Exchange Act of 1934, the Investment Company Act of 1940, and the Insider Trading and Securities Fraud Enforcement Act of 1988.

The Series 65 exam will include approximately 8 questions on the federal regulatory structure as it pertains to the issuance of securities and the registration of exchanges and broker/dealers who trade on these exchanges. ■

When you have completed this Unit, you should be able to:

■ **compare** and contrast the significant registration provisions and exemptions from the Securities Act of 1933;

■ **describe** the registration requirements of the Securities Exchange Act of 1934 regarding exchanges, broker/dealers, and agents;

■ **describe** the principal provisions of the Investment Company Act of 1940;

■ **discuss** the disclosure requirements, antifraud provisions, and prohibitions against market manipulation under the Securities Exchange Act of 1934;

■ **list** prohibitions against market manipulation; and

■ **recognize** the application of the Insider Trading and Securities Fraud Enforcement Act of 1988.

THE SECURITIES ACT OF 1933

The **Securities Act of 1933** (also called the **Paper Act**, the **Truth in Securities Act**, and the **Prospectus Act**) regulates the issuing of corporate securities sold to the public (**initial public offerings** or **IPOs**) and through subsequent offerings. The act requires securities issuers to make full disclosure of all material information in their registration materials in order for investors to make fully informed investment decisions.

Issuer information must be disclosed to the Securities Exchange Commission (SEC) in a registration statement and published in a prospectus. In addition, the act prohibits fraudulent activity in connection with the sale, underwriting, and distribution of securities. The act provides for both civil and criminal penalties for violations of its provisions.

Even though registration under the Uniform Securities Act (the law that deals with regulation by the states) will be covered in detail in the next Unit, where appropriate, mention will be of the similarities and differences between certain federal and state definitions.

DEFINITIONS

Definitions under the Securities Act of 1933 are similar to those you will see under state securities law under the Uniform Securities Act (described in Unit 2). The most important definitions under the Securities Act of 1933 are those that follow.

Security

The definition of a *security* is very broad, but here are the terms most likely to be used on your exam.

The fundamental definition of a security was determined in a case heard before the US Supreme Court. That case, known as the Howey Case, defined an **investment contract** as a security if it met four conditions:

■ the investment of money;

■ in a common enterprise (pooling);

■ with an expectation of profits; and

■ that results solely from the efforts of others.

On the basis of Howey, a **security** is any of the following:

■ Stock

■ Bond

■ Debenture

■ Right or warrant

■ Note

- Put, call, or other option
- Limited partnership interests
- Certificate of interest in a profit-sharing arrangement

Issuer

Any person who issues or proposes to issue any security is an **issuer**. Most issuers are businesses, and the term *issuer* would also apply to a government entity.

Underwriter

Any person who has purchased from an issuer with a view to selling is an **underwriter**. This term does not include a brokerage firm earning a commission on a retail sale to the public.

Person

The term *person* is very broad and includes an individual, a corporation, a partnership, an association, a joint stock company, a trust, any unincorporated organization, or a governmental or political subdivision thereof. We will explain this in further detail when covering the Uniform Securities Act in the next Unit.

Prospectus

A **prospectus** is any notice, circular, advertisement, letter, or communication, written or broadcast by radio or television, that offers any security for sale or confirms the sale of a security. A **tombstone** advertisement (one that simply identifies the security, the price, and the underwriters) is not considered a prospectus. The term *prospectus* does not include oral communications.

Sale

The term *sale* or *sell* includes a contract for sale or the disposition of a security for value. An **offer to sell** refers to any attempt or offer to dispose of a security or an interest in a security for value or a solicitation of an offer to buy a security for value.

TAKE NOTE   The sale of a security does not include:

- preliminary negotiations or agreements between the issuer and underwriter; or
- a gift of securities.

Any security given or delivered with, or as a bonus on account of, any purchase of securities is presumed to constitute a part of that purchase and to have been offered and sold for value. In other words, when a bond is offered with warrants attached, the warrants are not considered to be a sale because they are considered to be part of the bond sale. However, when the warrant is exercised, that exercise is considered to be a sale of the security being purchased.

QUICK QUIZ 1.1

1. Which of the following meets the definition of a sale as described in the Securities Act of 1933?

    I. Your client, who owns 100 shares of XYZ common stock, receives an additional 50 shares of that stock from the issuer after the declaration of a 50% stock dividend.

    II. Your client exercises his conversion privilege by converting 10 ABC bonds into 100 shares of ABC common stock.

    III. A brokerage firm runs a special promotion this month giving 100 shares of Hot Shot Growth Fund to any client who purchases at least $5,000 worth of stock.

    A. I and II
    B. I and III
    C. II and III
    D. I, II and III

Quick Quiz answers can be found at the end of the Unit.

The SEC does not approve securities registered with it, does not pass on the investment merit of any security, and never guarantees the accuracy of statements in the registration statement and prospectus.

In its review process, the SEC merely attempts to make certain that all pertinent information is fully disclosed in the registration statement and prospectus by requiring that:

■ the issuer file a registration statement with the SEC before securities are offered or sold in interstate commerce;

■ a prospectus that meets the requirements of the act be provided to prospective buyers; and

■ penalties (civil, criminal, or administrative) be imposed for violations of this act.

EXEMPTED SECURITIES UNDER THE SECURITIES ACT OF 1933

The Securities Act of 1933 makes it unlawful to sell or deliver a security through any instrument of interstate commerce unless a registration statement is in effect. However, certain securities are exempted from the registration requirements of the act. The following issues qualify as exempted securities and are also exempt under the Uniform Securities Act (see Unit 2):

■ Any security issued or guaranteed by the United States, any state, or any political subdivision of a state (all federal government issues and municipal securities are exempted securities)

- Any commercial paper that has a maturity at the time of issuance of no more than nine months, with the stipulation that the proceeds are to be used by the issuer for current transactions (there is no minimum denomination or rating requirement similar to that found in the Uniform Securities Act)

- Any security issued by a religious, educational, charitable, or not-for-profit institution

- Any security issued by a federal or state bank, savings and loan association, building and loan association, or similar institution

- Any interest in a railroad equipment trust (for purposes of the law, *interest in a railroad equipment trust* means any interest in an equipment trust, lease, or other similar arrangement entered into, guaranteed by, or for the benefit of a common carrier to finance the acquisition of rolling stock, including motive power)

The following issues qualify as exempted securities but are not exempt under the Uniform Securities Act:

- Any insurance, endowment, or fixed annuity contract (variable life insurance or variable annuity contracts are considered to be securities and require registration)

- Any security exchanged by the issuer with its existing security holders exclusively, where no commission or other remuneration is paid or given directly or indirectly for soliciting such exchange (the standard example of this would be a stock split or stock dividend)

- Issues of small business investment companies (SBICs) which are privately owned and privately operated companies that have been licensed by the Small Business Administration to provide equity capital and long-term loans to small firms

- Regulation A issue: any security offered to the public when the total amount is $5 million or less during any 12-month period

For such issues, the SEC has adopted Regulation A, which exempts the issue from the standard registration requirements if certain specified conditions are met (such as the filing of an offering circular with the SEC). Regulation A offerings are bona fide registered interstate offerings. The best way to conceptualize the Regulation A limited exemption is to compare it to the standard Form 1040 tax filing with the Form 1040-EZ. Individuals with limited income are not exempt from filing a tax return; they just have a simpler filing. The same thing is true with registration under Regulation A.

- Rule 147 issue: any security offered and sold only to persons resident within a single state or territory, where the issuer of such security is a person resident and doing business within such state or territory

The Rule 147 exemption is available only if the entire issue is offered and sold exclusively to residents of a single state. If any sales take place to non-residents, the entire issue loses its exemption. The purpose of this exemption is to allow issuers to raise money on a local basis, provided the business was operating primarily within that state. The following conditions must be met in order to have a distribution qualify as an intrastate offering exempt from federal registration.

■ The securities must be offered or sold exclusively to persons resident in one state; persons purchasing the securities must have their principal residence within the state.

■ For nine months from the date of the last sale by the issuer of any part of the issue, resales of any part of the issue by any person will be made only to persons resident within the same state or territory. This will satisfy requirements that the issue come to rest in the state in order to claim the exemption.

■ At least 80% of the issuer's gross revenue must be derived from operations within the state.

■ At least 80% of the proceeds of the offering must be used for business purposes within the state.

■ At least 80% of the issuer's assets must be located within the state.

TEST TOPIC ALERT   Do you see why this is sometimes referred to as the "80-80-80 Rule"?

EXEMPTIONS UNDER THE SECURITIES ACT OF 1933 VERSUS UNIFORM SECURITIES ACT

There are three exemptions available under the Uniform Securities Act (see Unit 2) that are not available under the Securities Act of 1933.

■ Foreign government securities are not exempt under the Securities Act of 1933 but are exempt under the Uniform Securities Act.

■ Securities listed on a national exchange are not exempt under the Securities Act of 1933 but are exempt under the Uniform Securities Act (often called the blue-chip exemption).

■ Securities issued by insurance companies are not exempt under the Securities Act of 1933 but are exempt under the Uniform Securities Act (this refers to the securities issued by insurance companies, not their policies).

TAKE NOTE   No waivers may be granted by the purchaser agreeing to the seller's failure to comply with the Securities Act of 1933. It is important to remember that any such waivers are null and void.

EXEMPTED TRANSACTIONS UNDER THE SECURITIES ACT OF 1933

In addition to exempting certain securities, the act also exempts:

■ transactions by any person other than an issuer, underwriter, or dealer; and

■ transactions by an issuer that do not involve a public offering (private placement under Regulation D).

REGISTRATION OF SECURITIES

A security may be registered with the SEC by filing a registration statement in triplicate. The registration statement must be signed by the principal executive officer, the principal financial officer, and a majority of the board of directors.

All of the signers are subject to criminal and civil penalties for willful omissions and misstatements of material facts. The information required in the registration statement may be summarized as follows:

■ Purpose of issue

■ Public offering price (anticipated range)

■ Underwriter's commissions or discounts

■ Promotion expenses

■ Net proceeds of the issue to the company

■ Balance sheet

■ Earnings statements for the last three years

■ Names and addresses of officers, directors, underwriters, and stockholders owning more than 10% of the outstanding stock (i.e., control persons)

■ Copy of underwriting agreements

■ Copies of articles of incorporation

PROSPECTUS

A registration statement is normally a very long and complex document for an investor to read. The act requires the preparation of a shorter document called a **prospectus**. The prospectus summarizes the information contained in the registration statement. It must contain all the material facts in the registration statement, but in shorter form. The prospectus must be given to every person solicited and to every person who purchases or indicates an interest in purchasing securities. The purpose of a prospectus is to provide the investor with adequate information to analyze the investment merits of the security. Even if an investor does not intend to read a prospectus, it still must be given to him. It is unlawful for a company to sell securities before the effective date of the registration statement.

There is a specific SEC rule permitting investment companies to use what is known as an **omitting prospectus**. The rule is SEC Rule 482, which describes mutual fund advertisements. To comply with this rule, an omitting prospectus must meet the following conditions.

■ Any information in the advertisement must be taken substantially from the regular prospectus.

■ The advertisement must state conspicuously from whom a prospectus may be obtained.

■ The advertisement must urge investors to read the prospectus carefully before investing.

■ Any past performance data, such as yields or return, that are quoted in the advertisement must be accompanied by appropriate disclaimers and disclosures of load, if any.

■ The advertisement cannot be used to purchase the shares; purchase may be made only via an application found in the prospectus.

RED HERRING PROSPECTUS

A **red herring prospectus** is a preliminary prospectus. It is given to prospective purchasers during the minimum 20-day waiting period between the filing date of the registration statement and the effective date.

A red herring is used to acquaint investors with essential facts concerning the new issue. It is also used to solicit indications of buyer interest. However, it cannot be used:

■ as a confirmation of sale;

■ in place of a registration statement; or

■ to declare the final public offering price.

Under no circumstances may a broker/dealer or one of its agents accept money or orders prior to the effective date.

The term *red herring* was given to the prospectus because the front page contains the following statement printed in red ink.

A Registration Statement relating to these securities has been filed with the Securities and Exchange Commission but has not yet become effective. Information contained herein is subject to completion or amendment. These securities may not be sold nor may offers to buy be accepted prior to the time the Registration Statement becomes effective. The Prospectus shall not constitute an offer to sell or the solicitation of an offer to buy, nor shall there be any sale of these securities in any State in which such offer, solicitation, or sale would be unlawful prior to registration or qualification under the securities laws of any such State.

A registered representative is not allowed to make marks on a preliminary prospectus under any circumstances. He cannot write short summaries or reviews on the preliminary prospectus. The preliminary prospectus must be given to customers without any alterations because, as stated above, information is subject to change.

PERIOD BETWEEN FILING DATE AND EFFECTIVE DATE OF REGISTRATION STATEMENT

Unless an exemption applies, it is unlawful for any person to use the mail or any other instrument of interstate commerce to offer a security for sale unless a registration statement has been filed with the SEC. It is unlawful under the act to sell a security unless the registration statement has become effective.

Therefore, during the period between the filing date and the effective date of the registration statements, the following must occur.

- No sales of the security may take place.

- Offers of the security may take place, but written offers may be made only through a preliminary prospectus or red herring prospectus (tombstone advertising is permitted during this period). The red herring may be sent to prospective purchasers who have not specifically requested it.

- Registered representatives may answer unsolicited requests for information by sending out a preliminary prospectus.

- Subscription payments may not be accepted, even if the money is held in escrow until the registration is effective.

Effective Date of Registration Statement

On the date a registration statement becomes effective, securities may be sold to the public by the investment bankers. The effective date of a registration statement is the 20th day after filing the registration statement with the SEC, provided the registration statement is in proper form. The 20-day waiting period before the registration becomes effective is called the **cooling-off period**.

The purpose of the cooling-off period is to allow the SEC sufficient time to study the information in the registration statement and prospectus. The SEC may accelerate the effective date of a registration statement if it finds that adequate information with respect to the issuer is available and it is in the public interest to do so.

A copy of the final (effective) prospectus must be delivered to each purchaser before or at the time of the sale. This is normally accomplished by including the prospectus along with a confirmation of the trade. Additional sales literature may be used by the firm as long as the sales literature is preceded or accompanied by a prospectus. Money may be accepted by the broker/dealer from customers at this time.

Every prospectus always has the following statement in bold print on the front page.

> THESE SECURITIES HAVE NOT BEEN APPROVED OR DISAP-PROVED BY THE SECURITIES COMMISSION NOR HAS THE SECURITIES AND EXCHANGE COMMISSION PASSED UPON THE ACCURACY OR ADEQUACY OF THIS PROSPECTUS. ANY REPRESENTATION TO THE CONTRARY IS A CRIMINAL OFFENSE.

This statement is known as the SEC **disclaimer** and should be self-explanatory.

If an underwriter pays for the publication of any description of a security offered (other than a tombstone), the act requires that the publisher disclose the fact that payment was made and the amount of the payment.

LIABILITIES UNDER THE SECURITIES ACT OF 1933

The Securities Act of 1933 provides penalties for false and misleading statements contained in the registration statement or prospectus. If misrepresentations were intentionally made, the individuals responsible are subject to criminal prosecution. The civil liabilities codes allow a purchaser of a security under a registration statement containing a false statement of a material fact or omission of a material fact to sue:

- every person who signed the registration form;

- all directors of the issuer;

- attorneys;

- accountants;

- appraisers or other experts;

- underwriters; and

- parent companies.

A person would be exempt from liability if he could prove he had reasonable grounds to believe, after investigation, that the statements contained in the registration statement are accurate. The statute of limitations for bringing action is the earlier of one year after discovery of the violation or three years after the date of the action. Compare this statute with the statute of limitations in Unit 2, which is almost the same, except that the time limit is two years after discovery. This is one of the rare cases where the time period in the Uniform Securities Act is greater than that in federal law.

STOP ORDERS

The SEC will issue a **stop order**, sometimes called a **cease and desist order**, when it feels that a registration statement is not complete or is inadequate in a material way. A stop order requiring an amendment to the registration statement may be issued before the effective date. When the amendment has been filed properly, the SEC will state this to the issuer. The registration statement will be effective on the effective registration date or the date the amendment has been filed properly, whichever is later.

The SEC may issue a stop order to suspend the effectiveness of the registration even after the effective registration date. The SEC will take this action if they feel the registration statement includes any untrue statement of a material fact. The SEC may subpoena the issuing corporation's records to determine whether a stop order is necessary.

Other powers of the SEC include the ability to:

■ make, amend, and rescind rules;

■ administer oaths;

■ subpoena witnesses and other records for evidence;

■ seek injunctions or restraining orders in the appropriate court; and

■ turn over evidence to the attorney general of the United States for possible criminal prosecution.

If a person is found guilty in court, civil penalties can be severe, including a substantial fine as well as being barred from serving as an officer or director of a public corporation for a number of years. If the case involves criminal prosecution, the penalties may include a fine, a prison term, or both.

SEC REGULATION D (PRIVATE PLACEMENT EXEMPTION)

In a major effort aimed at facilitating the capital formation needs of small businesses, the SEC has adopted Regulation D, which contains SEC Rule 506. **SEC Rule 506** provides an exemption for offers and sales to no more than 35 purchasers. Accredited investors, however, do not count toward that limit. The 35 persons, other than accredited investors, must meet certain sophistication standards. Unsophisticated investors may participate in the offering if a purchaser representative (accountant or lawyer) is representing the unsophisticated investor. To remain exempt, the law prohibits any general solicitation or general advertising.

SEC Rule 501 classifies an accredited investor for the purposes of Regulation D into separate categories. Investors are considered to be accredited under the rule only if the issuer or any person acting on the issuer's behalf has reasonable grounds to believe, and does believe after reasonable inquiry, that the investors are included in one of the categories in the definition.

The separate categories of accredited investors under Regulation D include:

- institutional investors (banks, insurance companies, investment companies, broker/dealers purchasing for their own accounts, employee benefit plans managed by banks, insurance companies, or investment advisers or employee benefit plans with assets in excess of $5 million);

- directors, executive officers, and general partners of the issuer;

- any natural person whose individual net worth, or joint net worth with that person's spouse, at the time of his purchase exceeds $1 million;

- any natural person who had an individual income in excess of $200,000 in each of the two most recent years or joint income with that person's spouse in excess of $300,000 in each of those years and has a reasonable expectation of reaching the same income level in the current year; and

- entities made up of accredited investors.

The term *accredited investor* applies only to private placements.

QUICK QUIZ 1.2

1. Which of the following statements about accredited investors is TRUE?

A. Taxpayers who report an income in excess of $200,000 on a joint return in each of the last two years and who reasonably expect the same for the current year are included in the definition.

B. An officer, director, or greater than 10% shareholder of any company listed on the NYSE would be considered an accredited investor for purposes of acquiring a private placement your firm is selling.

C. The term includes an employee benefit plan with assets in excess of $2 million.

D. Purchases of securities by accredited investors do not count toward the 35-investor limitation found in Rule 506 of Regulation D.

SEC RULE 144 (SALE OF RESTRICTED AND CONTROL SECURITIES)

SEC Rule 144 was created so that certain resales of already existing securities could be made without having to file a complete registration statement with the SEC. The time and money involved in having to file such a registration are usually so prohibitive as to make it uneconomical for the individual seller.

Restricted Securities

Restricted securities are unregistered securities purchased by an investor in a private placement. They are also called **letter securities** (or **legend securities**), which refers to the fact that purchasers must sign an investment letter attesting to their understanding of the restriction upon resale and to the legend placed on the certificates indicating restriction upon resale.

Control Person

A corporate director, officer, greater than 10% voting stockholder, or the spouse of any of the preceding is a **control person**. They are loosely referred to as **insiders** or **affiliates** because of their unique status within the issuer.

Control Stock

Control stock is stock held by a control person. What makes it control stock is who owns it, not how he acquired it.

Nonaffiliate

An investor who is not a control person and has no other affiliation with the issuer other than as an owner of securities is a **nonaffiliate**.

 QUICK QUIZ 1.3

1. A man owns 15% of the stock of a company. His wife owns 5% of the stock of a company. If the wife wishes to sell some of the stock she owns, which of the following statements are TRUE?

    I.   Both the husband and the wife are affiliates.
    II. He is an affiliate, but she is not.
    III. She must file under Rule 144.
    IV. She does not have to file under Rule 144.

    A. I and III
    B. I and IV
    C. II and III
    D. II and IV

THE SECURITIES EXCHANGE ACT OF 1934

The Securities Exchange Act created the SEC. The act grants the SEC authority over all aspects of the securities industry, including the power to register, regulate, and oversee brokerage firms, transfer agents, and clearing agencies as well as the nation's securities self-regulatory organizations (SROs).

The various stock exchanges, such as the New York Stock Exchange (NYSE), American Stock Exchange (AMEX), and Nasdaq, are SROs. The largest SRO is NASD, the organization to which virtually all broker/dealers belong.

The act also identifies and prohibits certain types of conduct in the markets and confers to the SEC disciplinary powers over regulated entities and the persons associated with them.

The act also empowers the SEC to require periodic reporting of information by companies with publicly traded securities.

THE SECURITIES AND EXCHANGE COMMISSION (SEC)

The SEC consists of five people, with one serving as chair, appointed by the president with the advice and consent of the Senate. The SEC administrates all federal laws regulating the securities industry except those regulating the extension of credit. SEC commissioners are appointed for five-year terms and may have no other business or employment other than this job. The terms are staggered so that a new commissioner is appointed each year. To minimize political shenanigans, no more than three of the five commissioners may belong to the same party. Therefore, if there are three Republicans and two Democrats and a Democrat's term expires, the president must appoint another Democrat. Because of the sensitive nature of the employment, SEC commissioners may not engage in any personal securities transactions other than in US government issues. All securities positions they had when appointed are placed into a blind trust.

DEFINITIONS

The act defines many important terms, such as *broker, dealer,* and *exchange*. Many of these terms are also used in the Uniform Securities Act, which is model legislation that the states use to draft their securities laws.

Broker

A **broker** is any person engaged in the business of effecting transactions in securities for the account of others. Banks are not included in this definition.

Dealer

A **dealer** is any person regularly engaged in the business of buying and selling securities for his own account. Banks, insurance companies, investment companies, and any persons engaged in investing, reinvesting, or trading in securities for their own account, either individually or in some fiduciary capacity, but not as part of a regular business, are not included in this definition.

Person Associated with a Broker/Dealer

A **person associated with a broker/dealer** is any partner, officer, or director of the broker/dealer (or any person performing similar functions) or any person directly or indirectly controlling or controlled by the broker/dealer, including any employees of the broker/dealer, except that with regard to registration requirements, persons associated with a broker/dealer whose functions are clerical or administrative are not included in the meaning of the term.

Market Maker

A **market maker** is a dealer who holds himself out as being willing to buy and sell a particular security for his own account and on a regular or continuous basis. This holding out may be by entering quotations in an interdealer communications system or otherwise.

Securities Information Processor

A **securities information processor** is any person engaged in the business of:

■ collecting, processing, or preparing for distribution or publication information with respect to transactions in, or quotations for, any nonexempt security; or

■ distributing or publishing (whether by means of a ticker tape, a communications network, a terminal display device, or otherwise), on a current and continuing basis, information with respect to such transactions or quotations.

Some of the obvious securities information processors are:

■ The Consolidated Ticker Tape;

■ Bloomberg and Reuters;

■ Nasdaq; and

■ The *Pink Sheets*

The term *securities information processor* does not include:

■ a bona fide newspaper, news magazine, or business or financial publication of general or regular circulation, such as *The Wall Street Journal*;

■ any SRO (other than Nasdaq);

■ any bank or broker/dealer supplying quotation and transaction information as part of its customary banking or brokerage business; or

■ any common carrier subject to the jurisdiction of the Federal Communications Commission or a state commission (radio and television stations).

Transfer Agent

A **transfer agent** is any person who engages on behalf of an issuer of securities in:

■ countersigning the certificates;

■ registering the transfer of the issuer's securities;

■ exchanging or converting the issuer's securities; and

■ transferring record ownership of securities by bookkeeping entry without physical issuance of securities certificates.

The term *transfer agent* does not include:

■ any insurance company or separate account that performs these functions solely with respect to variable annuity contracts or variable life policies that it issues; or

■ any registered clearing agency (e.g., Options Clearing Corporation) that performs these functions solely with respect to options contracts that it issues.

Exchange

An **exchange** is an organization, association, or group of persons providing a marketplace or facilities for bringing together purchasers and sellers of securities. The term includes the marketplace and the facilities.

Exchanges must be registered. Registration is accomplished by filing an application with the SEC, which will be accepted or denied within 90 days of application. The exchange must be prepared to demonstrate the following.

■ Formation of the exchange is in the public interest.

■ The exchange will have compliance enforcement ability—that is, the ability to enforce both the SEC's and its own rules.

■ The board of directors will be represented by at least one member representing the investing public and at least one member representing listed companies. The balance of the board is usually made up of directors representing the membership of the exchange.

■ Membership in the exchange may only be offered to registered broker/dealers or associated persons.

Self-Regulatory Organization

A **self-regulatory organization (SRO)** is a national securities exchange or a registered securities association, such as NASD.

Security

The definition of a security is similar to the definition given in the Securities Act of 1933 and in the Uniform Securities Act, which will be discussed in Unit 2.

Equity Security

Equity security is defined as a stock or similar security. **Stock** means common or preferred stock. **Similar security** would include:

■ a security convertible into stock (e.g., convertible bond);

■ any security with a warrant or right attached to subscribe to or buy stock (e.g., a bond with warrants attached); and

■ any warrant or right to purchase stock.

Municipal Securities

Municipal securities are securities that are direct obligations of, or obligations guaranteed as to principal or interest by, a state or any political subdivision thereof, or any agent or instrumentality of a state or any political subdivision thereof. The most common example of municipal securities are municipal bonds.

Government Securities

Government securities are securities that are direct obligations of, or obligations guaranteed as to principal or interest by, the US government. The term also includes government agency securities, such as those issued by the Federal National Mortgage Association (Fannie Mae).

Statutory Disqualification

A person is subject to a **statutory disqualification** with respect to membership or participation in, or association with a member of, an SRO if that person:

- has been or is expelled or suspended from membership or being associated with a member of any SRO, commodities market, or futures trading association;

- is subject to an order of the SEC or other appropriate regulatory agency denying, suspending for a period not exceeding 12 months, or revoking his registration as a broker/dealer, or barring or suspending for a period not exceeding 12 months his association with a broker or dealer;

- by his conduct while associated with a broker or dealer, has been found to be a cause of any effective suspension, expulsion, or order of the type described in the two points above;

- has associated with any person who is known, or with the exercise of reasonable care should be known, to him to be a person described by one of the three points above;

- has been convicted within the past 10 years of a securities violation or a misdemeanor involving finance or dishonesty, bribery, embezzlement, forgery, theft, and so forth, or any felony;

- is subject to a temporary or permanent injunction from a competent court of jurisdiction prohibiting him from engaging in any phase of the securities business;

- has willfully violated any federal securities law; or

- has made a false or misleading statement in any filing with information requested by an SRO (omitting important facts is cause as well).

Loss of a civil lawsuit, even involving securities, is not a cause for statutory disqualification.

The effect of statutory disqualification is a prohibition against association of any kind with a member firm or any investment adviser.

Appropriate Regulatory Authority

The SEC is the appropriate regulatory agency for the following:

- National securities exchanges

- Registered securities associations

- Members of an exchange or association

- Persons associated with a member

- Applicants to become a member or person associated with a member

The SEC is also the appropriate regulatory agency for the Municipal Securities Rulemaking Board (MSRB). However, the SEC has no jurisdiction over banks and other similar financial institutions that are regulated by their functional regulators, including the:

- Federal Reserve Board;

- Office of the Controller of the Currency; and

- Federal Deposit Insurance Corporation (FDIC).

Investment Discretion

A person exercises **investment discretion** with respect to an account if, directly or indirectly, that person is authorized to determine:

- which securities will be purchased or sold by or for the account;

- the amount of the securities to be bought or sold for the account; or

- whether the transaction will be a purchase or sale.

Investment discretion does not include the decision as to the time or price of a particular transaction.

TAKE NOTE   The board of governors of the Federal Reserve was authorized by the act to establish regulations governing the use of credit for the purchase or carrying of securities. The Federal Reserve has issued Regulations T and U covering such credit.

REGISTRATION UNDER THE SECURITIES EXCHANGE ACT OF 1934

The Securities Exchange Act of 1934 requires many different groups and organizations to register with the SEC. Among them are:

- brokers and dealers operating in interstate commerce, including those operating on exchanges and in the over-the-counter markets (broker/dealers file application for membership on **Form BD**, and the SEC has 45 days to accept or deny the registration);

- securities exchanges (as mentioned earlier, the SEC has 90 days to accept or deny registration of an exchange);

- national securities associations, such as NASD and the MSRB (the Maloney Act of 1938 amended the Securities Exchange Act of 1934 and led to the creation of NASD, and the MSRB was created out of the Securities Acts Amendments of 1975, which means that both associations were created by the Securities Exchange Act of 1934, as amended); and

- corporations with listed securities (a security may be registered on a national securities exchange by the issuer filing an application with the exchange and filing with the SEC as well). The application for registration must include:

  — the organization, the financial structure, and nature of the business,

  — the terms, position, rights, and privileges of the different classes of outstanding securities,

  — the terms on which their securities are to be, and during the preceding three years have been, offered to the public,

  — the directors, officers, and underwriters, and each security holder of record holding more than 10% of any class of equity security of the issuer, including their remuneration and their interests in the securities and their material contracts with the issuer and any person directly or indirectly controlling or controlled by the issuer,

  — remuneration to individuals other than directors and officers exceeding $20,000 per year,

  — bonus and profit-sharing agreements,

  — management and service contracts,

  — options existing or to be created regarding their securities,

  — material contracts and patents,

  — certified balance sheets for the previous three fiscal years prepared by independent public accountants, and

  — certified profit and loss statements for the preceding three fiscal years prepared by independent accountants.

INSIDER TRANSACTIONS UNDER THE SECURITIES EXCHANGE ACT OF 1934

This act regulates securities transactions by insiders who generally own large amounts of their companies' stock. Certain persons must file a statement with the SEC concerning the amount of equity securities owned. These persons are:

■ every person who is directly or indirectly the beneficial owner of more than 10% of any class of equity security (other than exempt securities) registered on a national securities exchange; and

■ officers or directors of the issuers of such securities.

The SEC must be notified of any changes in the ownership of such securities. Such individuals are prohibited from selling short and from engaging in short-term transactions. Stockholders are permitted to sue to recover any short-term profits improperly realized by such insiders.

SCHEDULE D FILINGS

Section 13(d)—5% Beneficial Owners generally requires a beneficial owner of more than 5% of a class of equity securities registered under the Securities Exchange Act of 1934 (equity securities of publicly traded companies) to file a report with the issuer, SEC, and the securities markets where those securities trade within 10 days of any transaction that results in beneficial ownership of more than 5%. The reporting requirement of this section is fulfilled by filing Schedule 13D.

Schedule 13D requires information about the acquiring person, including:

■ the name and background of the person or entity (including partners, executive officers, directors, and controlling persons);

■ the origin of the money for the acquisition of the securities; and

■ the purpose of acquiring the securities, such as to acquire control of the business of the issuer, and plans or proposals that such persons may have to liquidate the issuer, to sell its assets to or merge it with any other persons, or to make any other change to its business or corporate structure.

SECTION 13(f) FILINGS

Section 13(f) of the Securities Exchange Act of 1934 requires that any institutional investment manager that uses the mail or any means or instrumentality of interstate commerce in the course of its business as a institutional investment manager, and that exercises investment discretion over an equity portfolio with a market value on the last trading day in any of the preceding 12 months of $100 million or more, must file a **Form 13F** with the SEC quarterly, within 45 days of the end of each quarter.

The purpose of this rule is to require institutional investment managers who exercise investment discretion over accounts holding certain levels of securities to make periodic public disclosures of significant portfolio holdings.

SCHEDULE G FILINGS

Regulation 13G was adopted to ease the beneficial ownership requirements for passive investors. Rather than filing a Schedule 13D, a passive investor whose beneficial ownership exceeds 5% of any registered security may file a Schedule 13G. A **passive investor** is defined as any person who can certify that they did not purchase or do not hold the securities for the purpose of changing or influencing control over the issuer and hold no more than 20% of the issuer's securities. Passive investors who choose to file a Schedule 13G must do so within 10 calendar days after crossing the 5% threshold just as with a Schedule 13D. Passive investors must amend their Schedule 13G within 45 days after the end of the calendar year to report any changes in the information previously reported.

SECTION 16 FILINGS

Section 16(a) of the Securities Exchange Act of 1934 requires executive officers, directors and greater than 10% stockholders (i.e., insiders) to file transaction reports before the end of the second business day following the day on which a transaction has been executed in an equity security where they are considered an insider.

CREDIT REQUIREMENTS (MARGIN)

As mentioned earlier, Regulation T of the Federal Reserve Board is a part of the Act of 1934. It delegates the board of governors of the Federal Reserve System to set margin requirements. These margin requirements determine how much credit may be extended by broker/dealers to their customers to purchase certain securities. During the stock market crash of 1929, the margin requirements were 10%. Today they are 50%. This means that, in 1929, an investor could purchase $20,000 worth of stock with cash equity of only $2,000. Today, that same purchase of $20,000 of stock would require a cash down payment of $10,000. It should be obvious from this example that one of the purposes of Regulation T is to prevent the excessive use of credit.

One specific type of security on which credit may not be extended is a new issue. The underwriting syndicate must receive full payment for any new issue within 35 days of the purchase. Since mutual funds are a continuous new issue, their shares may NOT be purchased on margin. However, as with all new issues, once the shares have been owned in the account for 30 days, they may be used as collateral for a margin loan.

MARKET MANIPULATION

The act outlaws the use of any manipulative, deceptive, or other fraudulent devices. The intent is to prevent any manipulation of securities markets. Some of the specific devices prohibited are listed below.

- **Churning** can be described as a broker/dealer effecting transactions in a discretionary account that are excessive in size or frequency, in view of the financial resources, objectives, and character of the account.

- **Wash sales** are prohibited under the act. A wash sale occurs when a customer enters a purchase order and a sale order at the same time through the same broker/dealer. This would normally be done to create an appearance of activity in a security. A wash sale for tax purposes is not related to this in any way. A wash sale for tax purposes occurs when a customer sells a security and repurchases it within 30 days after the sale and is covered in Unit 5 of this course.

- **Matched orders** are illegal under the act. Matched orders occur when a customer enters a purchase order and a sale order at the same time and at the same price. In the case of matched orders, the customer places the orders through different broker/dealers. As is the case with wash sales, no change in ownership takes place as a result of the transaction.

- **Pegging, fixing, and stabilizing** are prohibited, except when specifically permitted by the SEC rules. Such operations attempt to create a price level different from that which would result from the forces of supply and demand.

Accurate recording of orders and subsequent trades is one way the regulators monitor for attempts to manipulate the market.

Order Tickets

SEC rules require preparation of order tickets before order entry. Required disclosures include:

- the account number;

- whether the order is solicited, unsolicited, or discretionary;

- if a sale, whether long or short;

- if a bond, aggregate par value (but not rating); and

- time stamp showing the time the order was entered.

INSIDER TRADING AND SECURITIES FRAUD ENFORCEMENT ACT OF 1988 (ITSFEA)

An **insider** or **control person** or **affiliate** is defined as an officer, director, or owner of more than 10% of the voting stock of the company, or the immediate family of any of these persons. After the tremendous insider abuses of the mid-1980s, the SEC took steps to beef up its enforcement of insider trading, hence this act. This act incorporated all of the other prohibitions against the activities of insiders and the use of inside information and also increased the penalties that could be levied and made the recipient of inside information as guilty as the insider who passed on that information. In other words, the tippee would be just as guilty as the tipper.

An insider is in violation of SEC rules when he trades securities on the basis of material, nonpublic information or when he passes on this information to another who subsequently acts on this information. It is critical to remember that the insider is just as liable as the person to whom he passes the information.

Even persons who do not meet the definition of an insider are subject to the rules governing the use of nonpublic information and could be liable for any actions taken. When it comes to who could potentially be an insider—that is, who could possibly possess material inside information—the list is virtually endless. One could therefore say that a potential insider could be anyone coming across information dealing with a company, other than those individuals who, by virtue of their title or other circumstance, are definitely insiders.

The Insider Trading and Securities Fraud Enforcement Act of 1988 gave the SEC authority to seek *civil* penalties against persons violating the provisions of the act in amounts up to the greater of $1 million or treble damages. **Treble damages** means that the guilty party could be fined up to three times any ill-gotten gains or up to three times any losses avoided by using inside information to get out before a market drop. From this fine, the SEC is authorized to award bounties to informants. If the SEC should elect to pursue *criminal* action, then, of course, penalties would include potential jail time with a maximum sentence of 20 years.

Private Rights of Action for Contemporaneous Trading

Any person who violates the rules or regulations by purchasing or selling a security while in possession of material, nonpublic information shall be liable in an action in any court of competent jurisdiction to any person who, contemporaneously with the purchase or sale of securities that is the subject of such violation, has purchased (where such violation is based on a sale of securities) or sold (where such violation is based on a purchase of securities) securities of the same class.

■ **Limitations on liability**

The total amount of damages imposed will not exceed the profit gained or loss avoided in the transaction or transactions that are the subject of the violation.

■ **Statute of limitations**

No action may be brought under this section more than 5 years after the date of the last transaction that is the subject of the violation.

Powers of the SEC

The SEC has the authority to investigate possible violations of the federal securities laws. In addition, the SEC may also investigate possible violation of the rules of the SROs, specifically those of:

- a national securities exchange;

- the NASD; and

- the MSRB.

The fact that these SROs have their own procedures for enforcing the rules in no way limits the SEC's powers to investigate and/or obtain a court injunction.

In the course of these investigations, the SEC has the power to:

- administer oaths;

- subpoena witnesses;

- compel attendance;

- require books and records to be produced;

- summarily suspend trading in any nonexempt security for up to 10 days without prior notice; and

- suspend trading on an entire exchange for up to 90 days (in order to do this, the SEC must give prior notification to the president of the United States).

FINANCIAL RESPONSIBILITY RULES UNDER THE SECURITIES EXCHANGE ACT OF 1934

The SEC adopted SEC Rule 15c3-1 **(Uniform Net Capital Rule)**, which establishes minimum net capital requirements for broker/dealers. The term *net capital* refers to net liquid assets of a firm. In other words, a broker/dealer must at all times maintain a minimum amount of net capital for the protection of its customers. If a firm does not have the required net capital under the rule, the SEC does not allow it to operate. Therefore, the purpose of the net capital rule is to protect the customers of the firm by imposing minimum net capital requirements.

The SEC also requires all broker/dealers to maintain a fidelity bond to protect against misappropriation, forgery, and similar violations of the firm and its associated persons. The amount of the fidelity bond is based on the firm's required net capital, with a minimum bond of $25,000. The major wirehouses have fidelity bonds worth millions of dollars. There are no net capital requirements for investment advisers, and bonding requirements, if any, are determined by the states under the Uniform Securities Act.

SECURITIES ACTS AMENDMENTS OF 1975

The Securities Acts Amendments of 1975 was signed into law by President Ford on June 4, 1975. The act amended certain parts of the Securities Exchange Act of 1934 and the Securities Act of 1933. This act represents the most important changes in the regulation of securities markets since the Securities Exchange Act was passed by Congress in 1934.

The main purpose of the act was to remove any barriers to competition in the securities industry. The SEC was given much greater power to regulate the securities industry. The following is a summary of the main provisions of the Securities Acts Amendments of 1975.

■ Fixed-commission rates were abolished in favor of negotiated commissions on public orders.

■ The act directed the SEC to develop a national market system. This has led to increased efficiency resulting from a vast improvement in the flow of information. One of the goals of the national market system is to lessen the reliance on dealers and have more trades take place in an agency capacity.

■ The SEC was given the power to approve any proposed rule changes by the exchanges, NASD, or the MSRB and may refuse to approve any that are a burden on competition.

■ The act required registration of municipal securities dealers with the SEC. Previously, these broker/dealers were exempt from registration with the SEC. This amendment gave rise to the MSRB. It is important to remember that the existence of the MSRB does not in any way limit the power of the SEC to regulate the securities business. However, many MSRB members are banks that are beyond the jurisdiction of the SEC and are regulated by the various banking authorities.

■ The SEC was given the power to regulate the activities of clearing corporations, securities depositories, and transfer agents.

QUICK QUIZ 1.4

1. Under the Securities Exchange Act of 1934, as amended, registration with the SEC would be required of

    I.   a broker/dealer whose business was strictly municipal securities
    II. a broker/dealer registered with the SEC opening a new department for municipal underwriting
    III. a financial institution dealing in municipal bonds

    A. I and II
    B. I and III
    C. II and III
    D. I, II and III

INVESTMENT COMPANY ACT OF 1940

Under the Investment Company Act of 1940, an **investment company** is defined as any issuer that is or holds itself out as being engaged primarily in the business of investing, reinvesting, or trading in securities. A company is considered to be primarily in the business of investing if more than 40% of the value of the issuer's total assets is invested in investment securities. It is important for you to know that the definition of investment company does not include:

- broker/dealers and underwriters;

- banks and savings and loans;

- insurance companies;

- holding companies;

- issuers whose securities are beneficially owned by no more than 100 persons; and

- issuers who trade in investments other than securities.

TYPES OF INVESTMENT COMPANIES

The Investment Company Act of 1940 defines three types of investment companies.

- **Face-amount certificate company:** a face-amount certificate company is an investment company that issues face-amount certificates on the installment plan. A face-amount certificate is a security that represents an obligation on the part of its issuer to pay a stated sum at a fixed date more than 24 months after the date of issuance, in consideration of the payment of periodic installments of a stated amount. If the investor discontinues the plan and cashes in the certificate before maturity, he will probably lose money.

- **Unit investment trust:** a unit investment trust (UIT) is an investment company that does not have a board of directors and issues only redeemable securities, each of which represents an undivided interest in a unit of specified securities. An example of a UIT is the municipal bond trust. Another common example of a UIT is the separate account for an insurance company variable annuity. The ownership interests of variable annuity owners is typically **shares of beneficial interest (SBIs)** in the separate account.

- **Management company:** a management company is any investment company other than a face-amount certificate company or a UIT. Management companies are often referred to as mutual fund companies.

QUICK QUIZ 1.5

1. Which of the following would be considered investment companies under the Act of 1940?

    I.   Face-amount certificate company
    II. Unit investment trust
    III. Management company
    IV. Holding company
    V.   Insurance company

    A. I, II and III
    B. I, II, III and IV
    C. I, II, III and V
    D. I, II, III, IV and V

SUBCLASSIFICATION OF INVESTMENT COMPANIES

For the purpose of the Investment Company Act of 1940, management companies are divided into **open-end** and **closed-end** companies as follows.

■ An **open-end** company is a management company that is offering for sale, or has outstanding, any redeemable security of which it is the issuer. The term *open-end company* is synonymous with *mutual fund*. The redemption price is the net asset value, which is calculated every business day as of the close of the market. Purchases of mutual funds are always at net asset value plus a sales charge (if any).

■ A **closed-end** company is any management company other than an open-end company. Closed-end companies generally have a onetime offering of shares and do not redeem their outstanding shares. Pricing of closed-end companies is not like that of open-end companies. The pricing is not based on net asset value—it is based on supply and demand. Therefore, shares may be purchased or sold in the marketplace at a price above, below, or at the net asset value. When a closed-end company is selling at a price above the net asset value, it is said to be selling at a premium; selling below the net asset value is called selling at a discount.

Management companies are further subclassified into **diversified** and **nondiversified** companies, defined as follows.

■ A **diversified company** is any management company for which at least 75% of the value of its total assets is invested so that the securities of any one issuer are not greater than 5% of the total assets, and no more than 10% of the outstanding voting securities of any issuer are held. There are no other specific requirements for the other 25% of total assets; they can be invested in any fashion.

■ A **nondiversified company** is any management company other than a diversified company.

1. ABC Investment Company, with $30 million in net assets, is a diversified investment company. All of the following statements are correct EXCEPT

    A. ABC could own more than 10% of the outstanding voting securities of a particular issuer

    B. ABC could not have more than $1.5 million invested in securities of a particular issuer

    C. ABC could have as much as $9 million invested in the securities of a particular issuer

    D. ABC could be either an open-end or closed-end company

REGISTRATION OF INVESTMENT COMPANIES

Investment companies must register as such by filing with the SEC. The registration statement used by open-end investment companies to file with the SEC is the **Form N-1A**. In the registration statement, the registrant describes all of the important information, such as objective, sales loads, whether they will be concentrating investments in a particular industry or group of industries, and so on.

INELIGIBILITY OF CERTAIN AFFILIATED PERSONS AND UNDERWRITERS

The Investment Act of 1940 prohibits people who have committed certain acts from serving in certain sensitive positions with an investment company, its adviser, or its principal underwriter. Specifically, no one may serve as a director, employee, investment adviser, member of an advisory board, officer, or principal underwriter if that person has been:

■ convicted, within the previous 10 years, of any felony or misdemeanor involving the purchase or sale of any security or arising out of that person's conduct as an underwriter, broker/dealer, investment adviser, or affiliated person, salesman, or employee of any investment company; or

■ permanently or temporarily enjoined by order, judgment, or decree of any court of competent jurisdiction from acting in any phase of the securities business.

Any person who is ineligible, because of a conviction for felony or misdemeanor, to serve or act as stated above may file with the SEC an application to become eligible again. The SEC may grant the request, either unconditionally or on an appropriate temporary or other conditional basis, if it feels that it is not against the public interest or protection of investors to allow that person back into the business.

In general, investment companies cannot have a board of directors that consists of more than 60% of persons who meet the definition of interested persons of the investment company.

RULE 12b-1

Rule 12b-1 is titled Payment of Asset-Based Sales Loads by Registered Open-End Management Investment Companies. This rule permits a mutual fund to act as a distributor of its own shares without the use of an underwriter and with an asset-based sales load. An **asset-based sales load** is any direct or indirect financing by a mutual fund of sales or promotional services or activities in connection with the distribution of shares. This basically permits no-load funds to pay commissions (sometimes called **trails**) to broker/dealers who sell or otherwise promote the sale of their fund shares. The mutual fund may not use the term *no-load* if its 12b-1 fee exceeds .25% (25 basis points).

The mutual fund may act as a distributor of the shares of which it is the issuer, provided that any asset-based sales load paid by the company is paid according to a written plan describing all material aspects of the financing of the distribution. This written plan must meet the following requirements.

- The plan has been approved initially by a vote of a majority of the shareholders.

- The plan, together with any related agreements, has been approved initially and reapproved at least annually by a vote of the board of directors of the company, and of the directors who are not interested persons of the company and have no direct or indirect financial interest in the operation of the 12b-1 plan or in any related agreements.

The directors who vote in favor of implementation or continuation of the plan must believe that:

- it is likely that the plan will benefit the company, existing shareholders, and future shareholders;

- given the circumstances, the amounts payable under the plan and related agreements represent charges within the range of what would have been negotiated at arms length as payment for the specific sales or promotional services and activities to be financed under the plan; and

- the plan may be terminated at any time by a vote of the majority of the members of the board of directors of the company who are not interested persons of the company and have no direct or indirect financial interest in the operation of the plan or in any related agreements, or by a vote of the majority of the shareholders of the company.

TAKE NOTE

Recent legislation (facing a court challenge at the time of this writing) calls for any fund operating pursuant to a 12b-1 plan to have at least 75% of its board of directors be noninterested persons, with an independent chairperson.

QUICK QUIZ 1.7

1. All of the following statements regarding a 12b-1 company are true EXCEPT
   A. the plan must be initially approved by a majority of the fund's shareholders
   B. the plan must be renewed by a majority of the fund's directors
   C. the plan may be terminated by a vote of the majority of shareholders or a majority of the board of directors
   D. the rule only applies to open-end investment companies

PROHIBITED ACTIVITIES OF INVESTMENT COMPANIES

Investment companies are prohibited from engaging in several activities. Investment companies may not:

- purchase any security on margin;

- participate on a joint basis in any trading account in securities (i.e., an investment company cannot have a joint account with someone else);

- sell any security short; or

- acquire more than 3% of the shares of another investment company.

There are exceptions to the above prohibitions, but, for the purposes of the exam, you may disregard any exceptions.

QUICK QUIZ 1.8

1. The Investment Company Act of 1940 prohibits registered investment companies from engaging in any of the following practices EXCEPT
   A. issuing common stock
   B. selling short or purchasing securities for the company's portfolio on margin
   C. owning more than 3% of the shares of another investment company
   D. opening a joint account with another investment company

CHANGES IN INVESTMENT POLICY

In order for an investment company's board to make fundamental investment policy changes, a majority vote of the outstanding voting stock is required. Examples of fundamental changes would include:

- a change in subclassification, such as from an open-end to a closed-end company or from a diversified to a nondiversified company;

- deviation from any fundamental policy in its registration statement, including a change in investment objective; and

- changing the nature of its business so as to cease to be an investment company.

In other words, since the investment company is supposed to function for the benefit of the shareholders, any of these changes would require the vote of a majority of the shareholders.

Size of Investment Companies

No registered investment company is permitted to make a public offering of securities unless it has a net worth of at least $100,000 and more than 100 shareholders.

Investment Advisory and Underwriter Contracts

It is unlawful for any person to serve or act as investment adviser of a registered investment company, or as principal underwriter, except pursuant to a written contract that has been approved by a majority of the shareholders and that:

- precisely describes all compensation to be paid;

- will be approved at least annually by the board of directors or by majority vote of the shareholders if it is to be renewed after the first two years;

- provides that it may be terminated at any time, without penalty, by the board of directors or by majority vote of the shareholders on not more than 60 days' written notice to the investment adviser; and

- provides for its automatic termination in the event of its assignment.

In addition, it is unlawful for any registered investment company to enter into or renew any contract with an investment adviser or principal underwriter unless the terms have been approved by majority vote of directors who are not parties to such contract as affiliated persons (i.e., directors who are not affiliated with the adviser or the underwriter, who in the aggregate must comprise at least 40% of the directors).

Transactions of Certain Affiliated Persons and Underwriters

It is unlawful for any affiliated person of, or principal underwriter for, a registered investment company to:

- knowingly sell any security to that investment company unless it is a sale only of shares issued by that company itself (redemption of the fund's shares) or a sale of securities of which the seller is the issuer and which are part of a general public offering;

- borrow money or any other property from the fund; or

- knowingly purchase from that investment company any security other than the fund's shares.

Any person may file with the SEC an application for an order exempting a proposed transaction of the applicant from one or more of the above provisions. The SEC will grant the application and issue that order of exemption if it feels that the terms of the proposed transaction are reasonable and fair, that the proposed transaction is consistent with the policy of the investment company, and that the proposed transaction is consistent with the purposes of the Investment Company Act of 1940.

TEST TOPIC ALERT

An **affiliated person** is defined as any person directly or indirectly owning, controlling, or holding with power to vote, **5%** or more of the outstanding shares of the investment company. An affiliated person also includes any person directly or indirectly controlling, controlled by, or under common control with the investment company or any officer, director, partner or employee of the investment company. However, while technically considered an affiliated person, no person is deemed to be an "interested person" for purposes of the maximum percentage of interested persons on the board solely by reason of his being a member of the fund's board of directors or an owner of its securities. A person is deemed to be a **control** person when owning or controlling more than **25%** of the outstanding shares.

QUICK QUIZ 1.9

1. ABC is an NASD member broker/dealer. Among other functions, it serves as the principal underwriter of the XYZ Mutual Fund. Which of the following transactions of ABC would be prohibited unless exemptive relief was offered by the SEC?
    A. ABC tenders, from its investment account, 500 shares of the XYZ Mutual Fund for redemption.
    B. ABC purchases, for its investment account, 500 shares of XYZ Mutual Fund.
    C. ABC purchases some securities directly from XYZ's portfolio.
    D. All of the above.

SALE OF REDEEMABLE SECURITIES

This section deals with prices at which mutual fund shares may be sold. The rule basically requires that the public offering price, as stated in the prospectus, be upheld for all buyers. There are, however, several ways in which fund shares may be sold to investors at a reduced sales charge and even at no sales charge.

The most important way in which a reduction of sales charge may be made available is by use of a **breakpoint**. This is the quantity level stated in the prospectus at which investors receive a reduction in load. This breakpoint is available to any person who purchases in the stated quantity. In this case, however, the definition of any person is somewhat limited. It includes:

■ an individual, spouse, and dependent children under age 21 purchasing in one or more accounts;

■ any legitimate entity purchasing for its own account, as long as the entity was not formed for the purposes of making this purchase; and

■ the trustee purchasing on behalf of a qualified employee benefit plan, such as a pension or profit-sharing plan.

It does not include:

■ purchases made for the account of an investment club; and

■ purchases made on behalf of any entity or group that does not have a common purpose, other than making this investment.

Under what circumstances are the shares available at no sales charge?

■ Sales made to related persons of the fund, such as officers and other employees of the fund, the adviser, or the principal underwriter

■ Sales made to a plan company purchasing the shares as the underlying investment to a contractual plan (these plans were popular in the 1960s and 1970s but are almost extinct today because of investor concerns with their very high sales charges)

QUICK QUIZ 1.10

1. Under which of the following circumstances would a purchase of mutual fund shares at a price below the public offering price be allowable?

   I. The purchase is made by the designated agent of an incorporated investment club that reaches the breakpoint.
   II. A parent buys enough to reach the breakpoint but places half the order in his account and the other half in an account for which his wife is designated as custodian for their son.
   III. The receptionist for the XYZ Growth Fund purchases $100 of that fund.
   IV. A financial planner bunches his clients' orders and turns them in as one in an amount sufficient to reach the breakpoint.

   A. I and II
   B. I and III
   C. II and III
   D. II, III and IV

PERIODIC AND OTHER REPORTS

All investment companies must file annual financial reports with the SEC. These reports contain an audited balance sheet and income statement.

Shareholder Reports

At least semiannually, shareholders must be mailed reports, including:

■ a balance sheet;

■ an income statement;

■ a listing of the amounts and values of securities owned;

■ a statement of purchases and sales; and

■ a statement of the remuneration paid by the investment company during the period covered by the report to officers and directors, as well as any person of whom any officer or director of the company is an affiliated person.

DESTRUCTION AND FALSIFICATION OF REPORTS AND RECORDS

It is unlawful for any person, except as permitted by SEC rules or orders, to willfully destroy, mutilate, or alter any account, book, or other document required to be preserved under the act.

Unlawful Representations and Names

It is unlawful for any person, in issuing or selling any security of which a registered investment company is the issuer, to represent or imply in any manner whatsoever that such security or company has been guaranteed, sponsored, recommended, or approved by the US government or any agency thereof. This is a parallel requirement to the SEC disclaimer found on the front of every prospectus.

Larceny and Embezzlement

Whoever steals, unlawfully and willfully converts to his own use or to the use of another, or embezzles any of the monies, funds, securities, or assets of any registered investment company will be deemed guilty of a crime and, upon conviction thereof, will be subject to the penalties of a fine of a maximum of $10,000, imprisonment for up to five years, or both. In addition to these penalties, officers and directors of investment companies may be subject to civil action by the SEC for various violations of the Investment Company Act of 1940. If found guilty, you have the right to appeal within 60 days to the Federal Court of Appeals for the District in which the case was heard.

MONEY LAUNDERING

Money laundering involves disguising financial assets so they can be utilized without detecting the illegal activity that produced them. Through money laundering, a criminal transforms the proceeds of illicit activities into funds that appear to have been generated by legal means. Money laundering enables criminals to hide and legitimize the proceeds derived from illegal ventures.

CURRENCY TRANSACTION REPORTS (CTRs)

The Bank Secrecy Act requires every financial institution to file a currency transaction report (CTR) on FinCEN Form 104 for each cash transaction that exceeds $10,000. This requirement applies to cash transactions used to pay off loans, the electronic transfer of funds, or the purchase of certificates of deposit, stocks, bonds, mutual funds, or other investments. The act also requires the reporting of wire transfers in excess of $3,000.

Structured transactions are also included in this requirement. Structured transactions are a series of small deposits totaling more than $10,000 made over a short period, in an attempt to circumvent the $10,000 reporting requirement.

Structured transactions may involve cash deposits, account transfers, wire transfers, or ATM or securities transactions, each of which falls below the $10,000 threshold. Consequently, a CTR should be filed if a customer appears to be structuring transactions. Additionally, extra care should be taken when monitoring a client who has numerous accounts with a firm because it may be easier to construct multiple transactions that exceed the $10,000 reporting requirement. The following is an illustration of how a structured transaction might work.

EXAMPLE

Al is involved in illegal activities that have generated revenues of $150,000 in cash. To effectively launder these funds, Al and his accomplices open new accounts, each for less than $10,000, at several different financial institutions. The funds are then, one by one, transferred to another account through check deposits and wire transfers in amounts under the $10,000 threshold. Al then has the collected funds wired to a different financial institution, where he withdraws the funds, avoiding detection.

HOTSHEETS

For your convenience, Unit HotSheets summarizing the key points are located at the end of the manual on perforated pages.

UNIT TEST

1. The Securities Act of 1933 covers which of the following?

   I. The sale of new issues to the public
   II. Sending deficiency letters
   III. Insider trading
   IV. Trading on national securities exchanges

   A. I and II
   B. I, III and IV
   C. III and IV
   D. I, II, III and IV

2. All of the following are exempt from registration under the Securities Act of 1933 EXCEPT

   A. an intrastate offering
   B. a Regulation A offering
   C. a US government security
   D. an interstate offering of preferred stock

3. Which of the following acts regulates insider trading?

   A. Securities Act of 1933
   B. Securities Amendments Act of 1975
   C. Securities Exchange Act of 1934
   D. Investment Advisers Act of 1940

4. A broker/dealer effecting transactions in a discretionary account that are excessive in size or frequency in view of the financial resources and character of the account is considered to be

   A. churning
   B. matching orders
   C. pegging, fixing, and stabilizing
   D. successful

5. Under which of the following cases could an agent make an offering of a security?

   I. A registration statement has been filed with the SEC but has not yet become effective.
   II. A registration statement has been filed with the SEC and has become effective.
   III. The agent is aware of negotiations going on between an issuer and his firm's investment banking department.

   A. I and II
   B. I and III
   C. II only
   D. II and III

6. Under the Securities Act of 1933, the SEC

   A. approves securities registered with it
   B. attempts to make certain that all pertinent information is fully disclosed
   C. passes on the investment merit of the security
   D. guarantees that the statements made in the prospectus and registration statement are accurate

7. The Securities Exchange Act of 1934 does all of the following EXCEPT

   A. require that all securities listed on a national exchange be registered with the SEC
   B. prohibit manipulative practices such as wash sales and misleading statements
   C. prevent fraud in the sale of new issues
   D. require disclosure of information about a listed security

8. An exemption from registration under the Securities Act of 1933 is available to securities that are

   A. offered to the public only when the total amount is more than $4 million
   B. sold in more than one state by persons resident in those states
   C. sold only to persons resident in one state when the issuer is a resident doing business within that state
   D. listed on national exchanges

9. The Securities Exchange Act of 1934 does all of the following EXCEPT

    A. require the registration of new securities
    B. require publicly held corporations to provide annual reports for their shareholders
    C. provide for the regulation of credit in securities transactions
    D. provide for establishment of the Securities and Exchange Commission

10. Among the groups and organizations required to register with the SEC by the Securities Exchange Act of 1934 are

    A. corporations with listed securities
    B. securities exchanges and securities traded on exchanges
    C. brokers and dealers operating in interstate commerce and national securities associations
    D. all of the above

11. A principal purpose of the Securities Exchange Act of 1934 is generally considered to be to

    A. establish specific statutory standards for contractual agreements between corporations issuing bonds and the representatives of investors who own the bonds
    B. protect the public against unfair and inequitable practices in the over-the-counter market and on stock exchanges
    C. reimburse customers of failed broker/dealers
    D. establish standards to govern activities of organizations that engage in the business of providing securities investment advice

12. Under federal law, an application for becoming an associated person of an investment adviser would be denied for an individual

    I. convicted of a felony 122 months ago
    II. pleading no contest to a misdemeanor involving bribery 65 months ago
    III. accused of a securities-related felony 110 months ago

    A. I and II
    B. I and III
    C. II only
    D. II and III

13. An agent who violates federal securities laws may be subject to which of the following?

    I. Suspension
    II. Revocation
    III. Civil liabilities
    IV. Criminal penalties

    A. I and II
    B. I and III
    C. II, III and IV
    D. I, II, III and IV

14. A securities order that is initiated by a client and includes all the details as to time and price is what type of order?

    A. Nondiscretionary
    B. Unsolicited
    C. Discretionary
    D. Solicited

15. A manufacturing company whose debt securities are consistently rated AAA wishes to issue $20 million in 6-month commercial paper. The proceeds will be used to acquire the latest in computer-controlled lathes. Under the Securities Act of 1933, this issue

    A. is exempt from registration
    B. is not exempt from registration
    C. would only be exempt from registration if the denominations were a minimum of $50,000
    D. is straddling a commingled arbitrage

16. The requirement that each securities purchase recommended to a customer be consistent with that customer's objectives, financial situation, and needs falls under the general heading of

    A. suitability
    B. due diligence
    C. financial planning
    D. caveat emptor

17. Under federal securities laws, which of the following are considered to be securities?

    I. Treasury stock
    II. An investment contract
    III. A voting trust certificate
    IV. Debenture

    A. I and II
    B. I, III and IV
    C. III and IV
    D. I, II, III and IV

18. An objective of the Investment Company Act of 1940 is to

    A. control the size of individual investment companies and particularly their impact on the securities markets
    B. require minimum financial and accounting standards of brokers and dealers engaged in interstate commerce
    C. ensure that the individual investing in an investment company is fully informed as to company affairs and fairly treated by its management
    D. all of the above

19. The Investment Company Act of 1940 permits a reduction in sales charge when reaching a breakpoint for

    A. a designated agent of an investment club
    B. purchasers meeting the definition of *any person*
    C. clients of fee-only investment advisers
    D. a mother and her 35-year-old son purchasing separate accounts

20. Among the provisions of the Investment Company Act of 1940 designed to protect the interests of investors is the provision that

    A. any change in fundamental investment policy must be approved by stockholders
    B. advertising and sales literature must be approved by NASD before its use
    C. selection of company investments must be approved by SEC
    D. for diversification purposes, an investment company may own up to 10% of the shares of another investment company

21. Which of the following statements under the Investment Company Act of 1940 are TRUE?

    I. An investment adviser with discretion over more than 100 accounts using pooled client funds might be running an investment company.
    II. Investment companies are prohibited from owning more than 3% of another investment company's shares.
    III. Mutual funds must file semiannual reports with their shareholders and the SEC.

    A. I and II
    B. I and III
    C. II and III
    D. I, II and III

22. A securities salesperson may indicate to a prospective customer that the SEC has approved a securities issue if

    A. the SEC has not initiated action against either the company or the underwriters of the issue
    B. the SEC has not opened an investigation of the company, the underwriter, or the market makers of the security
    C. a registration statement is in effect with the SEC
    D. none of the above

23. For regulatory purposes, open-end funds are subject to the provisions of

    I. the Investment Company Act of 1940
    II. the Securities Act of 1933
    III. the Securities Act of states in which the fund is sold

    A. I only
    B. I and II
    C. I and III
    D. I, II and III

24. Which of the following terms are defined in the Securities Exchange Act of 1934?

    I. Securities information processor
    II. Transfer agent
    III. Market maker
    IV. Prospectus

    A. I and II
    B. I and III
    C. I, II and III
    D. I, II, III and IV

25. Which of the following statements may NOT be made by an agent in regard to a security registered with the SEC under the Act of 1933?

    A. "The SEC has approved of this issue and that's why I'm so glad to be able to offer it to you."
    B. "This issue is lawful for sale."
    C. "This issue is suitable for you on the basis of your objectives and the personal profile you have provided me."
    D. None the above.

26. Under the Securities Exchange Act of 1934, the term *municipal security* would include a(n)

    I. New Jersey Turnpike revenue bond
    II. Illinois Tool Company debt issue backed by their full faith and credit
    III. State of Texas general obligation bond

    A. I and II
    B. I and III
    C. II and III
    D. I, II and III

27. Under the Securities Exchange Act of 1934, the term *municipal security* would NOT include a(n)

    I. City of Chicago school district bond
    II. US Treasury Bill
    III. Province of Ontario library construction bond

    A. I and II
    B. I and III
    C. II only
    D. II and III

ANSWERS AND RATIONALES

1. **A.** Insider trading is covered primarily in the Insider Trading and Securities Fraud Enforcement Act of 1988, as well as the 10(b) sections of the Securities Exchange Act of 1934. Of course, it is the Securities Exchange Act of 1934 that deals with securities exchanges. A deficiency letter is used by the SEC to extend the 20-day cooling-off period when something is missing from the registration statement.

2. **D.** Intrastate issues are exempt from the Securities Act of 1933 under Rule 147. US government securities are always exempt. Regulation A exempts issues of $5 million or less during a 12-month period from standard registration, although an offering circular is filed with the SEC regional office.

3. **C.** The 10(b) sections of the Securities Exchange Act of 1934 cover insider trading. The Insider Trading and Securities Fraud Enforcement Act of 1988 is considered a part of the Securities Exchange Act of 1934.

4. **A.** This is the definition of churning.

5. **A.** An offer can always be made with an effective prospectus. The Securities Act of 1933 also permits an offering to be made by use of a red herring preliminary prospectus, which is published when the issue is filed with the SEC and is used until the effective date. Only an offer can be made with a red herring, not a sale.

6. **B.** Every prospectus carries the SEC disclaimer on the front cover in bold type. All the SEC can hope for is full disclosure of the pertinent information.

7. **C.** Although there are antifraud provisions in the Securities Exchange Act of 1934, they have nothing to do with new issues.

8. **C.** These securities are eligible for the intrastate exemption afforded under Rule 147. They might have to register in that particular state, depending on whether they met the exemption requirements in that state for that type of issue. Only under the NSMIA and the Uniform Securities Act do securities listed on a national stock exchange receive a registration exemption (the blue-chip exemption).

9. **A.** New issues are included in the Securities Act of 1933. Regulation of credit is found in Regulation T, which is part of the Securities Exchange Act of 1934.

10. **D.** The Securities Exchange Act of 1934 requires registration of securities exchanges, as well as the securities listed on those exchanges. It also requires registration of corporations whose securities are listed. All broker/dealers (other than intrastate) must register, as well as SROs, such as NASD and the MSRB.

11. **B.** Choice A relates to the Trust Indenture Act of 1939; Choice C relates to SIPA of 1970, which created SIPC; and Choice D relates to the Investment Advisers Act of 1940.

12. **C.** An individual who is convicted of, or has pleaded guilty or no contest to, any felony or certain misdemeanors in the previous 10 years (120 months) is subject to statutory disqualification. A conviction made more than 10 years ago is part of the record but not cause for disqualification. A misdemeanor involving bribery within the past 10 years is not allowed. Accusation is not the same as conviction.

13. **D.** The maximum period of suspension is 12 months. Revocation of registration is indefinite and may be permanent. Violations could lead to civil or criminal penalties or both.

14. **B.** This is the definition of an unsolicited transaction.

15. **B.** Under the Securities Act of 1933, there are two requirements for commercial paper to be exempt from registration: maturity may not exceed 270 days and proceeds must be used for current operational needs.

    Acquiring machinery would not be considered current because the result is new fixed assets. Rating and denominations are only important under the Uniform Securities Act.

16. **A.** Suitability requires that every recommendation be consistent with the customer's objectives, situation, and needs.

17. **D.** Stock, voting trust certificates, debentures, and investment contracts are all included in the definition of the term *security*. This topic appears frequently on the exam, and it is advisable that you learn the short list of items that are not securities.

18. **C.** Nothing in the Investment Company Act of 1940 controls the size or impact of investment companies. The act has nothing to do with broker/dealer accounting. Investment companies are required to keep shareholders fully informed by providing semiannual reports, which include balance sheets and statements of portfolio changes.

19. **B.** The term *any person* does not include the designated agent of an investment club. The other groupings could not legally combine purchases to reach a breakpoint.

20. **A.** An investment company may own up to 3% of another investment company. Even though NASD rules do require approval of investment company advertisements (not sales literature), such approval is not part of the Investment Company Act of 1940.

21. **A.** Section 30(d) of the act requires semiannual reports from the fund. Although filing is required with the SEC, the company does not file with its shareholders.

22. **D.** The SEC does not approve securities.

23. **D.** The prospectus requirements are found in the Securities Act of 1933. Open-end investment companies (mutual funds) are always a new issue. Almost every other regulation arises from the Investment Company Act of 1940. These funds are securities in each state in which they are offered and, under the Uniform Securities Act, must comply with the rules of the state. In most cases, these funds are known as federal covered investment companies and do not register with the state, although they may pay fees and are subject to the antifraud statutes.

24. **C.** A prospectus deals with new issues, so the term is defined in the Securities Act of 1933.

25. **A.** The SEC never approves of an issue. The other statements are permissible.

26. **B.** The Illinois Tool Company is a corporation, even though it has a state in its name.

27. **D.** Treasury bills are defined as government securities, not municipal securities. Under federal law, Canadian cities (or provinces) are not municipal securities.

QUICK QUIZ ANSWERS

Quick Quiz 1.1

1. **C.** Shares received from a stock dividend or stock split would never be considered a sale because, for sale to take place, there must be an exchange of something for value. Exercise of a right, warrant, or other convertible privilege is considered to be a sale at that time, as is any security given as a bonus for the purchase of another security.

Quick Quiz 1.2

1. **D.** One of the benefits of this term is that these investors do not count in the numerical limitation placed on private placements. When filing a joint return, the income requirement is $300,000, and an employee benefit plan must have assets in excess of $5 million. Insiders are only considered accredited investors when it is that issuer's security being offered.

Quick Quiz 1.3

1. **A.** His 15% ownership is control. Her 5% is not, but the fact that she is the spouse of an affiliate makes her one, causing this to be a sale of control stock. All sales of control stock (unless an exemption applies) must be accompanied by a Rule 144 filing.

Quick Quiz 1.4

1. **A.** The 1975 Amendments required, for the first time, that any firm engaged in the municipal securities business be registered with the SEC. However, firms that were already registered as broker/dealers with the SEC did not have to reregister or requalify to handle municipals. Banks (financial institutions) are members of the MSRB but are exempt from SEC registration.

Quick Quiz 1.5

1. **A.** Holding companies and insurance companies are specifically excluded from the definition of an investment company.

Quick Quiz 1.6

1. **B.** The 5% and 10% limitations apply only to an identified 75% of the total assets. The other 25% can be invested in any fashion desired. Therefore, a diversified company could have as much as 30% of its assets invested in the securities of a particular issuer, and with that free 25%, could own significantly more than 10% of the voting stock of any particular company. The term *diversified company* applies to either an open-end or a closed-end company.

Quick Quiz 1.7

1. **C.** The plan may be terminated by a majority vote of the shareholders or a majority vote of the board of directors who are noninterested directors of the fund.

Quick Quiz 1.8

1. **A.** The one thing that all investment companies must do is issue common stock. That is the form of ownership. All of the other activities are prohibited.

Quick Quiz 1.9

1. **C.** Without an exemptive order from the SEC, it would be a violation of the Investment Company Act of 1940 for any affiliated person to purchase any security from an investment company other than shares of the fund itself.

Quick Quiz 1.10

1. **C.** Any family unit may combine purchases in as many accounts as it wishes to reach the breakpoint for reduced sales charges. If an employee of the fund (the receptionist) purchases for his own account, the sales charge is usually eliminated altogether. A purchase made for a group, such as an investment club or multiple clients with no common purpose other than investment, is not eligible for a reduction.

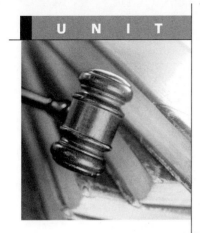

2

State Regulation Under the Uniform Securities Act (USA)

The Uniform Securities Act (USA) is model legislation that arose in an effort to unify numerous state securities laws, known as **blue-sky laws**. Under the USA, the state Administrator has jurisdiction over securities transactions that originate in, are directed into, or are accepted in the Administrator's state. For those persons or transactions that fall within the jurisdiction of the Administrator, the Administrator has power to make rules and orders; conduct investigations and issue subpoenas; issue cease and desist orders; and deny, suspend, cancel, or revoke registrations.

The USA provides both civil liabilities and criminal penalties for violating the act. Civil liabilities enable an investor to recover attorney's fees, court costs, and losses resulting from securities sold in violation of the USA. Criminal penalties may be levied in addition to the civil liabilities against those who engage in fraudulent activities under the act.

The Series 65 exam will include approximately 25 questions on the material presented in this Unit. ■

When you have completed this Unit, you should be able to:

■ **recognize** the jurisdiction of the state securities Administrator;

■ **list** the powers of the Administrator within its jurisdiction;

■ **discuss** the different methods of state securities registration;

■ **identify** instruments that are defined under the USA as securities;

■ **identify** securities that are defined as exempt under the USA;

■ **define** exempt transactions and provide examples;

■ **define and understand** the differences between broker/dealer, agent, investment adviser, and investment adviser representative;

■ **identify** for each category of professional, the procedures and requirements for registration in a state;

■ **understand** the antifraud provisions of the USA;

■ **recognize** specific fraudulent activities, unethical practices prohibited practices, and various forms of deceptive market manipulation;

■ **identify** what is and what is not considered a person;

■ **understand** the differences between exclusions from a definition and exemptions from provisions of the USA;

■ **recognize** what is and what is not a security;

■ **determine** who is and is not a security issuer;

■ **describe** the requirements for exemption from registration for private placements;

■ **understand** the relationship between state and national securities laws;

■ **describe** the civil rights of recovery for a security's sale or for investment advice purchased in violation of the USA; and

■ **contrast** civil and criminal penalties for violation of the act.

SCOPE OF THE ACT

After the Civil War, financial markets developed along with the rapid industrialization of the United States. As a result of new commercial opportunities, corporations issued securities to the public to fund their growth and development. Each state, in turn, enacted securities laws to regulate the sale of these securities within their states.

STATE SECURITIES LAWS (BLUE-SKY LAWS)

The first state to enact a securities law, known as a **blue-sky law**, was Kansas in 1911. The term *blue sky* was coined by a Kansas Supreme Court justice who considered some of these newly issued securities as nothing more than "speculative schemes that have no more basis than so many feet of blue sky."

After the adoption of the first act, the idea of securities regulation began to spread, and by 1913, 23 other jurisdictions had adopted securities acts. By the time of the Great Depression in 1929, virtually all of the states had some form of securities act. The stock market crash of 1929 precipitated a movement to create a federal securities agency that could deal with schemes involving interstate commerce. This movement culminated in the passage of the Securities Act of 1933 and the Securities Exchange Act of 1934 discussed in Unit 1.

THE USA IS MODEL STATE SECURITIES LEGISLATION

With the enactment of numerous state blue-sky laws, the need for uniformity in securities laws among the states arose. In 1956, the **National Conference of Commissioners on Uniform State Laws (NCCUSL)**, a national organization of lawyers devoted to unifying state laws, drafted the original Uniform Securities Act (USA) as model legislation for the separate states to adopt. As model legislation, the USA is not actual legislation; the USA is a template or guide that each state uses in drafting its securities legislation. The securities laws of most states follow the USA very closely, and, in many cases, almost exactly.

TEST TOPIC ALERT   The exam will test your knowledge of the USA, not the specifics of your state's securities legislation. The USA is periodically updated to adjust to developments in the securities markets. You will be tested on the latest version of the USA used by the **North American Securities Administrators Association (NASAA)**, the advisory body of state securities regulators responsible for the content of the exam. The Series 65 exam requires that you not only know what the USA says, but also are able to apply the law to concrete situations. General knowledge of the law is not enough to pass the exam; you will be asked to apply the law to situations that may arise in the course of business.

DEFINITION OF PERSON IN SECURITIES LAW

In securities legislation, such as the USA, terms that you are familiar with in normal speech have slightly different meanings under the law. The term *person* is one such example. Under the USA, person is used to refer to:

■ an individual human being or natural person; or

■ a legal person, such as a corporation or partnership.

A **natural person** means an individual person (human being) as the term is used in common, nonlegal conversation. Individual human beings subject to the act are agents and investment adviser representatives.

Legal persons (legal entities) are creatures of law. For example, a corporation or partnership is formed under the provisions of state law and therefore is a creature of law. For a legal entity to be sued in court, it must have legal existence or legal identity.

Legal entities such as broker/dealers or investment advisory partnerships can conduct business, commit criminal acts, bear civil liabilities, and be sued in court. They are legal persons subject to the USA. In the context of securities regulation, natural persons (individual agents) work for legal persons, such as broker/dealers and investment advisory firms.

TAKE NOTE   There are other legal persons included in the USA's definition of *person*, such as trusts, associations, joint-stock companies, governments, and political subdivisions of governments.

TEST TOPIC ALERT   Although there are a wide variety of entities that may be defined as persons, on the exam, there are only three nonpersons. Those are:

■ minors (anyone unable to enter into contracts under the laws of the state);
■ deceased individuals; and
■ individuals legally declared mentally incompetent.

EXCLUSION FROM DEFINITIONS AND EXEMPTION FROM REGISTRATION

Understanding terms is not a mere semantic exercise. Definitions create jurisdiction. Jurisdiction means that a person or security is covered or subject to the law. Exemptions and exclusions affect persons covered by the act but provide for exemptions and exclusions from provisions of the act. These distinctions must be kept in mind.

Exclusion from a Definition

Exclusion means excluded from, or not included in, a definition. For the purposes of the USA, if a person is excluded from the definition of an agent, that person is not subject to provisions of state law that refer to agents. *Agent,* which will be more fully defined later in this Unit, is any individual other than a broker/dealer who represents a broker/dealer or issuer in effecting transactions in securities.

There are, however, situations in which a person who is representing an issuer in securities transactions is not, by definition, an agent for purposes of the USA. How is this accomplished? By excluding that person from the definition. Here is what the act says:

Agent does not include an individual who represents an issuer in . . . (1) effecting transactions in a security exempted by [the act] . . . or . . . (2) effecting transactions exempted [by the act] or (3) effecting transactions with existing employees, partners, or directors of the issuer if no commission or other remuneration is paid or given directly or indirectly for soliciting any person in this state.

This means when a person performs the functions of an agent for an issuer (effecting transactions in securities on behalf of a company issuing shares to the public), that person is not defined as an agent by the act in three specific circumstances: (1) when effecting transactions in securities exempt from registration; (2) in transactions that are exempt from registration; and (3) when effecting transactions with existing employees, when no commissions are paid.

TAKE NOTE

Keep in mind that an individual who works for an issuer of securities is excluded from the definition of an agent when engaging in transactions involving the issuer's securities, provided that the individual is not compensated for such participation by commissions or other remuneration based either directly or indirectly on the amount of securities sold. In other words, salaried employees engaged in distributing their employers' shares as part of an employee benefit plan would not be required to register as agents because they are by definition excluded from the definition. If such employees were compensated on the basis of the number of shares sold, they would be defined as agents and therefore subject to registration.

Exemption from Registration Under the Act

Exemption in the USA means not being subject to a registration provision of the act even though that person is otherwise covered by the act. For example, a person defined as an agent can be exempt from registration requirements as an agent because that person enjoys an exemption from registration under federal law.

When federal law, such as the Securities Act of 1933, exempts a person or security from registration, the individual states cannot then require that person or security to register under state law. Such person or security is **exempt**. The same logic holds true for exclusion. If a person is excluded from a definition under federal securities law, the states cannot then include that person in the definition to subject that person to state law. Such person or security is excluded.

The logic here should be obvious: if the separate states could require persons that are excluded from a definition or exempt from registration under federal law, then state securities laws would be in conflict with federal securities laws. Remember, the National Securities Markets Improvement Act was enacted to eliminate duplications and conflicts between state and federal securities regulations.

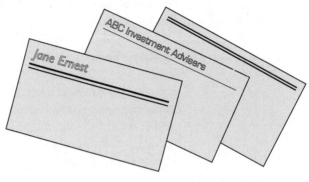

Individual   or   Business   or   Government

QUICK QUIZ 2.1   True or False?

_____   1. A corporation is not a person and therefore the state Administrator does not have jurisdiction over its securities activities.

_____   2. An individual is a natural person and not a legal person subject to the jurisdiction of the Uniform Securities Act.

Quick Quiz answers can be found at the end of the Unit.

PERSONS SUBJECT TO STATE REGISTRATION

Now that the terms *exclusion* and *exemptions* have been addressed, attention must now be directed to those persons who are not excluded or exempted from provisions of the act. The following are the four classes of persons that fall under the jurisdiction of state securities laws:

■ Broker/dealers—generally legal persons

■ Agents—always individuals

■ Investment advisers—generally legal persons

■ Investment adviser representatives—always individuals

TEST TOPIC ALERT

On your exam, always keep in mind which of the four categories of persons is the subject of the question. Rules that apply to agents, for example, are not the same as those that apply to broker/dealers. You will be tested on your understanding of the distinctions between each class of person defined in this Unit.

BROKER/DEALER

A **broker/dealer** is defined in the USA as any person (legal entity) engaged in the business of effecting transactions in securities for the accounts of others or for its own account. Any legal person (e.g., a securities firm) with an established place of business (an office) in the state that is in the business of buying and selling securities for the accounts of others (customers) and/or for its own proprietary account is a broker/dealer and must register in the state as such.

In other words, broker/dealers are firms for which registered representatives (agents) work. They are firms that engage in securities transactions, such as sales and trading. When acting on behalf of their customers—that is, buying and selling securities for their clients' accounts—broker/dealers act in an agency capacity. When broker/dealers buy and sell securities for their own accounts, called proprietary accounts, they act in a principal capacity as dealers.

TAKE NOTE

Individuals who buy and sell securities for their own accounts are not broker/dealers because they are engaged in personal investment activity, not the business of buying and selling securities for others. They are individual investors, not securities dealers.

Exclusions from the Definition of Broker/Dealer

Broker/dealers are firms that buy and sell securities for others or themselves as a business. There are, however, many persons, legal and natural, that effect securities transactions that are excluded from the definition of broker/dealer for purposes of state regulation. Persons not included in the definition of broker/dealer are:

- agents;

- issuers; and

- banks, savings institutions, and trust companies (not engaged in broker/dealer activities).

Domestic commercial banks and other financial institutions are generally excluded from the definition of a broker/dealer. However, with the adoption of the Gramm-Leach-Bliley Act in 1999, also known as the Financial Modernization Act, federal securities law adopted a functional approach to the regulation of financial institutions. Under the functional approach, those financial institutions that engage in brokerage-related securities activities are subject to SEC registration as broker/dealers as well as to applicable provisions of state securities law—the USA—that relate to broker/dealers.

Today most banks and other financial institutions engage in securities activities through broker/dealer subsidiaries. The broker/dealer subsidiaries of banks are, as a result, not excluded from the definition of a broker/dealer and therefore subject to the same securities regulations as other broker/dealers. Keep in mind that formation of these subsidiaries eliminates the need for the bank holding companies to register as broker/dealers. Their broker/dealer subsidiaries must, of course, register.

TAKE NOTE   Keep in mind the distinction between a bank holding company and a wholly owned commercial bank subsidiary. Commercial banks, the subsidiaries of bank holding companies, do not have to register because they are exempt. When engaged in securities transactions with the public, bank subsidiaries are subject to securities legislation as any other broker/dealer.

No Place of Business in the State

There is another exclusion from the definition of broker/dealer. This exclusion relates to the location of the broker/dealer's place of business. States exclude from the definition of broker/dealer those broker/dealers that:

- have no place of business in the state and deal exclusively with issuers, other broker/dealers, and other financial institutions, such as banks, savings and loan associations, trust companies, insurance companies, investment companies, and pension or profit-sharing trusts; and

- have no place of business in the state, but are licensed in a state where they have a place of business, and offer and sell securities in the state only with persons in the state who are existing customers and who are not residents of the state. This is sometimes referred to as the *snowbird exemption.*

In other words, the USA excludes broker/dealers with no place of business in the state from the definition of a broker/dealer to allow those firms that deal exclusively with other financial institutions to operate in the state without registering. The reason for this exclusion is that broker/dealers who transact business solely with financial institutions are already subject to securities regulations by their functional regulators. Duplicate regulation is thereby eliminated.

The USA also allows broker/dealers to do business with existing customers who are temporarily in a state to avoid unnecessary multiple registrations. In most states, when an existing client legally changes residence to another state in which the broker/dealer is not registered, the firm has 30 days during which it may continue to do business with that client without registration in the new state. Should it wish to continue to maintain that client, the broker/dealer would have to register in that state.

Notice how important language is here: If broker/dealers with no place of business in the state were defined as broker/dealers, they would be subject to state registration. But if such broker/dealers with no place of business in the state are not defined as broker/dealers, those broker/dealers are not subject to the registration requirements of that state. Language and definitions determine jurisdiction. If a person or entity is defined as a broker/dealer, that person is covered by (subject to) the provisions of the act. If a person or entity is excluded from a definition, that person is not subject to (covered by) the act.

TEST TOPIC ALERT   The exam focuses more on the exclusions from the definition of broker/dealer than on the definition itself. Know these exclusions well.

CASE STUDY   **Exclusion from the Definition of Broker/Dealer**

Situation: First Securities Corporation is a registered broker/dealer with offices in Illinois. Mr. Thompson, an agent in the Illinois office of First Securities, recommends the purchase of ABC Shoes stock to his customer, Mr. Bixby, an Illinois resident, who is temporarily on vacation in Hawaii. Mr. Bixby agrees to the purchase of ABC Shoes, as well as other securities, while in Hawaii.

The Hawaiian state securities Administrator does not issue a cease and desist order against First Securities for unlawfully selling securities as an unregistered broker/dealer in Hawaii.

Analysis: The Hawaiian securities Administrator acted correctly by not issuing a cease and desist order against First Securities. Under the USA, First Securities is not required to register as a broker/dealer in Hawaii because it limits its business to an existing customer, Mr. Bixby, who is temporarily in the state. Because First Securities is properly registered in Illinois, it need not register in Hawaii, provided, of course, Mr. Bixby does not take up permanent residence there. In this case, First Securities does not fall under the definition of broker/dealer in Hawaii because it does not do business in Hawaii other than with one existing customer temporarily in the state. In this situation, First Securities is not defined as a broker/dealer in the state of Hawaii and therefore does not have to register as a broker/dealer in Hawaii. Definitions determine jurisdiction.

TAKE NOTE   A broker/dealer registered in Canada that does not have a place of business in this state is permitted to effect transactions in securities with a client from Canada who now lives in this state if those transactions are in a self-directed, tax-advantaged retirement plan (similar to an IRA), of which the individual client is the holder or contributor in Canada.

Broker/Dealer Registration Requirements

Under the USA, if a person is included in the definition of a broker/dealer, that person must register as a broker/dealer in the states where it does business. The USA is clear about broker/dealer registration. It states, "It is unlawful for any person to transact business in this state as a broker/dealer . . . unless he is registered under this Act."

This means every person (legal entity) that falls within the definition of a broker/dealer must register with the Administrator of the state. Again, keep in mind that if a person falls under one of the exclusions from the definition, that person or legal entity does not have to register in the state.

TAKE NOTE

In addition, at the time of registration of a broker/dealer, any partner, officer, or director of the broker/dealer is automatically registered as an agent of the broker/dealer.

CASE STUDY

Who Is a Broker/Dealer?

Situation: First Securities Corporation of Illinois sells municipal bonds and equity securities to both the general public and other securities firms. First Securities sells many of its municipal bonds to its biggest customer, Transitions Broker/Dealers, Inc., located in Indiana. Transitions Broker is a wholesale broker/dealer with no offices in Illinois that trades exclusively with other broker/dealers.

First Securities discovers that Transitions Broker/Dealers is not registered in Illinois but does business with other broker/dealers in Illinois. The president of First Securities asks the president of Transitions Broker why his firm is not registered in Illinois; the president of Transitions answers that it is because they are not broker/dealers in Illinois. The president of First Securities is baffled—it appears to him that Transitions is indeed a broker/dealer.

Analysis: First Securities sells both exempt securities (municipal bonds) and nonexempt securities (equities) to the general public and to other broker/dealers. First Securities is a broker/dealer because it is a legal entity with a place of business in the state that effects securities transactions for itself and for the accounts of others and so must register in Illinois.

Like First Securities, Transitions Broker/Dealers conducts broker/dealer activities. However, in Illinois it confines the business to transactions between itself and other broker/dealers, such as First Securities. The USA specifically excludes from the definition of *broker/dealer* out-of-state broker/dealers who deal exclusively with other broker/dealers and have no place of business in the state.

Although Transitions Broker is, in fact, conducting operations of a broker/dealer in Illinois, it does not meet the definition as stated in the USA and, therefore, is not subject to registration with the Illinois securities Administrator. If Transitions Broker were located or had an office in Illinois, it would be a broker/dealer by definition and have to register as such in Illinois.

What about the Indiana Administrator? Which of the firms must register? Even though Transitions Broker only does a wholesale business, because it has an office in the state of Indiana, it would meet the definition of broker/dealer and would have to register as such. What about First Securities? Well, it depends on several factors we haven't been told. Does First Securities maintain an office in Indiana? If it does, registration is required. If it doesn't and the only securities business it does is with other broker/dealers and financial institutions, then it does not have to register in Indiana.

Financial Requirements

The Administrator may establish net **capital requirements** for broker/dealers. Think of net capital as the broker/dealer's liquid net worth. Net capital requirements of the states may not exceed those required by federal law, in this case, the Securities Exchange Act of 1934. The Administrator of a state may, however, require those broker/dealers that have custody of, or discretionary authority over, clients' funds or securities to post **surety bonds**. The amount of surety bonds required by the states is limited to the amount set by the Securities Exchange Act of 1934. The Administrator may not require a bond of a broker/dealer whose net capital is in excess of that required by the SEC.

In lieu of a surety bond, the Administrator will accept deposits of cash or securities.

Broker/Dealer Postregistration Requirements

Once registered, broker/dealers are subject to numerous administrative requirements to keep their registrations current and in good order.

Books and Records

Every registered broker/dealer must make and keep such accounts, blotters, correspondence, memoranda, papers, books, and other records as the state Administrator by rule prescribes. All records so required must be preserved for three years unless the Administrator specifies otherwise. These records must be current, complete, and accurate. Broker/dealers are obligated to promptly file correcting amendments. State securities Administrators cannot impose recordkeeping requirements that are in excess of those prescribed by the SEC.

The records broker/dealers are required to maintain are subject to periodic, special, or other examinations by representatives of the Administrator of the broker/dealer's state or of any other state as the Administrator deems necessary or appropriate in the public interest.

TAKE NOTE

To avoid unnecessary duplication of examinations, the Administrator may cooperate with the securities administrators of other states, the SEC, and any national securities exchange or national securities association registered under the Securities Exchange Act of 1934.

QUICK QUIZ 2.2

True or False?

_____   1.   In general, a person who effects transactions in securities for itself or for the account of others in the course of business must register in the state as a broker/dealer.

_____   2.   Under the Uniform Securities Act, an out-of-state firm that transacts business with an established customer who is on vacation is not considered a broker in the state in which the customer is on vacation.

_____   3.   A person not defined as a broker/dealer in the state under the USA need not register as such.

AGENT

The USA defines an **agent** as any individual who represents a broker/dealer (legal entity) or an issuer (legal entity) in effecting (or attempting to effect) transactions in securities.

Agents are individuals in a sales capacity who represent broker/dealers or issuers of securities. As agents, they act, usually on a commission basis, on behalf of others. Other than on this exam, agents are often referred to as **sales representatives** or **registered representatives**, whether they sell registered securities or securities exempt from registration.

The use of the term *individual* here is important. Only an individual, or a natural person, can be an agent. A corporation, such as a brokerage firm, is not a natural person—it is a legal entity. The brokerage firm is the legal person (legal entity) that the agent (natural person) represents in securities transactions.

Exclusions from Definition of Agent for Administrative Personnel

Clerical and administrative employees of a broker/dealer are generally not included in the definition of agent and, therefore, are not required to be registered. The logic for this exclusion from the definition should again be obvious. Clerical and administrative employees do not effect securities transactions with the public. They attend to the administration of the broker/dealer as a business organization. Under these circumstances, they are like employees of any other corporation.

The situation changes when administrative personnel take on securities-related functions. When they do so, they lose their exemption and must register as an agent.

TAKE NOTE   Secretaries and sales assistants (known as ministerial personnel) are not agents if their activities are confined to administrative activities, including responding to an existing client's request for a quote. However, if secretaries or sales assistants accept customer transactions or take orders over the phone, they are engaging in securities transactions and are subject to registration as agents.

Exclusions from the Definition of Agent for Personnel Representing Issuers

In many cases, individuals who represent issuers of securities are agents and therefore must register as such in the states in which they sell the issuers' securities. As discussed under the general topic of exemptions and exclusions, there are three exclusions from the definition of agent for individuals when representing issuers. They are repeated here for emphasis. Individuals are excluded from the definition of agent, when representing issuers in effecting transactions:

■ in exempt securities;

■ exempt from registration;

■ with existing employees, partners, or directors of the issuer when no commission or other remuneration is paid or given directly or indirectly for soliciting any person in this state.

Effecting Transactions in Exempt Securities

Securities exempt from registration are called **exempt securities**. An employee of an issuer is not an agent when representing an issuer in the following exempt securities:

■ US government and municipal securities

■ Securities of governments with which the United States has diplomatic relationships

■ Securities of US commercial banks and savings institutions or trust companies (when not engaged in securities-related broker/dealer activities)

■ Commercial paper rated in the top three categories by the major rating agencies with denominations of $50,000 or more with maturities of nine months or less

■ Investment contracts issued in connection with employee's stock purchase, savings, pensions, or profit-sharing plans

Once again, the exclusion from the definition of agent only applies when the individual does not receive compensation that is related to the amount or type of sales made.

Effecting Exempt Transactions

Transactions exempt from registration are called **exempt transactions.** They are:

■ isolated nonissuer transactions;

■ transactions between issuer and underwriters;

■ transactions between savings institutions or trust companies; or

■ private placements.

Exempt security and exempt transaction will be covered in thorough detail later in this Unit.

TAKE NOTE   An employee of an issuer is not an agent when representing an issuer if the issue is exempt from registration (e.g., banks, financial institutions, and governments). Additionally, the employee is not an agent when representing an issuer in exempt transactions (e.g., transactions between an underwriter and issuer). If the individual receives compensation that is based on sales, registration as an agent is required.

Agent Registration Requirements

The registration requirements for an agent that is not exempt are similar to those for a broker/dealer. The USA states, "It is unlawful for any person to transact business in this state as an agent unless he is registered under this act." In other words, an individual may not conduct securities transactions in a state unless that person is properly registered in the state where he conducts business. Furthermore, the act makes it unlawful for any broker/dealer or issuer to employ an agent unless the agent is registered.

An agent's registration is not effective during any period when the agent is not associated with a broker/dealer registered in the state. When an agent begins or terminates a connection with a broker/dealer or issuer, or begins or terminates those activities that make him an agent, the agent and the broker/dealer or issuer must promptly notify the Administrator.

Financial Requirements

There are no financial requirements, or **net worth requirements**, to register as an agent. The Administrator may, however, require an agent to be bonded, particularly if the agent has discretion over a client's account.

CASE STUDY

Agent as Defined by the USA

Situation: The City of Chicago issues bonds for the maintenance of local recreational facilities. Purchasers have two choices: they can purchase the bonds directly from the city through Ms. Stith (an employee of the city responsible for selling the bonds), or they can purchase them from Mr. Thompson (an employee of First Securities Corporation of Chicago). Neither Ms. Stith nor Mr. Thompson charges a commission, although First Securities is remunerated with an underwriting fee.

Analysis: The City of Chicago is an issuer of exempt securities (municipal bonds). Ms. Stith, as an employee of the issuer (City of Chicago), is not an agent as defined in the USA because she is representing the issuer in the sale of an exempt security and is not receiving sales-based compensation. Therefore, Stith does not need to register as an agent with the Administrator of Illinois. However, Thompson, as a representative of First Securities, must register with the Administrator because he represents a broker/dealer in effecting securities transactions in the state. Representatives (agents of broker/dealers) must register in the states where they sell securities.

Exemptions from registration as an agent generally apply to representatives of issuers, rather than to representatives of broker/dealers.

If Ms. Stith received a bonus based on sales production, the USA would consider that as commission compensation and Ms. Stith would have to register as an agent.

Fee and Commission Sharing

Multiple Registrations

An individual may not act at any one time as an agent for more than one broker/dealer or for more than one issuer, unless the broker/dealers or issuers for whom the agent acts are affiliated by direct or indirect common control or the Administrator grants an exception.

Registered agents of broker/dealers may share fees or split commissions with others provided they are registered as agents for the same broker/dealer or for a broker/dealer under common ownership or control.

Limited Registration of Canadian Broker/Dealers and Agents

Provided the limited registration requirements enumerated below are met, a broker/dealer domiciled in Canada that has no office in this state may effect transactions in securities with or for, or attempt to induce the purchase or sale of any security by:

■ a person from Canada who is temporarily a resident in this state who was already a client of the broker/dealer; or

■ a person from Canada who is a resident in this state, whose transaction is in a self-directed, tax-advantaged retirement plan in Canada of which the person is the holder or contributor.

An agent who will be representing a Canadian broker/dealer who registers under these provisions may effect transactions in securities in this state on the same basis as permitted for the broker/dealer.

For the Canadian broker/dealer to register in this fashion, it must:

■ file an application in the form required by the jurisdiction where it has its principal office in Canada;

■ file a consent to service of process;

■ provide evidence that it is registered in good standing in its home jurisdiction; and

■ be a member of an SRO or stock exchange in Canada.

Requirements for agents are the same, except that membership in an SRO or stock exchange is not relevant.

However, just as with domestic broker/dealers, if there is no place of business in the state, there are no registration requirements if the only securities transactions are with issuers, other broker/dealers, and institutional clients.

TAKE NOTE   Renewal applications for Canadian broker/dealers and agents who file for limited registration must be filed before December 1 each year.

QUICK QUIZ 2.3

Write **A** if the person is an agent and **B** if not.

_____ 1. Person who effects transactions in municipal securities on behalf of a broker/dealer

_____ 2. An agent's salaried secretary who takes orders

_____ 3. An employee of a bank that is issuing shares who receives a commission for selling the bank's securities

_____ 4. Individual who represents her nonexempt employer in the sale of its securities to existing employees for a commission

_____ 5. Person who represents an issuer in effecting transactions with underwriters

INVESTMENT ADVISER

Under the USA, an **investment adviser** is defined as any person who, for compensation and as part of a regular business, engages in the business of advising others as to the value of securities or as to the advisability of investing in or selling them. The advice can be delivered in person, through publications or writings, or through research reports concerning securities.

Advice given on investments not defined as securities, such as rare coins, art, and real estate, is not investment advice covered by the USA or other securities legislation. As a result, persons providing such advice are not investment advisers. Again, definitions are crucial for determining whether an activity is subject to securities law or not.

To be an investment adviser under both state and federal securities law, a person must:

- provide advice about securities (not about jewelry, rare coins, or real estate);

- provide that advice as part of an ongoing business (hang out a shingle and have an office for conducting business); and

- receive compensation (actually get paid for the advice).

TAKE NOTE

In most cases, investment advisers are legal persons—that is, partnerships or corporations that provide investment advice or portfolio management services on an ongoing basis. An individual can be an investment adviser if he operates as a sole proprietorship.

Investment Adviser Representative

An **investment adviser representative** is any individual who represents a state-registered investment adviser or federal covered investment adviser performing duties related to the giving of or soliciting for advisory services.

TAKE NOTE

The subject of investment advisers and their representatives will be covered in greater detail in the next Unit.

GENERAL REGISTRATION PROCEDURES

Any person who meets the definition of broker/dealer, agent, investment adviser, or investment adviser representative must register with the state. To register with the state securities Administrator, a person must:

- submit an application;

- provide a consent to service of process;

- pay filing fees;

- post a bond (if required by the Administrator); and

- take and pass an examination if required by the Administrator. The examination may be written, oral, or both.

SUBMIT APPLICATION

All persons must complete and submit an **initial application** (as well as renewals) to the state securities Administrator. The application must contain whatever information the Administrator may require by rule, and may include:

- form and place of business (broker/dealers and investment advisers);

- proposed method of doing business;

- qualifications and business history (broker/dealers and investment advisers must include the qualifications and history of partners, officers, directors, and other persons with controlling influence over the organization);

- injunctions and administrative orders;

- convictions of misdemeanors involving a security or any aspect of the securities business;

- felony convictions, whether securities related or not;

- financial condition and history; and

- Form ADV, if an investment adviser.

The Administrator also may require that an applicant publish an announcement of the registration in one or more newspapers in the state.

T A K E N O T E
If an agent terminates employment with a broker/dealer, both parties must notify the Administrator promptly.

If an agent terminates employment with one broker/dealer to join another broker/dealer, all three parties must notify the Administrator. If an investment adviser representative terminates employment with an investment adviser, notification depends on how the investment adviser is registered.

If it is a state-registered adviser, then the firm must notify the Administrator. If it is a federal covered adviser, then the investment adviser representative must be the one to notify the Administrator.

PROVIDE CONSENT TO SERVICE OF PROCESS

New applicants for registration must provide the Administrator of every state in which they intend to register with a **consent to service of process**. The consent to service of process appoints the Administrator as the applicant's attorney to receive and process noncriminal securities-related complaints against the applicant. Under the consent to service of process, all legal documents (e.g., subpoenas or warrants) received by the Administrator have the same legal effect as if they had been served personally on the applicant.

T A K E N O T E
The consent to service of process is submitted with the initial application and remains in force permanently. It does not need to be supplied with each renewal of a registration.

PAY INITIAL AND RENEWAL FILING FEES

States require **filing fees** for initial applications as well as for renewal applications. If an application is withdrawn or denied, the Administrator is entitled to retain a portion of the fee. Filing fees for broker/dealers, investment advisers, and their representatives need not be identical. Broker/dealers and investment advisers may file an application for registration of a successor, whether or not the successor is then in existence, for the unexpired portion of the year. Please note that the successor pays no registration fee until renewal of the firm's license.

The renewal date for all registrations is December 31.

T A K E N O T E
The Administrator's authority does not stop at the state line. The Administrator of any state where the registrant is registered may demand an inspection during reasonable business hours with whatever frequency the Administrator deems necessary.

EFFECTIVENESS OF REGISTRATION

Unless a legal proceeding is instituted or the applicant is notified that the application is incomplete, the license of a broker/dealer, agent, investment adviser, or investment adviser representative becomes effective at noon, 30 days after the later of the date an application for licensing is filed and is complete or the date an amendment to an application is filed and is complete. An application is complete when the applicant has furnished information responsive to each applicable item of the application. By rule or by order, the Administrator may authorize an earlier effective date of licensing. In other words, there could be an occasion where, in effect, a person was the subject of a rush order.

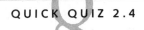

QUICK QUIZ 2.4   True or False?

_____   1.   A consent to service of process must be submitted with each renewal application.

_____   2.   An Administrator may establish net capital requirements for investment adviser representatives.

_____   3.   When a securities professional registers in a state, he must provide the state Administrator with a list of all the states where he intends to register.

WHAT IS A SECURITY UNDER THE UNIFORM SECURITIES ACT?

Perhaps the most important term in the USA is the term *security*. Why is it so important? The reason is simple: the USA applies only to those financial instruments that are securities. The purchase, sale, or issuance of anything that is not a security is not covered by the act. The definition of a security, however, is complex. Over the years, courts have determined case by case what constitutes a security. The US Supreme Court, in the Howey decision, defined the primary characteristics of what constitutes a security. For an instrument to be a security, the court held, it must constitute (1) an investment of money, (2) in a common enterprise, (3) with the expectation of profits, (4) to be derived primarily from the efforts of a person other than the investor. A **common enterprise** means an enterprise in which the fortunes of the investor are interwoven with those of either the person offering the investment, a third party, or other investors.

LIST OF SECURITIES UNDER THE UNIFORM SECURITIES ACT

The USA does not define the term but provides a comprehensive list of financial instruments that are securities under the act and therefore covered by its provisions. Under the USA, *securities* include:

■   notes;

- stocks;

- treasury stocks;

- bonds;

- debentures;

- evidence of indebtedness;

- certificates of interest or participation in a profit-sharing agreement;

- collateral trust certificates;

- preorganization certificates or subscriptions;

- transferable shares;

- investment contracts;

- voting trust certificates;

- certificates of deposit for a security;

- fractional undivided interests in oil, gas, or other mineral rights;

- puts, calls, straddles, options, or privileges on a security;

- certificates of deposit or groups or indexes of securities;

- puts, calls, straddles, options, or privileges entered into on a national securities exchange relating to foreign currency;

- any interest or instrument commonly known as a security; or

- certificates of interest or participation in, receipts of, guarantees of, or warrants or rights to subscribe to or purchase, any of the above.

The following six items are not securities under the act:

- An insurance or endowment policy or annuity contract under which an insurance company promises to pay a fixed sum of money either in a lump sum or periodically

- Interest in a retirement plan, such as an IRA or Keogh plan

- Collectibles

- Commodities such as precious metals and grains

- Condominiums used as a personal residence

- Currency

TEST TOPIC ALERT   The exam will want you to know what is and what is not a security. We suggest that you concentrate on learning the six that are NOT securities because they are much easier to remember, and you will still be able to answer the questions correctly.

Examples of Nonsecurity Investments Versus Securities Investments

Although collectibles, precious metals, grains, real estate, and currencies can be attractive investments, they are not securities. Because these items are not securities, their sale is not regulated by state securities law. Furthermore, if a registered agent commits fraud in the sale of any of these items, he has not committed a violation of the any state securities law. He has violated the antifraud provisions of another act prohibiting fraudulent commercial transactions.

EXAMPLE   An individual farmer's direct ownership of a cow is not a security—it is just owner-ship of a cow. However, if the farmer makes an investment of money in a tradable interest in a herd of cattle, on which he expects to earn a profit solely as the result of the breeder's efforts, he has purchased a security. In the same manner, if a condominium is purchased in a resort area with the goal of renting it out most of the year, and it is used only for personal vacation time, the condo is considered a security because there is a profit motive, typically reliant on the efforts of a third party—the rental agent. On the other hand, if you have chosen to live in a condominium as a personal residence, that's a home, not a security.

TAKE NOTE   Annuities with fixed payouts are not securities, but variable annuities are because they are dependent on the investment performance of securities within the annuity.

NONEXEMPT SECURITY

A nonexempt security is a security subject to the registration provisions mandated by the USA. *Exempt* means not subject to registration. If a security is not registered or exempt from registration, it cannot be sold in a state unless it is sold in an exempt transaction. As you will see, the sale of an unregistered nonexempt security is a prohibited practice under the USA and may subject an agent to criminal penalties.

TAKE NOTE   The methods of registration discussed in this Unit refer to nonexempt securities. Think of what the legal terms actually mean in everyday usage. For example, a registered nonexempt security is most likely a common stock properly registered for sale in a state.

ISSUER

An **issuer** is any person who issues (distributes) or proposes to issue a security. The most common issuers of securities are companies or governments (federal, state, and municipal governments and their agencies and subdivisions).

If an issuer is nonexempt, it must register its securities in the states where they will be sold under one of the registration methods described in the Unit.

EXAMPLE   ABC Shoe Co. (a retail chain store) issues shares to the public. Mr. Bixby (an investor) buys the shares through his broker, Mr. Thompson, at First Securities Corporation. ABC Shoe is the issuer; Mr. Bixby is the investor; First Securities is the broker/dealer; and Mr. Thompson is the registered representative, known under the USA as an agent.

Issuer Transaction

An **issuer transaction** is one in which the proceeds of the sale go to the issuer. All newly issued securities are issuer transactions. In other words, when a company raises money by selling (issuing) securities to investors, the proceeds from the sale go to the company itself.

Nonissuer Transaction

A **nonissuer transaction** is one in which the proceeds of the sales do not go, directly or indirectly, to the entity that originally offered the securities to the public. The most common instance of this is everyday trading on exchanges such as the New York Stock Exchange or Nasdaq. In a nonissuer transaction, the proceeds of the sale go to the investor who sold the shares.

TAKE NOTE   If Mr. Bixby, an investor, sells 100 shares of stock he owns in ABC Shoe Co. (the securities issuer) on the New York Stock Exchange (NYSE), Mr. Bixby receives the proceeds from the sale, not ABC Shoes. This is a nonissuer transaction.

Nonissuer transactions are also referred to as **secondary transactions** or transactions between investors.

INITIAL OR PRIMARY OFFERING

An issuer transaction involving new securities is called a **primary offering**. If it is the first time an issuer distributes securities to the public, it is called an **initial public offering (IPO)**. Initial or primary offerings are issuer transactions because the issuer (the company) receives the proceeds from the investor investing in the company.

EXAMPLE   The first time that ABC Shoe Co. issued shares to the public, ABC Shoe engaged in an IPO or a primary offering because it received the proceeds from distributing its shares to the public. After ABC Shoe went public, transactions between investors executed on exchanges through brokerage agents were secondary transactions in nonissuer securities.

QUICK QUIZ 2.5

1. Which of the following instruments are NOT securities?

    A. Stock, treasury stock, rights, warrants, and transferable shares
    B. Voting trust certificates and interests in oil and gas drilling programs
    C. Commodity futures contracts and fixed payment life insurance contracts
    D. Commodity options contracts and interests in multilevel distributorship arrangements

2. The US Supreme Court defined an investment contract as having four components. Which of the following is NOT part of the four-part test for an investment contract?

    A. An investment of money
    B. An expectation of profit
    C. Management activity by owner
    D. Solely from the efforts of others

3. Nonexempt securities

    A. need not be registered in the state in which they are sold
    B. must always be registered in the state in which they are sold
    C. need not be registered if sold in an exempt transaction
    D. need not be registered if sold in a nonexempt transaction

4. A nonissuer transaction is a transaction

    A. between two corporations where one is issuing the stock and the other is purchasing
    B. in which the issuing corporation will not receive the proceeds from the transaction
    C. where a mutual fund purchases a Treasury bond directly from the government
    D. in which the security must be registered

REGISTRATION OF SECURITIES UNDER THE UNIFORM SECURITIES ACT

Under the USA, it is unlawful for any person to offer or sell a security in a state unless the security, transaction, or offer is exempt from the USA's registration requirements. If the security is not exempt or is not a federal covered security as defined by the National Securities Markets Improvement Act, it must be registered in the state or it cannot be lawfully sold in the state.

NATIONAL SECURITIES MARKETS IMPROVEMENT ACT OF 1996 (NSMIA)

The US Congress, through its passage of the NSMIA, established the SEC as the regulator of nationally based securities activities, leaving the states with authority over state-based securities activities. Defining this relationship between state and federal regulation was accomplished under the NSMIA with the concept of federal covered securities.

A **federal covered security** is simply a security that has a federally imposed exemption from state regulation. Most securities sold today are federal covered securities.

CATEGORIES OF FEDERAL COVERED SECURITIES

The major categories of federal covered securities (securities covered by federal securities laws), which therefore cannot be regulated by state securities Administrators, include:

- **nationally traded securities** and those specific securities equal to or senior to them, such as

  — securities listed or authorized for listing on the NYSE and other SEC registered exchanges, and

  — securities included or qualified for inclusion in the Nasdaq Stock Market; and

- **investment company securities** registered under the Investment Company Act of 1940, such as

  — open-end management investment companies (mutual funds),

  — closed-end management investment companies,

  — unit investment trusts,

  — face-amount certificates; and

- **offers and sales of certain exempt securities,** such as

  — securities offered to qualified purchasers under Regulation D of the Securities Act of 1933 (private placement), and

  — securities offered by a municipal/governmental issuer unless the issuer is located in the state where the securities are being offered.

Nationally traded securities are securities that trade on the major exchanges regulated by the SEC. These exchanges register with the SEC and, in addition, are regulated by various self-regulatory organizations (SROs). The SEC, NASD, and the exchanges regulate nationally traded securities, so, as required by the NSMIA, states may not require registration. Such state regulation would be duplicative of federal registration.

Exempt securities (securities exempt from federal registration) are federal covered securities that states may not regulate. The most notable categories of exempt securities not subject to registration in the states are federal government securities, municipal securities and private placements (Regulation D securities).

TAKE NOTE   Although investment company securities are federal covered securities, the Uniform Securities Act allows states to impose filing fees on them under a process called notice filing, as described below.

Bonds issued by municipalities—for example, the City of New York bonds due 2020—are federal covered securities exempt from registration requirements in the states, but there is an exception to the rule. States may require registration of some types of municipal securities of their own states, but they may not require registration of municipal securities issued by other states. Why? Because municipal securities of other states are covered securities exempt from state registration. Municipal securities issued in an Administrator's state are not covered securities; they are not covered by the exemption (states retain authority over the issue of the municipal securities by their own municipalities).

TAKE NOTE   Effective July 3, 2006, Nasdaq renamed the Nasdaq National Market as the Nasdaq Global Market. In addition, they created an even higher tier known as the Nasdaq Global Select Market. On May 24, 2007, the SEC added Nasdaq Capital Market securities to the list of federal covered securities. The effect of these changes is that any security included any Nasdaq listing is considered to be federal covered.

METHODS OF STATE REGISTRATION OF SECURITIES

The USA provides three methods for securities issuers to register their securities in a state. They are:

- notification, or filing;
- coordination; and
- qualification.

NOTIFICATION (FILING)

The **notification** method of registering an issue—sometimes called **registration by notification** or **registration by filing**—applies to issuers who have registered their securities with the SEC under the Securities Act of 1933 but are not exempt from registration with the states where they intend to distribute their shares. Such securities are nonlisted securities that trade interstate, as opposed to within one state (intrastate), and as such they must register by filing.

State registration under this method is accomplished by filing with the state copies of all records filed with the SEC (including amendments). Securities filed under this method are federally registered but are not federal covered securities.

TAKE NOTE
States can require the registration of the securities of public offerings by nonbank, nongovernment issuers whose issues are traded in uncovered marketplaces such as the *Pink Sheets* or the OTC Bulletin Board. Notwithstanding the preemptive provisions of the NSMIA, state securities Administrators may require certain issuers whose securities are not traded on SEC-registered exchanges or the Nasdaq Stock Market to file copies of those documents filed with the SEC for notice purposes.

Qualifications for Notification

To qualify for registration by filing, the issuer must have filed a registration statement with the SEC and:

■ be organized under the laws of the United States or a state or have a designated American agent;

■ have been in continuous operation for at least three years and have filed all required reports with the SEC during that time;

■ have a class of equity securities of at least 400,000 shares held by at least 500 public shareholders—excluding securities held by officers and directors of the issuer, underwriters, and control persons owning 10% or more of that class of securities (warrants and options held by those persons cannot total more than 10% of the total number of shares);

■ have either

— total net worth of $4 million, or

— total net worth of $2 million and net pretax income from operations for two of the last three years;

■ not have defaulted in the payment of principal, interest, or dividends in the current fiscal year;

■ for 30 days during the preceding three months, have at least four registered market makers; and

■ each underwriter of the security must be an NASD member who has agreed to a maximum commission of 10% of the offering price (offering price must be at least $5 per share).

Required Documentation for Notification

To register a security in a state by **notification**, consent to service of process and the following documentation are required:

- A statement demonstrating eligibility for registration by filing

- The name, address, form of organization of the issuer, the amount of securities to be offered in the state, the states in which the offering will be registered, any adverse judgments pending, and a description of the security

- If part of the offering is made on behalf of a nonissuer, the name, address, amount of securities held by that nonissuer and the reasons for making the offering

- A copy of the latest prospectus filed with the registration statement

If no stop order is in effect and no proceeding is pending, the documentation has been on file with the Administrator for five days, and the filing fee was paid before the effectiveness of the federal registration statement, the registration becomes effective concurrently with the federal registration.

If the federal registration statement becomes effective before conditions are met on the state level, the registration statement becomes effective when the conditions are satisfied.

Notice Filing for Federal Covered Investment Companies

Although states are prohibited from requiring filings by federal covered issuers, an exemption was made for investment companies. This exemption was made to allow state securities administrative departments to collect fees from investment companies to offset state costs of the prosecution of fraudulent securities practices in their states.

Under the notice filing procedure, state Administrators may require the issuer to file the following documents as a condition for sale of their securities in the state:

- Documents filed along with their registration statements filed with the SEC

- Documents filed as amendments to the initial federal registration statement

- A report as to the value of such securities offered in the state

- Consent to service of process

TEST TOPIC ALERT

Before the initial offer of any federal covered security in this state, the Administrator, by rule or order, may require the filing of all documents that are part of a federal registration statement filed with the US Securities and Exchange Commission under the Securities Act of 1933, together with a consent to service of process signed by the issuer.

REGISTRATION BY COORDINATION

A security may be **registered by coordination** if a registration statement has been filed under the Securities Act of 1933 in connection with the same offering.

In coordinating a federal registration with state registration, issuers must supply the following records in addition to the consent to service of process:

- Copies of the latest form of prospectus filed under the Securities Act of 1933, if the Administrator requires it

- Copy of articles of incorporation and bylaws, a copy of the underwriting agreement, or a specimen copy of the security

- If the Administrator requests, copies of any other information filed by the issuer under the Securities Act of 1933

- Each amendment to the federal prospectus promptly after it is filed with the SEC

Effective Date

Registration by coordination becomes effective at the same time the federal registration becomes effective, provided:

- no stop orders have been issued by the Administrator and no proceedings are pending against the issuer;

- the registration has been on file for at least the minimum number of days specified by the Administrator, a number that currently ranges from 10 to 20 days, depending on the state; and

- a statement of the maximum and minimum offering prices and underwriting discounts have been on file for two business days.

Registration by coordination is by far the most frequently used method.

REGISTRATION BY QUALIFICATION

Any security can be **registered by qualification**. Registration by qualification requires a registrant to supply any information required by the state securities Administrator. Securities not eligible for registration by another method must be registered by qualification. In addition, securities that will be sold only in one state (intrastate) will be registered by qualification.

To register by qualification, an issuer must supply a consent to service of process and the following information:

- Name, address, form of organization, description of property, and nature of business

■ Information on directors and officers and every owner of 10% or more of the issuers securities, and the remuneration paid to owners in the last 12 months

■ Description of issuers' capitalization and long-term debt

■ Estimated proceeds and the use to which the proceeds will be put

■ Type and amount of securities offered, offering price, and selling and underwriting costs

■ Stock options to be created in connection with the offering

■ Copy of any prospectus, pamphlet, circular, or sales literature to be used in the offering

■ Specimen copy of the security along with opinion of counsel as to the legality of the security being offered

■ Audited balance sheet current within four months of the offering with an income statement for three years before the balance sheet date

The Administrator may require additional information by rule or order. The Administrator may require that a prospectus be sent to purchasers before the sale and that newly established companies register their securities for the first time in a state by qualification.

Effective Date

Unlike coordination, where the effective date is triggered by SEC acceptance of the registration, a registration by qualification becomes effective whenever the state Administrator so orders.

Regardless of the method used, every registration statement is effective for one year from its effective date. Unlike agent and broker/dealer registrations, the date December 31 is of no consequence. One interesting facet of the law is that the registration may continue in effect past the first anniversary if there are still some unsold shares remaining, as long as they are still being offered at the original public offering price by either the issuer or the underwriter.

QUICK QUIZ 2.6

True or False?

_____ 1. ABC Shoe Company, a new retail shoe store chain, has applied for the registration of its securities with the SEC as required by the Securities Act of 1933 and wants to register its securities in the state of Illinois. Simus would most likely register by coordination.

_____ 2. Any company may register by qualification whether or not it files a statement with the SEC.

EXEMPTIONS FROM REGISTRATION

In certain situations, the USA exempts both securities and transactions from registration and filing requirements of sales literature. A security, a transaction, or both, can be exempt.

An **exempt security** retains its exemption when initially issued and in subsequent trading. However, an **exempt transaction** must be established before each transaction. The two are not mutually exclusive.

The USA provides for a number of categories of exempt securities and even more categories of exempt transactions. Those securities that are **nonexempt** must register. Certain federal covered securities do not register with the Administrator but file a notice with the Administrator. As mentioned above, an **exempt security** retains its exemption at its initial issue and in subsequent trading.

An exemption for a transaction, on the other hand, must be established with each transaction. Provided it is in the public interest, the state Administrator can deny, suspend, or revoke any securities transaction exemption other than that of a federal covered security.

TAKE NOTE

A security is exempt because of the nature of the issuer, not the purchaser.

An **exempt transaction** is exempt from the regulatory control of the state Administrator because of the manner in which a sale is made or because of the person to whom the sale is made. A transaction is an action and must be judged by the merits of each instance.

The USA prohibits the sale of securities in the state unless they are registered in the state, exempt from registration in the state, or subject to an exempt transaction. For example, an agent can sell a security that is not exempt in the state if the purchaser of the security is a bank or other institutional buyer. Because the sale is an exempt transaction, the sale can be made without registration. This means that the securities sold in exempt transactions do not have to be registered in the state. If such securities were not sold in exempt transactions, such as to an individual investor, they would have to be registered in the state.

EXEMPT SECURITIES

Securities exempt from state registration are also exempt from state filing of sales literature. Exempt securities include the following.

- **US and Canadian government and municipal securities**. These include securities issued, insured, or guaranteed by the United States or Canada, by a state or province, or by their political subdivisions.

- **Foreign government securities**. These include securities issued, insured, or guaranteed by a foreign government with which the United States maintains diplomatic relations.

- **Depository institutions**. These include securities that are issued, guaranteed by, or are a direct obligation of a depository institution (depository institution means any bank, savings institution, or trust company organized and supervised under the laws of the United States or any state). Securities issued by a savings and loan association are exempt only if the institution is authorized to do business in the state.

- **Insurance company securities**. These include securities issued, insured, or guaranteed by an insurance company authorized to do business in the state. Insurance company securities refer to the stocks or bonds issued by insurance companies, not the variable policies sold by the companies. Fixed insurance and annuity policies are not securities.

- **Public utility securities**. These include any security issued or guaranteed by a public utility or public utility holding company, or an equipment trust certificate issued by a railroad or other common carrier regulated in respect to rates by federal or state authority; or regulated in respect to issuance or guarantee of the security by a governmental authority of the United States, any state, Canada, or any Canadian province.

- **Federal covered securities.** These include any security of that issuer equal to or senior to it. This would include rights, warrants, preferred stock, and any debt security.

- **Securities issued by nonprofit organizations**. These include securities issued by religious, educational, fraternal, charitable, social, athletic, reformatory, or trade associations.

- **Securities issued by cooperatives**. These include securities issued by a nonprofit membership cooperative to members of that cooperative.

- **Securities of employee benefit plans**. This includes any investment contract issued by an employee stock purchase, saving, pension, or profit-sharing plan.

- **Certain money market instruments**. Commercial paper and banker's acceptances are the two most common examples.

TAKE NOTE

A promissory note (commercial paper), draft, bill of exchange, or banker's acceptance that matures within nine months, is issued in denominations of at least $50,000, and receives one of the three highest ratings by a nationally recognized rating agency is exempt from registration requirements. Please note that this is the only case where a security's rating is part of the registration or exemption under the Uniform Securities Act.

QUICK QUIZ 2.7

1. Which of the following securities are exempt from registration and advertising filing requirements under the USA?

    I.   Shares of investment companies registered under the Investment Company Act of 1940
    II.   Shares sold on the Nasdaq Global Market System
    III. AAA rated promissory notes of $100,000 that mature in 30 days
    IV.   Shares sold on the New York Stock Exchange

    A. I only
    B. II, III and IV
    C. II and IV
    D. I, II, III and IV

2. Which of the following securities is NOT exempt from the registration and advertising requirements of the USA?

    A. Shares of Commonwealth Edison, a public utility holding company
    B. Securities issued by the Carnegie Endowment for Peace
    C. Securities issued by a bank that is a member of the Federal Reserve System
    D. Variable annuity contract issued by Prudential Insurance

EXEMPT TRANSACTIONS

Before a security can be sold in a state, it must be registered unless exempt from registration, or traded in an exempt transaction. This section covers exemptions for transactions that take place in a state.

There are many different types of **exempt transactions**. We begin by focusing on those most likely to be on your exam and finish with several others.

- **Isolated nonissuer transactions.** Isolated nonissuer transactions include secondary (nonissuer) transactions, whether effected through a broker or not, that occur infrequently (very few transactions per broker per year; the exact number varies by state). However, these usually do not involve securities professionals. In the same manner that individuals placing a "for sale by owner" sign on their front lawns do not need a real estate license, one individual selling stock to another in a one-on-one transaction is engaging in a transaction exempt from the oversight of the Administrator, because the issuer is not receiving any of the proceeds, and the parties involved are not trading as part of a regular practice.

- **Unsolicited brokerage transactions.** These include transactions initiated by the client, not the agent. This is probably the most common of the exempt transactions. If a client calls a registered agent and requests that the agent buy or sell a security, the transaction is an unsolicited brokerage transaction exempt from state registration.

- **Underwriter transactions.** These include transactions between issuer and underwriter as well as those between underwriters themselves.

- **Bankruptcy, guardian, or conservator transactions.** Transactions by an executor, administrator, sheriff, or trustee in bankruptcy are exempt transactions. Please note that a custodian under UGMA or UTMA is not included in this list.

- **Institutional investor transactions.** These are primarily transactions with financial institutions.

- **Limited offering transactions.** These include any offering, called a private placement, directed at not more than 10 persons other than institutional investors during the previous 12 consecutive months, provided that

  — the seller believes that all of the noninstitutional buyers are purchasing for investment purposes only,

  — no commissions or other remuneration is paid for soliciting noninstitutional investors, and

  — no general solicitation or advertising is used.

Unlike federal law, where the private placement rule restricts the number of purchasers, the USA restricts the number of offers that may be made.

- **Preorganization certificates.** An offer or sale of a preorganization certificate or subscription is exempt if

  — no commission or other renumeration is paid or given directly or indirectly for soliciting any subscriber,

  — the number of subscribers does not exceed 10, and

  — no payment is made by any subscriber.

A preorganization certificate is a certificate to subscribe to an issue of securities. The certificate is issued before the organization of the issuer itself.

- **Transactions with existing security holders.** A transaction made under an offer to existing security holders of the issuer (including persons who are holders of convertible securities, rights, or warrants) is exempt as long as no commission or other form of remuneration is paid directly or indirectly for soliciting that security holder.

- **Specified nonissuer transactions.** These include nonissuer transactions by a registered agent, provided that the security has been outstanding in the public's hands for at least 90 days and the issuer has

  — registered a class of securities under the Securities Exchange Act of 1934, or

  — filed and maintained information comparable to that required under the Securities Exchange Act of 1934 with the Administrator for 180 days.

Most transactions that occur in federal covered securities, including securities of Investment Companies registered under the Investment Company Act of 1940, are traded in exempt transactions.

The following are examples of exempt transactions that are unlikely to be on your exam.

- **Nonissuer transactions by pledgees.** A nonissuer transaction executed by a bona fide pledgee (i.e., the one who received the security as collateral for a loan), as long as it was not for the purpose of evading the act, is a nonissuer transaction.

- **Unit secured transactions.** These include transactions in a bond backed by a real mortgage or deed of trust provided that the entire mortgage or deed of trust is sold as a unit.

- **Control transactions.** This includes mergers, consolidations, or reorganization transactions to which the issuer and the other person or its parent or subsidiary are parties.

- **Rescission offers.** These include offers made to rescind an improper transaction.

TEST TOPIC ALERT

Remember the distinction between an accredited investor and institutional investor. An **accredited investor** is an investor who meets the accredited investor standards of Regulation D. Rule 501 of Regulation D considers an individual with net worth greater than $1 million on the date of purchase, singly or with a spouse, including principal residence, to meet the definition of accredited investor. Alternatively, one may qualify with earnings greater than $200,000 per year ($300,000 if including spouse) in each of the previous two years and a reasonable expectation of reaching that level in the current year. This term only applies to federal law, not the USA, and will probably never be the correct answer to a USA question.

An **institutional investor** is an investor that manages large amounts of money for other people, such as a mutual fund, an insurance company, a bank, or a pension fund.

Administrator's Powers

The USA grants the Administrator the authority, by rule or order, to exempt a security, transaction, or offer from the USA's registration and filing requirements. In addition, the Administrator may waive a requirement for an exemption of a transaction or security.

The Administrator may, by rule or order, deny or revoke any exemption with respect to a security or transaction, other than that of a federal covered security, upon prior notice to the interested parties. The Administrator must also provide an opportunity for a hearing within 15 days of a written request. The Administrator also has the power to summarily deny or revoke exemptions pending final determination of any proceedings.

Under the USA, the burden of providing an exemption or an exception from a definition falls upon the person claiming it.

QUICK QUIZ 2.8

Indicate an exempt transaction with **Y** and a nonexempt transaction with **N**.

_____ 1. Mr. Thompson, an agent with First Securities, Inc. (a broker/dealer), receives an unsolicited request to purchase a security for Mary Gordon, a high net worth individual

_____ 2. The sale of an unregistered security in a private, nonpublicly advertised transaction, offered to 10 or fewer investors over the last 12 months

_____ 3. The sale of unclaimed securities by the Administrator of securities for the state of New Mexico

_____ 4. Sale of stock of a privately owned company to the public in an initial public offering

5. Which of the following are exempt transactions?

 I. A nonissuer transaction with a bank in a Nasdaq Capital Market Security
 II. An unsolicited request from an existing client to purchase a nonexempt security
 III. The sale of an unregistered security in a private, nonpublicly advertised transaction to 10 noninstitutional purchasers over a period not exceeding 12 months
 IV. The sale of unlisted securities by a trustee in bankruptcy

 A. I and II
 B. I, II and III
 C. I, II and IV
 D. I, II, III and IV

STATE SECURITIES REGISTRATION PROCEDURES

The first step in the registration procedure is for the issuer or its representative to pick up a registration statement or application from the state securities Administrator. The person registering the securities is known as the **registrant**.

TEST TOPIC ALERT

Although most registration statements are filed by the issuer, the exam may require you to know that they may also be filed by any selling stockholder, such as a large block sale by an insider, or a broker/dealer.

FILING THE REGISTRATION STATEMENT

State Administrators require every issuer to supply the following information on their applications:

■ Amount of securities to be issued in the state

■ States in which the security is to be offered, but not the amounts offered in those other states

■ Any adverse order or judgment concerning the offering by regulatory authorities, court, or the SEC

When filing the registration statement with the Administrator, an applicant may include documents that have been filed with the Administrator within the last five years, provided the information is current and accurate. The Administrator may, by rule or order, permit the omission of any information it considers unnecessary.

Filing Fee

The issuer (or any other person on whose behalf the offering is to be made) must pay a filing fee, as determined by the Administrator, when filing the registration. The filing fees are often based on a percentage of the total offering price.

If the registration is withdrawn or if the Administrator issues a stop order before the registration is effective, the Administrator may retain a portion of the fee and refund the remainder to the applicant.

Ongoing Reports

The Administrator may require the person who filed the registration statement to file reports to keep the information contained in the registration statement current and to inform the Administrator of the progress of the offering.

TEST TOPIC ALERT　　　These reports cannot be required more often than quarterly.

Escrow

As a condition of registration, the Administrator may require that a security be placed in **escrow** if the security is issued:

■ within the past three years;

■ at a price substantially different than the offering price; or

■ to any person for a consideration other than cash.

Special Subscription Form

The Administrator may also require, as a condition of registration, that the issue be sold only on a form specified by the Administrator and that a copy of the form or subscription contract be filed with the Administrator or preserved for up to three years.

Withdrawal of Registration Statement

A registration statement may not be withdrawn until one year after its effective date, if any securities of the same class are outstanding, and may be withdrawn only with the approval of the Administrator.

The Administrator has the power under the USA to deny, suspend, or revoke the registration of a security; however, the Administrator can invoke these powers only if it is in the public's interest and:

■ the applicant files a false or incomplete statement;

■ the applicant is in violation of the USA;

■ the applicant is engaged in a method of business that is illegal;

■ the applicant has prepared a fraudulent registration;

■ the underwriter charges unreasonable fees; or

■ the issue is subject to a court injunction.

In addition, the Administrator may deny a registration if the applicant fails to pay the filing fee. When the fee is paid, the denial order will be removed provided the applicant is in compliance with all registration procedures.

QUICK QUIZ 2.9

1. With regard to the registration requirements of the Uniform Securities Act, which of the following are TRUE?

   I. Only the issuer itself can file a registration statement with the Administrator.
   II. An application for registration must indicate the amount of securities to be issued in the state.
   III. The Administrator may require registrants to file quarterly reports.

   A. I and II
   B. I and III
   C. II and III
   D. I, II and III

ANTIFRAUD PROVISIONS OF THE USA

Fraudulent activity may occur when conducting securities sales or when providing investment advice. Each of these categories is discussed separately. In general, **fraud** means the deliberate or willful attempt to deceive someone for profit or gain.

FRAUDULENT AND PROHIBITED PRACTICES IN THE SALE OF SECURITIES

Under the USA, state securities Administrators can prohibit those business practices that securities industry self-regulatory agencies, such as NASD, prohibit. The North American Securities Administrators Association (NASAA), in their policy statements, publish lists of fraudulent and unethical business practices that agents and representative must not engage in. See Appendix C of this license exam manual for the important policy statement regarding the ethical behavior of broker/dealers and agents. Appendix C is an integral part of this course and should be studied carefully.

State securities laws modeled on the USA address fraud by making it unlawful for any person, when engaged in the offer, sale, or purchase of any security, directly or indirectly, to:

■ use any device, scheme, or artifice to defraud;

■ make any untrue statement of a material fact or omit to state a material fact necessary to make a statement not misleading; or

■ engage in any act, practice, or course of business that operates as a fraud or deceit on a person.

TAKE NOTE   There are no exceptions to the antifraud provisions of state securities laws. They pertain to any person or transaction whether the person or transaction is registered, exempt, or federal covered. Prevention of fraud is one of the few areas of securities law where the states have full authority to act.

Although the USA does not list the prohibited practices, the following have been held by courts, regulatory agencies, and state Administrators to be fraudulent, dishonest, or unethical practices that will be prosecuted by state securities regulators.

The major categories of fraudulent and unethical behavior include:

■ misleading or untrue statements;

■ failure to state material facts;

■ using inside information;

■ making unsuitable investment recommendations;

■ exercising discretion without previous written authority;

■ loaning money to or borrowing money or securities from clients;

■ commingling customer funds and securities with those of the broker/dealer or agent;

■ guaranteeing client profits;

■ sharing in client accounts; and

■ market manipulation.

Misleading or Untrue Statements

Securities laws prohibit any person from making any **misleading** or **untrue statements of material fact** in connection with the purchase or sale of a security. Not all facts are material. The law defines **material** as information that is used by a prospective purchaser to make an investment decision. In other words, when selling securities to their clients, agents must not deliberately conceal a material fact to encourage a client to buy or sell a security. Such an act would constitute deliberate deceit for personal gain.

An agent who inadvertently provides a client with an inaccurate address of a company whose shares the client was interested in purchasing would not likely be making an untrue statement of a material fact. Investors do not purchase shares on the basis of the company's street address. On the other hand, investors do make investment decisions based on the qualifications of a company's management. Deliberately misstating those qualifications would therefore be material fact. To misstate them is fraud.

The following are examples of material facts that constitute fraud if misstated by agents knowingly and willfully.

- **Inaccurate market quotations**. Telling a client the stock is up when the reverse is true is obviously an improper action. However, it would not be considered fraud if the inaccuracy were due to a malfunction of the quote machine or an unintended clerical error. To be considered fraud, the action must be deliberate.

- **Misstatements of an issuer's earnings or projected earnings or dividends**. Telling a client that earnings are up, or that the dividend will be increased when such is not the case, is a fraudulent action. However, it would not be fraud if you were quoting a news release that was incorrect.

- **Inaccurate statements as to the amount of commissions, markup, or markdown**. There are circumstances where the amount of commission or markup may be higher than normal. That is permissible, as long as it is disclosed properly. But telling a client that it costs him nothing to trade with your firm because you never charge a commission, and not informing him that all trades are done on a principal basis with a markup or markdown, is fraud.

- **Telling a customer that a security will be listed on an exchange without concrete information concerning its listing status**. Years ago, before Nasdaq Global Market (NGM) securities, an announcement that a stock was going to be listed on the NYSE invariably caused its market price to jump. Even though it doesn't have the same significance today (a better example would be a Nasdaq Capital Market stock going NGM), any statement of this type relating to a change in marketplace for the security is only permitted if, in fact, you have knowledge that such change is imminent.

- **Informing a client that the registration of a security with the SEC or with the state securities Administrator means that the security has been approved by these regulators**. Registration never implies approval.

- **Misrepresenting the status of customer accounts.** This behavior is fraudulent. Many people are not motivated to pay strict attention to their monthly account statements, making it relatively easy for an unscrupulous agent to fraudulently claim increasing values in the account when the opposite is true. Doing so would be a fraudulent action.

- **Promising a customer services without any intent to perform them or without being properly qualified to perform them.** You say, "Yes, I can" to your client, even if you know you can't deliver. For instance, the client asks you to analyze her bond portfolio to determine the average duration. Even though you don't know how to do that, you agree to do so. Under the USA, you committed fraud.

- **Representing to customers that the Administrator approves of the broker/dealer or agent's abilities.** This is another case of using the word *approve* improperly. A broker/dealer or agent is registered, not approved.

TEST TOPIC ALERT

Merely learning the terms is not enough to get you through the exam. On the exam, you must be able to identify situations in which violations occur. Be able to apply the concepts of fraud and unethical behavior to scenarios that are likely to occur in conducting everyday business.

CASE STUDY

Making Leading or Untrue Statements

Situation: Mr. Thompson, a registered securities agent in Illinois, informs a long-standing client, Ms. Gordon, that her largest equity holding, First Tech Internet Services, Inc., will be listed on the New York Stock Exchange upon completion of its application for listing. In addition, he exaggerates the earnings by $1 per share to make her more comfortable and encourage her to buy more shares. Thompson is convinced the earnings will rise to that amount and does not want Ms. Gordon to sell because he believes the stock will appreciate in price once listed on the exchange. He also tells her that, because his firm will not be charging her any commission on the trade as they already have the stock in inventory, she will be ahead from the start.

Analysis: Mr. Thompson violated the USA by deliberately misrepresenting the earnings of First Tech Internet Services. Although Mr. Thompson's motives may have been good, he must be truthful in his effort to encourage clients to purchase more stock—his conviction that stock would rise upon its listing on the NYSE is not sufficient. No violation of the act occurred with respect to First Tech's exchange listing because Mr. Thompson knew that the stock was in registration to be listed on the NYSE. Stating that the firm will not charge a commission, but failing to state that a sale from inventory would include a markup, is a fraudulent act.

Failure to State Material Facts

The USA does not require an agent to provide all information about an investment, only the information that is material to making an informed investment decision. However, the agent must not fail to mention material information that could have an impact on the price of the security. In addition, the agent may not state facts that in and of themselves are not untrue but, as a result of deliberately omitting others, render the recommendation misleading under the circumstances.

CASE STUDY | **Failure to State Material Facts**

Situation: Upon NYSE acceptance of the listing application, there is an announcement that First Tech Internet Services will publish its financial statements in a newspaper advertisement. Mr. Thompson deliberately failed to mention this advertisement to Ms. Gordon.

After its listing on the NYSE, the research department in Mr. Thompson's firm prepares a negative report on First Tech. The research department discovered a change in accounting practices that will have a detrimental affect on subsequent earnings reported by First Tech. Mr. Thompson continues to recommend the stock to Ms. Gordon because he believes the increased exposure gained by the exchange listing will outweigh the future decline in earnings. As a result, Thompson neglects to inform Ms. Gordon of the change before her purchase of additional shares.

Analysis: Mr. Thompson violated the USA even though he made no misleading statements to Ms. Gordon with respect to First Tech. Mr. Thompson did not have to mention the advertisement in the paper because it is not material, yet he violated the act when he failed to mention the accounting change that would result in significantly lower earnings. Although an accounting change is not ordinarily a material fact, in this case it was because it would have a detrimental impact on the company's earnings and its market price.

Using Inside Information

Making recommendations based on material inside information about an issuer or its securities is prohibited. Should an agent come into possession of inside information, the agent must report the possession of the information to a supervisor or compliance officer.

TAKE NOTE | Material inside information under securities law is any information about a company that has not been communicated to the general public and that would likely have an impact on the value of a security.

CASE STUDY | **Using Inside Information**

Situation: Mr. Thompson is a friend and neighbor of Ms. Cage, president and owner of more than half of First Tech's securities. Ms. Cage discloses to Mr. Thompson that the company has just discovered a new technology that will double First Tech's earnings within the next year. No one outside of the company, except for Mr. Thompson, knows of this discovery. On this basis, Mr. Thompson buys additional shares of First Tech for his client, Ms. Gordon.

Analysis: The information on First Tech's new technology is material inside information that has not been made public. It is material information that only Mr. Thompson and company officials know. Mr. Thompson violated the USA in acting on this information. Mr. Thompson should have communicated the possession of the information to his compliance officer and refrained from making recommendations on the basis of this information.

Making Unsuitable Investment Recommendations

Agents must always have reasonable grounds for making recommendations to clients. Before making recommendations, the agent must inquire into the client's financial status, investment objectives, and ability to assume financial risk.

The following practices violate the suitability requirements under the USA as well as the rules of fair practice that regulatory agencies have developed. A securities professional may not:

- recommend securities transactions without regard to customer financial situation, needs, or investment objectives;

- induce transactions solely to generate commissions (i.e., churning, which is defined as transactions in customer accounts that are excessive in size or frequency, in relation to the client's financial resources, objectives, or the character of the account);

- recommend a security without reasonable grounds; or

- fail to sufficiently describe the important facts and risks concerning a transaction or security.

 C A S E S T U D Y

Making Unsuitable Investment Recommendations

Situation: Mr. Thompson has a wide variety of clients: high net worth individuals, trusts, retirees with limited incomes and resources, and college students. Mr. Thompson has strong beliefs about First Tech, a growth stock that pays no dividends. He forcefully recommends the stock to all his clients without informing them of the volatility of First Tech and the research department's pending downgrade in earnings. He also informs his clients of the new technology breakthrough that Ms. Cage, the president of First Tech, had revealed to him in confidence.

Analysis: Mr. Thompson has violated the USA on several counts. First, he made a recommendation without regard to the separate financial conditions, needs, and objectives of his diverse client base. The recommendation is unsuitable for the investment objectives of his retired clients with fixed incomes and limited financial resources. In addition, he made the recommendation in an unsuitable manner by failing to reveal the earnings volatility or risk and the downgrade in earnings, and then he revealed inside information to clients while making recommendations based on that information.

Exercising Discretion Without Prior Written Authority

Agents of broker/dealers may not exercise discretion in an account without **prior written authority (power of attorney)** from the client. Prior written authority is also known as **trading authorization.**

Discretion is given to an agent by the client when the client authorizes (in writing) the agent to act on his own, to use his discretion, in deciding the following for the client:

- Asset (security)

- Action (buy or sell)

- Amount (how many shares)

However, merely authorizing an agent to determine the best price or time to trade a security is not considered to be discretion.

CASE STUDY

Discretionary Trading Authorization

Situation: Mr. Thompson's client, Mr. Bixby, has indicated over the phone that he authorizes Mr. Thompson to make trades for him. Mr. Bixby's family lawyer, Ms. Derval, has specific power of attorney over some of Mr. Bixby's businesses. Mr. Bixby promised Mr. Thompson that he would send in the trading authorization within the next day or two to give Thompson discretion over the account. However, Mr. Thompson immediately executed trades in First Tech for Mr. Bixby to take advantage of its impending NYSE listing.

The following week, Mr. Thompson received Mr. Bixby's written discretionary trading authorization. On the day after the authorization arrived, Mr. Bixby's attorney, Ms. Derval, indicated that Mr. Bixby would like to buy shares in XYZ Corp. Because Ms. Derval has power of attorney for Mr. Bixby, Mr. Thompson bought the shares.

Analysis: Mr. Thompson violated the USA by trading in Mr. Bixby's account before receipt of the written trading authorization. Having authorization in the mail is not sufficient. Mr. Thompson also violated the USA by accepting the order from Ms. Derval because although she is Bixby's attorney, she was not specifically authorized to trade in Mr. Bixby's securities account. The trading authorization signed by Mr. Bixby only gave authority to Mr. Thompson. Had Ms. Derval provided Thompson with specific written third-party trading authorization from Mr. Bixby, Mr. Thompson then could have accepted the order for XYZ Corp. without a violation of the act.

Loaning Money to or Borrowing Money or Securities from Clients

Securities professionals may not borrow money or securities from a client unless the client is a broker/dealer, an affiliate of the professional, or a financial institution engaged in the business of loaning money.

Securities professionals may not loan money to clients unless the firm is a broker/dealer or financial institution engaged in the business of loaning funds or the client is an affiliate.

Borrowing Money or Securities from Clients

Situation: On occasion, Mr. Thompson borrows cash from his discretionary client, Mr. Bixby, when Mr. Bixby's account is not invested fully. Mr. Bixby has given Mr. Thompson much latitude because Mr. Thompson has done well in managing the account and Mr. Thompson always repays the money in time to reinvest Mr. Bixby's funds in new securities purchases. Thompson justifies these borrowings as being within the discretionary power Mr. Bixby had granted him. The First National Bank is also a client of Mr. Thompson, but he does not borrow from the bank because it charges unusually high interest rates.

Analysis: Mr. Thompson has engaged in a prohibited practice because securities professionals may not borrow from customers who are not in the business of lending money. Furthermore, Mr. Thompson violated the USA in exceeding the specific discretionary authority that Mr. Bixby had authorized. Mr. Bixby had authorized Mr. Thompson to trade in securities—not to take his money for personal use. Had Mr. Thompson decided to borrow from The First National Bank, that would have been permitted because the bank is an entity engaged in the business of lending money.

Commingling Customer Funds and Securities

Securities that are held in customer name must not be **commingled** (mixed) with those of the firm.

If a firm has 100,000 shares of XYZ Corp. stock in its own proprietary account and its clients separately own an additional 100,000 shares, the firm may not place customer shares in the firm's proprietary account.

To mix shares together would give undue leverage or borrowing power to a firm and could jeopardize the security of client securities in the event of default.

Guaranteeing Client Profits

Securities professionals may not guarantee a certain performance, nor may they guarantee against a loss by providing funds to the account.

The term *guaranteed* under the USA means "guaranteed as to payment of principal, interest, or dividends." It is allowable to refer to a guaranteed security when an entity other than the issuer is making the guarantee. However, the regulatory agencies of the securities industry prohibit securities professionals from guaranteeing the performance returns of an investment or portfolio.

Sharing in Client Accounts

Agents cannot share in the profits or losses of client accounts unless the client and the broker/dealer supply prior written approval and the account is jointly owned. Furthermore, the gains and losses must be in proportion to the funds invested. In such a situation, it would be permissible to commingle the agent's and the customer's funds.

An agent and a customer can have a joint account in which they share profits and losses in proportion to the amount invested. However, clients and a broker/dealer cannot have joint accounts.

Market Manipulation

Securities legislation is designed to uphold the integrity of markets and transactions in securities. However, market integrity is violated when transactions misrepresent actual securities prices or market activity. The most common forms of market manipulation are **front running** and **matching purchases**.

Front running is the practice of entering an order for the benefit of a firm or a securities professional before entering customer orders.

If a securities professional receives an order from an institutional client to purchase a large number of shares, the securities representative or firm cannot enter a personal order before completing the customer's purchase in an effort to benefit from a likely price rise.

Matched purchases occur when market participants agree to buy and sell securities among themselves to create the appearance of activity or trading in a security. Increased volume in a security can induce unsuspecting investors to purchase the security, thereby bidding up the price. As the price rises, those who initiated the matched purchases sell their securities at a profit.

TAKE NOTE

Arbitrage is the simultaneous buying and selling of the same security in different markets to take advantage of different prices; it is not a form of market manipulation. Simultaneously buying a security in one market and selling it in another forces prices to converge and, therefore, provides uniform prices for the general public.

OTHER PROHIBITED PRACTICES WHEN ENGAGED IN THE SALE OF SECURITIES

Security industry regulatory agencies have determined that the following practices violate industry standards of fair practice and, as a result, are prohibited when engaged in selling securities:

- Deliberately failing to follow a customer's order

- Effecting transactions with customers not recorded on the books of the employing broker/dealer without express prior written consent

- Failing to bring written customer complaints to the attention of the employing broker/dealer

- Failing to inform customers that certain transactions involve larger than ordinary commissions, taxes, or transaction costs

- Soliciting orders for unregistered, nonexempt securities

- Spreading rumors

- Recommending transactions on the basis of rumors

- Failure to disclose capacity (whether the firm acted as a broker or a dealer) on a trade confirmation

- Dividing or otherwise splitting the agent's commissions for the purchase or sale of securities with any person not also registered as an agent for the same broker/dealer, or for an affiliated broker/dealer

- Backdating any records, including confirmations

- Attempting to obtain a written agreement for a customer that he will not sue the agent even though the sale of certain securities is in violation of state law; any such agreement or waiver is not valid

---

CASE STUDY

Practices—Trades Not on the Books

Situation: Mr. Thompson, a registered agent for First Securities, Inc., of Illinois, is also a part owner of Computer Resources, Inc., a privately held company in the state. Mr. Thompson is also a friend of Ms. Byers, the chairman of Aircraft Parts, Inc., a large manufacturing company traded on the New York Stock Exchange. Ms. Byers has an account with Mr. Thompson at First Securities.

Mr. Thompson decides to sell his shares in Computer Resources to one of his clients. Because the shares are not publicly traded, Mr. Thompson completes the trades without informing First Securities or recording the transaction on their books. Mr. Thompson believes there is no need to inform his employer because the transaction was private. On the following day, Ms. Byers calls Mr. Thompson and indicates that she would like to sell her shares in Aircraft Parts. Mr. Thompson, who now has plenty of liquid assets from the sale of his shares in Computer Resources, decides to buy the shares directly from Ms. Byers. Mr. Thompson does not record the trade on the records of First Securities because he considers it a private transaction between himself and Ms. Byers.

Analysis: In both cases, Mr. Thompson has engaged in a prohibited practice. A registered agent may not conduct transactions with customers of his employing broker/dealer that are not recorded on the books without prior written consent. It makes no difference whether the shares Mr. Thompson sold were privately held—when an agent effects trades with clients of the firm, they must be recorded on the books of the firm unless prior written authorization is obtained from the firm.

CASE STUDY

Practices—Customer Complaints and Front Running

Situation: Upon completion of the sale of her shares in Aircraft Parts, Inc., Ms. Byers has considerable funds to invest. Mr. Thompson then recommends to Ms. Byers that she purchase ABC Shoes, a thinly traded chain store that analysts with First Securities have highly recommended subsequent to its initial public offering. Ms. Byers agrees. Just before entering Ms. Byers's order, Mr. Thompson purchases several hundred shares for himself. Ms. Byers learned of Mr. Thompson's purchase and wrote him a stinging letter of complaint about it. Because Mr. Thompson considered the transaction a private matter, he did not think it necessary to bring the letter to the attention of First Securities. A few days later, Mr. Thompson personally apologized to Ms. Byers and took her out for a drink.

Analysis: Mr. Thompson has engaged in two practices that violate industry practice. First, although the recommendation of ABC Shoes was perfectly appropriate, it was not appropriate for Mr. Thompson to enter his personal order for the same shares before completing Ms. Byers's purchase. This is known as **front running**, a prohibited practice. Additionally, Mr. Thompson (as a registered agent) must bring all written complaints to the attention of his employer. Had Ms. Byers simply lodged a verbal complaint, Mr. Thompson would not have been under an obligation to bring it to the attention of the manager of his office. Taking Ms. Byers out for a drink did not violate industry standards.

TEST TOPIC ALERT

Know how to recognize fraudulent, unethical, and prohibited practices. On your exam, you will be given various situations or scenarios and asked to determine which of NASAA's policy statements on ethical practices is violated. NASAA policy statements are contained in the Appendixes B and C to this learning exam manual. Review them carefully before your take your exam.

QUICK QUIZ 2.10

Write **U** for unlawful or prohibited activities and **L** for lawful activities.

_____ 1. An agent guarantees a client that funds invested in mutual funds made up of government securities cannot lose principal.

_____ 2. A nondiscretionary customer calls his agent and places a buy order for 1,000 shares of any hot Internet company. Later in the day, the representative enters an order for 1,000 shares of Global Internet Services.

_____ 3. An agent receives a call from his client's spouse advising him to sell her husband's securities. Her husband is out of the country and requested that his wife call the agent. The agent refuses because the wife does not have trading authorization and she complains vigorously to his manager.

_____ 4. A client writes a letter of complaint to his agent regarding securities that the agent had recommended. The agent calls the client to apologize and then disposes of the letter because the client seemed satisfied.

_____ 5. A registered agent borrows $10,000 from a credit union that is one of her best customers.

_____ 6. An agent is convinced that Internet Resources will rise significantly over the next 3 months. She offers to buy the stock back from her customers at 10% higher than its current price at any time during the next 3 months.

_____ 7. An agent receives an order for the purchase of an obscure foreign security. The agent informs the client that the commissions and charges on this purchase will be much higher than those of domestic securities.

_____ 8. An agent who works for a small broker that employs no securities analysts assures her clients that she can analyze any publicly traded security better than any analyst and that she will do it personally for each security purchased by a client, regardless of the industry.

_____ 9. A securities sales agent recommends that her client buy 1,000 shares of Internet Consultants, Inc., an unregistered nonexempt security with a bright future.

JURISDICTION AND POWERS OF THE STATE ADMINISTRATOR

The jurisdiction and powers of the Administrator extend to activities related to securities transactions originated in the state, directed to the state, and accepted in the state.

SALE OR SELL AND OFFER OR OFFER TO SELL

Sale or Sell

The USA defines **sale** or **sell** as every contract of sale, contract to sell, and disposition of a security or interest in a security for value. This means that any transfer of a security in which money or some other valuable consideration is involved is covered by this definition and subject to the act.

Offer or Offer to Sell

The USA defines **offer** or **offer to sell** as every attempt or offer to dispose of, or solicitation of an offer to buy, a security or interest in a security for value. These terms include any:

■ security given or delivered with, or as a bonus on account of, any purchase of securities or other items constituting part of the purchase;

■ gift of assessable stock (assessable stock is stock issued below par for which the issuer or creditors have the right to assess shareholders for the balance of unpaid par); or

■ warrant or right to purchase or subscribe to another security (an offer of the other security is considered to be included in the warrant or right).

If a car dealer, as an essential part of a sale, offers $1,000 in corporate bonds as an incentive, this would be considered a bonus under the act and, therefore, this sale falls under the jurisdiction of the state securities Administrator. As a result, to do this, the car dealer would have to register with the state as a broker/dear.

When assessable stock is given as a gift, the Administrator has jurisdiction over the transaction because there is a potential future obligation in that either the issuer or, more likely, creditors can demand payment for the balance of the par value.

TAKE NOTE

If an individual owned assessable stock and felt that the issuer was on the verge of bankruptcy, that person could give the stock as a present. If the bankruptcy occurred, the new owner would then be subject to the assessment.

TEST TOPIC ALERT

There is no longer any assessable stock in existence, but the exam may ask about it anyway.

The terms *offer* or *offer to sell* do not include any:

- bona fide pledge or loan;

- gift of nonassessable stock;

- stock dividend or stock split, if nothing of value is given by the stockholders for the additional shares;

- class vote by stockholders, pursuant to the certificate of incorporation or the applicable corporation statute, or a merger, consolidation, reclassification of securities, or sale of corporate assets in consideration of the issuance of securities of another corporation; or

- act incident to a judicially approved reorganization with which a security is issued in exchange for one or more outstanding securities, claims, or property interest, or partly in such exchange and partly for cash.

JURISDICTION OF THE ADMINISTRATOR

Under law, for any agent of a state (e.g., the Administrator) to have authority over an activity such as a sale or offer of securities, it must have **legal jurisdiction** to act. Jurisdiction under the USA specifically means the legal authority to regulate securities activities that take place in the state.

The USA describes those activities considered to have taken place in the state as any offer to buy or sell a security, as well as any acceptance of the offer, if the offer:

- **originated in** the Administrator's state;

- is **directed to** the Administrator's state; or

- is **accepted in** the Administrator's state.

TAKE NOTE   Because securities transactions often involve several states, more than one Administrator may have jurisdiction over a security or a transaction.

CASE STUDY   **Offer Originated in Administrator's State**

Situation: Mr. Thompson (a registered agent in Illinois), on the recommendation of his best client (Mr. Bixby), phones a friend of Mr. Bixby's in Indiana. Mr. Thompson sells a security to Mr. Bixby's friend, Ms. Gordon, who then mails payment to Mr. Thompson's office in Illinois.

Analysis: The Administrators of both Illinois and Indiana have jurisdiction—the Administrator of Illinois has jurisdiction because the call (offer) originated in Illinois, and the Administrator of Indiana has jurisdiction because the offer was accepted by Ms. Gordon in Indiana.

CASE STUDY   **Offer Directed to Administrator's State**

Situation: The day after he completes his first transaction with Ms. Gordon, Mr. Thompson mails sales offering materials to her home address in Indiana. Ms. Gordon is not in a position to buy any more securities, so she discards the material without reading it.

Analysis: By sending sales materials to Ms. Gordon's home address in Indiana, Mr. Thompson directed the offer to Indiana. Even though Ms. Gordon discarded the information, the Administrator in Indiana has jurisdiction because the sales offer was directed to Indiana. The Administrator of Illinois also has jurisdiction because the offer originated in Illinois.

CASE STUDY   **Offer Accepted in an Administrator's State**

Situation: Mr. Thompson sends additional offers to Ms. Gordon in Indiana, who is now on a three-month summer vacation in Florida. Ms. Gordon has her mail forwarded to her in Florida. Upon receiving Mr. Thompson's materials in Florida, she decides to purchase the securities. She pays for the securities by mailing a check to Mr. Thompson drawn on her local bank in Indiana.

Analysis: The offer is accepted by Ms. Gordon while she was in Florida; therefore, the Administrator of Florida has jurisdiction. Additionally, the Administrator in Illinois has jurisdiction because the offer originated in Illinois, and the Administrator in Indiana has jurisdiction because the offer was directed to Indiana. This is a situation where the Administrators of three different states have jurisdiction.

PUBLISHING AND BROADCAST EXCEPTIONS TO JURISDICTION

There are special rules regarding the Administrator's jurisdiction over offers made through a TV or radio broadcast or through a bona fide newspaper.

The USA specifies that an offer would not be made in an Administrator's state and, therefore, the Administrator would not have jurisdiction if it were made in:

■ a television or radio broadcast that originated outside of the state;

■ a bona fide newspaper or periodical published outside of the state; or

■ a newspaper or periodical published inside the state but with more than two-thirds (66%) of its circulation outside the state in the last year.

TAKE NOTE

A bona fide newspaper is a newspaper of general interest and circulation, such as *The New York Times*. Private investment advisory newsletters, usually distributed by subscription, are not bona fide newspapers and therefore do not fall under the publishing exception.

CASE STUDY

Publishing and Broadcast Exemptions

Situation: First Securities & Co., broker/dealers with offices in New York state and Illinois, offers to sell shares in a new retail shoe chain store located in New York. First Securities advertises the offering to residents of New York in the local newspaper, the *New York Gazette*. First Securities also advertises through the *Gazette's* wholly owned radio station. The *Gazette* and its radio station are both located in western New York near the Pennsylvania border. About 55% of the *Gazette's* readers and listeners live in Pennsylvania.

Analysis: Although more than half the readers and listeners of the *Gazette* live in Pennsylvania, under the terms of the publishing and broadcasting exemption of the USA, the offer is not made in Pennsylvania because the paper is not published in Pennsylvania, so the Administrator of New York state has sole jurisdiction over the offering. No dual or multiple jurisdiction applies in this case unless the offer is actually accepted in Pennsylvania. The fact that First Securities is registered in Illinois in addition to New York is not relevant to this offering because no securities were sold there, nor were any offers or advertising directed to the state.

QUICK QUIZ 2.11

1. A state's securities Administrator has jurisdiction over a securities offering if it was
   A. directed to residents of that state
   B. originated in that state
   C. accepted in that state
   D. all of the above

2. An Administrator has jurisdiction over an offer to sell securities if it is made in a newspaper published within the state with no more than
   A. ⅓ of its circulation outside the state
   B. ½ of its circulation outside the state
   C. ⅔ of its circulation outside the state
   D. 90% of its circulation outside the state

POWERS OF THE ADMINISTRATOR WITHIN ITS JURISDICTION

The USA not only establishes the jurisdiction of the Administrator but also outlines the powers that the Administrator has within its jurisdiction.

The four broad powers the Administrator has to enforce and administer the act in its state are to:

■ make, amend, or rescind rules and orders;

■ conduct investigations and issue subpoenas;

■ issue cease and desist orders and seek injunctions; and

■ deny, suspend, cancel, or revoke registrations and licenses.

Although the Administrator has powers to enforce the act for the benefit of the public, the Administrator and his employees have the obligation not to misuse the office for personal gain. Administrators are, as a result, prohibited from using for their own benefit any information derived from their official duties that has not been made public.

MAKE, AMEND, OR RESCIND RULES AND ORDERS

To enforce the USA, the Administrator has authority to **make**, **amend**, or **rescind rules** and orders necessary to administer the act. The Administrator may also issue interpretive letters. The USA requires that all rules and orders be published. A rule or order of the Administrator has the same authority as a provision of the act itself, but these rules and orders are not part of the USA itself. The difference between a rule and an order is that a **rule** applies to everyone, whereas an **order** applies to a specific instance.

EXAMPLE   The Administrator may decide to issue a ruling requiring all agents to pay an annual registration fee of $250. That applies to everyone. Or, the Administrator may find that a specific agent has violated a provision of the law and order a 30-day suspension. That order applies only to that particular agent.

A person may challenge an order of the Administrator in court within 60 days of order issuance.

Although the Administrator has the power to make and amend rules for compliance with his state's blue-sky laws, he does not have the power to alter the law itself.

The composition or content of state securities law is the responsibility of the state legislature and not that of administrative agencies. Rules for administration and compliance with the law are the responsibility of the securities Administrator.

CASE STUDY

Rules and Orders of the Administrator

Situation: The Iowa state securities Administrator requires by rule that all companies registering their securities in Iowa must supply financial statements in a specific form and with content prescribed by the Administrator. However, the Administrator does not publish the rule because the rule is too long and complex.

Analysis: The USA allows state Administrators to issue rules and orders in carrying out their regulatory functions, and the Iowa Administrator acted properly in designing the form and content for financial reports. However, it is required by the USA that Administrators publish all rules and orders. The Administrator, despite the latitude given him in administering the USA, cannot suspend any provision of the USA itself. The Iowa Administrator acted within his authority in designing the forms but acted without authority—that is, he violated the USA—by suspending the requirement that all rules and orders be published.

CONDUCT INVESTIGATIONS AND ISSUE SUBPOENAS

The Administrator has broad discretionary authority to **conduct investigations** and **issue subpoenas**. These investigations may be made in public or in private and may occur within or outside of the Administrator's state. These investigations are open to the public normally, but when, in the opinion of the Administrator and with the consent of all parties, it is felt that a private investigation is more appropriate, that investigation will be conducted without public scrutiny.

In conducting an investigation, the Administrator, or any officer designated by him, has the power to:

■ require statements in writing, under oath, as to all matters relating to the issue under investigation;

■ publish and make public the facts and circumstances concerning the issue to be investigated;

■ subpoena witnesses and compel their attendance and testimony; and

■ take evidence and require the production of books, papers, correspondence, and any other documents deemed relevant.

In addition to the power to conduct investigations, the Administrator may enforce subpoenas issued by Administrators in other states on the same basis as if the alleged offense took place in the Administrator's state.

ISSUE CEASE AND DESIST ORDERS

If an Administrator determines that a person is about to engage in an activity that constitutes a violation of the USA, the Administrator may issue a **cease and desist order** without a hearing. The Administrator is granted this power to prevent potential violations before they occur.

Although the Administrator has the power to issue cease and desist orders, he does not have the legal power to compel compliance with the order. To compel compliance in the face of a person's resistance, the Administrator must apply to a court of competent jurisdiction for an **injunction**. Only the courts can compel compliance by issuing injunctions and imposing penalties for violation of them. If a temporary or permanent injunction is issued, upon request of the Administrator, a receiver or conservator may be appointed over the defendant's assets.

Cease and desist orders are not the same as stop orders. Cease and desist orders are directed at persons, requiring them to cease activities. Stop orders are directed to registration applications.

CASE STUDY   **Cease and Desist Orders**

Situation: Mr. Thompson is registered to conduct business in the state of Illinois and makes plans to sell a security within the next few days. The Administrator considers this security ineligible for sale in the state. The Administrator orders Thompson to stop his sales procedures immediately.

Analysis: The Administrator of Illinois issued a cease and desist order to Thompson because there was not sufficient time to conduct a public hearing before the sale to determine whether the security was eligible for sale in the state.

DENY, SUSPEND, CANCEL, OR REVOKE REGISTRATIONS

The Administrator has the power to deny, suspend, cancel, or revoke the registration of broker/dealers, investment advisers, and their representatives.

Broker/Dealers, Advisers, and Their Representatives

To justify a denial, revocation, or suspension of the license of a **securities professional**, the Administrator must find that the order is in the public interest and also find that the applicant or registrant, or in the case of a broker/dealer or investment adviser, any partner, officer, or director, or any person occupying a similar status or performing similar functions:

- has filed an incomplete, false, or misleading registration application;

- willfully violated the USA;

- has been convicted of a securities-related misdemeanor within the last 10 years;

- has been convicted of any felony within the last 10 years;

- has been enjoined by law from engaging in the securities business;

- is subject to another Administrator's denial, revocation, or suspension;

- is engaged in dishonest or unethical securities practices;

- is insolvent;

- is the subject of an adjudication that the broker/dealer has willfully violated the Securities Act of 1933, the Securities Exchange Act of 1934, the Investment Advisers Act of 1940, the Investment Company Act of 1940, or the Commodities Exchange Act;

- has failed to reasonably supervise his agents or employees;

- has failed to pay application filing fees; or

- is not qualified on the basis of training, lack of experience, and knowledge of the securities business.

TAKE NOTE

An Administrator may not base a denial of an person's registration solely on the person's lack of experience. However, the USA allows the Administrator to restrict an applicant's registration for an investment adviser's license to that of a broker/dealer if that person is not qualified to function as an investment adviser.

TAKE NOTE

The public's best interest is not reason enough for the denial, suspension, or revocation of a registration. There must be a further reason, as described above.

The Administrator must notify the registrant of any reason to deny, suspend, revoke, or cancel a registration, and if asked in writing, must provide a hearing within 15 days. The Administrator may not stop a registration on the basis of facts that were known to the Administrator at the time the registration became effective (unless the proceedings are initiated within 30 days).

QUICK QUIZ 2.12

1. With regard to the powers of the Administrator, which of the following statements are NOT true?

    I. The Administrator must seek an injunction to issue a cease and desist order.
    II. The USA requires an Administrator to conduct a full hearing, public or private, before issuing a cease and desist order.
    III. The USA grants the Administrator the power to issue injunctions to force compliance with the provisions of the act.

    A. I and II
    B. I and III
    C. II and III
    D. I, II and III

2. Although the Administrator has great power, the USA does place some limitations on the office. Which of the following statements regarding those powers are TRUE?

   I. In conducting an investigation, an Administrator can compel the testimony of witnesses.

   II. Investigations of serious violations must be open to the public.

   III. An Administrator in Illinois may only enforce subpoenas from South Carolina if the violation originally occurred in Illinois.

   IV. An administrator may deny the registration of a securities professional who has been convicted of any felony within the past 10 years, but must provide a hearing, if requested in writing, within 15 days.

   A. I, II and IV
   B. I, III and IV
   C. I and IV
   D. II and III

NONPUNITIVE TERMINATIONS OF REGISTRATION

A registration can be terminated even if there has not been a violation of the USA. A request for withdrawal and lack of qualification are both reasons for cancellation.

Withdrawal

A person may request on his own initiative a withdrawal of a registration. The withdrawal is effective 30 days after the Administrator receives it, provided no revocation or suspension proceedings are in process against the person making the request. In that event, the Administrator may institute a revocation or suspension proceeding within one year after a withdrawal becomes effective.

Cancellation

If an Administrator finds that an applicant or a registrant no longer exists or has ceased to transact business, the Administrator may cancel the registration.

TEST TOPIC ALERT   You may encounter this type of question regarding cancellation: "What would the Administrator do if mailings to a registrant were returned with no forwarding address?" The answer is, "Cancel the registration."

The Administrator may also cancel a registration if a person is declared mentally incompetent.

TAKE NOTE

Be familiar with the distinctions between cancellation and denial, suspension, or revocation. Cancellation does not result from violations or a failure to follow the provisions of the act. Cancellation occurs as the result of death, dissolution, or mental incompetency.

QUICK QUIZ 2.13

1. Which of the following statements relating to termination of registration is TRUE?
   A. A registration, once in effect, may never be voluntarily withdrawn.
   B. An Administrator may not cancel a registration of a securities professional who is declared mentally incompetent.
   C. An Administrator may revoke the registration of a securities professional who is declared mentally incompetent.
   D. An Administrator may cancel the registration of a registrant no longer in business.

PENALTIES FOR VIOLATIONS OF THE UNIFORM SECURITIES ACT

The USA provides both civil liabilities and criminal penalties for persons who violate the USA. In addition, the act provides for recovery by a client of financial loss that results from the fraudulent sale of a security or investment advice.

CIVIL LIABILITIES

Persons who sell securities or offer investment advice in violation of the USA are subject to **civil liabilities** (as well as criminal penalties).

The purchaser of securities sold in violation of the act may sue the seller to recover financial loss.

The purchaser may sue for recovery if:

■ the securities were sold in violation of the registration provisions of USA;

■ the securities professional omits or makes an untrue statement of material fact;

■ the securities were sold by an agent who should have been but was not registered under the act; or

■ the securities were sold in violation of a rule or order of the securities Administrator.

Statute of Limitations

The time limit, or statute of limitations, for violations of the civil provisions of the USA is three years from the date of sale (or rendering of the investment advice) or two years after discovering the violation, whichever comes first.

Rights of Recovery from Improper Sale of Securities

If the seller of securities discovers that they have made a sale in violation of the USA, the seller may offer to repurchase the securities from the buyer. In this case, the seller is offering the buyer the **right of rescission**. To satisfy the buyer's right of rescission, the amount paid back to the buyer must include the original purchase price and interest, as determined by the Administrator.

By offering to buy back the securities that were sold in violation of the act, the seller can avoid a lawsuit through a **letter of rescission**. The buyer has 30 days after receiving the letter of rescission to respond. If the buyer does not accept or reject the rescission offer within 30 days, the buyer gives up any right to pursue a lawsuit at a later date.

If the buyer accepts the rescission offer, he may recover:

- the original purchase price of the securities; plus

- interest at a rate determined by the Administrator; plus

- all reasonable attorney's fees; minus

- any income received while the securities were held.

Rights of Recovery from Improper Investment Advice

A person who buys a security as the result of investment advice received in violation of the USA also has the right of rescission. In the case of securities purchased as a result of improper investment advice, the buyer may recover:

- cost of the advice; plus

- loss as a result of the advice; plus

- interest at a rate determined by the Administrator; plus

- any reasonable attorney's fees.

When securities are sold improperly, the buyer can recover the original purchase price in addition to other losses. When improper investment advice is offered, the purchaser of the advice is entitled to recover the cost of the advice and losses incurred but is not entitled to recover the original purchase price from the adviser.

CRIMINAL PENALTIES

Persons found guilty of a fraudulent securities transaction are subject to **criminal penalties** (as well as civil liabilities). Upon conviction, a person may be fined, imprisoned, or both. To be convicted of fraud, the violation must be willful, and the registrant must know that the activity is fraudulent.

Fraud is the deliberate or willful concealment, misrepresentation, or omission of material information or the truth to deceive or manipulate another person for unlawful or unfair gain. Under the USA, fraud is not limited to common-law deceit.

Statute of Limitations

The statute of limitations for criminal offenses under the USA is five years from the date of the offense.

TAKE NOTE

Remember the sequence 5-5-3 for the application of criminal penalties: 5-year statute of limitations, $5,000 maximum fine, and imprisonment of no more than 3 years.

Under the civil provisions, the statute of limitations runs for 2 years from the discovery of the offense or to 3 years after the act occurred, whichever occurs first.

CASE STUDY

Fraudulent Sale of Securities

Situation: Mr. Thompson, the registered sales agent, knowingly omitted the fact that the shares of a company he sold to his client, Mr. Bixby, were downgraded to speculative grade and that their bonds were placed on a credit watch by one of the major credit rating agencies. A month after the sale, the shares became worthless.

Analysis: Mr. Thompson sold these securities to Mr. Bixby in violation of the USA because he deliberately or knowingly failed to mention material information—information that was important for Mr. Bixby to know for him to make an informed investment decision. Mr. Bixby has the right to recover the financial losses that result from the sale.

Under the USA, the actual seller of the securities or the advice is not the only person liable for the violation of the act. Every person who directly or indirectly controls the person who sold the securities or the advice, or is a material aid to the transaction, is also liable to the same extent as the person who conducted the transaction.

JUDICIAL REVIEW OF ORDERS (APPEAL)

Any person affected by an order of the Administrator may obtain a review of the order in an appropriate court by filing a written petition within 60 days. In general, filing an appeal does not automatically act as a stay of the penalty. The order will go into effect as issued unless the court rules otherwise.

QUICK QUIZ 2.14

1. Which of the following statements relating to penalties under the USA is TRUE?

    A. Unknowing violation of the USA by an agent is cause for imprisonment under the criminal liability provisions of the act.

    B. A purchaser of a security where a violation of the USA occurred may recover the original purchase price plus legal costs plus interest, less any earnings already received.

    C. A seller who notices that a sale was made in violation of the act may offer a right of rescission to the purchaser; this must be accepted within the sooner of two years after notice of the violation or three years after the sale.

    D. Any person aggrieved by an order of the Administrator may request an appeal of the order within 15 days, which, in effect, functions as a stay of the order during the appeal period.

HOTSHEETS

For your convenience, Unit HotSheets summarizing the key points are located at the end of the manual on perforated pages.

UNIT TEST

1. Which of the following would be an agent under the terms of the USA?

   I. A sales representative of a licensed broker/dealer who sells secondary securities to the general public
   II. An assistant to the president of a broker/dealer who, for administrative purposes, accepts orders on behalf of the senior partners
   III. A subsidiary of a major commercial bank registered as a broker/dealer that sells securities to the public
   IV. An issuer of nonexempt securities registered in the state and sold to the general public

   A. I and II
   B. I, II and III
   C. III and IV
   D. I, II, III and IV

2. A publicly traded corporation offers its employees an opportunity to purchase shares of the company's common stock directly from the issuer. A specific employee of the company is designated to process any orders for that stock. Under the USA, the employee

   A. must register as an agent of the issuer
   B. need not register as an agent of the issuer under any circumstances
   C. may receive commissions without registration
   D. must register as an agent if he will receive commissions or remuneration, either directly or indirectly

3. Which of the following persons is defined as an agent by the Uniform Securities Act?

   A. Silent partner of a broker/dealer
   B. Secretary of a branch office sales manager
   C. Clerk at a broker/dealer who is authorized to take orders
   D. Broker/dealer executive who does not solicit or transact business

4. Under the Uniform Securities Act, an agent is a(n)

   A. broker/dealer who sells registered securities to the general public
   B. individual who represents an issuer in a transaction exempt from the act
   C. individual representing a broker/dealer who sells federal covered securities exempt from registration under the act
   D. individual who represents an issuer in an exempt transaction in which no commissions are paid

5. According to the Uniform Securities Act, which of the following is(are) considered a broker/dealer?

   I. An agent who issues securities for his own account and for clients of his employer
   II. An issuer of securities that are traded on SEC-registered exchanges
   III. A corporation that specializes in the sale of various oil and gas limited partnerships
   IV. A credit union that issues its own stock to depositors in proportion to the amount of the funds on deposit

   A. I only
   B. I and IV
   C. II and III
   D. III only

6. Under the Uniform Security Act, the term *person* would include all of the following EXCEPT

   I. an unincorporated association
   II. a child prodigy, gifted in math, in the custody of his parents, for whom his parents opened an account at a major securities firm
   III. a political subdivision
   IV. an individual

   A. I, II and IV
   B. II only
   C. II and III
   D. III and IV

7. Under the USA, which of the following is considered a broker/dealer in a state?

   A. First Federal Company Trust
   B. XYZ broker/dealer with an office in the state whose only clients are insurance companies
   C. An agent effecting transactions for a broker/dealer
   D. A broker/dealer with no place of business in the state who only does business with other broker/dealers

8. Which of the following must register as an agent?

   I. An individual representing a broker/dealer who sells commercial paper
   II. An individual who sells commercial paper for ABC National Bank
   III. An employee of the Fed whose job is selling Treasury bonds to the public
   IV. An individual who is paid a commission to sell certificates of deposit for ABC National Bank

   A. I only
   B. I, II and III
   C. I, III and IV
   D. I, II, III and IV

9. Which of the following is defined as a security under the Uniform Securities Act?

   A. A guaranteed, lump-sum payment to a beneficiary
   B. Fixed, guaranteed payments made for life or for a specified period
   C. Commodity futures contracts
   D. An investment contract

10. Under the Uniform Securities Act, which of the following persons is responsible for proving that a securities issue is exempt from registration?

    A. Underwriter
    B. Issuer
    C. State Administrator
    D. There is no need to prove eligibility for an exemption.

11. Registration is effective when ordered by the Administrator in the case of registration by

    A. coordination
    B. integration
    C. notice filing
    D. qualification

12. The US Supreme Court, in the Howey decision, ruled that an instrument that represents the investment of money in a common enterprise with an expectation of profit solely through the managerial efforts of others is a security. In following the Howey decision, the USA would consider which of the following a security?

    A. Purchase of a house in a desirable real estate market with the expectation that the house will be resold at a profit within a few years
    B. Purchase of jewelry for speculative purposes as opposed to personal use
    C. Investment in options to acquire a security
    D. Investment in commodities futures

13. Under the Uniform Securities Act, which of the following would be considered an exempt transaction?

    I. An existing client calls you to purchase 1,000 shares of a common stock that is not registered in this state
    II. Shares that are part of a registered secondary of a NYSE-listed company are sold to an individual client
    III. Shares of a bank's IPO are sold to an institutional client
    IV. Shares of an insurance company's IPO are sold to an individual client

    A. I and III
    B. I, III and IV
    C. II and IV
    D. I, II, III and IV

14. Which of the following securities is(are) exempt from the registration provisions of the USA?

    I. Issue of a savings and loan association
    II. General obligation municipal bond
    III. Bond issued by a company that has common stock listed on the American Stock Exchange

    A. I only
    B. II only
    C. II and III
    D. I, II and III

15. A primary issue is
    A. the first transaction between two parties in the over-the-counter market
    B. a sale between investors of securities traded on the New York Stock Exchange
    C. a new offering of an issuer sold to investors
    D. a secondary market transaction in a security recently offered to the public

16. All of the following describe exempt transactions EXCEPT
    A. ABC, a broker/dealer, purchases securities from XYZ Corporation
    B. First National Bank sells its entire publicly traded bond portfolio to Amalgamated National Bank
    C. Amalgamated National Bank sells its publicly traded bond portfolio to ABC Insurance Company
    D. Joe Smith, an employee of Amalgamated National Bank, buys securities from ABC Brokerage Corporation

17. Under the USA, all of the following are exempt securities EXCEPT
    I. US government securities
    II. unsolicited transactions
    III. transactions between issuers and underwriters
    IV. securities of credit unions

    A. I, II and IV
    B. I and IV
    C. II and III
    D. IV only

18. Registration statements for securities under the Uniform Securities Act are effective for
    A. a period determined by the Administrator for each issue
    B. 1 year from the effective date
    C. 1 year from the date of issue
    D. 1 year from the previous January 1

19. Under the Uniform Securities Act, an issuer is any person who issues, or proposes to issue, a security for sale to the public. According to the USA, which of the following is NOT an issuer?
    I. The City of Chicago, which is involved in a distribution of tax-exempt highway improvement bonds
    II. A partner in the AAA Oil and Gas Partnership sells his interest in the investment
    III. The AAA Manufacturing Company, which proposes to offer shares to the public but has not completed the offering
    IV. The US government, which proposes to offer Treasury bonds

    A. I only
    B. II only
    C. I, II and III
    D. I, II and IV

20. Which of the following transactions are exempt from registration under the USA?
    I. A trustee of a corporation in bankruptcy liquidates securities to satisfy debt holders.
    II. An offer of a securities investment is directed to 10 individuals in the state during a 12-month consecutive period.
    III. An agent frequently engages in nonissuer transactions in unregistered securities in his own account.
    IV. Agents for an entrepreneur offer pre-organization certificates to fewer than 10 investors in the state for a modest commission.

    A. I and II
    B. I, III and IV
    C. II and IV
    D. I and IV

21. Which of the following is(are) primary transactions?

    I. John inherited securities of the XYZ Corporation from his father who, as a founder to the company, received the shares directly from the company as a result of stock options.

    II. John sold the securities he had inherited from his father to his neighbor, Peter, at the market price without charging a commission.

    III. John's father, a founder of XYZ corporation, purchased shares of XYZ directly from the corporation subsequent to its founding without paying a commission.

    IV. John purchased shares in XYZ Corporation in a third-market transaction.

    A. I only
    B. I and II
    C. III only
    D. I, II, III and IV

22. XYZ Corporation has been in business for over 20 years. They need additional capital for expansion, and determine that a public offering in their home state and neighboring states is appropriate. Which method of securities registration would most likely be used to register this initial public offering?

    A. Coordination
    B. Notice filing
    C. Qualification
    D. Any of the above

23. Which of the following meet the USA's definition of an exempt transaction?

    I. Transactions by an executor of an estate
    II. Transactions with an investment company registered under the Investment Company Act of 1940
    III. An unsolicited sale of a Bulletin Board stock
    IV. Sale of a new issue to an individual customer

    A. I and II
    B. I, II and III
    C. IV only
    D. I, II, III and IV

24. Market manipulation is one of the prohibited practices under the Uniform Securities Act. Which of the following is an example of a broker/dealer engaging in market manipulation?

    I. Churning
    II. Arbitrage
    III. Front running
    IV. Matched trades

    A. I and II
    B. I, III and IV
    C. III and IV
    D. IV only

25. Your customer called to check on her account value at 9:00 am. You were unavailable at the time. It is now 2:00 pm, and you are able to call her back. Between 9:00 am and 2:00 pm, her account value dropped from $11,500 to $10,000. What should you say to her?

    A. "At the time that you called, your account had a value of $11,500."
    B. "Your account value cannot be determined until the market closes."
    C. "Your account is valued at $10,000 at this time."
    D. "Your account was down to $9,700 earlier today but is up to $10,000."

26. All of the following are prohibited practices under the USA EXCEPT

    I. borrowing money or securities from the account of a former banker with express written permission
    II. failing to identify a customer's financial objectives
    III. selling rights
    IV. supplying funds to a client's account only when or if it declines below a previously agreed-upon level

    A. I and II
    B. I, II and III
    C. II and IV
    D. III only

27. A customer is upset with her agent for not servicing her account properly and sends him a complaint letter about his actions. Under the Uniform Securities Act, the agent should

 A. call the customer, apologize, and attempt to correct the problem
 B. tell the customer he is willing to make rescission
 C. do nothing
 D. bring the customer complaint to his employer immediately

28. Under the USA, the Administrator may deny or revoke a registration if an agent

 I. borrows money from his wealthy clients' accounts
 II. solicits orders for nonexempt unregistered securities
 III. buys and sells securities in accounts to generate a high level of commissions
 IV. alters market quotations to induce a client to invest in an attractive growth stock

 A. I, II and III
 B. I and III
 C. I and IV
 D. I, II, III and IV

29. According to the USA, which of the following is an example of market manipulation?

 A. Creating the illusion of active trading
 B. Omitting material facts in a presentation
 C. Guaranteeing performance of a security
 D. Transactions in excess of a customer's financial capability

30. Registration as an investment adviser under the USA would be required for any firm in the business of giving advice on the purchase of

 A. convertible bonds
 B. gold coins
 C. rare convertible automobiles
 D. apartments undergoing a conversion to condominiums

31. Which of the following practices is prohibited under the USA?

 A. Participating in active trading of a security in which an unusually high trading volume has occurred
 B. Offering services that an agent cannot realistically perform because of his broker/dealer's limitations
 C. Altering the customer's order at the request of a customer, which subsequently results in a substantial loss
 D. Failing to inform the firm's principal of frequent oral customer complaints

32. An agent hears a rumor concerning a security and uses the rumor to convince a client to purchase the security. Under the USA, the agent may

 A. recommend the security if it is an appropriate investment
 B. recommend the investment if the rumor is based on material inside information
 C. recommend the security if the source of the rumor came from a reliable source
 D. not recommend the security

33. If an agent thought that a technology stock was undervalued and actively solicited all customers, the agent

 I. did not violate the USA if all material facts were disclosed
 II. committed an unethical sales practice because the firm has not recommended this technology stock
 III. committed an unethical business practice
 IV. did not commit a violation if all clients were accurately informed of the price of the stock

 A. I, II and IV
 B. I and IV
 C. III only
 D. I, II, III and IV

34. Which of the following transactions are prohibited?
    I.   Borrowing money or securities from a high net-worth customer
    II. Selling speculative or hot issues to a retired couple of modest means on a fixed income
    III. Failing to follow a customer's orders so as to prevent investment in a security not adequately covered by well-known securities analysts
    IV. Backdating confirmations for the benefit of the client's tax reporting

    A. I and II
    B. I, II and III
    C. II and III
    D. I, II, III and IV

35. It is legal under the USA for a registered investment adviser to tell a client that

    A. a registered security may lawfully be sold in that state
    B. an exempt security is not required to be registered because it is generally regarded as being safer than a nonexempt security
    C. her qualifications have been found satisfactory by the Administrator
    D. a registered security has been approved for sale in the state by the Administrator

36. An agent omits facts that a prudent investor requires to make informed decisions. Under the Uniform Securities Act, this action is

    A. fraudulent for nonexempt securities only
    B. fraudulent for exempt securities only
    C. fraudulent for both exempt and nonexempt securities
    D. not fraudulent if there was willful intent to omit the information

37. Which of the following actions is NOT a prohibited practice under the USA?

    A. A market maker fills his firm's order ahead of a customer order at the same price.
    B. A specialist buys and sells stock as principal.
    C. A principal of a broker/dealer allows a rumor to leak out that ABC is going to acquire LMN; after a few days, the broker/dealer sells ABC short for its own account.
    D. An agent sells a customer's stock at the bid price and makes up the difference with a personal check.

38. Which of the following is(are) prohibited under the USA?

    I.   Recommending tax shelters to low-income retirees
    II. Stating that a state Administrator has approved an offering on the basis of the quality of information found in the prospectus
    III. Soliciting orders for unregistered, nonexempt securities
    IV. Employing any device to defraud

    A. I only
    B. I and II
    C. I, II and III
    D. I, II, III and IV

39. According to the USA, which of the following is a prohibited activity?

    A. The agent enters into an agreement to share in the profits/losses of the customer's account without an investment in the account.
    B. The agent and his spouse jointly own their own personal trading account at the firm.
    C. The agent, with his firm's and the client's permission, participates in the profits and losses of the account in proportion to his investment in the account.
    D. An agent refuses a client's request to share in the performance of the client's account.

40. A registered broker/dealer is under common control with a registered investment adviser. An individual who is an agent of the broker/dealer and an investment adviser representative of the adviser has a client with $250,000 under an asset management program. This individual calls the client and suggests the purchase of 500 shares of RMBM common stock as an appropriate addition to the portfolio. The broker/dealer is a market maker in RMBM, and the sale will be made as a principal, a fact that is disclosed to the client on the trade confirmation. In this situation, the registered person has acted

A. lawfully in that the disclosure of capacity was made on the confirmation
B. lawfully in that disclosure of capacity is not necessary when executing trades in managed accounts
C. unlawfully in that any stock the broker/dealer is a market maker in is probably not suitable for a managed money client
D. unlawfully in that investment advisers are required to make written disclosure in advance of a trade where the firm or an affiliate will be acting in a principal capacity and receive the client's consent

41. If convicted of a willful violation of the Uniform Securities Act, an agent is subject to

A. imprisonment for 5 years
B. a fine of $5,000 and/or imprisonment for 3 years
C. a fine of $10,000
D. disbarment

42. To protect the public, the Administrator may

I. deny a registration if the registrant does not have sufficient experience to function as an agent
II. limit a registrant's functions to that of a broker/dealer if, in the initial application for registration as an investment adviser, the registrant is not qualified to act as an adviser
III. take into consideration that the registrant will work under the supervision of a registered investment adviser or broker/dealer in approving a registration
IV. deny a registration, although denial is not in the public's interest, if it is prudent in view of a change in the state's political composition

A. I and II
B. II and III
C. III and IV
D. I, II, III and IV

43. Aaron is a client of XYZ Financial Services. Over the past several years, Aaron has been suspicious of possible churning of his account, but has taken no action because account performance has been outstanding. After reviewing his most recent statement, Aaron suspects that excessive transactions have occurred. He, consults his attorney, who informs him that under the USA, any lawsuit for recovery of damages under the USA must be started within

A. 1 year of occurrence
B. 2 years of occurrence
C. 3 years of occurrence or 2 years of discovery, whichever occurs first
D. 2 years of occurrence or 3 years of discovery, whichever occurs last

44. Which of the following accurately describes a cease and desist order as authorized by the USA?

A. An order that a federal agency issued to a brokerage firm to stop an advertising campaign
B. An Administrator's order to refrain from a practice of business believed by that Administrator to be unfair
C. A court-issued order requiring a business to stop an unfair practice
D. An order from one brokerage firm to another to refrain from unfair business practices

45. A customer living in one state receives a phone call from an agent in another state. A transaction between the two occurs in yet another state. According to the Uniform Securities Act, under whose jurisdiction does the transaction fall?

    A. Administrator of the state in which the customer lives
    B. Administrator of the state from which the agent made the call
    C. Administrator of the state in which the transaction took place
    D. Administrators of all 3 states involved

46. The Administrator may, by rule,

    A. forbid an adviser from taking custody of client funds
    B. allow an agent to waive provisions of the USA
    C. suspend federal law if the Administrator believes it to be in the public interest
    D. suspend the registration of a federal covered adviser because the contract did not meet the requirements for a state-sanctioned investment advisory contract

47. If it is in the public interest, the Uniform Securities Act provides that the state Administrator may deny the registration of a person for all of the following reasons EXCEPT

    A. the applicant is not qualified owing to lack of experience
    B. a willful violation of the Uniform Securities Act has taken place
    C. the applicant is financially insolvent
    D. the applicant is enjoined temporarily from engaging in the securities business

48. If an agent chooses to appeal an Administrator's order, when must the agent file for review of the order with the appropriate court?

    A. Immediately
    B. Within 30 days after the entry of the order
    C. Within 60 days after the entry of the order
    D. Within 180 days after the entry of the order

49. An Administrator may summarily suspend a registration pending final determination of proceedings under the USA. However, the Administrator may not enter an order without

    I. appropriate prior notice to the applicant as well as the employer or prospective employer of the applicant
    II. opportunity for a hearing
    III. findings of fact and conclusions of law
    IV. prior written acknowledgment of the applicant

    A. I only
    B. I and II
    C. I, II and III
    D. I, II, III and IV

50. The Administrator has authority to

    I. issue a cease and desist order without a hearing
    II. issue a cease and desist order only after a hearing
    III. suspend a securities registration upon discovering an officer of the registrant has been convicted of a nonsecurities related crime
    IV. sentence violators of the USA to 3 years in prison

    A. I only
    B. I and IV
    C. II and III
    D. II and IV

ANSWERS AND RATIONALES

1. **A.** Under the USA, only individuals can be agents. A person who sells securities for a broker/dealer is an agent. An administrative person, such as the assistant to the president of a broker/dealer, is considered an agent if he takes securities orders from the public. Corporate entities are excluded from the definition of an agent. Broker/dealers and issuers are not agents.

2. **D.** Under the USA, an individual is an agent when effecting transactions with an issuer's existing employees if commissions are paid. Therefore, Choice B is not correct because there are cases where the employee would have to register as an agent.

3. **C.** Anyone who solicits or receives an order while representing a broker/dealer is an agent. Silent partners, administrative personnel, and executives of broker/dealers are not agents under the terms of the USA because they do not solicit or receive orders. Remember, broker/dealers are not agents; agents represent broker/dealers. If, however, any of these individuals were authorized to accept orders, registration as an agent would be required.

4. **C.** An individual employed by a broker/dealer who sells securities to the public is an agent under the Uniform Securities Act. The USA defines an agent as "any individual other than a broker/dealer who represents a broker/dealer or issuer in effecting or attempting to effect purchases or sales of securities." The law excludes those individuals from the definition of an agent who represent an issuer in exempt transactions, exempt securities, and transactions with issuers' employees when no commission is paid. There is virtually no case in which a salesperson representing a broker/dealer is not an agent.

5. **D.** A corporation that sells securities to the public, in this case an oil and natural gas partnership, is a broker/dealer as defined by the USA. Agents and securities issuers are not included in the definition of broker/dealer. Credit unions are not considered broker/dealers under the USA.

6. **B.** The term *person* is extremely broad. Excluded from the term would be a minor, a deceased individual, and one who has legally been determined incompetent.

7. **B.** Any broker/dealer with an office in the state, regardless of the nature of its clients, is defined as a broker/dealer under the USA. If the firm did not have an office in the state and its only clients were institutions such as insurance companies, or other broker/dealers as in Choice D, it would be excluded from the definition. Banks or trust companies and agents are never broker/dealers.

8. **A.** An individual who represents a broker/dealer and sells commercial paper must register under the USA. The securities (commercial paper) are exempt; nevertheless the representative must be registered as an agent of the broker/dealer. An individual who sells commercial paper for ABC National Bank would not have to register because the bank is excluded from the definition of broker/dealer and both the transaction and security are exempt from state registration requirements. An employee of the federal government need not register with the state because he represents an exempt issuer and is selling exempt securities without receiving compensation tied to sales. An individual who is paid a commission to sell certificates of deposit for a commercial bank does not have to register as an agent because he is not selling a security.

9. **D.** Investment contracts are defined as a security under the Uniform Securities Act. In fact, the term is often used as a synonym for a security. A guaranteed, lump-sum payment to a beneficiary is an endowment policy excluded from the definition of a security. Fixed, guaranteed payments made for life or for a specified period are fixed annuity contracts not defined as securities. Commodity futures contracts and the commodities themselves are not securities. It is much easier to remember what is not a security than what is.

10. **B.** The burden of proof for claiming eligibility for an exemption falls to the person claiming the exemption. In the event the registration statement was filed by someone other than the issuer (such as selling stockholders or broker/dealer), that person must prove the claim.

11. **D.** Registration by qualification is the only registration method where the Administrator sets the effective date. The effective date under registration by coordination is set by the SEC, and notice filing is merely the filing of certain documents for the registrant to be able to offer securities in that state. Registration is effective on filing.

12. **C.** The investment in options is the only choice that meets the definition of a security. It is an investment in a common enterprise with the expectation that the owner will profit as a result of the managerial efforts of others. The purchase of a house or jewelry is a purchase of a real asset or product that may result in a profit for the owner but not as a result of the managerial efforts of a third party. Commodities futures contracts are specifically excluded from the definition of a security. Note that options on futures, however, are securities under the USA. Remember the items listed that are not securities.

13. **A.** A client calling to purchase stock is an unsolicited transaction, probably the most common of the exempt transactions. Any sale to an institutional client is an exempt transaction, whereas those to individuals, unless unsolicited, generally are not.

14. **D.** The USA exempts from registration a number of different issues. Included in that group are securities issued by a bank or anything that looks like a bank (a savings and loan or a credit union). Securities issued by a governmental unit are always exempt. Securities listed on the American Stock Exchange are part of a group known as federal covered securities that also includes those listed on the New York Stock Exchange and Nasdaq Stock Market issues.

15. **C.** A primary issue is a new offering of securities by an issuer sold to investors. Transactions between two investors in the over-the-counter market refers to a secondary transaction (the market between investors). A sale between investors of securities traded on the New York Stock Exchange is another example of a secondary transaction.

16. **D.** The purchase of securities from a broker/dealer by an employee of a bank is a nonexempt transaction—it is a sale of a security by a broker/dealer to a member of the public and is therefore not exempt. Transactions between brokers and issuers; transactions between banks; and transactions between banks and insurance companies are exempt because they are transactions between financial institutions. Exempt transactions are most often identified by who the transaction is with rather than what type of security is involved.

17. **C.** Both unsolicited transactions and transactions between issuers and underwriters are exempt transactions, not exempt securities. US government securities and securities of credit unions are exempt securities, not exempt transactions.

18. **B.** Securities registration statements are effective for 1 year from the effective date.

19. **B.** Under the Uniform Securities Act, an issuer is any person who issues, or proposes to issue, a security. Examples of issuers are a municipality such as the city of Chicago, which issues tax-exempt highway improvement bonds; the AAA Manufacturing Company, which proposes to offer shares to the public even though it has not completed the offering; and the United States government, when it proposes to offer Treasury bonds. Oil, gas, and mining partnerships are not issuers under the terms of the Uniform Securities Act; however, certificates of interest in them are securities. The resale of a partnership interest by an investor is a nonissuer sale because the investor is not the issuer.

20. **A.** Transactions by fiduciaries, such as a trustee in a bankruptcy reorganization, are exempt from registration. An offer of a securities investment to 10 or fewer individuals (called a private placement) is also exempt from registration. Engaging in nonissuer transactions on a regular basis is not exempt from registration. That exemption is only granted in the case of isolated transaction, the opposite of regular. Offers of pre-organization certificates are not exempt when commissions are charged.

21. **C.** A primary transaction is one where the issuer of the securities receives the proceeds of the sale. John's father, although a founder of the company, purchased shares directly from the company. This transaction is a primary transaction because the firm received the funds from the sale of the shares. In all the other instances, the firm, the original issuer of the securities, did not receive the proceeds of the transaction. These transactions are called nonissuer transactions.

22. **A.** Because this offering is being made in more than one state, SEC registration is necessary. The state registration method would be coordination, which is the simultaneous registration of a security with both the SEC and the states.

23. **B.** Transactions by a fiduciary, such as the executor of an estate, are included in the definition of exempt transaction. So are transactions with certain institutional clients like investment companies and insurance companies. The Bulletin Board is an electronic medium for the trading of highly speculative, thinly capitalized issues. Because the order is an unsolicited one, the transaction is exempt. Sale of a new issue of stock to an individual client would not be an exempt transaction.

24. **C.** Front running, the practice of entering an order for the benefit of the firm ahead of a customer order, is a form of market manipulation. Matched trades or matched purchases occur when market participants agree to buy and sell securities among themselves to create the appearance of heightened market activity; this is also a form of market manipulation. Although churning is a prohibited practice, it does not involve manipulating the market, and arbitrage is the perfectly legal practice of buying a security in one marketplace and simultaneously selling it in another to benefit from a price disparity.

25. **C.** All other choices are clearly a misrepresentation of account status.

26. **D.** It is permissible to sell rights, which are securities. Borrowing money or securities from other than a bank or broker/dealer in the business of lending, failing to identify a customer's financial objectives, and guaranteeing a customer's account against losses are all prohibited practices.

27. **D.** Failure to bring customers' written complaints to the attention of the agent's broker/dealer is prohibited.

28. **D.** An Administrator may deny or revoke an agent's registration if the agent engages in prohibited practices such as those described in each of the choices in the question.

29. **A.** Creating the illusion of trading activity is market manipulation. Guaranteeing performance of a security and omitting material facts are prohibited practices but do not constitute market manipulation. Trades too large for a customer are also prohibited because they are not suitable.

30. **A.** Only those in the business of giving advice on securities are required to register as investment advisers. Only the convertible bonds are securities.

31. **B.** An agent may not offer services that he cannot perform. An agent may participate actively in trading a security in which an unusually high trading volume has occurred, provided the trading is not designed to create a false appearance of high volume. At the client's request, an agent can alter a client's order, even if the change results in a loss. An agent is only required to report written complaints to his employing principal, although it would be wise to report repeated oral complaints.

32. **D.** The use of information, such as a rumor, that has no basis in fact is prohibited.

33. **C.** Agents must always determine suitability before soliciting purchases or sales. The key here is that the agent recommended this stock to all clients. One investment cannot be suitable for all of your clients.

34. **D.** All of the practices are prohibited. An agent may not borrow money or securities from a customer unless that customer is a bank or broker/dealer in the business of lending money and/or securities. Selling speculative or hot issues to a retired couple of modest means is an unsuitable transaction because it is not consistent with the objectives of the client. An agent must follow legal orders of the customer, even if the agent believes the order is an unwise one. An agent may not backdate confirmations for the benefit of the client.

35. **A.** An agent may indicate that a security is registered or is exempt from registration. All of the other statements are illegal.

36. **C.** Material facts are facts that an investor relies on to make investment decisions. The omission of a material fact in the sale, purchase, or offer of a security is fraudulent. This applies whether the security offered is exempt or nonexempt.

37. **B.** The function of the specialist is to act as a broker for orders that other broker/dealers left with him and to act as a dealer in buying and selling for his own account. His activity is not prohibited. Allowing a rumor to leak out and then trade on it is a prohibited practice. Selling stock at the bid price and making up the difference with a personal check is a prohibited practice. Filling a firm's proprietary order ahead of a customer's order is a prohibited practice called front running.

38. **D.** Recommending tax shelters to low-income retirees is an example of an unsuitable transaction. Stating that an Administrator has approved an offering on the basis of the quality of information in the prospectus, soliciting orders for unregistered nonexempt securities, and employing a device to defraud are all prohibited practices under the USA.

39. **A.** It is a prohibited practice under the USA for an agent to share in the profits or losses of a customer's account unless the customer and the employer have given written consent and the percentage of participation is proportionate to the percentage of the agent's personal funds in the account. An agent is permitted to jointly own a personal account at the firm and can refuse to share in a customer's account.

40. **D.** The rules regarding investment advisers and account trading are much stricter than those for broker/dealers because of the fiduciary responsibility of the adviser. Any action that results in a transaction in which the firm or an affiliate acts in either a principal or agency capacity requires prior written disclosure of that fact to the client and approval of the client.

41. **B.** Under the USA, the maximum penalty is a fine of $5,000 and/or 3 years in jail.

42. **B.** The Administrator can deny, suspend, or revoke a registration for many reasons, but they must be in the interest of the public. The Administrator may not deny the registration simply because it is prudent. The Administrator may determine that an applicant, in his initial application for registration for an investment adviser, is not qualified to act as an adviser and thus limit the registration to that of a broker/dealer; the Administrator can also take into consideration whether the registrant will work under the supervision of a registered investment adviser or broker/dealer when approving an application. Lack of experience is insufficient for denial.

43. **C.** Under the USA, the lawsuit for recovery of damages must commence within the sooner of 3 years of occurrence of the offense or 2 years of its discovery.

44. **B.** A cease and desist order is a directive from an administrative agency to immediately stop a particular action. The order can come from a federal, state, or judicial body; it is not exclusive to any one. Administrators may issue cease and desist orders with or without a hearing. Brokerage houses cannot issue cease and desist orders to each other.

45. **D.** Under the scope of the Uniform Securities Act, if any part of a transaction occurs in a state, the transaction falls under the jurisdiction of the state Administrator. The transaction is under the control of the Administrator of the state in which the customer lives as the offer was received there, the Administrator of the state in which the agent is calling as the offer was made from that state, and the Administrator of the state in which the transaction took place.

46. **A.** The Administrator has considerable discretion to make rules or issue orders. Specifically, the USA allows the Administrator to prohibit custody by rule. However, the USA does not allow the Administrator to waive provisions of the USA, nor can the Administrator suspend federal law.

47. **A.** If the person qualifies by virtue of training or knowledge, registration cannot be denied for lack of experience only. Registration may be denied if the applicant willfully violates the Uniform Securities Act, is financially insolvent, or has been enjoined from engaging in the securities business.

48. **C.** Under the USA, a registered person has up to 60 days to appeal any disciplinary finding by the state Administrator.

49. **C.** With the exception of those proceedings awaiting final determination, the Administrator must provide an appropriate prior notice to the applicant as well as the employer or prospective employer of the applicant and provide the opportunity for a hearing. In addition, the Administrator may only issue a final stop order after findings of fact and conclusions of law. An applicant is not required to provide written acknowledgment before an order is issued.

50. **A.** The Administrator may issue a cease and desist order without a hearing, but does not have the authority to convict violators of the 1933 Securities Act in criminal prosecutions or sentence violators of the USA. The Administrator may not suspend a security's registration upon discovering in subsequent years that an officer of the firm has been convicted of a nonsecurities-related crime.

QUICK QUIZ ANSWERS

Quick Quiz 2.1

1. **F.** A corporation is a person under the law and subject to the jurisdiction of the state Administrator with respect to securities transactions.

2. **F.** An individual is a natural person and, just like a legal person (e.g., a corporation), may be subject to the Uniform Securities Act.

Quick Quiz 2.2

1. **T.** A person who effects transactions in securities for itself or for the account of others must register in the state as a broker/dealer unless specifically excluded from the definition.

2. **T.** A firm with an out-of-state registration is not considered a broker/dealer in that state if transacting business with a customer who is passing through the state on vacation.

3. **T.** If a person is excluded from the definition, that person need not register as a broker/dealer; however, if they are not excluded, they must register.

Quick Quiz 2.3

1. **A.** Persons must be registered as agents when they effect transactions on behalf of broker/dealers whether or not the securities are exempt.

2. **A.** Any individual taking orders effecting transactions on behalf of a broker/dealer must be registered whether or not they receive a commission.

3. **A.** An employee who represents an issuer of exempt securities (a bank) in selling its securities must register as an agent if they receive commissions. If no compensation were involved, then registration would not be required because such an individual is not an agent.

4. **A.** A person who represents an employer in selling securities to employees must register as an agent if the person receives a commission. If no commission is paid, registration is not necessary.

5. **B.** Persons who represent issuers in securities transactions with underwriters need not register as agents as long as no compensation is paid. In the absence of a statement to the contrary, assume that there is no compensation.

Quick Quiz 2.4

1. **F.** A consent to service of process is filed with the initial application and permanently remains on file with the Administrator.

2. **F.** The term *net capital requirement* refers to the financial requirements of a broker/dealer, not an investment adviser representative. Investment adviser representatives may be required to post a bond if they maintain discretion.

3. **F.** A list of other states in which a securities professional intends to register is not required on a state application for registration.

Quick Quiz 2.5

1. **C.** Commodity futures contracts and fixed payment life insurance contracts are included in our list of 6 items that are not securities. Commodity option contracts are securities.

2. **C.** Management activity on the part of the owner is not part of the Howey, or four-part, test for an instrument to be a security. The four parts are: (1) an investment of money in (2) a common enterprise with (3) an expectation of profit (4) solely from the effort of others.

3. **C.** Nonexempt securities usually are required to be registered, but not always. If the nonexempt security is sold in an exempt transaction, registration may not be required.

4. **B.** A nonissuer transaction is one where the company that is the issuer of the security does not receive the proceeds from the transaction. A nonissuer transaction is a transaction between two investors and may or may not require the security to be registered. Whenever the proceeds go to the issuer, it is an issuer transaction.

Quick Quiz 2.6

1. **T.** Registration by coordination involves coordinating a state registration with that of a federal registration.

2. **T.** Any company may register by qualification. Companies that are not established or that intend to offer their securities in one state register by qualification.

Quick Quiz 2.7

1. **D.** All of the securities are federal covered securities and therefore not subject to the registration and advertising filing requirements of the USA.

2. **D.** Variable annuities (whose performance depends on the securities in a segregated fund) are nonexempt, which means they are covered by the act and have to register. Shares in public utilities, charitable foundations, and banking institutions that are members of the Federal Reserve System are included in our list of exempt securities.

Quick Quiz 2.8

1. **Y.** Mr. Thompson's receipt of an unsolicited order from Ms. Gordon is an exempt transaction.

2. **Y.** The sale of an unregistered security in a private, nonpublicly advertised transaction to 10 or fewer offerees over the last 12 months is an exempt transaction (a private placement).

3. **Y.** The sale of unclaimed securities by the Administrator of securities for the state of New Mexico is an exempt transaction.

4. **N.** The sale of stock of a privately owned company to the public in an initial public offering is not an exempt transaction.

5. **C.** Choice III is not an exempt transaction because the private placement exemption is limited to 10 offerees, not 10 purchasers. The Administrator would be suspicious of anyone with a 100% closing ratio. All of the others are included in our list of exempt transactions.

Quick Quiz 2.9

1. **C.** The USA requires that any application for registration include the amount of securities to be sold in that state. The Administrator has the power to request regular filings of reports, but no more frequently than quarterly. Although the issuer is most commonly the registrant, selling stockholders and broker/dealers may also make application.

Quick Quiz 2.10

1. **U.** It is unlawful to guarantee the performance of any security. Government securities, although default free, have interest rate risk or market price risk that an agent may not guarantee.

2. **U.** It is unlawful to exercise discretion without prior written authorization. Since the client was a nondiscretionary client, the agent could not, on his own initiative, select which Internet company to invest in.

3. **L.** An agent must refuse orders from anyone other than the customer unless that person has prior written trading authority.

4. **U.** All written customer complaints must be forwarded to a principal of the agent's employing broker/dealer.

5. **L.**   Agents may borrow from banks or financial institutions that are in the business of lending money to public customers. Agents may not borrow money from their customers who are not in the business of lending money.

6. **U.**   An agent may not guarantee the performance of a security.

7. **L.**   It is lawful to charge extra transaction fees when justified as long as the customer is informed before the transaction.

8. **U.**   It is unlawful to promise services that an agent cannot reasonably expect to perform or that the agent is not qualified to perform.

9. **U.**   It is unlawful to solicit unregistered nonexempt securities.

Quick Quiz 2.11

1. **D.**   The Administrator has jurisdiction over a security offering if it was directed to, originated in, or was accepted in that state.

2. **C.**   A state Administrator has jurisdiction over a securities offering made in a bona fide newspaper published within the state, but only whose circulation is less than ⅔ outside the state.

Quick Quiz 2.12

1. **D.**   The Administrator need not seek an injunction to issue a cease and desist order. The USA does not require that an Administrator conduct a public or private hearing before issuing a cease and desist order. When time does not permit, the Administrator may issue a cease and desist before a hearing to prevent a pending violation. The USA does not grant the Administrator the power to issue injunctions to force compliance with the act. The act permits the Administrator to issue cease and desist orders, and, if they do not work, the Administrator may seek an injunction from a court of competent jurisdiction. A cease and desist order is an administrative order, whereas an injunction is a judicial order.

2. **C.**   An Administrator may compel the testimony of witnesses when conducting an investigation. Investigation of serious violations need not be held in public. An Administrator in Illinois may enforce subpoenas from South Carolina whether or not the violation occurred in Illinois. Conviction for any felony within the past 10 years is one of a number of reasons that the Administrator has for denying a license. However, upon notice of the denial, a written request may be made for a hearing. That request must be honored within 15 days.

Quick Quiz 2.13

1. **D.**   An administrator may cancel the registration of a registrant that is no longer in existence. A person may request a withdrawal of a registration. Withdrawals become effective after 30 days if there are no revocation or denial proceedings in process. An Administrator does not revoke the registration of a person who is declared mentally incompetent but instead cancels his registration; this is a nonpunitive administrative action.

Quick Quiz 2.14

1. **B.**   To be subject to time in prison, a sales agent must knowingly have violated the USA. A client who purchased a security in violation of the USA may recover the original purchase price plus costs involved in filing a lawsuit. In addition, the purchaser is entitled to interest at a rate stated by the Administrator, less any earnings already received on the investment. The right of rescission must be accepted within 30 days of receipt of the letter of rescission. Although any person aggrieved by an order of the Administrator may request an appeal of the order within 60 days, such appeal does not function as a stay order during the appeal process. The person who is the subject of the order must comply with the order during the period unless a stay is granted by the court.

3

Federal and State Regulation of Investment Advisers and Their Representatives

Investment advisers and their representatives are defined by federal and state securities laws. A person that performs the functions of an investment adviser, as the term is defined in the Investment Advisers Act of 1940 and more fully described in SEC Release IA-1092, is by definition an investment adviser. Advisers and their representatives must conduct business within the regulatory framework prescribed in federal and state securities laws.

The Series 65 exam will include approximately 12 questions on the material presented in this Unit. ■

When you have completed this Unit, you should be able to:

- **define** federal covered investment adviser and list exemptions and exclusions under the Investment Advisers Act of 1940 and the Uniform Securities Act;

- **describe** the investment adviser registration process, required postregistration filings, and business activities;

- **identify** required elements of the investment advisory contract, client disclosure brochure, wrap-fee programs, and solicitor's brochure;

- **list** the important ethical considerations and fiduciary responsibilities in providing investment advisory services;

- **explain** the impact of SEC Release IA-1092 on the definition of investment advisers and their activities; and

- **understand** the implications of NASAA's Statement of Policy in Unethical Business Practices of Investment Advisers.

INVESTMENT ADVISERS ACT OF 1940

The **Investment Advisers Act of 1940** is the federal legislation that defines the term *investment adviser* and requires persons that fall within the definition to register with the **Securities and Exchange Commission (SEC)** or with the **states** in which they do business. Under the **National Securities Markets Improvement Act of 1996 (NSMIA)**, investment advisers who are registered with the SEC or are exempt from registration under the Investment Advisers Act of 1940 do not have to register with state securities Administrators.

The two primary purposes of the Investment Advisers Act of 1940 are:

- the regulation of persons, both natural and legal, in the business of giving investment advice; and

- the establishment of standards of ethical business conduct for the industry.

DEFINITIONS

To understand the application of this act, it is necessary to understand the definitions that follow. Although these definitions come from the Investment Advisers Act of 1940—federal legislation—the same terms are used in the Uniform Securities Act (USA), model legislation that most states use for drafting state securities laws, known as blue-sky laws, as discussed in Unit 2.

Broker

A **broker** means any person engaged in the business of effecting transactions in securities for the account of others.

Dealer

A **dealer** is any person regularly engaged in the business of buying and selling securities as principal for his own account, but does not include a bank, insurance company, or an investment company.

Fiduciary

A **fiduciary** is a person legally appointed and authorized to hold assets in trust for another person. The fiduciary manages the assets for the benefit of the other person rather than for his or her own profits and must exercise a standard of care imposed by law. Examples include an executor of an estate, a trustee, and, in this exam, an investment adviser.

Person

Although the definition of person (see Unit 2, page 48) under the USA is somewhat broader than that found in federal law, for purposes of the exam, the slight differences are not relevant.

Person Associated with an Investment Adviser

Person associated with an investment adviser means any partner, officer, or director of the investment adviser (or any person performing similar functions) or any person directly or indirectly controlling or controlled by the investment adviser, including any employees of the investment adviser, except that as far as registration requirements are concerned, persons associated with investment advisers whose functions are clerical or administerial are not included in the meaning of the term. Most students taking this course are included in the definition of an investment adviser representative.

QUICK QUIZ 3.1

1. A person who acts in a principal capacity while engaging in the securities business would be known as a(n)

   A. agent
   B. broker
   C. dealer
   D. bank

Quick Quiz answers can be found at the end of the Unit.

WHO ARE INVESTMENT ADVISERS?

An **investment adviser** is defined under both the Investment Advisers Act of 1940 and the USA as "any person who, for compensation, engages in the business of advising others as to the value of securities or the advisability of investing in securities or, as part of a regular business, issues analyses or reports concerning securities."

SEC RELEASE IA-1092

As a result of the proliferation of persons offering investment advice, Congress directed the SEC to define the activities that would subject a person to the 1940 Investment Advisers Act. The SEC did so in SEC Release IA-1092.

SEC Release IA-1092 interprets the definition of investment adviser under the Investment Advisers Act of 1940 to include financial planners, pension consultants, and others who offer investment advice as part of their financial practices.

Release IA-1092, in short, identifies as an investment adviser anyone who:

■ provides investment advice, reports, or analyses with respect to securities;

■ is in the business of providing advice or analyses; and

■ receives compensation, directly or indirectly, for these services.

TAKE NOTE

If a person engages in these three activities, that person is an investment adviser subject to the Investment Advisers Act of 1940. As an investment adviser, this person must register with either the SEC or the states.

Provide Investment Advice

In Release IA-1092, the SEC maintains that a person who gives advice and issues reports, analyses, and recommendations about specific securities is an investment adviser if that person is in the business of doing so and receives compensation for the advice. This definition of an investment adviser includes financial planners, pension consultants, and sports and entertainment representatives.

Financial Planners

Financial planners who make recommendations regarding a person's financial resources or perform analyses that concern securities are investment advisers if such services are performed as part of a business and for compensation. Under this interpretation, the SEC even includes those financial planners who advise clients as to the desirability of investing in securities as an alternative to other investments, such as real estate, intangibles, or other assets.

Pension Consultants

Consultants who advise employee benefit plans on how to fund their plans with securities are also considered investment advisers by the SEC. In addition, under Release IA-1092, the SEC considers pension consultants who advise employee benefit plans on the selection, performance, and retention of investment managers to be investment advisers.

Sports and Entertainment Representatives

Persons who provide financially related services to entertainers and athletes that include advice related to investments, tax planning, budgeting, and money management are also investment advisers.

A sports agent who secures a favorable contract for a football player and receives a commission of 10% of the player's salary is not necessarily an investment adviser. However, if the sports agent advises the football player to invest his money in specific securities, the agent is then in the business of offering investment advice and would then be subject to the Investment Advisers Act of 1940.

In the Business of Providing Advice

A person is in the business of providing advice and subject to regulation as an investment adviser if he:

■ gives advice on a regular basis such that it constitutes a business activity conducted with some regularity (although the frequency of the activity is a factor, it is not the only determinant in whether one is in the business of giving advice, and providing advice does not have to be the person's principal activity); and

■ advertises investment advisory services and presents himself to the public as an investment adviser or as one who provides investment advice.

A person is in the business of giving investment advice if he receives separate compensation that represents a charge for giving the advice.

A person is in the business if he provides investment advice or issues reports on anything other than rare, isolated, and nonperiodic instances. In this context, a person is an investment adviser if he recommends that a client allocate funds to specific assets, such as high-yield bonds, technology stocks, or mutual funds.

A person whose business is to offer only nonspecific investment advice, through publication of a general newsletter, for instance, is not covered by the act. However, such a person would be included if he acted as a representative of a broker/dealer and then made specific securities recommendations to clients.

Compensation

A person who receives any economic benefit as a result of providing investment advice is an investment adviser. Compensation includes advisory fees, commissions, or other types of fees relating to the service rendered. A separate fee for the advice need not be charged; the fee can be paid by a third party on behalf of the beneficiary of the advice.

Fees that an investment adviser receives from a corporation for advice given to the corporation's employees or retirees are considered compensation. A financial planner who designs a comprehensive financial plan for the corporation's employees without charging a fee but receives commissions on insurance policies sold as part of the plan is acting as an investment adviser representative. Even though that compensation is indirect, it meets the release's definition of compensation for investment advice.

EXCLUSIONS FROM DEFINITION OF INVESTMENT ADVISER UNDER FEDERAL LAW

Although the definition of an investment adviser is broad, certain exclusions apply. There are five primary exclusions from the definition of an investment adviser.

- Any bank or bank holding company, as defined in the Bank Holding Company Act of 1956, is excluded.

- Any **lawyer, accountant, teacher,** or **engineer** whose advice is solely incidental to the practice of his profession is excluded. This exclusion is not available to any of these who have established a separate advisory business. Also, the exclusion would not be available to any of these who holds himself out as offering investment advice.

- Any broker/dealer whose performance of such services is solely incidental to the conduct of his business as a broker or dealer and who receives no special compensation is excluded. The exclusion also applies to registered representatives of broker/dealers.

- The definition of investment adviser encompasses publishers as well as authors. However, the act excludes from the definition of investment adviser the publisher of any bona fide newspaper, news magazine, or business or financial publication of general and regular circulation. This exception is applicable only where, on the basis of the content, advertising material, readership, and other relevant factors, a publication is not primarily a vehicle for distributing investment advice. For example, newspapers of general circulation would be eligible for the exclusion.

- Any person whose advice relates solely to securities issued or guaranteed by the federal government is excluded.

QUICK QUIZ 3.2

1. The Investment Advisers Act of 1940 excludes certain persons from the definition of an investment adviser if their performance of advisory services is solely incidental to their professions. This exclusion would apply to all of the following EXCEPT

   A. an accountant
   B. an economist
   C. an electrical engineer
   D. a college professor teaching a course on economics

2. Which of the following would be excluded from the definition of investment adviser under the Investment Advisers Act of 1940?

   I.   A bank offering advice through its trust department
   II. A geologist giving advice on the potential prospects of an oil and gas limited partnership program
   III. A person whose only clients are individuals and whose only advice deals with securities which are direct obligations of the US government

   A. I and II
   B. I and III
   C. II and III
   D. I, II and III

EXCLUSIONS FROM THE DEFINITION OF INVESTMENT ADVISER UNDER STATE LAW

Below are the exclusions from the definition of investment adviser under state law.

- Banks, savings institutions, and trust companies are excluded.

- Any lawyer, accountant, teacher or engineer whose advice is solely incidental to the practice of his profession is excluded. This exclusion is not available to any of these who have established a separate advisory business. Also, the exclusion would not be available to any of these who holds himself out as offering investment advice.

- Any broker/dealer or its agents whose performance of such services is solely incidental to the conduct of his business as a broker/dealer and who receives no special compensation is excluded.

- The definition of investment adviser encompasses publishers as well as authors. However, the act excludes from the definition of investment adviser a publisher of any bona fide newspaper, news column, newsletter, news magazine, or business or financial publication or service, whether communicated in hard copy form, or by electronic means, or otherwise, that does not consist of the rendering of advice on the basis of the specific investment situation of each client.

- Investment adviser representatives are excluded.

- Any person who is a federal covered adviser is excluded.

- Any person excluded by the Investment Advisers Act of 1940 is also excluded.

- Any other person the Administrator specifies is excluded.

As you can see, the first four exclusions are virtually identical under both federal and state law. The only real difference is that under the USA, publishers will only be considered investment advisers if their advice is specific to each and every subscriber.

Then we have some important differences. There is no stated exclusion under the USA for those giving advice solely on US government securities, but, they are excluded under the sixth item. The state law specifically excludes investment adviser representatives and, of course, federal covered advisers.

TAKE NOTE

For purposes of the exclusion, under both state and federal law, the term "bank" does not include a savings and loan association or a foreign bank.

TAKE NOTE

In 2005, the SEC issued Rule 202(a)(11)-1 to the Investment Advisers Act of 1940. This rule (known in the industry as the *Merrill Lynch Rule*) modified the broker/dealer exclusion from the definition of investment adviser. On March 30, 2007, the US Court of Appeals for the District of Columbia Circuit overturned the rule so it is unlikely that there will be questions dealing with it on your exam.

REGISTRATION REQUIREMENTS UNDER THE INVESTMENT ADVISERS ACT OF 1940

The Investment Advisers Act of 1940 makes it unlawful for a nonregistered investment adviser to use the mail or any instrumentality of interstate commerce in connection with his business. Unless an exemption is available, registration with the SEC or with a state is required.

TAKE NOTE

In the following section, *exemption from registration* refers to persons who meet the definition of investment advisers but who do not have to register.

EXEMPTION FROM THE REGISTRATION REQUIREMENTS UNDER FEDERAL LAW

The Investment Advisers Act of 1940 exempts the following classes of investment advisers from the registration requirements.

- Advisers whose clients are residents of the state in which the adviser has its principal office and place of business and who do not give advice dealing with securities listed on any national exchange are exempt. For example, an adviser would be exempted under this provision if all of its clients were Georgia residents, its only places of business were in Georgia, and it did not give advice on securities listed on any national exchange.

- Advisers whose only clients are insurance companies are exempt.

- Advisers who, during the course of the preceding 12 months, had fewer than 15 clients, none of which is an investment company registered with the SEC, and do not hold themselves out generally to the public as investment advisers are exempt. This is known as the **de minimis** exemption.

A person is considered to be holding himself out generally to the public as an investment adviser if, among other things, he lets it be known by word of mouth through existing clients or otherwise that he is willing to take on clients. Thus, the exemption is not ordinarily available to a person who maintains a listing as an investment adviser in a telephone or business directory or who uses stationery indicating that he is an investment adviser.

TAKE NOTE

The SEC has applied the 15-client rule to investment clubs. When determining the number of clients receiving advice, the individual members of an investment club are counted separately, rather than the club as a single client.

An exemption is granted on the basis of who you advise, not on what you advise. Note also that **exclusion** means exclusion from a definition, whereas **exemption** means not subject to registration.

QUICK QUIZ 3.3

1. Which of the following investment advisers are exempt from registration under the Investment Advisers Act of 1940?

   I.   An adviser whose only clients are insurance companies
   II. An adviser who maintains offices in only one state, advises only residents of that state, and gives advice relating to only tax-exempt municipal bonds
   III. An adviser whose only clients are banks

   A. I and II
   B. I and III
   C. II and III
   D. I, II and III

FEDERAL COVERED ADVISERS

The National Securities Markets Improvement Act of 1996 (NSMIA) made major changes in the way investment advisers register. The NSMIA divided registration responsibilities between the SEC and the states' securities departments. Basically, the largest firms are required to register with the SEC, and the smaller ones are required to register with the states.

Advisers registered with the SEC are known as **federal covered investment advisers**. Federal covered advisers are those:

- required to be registered or registered as an investment adviser with the SEC;

- excluded from the definition of an investment adviser by the Investment Advisers Act of 1940; or

- under contract to manage an investment company registered under the Investment Company Act of 1940, regardless of the amount of assets under management.

TAKE NOTE

Because so much of this exam deals with interpreting the laws, it is sometimes necessary to review some legal concepts with you. For example, if a person is excluded from the definition of investment adviser under the Investment Advisers Act of 1940, the states, under the NSMIA, cannot define such person as an investment adviser because federal law excluded that person from the definition. In other words, if the separate states could define those persons who were excluded from the federal definition as investment advisers, the federal law would have no meaning.

EXEMPTIONS FROM THE REGISTRATION REQUIREMENTS UNDER THE UNIFORM SECURITIES ACT

Exemption from Registration for Investment Advisers

The USA exempts from registration certain persons who, although they fall within the definition of an investment adviser, do not have to register as such in the state.

The advisers exempt from registration with the state Administrator are those who have no place of business in the state but are registered in another state, provided their only clients in the state are:

- broker/dealers registered under the act;

- investment advisers;

- institutional investors, including employee benefit plans with assets of not less than $1 million;

- existing clients who are not residents but are temporarily in the state;

- limited to five or fewer clients, other than those listed above, resident in the state during the preceding 12 months (called the de minimis exemption); or

- any others the Administrator exempts by rule or order.

CASE STUDY

Out-of-State Advice

Situation: A California-registered investment adviser with no offices located in any other state has directed investment advice on five separate occasions over the past year to individual residents of the state of Nevada. Is the investment adviser required to register in the state of Nevada?

Analysis: The answer is no. Registration is not required because the investment adviser does not have an office in Nevada and directs business to five or fewer individual residents of the state during the year. If the firm had an office in Nevada, registration would be required in that state. Also, even if the firm had no office in Nevada, registration would be required if business had been transacted with six or more individual residents of the state during the previous 12 months.

If the business had been transacted with other investment advisers, broker/dealers, or institutional investors, there is no limit as long as there is no office in the state.

TAKE NOTE

The NSMIA eliminated state registration requirements for advisers with $30 million or more in assets under management. Advisers with at least $25 million but less than $30 million have the option to register with either the state or the SEC. Advisers with less than $25 million must register with the state. The NSMIA stated that pension consultants with assets under control of at least $50 million would also be federal covered advisers.

Investment advisers exempt from state registration are not exempt from paying state filing fees and giving notice to the Administrator. The procedure followed is called **notice filing.**

CASE STUDY

Exclusion from Definition and Exemptions from Registration

Situation: Charles & Goode, a partnership located in Illinois, has been in the business of selling investment advice in the form of research reports and managing securities portfolios for the past 20 years. The partnership has earned a good reputation among investors and has managed less than $25 million until this year. This year they gained several new clients and now have $50 million in assets under management.

Most of Charles & Goode's clients are wealthy individuals and residents of Illinois, but they have three clients who are residents of Wisconsin and 30 clients who live in Indiana. The principals of Charles & Goode have also formed a separate partnership called C&G Mutual Fund Advisers, Inc., which manages a small investment company with assets of $15 million. The partners in Charles & Goode are uncertain about what they must do to be in compliance with the Uniform Securities Act.

Analysis: As a partnership in the business of managing money for individual clients, Charles & Goode falls within the definition of an investment adviser and must so register with the Illinois securities Administrator until it manages $25 million or more in assets. However, with the addition of new clients as of the current year, Charles & Goode will be exempt from registration with Illinois, because it is now excluded from the definition of an investment adviser. Charles & Goode is now a federal covered adviser that must register with the SEC because it has crossed the threshold of $30 million of assets under management.

Before becoming a federal covered adviser, Charles & Goode need not register in Wisconsin because they have five or fewer clients in the state; however, they would have to register in Indiana because they have more than five clients there. After becoming a federal covered adviser, Charles & Goode does not have to register in Indiana, Wisconsin, or Illinois—after it manages more than $30 million it only has to register with the SEC, not the state Administrator. An adviser with assets of least $25 million but less than $30 million may register with either the state or the SEC. Advisers with $30 million or more of assets under management must register with the SEC only.

The separate partnership, C&G Mutual Fund Advisers, Inc., which manages only $15 million, is exempt from registration in Illinois (or any other state) because those persons who operate as investment advisers to investment companies registered under the Investment Company Act of 1940, regardless of the size of the investment company, are included in the definition of federal covered adviser. Both C&G Mutual Fund Advisers Inc. and the fund they manage may have to pay state filing fees under a procedure called *notice filing*.

TAKE NOTE

As a general rule, the SEC or federal rules involve bigger numbers than the state rules—that is, large investment advisers must register with the SEC, whereas small investment advisers must register with the state.

Adviser managing . . .

. . . $30 million or more—**SEC** registration

$30 million

$25 million

. . . at least $25 million but less than $30 million—**SEC** or **state** registration

. . . less than $25 million—**state** registration

$0 million

Write **A** if the phrase describes an investment adviser that must register under the USA and **B** if it does not.

_____   1. Publisher of a newspaper that renders general financial advice

_____   2. Broker/dealer that charges a fee for providing investment advice over and above commissions from securities transactions

_____   3. Investment adviser that manages $10 million in assets

---

REGISTRATION REQUIREMENTS UNDER FEDERAL LAW

The standard registration form under the Investment Advisers Act is **Form ADV**. This form consists of two parts: Part I asks for information used to review the application. Part II asks for the background and business practices of the investment adviser. Only Part I is filed with the SEC. Part II must be kept on file, readily accessible at the adviser's principal office. The SEC has 45 days after the ADV is filed in which to either grant registration or begin proceedings to deny it. Once an ADV has been filed, it is part of the adviser's permanent record. From time to time, it becomes necessary to update the ADV, which is accomplished by amending the form. Amending the ADV requires completing the first page of the ADV Part I and the entire page containing the updated items.

There are no educational qualifications specified in the Advisers Act as a condition for registration as an investment adviser. However, the SEC staff has stated that a person holding himself out as an investment adviser represents that he has adequate qualifications by his educational background or experience to engage in that activity.

Schedule I

SEC registration is prohibited unless the adviser proves on Schedule I of the ADV that it has at least $25 million under management. Investment advisers may register with the SEC if the adviser expects to have $25 million under management within the next 120 days. There is an exception for advisers domiciled in a state that does not have provisions for registration of investment advisers (only one at the time of this printing). Another exception applies to an adviser to a registered investment company. Even if the assets of an adviser to a registered investment company are less than $25 million, the adviser, as a federal covered adviser, must register with the SEC. There is another way for an investment adviser with assets under management less than $25 million to register with the SEC. If the entity does such a widespread business that it functions as an investment adviser under the laws of at least 30 states and, were it not for this rule, would have to register in at least 25 of them, the SEC will allow federal registration.

Every investment adviser who is registered under the act on the last day of its fiscal year is required to file **Form ADV-Schedule I** no later than 90 days after the end of the adviser's fiscal year. This Schedule I verifies the adviser's continued eligibility to register with the SEC by having at least $25 million under management (or one of the other qualifications). It is important to remember that the filing of the Form ADV-Schedule I does not relieve the adviser of any requirements to properly amend its ADV. The Schedule I is always used for renewal and not for amendments.

Updating

Certain changes to the ADV require prompt updating, whereas others require updating within 90 days of the end of the fiscal year. Changes requiring prompt updating are:

- change of the registrant's name;

- change in the principal business location;

- change in the location of books and records, if they are kept somewhere other than at the principal location;

- change to the contact person preparing the form;

- change in organizational structure from partnership to corporation and so on;

- change to any of the questions regarding disciplinary actions;

- change in policy regarding custody of the customer funds and/or securities; and

- any material changes to either Part I or Part II of the ADV.

TAKE NOTE   An investment adviser registered under state law whose annual filing reveals $30 million under management has 90 days to register with the SEC. A federal covered investment adviser whose annual filing discloses less than $25 million in assets under management no longer qualifies for SEC registration and has 180 days to register with the state(s).

Fees

Even though registration under Form ADV remains in effect until it is withdrawn by the registrant or canceled or revoked by the SEC, there is a requirement for annual renewal. There are fees for the initial filing and renewals. If an investment adviser changes its form of business organization (e.g., from a sole proprietorship to a corporation), a new ADV, but no fees, would be required.

Form ADV-W

If an adviser no longer desires to engage in the business, application to withdraw registration is accomplished by filing **Form ADV-W**. Form ADV-W must be filed in order to withdraw the registration voluntarily. The request to withdraw from registration accompanied by properly filed Form ADV-W becomes effective 60 days after filing with the SEC.

QUICK QUIZ 3.5

1. John Oldman has been responsible for keeping the firm's Form ADV updated for the last 40 years. John has suddenly announced his immediate retirement. This would require

   A. prompt filing of an amended ADV with the SEC indicating the change in contact person
   B. prompt filing of an ADV-W with the SEC indicating the change of contact person
   C. filing of amended ADV within 90 days of the end of the adviser's fiscal year giving notice of the change of contact person
   D. filing of the ADV-W within 90 days of the end of the adviser's fiscal year giving notice of the change of contact person

---

TEST TOPIC ALERT

Under the Investment Advisers Act of 1940 as well as NASAA's Model Rule, any person that directly or indirectly has the right to vote more than 25% of the voting securities, or is entitled to more than 25% of the profits, of an investment adviser is presumed to control that investment adviser.

CANCELLATION OF REGISTRATION

The SEC has the power to cancel the registration of any adviser upon finding that the adviser is no longer in existence, is not engaged in business as an investment adviser, or does not meet the necessary dollar standards to remain SEC registered. If not withdrawn by the adviser or canceled or revoked by the SEC, registration continues indefinitely.

INVESTMENT COUNSEL

The Investment Advisers Act of 1940 prohibits a person registered under the Investment Advisers Act from representing that he is an investment counsel or using the term *investment counsel* as descriptive of his business unless:

- his principal business consists of acting as investment adviser; and

- a substantial part of his business consists of rendering investment supervisory services. The act defines **investment supervisory services** as the giving of continuous advice as to the investment of funds on the basis of the individual needs of each client.

QUICK QUIZ 3.6

1. Which of the following investment advisers would be permitted to use the term *investment counsel*?

    A. A financial planner offering a wide range of services to his clients, including tax planning, estate planning, and insurance planning, as well as investment advice
    B. A professional providing a market timing service with an annual subscription fee of $495 (this service attempts to maximize profits by suggesting entry and exit points for over 100 listed stocks)
    C. A firm whose exclusive business is placing their client's assets into model portfolios
    D. All of the above

REGISTRATION AS AN INVESTMENT ADVISER UNDER THE USA

For those investment advisers where state registration is required, the procedure is the same as that previously described in Unit 2. Filing of the ADV Part I (some states also require that Part II be filed as well), accompanied by a consent to service of process and the required fees, is the standard.

TEST TOPIC ALERT

Successor firm:

Under both federal and state law, a successor firm registers by filing a new application and, in the case of the SEC, paying the appropriate fee and, under the USA, without additional fee. Please note the difference—one case involves a fee, the other does not.

Financial Requirements

Under the Investment Advisers Act of 1940, no specific financial requirements are spelled out. It is, of course, required that any federal covered investment adviser notify clients of any financial situation that might impair its ability to perform the functions for which it has been contracted.

Under the Uniform Securities Act, the Administrator may, by rule or order, establish minimum financial requirements for an investment adviser registered in the state. The Administrator may require an adviser who has custody of client funds or securities or has discretion over a client's account to post a surety bond or maintain a minimum net worth. Usually, the requirement is higher for custody than for discretion. Typically, the net worth required of investment advisers with discretionary authority is $10,000, and that for those taking custody is $35,000. If the adviser is using a surety bond instead, the requirement in either case is $35,000. An adviser who does not exercise discretion and does not maintain custody, but does accept prepayment of fees of more than $500, six or more months in advance, must maintain a positive net worth at all times.

TAKE NOTE

Because the USA is only a template, some states have higher net worth or bonding requirements. The exam may want you to know that if an IA meets the net worth or surety bonding requirements of the state where its principal office is located, that is sufficient in any other state in which it may be registered.

One exception to all this is the case of an investment adviser whose only type of custody is direct deduction of fees. If this adviser meets all of the safeguards required by the Administrator, then the adviser is exempt from the net worth or bonding requirements.

The USA specifies the action to be taken by a registered investment adviser whose net worth falls below the required minimum. By the close of business on the next business day, the adviser must notify the Administrator that the investment adviser's net worth is less than the minimum required. After sending that notice, the adviser must file a financial report with the Administrator by the close of business on the next business day.

QUICK QUIZ 3.7

1. All of the following statements regarding the USA's minimum financial requirements of an investment adviser are correct EXCEPT

   A. advisers maintaining custody of customer funds and/or securities must have a net worth of $35,000
   B. advisers maintaining discretion over client accounts must have net worth of $35,000
   C. advisers accepting substantial prepayments of fees must have a positive net worth
   D. advisers whose only custody of client funds is the ability to have direct deduction of fees are exempt from the net worth and bonding requirements

2. A registered investment adviser has discretionary authority over client accounts. Its accounting department has just discovered that the firm's net worth is $8,500. Under the Uniform Securities Act, they

   I. must notify the administrator of the net worth deficiency by the close of that day
   II. must notify the administrator of the net worth deficiency by the close of the next business day
   III. must file a financial report with the Administrator by the first business day following notice
   IV. may no longer exercise discretion until they increase their net worth

   A. I and III
   B. I and IV
   C. II and III
   D. II and IV

3. XYZ Advisers has its principal office in State A. XYZ maintains custody of customer securities and they wish to open an office in State B. They have been informed that the Administrator of State B requires all investment advisers that take custody to maintain a minimum net worth of $65,000. Which of the following statements is CORRECT?

    A. XYZ will have to meet State B's net worth requirements if it wishes to register there.
    B. XYZ can register in State B only if they cease taking custody.
    C. As long as XYZ meets the net worth requirements of State A, it can register in any other state.
    D. In lieu of meeting State B's requirements, a surety bond may be posted.

INVESTMENT ADVISER REPRESENTATIVE

An **investment adviser representative** means any individual (other than an investment adviser) who represents a state-registered investment adviser or federal covered investment adviser when:

■ making investment recommendations;

■ managing accounts or client portfolios;

■ soliciting investment advisory services; or

■ supervising employees who perform any of these duties.

Partners, officers, directors, or other employees controlled by an investment adviser who provide the above services are, for state regulatory purposes, investment adviser representatives.

Investment Adviser: Business or Individual

Investment Adviser Representative:
Individual Only

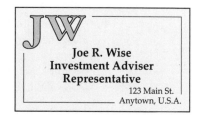

Exclusions from the Definition of Investment Adviser Representative

Employees of investment advisory firms are excluded from the term *investment adviser representative*, provided their activities are confined to clerical duties or those activities that are solely incidental to the investment advisory services offered. Should the investment advisory employee receive specific compensation for offering these services, the employee would then have to register as an investment adviser representative. Exclusion criteria for administrative employees of investment advisers are much the same as those for administrative personnel of broker/dealers.

Registration of an investment adviser also leads to automatic investment adviser representative registration of partners, officers, or directors active in the business and anyone else performing a similar function. What does that really mean? Since an investment adviser representative can only be registered as a representative of a registered adviser, those individuals holding the positions mentioned above are in limbo until the adviser's registration becomes effective. At that time, their individual registrations go into effect. It does not mean that these people do not have to file applications and don't have to take the appropriate examinations.

Many independent financial planners operate as independent contractors, not employees of investment advisory firms or broker/dealers. Regardless, they are required to be registered as investment adviser representatives of the firm and must be placed under the same level of supervisory scrutiny as employees. Their business cards may contain the name of their separate planning entity, but must also disclose the name of the entity registered as the investment adviser.

TEST TOPIC ALERT

Registered investment advisers are responsible for the supervision of those individuals registered as investment adviser representatives, but acting in the capacity of independent contractors, to the same extent as those who are actual employees of the firm.

QUICK QUIZ 3.8

True or False?

_____ 1. An investment adviser representative must register with the SEC if she has clients with assets of $30 million or more under management.

_____ 2. A state-registered investment adviser maintaining custody of a customer's securities or funds and exercising discretion in the account is generally required to maintain a minimum net worth of $35,000.

_____ 3. An employee of an investment advisory firm is an investment adviser representative if his duties are confined to clerical activities.

_____ 4. An administrative employee who receives specific compensation for offering investment advisory services is not an investment adviser representative.

_____ 5. An employee of an investment advisory firm is an investment adviser representative if his duties involve making investment recommendations.

BOOKS AND RECORDS REQUIRED BY FEDERAL AND STATE LAW

The Uniform Securities Act virtually duplicates the first 12 items of the recordkeeping requirements of the Investment Advisers Act of 1940. The major exception is that on the eleventh bullet (a copy of each notice), NASAA's Model Rule requires a copy when the material is distributed to two or more persons, not 10 or more as is the case under federal law.

BOOKS AND RECORDS REQUIRED BY THE INVESTMENT ADVISERS ACT OF 1940

The Investment Advisers Act requires every adviser (other than one specifically exempted from registration) to make, keep, and preserve such records, and for such periods as the SEC may prescribe as necessary or appropriate in the public interest or for the protection of investors. By rule, the SEC has set forth various recordkeeping requirements for investment advisers. Moreover, the act makes it unlawful for any person to willfully make any untrue statement of a material fact in any report filed with the SEC or to willfully omit to state in a report any material fact required to be stated therein.

The SEC and the states require investment advisers to maintain the following books and records:

- A journal, including cash receipts and disbursement records

- General and auxiliary ledgers reflecting asset, liability, reserve, capital, income, and expense accounts

- A memorandum of each order given by the adviser for the purchase or sale of any security, or any instruction received by the adviser from the client concerning the purchase, sale, receipt, or delivery of a security, and of any modification or cancellation of any such order or instruction

- All checkbooks, bank statements, canceled checks, and cash reconciliations

- All bills or statements (or copies thereof) paid or unpaid

- All trial balances, financial statements, and internal audit working papers

- Originals of all written communications received and copies of all written communications sent by the adviser related to any recommendation or advice given or proposed to be given; any receipt, disbursement, or delivery of funds or securities; or the placing or execution of any order to purchase or sell any security

- A record of all accounts in which the adviser is vested with any discretionary power with respect to the funds, securities, or transactions of any client

- All powers of attorney and other evidences of the granting of any discretionary authority by any client to the adviser, or copies thereof

■ All written agreements (or copies thereof) entered into by the adviser with a client or otherwise relating to his investment advisory business

■ A file containing a copy of each notice, circular, advertisement, newspaper article, investment letter, bulletin, or other communication, including by electronic media (email), that the investment adviser circulates or distributes, directly or indirectly, to 10 or more persons (other than persons connected with the investment adviser); if the item, including communications by electronic media recommends the purchase or sale of a specific security and does not state the reasons for the recommendation, the adviser must prepare a memorandum indicating the reasons for that recommendation

■ With certain exceptions, a record of all securities transactions in which an investment adviser or any advisory representative has, or by reason of such transaction acquires, any direct or beneficial ownership

In practice, the recordkeeping rule has served as a deterrent to the practice of scalping because it requires all advisory representatives to report all of their security transactions to their affiliated advisory firms on a regular basis; these reports are subject to SEC examination. **Scalping** is the practice whereby an investment adviser, before the dissemination of a securities recommendation, trades on the anticipated short-run market activity that may result from the recommendation.

Investment Adviser Code of Ethics

There are some additional recordkeeping requirements under federal law because of the need for federal covered advisers to institute a code of ethics. This text will include the most testable items relating to that code. Rule 204A-1, Investment Adviser Code of Ethics, requires:

■ a copy of the investment adviser's code of ethics adopted and implemented pursuant to the Investment Advisers Act of 1940;

■ a record of any violation of the code of ethics and of any action taken as a result of the violation;

■ a record of all written acknowledgments, as required by the code of ethics rule, for each person who is currently, or within the past five years was, a supervised person of the investment adviser; and

■ each adviser's code of ethics to require an adviser's access persons (defined below) to periodically report their personal securities transactions and holdings to the adviser's chief compliance officer or other designated persons. The code of ethics must also require the adviser to review those reports. Reviewing these reports will allow advisers as well as the SEC's examination staff to identify improper trades or patterns of trading by access persons.

Personal Trading Procedures

Advisory firms should include the following elements, or address the following issues, when crafting their procedures for employees' personal securities trading:

- Prior written approval before access persons can place a personal securities transaction (i.e., preclearance)

- Maintenance of lists of issuers of securities that the advisory firm is analyzing or recommending for client transactions, and prohibitions on personal trading in securities of those issuers

- Maintenance of restricted lists of issuers about which the advisory firm has inside information, and prohibitions on any trading (personal or for clients) in securities of those issuers

- Blackout periods when client securities trades are being placed or recommendations are being made and access persons are not permitted to place personal securities transactions

- Reminders that investment opportunities must be offered first to clients before the adviser or its employees may act on them, and procedures to implement this principle

- Prohibitions or restrictions on short-swing trading and market timing

- Requirements to trade only through certain brokers, or limitations on the number of brokerage accounts permitted

- Requirements to provide the adviser with duplicate trade confirmations and account statements

- Procedures for assigning new securities analyses to employees whose personal holdings do not present apparent conflicts of interest

The rule permits three exceptions to personal securities reporting. No reports are required:

- with respect to transactions effected pursuant to an automatic investment plan, in which regular periodic purchases (or withdrawals) are made automatically in (or from) investment accounts in accordance with a predetermined schedule and allocation (an automatic investment plan includes a dividend reinvestment plan; however, any transaction that overrides the preset schedule or allocations of the automatic investment plan must be included in a quarterly transaction report);

- with respect to securities held in accounts over which the access person had no direct or indirect influence or control; or

- in the case of an advisory firm that has only one access person, so long as the firm maintains records of the holdings and transactions that the rule would otherwise require to be reported.

The rule treats all securities as reportable securities, with five exceptions designed to exclude securities that appear to present little opportunity for the type of improper trading that the access person reports are designed to uncover:

- Transactions and holdings in direct obligations of the Government of the United States

- Money market instruments—that is, bankers' acceptances, bank certificates of deposit, commercial paper and other high quality short-term debt instruments

- Shares of money market funds

- Transactions and holdings in shares of other types of mutual funds, unless the adviser or a control affiliate acts as the investment adviser or principal underwriter for the fund

- Transactions in units of a unit investment trust if the unit investment trust is invested exclusively in unaffiliated mutual funds

The rule thus requires access persons to report shares of mutual funds advised by the access person's employer or an affiliate, and is designed to help advisers (and the SEC) identify abusive trading by personnel with access to information about a mutual fund's portfolio.

An **access person** is any of the adviser's supervised persons who (1) has access to nonpublic information regarding any clients' purchase or sale of securities, or nonpublic information regarding the portfolio holdings of any reportable fund, or (2) is involved in making securities recommendations to clients, or who has access to such recommendations that are nonpublic. If providing investment advice is the adviser's primary business, all of the firm's directors, officers and partners are presumed to be access persons.

The following records are required under Rule 204A-1, Investment Adviser Code of Ethics:

- A record of each report made by an access person

- A record of the names of persons who are currently, or within the past five years were, access persons of the investment adviser

- A record of any decision, and the reasons supporting the decision, to approve the acquisition of securities by access persons, for at least five years after the end of the fiscal year in which the approval is granted

TIME PERIOD FOR MAINTENANCE OF RECORDS

The Investment Advisers Act of 1940, as well as the Uniform Securities Act, requires that an investment adviser's books and records be maintained in a readily accessible place for five years. The five-year period will run from the end of the fiscal year during which the last entry was made on the record. During the first two years of the five-year period, the rule requires that the records be maintained in an appropriate office of the adviser. However, after this initial two-year period, the records may be preserved in the form of microfilm in compliance with the act.

Partnership articles and any amendments thereto, articles of incorporation, charters, minute books, and stock certificate books of the investment adviser and of any predecessor must be maintained in the principal office of the investment adviser and preserved until at least three years after termination of the enterprise.

TEST TOPIC ALERT

Because the Uniform Securities Act is only a template, some states have more stringent recordkeeping requirements than others. The exam will want you to know that as long as the investment adviser complies with the requirements of the state in which its principal office is located, it will not have to meet the requirements of any other state.

QUICK QUIZ 3.9

1. Under the Investment Advisers Act of 1940, all of the following are true regarding adviser recordkeeping EXCEPT

    A. it must keep records of transactions made for its own account as well as the account of investment adviser representatives to lessen the likelihood of scalping

    B. computer-generated records may be stored in that format

    C. client account records must be maintained, including a list of recommendations made

    D. records must be maintained for a period of 2 years from the end of the fiscal year in which the last entry was made

BROCHURE RULE

Generally, both acts require investment advisers, when entering into an advisory contract, to deliver to their current and prospective clients a written disclosure statement containing information concerning their background and practices. Regarding prospective clients, the written disclosure statement must be delivered when entering into an advisory contract. However, advisers must deliver a brochure to current clients when those clients enter into a substantially revised advisory contract.

The brochure rule permits the required disclosure to be made in one of two ways.

■ The adviser may use Part II of Form ADV as the written disclosure statement.

■ An adviser may use a written document containing the information required by Part II of Form ADV.

The information contained in the separate written disclosure need not follow the same format as Part II of Form ADV. It is sufficient if the written statement contains a fair representation of the information required. However, it is the responsibility of the adviser to prepare these written statements in a meaningful and fair manner. Moreover, the SEC has encouraged advisers to set out this information in a readable and informative manner.

The brochure rule requires advisers to deliver the brochure to the client at least 48 hours before entering into an advisory contract or at the time of entering into an advisory contract, if the advisory client has the right to terminate the contract without penalty within five business days after entering into the contract. Some advisers charge a start-up or set-up fee. Any new client who does not receive a brochure at least 48 hours before entering into an advisory agreement may terminate the agreement and be refunded the set-up fee. However, it would not be considered a penalty for the adviser to make a pro rata charge for management services rendered during that five-business-day period.

EXEMPTIONS FROM THE BROCHURE RULE

There are two exemptions from the initial delivery requirements of the rule.

- Contracts with a registered investment company are exempted. The Investment Company Act of 1940 requires investment advisers to furnish information to the board of directors of a registered investment company to enable the board to evaluate the terms of the proposed contract. Under these circumstances, the SEC thought it unnecessary to require the adviser to deliver a brochure to the investment company.

- Advisers entering into a contract providing solely for impersonal advisory services—that is, publishers of market letters—are exempt from the rule's initial delivery requirements. If the annual charge for this service is $200 or greater, delivery of the brochure must be offered with the same two timing options listed above.

TEST TOPIC ALERT   The brochure rule requires advisers to annually deliver, or to offer in writing to deliver without charge to each of their clients, a written disclosure statement meeting the requirements of the brochure rule.

QUICK QUIZ 3.10
1. With regard to the brochure rule of the Investment Advisers Act of 1940, which of the following are exempt from the delivery requirements of that rule?
    A.   An adviser whose only clients are registered investment companies
    B.   An adviser whose only clients are insurance companies
    C.   An adviser who only provides impersonal advisory services
    D.   All of the above

2. Which of the following statement regarding the Form ADV Part II is CORRECT?
    A.   It must be delivered no later than 48 hours before entering into an advisory contract.
    B.   It must be delivered no later than upon receipt of a client's funds.
    C.   It must accompany the ADV Part I with any initial filing for registration.
    D.   An investment adviser must deliver or offer to deliver to each client, a copy of the most recent ADV Part II no less frequently than annually.

WRAP FEE PROGRAMS

The rules on disclosure are somewhat different for wrap fee programs. A **wrap fee program** is a program under which a client is charged a specified fee, or fees not based directly on transactions in a client's account, for investment advisory services (which may include portfolio management or advice concerning the selection of other investment advisers) and for execution of client transactions.

Any registered investment adviser compensated under a wrap fee program for sponsoring, organizing, or administering the program, or for selecting, or providing advice to clients regarding the selection of, other investment advisers in the program, does not use the normal brochure or Part II of the ADV. Instead, that adviser furnishes clients and prospective clients a document containing at least the information required by Schedule H of Form ADV.

If the investment adviser is offering wrap fee programs, Schedule H requires that the wrap fee document be filed with the SEC and, if applicable, the Administrator. If the firm prepared separate wrap fee brochures for different programs, each brochure must be filed. In the event that a client receives a brochure from one of the advisers involved in the program, it is unnecessary for any other adviser to furnish another brochure.

If information contained in the wrap fee brochure becomes inaccurate in a material manner, the investment adviser must promptly file an amended brochure with the SEC and/or Administrator correcting the information. An investment adviser may update the brochure by using a supplement or sticker that indicates what information is being added or updated and states the new or revised information. Nonmaterial changes are filed within 90 days after the adviser's fiscal year-end.

Some of the required disclosures required under Schedule H include:

- the amount of the wrap fee charged for the program;

- whether the fees are negotiable;

- the portion of the total fee paid to persons providing advice to clients regarding the purchase or sale of specific securities under the program;

- the services provided under the program, including the types of portfolio management services;

- a statement that the program may cost the client more or less than purchasing these services separately; and

- a description of the nature of any fees that the client may pay in addition to the wrap fee.

RULES ON CUSTODY OF FUNDS AND SECURITIES

In April of 2004, compliance with new SEC rules regarding an investment adviser's custody of customer's funds and securities went into effect. NASAA published its rules on custody later that same month. For the most part, the rules are identical. Our text will focus on the rule stated in the Investment Advisers Act of 1940 and, where the NASAA model rule differs, a notation will be made.

Safekeeping required. If you are an investment adviser registered or required to be registered under either federal or state law, it is a fraudulent, deceptive, or manipulative act, practice, or course of business within the meaning of the act for you to have custody of client funds or securities unless the following conditions are met.

■ You have a qualified custodian. A qualified custodian maintains those funds and securities in a separate account for each client under that client's name, or in accounts that contain only your clients' funds and securities, under your name as agent or trustee for the clients.

■ You give notice to your clients. If you open an account with a qualified custodian on your client's behalf, either under the client's name or under your name as agent, you must notify the client in writing of the qualified custodian's name and address and the manner in which the funds or securities are maintained, promptly when the account is opened and following any changes to this information.

■ Account statements are delivered to clients, either:

— by qualified custodian (you have a reasonable basis for believing that the qualified custodian sends an account statement, at least quarterly, to each of your clients for which it maintains funds or securities, identifying the amount of funds and of each security in the account at the end of the period and setting forth all transactions in the account during that period), or

— by adviser you send a quarterly account statement to each of your clients for whom you have custody of funds or securities, identifying the amount of funds and of each security of which you have custody at the end of the period and setting forth all transactions during that period. An independent public accountant must verify all of those funds and securities by actual examination at least once during each calendar year, at a time that is chosen by the accountant without prior notice or announcement to you and that is irregular from year to year, and file a copy of the auditor's report and financial statements with the SEC/Administrator within 30 days after the completion of the examination, stating that it has examined the funds and securities and describing the nature and extent of the examination: If the independent public accountant finds any material discrepancies during the course of the examination, it must notify the SEC/Administrator within one business day of the finding, by means of a facsimile transmission or electronic mail, followed by first class mail, directed to the attention of the Director of the Office of Compliance Inspections and Examinations/Administrator.

■ The client designates an independent representative. A client may designate an independent representative to receive, on his behalf, notices and account statements as required above.

Under the NASAA model rule, the investment adviser notifies the Administrator promptly in writing on Form ADV that the investment adviser has or may have custody.

Exceptions to this rule. Some exceptions include the following.

■ Shares of mutual funds—with respect to shares of an open-end company (mutual fund), you may use the mutual fund's transfer agent in lieu of a qualified custodian since the mutual fund's transfer agent maintains the securities for the client on the mutual fund's books.

■ Certain privately offered securities—you are not required to comply with this section with respect to securities that are:

— acquired from the issuer in a transaction or chain of transactions not involving any public offering,

— uncertificated, and ownership thereof is recorded only on books of the issuer or its transfer agent in the name of the client, and

— transferable only with prior consent of the issuer or holders of the outstanding securities of the issuer.

■ Registered investment companies—you need not comply with the rule with respect to clients that are registered investment companies. Registered investment companies and their advisers must comply with the strict requirements of the Investment Company Act of 1940, and the custody rules adopted under that act.

Definitions. For the purposes of this rule **custody** means holding, directly or indirectly, client funds or securities, or having any authority to obtain possession of them. Custody also includes:

■ possession of client funds or securities (but not of checks drawn by clients and made payable to third parties) unless you receive them inadvertently and you return them to the sender promptly but in any case within three business days of receiving them: therefore, you should remember that the SEC never considers the receipt of a third-party check to constitute custody, while the Administrator will if the check is not sent on within 24 hours (NASAA—Under state law, the receipt of checks drawn by clients and made payable to unrelated third parties is considered custody unless forwarded to the third party within 24 hours of receipt and the adviser maintains a record of the event).

■ any arrangement (including a general power of attorney) under which you are authorized or permitted to withdraw client funds or securities maintained with a custodian upon your instruction to the custodian; and

■ any capacity (such as general partner of a limited partnership, managing member of a limited liability company, or a comparable position for another type of pooled investment vehicle, or trustee of a trust) that gives you or your supervised person legal ownership of or access to client funds or securities.

An **independent representative** is a person that:

■ acts as agent for an advisory client, including in the case of a pooled investment vehicle, for limited partners of a limited partnership (or members of a limited liability company, or other beneficial owners of another type of pooled investment vehicle) and by law or contract is obliged to act in the best interest of the advisory client or the limited partners (or members, or other beneficial owners);

- does not control, is not controlled by, and is not under common control with you; and

- does not have, and has not had within the past two years, a material business relationship with you.

A **qualified custodian** is a bank or savings association that has deposits insured by the Federal Deposit Insurance Corporation under the Federal Deposit Insurance Act, a registered broker-dealer holding the client assets in customer accounts, and a foreign financial institution that customarily holds financial assets for its customers, provided that the foreign financial institution keeps the advisory clients' assets in customer accounts segregated from its proprietary assets.

TAKE NOTE

There are two major benefits to an investment adviser using a qualified custodian.

- Since the custodian is sending the quarterly reports to the client, that administrative burden is lifted from the investment adviser.

- There is no requirement for a surprise annual audit by an independent accountant.

The NASAA model rule also adds language dealing with direct fee deduction. An adviser who has custody because the adviser's fees are directly deducted from client's accounts must also provide the following safeguards.

- Written authorization—the adviser must have written authorization from the client to deduct advisory fees from the account held with the qualified custodian.

- Notice of fee deduction—each time a fee is directly deducted from a client account, the adviser must concurrently:

  — send the qualified custodian notice of the amount of the fee to be deducted from the client's account, and

  — send the client an invoice itemizing the fee. Itemization includes the formula used to calculate the fee, the amount of assets under management the fee is based on, and the time period covered by the fee.

- Notice of safeguards—the investment adviser notifies the Administrator in writing on Form ADV that the adviser intends to use the safeguards provided above.

- Waiver of net worth or bonding requirements—an investment adviser with custody solely because of direct fee deduction and who complies with these safeguards will not be required to meet the $35,000 bonding or net worth standard.

Other Differences Between SEC and NASAA Rules

In addition to the differences pointed out above, there are two more very important areas in which the NASAA rule diverges from the federal law. The first of these deals with the requirement to make an annual audited balance sheet part of the adviser's brochure. Federal covered advisers using a qualified custodian do not have to include the balance sheet in their brochure, whereas the NASAA rule does not exempt state registered advisers.

The second difference deals with sending advisory clients a billing statement. If a federal covered adviser uses a qualified custodian, the rule under the Investment Advisers Act of 1940 does not require the adviser to send invoices or fee calculation statements when deducting fees from client's accounts. On the other hand, NASAA's position is that the qualified custodian merely performs a safekeeping function, which should not be confused with the adviser's fiduciary duty and books and records requirements that all investment advisers send billing statements to their clients.

EXAMPLE

Let's look at three examples of custody given by the SEC.

■   An adviser that holds clients' stock certificates or cash, even temporarily, puts those assets at risk of misuse or loss. The rule, however, expressly excludes inadvertent receipt by the adviser of client funds or securities, so long as the adviser returns them to the sender within three business days of receiving them. The rule does not permit advisers to forward clients' funds and securities without having custody, although advisers may certainly assist clients in such matters. In addition, the rule makes clear that an adviser's possession of a check drawn by the client and made payable to a third party is not possession of client funds for purposes of the custody definition. (Note, this is only true under NASAA rules if forwarded within 24 hours).

■   An adviser has custody if it has the authority to withdraw funds or securities from a client's account. An adviser with power of attorney to sign checks on a client's behalf, to withdraw funds or securities from a client's account, or to dispose of client funds or securities for any purpose other than authorized trading has access to the client's assets. An adviser authorized to deduct advisory fees or other expenses directly from a client's account has access to, and therefore has custody of, the client funds and securities in that account. These advisers might not have possession of client assets, but they have the authority to obtain possession.

■   An adviser has custody if it acts in any capacity that gives the adviser legal ownership of, or access to, the client funds or securities. One common instance is a firm that acts as both general partner and investment adviser to a limited partnership. By virtue of its position as general partner, the adviser generally has authority to dispose of funds and securities in the limited partnership's account and thus has custody of client assets.

QUICK QUIZ 3.11

1.   Which of the following advisers would be deemed to have custody of customer funds or securities as defined in the Investment Advisers Act of 1940?

A.   The adviser receives the proceeds of sales in the customer's account.

B.   The adviser receives a fee of $1,000 as a prepayment for the next contract year.

C.   The adviser has investment discretion over the account.

D.   All of the above.

2. Which of the following registered investment advisers would be required to furnish an audited balance sheet as part of its disclosure statement?

    I.   The adviser's fee is automatically debited from the client's account.
    II. The adviser receives his fee each quarter in advance in the amount of $900.
    III. The client's securities are held by a broker/dealer with whom the adviser has an affiliate relationship.

    A. I and II
    B. I and III
    C. II and III
    D. I, II and III

3. An investment adviser registered with the state wishes to take custody of client's funds or securities. Which of the following statements best describes NASAA rules regarding notification to the Administrator?

    A. The adviser must supply prompt notification to the Administrator by immediately updating its Form ADV.
    B. The adviser must notify the Administrator within 90 days of the end of its fiscal year by updating its Form ADV.
    C. If the adviser will be using a qualified custodian, no notification is necessary.
    D. Prompt notification to the Administrator is made by the independent accounting firm performing the adviser's annual surprise audit.

4. An investment adviser takes custody of client's funds and securities. Client account statements must be sent no less frequently than

    A. monthly
    B. quarterly
    C. semiannually
    D. annually

5. A federal covered investment adviser inadvertently receives securities from a client. The custody rules of the Investment Advisers Act of 1940 would require the adviser to

    A. forward those securities to the qualified custodian within 3 business days after receipt
    B. keep those securities in its vault
    C. notify the SEC promptly
    D. return those securities to the sender within 3 business days after receipt

6. What type of qualified custodians do NASAA rules permit to hold investment advisory clients' funds or securities?

    I.   Banks and savings associations
    II. Federal covered investment advisers
    III. Registered broker/dealers
    IV. Transfer agents for NYSE listed corporations

    A. I and III
    B. I and IV
    C. II and III
    D. II and IV

Just because an adviser does not maintain custody or require prepayments and is not required to file the balance sheet with the SEC does not mean he has no obligation to maintain true, accurate, and current books.

FIDUCIARY RESPONSIBILITIES OF INVESTMENT ADVISERS

Investment advisers are fiduciaries who owe a duty of undivided loyalty to their clients and must deal fairly and honestly with them. This fiduciary relationship between an adviser and his client imposes on an adviser an affirmative duty of utmost good faith and full and fair disclosure, as well as an affirmative obligation to employ reasonable care to avoid misleading his clients.

Both state and federal law reflect a recognition of the delicate fiduciary nature of an investment advisory relationship, as well as an intent to eliminate or at least expose all conflicts of interest that might incline an adviser to render advice that was not disinterested. A key difference between investment advisers and broker/dealers is that, as fiduciaries, the former have a defined legal obligation to always place the interests of the client first.

Moreover, the relationship between an investment adviser and his client is governed not only by statutory law, but also by common law principles applicable to fiduciary relationships.

DISCLOSURE AND CONSENT

Both acts prohibit an investment adviser from effecting transactions as a principal with his clients or as an agent for his clients, unless his clients receive full written disclosure as to the capacity in which the adviser proposes to act and consent to do so before the completion (settlement) of the proposed transaction. This is unlike a broker/dealer who, when acting as a principal in a trade with a customer or as the customer's agent, need only indicate that capacity on the trade confirmation; consent is not required.

To provide some assurance that the act will not be violated, the regulators have recommended that each of the adviser's advisory clients be given in advance a written statement (brochure) prepared by the adviser that makes all appropriate disclosures. The disclosure statement should include the nature and extent of any adverse interest of the adviser, including the amount of compensation he would receive in connection with the account. This is particularly important if the adviser will be receiving compensation from sources other than the agreed-upon advisory fee. Furthermore, the adviser should obtain a written acknowledgement from each of his clients of their receipt of the disclosure statement.

The securities laws do not prohibit a registered investment adviser representative from being an employee of a registered broker/dealer. However, there would be a duty on the part of both the broker/dealer and the soliciting advisers to inform advisory clients of their ability to seek execution of transactions with broker/dealers other than those who have employed the advisers.

Disclosure must be made to all current clients and to prospective clients regarding material disciplinary action. The broadest definition of *material* would include any actions taken against the firm or management persons by a court or regulatory authority within the past 10 years. Required disclosure would include the following:

■ State or regulatory proceedings in which the adviser or a management person was found to have violated rules or statutes that led to the denial, suspension, or revocation of the firm's or the individual management person's registration

■ Court proceedings, such as a permanent or temporary injunction, against the firm or management person pertaining to an investment-related activity or any felony

■ SRO proceedings in which the adviser or management person caused the business to lose its registration or the firm or individual was barred, suspended, or expelled, or a fine in excess of $2,500 or a limitation was placed on the adviser or management person's activities

During routine inspections, the regulators review an adviser's filings with the SEC or Administrator and other materials provided to clients to ensure that the adviser's disclosures are accurate, timely, and do not omit material information. Examples of failures to disclose material information to clients would include the following.

■ An adviser fails to disclose all fees that a client would pay in connection with the advisory contract, including how fees are charged and whether fees are negotiable.

■ An adviser fails to disclose its affiliation with a broker/dealer or other securities professionals or issuers.

■ If an adviser has discretionary authority or custody over a client's funds or securities, or requires prepayment of advisory fess of more than $500 from a client, six or more months in advance, the adviser fails to disclose a financial condition that is reasonably likely to impair the ability of the adviser to meet contractual commitments to those clients.

■ An adviser may defraud its clients when it fails to use the average price paid when allocating securities to accounts participating in bunched trades and fails to adequately disclose its allocation policy. This practice violates the act if securities that were purchased at the lowest price or sold at the highest price are allocated to favored clients without adequate disclosure.

■ Any material legal action against the adviser must be disclosed to existing clients promptly. If the action occurred within the past 10 years, it must be disclosed to prospective clients not less than 48 hours before entering into the contract, or no later than the time of entering into such contract if the client has the right to terminate the contract without penalty within five business days.

QUICK QUIZ 3.12

1. The BJS Advisory Service maintains no custody of customer funds or securities, requires no substantial prepayments of fees, and does not have investment discretion over clients' accounts. Which of the following would have to be promptly disclosed to clients?

   I. The SEC has entered an order barring the executive vice president of the firm from association with any firm in the investment business.
   II. BJS has just been fined $3,500 by the NYSE.
   III. A civil suit has just been filed against BJS by one of its clients alleging that BJS made unsuitable recommendations.

   A. I and II
   B. I and III
   C. II and III
   D. None of the above

HEDGE CLAUSES

A constant concern of the regulators is any attempt by an investment adviser to waive the implied fiduciary responsibilities inherent in the client/adviser relationship. One of the most common methods of doing so is through the use of the hedge clause. This is not a new issue. In 1951, the SEC addressed it in a release that simply states that "the anti-fraud provisions of the Securities and Exchange Commission statutes are violated by the employment of any legend, hedge clause, or other provision which is likely to lead an investor to believe that he has in any way waived any right of action he may have." This test is consistent with the Investment Advisers Act of 1940 which states that "any condition, stipulation, or provision binding any person to waive compliance with any provision of this Act or with any rule, regulation or order thereunder shall be void."

What does that mean as far as the exam is concerned? Both the SEC and the US Supreme Court have held that the common law standards embodied in the antifraud statutes hold advisers to an affirmative duty of utmost good faith and full and fair disclosure when dealing with clients. Even a negligent misrepresentation or failure to disclose material facts (especially in the case of a conflict or potential conflict of interest) places the adviser in violation of the antifraud provision whether or not there is specific intent or gross negligence or malfeasance. Perhaps viewing several SEC and USA examples will help give you a good idea of what to look for.

In several advisory interpretations made publicly available, the SEC has applied the analytical framework discussed above in determining the legality of a particular hedge clause or waiver. For example, in a 1972 letter, the SEC opined that a hedge clause that attempted to waive liability for acts constituting "ordinary negligence" was misleading, notwithstanding further language in the advisory agreement that specifically disclaimed any waiver for "acts or omissions which constitute fraudulent representations under applicable State or Federal common law or statute, gross negligence, willful misconduct or violations of the Investment Advisers Act of 1940, [or] any other applicable State or Federal statute or regulation thereunder."

Similarly, the SEC has found to be misleading another hedge clause that sought to limit liability to acts done in bad faith or pursuant to willful misconduct but also explicitly provided that rights under state or federal law cannot be relinquished. In reaching this conclusion, it was noted that "it is unlikely that a client who is unsophisticated in the law would realize that he may have a right of action under federal or state law even where his adviser has acted in good faith."

Several recent investment adviser applications filed with the states have contained advisory contracts with hedge clauses that the Administrator believed would be potentially misleading to clients. For example, one agreement stated that "adviser shall not be liable for any loss or depreciation in the value of the account unless it shall have failed to act in good faith or with reasonable care." The state advised the applicant that this clause could be construed as inconsistent with the USA since under both state and federal law, an investment adviser is a fiduciary who may be subject to civil liability even when he or she acts in good faith and with reasonable care.

Another advisory contract contained the following provision: "While [Adviser] agrees to use its best efforts in the management of the portfolio, [Adviser] shall not be responsible for errors in judgment or losses incurred on investments made in good faith, and its liability shall be limited expressly to losses resulting from fraud or malfeasance, or from violation of applicable law."

Again, the state viewed this language as potentially misleading to clients, given the adviser's duties as a fiduciary. Moreover, the adviser's statement that it assumes liability for "violation of applicable law" only compounded the problem since it was unlikely that the client would realize that "applicable law" does, under several circumstances, provide a right of action for even good faith "errors in judgment." For similar reasons, the state took issue with a contract that stated: "It is understood that we will expend our best efforts in the supervision of the portfolio, but we assume no responsibility for action taken or omitted in good faith if negligence, willful or reckless misconduct, or violation of applicable law is not involved."

Although this hedge clause correctly excepts from its coverage acts involving "negligence, willful or reckless misconduct, or violation of applicable law," it is still misleading to waive liability for "action taken or omitted in good faith." As noted earlier, an investment adviser is a fiduciary subject, under certain circumstances, to liability even when he has acted in good faith and without evil intent. Moreover, since it is "applicable law" itself that holds that advisers are fiduciaries, such a provision is nonsensical and confusing.

When drafting agreements that seek to limit an adviser's civil liability, applicants and their counsel should bear in mind that as fiduciaries, investment advisers are held to an affirmative duty of utmost good faith and full and fair disclosure when dealing with clients. Moreover, under both state and federal laws, advisers are held to a strict liability standard for certain violations of those acts. Thus, language that seeks to limit liability to negligence or fraud would be misleading and untrue, even when qualified by a statement that excepts violations of state and federal law.

This is not to say that the acts prohibit the use of all hedge clauses. For example, the SEC has not objected to clauses that limit the investment adviser's liability for losses caused by conditions and events beyond its control, such as war, strikes, natural disasters, new government restrictions, market fluctuations, communications disruptions, and so forth. Such provisions are acceptable since they do not attempt to limit or misstate the adviser's fiduciary obligations to its clients.

QUICK QUIZ 3.13

1. An investment adviser runs an advertisement in the business section of the local newspaper. The ad describes the nature of the firm's model portfolio and indicates that it has outperformed the overall market by 800% over the past 10 years, and, therefore, they guarantee that their clients will more than keep pace with inflation. At the bottom of the ad, in smaller print is the following statement: Results are not guaranteed. Past performance is not indicative of future results. These results are not normal and cannot be expected to be repeated. This is an example of a (an)

    A. properly worded disclaimer
    B. improper hedge clause
    C. violation of an investment adviser's fiduciary responsibility
    D. wrap fee account

2. Which of the following statements regarding the use of a hedge clause by an investment adviser is CORRECT?

    A. The adviser's brochure must always contain at least one hedge clause.
    B. A properly worded hedge clause may be used to minimize the investment adviser's fiduciary responsibility.
    C. A hedge clause that limits the investment adviser's liability for losses caused by conditions and events beyond its control, such as war, strikes, and natural disasters, would generally be acceptable to the Administrator.
    D. A hedge clause that limits liability to acts done in bad faith or pursuant to willful misconduct but also explicitly provides that rights under state or federal law cannot be relinquished would generally be acceptable to the Administrator.

ADVERTISING

Under both laws, it is unlawful for an adviser to engage in any act, practice, or course of business that is fraudulent, deceptive, or manipulative. These prohibitions apply to advertising. The USA's rule on investment adviser advertising merely states that it is unlawful for any investment adviser to publish, circulate or distribute any advertisement that does not comply with the rules under the Investment Advisers Act of 1940.

The SEC has defined the term *advertisement* to include any notice, circular, letter, or other written communication addressed to more than one person, or any notice or other announcement in any publication or by radio or television, that offers:

■ any analysis, report, or publication concerning securities;

- any graph, chart, formula, or other device to be used in making any determination concerning securities; or

- any other investment advisory service with regard to securities.

The term *advertisement* has generally been broadly construed. For example, an investment adviser's proposed publication of lists of past securities recommendations for a specific period constitutes an advertisement. Similarly, investment advisory material that promotes advisory services for the purpose of inducing potential clients to subscribe to those services is advertising material.

The act provides that it is unlawful for an investment adviser to publish, circulate, or distribute any advertisement that:

- makes use of testimonials, including any statement of a client's experience with the adviser or a client's endorsement of the adviser (testimonials are prohibited under the Advisers Act);

- represents or implies that the adviser has been sponsored, recommended, or approved, or that its abilities or qualifications have in any respect been passed upon by the SEC or the Administrator (the SEC has taken the position that the use of the initials *R.I.A.* following a name on printed materials would be misleading because, among other things, it suggests that the person to whom it refers has a level of professional competence, education, or other special training, when in fact there are no specific qualifications for becoming a registered investment adviser; the term *registered investment adviser* may be used, but not the initials);

- makes reference to past, specific, profitable recommendations made by the adviser, without the advertisement setting out a list of all recommendations made by the adviser, both profitable and unprofitable, within the preceding period of not less than one year, and cautions the reader that is should not be assumed that recommendations made in the future will be profitable or will equal the performance of previous recommendations;

- represents that any graph, chart, formula or other device can, in and of itself, be used to determine which securities to buy or sell, or when to buy or sell such securities, or can assist persons in making those decisions, without the advertisement prominently disclosing the limitations and the difficulties regarding its use; or

- represents that a report, analysis, or other service was provided without charge, when the report, analysis, or other service was provided with some obligation.

TEST TOPIC ALERT   Although use of the initials *R.I.A.* is unethical, the exam will frequently refer to investment advisers as *IAs* and adviser representatives as *IARs*.

QUICK QUIZ 3.14

1. Which of the following statements is(are) TRUE regarding advertising by an investment adviser?

    I.   Free offers must be free of cost or any other obligation.

    II. All advertisements where the copy will be seen by 10 or more people must be filed with the SEC.

    III. Past specific recommendations may be shown, but only if they include all recommendations of the same asset class for at least the previous 12 months and make very clear that past performance is not any assurance of the future.

    A. I only
    B. I and II
    C. I and III
    D. II and III

INVESTMENT ADVISORY CONTRACTS

The primary relationship between a client and an investment adviser is determined by an investment advisory contract. The major difference between the two acts is that the USA prohibits entering into, extending, or renewing any investment contract, other than a contract for impersonal advisory services, unless the contract is in writing. Federal law states that the contract may be written or oral.

Under both acts, the contract must disclose:

- the services to be provided;

- the term of the contract;

- the amount of the advisory fee or the formula for computing the fee;

- the amount or manner of calculation of the amount of any prepaid fee to be returned in the event of contract termination;

- whether the contract grants discretionary power to the adviser or its representatives;

- that no assignment of the contract may be made by the adviser without the consent of the other party to the contract; and

- that, if the adviser is organized as a partnership, any change to a minority interest in the firm will be communicated to advisory clients within a reasonable period of time. A change to a majority of the partnership interests would be considered an assignment.

The acts also prohibit certain performance fee arrangements contingent on capital gains or appreciation in the client's account. There is an exception, however, from the performance fee provisions for contracts with:

- a registered investment company;

■ certain clients with more than $1 million in managed assets (usually institutions); or

■ clients with $750,000 under the adviser's management or a net worth of at least $1.5 million (usually individuals).

A fee based on the average amount of money under management over a particular period is not considered to be a performance fee.

The most common type of performance fee is known as a fulcrum fee. In this case, the fee is averaged over a specified period (at least 12 months) with an increase or decrease in proportion to the investment performance in relation to the performance of a specified securities index (usually the S&P 500). For example, for each 5% that the client's account outperforms the specified index, the adviser would receive an increase to the fee of 10 basis points. Of course, negative performance would have the same results.

TAKE NOTE

It is necessary for you to understand the technical definition of *assignment* as used in the acts. Assignment includes any direct or indirect transfer or pledge of an investment advisory contract by the adviser or of a controlling block of the adviser's outstanding voting securities by a stockholder of the adviser. If the investment adviser is a partnership, no assignment of an investment advisory contract is considered to result from the death or withdrawal of a minority of the partners or from the admission to the adviser of one or more partners who, after admission, will be only a minority interest in the business while a change to a majority would be considered an assignment. However, a reorganization or similar activity that does not result in a change of actual control or management of an investment adviser is not an assignment

---

QUICK QUIZ 3.15

1. The Investment Advisers Act of 1940 would permit investment advisory contracts to provide for

    I.   assignment without the client's consent
    II. changes to be made in a partnership with notification to clients within a reasonable period of time
    III. compensation based on average assets of the management over a particular time period

    A. I and II
    B. I and III
    C. II and III
    D. I, II and III

2. Which two of the following statements regarding investment advisory contracts demonstrate compliance with the Uniform Securities Act?

    I.   ABC Investment Advisers, organized as a partnership with 5 equal partners, admits 2 additional partners on a proportionate basis, but fails to obtain consent of its clients.

    II. DEF Investment Advisers, organized as a partnership with 7 equal partners, has 4 of those partners simultaneously leave, but the firm continues to operate as before while failing to obtain consent of its clients.

    III. GHI Investment Advisers, organized as a corporation with 5 equal shareholders, has 3 of them pledge their GHI stock as collateral for a bank loan, but the firm fails to obtain consent of its clients.

    IV. JKL Investment Advisers, organized as a corporation with 5 equal shareholders, has 3 of them sell their shares to the remaining 2 owners, but the firm fails to obtain consent of its clients.

    A. I and III
    B. I and IV
    C. II and III
    D. II and IV

CASE STUDY

Assignment and Notification of Change in Membership

Situation: Mr. Bixby withdrew $10 million from his account at the end of the year, leaving less than $750,000 under management with Market Tech Advisers, Inc., an advisory company incorporated in Illinois. During the course of the year, three officers left the firm. As a matter of corporate policy, Market Tech did not advise Mr. Bixby of these changes.

The following year, Market Tech (without notifying Mr. Bixby) assigned his account to Associated Investment Partners, a small partnership located in California, and Mr. Bixby was happy with the new partnership. Shortly after the assignment, Mr. Bixby learned of the death of one of the major partners through an article in the newspaper. He retained his account at Associated even though he had not been informed by them of the partner's death.

Analysis: Market Tech Advisers, Inc., was under no obligation to inform Mr. Bixby of the change in officers because it is a corporation and not a partnership. However, they did violate the USA by assigning Mr. Bixby's account to Associated Partners without his consent. Additionally, the USA requires partnerships to inform clients of any change in partner membership within a reasonable amount of time after the change, which means that Associated Partners violated the USA by not informing Mr. Bixby of the partner's death.

CASE STUDY

Investment Advisory Fees

Situation: Using the same client information as above, Market Tech Advisers, a registered investment advisory company, charges clients a fee of 1% of their assets managed by the firm, on the basis of the average amount of funds in the account each quarter. In addition, for some of their high net worth clients, Market Tech charges a fee based on the degree to which their performance exceeds that of the S&P 500. Last quarter, Market Tech's performance was extremely good, and, as a result, the fees of one of its largest clients, Mr. Bixby, more than doubled. Next quarter, the value of the account dropped by 25%, and so did the fee. Mr. Bixby complained that Market Tech was sharing in his capital appreciation in violation of the USA, because he no longer had the required funds on deposit in the account.

Analysis: Market Tech is in compliance with the USA. Market Tech charged Mr. Bixby a 1% fee based on the total assets in the account over a designated period as well as the stated performance fee. Because the assets increased and the performance beat the benchmark, so did the fee. Market Tech based its fees on the average value of funds under management and on a percentage of Mr. Bixby's capital gains—a practice in compliance with the USA for investors with a net worth at his level. Even though he no longer had $750,000 at the firm, his net worth was still in excess of $1.5 million. In the subsequent quarter, Market Tech's fee declined by 25% as a result of market deterioration. More than likely, there was no incentive fee earned in this quarter.

AGENCY CROSS TRANSACTIONS

Unlike broker/dealers, investment advisers are required to obtain the client's written consent, before the completion of the transaction, to act as principal or agent for that client. In an **agency cross transaction**, the adviser acts as agent for both its advisory client and the party on the other side of the trade. Both acts will permit an adviser to engage in these transactions provided the adviser obtains prior consent for these types of transactions from the client that discloses the following.

■ The adviser will be receiving commissions from both sides of the trade.

■ There is a potential conflict of interest because of the division of loyalties to both sides.

■ On at least an annual basis, the adviser furnishes a statement or summary of the account identifying the total number of such transactions and the total amount of all remuneration from these transactions.

■ The disclosure document conspicuously indicates that this arrangement may be terminated at any time.

■ No transaction is effected in which the same investment adviser or an investment adviser and any person controlling, controlled by, or under common control with that investment adviser recommended the transaction to both any seller and any purchaser.

These requirements do not relieve advisers of their duties to obtain best execution and best price for any transaction.

EXAMPLE

An adviser has a client who is conservative and another who generally looks for more aggressive positions. The conservative client calls and expresses concerns about the volatility of First Tech Internet Services, Inc., stating that he thinks this may be the best time to exit his position. The adviser agrees and mentions that he has a risk-taking client for whom First Tech is suitable and he'd like to "cross" the security between the two clients, charging a small commission to each of them. With the permission of both parties, this is not a violation.

In an agency cross transaction, the adviser may not recommend the transaction to both parties of the trade.

An exception to the prior written consent requirement is made when an investment adviser only provides what is called **impersonal investment advice.** This is typically the case with investment newsletters where the publisher discloses that they may have a position in the securities being recommended.

CASH REFERRAL FEES

The SEC has not prohibited payment of cash referral fees by investment advisers to persons who solicit business for them. The Investment Advisers Act of 1940 prohibits payment of cash referral fees to solicitors unless four conditions are met. The first three conditions apply to all cash referral fee payments.

The first condition requires that the investment adviser be registered under the Advisers Act. Thus, the rule prohibits cash referral fee payments to a solicitor by an investment adviser required to be registered but who is not registered. The second condition prohibits payment of cash referral fees to a solicitor who is subject to a statutory disqualification (e.g., a solicitor who is subject to an SEC order or convicted of certain crimes within a 10-year period). The third condition requires cash referral fees to be paid pursuant to a written agreement to which the investment adviser is a party.

Even if the first three conditions are satisfied, cash referral fee payments are prohibited unless they are made in one of three circumstances. In the first circumstance, payments are for the provision of impersonal advisory services. The second circumstance is where the adviser pays a referral fee to a person affiliated with the adviser (e.g., a partner, officer, director, or employee of the adviser). The third circumstance in which cash referral fees may be paid involves third-party solicitors who are not persons affiliated with the adviser.

When the cash referral fees are paid to third-party solicitors who are not affiliated with the adviser, the following disclosures must be made:

■   Unless for impersonal advisory services, the fact that it is a third party must be disclosed (this is usually accomplished by requiring that a separate solicitor brochure be delivered along with the adviser's brochure).

■   Any script or sales approach used by the third party is the responsibility of the adviser.

According to the SEC staff, failure to adequately inform clients of a referral fee arrangement may violate the act. The amount of the remuneration and the basis on which it is paid should be disclosed, together with the fact that the finder is being compensated specifically for referring clients to the adviser.

1. Which of the following statements regarding cash referral fees to solicitors are CORRECT under the Investment Advisers Act of 1940?

    I.   If the solicitation involves anything other than impersonal advisory services, disclosure must be made to the client regarding any affiliation between the adviser and the solicitor.

    II. The agreement must be in writing.

    III. The solicitor must not be subject to a statutory disqualification.

    IV. The adviser's principal business activity must be the rendering of investment advice.

    A. I and II
    B. I, II and III
    C. II and III
    D. I, II, III and IV

FRAUDULENT AND PROHIBITED PRACTICES WHEN PROVIDING INVESTMENT ADVICE

Both acts make it unlawful for any person who receives compensation (directly or indirectly) for advising another person (whether through analyses or reports) as to the value of securities to use any device, scheme, or artifice to defraud the other person. Additionally, they may not engage in any act, practice, or course of business that operates or would operate as a fraud or deceit upon the other person or engage in dishonest or unethical practices.

TAKE NOTE

Prohibitions are determined by the nature of the activity, not the registration status of the person engaged in the activity. Broker/dealers and their agents may give investment advice, yet not be included in the definition of investment adviser. Nevertheless, broker/dealers and their agents are subject to the antifraud provisions of the act when in the act of providing advice. Why? The antifraud provisions refer to "any person" who commits fraud when selling securities or when providing investment advice with respect to securities.

The following are examples of prohibited practices when providing investment advice:

■ Disclosing the identity or investments of a client without consent of the client, unless required by law (an example of forced disclosure would be a subpoena to testify in a divorce case or a demand by the IRS to provide information about a client who is the subject of an audit)

■ Using third-party prepared materials without proper attribution (reports that are purely statistical in nature are excluded from this requirement, but a research report or market letter prepared by another entity could only be used if its authorship were disclosed)

- Use of any advertisement (defined as a communication to more than one person) that uses any testimonial (an advertisement may make reference to specific past performance of the adviser's recommendations as long as all recommendations of the same type of security for at least the past 12 months are included—not only the winners, but the losers as well)

- Calculating advisory fees using a methodology different than that agreed to in the contracts

- Failing to comply with clients' wishes concerning directed brokerage arrangements

- Causing clients to invest in securities that are inconsistent with the level of risk that clients have agreed to assume

- Allocating client brokerage to a broker in exchange for client referrals without full disclosure of either the practice or the fact that clients pay higher brokerage commissions and do not obtain the best price and execution

- Allocating client brokerage to a broker in exchange for research or other products without disclosure

- Trading in securities for personal accounts, or for accounts of family members or affiliates, shortly before trading the same securities for clients (i.e., front-running), and thereby receiving better prices

- Directing clients to trade in securities in which the adviser has an undisclosed interest, causing the value of those securities to increase to the adviser's benefit

- Indicating in an advisory contract, any condition, stipulation, or provisions binding any person to waive compliance with any provision of the Uniform Securities Act or the Investment Advisers Act of 1940 (e.g., the use of certain hedge clauses)

- Unfairly criticizing work done by a client's professional advisers, such as accountants and lawyers (e.g., "Your attorney drew up a very poor estate plan", or "Your CPA missed many tax saving opportunities on your income tax return" are statements that may be considered unethical)

If you are an investment adviser registered or required to be registered under the Investment Advisers Act of 1940, it is unlawful for you to provide investment advice to clients unless you:

- adopt and implement written policies and procedures reasonably designed to prevent violation, by you and your supervised persons, of the act and the rules that the SEC has adopted under the act;

- review, no less frequently than annually, the adequacy of the policies and procedures established pursuant to this act and the effectiveness of their implementation; and

- designate an individual (who is a supervised person) responsible for administering the policies and procedures that you adopt, as noted above.

For a complete listing of those practices considered unethical, please review Appendix B, which contains NASAA's Statement of Policy on Unethical Business Practices of Investment Advisers. Pay particular attention to NASAA's comments since they use those to derive actual test questions.

Section 28(e) Safe Harbor

Research is the foundation of the money management industry. Providing research is one important, long-standing service of the brokerage business. Soft dollar arrangements have developed as a link between the brokerage industry's supply of research and the money management industry's demand for research. What does that mean and how does it work? To find the answers, we must review the provisions of Section 28(e) of the Securities Exchange Act of 1934.

Broker/dealers typically provide a bundle of services, including research and execution of transactions. The research provided can be either proprietary (created and provided by the broker/dealer, including tangible research products as well as access to analysts and traders) or third party (created by a third party but provided by the broker/dealer). Because commission dollars pay for the entire bundle of services, the practice of allocating certain of these dollars to pay for the research component has come to be called *soft dollars*. The SEC has defined soft dollar practices as arrangements under which products or services other than execution of securities transactions are obtained by an adviser from or through a broker/dealer in exchange for the direction by the adviser of client brokerage transactions to the broker/dealer, frequently referred to as *directed transactions* on the exam. Under traditional fiduciary principles, a fiduciary cannot use assets entrusted by clients to benefit itself. As the SEC has recognized, when an adviser uses client commissions to buy research from a broker/dealer, it receives a benefit because it is relieved from the need to produce or pay for the research itself. In addition, when transactions involving soft dollars involve the adviser paying up or receiving executions at inferior prices, advisers using soft dollars face a conflict of interest between their need to obtain research and their clients' interest in paying the lowest commission rate available and obtaining the best possible execution.

Soon after May 1, 1975 (May Day), when the SEC abolished fixed commission rates, Congress created a safe harbor under Section 28(e) of the Securities Exchange Act of 1934 to protect advisers from claims that they had breached their fiduciary duties by causing clients to pay more than the lowest available commission rates in exchange for research and execution. Because of the conflict of interest that exists when an investment adviser receives research, products, or other services as a result of allocating brokerage on behalf of clients, the SEC requires advisers to disclose soft dollar arrangements to their clients. Section 28(e) provides that a person who exercises investment discretion with respect to an account will not be deemed to have acted unlawfully or to have breached a fiduciary duty solely by reason of his having caused the account to pay more than the lowest available commission if such person determines in good faith that the amount of the commission is reasonable in relation to the value of the brokerage and research services provided.

In adopting Section 28(e), Congress acknowledged the important service broker/dealers provide by producing and distributing investment research to money managers. Section 28(e) defines when a person is deemed to be providing brokerage and research services, and states that a person provides brokerage and research services insofar as he:

■ furnishes advice directly or through publications or writing about the value of securities, the advisability of investing in, purchasing, or selling securities, or the availability of purchasers or sellers of securities;

■ furnishes analyses and reports concerning issuers, industries, securities, economic factors and trends, portfolio strategy, and performance of accounts; or

■ effects securities transactions and performs functions incidental thereto (such as clearance, settlement, and custody).

Finally, Section 28(e)(2) grants the SEC rulemaking authority to require that investment advisers disclose their soft dollar policies and procedures

An adviser is obligated under both the Investment Advisers Act of 1940 and state law to act in the best interests of its client. This duty generally precludes the adviser from using client assets for its own benefit or the benefit of other clients, without obtaining the client's consent based on full and fair disclosure. In such a situation, the antifraud provisions of the federal securities laws also would require full and fair disclosure to the client of all material facts concerning the arrangement. As the SEC has stated, "the adviser may not use its client's assets for its own benefit without prior consent, even if it costs the client nothing extra." Consent may be expressly provided by the client; consent also may be inferred from all of the facts and circumstances, including the adviser's disclosure in its Form ADV.

It also should be noted that Section 28(e) only excuses paying more than the lowest available commission. It does not shield a person who exercises investment discretion from charges of violations of the antifraud provisions of the federal securities laws arising from churning an account, failing to obtain the best price or best execution, or failing to make required disclosure.

Section 28(e) does not relieve investment advisers of their disclosure obligations under the federal securities laws. Disclosure is required whether the product or service acquired by the adviser using soft dollars is inside or outside of the safe harbor. Advisers are required to disclose, among other things, the products and services received through soft dollar arrangements, regardless of whether the safe harbor applies.

Registered investment advisers must disclose certain information about their brokerage allocation policies to clients in Items 12 and 13 of Part II of Form ADV. Specifically, if the value of products, research, and services provided to an investment adviser is a factor in selecting brokers to execute client trades, the investment adviser must describe in its Form ADV:

■ the products, research, and services;

■ whether clients may pay commissions higher than those obtainable from other brokers in return for the research, products, and services;

■ whether research is used to service all accounts or just those accounts paying for it; and

■ any procedures that the adviser used during the last fiscal year to direct client transactions to a particular broker in return for products, research and services received.

The purpose of this disclosure is to provide clients with material information about the adviser's brokerage selection practices that may be important to clients in deciding to hire or continue a contract with an adviser and that will permit them to evaluate any conflicts of interest inherent in the adviser's policies and practices. In this respect, the SEC and courts have stated that disclosure is required, even when there is only a potential conflict of interest.

It is important to note, however, that disclosure in the Form ADV may not satisfy an adviser's full obligation to disclose soft dollar arrangements. For example, Part II of Form ADV, or the adviser's brochure, must be delivered only at the commencement of the advisory relationship, and offered to be delivered only annually thereafter. Thus, an adviser may have to update Part II and provide existing clients with additional disclosure whenever material changes occur in its soft dollar practices.

TEST TOPIC ALERT

What this all comes down to is knowing what is and what is not included in the safe harbor. Here are some of the items that, if received as soft dollar compensation, would likely fall under 28(e)'s safe harbor:

■ research reports analyzing the performance of a particular company or stock;

■ financial newsletters and trade journals could be eligible research if they relate with appropriate specificity;

■ quantitative analytical software;

■ seminars or conferences with appropriate content; and

■ effecting and clearing securities trades

Likely to fall out of the safe harbor would be:

■ telephone lines;

■ office furniture, including computer hardware;

■ travel expenses associated with attending seminars;

■ rent;

■ any software that does not relate directly to analysis of securities;

■ payment for training courses for this exam; and

■ Internet service.

QUICK QUIZ 3.17

1. Which of the following would NOT be included in the safe harbor provisions of Section 28(e) of the Securities Exchange Act of 1934?

A. Proprietary research
B. Third-party research
C. Rent
D. Seminar registration fees

2. When an investment adviser with discretion over a client's account directs trade executions to a specific broker/dealer and uses the commission dollars generated to acquire software that analyzes technical market trends, it is known as

   A. hard dollar compensation
   B. indirect compensation
   C. investment discretion
   D. soft dollar compensation

QUICK QUIZ 3.18

1. An investment advisory contract need NOT include

   A. the fees and their method of computation
   B. a statement prohibiting assignment of client accounts without client consent
   C. the states in which the adviser is licensed to conduct business
   D. notification requirement upon change in membership if an investment partnership

   True or False?

___ 2. An Administrator may not prevent custody of securities or funds if an adviser notifies the Administrator before taking custody.

___ 3. An adviser may not sell securities to its customers from its own proprietary account.

___ 4. Under USA antifraud provisions, an investment adviser is bound by the restrictions that apply to sales practices when engaged in sales activities.

COMPLIANCE PROGRAMS

We have just completed a very comprehensive description of the many rules and regulations imposed upon investment advisers. How do the regulators ensure compliance with these rules? Effective October 2004, the Investment Advisers Act of 1940 was amended to require each investment adviser registered with the SEC to adopt and implement written policies and procedures designed to prevent violation of the federal securities laws, review those policies and procedures **annually** for their adequacy and the effectiveness of their implementation, and designate a **chief compliance officer** (CCO) to be responsible for administering the policies and procedures. An adviser's chief compliance officer should be competent and knowledgeable regarding the Advisers Act and should be empowered with full responsibility and authority to develop and enforce appropriate policies and procedures for the firm. Thus, the compliance officer should have a position of sufficient seniority and authority within the organization to compel others to adhere to the compliance policies and procedures. In fact, the CCO's identity must be disclosed on the Form ADV. However, the SEC does not set a standard of competency such as a specific qualification exam or number of years of experience.

Under rule 206(4)-7, it is unlawful for an investment adviser registered with the Commission to provide investment advice unless the adviser has adopted and implemented written policies and procedures reasonably designed to prevent violation of the Advisers Act by the adviser or any of its supervised persons. The rule requires advisers to consider their fiduciary and regulatory obligations under the Advisers Act and to formalize policies and procedures to address them.

Each adviser, in designing its policies and procedures, should first identify conflicts and other compliance factors creating risk exposure for the firm and its clients in light of the firm's particular operations, and then design policies and procedures that address those risks. The SEC expects that an adviser's policies and procedures, at a minimum, should address the following issues to the extent that they are relevant to that adviser:

- Portfolio management processes, including allocation of investment opportunities among clients and consistency of portfolios with clients' investment objectives, disclosures by the adviser, and applicable regulatory restrictions;

- Trading practices, including procedures by which the adviser satisfies its best execution obligation, uses client brokerage to obtain research and other services ("soft dollar arrangements"), and allocates aggregated trades among clients;

- Proprietary trading of the adviser and personal trading activities of supervised persons;

- The accuracy of disclosures made to investors, clients, and regulators, including account statements and advertisements;

- Safeguarding of client assets from conversion or inappropriate use by advisory personnel;

- The accurate creation of required records and their maintenance in a manner that secures them from unauthorized alteration or use and protects them from untimely destruction;

- Marketing advisory services, including the use of solicitors;

- Processes to value client holdings and assess fees based on those valuations;

- Safeguards for the privacy protection of client records and information; and

- Business continuity plans.

Although the rule requires only annual reviews, advisers should consider the need for interim reviews in response to significant compliance events, changes in business arrangements, and regulatory developments.

ENFORCEMENT

Enforcement and administration of the Investment Advisers Act of 1940 is the responsibility of the SEC. There is no self-regulatory organization (SRO) for investment advisers. In other words, NASD, the NYSE, and the like have no jurisdiction over investment advisers; only the SEC does. If the SEC suspects a violation of the law or its rules, it may take the following actions:

- Subpoena witnesses

- Acquire evidence

- Subpoena books and records

- Administer oaths

- Go to a competent court of jurisdiction to obtain an injunction enjoining a person from continued activity until the results of a hearing

- Refer to the appropriate court for criminal prosecution

The SEC has the power to censure, place limitations on the activities, functions, or operations of, suspend for a period not exceeding 12 months, or revoke the registration of any investment adviser if it finds, after a hearing, that the penalty is appropriate. If it is necessary to go to court, all hearings are held in the federal court system. If a defendant is found guilty, he may appeal an SEC order against him by filing that appeal in the US Court of Appeals with jurisdiction where the violation occurred.

If the violation is one in which the SEC seeks criminal penalties, the act provides for a fine of no more than $10,000, imprisonment for no more than five years, or both.

Enforcement and administration of the USA is the responsibility of each individual Administrator. If the Administrator suspects a violation of the law or its rules, he may take all of the actions listed above.

However, there is nothing in the USA that specifies a maximum suspension as there is in the federal law. Another difference is that, in the case of an appeal, it is made through the state court system, not the federal one. In both cases, the appeal must be filed within 60 days of the court's decision.

Another difference is in the level of penalties. Under the USA, the maximum penalties for a criminal infraction are a fine of up to $5,000, or a prison sentence not to exceed 3 years, or both.

TEST TOPIC ALERT

You will be asked about either or both of these penalties on your exam and must be able to keep them straight. Federal law is $10,000 and 5 years. State law is $5,000 and 3 years.

HOTSHEETS

For your convenience, Unit HotSheets summarizing the key points are located at the end of the manual on perforated pages.

UNIT TEST

1. Which of the following advisers does NOT maintain custody as defined in the Investment Advisers Act of 1940?

   A. A client of the adviser has funds in a joint bank account with the adviser.
   B. Proceeds of sales of customer securities are held by the adviser for only a short time pending mailing instructions from the client.
   C. The adviser receives client securities several days before entering sell orders for those securities.
   D. Certain clients are required to prepay their advisory fees 1 year in advance.

2. Which of the following statements concerning the Investment Advisers Act of 1940 are TRUE?

   I. Investment advisers must keep certain books and records.
   II. Unless an exemption applies, all investment advisers must be registered.
   III. A written disclosure document must be given to clients by investment advisers concerning their background and practices in most instances.
   IV. Client funds and securities held by an investment adviser must be verified by an independent public accountant.

   A. I and III
   B. I, III and IV
   C. II and IV
   D. I, II, III and IV

3. An investment adviser owes an undivided loyalty to its clients and therefore is considered to be a(n)

   A. agent
   B. fiduciary
   C. principal
   D. custodian

4. Which of the following statements regarding provisions of the Investment Advisers Act of 1940 is TRUE?

   A. Big Gains Registered Investment Advisers must disclose its sources of information for specific recommendations they make to their clients.
   B. An investment adviser must obtain client permission to accept a buyout offer for all of the adviser's stock.
   C. Five Partners Advisers, Ltd., must inform all clients that one of the 5 partners has retired and been replaced by a new partner.
   D. Pledging a client's contract as collateral for a loan to the adviser would not be considered an assignment of the contract.

5. To be exempt from registration under the Investment Advisers Act of 1940 on the basis of the number of clients, an investment adviser must meet which of the following conditions?

   I. During the preceding 12 months, had fewer than 15 clients
   II. Does not hold himself out to the public as an investment adviser
   III. Does not act as an investment adviser to a registered investment company or a business development company
   IV. Has a graduate degree from an approved institution

   A. I and II
   B. I, II and III
   C. III and IV
   D. I, II, III and IV

6. Which of the following would be deemed to be an assignment of an investment advisory contract?

   I. All of the stock in NLT Advisers, a corporation, is acquired by MMS Advisers, Inc.

   II. The Lucky Seven Partnership is an investment adviser with 7 partners. Four of the partners make a fortune and decide to retire. They are replaced by new partners.

   III. Albert is an investment adviser. His clients' accounts are automatically debited monthly for his fee. Because of this steady cash flow, his banker readily accepts a pledge of these accounts as collateral for a loan.

   A. I and II
   B. I and III
   C. II and III
   D. I, II and III

7. Which of the following are exempt from registration as an investment adviser under the act?

   I. An adviser whose clients consist solely of insurance companies

   II. An adviser with only 7 individual clients during the preceding 12 months who does not hold himself out to the public as an investment adviser

   III. An adviser in Georgia who deals only with Georgia residents and does not deal in securities listed on any national securities exchange

   IV. An adviser in Florida with only 10 Florida clients who advertises in telephone and business directories and specializes in dealing in New York Stock Exchange issues

   A. I and II
   B. I, II and III
   C. III and IV
   D. I, II, III and IV

8. Which of the following are unlawful or prohibited practices for an investment adviser under the act?

   I. To make an untrue statement of a material fact in a registration application with the SEC

   II. To state that his ability and qualifications have been approved by the US government

   III. To state that he is registered under the Investment Advisers Act of 1940

   IV. To represent that he is an investment counselor when he does not normally render investment advice

   A. I, II and IV
   B. I and III
   C. II and IV
   D. I, II, III and IV

9. Under the Investment Advisers Act of 1940, an investment adviser is required to

   I. submit justification for continued registration to the SEC if his client base drops below 15 individuals for any consecutive 12-month period

   II. disclose, in his brochure, the number of clients he serves

   III. disclose, in his brochure, the formal education after high school of each individual who supervises persons determining general investment advice given to clients

   A. I and II
   B. I and III
   C. II and III
   D. III only

10. Which of the following statements concerning investment advisers are TRUE?

   I. An investment adviser who is exempt from registration is also exempt from the antifraud provisions of the act.

   II. The SEC can cancel the registration of any investment adviser if it finds that the adviser is no longer in business.

   III. An investment adviser who represents that his qualifications and methods of security analysis have been passed on by the SEC has violated the act.

   A. I and II
   B. I and III
   C. II and III
   D. I, II and III

11. Which of the following statements regarding investment advisers are NOT true?

   I. There are specific educational requirements that all investment advisers must meet.

   II. The term *scalping* is the practice whereby an investment adviser, before the dissemination of a securities recommendation, trades on the anticipated short-run market activity that may result from the recommendations.

   III. An investment adviser's books and records must be maintained in an easily accessible place for 3 years under the act.

   A. I and II
   B. I and III
   C. II and III
   D. I, II and III

12. Which of the following people would NOT meet the definition of a person associated with an investment adviser?

   A. An individual who solicits potential clients to open advisory accounts
   B. A vice president of a registered investment adviser
   C. A brokerage firm that is considered to be the parent of a registered investment adviser
   D. The typist responsible for operating the desktop publishing system that prepares the investment adviser's weekly research bulletins

13. Under which of the following circumstances would the SEC be permitted to cancel or revoke an investment adviser's registration?

   I. A registered investment adviser has fewer than 5 clients.

   II. Schedule I has not been filed for the current fiscal year, and mail addressed to the investment adviser is returned with a notation "no forwarding address available."

   III. An investment adviser registered in 10 states has been enjoined by a competent court of jurisdiction in one of those states from engaging in the securities business.

   IV. A registered investment adviser is insolvent.

   A. I and II
   B. II and III
   C. II, III and IV
   D. I, II, III and IV

14. If an investment adviser registered under the Investment Advisers Act of 1940 maintains custody of customer funds or securities, which of the following is TRUE?

   A. A surety bond will be required.
   B. The auditing firm engaged to prepare the annual balance sheet must give appropriate notice to the adviser before doing the books.
   C. The adviser must, on an annual basis, provide his clients for whom he maintains custody a list of all securities held in custody by the firm.
   D. If the firm changes the location of safekeeping, all affected clients must be notified promptly.

15. A firm is registered as an investment adviser under the Investment Advisers Act of 1940. It has decided to raise its annual management fee from $600 to $1,000 and require that it be paid 1 year in advance instead of quarterly. The firm would

   A. need client permission to make this change
   B. need SEC permission to make this change
   C. now come under the balance sheet requirements of the ADV
   D. be in violation of the law that prohibits pre-payments more than 6 months in advance

16. Which of the following statements regarding the SEC's power to revoke the registration of an investment adviser is TRUE?

   A. If it is determined that an investment adviser is insolvent, the SEC may revoke the registration.
   B. Failure to adequately supervise a person associated with the adviser would be cause for the SEC to revoke the firm's registration.
   C. Revocation would occur, with appropriate notice, when a firm's Schedule I was received by the SEC 120 days after the end of the registrant's fiscal year.
   D. An investment adviser maintaining custody of funds for approximately 50% of its clients that fails to include a copy of its balance sheet in its brochure delivered to all clients on an annual basis would give the SEC cause for immediate revocation.

17. A person registered as an investment adviser under the Investment Advisers Act of 1940 could use the term *investment counsel* if

    I. his principal business consists of rendering investment advice
    II. a substantial portion of his business involves investment supervisory services
    III. he maintains full investment discretion

    A. I and II
    B. I and III
    C. II and III
    D. I, II and III

18. Which of the following is NOT a prohibited practice under the Investment Advisers Act of 1940?

    A. Scalping
    B. Failure to maintain a file of all advertisements circulated to 10 or more persons
    C. Maintaining required records easily accessible for only 5 years
    D. Maintaining required records easily accessible for only 2 years

19. A registered investment adviser runs a promotion offering free information to all who request it. Which of the following statements to people who respond do not comply with the advertising interpretation of the Investment Advisers Act of 1940?

    I. "The offer is yours, free of charge; all I need are the names of 5 friends who might be able to use our service."
    II. "Such a deal; our information about the market is free to anyone who makes only one trade with our broker/dealer affiliate."
    III. "Thank you for responding; if we can help you after you read our information, please let us know."

    A. I and II
    B. I and III
    C. II and III
    D. I, II and III

20. Although there are no experience requirements, a license could be revoked for

    A. failure to have proper training and knowledge about the business
    B. failure to obtain a high school diploma or GED
    C. not taking advantage of the apprenticeship provisions of the act
    D. filing a Schedule I with the SEC 120 days after the end of the registrant's fiscal year

21. The Investment Advisers Act of 1940 would permit an ADV to be filed by a(n)

    I. corporation
    II. partnership
    III. sole proprietorship
    IV. unincorporated association

    A. I and II
    B. I, II and III
    C. II and III
    D. I, II, III and IV

22. Which of the following statements made by an investment adviser would be fraudulent?

    A. "We believe that fundamental analysis is the best way to select stocks for our clients."
    B. "Our fees are nonnegotiable" (when ADV Part II clearly indicates otherwise).
    C. "We require any associated person determining general investment advice to be a CFA."
    D. All of the above.

23. Smith & Jones is a registered investment adviser under the Act of 1940. It has 1,000 active clients. The firm maintains custody for 200 of their clients and exercises investment discretion for 400 of them. When preparing its brochure for annual distribution, it would need to include an audited balance sheet prepared by an independent accountant for

    A. the 200 clients for whom it maintains custody
    B. the 200 clients for whom it maintains custody, as well as the 400 for whom it exercises investment discretion
    C. all of its clients because it is an integral part of its brochure once it maintains custody for even 1 client
    D. none of its clients because the balance sheet requirement is only important when a majority of the clients are subject to custody

24. A federal covered investment adviser is one who
    I.   has $30 million or more in assets under management
    II. manages an investment company registered under the Investment Company Act of 1940
    III. limits his advice to securities listed on the NYSE
    IV. is affiliated with a federally chartered bank

    A. I and II
    B. I and III
    C. II and III
    D. I, II, III and IV

25. Under the Uniform Securities Act, which of the following qualifies as an investment adviser representative?

    A. An employee, highly skilled in evaluating securities, who performs administrative or clerical functions for an investment adviser
    B. An individual who renders fee-based advice on precious metals
    C. A solicitor for an investment advisory firm who is paid a fee for his services
    D. An agent who offers incidental advice on securities as part of his sales commissions

26. Under the Uniform Securities Act, all of the following may provide investment advice incidental to their normal business without requiring registration as an investment adviser EXCEPT

    A. a teacher
    B. an economist
    C. a lawyer
    D. an engineer

27. Under the Uniform Securities Act, any partner, officer, or director of a registered investment adviser is an investment adviser representative if he
    I.   offers advice concerning securities
    II. manages client accounts or portfolios
    III. determines securities recommendations for representatives to disseminate
    IV. supervises personnel engaged in the above activities but does not sell these services to the public

    A. I only
    B. I and II
    C. I, II and III
    D. I, II, III and IV

28. Under SEC Release IA-1092, an investment adviser is all of the following EXCEPT
    I.   a broker/dealer who charges for investment advice
    II. a publisher of a financial newspaper
    III. a person who sells security analysis
    IV. a CPA who, as an incidental part of his practice, suggests certain tax-sheltered investments to his affluent clients

    A. I and II
    B. II and III
    C. II and IV
    D. III and IV

29. An Administrator can deny an investment adviser representative's registration for all of the following reasons EXCEPT

    A. lack of experience
    B. failure to post a surety bond
    C. failure to pass a written exam
    D. not meeting minimum financial standards

30. Which of the following would meet the definition of investment adviser under the Uniform Securities Act?
    I.   A broker/dealer making a separate charge for investment advice
    II. The publisher of a weekly magazine, sold on newsstands, that contains at least 5 stock recommendations per issue
    III. A civil damages attorney who advertises that he is available to assist clients in suggesting appropriate investments for their successful claims
    IV. A finance teacher at a local community college who offers weekend seminars on comprehensive financial planning at a very reasonable price

    A. I only
    B. I, II and III
    C. I, III and IV
    D. I, II, III and IV

31. Under the Uniform Securities Act, an investment adviser may legally have custody of money or securities belonging to a client if the

   I. adviser is not bonded
   II. Administrator has not prohibited custodial arrangements
   III. adviser does not also have discretionary authority over the account
   IV. adviser has notified the Administrator that he has custody

   A. I and III
   B. II only
   C. II and IV
   D. IV only

32. According to the Uniform Securities Act, an investment adviser may have custody of a customer's funds and securities if

   A. it has received the permission of the Administrator
   B. it has received permission from the SEC
   C. it does not share in the capital gains of the account
   D. the Administrator has been informed of the custody

33. Which of the following are prohibited practices?

   I. An investment advisory firm organized as a partnership failing to inform its clients of the departure of a partner with a very small interest in the partnership
   II. An investment advisory firm charging an annual fee equal to 2% of the first $250,000 in assets under management; 1% of the next $500,000; and .5% for everything in excess of $750,000
   III. The majority stockholder of a registered investment adviser pledging his stock as collateral for a loan taken out by the firm to expand its services without obtaining client consent for assignment of their contracts
   IV. Engaging in agency cross transactions

   A. I and III
   B. I and IV
   C. III and IV
   D. I, II, III and IV

34. One respect in which NASAA treats the handling of discretionary authorization by an investment adviser differently from the SEC is that

   A. NASAA has a requirement that all discretionary orders be approved before entry
   B. NASAA allows use of oral discretion for the first 10 business days after the date of the first transaction
   C. An investment adviser is prohibited from opening discretionary accounts without prior notification to the Administrator
   D. A federal covered adviser may not be cited for churning a discretionary account by an Administrator

35. The head of research for your firm has just prepared a very positive report on DEF Industries, Inc. The report will be placed on the firm's Website later today and copies mailed to clients for whom the security is deemed appropriate. Tonight, this analyst will be appearing on CNBC and will be describing why he has issued this "strong buy" recommendation. As an investment adviser representative, you would

   A. be permitted to contact your clients with this recommendation right now
   B. be permitted to contact your clients with this recommendation tomorrow
   C. not be permitted to contact your clients until it was ascertained that the report was general public knowledge
   D. be required to send your clients to the firm's Website before making any comments regarding this security

ANSWERS AND RATIONALES

1. **D.** Although there are cases where a prepayment of fees (more than $500 for 6 or more months in advance) would require filing of an audited balance sheet just as does custody, prepayments are not considered to be custody under either the Investment Advisers Act of 1940 or the Uniform Securities Act. In the other choices, the adviser clearly has control over either securities or money.

2. **D.** The books and records kept by an adviser must be readily available for 5 years after the end of the fiscal year in which the entry has been made. The 3 exemptions from registration for an investment adviser are intrastate, insurance company clients, and de minimis. The disclosure document referred to in Choice III is either ADV Part II or a brochure. The accountant's verification of client assets must be done on an annual basis as part of the annual audit.

3. **B.** Both federal and state law consider the relationship to be a fiduciary one.

4. **C.** No adviser is required to disclose his sources for a particular recommendation. If an adviser wants to sell his firm, he does not need client permission to do so. However, if the transaction results in a change that would be deemed to be an assignment, the adviser must obtain the client's consent to maintain his contracts. The regulatory bodies consider a pledge of clients' contracts to be an assignment. Both state and federal law require advisers operating as partnerships to notify their clients of changes in partners where it represents a minority interest in the firm.

5. **B.** This is directly from the law. There are no educational requirements to be an investment adviser.

6 **D.** It is deemed to be an assignment whenever a majority interest in an adviser changes hands. Pledging a client's contract is considered to be an assignment.

7. **B.** To qualify for the intrastate exemption, there is no numerical limitation and advertising on an intrastate basis is permitted. However, no advice may be given on securities traded on a national stock exchange.

8. **A.** One of the criteria for using the term *investment counsel* is that the adviser's primary business is providing investment advice. It is always prohibited to make an untrue statement, whether or not the fact is material, and one can never imply government approval of one's abilities.

9. **D.** Choice III is question 6 on ADV Part II and therefore must be disclosed to customers. Choice II is question 17 on ADV Part I, but Part I is not part of the brochure.

10. **C.** No one is ever exempt from antifraud provisions on the exam. The SEC may cancel the registration of an adviser for one of several reasons. Choice III states a violation.

11. **B.** There are no educational requirements, and books and records must be maintained for 5 years. Choice II describes scalping, a prohibited practice.

12. **D.** People in strictly clerical or administrative positions are not considered to be associated persons of an investment adviser. Expect to see several variations of this theme on the exam.

13. **B.** Reasons for cancellation do not include dropping below a minimum number of clients. Revocation of registration is usually connected with some form of disciplinary action. Insolvency is not cause for revocation or cancellation under the Investment Advisers Act of 1940, although it is cause under the Uniform Securities Act.

14. **D.** Surety bonds are never required under the Investment Advisers Act of 1940, although they may be required under the Uniform Securities Act. The audit must be a surprise. The adviser only informs the client about his securities, not everybody else's securities held by the adviser.

15. **C.** Prepayments in excess of $500 and for periods of 6 months or more require a firm to submit an annual audited balance sheet as part of its ADV Part II (and brochure). Previously, even though the firm's fee was in excess of $500, because it was collected on a quarterly basis, the firm did not fall under the balance sheet rule.

16. **B.** Insolvency is not a cause for revocation under the Investment Advisers Act of 1940. A late ADV Schedule I might be cause for some action but almost certainly not a revocation. It is not that serious an offense. In Choice D, the balance sheet would only have to be part of the disclosure statement (brochure) given to those for whom custody is maintained. Failure to supervise, if proven, is cause for revocation.

17. **A.** These are the 2 requirements for use of the term *investment counsel*. Discretion is meaningless here.

18. **C.** Five years is the required recordkeeping requirement.

19. **A.** If an advertisement claims to offer something for free, it must be free of any obligation. Choices I and II have strings attached and are not free.

20. **A.** This answer states the rule about registration requirements. In addition, the rule states that agents and investment adviser representatives who will work under supervision need not have the same qualifications as the firms that employ them. A late filing of ADV Schedule I (it is due within 90 days) is not cause for revocation.

21. **D.** Any entity meeting the definition of a person would be eligible to file for registration as an investment adviser on Form ADV.

22. **B.** An adviser may certainly state which method of analysis he thinks is best. A firm can also set whatever standards it wishes, even though none are required by the regulatory bodies. Stating an untruth would be considered fraud.

23. **A.** The balance sheet is required only when the adviser maintains custody or receives prepayments in excess of $500 for periods of 6 months or longer. Further, the Investment Advisers Act of 1940 only requires a brochure to include information found in ADV Part II that is relevant to the services provided by that adviser to that client.

24. **A.** Federal registration is required of any investment adviser managing at least $30 million in assets. It is optional at $25 million; anything less requires state registration. The NSMIA provides that any investment adviser under contract to a registered investment company under the Investment Company Act of 1940 is required to register with the SEC as a federal covered adviser. Providing advice on federal covered securities listed on the NYSE does not make the adviser a federal covered adviser. Banks and their representatives are always excluded from the definition of an investment adviser, federal covered or not.

25. **C.** A solicitor is considered an investment adviser representative under the Uniform Securities Act. An employee who performs only clerical or administrative functions is not an investment adviser representative. Precious metals are not securities and, therefore, a person advising on them is not considered an investment adviser representative. An agent is a representative of a broker/dealer, and as long as the only form of compensation is sales commissions, registration as an investment adviser representative is not required.

26. **B.** The Uniform Securities Act does not exclude economists from the definition of investment adviser as it does lawyers, accountants, teachers, and engineers who give advice that is incidental to the practice of their profession. Remember the acronym LATE—lawyers, accountants, teachers, and engineers. Do not be fooled by the **E** in *economist*.

27. **D.** The Uniform Securities Act defines persons associated with an investment adviser as an investment adviser representative, including any partner, officer, or director who offers advice concerning securities. Persons who manage client accounts or portfolios, determine securities recommendations, or supervise personnel engaged in the above activities are investment adviser representatives.

28. **C.** A publisher of a financial newspaper and a CPA who, as an incidental part of his practice, suggests tax-sheltered investments are not investment advisers. This answer would be the same under either the USA or federal law.

29. **A.** Lack of experience, by itself, is not cause for registration denial.

30. **C.** Publishers of general circulation newspapers and magazines are excluded from the definition of investment adviser, even if the entire publication is devoted to investment advice. A broker/dealer loses its exclusion the moment it offers advice for a separate charge, as does an attorney who holds himself out as offering investment advice. Normally, a teacher is excluded, but not when charging for advice as would appear to be the case here. On this examination, the term *comprehensive financial planning* always includes securities advice.

31. **C.** The Administrator may prohibit advisers from having custody of client funds or securities. If no such prohibition applies, the Administrator must be notified in writing if an adviser has custody. In almost all jurisdictions, a bond or sufficient net worth is required to maintain custody. Discretionary authority does not affect an adviser's ability to have custody.

32. **D.** As long as retaining custody of funds is not prohibited, an investment adviser may have custody of a customer's account after providing notice to the Administrator.

33. **A.** Any change in the ownership of an investment advisory firm organized as a partnership, no matter how small, requires notification to all clients within a reasonable amount of time. If the firm is structured as a corporation, pledging a controlling interest in the company's stock is viewed as an assignment of the contracts. This may not be done without the approval of the clients. Agency cross transactions— that is, where the adviser represents both sides of the trade—are permitted as long as the adviser makes the proper written disclosures and does not make the buy/sell recommendations to either party.

34. **B.** The SEC requires prior written discretionary authorization, whereas NASAA's Statement of Policy on Unethical Business Practices of Investment Advisers only requires that the written document be received no later than 10 business days after the first transaction in the account. Discretionary orders must be promptly reviewed, but not before placing the order. Even with the NSMIA, the Administrator has the power to take action against any federal covered adviser operating in the state where there is a belief that fraudulent action has taken place.

35. **A** A firm's internal research is not considered inside information. Clients may be contacted as soon as the IAR has access to the report. What is prohibited would be for the IAR to purchase this stock personally, prior to release of the report, and then contact clients.

QUICK QUIZ ANSWERS

Quick Quiz 3.1

1. **C.** By definition, a person (under the broad definition of this word) engaged in the securities business who trades for his own account and risk (principal) is known as a dealer.

Quick Quiz 3.2

1. **B.** The act specifically excludes accountants, lawyers, any professional engineer (aeronautical, civil, mechanical, or others), and teachers. Economists are not included in this listing.

2. **B.** There is an exclusion from the definition for all banks and bank holding companies, regardless of what they do. Also excluded are persons whose advice relates only to securities that are direct obligations of or guaranteed by the United States—it makes no difference who their clients are. A geologist is not excluded because the law only specifies 4 professional exclusions: accountants, attorneys, engineers, and teachers.

Quick Quiz 3.3

1. **A.** Advisers who only service insurance companies are exempt, as are advisers performing intrastate who do not give advice on listed securities (municipal bonds are not listed). Advising banks only does not qualify one for the exemption.

Quick Quiz 3.4

1. **B.** Publishers of newspapers and magazines of general circulation that offer general financial advice need not register.

2. **A.** Broker/dealers must register as investment advisers if they receive special or separate compensation for giving investment advice.

3. **A.** An investment adviser that manages less than $25 million in assets must register as an investment adviser under the USA. If the client is an investment company registered under the Investment Company Act of 1940, registration with the SEC is mandatory regardless of amount under management.

Quick Quiz 3.5

1. **A.** Because Mr. Oldman has been responsible for updating the ADV, it is logical to assume that he is the contact person for information regarding the form. His sudden retirement means the firm would have to appoint a new contact person. This is a change that the SEC deems necessary to promptly amend of the Form ADV. Amendments to the ADV may not be done using Form ADV-W—that is for withdrawal only.

Quick Quiz 3.6

1. **C.** In order to use the term *investment counsel*, both criteria must be met. The financial planner is not principally in the business of offering investment advice because he describes his service as offering a wide range of services, of which advice is only one part. The exam frequently uses that wording to indicate that advice is not the principal activity. While the publisher's principal business activity may be offering advice, nothing about the description indicates that individual client accounts are being monitored.

Quick Quiz 3.7

1. **B.** Advisers maintaining discretion over client accounts are required to have a minimum net worth of $10,000.

2. **C.** Under the USA, an investment adviser exercising discretion over client accounts must maintain minimum net worth of $10,000. If the adviser falls below that minimum, it must notify the Administrator by the close of business the following day. Then, a complete financial report must be furnished to the Administrator by the close of business the day following the sending of the notice. Unless otherwise instructed by the Administrator, the firm may continue to exercise discretion.

3. **C.** The USA requires advisers who take custody to maintain a minimum net worth of $35,000. Any Administrator is empowered to change that number, higher or lower. As long as an investment adviser meets the net worth requirements of the state where its principal office is located, there is no need to be concerned about any other state's requirements.

Quick Quiz 3.8

1. **F.** An investment adviser (not the investment adviser representative) must register with the SEC if the firm manages assets of $30 million or more. The individual would have to be registered as an investment adviser representative in the state in which her office is located.

2. **T.** An adviser maintaining custody, whether or not discretion is involved, is generally required to maintain a net worth of $35,000.

3. **F.** An employee of an investment advisory firm is not an investment adviser representative if his duties are confined to clerical activities.

4. **F.** Any administrative employee who receives specific compensation for offering investment advisory services is considered an investment adviser representative.

5. **T.** Any employee of an investment advisory firm is an investment adviser representative if his duties involve making investment recommendations.

Quick Quiz 3.9

1. **D.** This is the exception, since the records must be kept for 5 years. Nothing in the question asked about the 2-year requirement in the office. The 5-year requirement is that records be easily accessible whether in the office or not.

Quick Quiz 3.10

1. **D.** An adviser to investment companies and an adviser who provides only impersonal advisory services are specifically listed as being exempt from the delivery requirements of the brochure rule (impersonal advice with a charge of $200 or more would require an offer to deliver). An adviser who provides advice only to insurance companies is exempt from registration as an investment adviser and therefore would also be exempt from the requirements of the brochure.

2. **D** Annual delivery of the ADV Part II, or brochure, or an offer to deliver, must be made to each client. If a brochure is not delivered at least 48 hours before entering into a new advisory relationship, there must be a 5-business-day right of withdrawal without penalty. Only the ADV Part I is filed when registering.

Quick Quiz 3.11

1. **A.** Discretion and substantial prepayments are not considered custody. Access to funds in the client's account is one of the standard tenets of custody.

2. **B.** Generally speaking, with the exception stated above, automatic payment of advisory fees is considered to be custody. For a $900 prepayment (or anything in excess of $500) to be considered substantial, it must cover a period of at least 6 months. If an affiliated broker/dealer maintains custody, the adviser is covered under this requirement and must provide the balance sheet. However, if the broker/dealer had not been an affiliate, the adviser would not be deemed to have custody and no balance sheet would be required.

3. **A.**   Taking custody is considered to be of such significance that it requires prompt notification to the Administrator by the investment adviser by updating the Form ADV.

4. **B.**   Whether custody is maintained by the investment adviser itself or by a qualified custodian, statements must be sent at least quarterly.

5. **D.**   If the adviser does not return the securities to the sender within 3 business days, the adviser not only has actual custody, but has also violated the rule's requirement that client securities be maintained in an account with a qualified custodian.

6. **A.**   NASAA lists 3 acceptable qualified custodians. They are (1) a bank or savings association that has deposits insured by the Federal Deposit Insurance Corporation under the Federal Deposit Insurance Act; (2) a registered broker/dealer holding the client assets in customer accounts; and (3) a foreign financial institution that customarily holds financial assets for its customers, provided that the foreign financial institution keeps the advisory clients' assets in customer accounts segregated from its proprietary assets. If the transfer agent for a mutual fund is holding customer accounts, that is not considered to be custody, so no qualified custodian is necessary.

Quick Quiz 3.12

1. **A.**   Material disciplinary violations must be reported by all investment advisers, regardless of whether they keep custody. The first 2 answers fit the definition of material actions, but not the third. If the suit goes in favor of the client and the adviser is found guilty, disclosure would need to be made. Nothing in the rules refers at all to how much of the adviser's time must be spent giving advice. The only time there is a requirement that a substantial portion of the adviser's business be giving investment advice is when using the term *investment counsel*.

Quick Quiz 3.13

1. **B.**   Hedge clauses may not be used to disclaim statements that are inherently misleading.

2. **C.**   The regulators have not objected to clauses that limit the investment adviser's liability for losses caused by conditions and events beyond its control, such as war, strikes, natural disasters, new government restrictions, market fluctuations, communications disruptions, and so forth. Such provisions are acceptable since they do not attempt to limit or misstate the adviser's fiduciary obligations to its clients. Limiting liability to acts done in bad faith might cause the unsophisticated client to fail to understand that he still has a right to take action, even when the acts are committed in good faith. Fiduciary responsibility can not be limited by hedge clauses.

Quick Quiz 3.14

1. **C.**   Investment advisers never file anything with the SEC unless it relates to Form ADV. Past specific recommendations may be shown as long as they include all recommendations of the same type of asset, cover at least the prior 12-month period, and contain a disclaimer regarding any assurance of future results.

Quick Quiz 3.15

1. **C.**   A client's contracts, whether written or oral (technically, the Investment Advisers Act of 1940 does not require written contracts), may not be assigned without the client's consent under any circumstances. If the adviser is a partnership, notice must be made to clients of any changes in the membership of the partnership within a reasonable period. It is always permitted to charge a fee based on the average value of assets under management.

2. **B.** The addition of 2 equal partners to a 5-person firm does not constitute a majority change so all that is necessary is notice within a reasonable period of time, not consent. In the case of a corporation, a change in stock ownership is never required to be disclosed unless there is an actual change to the control or management of the adviser and such is not indicated here. Pledging a majority stock interest in an adviser structured as a corporation is considered an assignment and, therefore, requires client consent.

Quick Quiz 3.16

1. **B.** To make cash payments to solicitors, the agreement must:

   - be in writing;
   - provide for disclosure of any affiliations between the adviser and the solicitor (unless the solicitation is being made for impersonal advisory service);
   - provide that no one subject to statutory disqualification be compensated;
   - follow a script approved by the adviser (3rd party); and
   - provide that, in addition to the adviser's brochure, a solicitor brochure be delivered as well (3rd party).

   Nothing in the rules refers at all to how much of the adviser's time must be spent giving advice. The only time there is a requirement that a substantial portion of the adviser's business be giving investment advice is when using the term *investment counsel*.

Quick Quiz 3.17

1. **C** Section 28(e) provides a safe harbor for those expenses paid with soft dollars that offer a direct research benefit. Rent is not included in the list of acceptable items coming under that safe harbor.

2. **D.** Soft dollar compensation is when an investment adviser derives and economic benefit from the use of a client's commission dollars. Software of the type mentioned here is allowable under the safe harbor provisions of Section 28(e) of the Securities Exchange Act of 1934. It is true that this is indirect compensation and that this is a discretionary account, but the answer that best matches the question is soft dollar. Many times on the exam, you have to select best of the choices given.

Quick Quiz 3.18

1. **C.** The USA does not require investment advisers to include in their contracts a list of those states in which they are licensed to do business. The USA does require advisers to include their method of computing fees, a statement prohibiting assignment without client consent, and notification of change in membership of the investment partnership.

2. **F.** An Administrator may, by rule or order, prevent an adviser from taking custody. If an Administrator prevents custody, an adviser cannot overrule the Administrator by notifying the Administrator first.

3. **F.** An adviser may sell securities to clients from its own account provided disclosure is made upon receipt of written consent from the client before executing the trade.

4. **T.** Investment advisers are bound by the regulations that apply to sales activities as well as those that apply to advisory activities.

4

Equity and Debt Securities

The investment world is divided between owners (represented by stock or equity securities) and lenders (represented by bonds or debt securities).

Investors who buy stock in a company are its owners. Owners receive dividends. Investors who buy bonds in a government or corporation are lenders. Lenders receive interest payments.

The Series 65 exam will include approximately 12 questions on the material presented in this Unit. ∎

When you have completed this Unit, you should be able to:

- **compare** and contrast the basic features of common and preferred stock;

- **describe** and evaluate the basic features of government, municipal, and corporate debt; and

- **identify** the unique features of American depositary receipts (ADRs) and real estate investment trusts (REITs).

EQUITY SECURITIES

When individual investors become owners of a publicly traded company by purchasing common stock in that company, they can participate in the company's growth.

COMMON STOCK

Common stock is equity ownership in a corporation. A company issues stock to raise business capital, and investors who buy the stock also buy a share of ownership in the company's net worth. Whatever a business owns (its assets) less its creditors' claims (its liabilities) belongs to the businessowners (its stockholders).

Each share of stock entitles its owner to a portion of the company's earnings and dividends and a proportionate vote in major management decisions. Most corporations are organized in such a way that their stockholders regularly vote for and elect a few individuals to a board of directors to oversee company business. By electing a board of directors, stockholders have a say in the company's management but are not involved in the day-to-day details of its operations.

EXAMPLE

If a corporation issues 100 shares of stock, each share represents an identical 1/100—or 1%—ownership position in the company. An investor who owns 10 shares of stock would own 10% of the company; an investor who owns 50 shares of stock would own 50% of the company.

Corporations may issue two types of stock: common and preferred. When speaking of stocks, people generally mean common stock. **Preferred stock** also represents equity ownership in a corporation but usually does not have the same voting rights or appreciation potential as common stock. Preferred stock normally pays a fixed quarterly dividend and has priority claims over common stock; that is, the preferred is paid first if a company goes bankrupt, and common stockholders will never receive a dividend until the preferred shareholders have been paid theirs.

BENEFITS OF OWNING STOCK

Growth (Capital Gains)

An increase in the market price of securities is **capital appreciation**. Historically, owning common stock has provided investors with high real returns, although stock prices decline as well.

EXAMPLE

An investor buys shares of RST for $60 per share on January 1, 2003. On December 31, 2003, the shares are worth $90, an increase of 50% in the market price.

Income

Many corporations pay regular quarterly cash dividends to stockholders. A company's dividends may increase over time as profitability increases. Dividends, which can be a significant source of income for investors, are a major reason many people invest in stocks.

Issuers may also pay stock dividends in additional shares in the issuing company, or property dividends, shares in a subsidiary company, or in product.

EXAMPLE

RST paid a dividend of $2 per share during 2001, which provided the investor with a dividend yield of 3.3% ($2 ÷ $60 = 3.33%) in addition to the price appreciation.

TAKE NOTE

The increase in the price of RST stock in the example above is an unrealized gain until the stock is sold; when it is sold, it becomes a realized gain. Capital gains are not taxed until they are realized. Dividend income is taxed as ordinary income during the year when it is paid.

Voting Rights and Procedures

Common stockholders have the right to vote for corporate directors. Corporations usually provide for either statutory (regular) or cumulative voting. With statutory (regular) voting rights, if an investor owns 300 shares of common stock in a particular company and there are four vacancies on the board of directors, he may cast up to 300 votes for each of the four vacancies. With cumulative voting, if there are four positions to be filled, he could cast 1,200 votes (4 positions × 300 shares) any way he wanted—for instance, all 1,200 votes on one candidate; 600 on each of two candidates; 1,000 on one, 100 on each of two others; and so forth. He has 1,200 votes to vote as he pleases. Cumulative voting is beneficial to minority interests.

QUICK QUIZ 4.1

Here are two samples of how you might be asked about regular and cumulative voting on the exam.

1. By regular, or statutory, voting procedures, a stockholder with 100 shares would be able to vote for 6 directors in which of the following ways?

   A. 600 votes for any 1 director, no votes for the others
   B. 300 votes for any 2, none for the other 4
   C. 150 votes for any 4 candidates
   D. 100 votes for each of 6 candidates

2. A corporation features <u>cumulative</u> voting and a stockholder holds 200 shares of common stock. An election for 3 directors is being held. Which of the following combinations of votes could the stockholder cast?

A. 200 votes for each of these directors
B. 300 votes for any 2 directors
C. 600 votes for any 1 director
D. Any of the above

Quick Quiz answers can be found at the end of the Unit.

Proxy Voting

Frequently, it is not possible for the stockholder to attend the stockholder's meetings to personally cast his vote. An absentee ballot, known as a **proxy**, is made available for those shareholders who vote by mail.

They have the right to sell or give away their shares without permission of the corporation. Common stock is freely transferable to anyone who wants to buy it or receive it as a gift. Without this feature, there would be no stock markets.

Common stockholders have a right to limited access to the corporation's books. For the most part, common stockholders have the right to examine the minutes of meetings of the board of directors and the right to examine the list of the stockholders. Usually, this right is not exercised unless the performance of the corporation's management declines seriously. They also have the right to receive an audited set of financial statements of the company's performance each year (annual reports).

Common stockholders usually have the preemptive right to maintain their proportionate share of ownership in the corporation. The word *preempt* means to put oneself in front of another.

Essentially, common stockholders have a first right of refusal regarding any additional common stock to be issued by their company. For example, if the RAL Corporation has 1 million shares of common stock outstanding and an investor owns 10,000 shares, he owns 1% of the outstanding shares (10,000 ÷ 1 million = 1%). If RAL decides to issue 100,000 new shares of common stock, the company has to offer him the opportunity to buy 1,000 of the new shares before they are offered to the public, so that he can maintain his proportionate share of ownership. This right guarantees to stockholders that their ownership in the company will not be diminished against their wishes. An investor, of course, may refuse to buy these shares if he does not want them. However, if he refuses to buy the new shares, his proportionate share of ownership of RAL will be reduced.

Limited Liability

One of the most important features of equity ownership (common or preferred) is limited liability. In the event of the bankruptcy of a corporation, when corporate assets are not adequate to meet corporate obligations, personal assets are not at risk. One cannot be forced to sell any personal assets to help pay the debts of the business. If an individual invests $5,000 in the stock of a corporation that goes bankrupt, he may lose his entire $5,000 if the company is not salvaged, but he will not be forced to pay out any more monies to take care of additional debts. He is personally at risk only for the amount he has invested. A partner or sole proprietor risks not only the amount he has personally invested in his business, but also his personal assets should the business not be able to pay off its obligations.

RISKS OF OWNING STOCK

Regardless of their expectations, investors have no assurances that they will receive the returns they expect from their investments.

Market Risk

The chance that a stock will decline in price is one risk of owning common stock (known as **market risk**). A stock's price fluctuates daily as perceptions of the company's business prospects change and influence the actions of buyers and sellers. Investors have no assurance whatsoever that they will be able to recoup the investment in a stock at any time.

Decreased or No Income

A risk of stock ownership is the possibility of dividend income decreasing or ceasing entirely if the company loses money.

Low Priority at Dissolution

If a company enters bankruptcy, the holders of its bonds and preferred stock have priority over common stockholders. A company's debt and preferred shares are considered **senior securities**. Common stockholders have residual rights to corporate assets upon dissolution.

TAKE NOTE

In owning common equity, the investor stands to lose current income through dividend reduction or suspension, as well as capital loss, should the market price decline. In return, however, the shareholder has limited liability; that is, the liability is limited to the amount invested.

1. Which of the following represent(s) ownership in a company?

    I.   Corporate bonds
    II. Common stock
    III. Preferred stock
    IV. Mortgage bonds

    A. I and IV
    B. II only
    C. II and III
    D. I, II, III and IV

2. Among the benefits of owning common stock are

    I.   it has historically been a hedge against inflation
    II. voting rights
    III. access, as owners, to corporate earnings before the general public
    IV. dividends

    A. I and II
    B. I, II and IV
    C. II and IV
    D. I, II, III and IV

3. In which of the following ways may a company declare dividends?

    I.   Cash
    II. Stock
    III. Stock of another company

    A. I only
    B. I and II
    C. II and III
    D. I, II and III

4. Limited liability regarding ownership in a large, publicly held US corporation means all of the following EXCEPT

    A. investors might lose more than the amount of their investment
    B. investors might lose their investment
    C. investors' shares are nonassessable
    D. investors are not liable to the full extent of their personal property

5. Common stockholder rights include a

    I.   residual claim to assets at dissolution
    II. vote for the amount of stock dividend to be paid
    III. vote in matters of recapitalization
    IV. claim against dividends that are in default

    A. I only
    B. I and III
    C. II and III
    D. III and IV

6. All of the following are considered to be risks of owning common stock EXCEPT
   A. market risk
   B. possible decrease in dividend payments
   C. removal of voting rights
   D. low priority of claim at dissolution

PREFERRED STOCK

Preferred stock has features of both equity and debt securities and is an equity security because it represents ownership in the corporation. Like a bond, preferred stock is usually issued as a fixed-income security with a fixed dividend. Its price tends to fluctuate with changes in interest rates rather than with the issuing company's business prospects unless, of course, dramatic changes occur in the company's credit quality.

TAKE NOTE   Unlike common stock, most preferred stock is nonvoting.

TEST TOPIC ALERT   Like common stock, preferred stock represents ownership in a company, but its price reacts to the market more like a bond because its price is sensitive to interest rate changes.

Benefits of Preferred Stock

Although preferred stock does not typically have the same growth potential as common stock, preferred stockholders have two advantages over common stockholders.

■ When the board of directors declares dividends, owners of preferred stock receive their dividends before common stockholders.

■ If a corporation goes bankrupt, preferred stockholders have a priority claim over common stockholders on the assets remaining after creditors have been paid.

Because preferred stocks generally make fixed dividend payments, the shares trade like bonds in the secondary market. When interest rates rise, preferred share prices decline; when interest rates decline, preferred share prices rise.

Fixed Rate of Return

A preferred stock's fixed dividend is a key feature for income-oriented investors. Normally, a preferred stock is identified by its annual dividend payment stated as a percentage of its par value.

A preferred stock with a par value of $100 that pays $6 in annual dividends would be known as a 6% preferred. The dividend of preferred stock with no par value is stated in a dollar amount (e.g., a $6 no-par preferred).

Adjustable-Rate Preferred

Some preferred stocks are issued with adjustable (or variable) dividend rates. Such dividends are usually tied to the rates of other interest rate benchmarks, such as Treasury bills and money market rates, and can be adjusted as often as quarterly. Because the payment adjusts to current interest rates, the price of the stock remains relatively stable.

No Maturity Date or Set Maturity Value

Although it is generally regarded as a fixed-income investment, preferred stock, unlike debt securities, usually has no preset date at which it matures and no scheduled redemption date. Preferred stock is thus a perpetual security.

Types

Separate categories of preferred may differ in several ways, including dividend rate and profit participation privileges. However, all maintain preference over common stock. Preferred stock may have one or more of the following characteristics.

Straight (Noncumulative)

Straight preferred has no special features beyond the stated dividend payment. Missed dividends are not paid to the holder.

Cumulative Preferred

Cumulative preferred stock accrues payments due its shareholders in the event dividends are reduced or suspended. If the directors of a company in financial difficulty reduce or suspend dividend payments, the corporation will not make up any dividends missed by common stockholders.

Dividends due cumulative preferred stock accumulate on the company's books until the corporation can pay them. When the company resumes dividend payments, cumulative preferred stockholders receive current dividends plus the total accumulated dividends—dividends **in arrears**—before any dividends may be distributed to common stockholders.

EXAMPLE

In 2000, RST Corp. had both common stock and cumulative preferred stock outstanding. The common paid a dividend of $1, and the preferred paid a $2 dividend. Because of financial difficulties, the company stopped paying dividends during 2000. After resolving its problems in 2001, the company resumed dividend payments and paid the cumulative preferred holders an $8 dividend for the arrears in years 2000, 2001, 2002, and 2003 before paying any dividends to the common stockholders.

Callable Preferred

Corporations often issue **callable** (or **redeemable**) **preferred**, which a company can buy back from investors at a stated price after a specified date. The right to call the stock allows the company to replace a relatively high fixed dividend obligation with a lower one.

When a corporation calls a preferred stock, dividend payments and conversion rights generally cease on the call date. In return for the call privilege, the corporation may pay a premium exceeding the stock's par value at the call, such as $103 for a $100 par value stock.

Convertible Preferred

A preferred stock is **convertible** if the owner can exchange the shares for shares of common stock.

TAKE NOTE

Because the value of a convertible preferred stock is linked to the value of a common stock, the convertible preferred's price fluctuates in line with the common.

Convertible preferred may be issued with a lower stated dividend rate than nonconvertible preferred because the investor may have the opportunity to convert to common shares and enjoy greater capital gain potential.

QUICK QUIZ 4.3

1. Which of the following types of preferred stock typically has the highest stated rate of dividend (all other factors being equal)?

    A. Convertible
    B. Straight
    C. Cumulative
    D. Callable

2. Of straight and cumulative preferred, which would have the higher stated rate?

    A. Straight preferred
    B. Cumulative preferred

3. Which of the following types of preferred stock is most influenced by the price of an issuer's common stock?

A. Cumulative
B. Straight
C. Convertible
D. Callable

FOREIGN INVESTMENTS: AMERICAN DEPOSITARY RECEIPTS (ADRs)

American Depositary Receipts (ADRs), also known as American Depositary Shares (ADSs), facilitate the trading of foreign stocks in US markets because everything is done in English and in US dollars. An **ADR** is a negotiable security that represents a receipt for shares of stock in a non-US corporation, usually from 1 to 10 shares. ADRs are bought and sold in the US securities markets like stock.

Rights of ADR Owners

Most of the rights that common stockholders normally hold, such as the right to receive dividends, also apply to ADR owners.

Currency Risk

In addition to the normal risks associated with stock ownership, ADR investors are also subject to currency risk. **Currency risk** is the possibility that an investment denominated in one currency (such as the Mexican peso) could decline if the value of that currency declines in its exchange rate with the US dollar. Because ADRs represent shares of stock in companies located in foreign countries, currency exchange rates are an important consideration.

Custodian Bank

Domestic branches of large commercial US banks issue ADRs. A custodian, typically a bank in the issuer's country, holds the shares of foreign stock that the ADRs represent. The stock must remain on deposit as long as the ADRs are outstanding because the ADRs are the depositary bank's guarantee that it holds the stock.

Registered Owner

ADRs are registered on the books of the US banks responsible for them. The individual investors in the ADRs are not considered the stock's registered owners. Because ADRs are registered on the books of US banks, dividends are sent to the custodian banks as registered owners. The banks collect the payments, convert them into US funds for US owners, and withhold any required foreign tax payments.

TAKE NOTE   Although portions of dividends may be withheld to pay local taxes, owners of ADRs can claim a US tax credit for these withholdings.

TAKE NOTE   The exam will want you to know that ADRs are issued by domestic branches of American banks and that, even though they are traded in US dollars, they still bear currency risk.

RISKS OF INVESTING IN FOREIGN MARKETS

Although foreign securities offer investors the potential for substantial gains, they bear a variety of risks that are not present with domestic investments. There are two broad market classifications of foreign markets: emerging and developed.

Emerging Markets

Emerging markets are markets in lesser developed countries. They are generally associated with:

- low levels of income, as measured by the gross national product (GNP);
- low levels of equity capitalization;
- questionable market liquidity;
- potential restrictions on currency conversion;
- high volatility;
- prospects for economic growth and development;
- stabilizing political and social institutions;
- high taxes and commission costs for foreign investor; and
- restrictions on foreign ownership and on foreign currency conversion.

Despite primitive market infrastructures, many emerging markets have rapid growth rates that make their securities attractive to foreign investors whose local markets experience more modest growth.

Developed Markets

Developed markets are those associated with countries that have highly developed economies with stable political and social institutions. These are characterized by:

- large levels of equity capitalization;
- low commission rates;

■ few, if any, currency conversion restrictions;

■ highly liquid markets with many brokerage institutions and market makers; and

■ many large capitalization securities.

Whether investing in the securities of emerging or developed foreign markets, the investor faces several risks not present in domestic investing. These include:

■ country risk;

■ exchange controls;

■ currency risk; and

■ withholding, fees, and taxes.

Country Risk

Country risk is a composite of all the risks of investing in a particular country. These may include political risks, such as revolutions or military coups, and structural risks, such as confiscatory policies toward profits, capital gains, and dividends. Economic policies, interest rates, and inflation are also elements of risk of investing in emerging countries.

Exchange Controls

Foreign investors can also be subject to restrictions on currency conversion or movement.

Withholding, Fees, and Taxes

Some foreign countries may withhold a portion of dividends and capital gains for taxes. Some also impose heavy fees and taxes on securities that the investor must bear in addition to generally higher brokerage commissions.

QUICK QUIZ 4.4

1. ADRs are used to facilitate

   A. foreign trading of domestic securities
   B. foreign trading of US government securities
   C. domestic trading of US government securities
   D. domestic trading of foreign securities

2. Which 2 of the following risks would be of greatest concern to the holder of an ADR?

    I.   Currency
    II. Liquidity
    III. Market
    IV. Purchasing power

    A. I and II
    B. I and III
    C. II and IV
    D. III and IV

REAL ESTATE INVESTMENT TRUSTS (REITs)

A **real estate investment trust** (**REIT,** pronounced *reet*) is a company that manages a portfolio of real estate investments to earn profits for shareholders. REITs are normally publicly traded and serve as a source of long-term financing for real estate projects. A REIT pools capital in a manner similar to an investment company. Shareholders receive dividends from investment income or capital gains distributions. REITs normally:

■ own commercial property (**equity REITs**);

■ own mortgages on commercial property (**mortgage REITs**); or

■ do both (**hybrid REITs**).

REITs are organized as trusts in which investors buy shares or certificates of beneficial interest either on stock exchanges or in the over-the-counter market.

Under the guidelines of Subchapter M of the Internal Revenue Code, a REIT can avoid being taxed as a corporation by receiving 75% or more of its income from real estate and distributing 90% or more of its taxable income to its shareholders.

TEST TOPIC ALERT   Four important points to remember about REITs follow.

■ An owner of REITs holds an undivided interest in a pool of real estate investments.

■ REITs trade on exchanges and over the counter.

■ REITs are not investment companies (mutual funds).

■ REITs offer dividends and gains to investors but do not pass through losses like limited partnerships, and therefore are·not considered to be direct participation programs (DPPs).

RIGHTS AND WARRANTS

Rights and warrants allow investors to buy additional shares of stock under defined circumstances.

RIGHTS

Preemptive rights entitle existing stockholders to maintain their proportionate ownership shares in a company by buying newly issued shares before the company offers them to the general public.

A **rights offering** allows stockholders to purchase common stock below the current market price. The rights are valued separately from the stock and trade in the secondary market during the subscription period.

A stockholder who receives rights may:

■ exercise the rights to buy stock by sending the rights certificates and a check for the required amount to the rights agent;

■ sell the rights and profit from their market value (rights certificates are negotiable securities); or

■ let the rights expire and lose their value.

WARRANTS

A **warrant** is a certificate granting its owner the right to purchase securities from the issuer at a specified price, normally higher than the current market price. Unlike a right, a warrant is usually a long-term instrument that gives the investor the option of buying shares at a later date at the exercise price.

Origination of Warrants

Warrants are usually offered to the public as sweeteners in connection with other securities, such as debentures or preferred stock, to make those securities more attractive. Such offerings are often bundled as units.

QUICK QUIZ 4.5

1. Which of the following statements regarding warrants is TRUE?

    A. Warrants are only offered to current shareholders.
    B. Warrants have longer terms than rights.
    C. Warrants do not trade in the secondary market.
    D. At the time of issuance, the exercise price of a warrant is typically below the market value of the underlying stock.

2. Which of the following statements regarding rights is TRUE?

    A. Common stockholders do not have the right to subscribe to rights offerings.
    B. Preferred stockholders do not have the right to subscribe to rights offerings.
    C. Both common and preferred stockholders have the right to subscribe to rights offerings.
    D. Neither common nor preferred stockholders have the right to subscribe to rights offerings.

FIXED-INCOME OR DEBT SECURITIES

DEBT SECURITIES

Debt capital represents money loaned to a corporation by investors in that corporation's bonds. A **bond** is a certificate representing the corporation's indebtedness. It is a loan made to the corporation by an investor. These certificates state the corporation's obligation to pay back a specific amount of money on a specific date. They also state a corporation's obligation to pay the investor a specific rate of interest for the use of his funds. When an investor buys a bond, he is lending a corporation money for a set period of time at a fixed annual interest rate.

It is important to understand that debt capital refers to long-term debt financing. Long-term debt, frequently called funded debt on the exam, is money borrowed for a minimum of five years, although more frequently the length of time is 20–30 years.

Even though only corporations have been mentioned to this point, it is important to know that there are two other major issuers of debt securities. The largest issuer of debt securities is the US government. Substantial sums are also borrowed by state governments and those political entities that are subdivisions of a state, such as cities, counties, towns, and so forth. These issues from state and local political entities are called **municipal bonds**. Whenever the word *government* is used in conjunction with a security on the exam, it means the federal government. Whenever the word *municipal security* is used on the exam, it is referring to a security issued by a state or other municipality.

Role as Lender

The most important fact in discussing debt securities is the investor's position as lender: he is acquiring no ownership but is placing himself in the role of creditor.

Has anyone ever asked you to loan them money? If so, there were probably four questions that you needed to answer for yourself before you could agree to the loan.

■ How much am I lending?

■ How safe is my loan and how sure am I that I will get my money back?

- How much interest will I be paid for the use of my money?

- How and when will I get my money back?

Let's take a look at the first question because it's the simplest to answer. Although the overall size of the issue may be anywhere from several million dollars to billions of dollars in the case of government issues, the face amount, or par value, of each bond is always $1,000, unless otherwise specified. That is, loans in the form of bonds are always made in $1,000 units.

For common stock, par value is of no importance to the investor. With preferred stock, par value is the number on which the dividend is based. Par value is even more important with bonds because not only does it represent what the interest payment is based on, but it also represents the amount of principal to be repaid at maturity.

Safety of Principal-Corporate Debt

Corporate debt securities, like any other loan, may be either secured or unsecured. **Secured debt securities** are backed by various kinds of assets of the issuing corporation, whereas **unsecured debt securities** are backed only by the reputation, credit record, and financial stability of the corporation.

Mortgage Bonds

Just as the owner of a home pledges a real asset (the home and land) as collateral for the mortgage, a corporation will borrow money backed by real estate and physical assets of the corporation. Just as a home ordinarily would have a market value greater than the principal amount of its mortgage, the value of the real assets pledged by the corporation will be in excess of the amount borrowed under that bond issue. If the corporation develops financial problems and is unable to pay the interest on the bonds, those real assets pledged as collateral are generally sold to pay off the mortgage bondholders.

The principle is no different from having a mortgage on a home. Does the lender of a home mortgage feel his loan to a buyer is secure? If the buyer couldn't pay, could he sell the home for more than the mortgage? Probably so. A purchaser of a mortgage bond is in the same position of safety.

Equipment Trust Certificate

When an automobile is purchased, a down payment is made, and the remaining balance is financed for an estimated three or four years. Because the asset would decrease in value, the buyer would have to make a down payment so that the value of the collateral (the automobile) would not be less than the amount financed. The buyer would pay off this note with monthly installments so that the value of the automobile was never worth less than the amount owed to the lender. If payment could not be made, the lender would repossess the automobile since he had first claim on the buyer's asset.

Corporations, particularly railroads and other transportation companies, do the same thing. They finance the acquisition of their rolling stock and locomotives by issuing an equipment trust certificate. The railroad makes a down payment, usually 20% of the cost of the rolling stock, and finances the balance over the course of 15 years. Because the equipment does wear out, the railroad will pay off a portion of the loan on an annual basis. At no time, theoretically, is the value of the assets (the rolling stock, locomotives, or both) worth less than the amount of the principal remaining on the loan. When the railroad has finished paying off the loan, it receives clear title to its equipment from the trustee. If the railroad does not make the payments, the lender repossesses the collateral and sells it for his benefit.

Collateral Trust Bonds

Sometimes a corporation wants to borrow money and has neither real estate (for a mortgage) nor equipment (for an equipment trust) to use as collateral. Instead, it deposits securities it owns into a trust to serve as collateral for the lenders. The securities it deposits can be securities in that corporation or of any other corporation as long as the securities are marketable, that is, readily liquidated. Obviously, the better the quality of the securities deposited as collateral, the better the quality and rating of the bond.

Debenture

A **debenture** is a debt obligation of the corporation backed only by its word and general creditworthiness. Debentures are written promises of the corporation to pay the principal at its due date and interest on a regular basis. Although this promise is as binding as a promise for a mortgage bond, debentures are not secured by any pledge of property. They are sold on the general credit of the company; their security depends on the assets and earnings of the corporation. Although debentures are unsecured, there are issuers whose credit standing is so good that their debentures are safer than mortgage bonds of less creditworthy companies.

Guaranteed Bonds

A **guaranteed bond** is a bond that is guaranteed as to payment of interest, or both principal and interest, by a corporate entity other than the issuer. The value of the guarantee is only as good as the strength of the company making that guarantee. Guaranteed bonds were particularly popular in the railroad industry in which a major railroad seeking to lease trackage rights from a short line would guarantee that smaller company's debt. A more recent example is the ExxonMobil Corporation guaranteeing the debt issues of the Exxon Pipeline Company.

Senior

The word *senior* is used to describe the relative priority of claim of a security. Every preferred stock has a senior claim to common stock. Every debt security has senior claim to preferred stock. Secured bonds have a senior claim to unsecured bonds. The term *senior securities* means bonds and preferred stock, because they have a claim senior to common stock. If an exam question described a corporation as having issued senior bonds, the answer would have to state that there were mortgage or equipment trust certificates issued by that corporation with prior claim ahead of unsecured creditors.

Subordinated

The term *subordinated* means "comes behind" or "comes after." It is usually describing a debenture. A subordinated debenture has a claim that is behind (junior to) that of any other creditor. However, no matter how subordinated the debenture, it is still senior to any stockholder.

Safety of Principal—Municipal Bonds

The safety of principal of municipal bonds depends on the type of municipal issue.

General Obligation Bonds (GOs)

General obligation bonds are backed by a pledge of the issuer's full faith and credit for prompt payment of principal and interest. Most city, county, and school district bonds have the further distinction of being secured by a pledge of unlimited ad valorem (property) taxes to be levied against all taxable property. In most cases, if taxes are not paid, the delinquent property is sold at a tax sale, giving the bondholder a superior claim above mortgages, mechanic's liens, and similar encumbrances. Because GOs are geared to tax resources, they are normally analyzed in terms of the size of the resources being taxed. They are generally very safe.

Revenue Bond

Revenue bonds are payable from the earnings of a revenue-producing enterprise, such as a water, sewer, electric or gas system, toll bridge, airport, college dormitory, or other income-producing facility.

Authorities and agencies are created by states or their subdivisions to perform specific functions, such as the operation of water, sewer, or electric systems, bridges, tunnels, or highways and in some states, to construct schools or public facilities. In some cases, the authority has the right to levy fees and charges for its services. In other cases, it receives lease rentals, which may be payable from specific revenues or may be general obligations of the lessee. They are usually analyzed in terms of their earnings, historical or potential, compared with bond requirements. The yield, generally, is higher for this type of bond than for a GO (taxes are more secure than revenues), although many have built up a good record over a long period of time and are sometimes rated higher than GOs.

SAFETY OF PRINCIPAL—GOVERNMENT SECURITIES

Government bonds are the safest of all. There are two primary types of backing; direct government backing or guarantee, as in the case of Treasury issues, and the moral guarantee as in the case of federal agencies.

Although most government issues trade in what is known as the capital market—that is, the market for long-term securities, stocks, and bonds—there are several issues that trade in the money market. The money market is where short-term instruments, those that mature in one year or less, are traded. The money market will be discussed later. No discussion of Treasury issues would be possible, however, without describing the widely held bellwether of the money market known as US Treasury bills.

US Treasury Bills

Treasury bills are direct short-term debt obligations of the US government. They are issued every week by using a competitive bidding process. Each week, T-bills, as they are known, with maturities of 4 weeks, 13 weeks (three months), and 26 weeks (six months) are issued.

Treasury bills pay no interest; they are issued at a discount from their par value. An investor might purchase a $10,000, 26-week T-bill at a price of $9,800. He would receive no interest, but, at maturity, the Treasury would send him a check for $10,000. The difference between the $9,800 he paid and the $10,000 he received would be considered his interest income even though he never received a separate interest check.

TAKE NOTE   Key points to remember regarding T-bills include: (1) Treasury bills are the only Treasury security issued at a discount; (2) Treasury bills are the only Treasury security issued without a stated interest rate; (3) Treasury bills are highly liquid; and (4) Treasury bills are used in market analysis as the stereotypical "risk-free" investment.

QUICK QUIZ 4.6

1. A company realizes money from the sale of surplus equipment. They would like to invest this money but will need it in 4–6 months and must take that into consideration when selecting an investment. You would recommend

   A. preferred stock
   B. Treasury bills
   C. AAA rated bonds with long-term maturities
   D. common stock

US Treasury Notes

US Treasury notes are direct debt obligations of the US Treasury with the following characteristics.

- They pay semiannual interest as a percentage of the stated par value.

- They have intermediate maturities (2–10 years).

- They mature at par value.

US Treasury Bonds

US Treasury bonds are direct debt obligations of the US Treasury with the following characteristics.

■ They pay semiannual interest as a percentage of the stated par value.

■ They have long-term maturities, generally 10–30 years.

■ Older 30-year bonds are usually callable at par beginning 25 years after issue. However, the last callable 30-year bond was issued in November 1984.

■ They mature at par value.

Treasury Inflation Protection Securities (TIPS)

A relatively new type of Treasury issue, **Treasury Inflation Protection Securities (TIPS)**, helps protect investors against purchasing power risk. These notes are issued with a fixed interest rate, but the principal amount is adjusted semiannually by an amount equal to the change in the Consumer Price Index (CPI), the standard measurement of inflation.

The interest payment the investor receives every six months is equal to the fixed interest amount times the newly adjusted principal. During times of inflation, the interest payments increase, while during times of deflation, the interest payments fall. These notes are sold at lower interest rates than conventional fixed-rate Treasury notes because of their adjustable nature.

Like other Treasury notes, TIPS are exempt from state and local income taxes on the interest income generated, but are subject to federal taxation. However, in any year when the principal is adjusted for inflation, that increase is considered reportable income for that year even though the increase will not be received until the note matures.

TEST TOPIC ALERT

The Series 65 exam may ask questions similar to the following.

1. A customer wishes to buy a security providing periodic interest payments, safety of principal, and protection from purchasing power risk. The customer should purchase

   A. TIPS
   B. TIGRS
   C. CMOs
   D. STRIPS

   Answer: A. TIPS offer inflation protection and safety of principal because they are backed by the US government.

2. A client has a TIPS with a coupon rate of 4.5%. The inflation rate has been 7% for the last year. What is the inflation-adjusted return?

   A. –2.5%
   B. 4.5%
   C. 7.0%
   D. 11.5%

   Answer: B. Treasury Inflation Protection Securities (TIPS) adjust the principal value every 6 months to account for the inflation rate. Therefore, the real rate of return will always be the coupon.

US Federal Agency Securities

US federal agency securities are issued by US government agencies that have been authorized by Congress to issue debt securities to help meet their financial needs. Although the securities do not have direct Treasury backing, they are considered moral obligations of the US government. Most of the agency bonds are described by their titles. The two principal US government agencies that issue debt securities are the Federal Farm Credit Banks and the Federal Home Loan Bank (FHLB).

Federal Land Banks (FLB)

Federal land banks (FLBs) are supervised by the Farm Credit Administration. FLBs, through Federal Land Bank associations, make loans secured by mortgages to farmers and ranchers.

Federal Intermediate Credit Bank (FICB)

The FICB consists of 12 banks authorized to make loans to farmers for expenses, machinery, and livestock. The loans are intermediate in term, running no longer than 10 years to maturity.

Bank for Cooperatives

These are operated under the Farm Credit Administration. The banks make loans to farm cooperatives.

Federal Home Loan Banks (FHLB)

Operating under the supervision of the Federal Home Loan Bank board, FHLB is the agency that stands behind the nation's savings and loans (S&Ls). The FHLB lends to member S&Ls to augment the money that these S&Ls receive from their regular depositors. In a nutshell, the FHLB borrows money in the open market by issuing various debt securities, then relends it to S&Ls who relend it to home buyers.

Interest received by the investor on all of the above securities is exempt from state and local income taxes but not federal income tax.

Federal National Mortgage Association

The Federal National Mortgage Association (Fannie Mae) was a government-owned corporation that was converted into a privately owned corporation in 1968. The common stock of the private corporation is traded on the New York Stock Exchange. Fannie Mae purchases and sells real estate mortgages—primarily those insured by the Federal Housing Administration (FHA) or guaranteed by the Veterans Administration (VA). Fannie Mae issues mortgage-backed bonds that can be purchased by individual investors. All Fannie Mae securities are considered to be quite safe. They are issued at par and pay semiannual interest. Like the other federal issues, they come out in book entry form.

Government National Mortgage Association

In 1968, when the Federal National Mortgage Association was split into two corporations, one privately owned, the other wholly owned by the federal government, the privately owned corporation retained the original name. The new federally owned corporation became known as the Government National Mortgage Association (Ginnie Mae). Ginnie Maes are known as modified pass-through certificates. They represent an interest in pools of FHA-insured mortgages or VA or Farmers Home Administration-guaranteed mortgages. The term *pass-through* is used because, as the homeowners make their monthly mortgage payments, those payments are collected in the pool and the shares passes through to the investor. This payment received by the investor differs from most other securities in two respects.

First, payments are received monthly, because underlying the security is a pool of home mortgages, which are paid for monthly. Second, each monthly payment the investor receives consists partly of interest and partly of principal. Because payments on home mortgages consist of principal and some interest and, because that money goes into the pool for all the investors, as it is paid out monthly, some of each monthly payment to the investor represents principal, and the balance of each payment represents interest. Ginnie Maes carry a minimum denomination of $25,000 and, unlike the other agencies are backed by the full faith and credit of the federal government. The interest on both the Fannie Maes and Ginnie Maes is subject to state and local taxation. Ginnie Mae investors receive monthly, not semiannual, payments.

Ratings

The purchase of a debt security is only as safe as who the borrower is and what is received for collateral. Because safety of the bond will frequently be a very important consideration for clients, consult the rating services. The two primary rating organizations for debt securities are Standard & Poor's and Moody's. Both organizations have highly qualified personnel who analyze all the details of the debt issue and arrive at a letter rating indicating their opinion of the debt's quality (safety). The following chart should give you all the information you need for the exam.

Standard & Poor's Bond Ratings		Moody's Ratings	
AAA	Bonds of highest quality	Aaa	Bonds of highest quality
AA	High-quality debt obligations	Aa	Bonds of high quality
A	Bonds that have a strong capacity to pay interest and principal but may be susceptible to adverse effects	A	Bonds whose security of principal and interest is considered adequate but may be impaired in the future
BBB	Bonds that have an adequate capacity to pay interest and principal but are more vulnerable to adverse economic conditions or changing circumstances	Baa	Bonds of medium grade that are neither highly protected nor poorly secured
BB	Bonds of lower medium grade with few desirable investment characteristics	Ba	Bonds of speculative quality whose future cannot be considered well assured
B	Primarily speculative bonds with great uncertainties and major risk if exposed to adverse conditions	B	Bonds that lack characteristics of a desirable investment
CCC	Bonds in poor standing that may be defaulted	Caa	Bonds in poor standing that may be defaulted
C	Income bonds on which no interest is being paid	Ca	Speculative bonds that are often in default
D	Bonds in default	C	Bonds with little probability of any investment value (lowest rating)
Note: Plus (+) and minus (–) are used to show relative strength within a rating category.		Note: For ratings Aa through B, 1 indicates the high, 2 indicates the middle, and 3 indicates the low end of the rating class.	

Investment-Grade Debt

In the industry, bonds rated in the top four categories (BBB or Baa and higher) are referred to as investment grade. Investment-grade bonds are generally the only quality eligible for purchase by the institutions (e.g., banks or insurance companies) and by fiduciaries.

Some bonds are not rated. There are two major reasons a debt security is not rated.

■   The issuer does not want to pay the cost of receiving the rating.

■   The issuer does not have a sufficient credit history to enable the rater to make a fair judgment.

High-Yield Bonds

Lower-grade bonds, known in the industry as junk bonds, are now more commonly called high-yield bonds. Because of their lower ratings (BB or Ba or lower) and additional risk of default, high-yield bonds may be subject to substantial price erosion during slow economic times or when a bond issuer's creditworthiness is questioned. Their volatility is usually substantially higher than investment-grade bonds, but they may be suitable for sophisticated investors seeking higher returns and possible capital appreciation from speculative fixed-income investments.

The cost of money is determined by supply and demand. The most popular measurement of this supply and demand is the prime rate. This is the rate charged by major banks to their most creditworthy customers and is a leading indicator of money rates.

There is a critical relationship in all investments known as the risk-reward relationship. The more risk an investor takes, the greater must be his reward. When a bank is loaning money to a major corporation, such as AT&T or IBM, it takes little risk, and therefore it is willing to rent out the money at the lowest possible rates given the supply and demand situation at that time. The less creditworthy the borrower, the more risk to the lender, so the greater reward the lender must receive to compensate for that risk. That is why lower-rated bonds carry higher rates of return.

To make its creditworthiness a little more attractive, an issuer can pledge collateral. It is important to understand that when the raters evaluate a bond they look at all the factors, including collateral. A mortgage bond is not necessarily safer than any debenture.

Yield Computations

The interest rate will always be stated as a percentage of the par value. The interest stated on the face of the bond is called the **nominal yield**. Sometimes it is referred to as the coupon rate. To compute the annual interest payments in dollars, multiply this nominal yield by the face amount of the bond ($1,000 unless stated otherwise). A bond with a 5% coupon rate pays $50 per year. One with an 8% nominal yield pays $80 per year. One with a coupon of 13.5% pays $135 per year. Because, on any particular bond, this interest payment is the same every year, it is referred to as a fixed charge.

Current Yield

An investor will always want to know the return on his investment. The most straightforward way to do that is to actually place the return on the investment as follows.

$$\frac{\text{Return}}{\text{Investment}}$$

The return will always be the annual interest in dollars (if referring to a stock, the dividend in dollars) divided by the current market price (the amount of investment required to own the security). This calculation is called current yield or current return.

Although most bonds are issued with a face, or par, value of $1,000, bond prices do fluctuate in the market. As stated earlier, the interest a bond pays is called its coupon rate or nominal yield. Look at this example: The DBL 10s of '19. DBL is the name of the issuer, 10s means the nominal yield is 10%, and '19 means that the bonds mature in 2019. The letter s is added because it is easier to say "the 10s" than to say "the 10." These bonds pay $100 a year ($50 semiannually) for each $1,000 of face value. Regardless of what the market price of the bonds may be, DBL has an obligation to pay annual interest of 10% of the $1,000 face they borrowed.

If an investor were to buy these bonds for more than $1,000 or less than $1,000, the return on the investment would not be 10%. For example, if these bonds had a current market value of $800, their current yield would be 12.5% ($100 ÷ $800). Similarly, someone paying $1,200 for the bonds will receive a current yield of 8.33% ($100 ÷ $1,200). Please notice, the $100 interest received is the same in all cases regardless of the current market price.

Discount and Premium

When a bond is selling at a price above par (or face), it is selling at a premium; when it is selling below par, it is selling at a discount. Two critical statements to remember follow.

> If you pay more, you get less.
> If you pay less, you get more.

If an investor buys a bond at a premium, he will always receive a rate of return less than the coupon (or nominal) yield stated on the face of the bond (8.33% is less than 10%). Conversely, any time an investor purchases a bond at a discount, he will get more than the rate stated on the face of the bond (12.5% is greater than 10%).

In addition to being the dollar amount on which the annual interest was based, par value was also the dollar amount that would be returned to the investor at maturity. Therefore, an investor purchasing a bond at a discount knows that if he holds the bond until maturity date he will get back the par value, which will be more than what he paid for the bond. If an investor purchases a bond at a premium and holds it until the maturity date, he knows that he will receive back the par value, which is less than what he paid for the bond. To accurately reflect this gain or loss that an investor will have upon maturity, there is another yield to consider—the yield to maturity, or true yield.

Yield to Maturity or Basis

This measurement takes into account the gain or loss the investor will have when the bonds are redeemed at maturity. The person who buys the bonds mentioned above at $800 will get back $1,000 if he holds the bonds to maturity, in addition to receiving $100 per year interest (a current yield of 12.5% on his money). Consequently, this investor will have a gain of $200 on top of his annual interest. The individual paying $1,200 for the bonds will have a $200 loss at maturity when he gets back face value for them.

Whenever an investor pays less (buys at a discount), he will make a profit in addition to his annual interest, and whenever he pays more (buys at a premium), he will suffer a loss if he holds it to maturity.

- A bond is issued at par ($1,000) because that is how much the issuer is borrowing.

- The interest paid on the bond is always fixed as a percentage of the par (face) value.

- Regardless of changes in the market value of the bond, the interest checks remain the same.

- The current market price of a bond is determined by supply and demand.

- The current market price will fluctuate.

- The current market price may be at par, above par, or below par.

- A bond always matures at par.

- Purchasing a bond at par will always result in getting back the same as the original investment at maturity.

- Purchasing a bond at a discount (below par) will always result in getting back par, which means more (a profit) than the original investment.

- Purchasing a bond at a premium (above par) will always result in getting back par, which means less (a loss) than the original investment.

Tax Equivalent Yield

One final factor to be considered in the analysis of debt securities is taxability. Municipal bonds have one important characteristic that sets them apart from all other securities. Interest from municipal bonds is free of federal income tax. Although an investor must report interest received on municipal bonds on his federal income tax return, that interest is not included in his taxable income.

Assume an investor has $2,000 to invest. If he purchases, at par, one corporate or government bond of standard size ($1,000) with a 10% nominal yield, he would receive $100 per year paid by two semiannual interest checks of $50. For purposes of this example, assume that he is in the 28% federal income tax bracket. An individual in the 28% tax bracket pays tax on any additional income earned at a rate of 28%. Therefore, on the $100 in interest he received above, he would pay the IRS $28 (28%) and keep the other $72.

The other $1,000 he had available to invest was used to purchase a $1,000-par-value municipal bond with a 7.5% nominal yield. He would receive $75 annually on that bond. The 10% bonds, on which the interest is taxable, would net $72 per year after taxes. Of the $75 interest received for the 7.5% municipal, none of it is taxed; the whole amount is kept. Therefore, a client in the 28% bracket should purchase 7.5% municipals before 10% corporates. The taxable equivalent yield of a 7.5% tax-free bond for this investor in the 28% tax bracket would be the tax-free yield divided by (100% minus the tax bracket). In this case, 7.5 ÷ (100 – 28), or .72. That equals 10.42%, so it is obvious that the 7.5% municipal bond will provide a higher after tax return.

Bond Pricing

It is important to understand how the market prices of bonds are quoted. Look at the following examples to see how corporates, municipals, and governments are quoted.

Corporates and Municipal

■ Corporate and municipal bonds are quoted as a percentage of par.

■ Each bond point represents $10, and the fractions are in eighths: each ⅛ = $1.25.

— A bond quoted at 90¼ = $902.50.

— A bond quoted at 101¾ = $1,017.50.

Municipals are also quoted on a yield basis. The investor's actual cost is derived from the quoted yield. It makes comparing bonds easier.

Governments

■ Government bonds are quoted as a percentage of par.

■ Each point is $10, and each 0.1 represents ¹⁄₃₂ ($.3125).

— A government bond quoted at 90.8 = $902.50.

— A government bond quoted at 101.24 = $1,017.50.

Price/Yield Relationship

There are many reasons interest rates rise and fall. The main concern for the exam, at this point, is the effect that interest rates have on the price fluctuations of bonds. As a general rule, keep in mind that interest rates and bond prices move counter to each other. That is, when interest rates are going up, bond prices will be going down. When interest rates are going down, bond prices will be going up.

When most people hear this for the first time, they have difficulty understanding it. After all, it makes sense that when interest rates are up, bonds should become more valuable, more people will buy them, and the prices should move up. But this is not how it works.

Look at the example DBL 10s '19. Suppose that now, three years after they were issued, interest rates fall to an average of 8% for similar quality bonds. This means that if the DBL Corporation were issuing those bonds today, they would only have to pay 8% on them instead of the 10% it offered a few years back. Newly issued bonds of the same quality (rating) will be coming out with nominal yields of about 8%. Consequently, investors will start buying the DBL 10s to get the higher interest rate. As the demand for the 10s increases, the bond's market price will start moving up (supply vs. demand). The bond prices will move up until the current yield on the DBL 10s is about 8%. When these bonds reach a price of approximately $1,250, they will no longer be especially attractive, because the current yield will be 8% ($100 ÷ $1,250 = 8%), the same as new bonds. When the yield to maturity is calculated, taking the loss into consideration, the bonds will cease to be attractive even before the market price reaches $1,250. But just keep the basic principle in mind. The prices of bonds fluctuate so that the current yield and yield to maturity are similar to, or competitive with, newly issued bonds of equal quality.

Applying this principle, one can see that bond prices will fall when interest rates are moving higher. If interest rates rise to about 12% after the DBL 10s are issued, investors will be more interested in buying new 12% bonds being offered of similar quality than in buying the old 10s. Demand for the old bonds will decline until they reach a market price where their yield is competitive with the new issues. At a price of approximately $830, the DBL 10s will yield approximately 12% ($100 ÷ $830 = 12%). You may have a calculation of this kind on the exam; just understand the concept—when interest rates go up, existing bonds in the marketplace must fall in price so that they will return a yield to an investor approximately equal to what he could get on newly issued bonds. If interest rates go down, the market price of existing bonds will rise because, with a higher coupon, they are worth more than the newly issued bonds and will sell at a price that will return to an investor approximately the same yield as on a new bond.

Zero-Coupon Bonds

The nominal (coupon) rate on a zero-coupon bond is zero. Zero-coupon bonds are issued at a substantial discount from par. They pay no interest, but the difference between the discounted price paid and the par value received at maturity makes up for the lack of a current interest coupon. For example, if an investor were to purchase a new zero-coupon bond for $500 that matured at par in 10 years, he would receive a profit of $500 in 10 years or an average of $50 per year on an out-of-pocket expenditure of $500. Here are the key things to remember about zero-coupon bonds:

■ Always issued at a discount

■ No reinvestment risk, because there are no interest payments to worry about reinvesting

■ More volatile than other bonds of similar quality

In the case of zero-coupon corporate or municipal securities, there is a somewhat higher level of credit risk. (On a 20-year bond, the investor receives nothing until the maturity date, and if the issuer is insolvent at that time, the investor has received nothing during the entire 20 years.) However, no credit risk exists in the case of zero-coupon treasuries since the risk of default on a government security is nonexistent.

The major attraction of this type of investment is that it allows an investor to lock in a yield (or rate of return) for a predetermined, investor-selected time with no reinvestment risk. Because all zeroes are sold at discounts and have no current return, there is a great deal of price volatility.

REPAYMENT OF PRINCIPAL

Redemption Before Maturity

One of the concepts on the exam is the method by which debt securities are paid off before their maturity date.

Again, consider DBL 10s of 2019. Suppose that three years from now current conditions in the bond market are such that bonds of comparable quality are being issued with nominal yields of 12%. If that is the case, relative to par, the DBL 10s '19 will be selling at a discount; it is critical to remember that as interest rates go up, bond prices go down.

Callable Bonds

Most of the questions on the exam dealing with early payback of principal are about callable bonds. Bonds can be either callable or noncallable. Callability is a feature that permits the issuer to redeem its bonds (pay off the principal) before maturity if it so desires. An issuer would not be interested in redeeming its bonds in the previous example since, when interest rates have gone up and the bond prices have gone down, the cheapest way for the issuer to retire its debt is to buy it in the open market.

Refunding

While it is clear that an issuer would not be interested in calling its bonds when interest rates have increased, what about when rates drop? In this case, the issuer could take advantage.

Call Protection

Before purchasing a bond, determine the extent of its call protection. **Call protection** is the number of years into the issue before the issuer may exercise the call provision. The best call protection a bond may have is if a bond is noncallable; in other words, the issuer cannot call it early, and the investor has the best protection against a call.

Convertible Bonds

The exam also deals with bonds paid off before maturity that have a convertible feature. These convertible bonds are issued by corporations only. Since they may be converted or exchanged for the company's common stock, there are no convertible municipal or government bonds. The conversion privilege is exercised at the discretion of the investor. The ratio of conversion varies from one bond to another according to the terms set forth in the indenture at the time the bonds are issued. The exact number of shares (or method of computing same) that a particular bond will be convertible into at any point is printed in the bond indenture at the time of issue. Most convertibles are debentures.

In many cases, the indenture merely tells you the number of shares into which the bond is convertible. For example, the bond may be convertible into 50 shares; thus, it would have a conversion ratio of 50:1, 50 shares for one bond. If a bond is convertible into 25 shares, it would have a conversion ratio of 25:1.

Frequently, instead of telling the number of shares into which the bond is convertible, the indenture will give the conversion price. That conversion price is the price per share that the corporation will sell their stock in exchange for the bond one is holding. Regardless of the current market price of the bond, the bond always represents a debt of the corporation of $1,000. Therefore, if the conversion price is given, to compute the number of shares into which the bond is convertible, always divide the par value ($1,000) by the conversion price. For example, a bond convertible at $20 per share is convertible into 50 shares ($1,000 ÷ $20 = 50 shares).

If the bond has a conversion price of $50, the conversion ratio is 20 shares ($1,000 ÷ $50 = 20 shares). If the DBL 16s of '11, currently selling at 120, were convertible at $40, how may shares would one get when one converted the bond? The answer is not 30. The current market has nothing to do with the computation. The bond conversion is fixed at issuance, and the market fluctuates all the time. The correct answer is 25 shares ($1,000 ÷ $40 = 25 shares).

The bond's price will rise along with the stock. Most convertible bonds contain a call provision. If the market price of the bonds becomes sufficiently high, the company can force the investors to convert by exercising the call provision. This is known as forced conversion. The reason the bond price went up was because the underlying stock went up. If a bond is called at a price significantly lower than its current market, it will be to the bondholder's advantage to convert the bond into the stock. Once that occurs, the issuer owes nothing, since there is stock now where there once were bonds.

Advantages to Investors

Downside Protection. The investor is a creditor. If the company's business does not prosper and the stock does not go up or declines in value, the investor becomes, as a bondholder, a creditor. Interest must be paid currently, and the principal must be repaid at maturity. Thus, the investor has assured income, as long as the company is solvent, and has a bondholder's claim, in the event of financial difficulty. There is a market level to which the bond will drop and then drop no further, because it will sell on the basis of its coupon rate competitively with other bonds. Convertibles carry a lower interest rate than nonconvertibles because of the added bonus of the convertibility factor. If the underlying common stock declines to a point where the convertibility factor is worth nothing, then the bond will sell on the basis of its yield alone like any other debt security.

Upside Potential. If the company's business prospers, the underlying stock will increase in market value. Since the bondholder can convert to stock, the bond will go up parallel to the increase in the common stock price.

A convertible bondholder, therefore, has all the upside potential of the common stockholder without all the downside risk.

Disadvantages to Investors

The only disadvantages to investors in convertible bonds are that they receive a lower interest rate than a nonconvertible debt and, of course, the possibility that the convertible bond may be called away before one is ready to convert.

MONEY MARKET

The **money market** may be defined as the market for buying and selling short-term loanable funds in the form of securities and loans. It is called the money market because that is what is traded there, money not cash. The buyer of a money market instrument is the lender of the money; the seller of a money market instrument is the entity borrowing the money.

Although there are many different kinds of money market instruments, there are several common factors. For example, they all have a maturity date of one year or less. In fact, the majority of money market instruments mature in less than six months. Another factor that many (but not all) money market instruments share is that they are issued at a discount; they do not pay interest because debt securities generally pay interest semiannually and since most money market instruments have a maturity of six months or less, the administrative costs of paying out interest would be very high. Therefore, the solution is to issue the security at a discount with the investor being paid back par at maturity, that difference being what he is paid for the use of his money. Money market instruments are safe. Although some are not quite as safe as others (e.g., commercial paper is not as safe as a Treasury bill), they are all considered to be low-risk securities.

Treasury Securities

Treasury bills are the bellwether of the money market. Because there is so much Treasury debt outstanding, the level of activity in Treasury bills and other short-term government issues is by far the highest and most carefully watched. Governments with short terms also refer to US Treasury notes or US Treasury bonds that are in their last year before maturity since, at that time, they would trade like any other security with one year or less to maturity. There are a number of advantages to Treasuries. First and foremost is the absence of credit risk. A second advantage is the extremely high liquidity in the secondary markets: the more active a security, the narrower the spread. The huge market activity in Treasuries keeps the spreads very low, making it easy for the investor to get in and out at a reasonable cost. A third benefit of investing in Treasuries is that the interest is exempt from state income tax. Because of these factors, the yields on these Treasuries are normally the lowest in the money market.

Certificates of Deposit

Certificates of deposit (CDs) were created because the Federal Reserve Board had restrictions on the amount of money a bank could pay on savings and other time deposits (a time deposit has a fixed maturity) until 1986. Because the Fed's rules were somewhat restrictive, it was impossible for the banks to compete for money. If a corporation had $1 million that they would not need for several weeks, there was no way that a bank could pay them a rate competitive with other money market instruments until the introduction of negotiable CDs. These CDs are unsecured time deposits (no asset of the bank is pledged as collateral, and the money is being loaned to the bank for a specified period of time). Most CDs have fixed interest rates although recently, because of very volatile conditions in the money market, there has been an introduction of a variable rate CD. The bank that issues the CD redeems the CD at face value plus interest on maturity date. CDs do not pay periodic interest; the interest is paid in full at the maturity date. To be considered a negotiable CD, such CDs must have a face value of $100,000 or more, with $1 million and more being most common. Although most CDs have an original maturity of one to three months, there is no time limit.

Commercial Paper

Another money market instrument is commercial paper. This is short-term unsecured paper issued by corporations. As covered in Units 1 and 2, commercial paper is exempt from registration as long as the maximum maturity is 270 days.

MORTGAGE-BACKED SECURITIES

A fast-growing sector of the bond market is mortgage-backed securities. These are basically debt obligations backed by a pool of mortgages and usually have a pass-through feature. One of the most popular of all mortgage pass-through securities is the Ginnie Mae. An investor is said to have an undivided interest in the pool. That is, he does not own a specific mortgage, but has a proportionate share in the cash flow generated by the entire pool. That cash flow is passed through to the holder of the security in the form of multiple payments of interest, principal, and frequently prepayments of mortgages. Very few mortgages last the full scheduled term.

Securities guaranteed by the Government National Mortgage Association (GNMA), sometimes referred to as Ginnie Mae, comprise VA-guaranteed or FHA-insured mortgages and are backed by the full faith and credit of the US government. GNMA investors receive monthly payments.

Freddie Mac Participation Certificate (PC)

Another type of pass-through is issued by the Federal Home Loan Mortgage Corporation (FHLMC or Freddie Mac). This issue is sometimes called a participation certificate (PC). Freddie Mac PCs comprise qualifying

FHLMC, conventional, residential mortgages on single-family homes. These PCs are not backed by the full faith and credit of the US government, but their yield is slightly higher than those of GNMAs.

Fannie Mae also issues mortgage-backed securities. These securities are similar to the Freddie Mac PCs and consist of some conventional mortgages and FHA-insured mortgages. FNMAs are not backed by the full faith and credit of the US government, but it is unlikely that the US government would permit them to default. Their yields are comparable to the PCs and slightly higher than those of GNMAs.

Collateralized Mortgage Obligations (CMOs)

Collateralized mortgage obligations (CMOs) were first introduced in June 1983. These are bonds that are collateralized by mortgages or by mortgage-backed securities. A key difference between traditional pass-throughs and CMOs is the mechanics of the principal payment process. In a pass-through, each investor receives his proportionate distribution of the monthly principal and interest payments made by the homeowner. This means that the pass-through holder receives some return of his principal each month. He does not get all his principal back, and the pass-through does not mature, however, until the last mortgage in the pool has been paid off. The CMO is issued with a stated maturity: some have short terms, some intermediate, and some long terms. As the principal on the mortgages is being paid, it is used exclusively for the newest maturity in sequence until each maturity has been paid off. Most of the mortgages are private mortgages, not qualified under VA or FHA.

Benefits to Investors

The primary advantage of investing in mortgage-backed securities is that, compared with other debt securities with similar ratings, they pay a higher rate of return.

Risks to Investors

There are a number of risks faced by investors in these securities:

- they are among the most complicated instruments and are, therefore, difficult to understand;

- prepayment risk due to mortgages being refinanced when rates drop;

- reinvestment risk; and

- liquidity risk.

HOTSHEETS

For your convenience, Unit HotSheets summarizing the key points are located at the end of the manual on perforated pages.

UNIT TEST

1. Holders of each of the following are creditors EXCEPT investors owning
   - A. preferred stock
   - B. corporate bonds
   - C. municipal bonds
   - D. government bonds

2. Among the advantages of including preferred stock in an investor's portfolio are
   - I. dividends must be paid before any distribution to common stockholders
   - II. a rate of return that is likely to keep pace with inflation
   - III. the opportunity for capital gains if the issuer's profits increase
   - IV. a fixed rate of return that is likely higher than that for a debt security offered by the same issuer
   - A. I and II
   - B. I and IV
   - C. II and III
   - D. III and IV

3. In general, the type of security offering the greatest degree of safety to an investor is
   - A. common stock
   - B. debentures
   - C. mortgage bonds
   - D. preferred stock

4. A debenture is issued based on
   - A. the general credit of the corporation
   - B. a pledge of real estate
   - C. a pledge of equipment
   - D. the ability to levy taxes

5. When Treasury bills are issued, they are quoted at
   - A. a premium over par
   - B. 100% of the par value
   - C. par value with interest coupons attached
   - D. a discount from principal with no coupons attached

6. According to Standard and Poor's rating system, the 4 highest grades of bonds (from best to lowest grade) are
   - A. Aaa; Aa; A; Baa
   - B. A; Aa; Aaa; B
   - C. B; A; AA; AAA
   - D. AAA; AA; A; BBB

7. Municipal bonds are often called tax-exempts. This refers to the exemption of their income from
   - A. state, federal, and inheritance taxes
   - B. state income taxes
   - C. federal income taxes
   - D. inheritance taxes

8. The current yield on a bond with a coupon rate of 5.5% selling at 110 is
   - A. 2%
   - B. 5%
   - C. 5.5%
   - D. 6%

9. A bond is selling at a premium over par value. Therefore, its
   - A. current yield is less than its nominal yield
   - B. nominal yield is less than its current yield
   - C. yield to maturity is greater than its current yield
   - D. none of the above

10. A bond issue that may be retired in advance of maturity at the option of the issuer is said to have a
    - A. callable feature
    - B. optional reserve
    - C. conversion feature
    - D. put option feature

11. BFJ Corp's 5% convertible bond is trading at 120. The bond is convertible at $50. If one bought the bond now and immediately converted into common stock, he would receive
    - A. 24 shares
    - B. 20 shares
    - C. 2.4 shares
    - D. 20 shares plus cash for fractional shares

12. All of the following are true of government agency bonds EXCEPT

    A. they are considered relatively safe investments

    B. they are direct obligations of the US government

    C. they trade openly

    D. older ones have coupons attached, new ones are book entry

13. All of the following are true about GNMAs EXCEPT

    A. they are backed by the US government.

    B. they provide funds for residential mortgages.

    C. interest on GNMAs is not exempt from state and local taxes

    D. interest is paid semiannually

14. One of the more popular money market instruments is the negotiable CD. These normally are found in minimum denominations of

    A. $25,000

    B. $100,000

    C. $500,000

    D. $1,000,000

15. All of the following are risk generally associated with CMOs EXCEPT

    A. credit

    B. liquidity

    C. prepayment

    D. reinvestment

ANSWERS AND RATIONALES

1. **A.** Remember, all stockholders (even preferred stockholders) are owners of a corporation, not creditors.

2. **B.** Preferred stock carries a fixed dividend that must be paid before any distribution to common stockholders—hence the name preferred. However, unlike the interest on a debt security, there is no obligation to pay the dividend. Therefore, the yield on a company's preferred stock is invariably higher than that on its debt issues. Disadvantages of owning preferred stock are that the fixed return may not keep up with inflation and, regardless of corporate earnings, the dividend will not change, so there is little hope for capital gain.

3. **C.** The only one of these with pledged assets as security for the loan is the mortgage bond.

4. **A.** There are no assets behind a debenture, merely the credit standing of the corporation. It is a corporate IOU.

5. **D.** Treasury bills are always issued at a discount, they pay no interest. The investor profits by receiving back par value and makes the difference between the discounted purchase price and the par received at maturity. All government bonds are now book entry; there has not been a Treasury note or bond issued since July 1986 with interest coupons attached.

6. **D.** Choice A would be correct if the question referred to Moody's.

7. **C.** Although municipal bonds are sometimes exempt from state income tax (if issued in the state of residence of the taxpayer), all references to tax exemption refer to their exemption from federal income taxes.

8. **B.** $\dfrac{5.5}{110} = 5\%$

9. **A.** Any bond selling at a premium will yield less than the coupon rate (nominal yield). Conversely, of course, a bond trading at a discount will certainly yield more. Remember, there is an inverse relationship between bond prices and bond yields.

10. **A.** A bond that is callable has a provision that the issuer, at its option, may redeem that bond at a specified price known as the call or redemption price.

11. **B.** $\dfrac{\text{Par}}{\text{Conversion price}} = \text{Number of shares}$

    $\dfrac{\$1,000}{50} = 20 \text{ shares}$

12. **B.** The only government agency that is a direct obligation of the US government is the Ginnie Mae security. All of the others are moral obligations.

13. **D.** GMNAs make payment monthly, unlike virtually all other debt securities, which make payments semiannually.

14. **B.** Negotiable CDs, sometimes referred to as jumbo CDs, have a minimum denomination of $100,000. They are unsecured, interest-bearing obligations of banks.

15. **A.** CMOs generally carry AAA or AA ratings and thus have little credit risk.

QUICK QUIZ ANSWERS

Quick Quiz 4.1

1. **D.** 100 votes for each of 6 candidates is the correct answer.

2. **D.** Any of the above choices would be correct.

Quick Quiz 4.2

1. **C.** Owning either common or preferred stocks represents ownership (or equity) in a corporation.

2. **B.** One does not have access to insider information solely by becoming a shareholder. Even if one did receive material nonpublic information, such as prior access to earnings, no benefit may be received from that information. All of the other choices are among the reasons to purchase common stock.

3. **D.** Cash dividends are normally declared by corporations, but corporations can also declare stock dividends in additional shares of the issuing corporation, or property dividends.

4. **A.** An advantage of owning stock is that an investor's liability is limited to the amount of money he invested when the stock was purchased.

5. **B.** A residual claim to assets at dissolution and a vote in matters of recapitalization are common stockholder rights.

6. **C.** Owning common stock subjects one to market risk, the possibility that dividends may be reduced, and the fact that they have the last priority in claims against the assets of the corporation. The right to vote cannot be taken away.

Quick Quiz 4.3

1. **D.** Callable preferred. When the stock is called, dividend payments are no longer made. To compensate for that possibility, the issuer must pay a higher dividend.

2. **A.** Straight preferred. Cumulative preferred is safer, and there is always a risk reward trade-off. Because straight preferred has no special features, it will pay a higher stated rate of dividend.

3. **C.** Because convertible can be exchanged for common shares, its price is closely linked to the price of the issuer's common.

Quick Quiz 4.4

1. **D.** ADRs are tradable securities issued by banks, with the receipt's value based on the underlying foreign securities held by the bank.

2. **B.** ADRs represent ownership in a foreign security so there is always going to be currency risk. These ADRs trade in the market and have market risk. Since most ADRs are traded on the exchanges, there is little liquidity risk and, because they represent equity, they are usually a good hedge against inflation.

Quick Quiz 4.5

1. **B.** Warrants are issued with long-term maturities and may be used as sweeteners in an offering of the issuer's preferred stock or bonds. Warrants are not offered only to current shareholders. The exercise price of a warrant is typically above the market value of the stock at the time of issue.

2. **B.** Preferred stockholders have no right to maintain a percentage of ownership when new shares are issued (no preemptive rights). However, they do receive preference in dividend payment and company liquidation.

Quick Quiz 4.6

1. **B.** Treasury bills are a short-term investment.

5

Other Securities Products

In addition to equity and debt, other investments related to stocks and bonds are available to investors. Such investment products include packaged products such as mutual funds, insurance-related securities products, and derivative securities products.

The Series 65 exam will include approximately 14 questions on the material presented in this Unit. ■

When you have completed this Unit, you should be able to:

- **identify** the unique features of investment company securities, annuities, direct participation programs (limited partnerships), and options; and

- **explain** the use and suitability of these securities in client portfolios.

INVESTMENT COMPANY SECURITIES

An **investment company** is a corporation or a trust through which individuals invest in large, diversified portfolios of securities by pooling their funds with other investors' funds. People often invest in investment companies because they believe a professional money manager should be able to outperform the average investor in the market.

By investing through an investment company, individuals gain some of the advantages large investors enjoy, such as diversification of investments, lower transaction costs, professional management, and more.

Investment companies raise capital by selling shares to the public. Investment companies must abide by similar registration and prospectus requirements imposed by the Securities Act of 1933 on every other issuer.

Investment companies are also subject to regulations regarding how their shares are sold to the public. The **Investment Company Act of 1940** provides for Securities and Exchange Commission (SEC) regulation of investment companies and their activities.

TYPES OF INVESTMENT COMPANIES

The Investment Company Act of 1940 classifies investment companies into three broad types: face-amount certificate (FAC) companies, unit investment trusts (UITs), and management investment companies.

Face-Amount Certificate (FAC) Companies

A **face-amount certificate (FAC)** is a contract between an investor and an issuer in which the issuer guarantees payment of a stated (or fixed) sum to the investor at some set date in the future. In return for this future payment, the investor agrees to pay the issuer a set amount of money either as a lump sum or in periodic installments.

If the investor pays for the certificate in a lump sum, the investment is known as a **fully paid FAC**. Issuers of these investments are called **FAC companies**. Few FAC companies operate today because tax law changes have eliminated their tax advantages.

TAKE NOTE

Three important features of FACs follow.

■ FAC companies pay a fixed rate of return.

■ FAC companies do not trade in the secondary market; they are redeemed by the issuer.

■ FAC companies are classified as investment companies.

Unit Investment Trusts (UITs)

A **unit investment trust (UIT)** is an unmanaged investment company organized under a trust indenture. UITs:

- do not have boards of directors;

- do not employ an investment adviser; and

- do not actively manage their own portfolios (trade securities).

A UIT functions as a holding company for its investors. UIT managers typically buy other investment company shares or government and municipal bonds. They then sell redeemable shares, known as **units** or **shares of beneficial interest**, in this portfolio of securities. Each share is an undivided interest in the underlying portfolio. Because UITs are not managed, when securities in the portfolio are liquidated or called, the proceeds must be distributed.

A UIT may be fixed or nonfixed. A **fixed UIT** typically purchases a portfolio of bonds and terminates when the bonds in the portfolio mature. In the past, fixed UITs were almost exclusively a portfolio of bonds. Now, a significant percentage of fixed UITs consist of a portfolio of equities. Since the equities do not have a maturity date, a liquidation date is set in the offering documents. A **nonfixed UIT** purchases shares of an underlying mutual fund. Under the Act of 1940, the trustees of both fixed and nonfixed UITs must maintain secondary markets in the units, thus guaranteeing a measure of liquidity to shareholders.

TAKE NOTE

Know the following features of UITs.

- UITs are not actively managed; there is no board of directors (BOD) or investment adviser.

- UIT shares (units) must be redeemed by the trust.

- UITs are investment companies as defined under the Investment Company Act of 1940.

Management Investment Companies

The most familiar type of investment company is the **management investment company**, which actively manages a securities portfolio to achieve a stated investment objective. A management investment company is either closed-end or open-end. Initially, both closed- and open-end companies sell shares to the public; the difference between them lies in the type of securities they sell and how investors buy and sell their shares—in the primary or secondary market.

Closed-End Investment Companies

To raise capital, a closed-end investment company conducts a common stock offering. For the initial offering, the company registers a fixed number of shares with the SEC and offers them to the public for a limited time through an underwriting group. The fund's capitalization is fixed unless an additional public offering is made. Closed-end investment companies can also issue bonds and preferred stock.

Closed-end investment companies are commonly known as **publicly traded funds**. After the stock is distributed, anyone can buy or sell shares in the secondary market, either on an exchange or over the counter (OTC). Supply and demand determine the **bid price** (price at which an investor can sell) and the **ask price** (price at which an investor can buy). Closed-end fund shares may trade at a premium or discount to the shares' net asset value (NAV).

Open-End Investment Companies

An open-end investment company, or mutual fund, does not specify the exact number of shares it intends to issue. It registers an open offering with the SEC. The open-end investment company can raise an unlimited amount of investment capital by continuously issuing new shares. Any person who wants to invest in the company buys shares directly from the company or its underwriters at the public offering price (POP).

A mutual fund's **POP** is the NAV per share plus any applicable sales charges. A mutual fund's **NAV** is calculated by deducting the fund's liabilities from its total assets. NAV per share is calculated by dividing the fund's NAV by the number of shares outstanding.

An open-end investment company sells redeemable securities. When an investor sells shares, the company redeems them at their NAV. For each share an investor redeems, the company sends the investor money for the investor's proportionate share of the company's net assets. Therefore, a mutual fund's capital shrinks when investors redeem shares.

	Open-End	Closed-End
Capitalization	Unlimited; continuous offering of shares	Fixed; single offering of shares
Issues	Common stock only; no debt securities; permitted to borrow	May issue: common stock, preferred stock, debt securities
Shares	Full or fractional	Full only
Offering and trading	Sold and redeemed by fund only Continuous primary offering Must redeem shares	Initial primary offering Secondary trading OTC or on an exchange Does not redeem shares
Pricing	NAV + sales charge Selling price determined by formula in the prospectus	Current market value + commission Price determined by supply and demand
Shareholder rights	Dividends (when declared), voting	Dividends (when declared), voting, preemptive

Diversified and Nondiversified. Diversification provides risk management that makes mutual funds popular with many investors. Under the Investment Company Act of 1940, an investment company qualifies as a diversified investment company if it meets the following 75-5-10 test.

■ Seventy-five percent of total assets must be invested in securities issued by companies other than the investment company or its affiliates. Cash on hand and cash equivalent investments (short-term government and money market securities) are counted as part of the 75% required investment in outside companies.

■ Of this 75%, no more than 5% of total assets can be invested in any one corporation's securities.

■ Of this 75%, the investment company can own no more than 10% of an outside corporation's voting class securities (common stock).

TAKE NOTE

A **nondiversified investment company** will not meet the 75-5-10 test.

An investment company that specializes in one industry is not necessarily a nondiversified company. Some investment companies choose to concentrate their assets in one industry or geographic area, such as health care or technology. These are **specialized** or **sector funds**. An investment company that invests in a single industry can still be considered diversified provided it meets the 75-5-10 test.

QUICK QUIZ 5.1

Choose **A** for an open-end company or **B** for a closed-end company.

_____ 1. Trades in the secondary market

_____ 2. Investors may purchase fractional shares

_____ 3. Can issue common, preferred, and bonds

_____ 4. Issues a fixed number of shares

_____ 5. Does not trade in the secondary market; shares must be redeemed

_____ 6. Price is set by supply and demand

_____ 8. Usually called mutual funds

_____ 9. Selling price usually includes a sales charge

Quick Quiz answers can be found at the end of the Unit.

CHARACTERISTICS OF MUTUAL FUNDS

A **mutual fund** is a pool of investors' money invested in various securities determined by the fund's objective. Open-end investment management companies (mutual funds) have several unique characteristics.

A mutual fund must redeem shares at the NAV. Unlike other securities, mutual funds offer guaranteed marketability because there is always a willing buyer for the shares.

Each investor in the mutual fund's portfolio owns an undivided interest in the entire underlying portfolio. No one investor has a preferred status over any other investor because mutual funds issue only one class of common stock. Each investor shares mutually with other investors in gains and distributions derived from the investment company portfolio.

Each investor's share in the fund's performance is based on the number of shares owned. Mutual fund shares may be purchased in either full or fractional units, unlike stock, which may be purchased in full units only. Because mutual fund shares can be fractional, the investor can think in terms of dollars rather than number of shares owned.

EXAMPLE   If NavCo Mutual Fund shares are $15 per share, a $100 investment buys 6.667 shares ($100 ÷ $15 = 6.667).

An investment company's portfolio is elastic. Money is simultaneously invested into the fund and paid out when shares are redeemed. The mutual fund portfolio's value and holdings fluctuate as money is invested or shares redeemed and as the value of the securities held by the portfolio rises and falls. The investor's account value fluctuates proportionately with the mutual fund portfolio's value.

Sales Charges

NASD prohibits its members who underwrite fund shares from assessing sales charges in excess of 8.5% of the POP on customer mutual fund purchases. These underwriters are free to charge lower rates if they specify these rates in the prospectus.

Closed-End Funds

Closed-end funds do not carry sales charges. An investor pays a brokerage commission in an agency transaction or pays a markup or markdown in a principal transaction.

Open-End Funds

All sales commissions are paid from the sales charges collected. Sales charges include commissions for the managing underwriter, dealers, brokers, and registered representatives, as well as all advertising and sales literature expenses.

Mutual fund distributors use three different methods to collect the fees for the sale of shares:

■ Front-end loads (difference between POP and net NAV)

■ Back-end loads (contingent deferred sales loads)

■ 12b-1 sales charges (asset-based fees)

Front-End Loads. Front-end sales loads are reflected in a fund's public offering price. The charges are added to the NAV at the time an investor buys shares. They are frequently referred to as Class A shares.

Back-End Loads. A back-end sales load, also called a contingent deferred sales load, is charged at the time an investor redeems mutual fund shares. The sales load, a declining percentage charge that is reduced annually (for instance, 8% the first year, 7% the second, 6% the third, and so forth), is applied to the proceeds of any shares sold in that year. The back-end load is usually structured so that it drops to zero after an extended holding period. They are frequently referred to as Class B shares.

12b-1 Asset-Based Fees. Mutual funds cannot act as distributors for their own fund shares except under Section 12b-1 of the Investment Company Act of 1940. This provision permits a mutual fund to collect a fee for promotion or sales-related activities in connection with the distribution of its shares. The fee is determined as a flat dollar amount or as a percentage of the fund's average total NAV during the year. The fee is disclosed in the fund's prospectus.

The percentage of net assets charged must be reasonable (typically .5% of net assets—this annual fee cannot exceed .75% of net assets), and the fee must reflect the anticipated level of distribution services. If the fee exceeds .25%, the fund cannot use the term *no-load*.

The payments represent fees that would have been paid to an underwriter had sales charges been negotiated for sales, promotion, and related activities.

Classes of Fund Shares

Mutual funds may offer several classes of shares to allow investors to select how they pay the sales charges. The following is a typical method by which firms may classify fund shares by fee type: Class A, B, and C shares.

■ **Class A** shares (front-end load): investors pay the charge at the time of purchase.

■ **Class B** shares (back-end load): declines over time so investors pay the charge at redemption.

■ **Class C** shares (level load): investor pays the asset-based fee annually.

The class of shares determines the type of sales charge only. All other rights associated with mutual fund ownership remain the same across each class.

Reductions in Sales Charges

The maximum permitted sales charge is reduced if an investment company does not offer certain features. To qualify for the maximum 8.5% sales charge, the investment company must offer both of the following:

■ Breakpoints—a scale of declining sales charges based on the amount invested

■ Rights of accumulation

Breakpoints

The schedule of discounts a mutual fund offers is called the fund's **breakpoints**. Breakpoints are available to any person. For a breakpoint qualification, the term *person* includes married couples, parents and their minor children, and corporations. Investment clubs or associations formed for the purpose of investing do not qualify for breakpoints.

Sample Breakpoint Schedule

Purchase	Sales Charge
$1–$9,999	8.5%
$10,000–$24,999	7.5%
$25,000–$49,999	7%
$50,000 +	6.5%

An investor can qualify for breakpoints in several ways. A large, lump-sum investment is one method. Mutual funds offer additional incentives for an investor to continue to invest and qualify for breakpoints through a letter of intent or rights of accumulation.

Breakpoint Sales. NASD prohibits registered representatives from making higher commissions by selling investment company shares in a dollar amount just below the point at which the sales charge is reduced. This is known as a **breakpoint sale**. NASD considers this practice contrary to just and equitable principles of trade. It is the responsibility of the principal to prevent breakpoint selling.

Letter of Intent (LOI)

A person who plans to invest more money with the same mutual fund company may decrease overall sales charges by signing a **letter of intent (LOI)**. In the LOI, the investor informs the investment company that he intends to invest the additional funds necessary to reach the breakpoint within 13 months.

The LOI is a one-sided contract binding on the fund only. The customer must complete the intended investment to qualify for the reduced sales charge. The fund holds the extra shares purchased as a result of the reduced sales charge in escrow. If the customer deposits sufficient money to complete the LOI, he receives the escrowed shares. Appreciation and reinvested dividends do not count toward the LOI.

EXAMPLE

Using the sample breakpoint schedule, a customer investing $9,000 is just under the $10,000 breakpoint. The customer might sign a letter of intent promising an amount that will qualify for the breakpoint within 13 months from the date of the letter. An additional $1,000 deposited within 13 months qualifies the customer for the reduced sales charge. Each deposit is charged the reduced sales charge at the time of purchase.

If the customer has not completed the investment within 13 months, he will be given the choice of sending a check for the difference in sales charges or cashing in escrowed shares to pay the difference.

Backdating the Letter

A fund often permits a customer to sign an LOI as late as 90 days after an initial purchase. The LOI may be backdated by up to 90 days to include prior purchases but may not cover more than 13 months in total. This means that if the customer signs the LOI after 60 days, he has 11 months to complete the letter.

Rights of Accumulation

Rights of accumulation, like LOIs, allow an investor to qualify for reduced sales charges. The major differences are that rights of accumulation:

- are available for subsequent investment and do not apply to initial transactions;

- allow the investor to use prior share appreciation to qualify for breakpoints; and

- do not impose time limits.

The customer may qualify for reduced charges when the total value of shares previously purchased and shares currently being purchased exceeds a breakpoint amount. For the purpose of qualifying customers for breakpoints, the mutual fund bases the quantity of securities owned on:

- the current value of the securities at either NAV or POP;

- total purchases of the securities at the actual offering price; or

- the higher of current NAV or the total of purchases made to date.

EXAMPLE

A customer who originally invested $10,000 has seen her investment grow to $15,000. She now wishes to invest an additional $10,000. Under rights of accumulation, the customer is charged 7% on the additional $10,000 investment because the total NAV meets the $25,000 threshold. The original sales charge on the initial investment is not adjusted. Most funds do not limit the amount of time during which an investor can qualify for breakpoints under rights of accumulation.

Combination Privilege

A mutual fund company frequently offers more than one fund and refers to these multiple offerings as its **family of funds**. An investor seeking a reduced sales charge may be allowed to combine separate investments in two or more funds within the same family to reach a breakpoint.

EXAMPLE

Joe Smith has invested $15,000 in the ACE Growth Fund for retirement and $10,000 in the ACE Income Fund for his children's education. The sponsor may view the two separate expenditures as one investment totaling $25,000 when calculating the sales charge.

Exchanges Within a Family of Funds

Many investment companies offer exchange or conversion privileges within their families of funds. **Exchange privileges** allow an investor to convert an investment in one fund for an equal investment in another fund in the same family, often without incurring an additional sales charge.

TAKE NOTE

Any exchange of funds is considered a sale for tax purposes. Any gains or losses are fully reportable at the time of the exchange.

TAKE NOTE

Other mutual fund characteristics include the following.

- A **professional investment adviser** manages the portfolio for investors.
- Mutual funds provide diversification by investing in many different companies.
- A **custodian** holds a mutual fund's shares to ensure safekeeping.
- Most funds allow a minimum investment, often $500 or less, to open an account and allow additional investment for as little as $25.
- An investment company may allow investments at reduced sales charges by offering breakpoints, for instance, through a letter of intent or rights of accumulation.
- An investor retains voting rights, such as the right to vote for changes in the board of directors, approval of the investment adviser, changes in the fund's investment objective, changes in sales charges, and liquidation of the fund.
- All funds offer automatic reinvestment of capital gains and dividend distributions without a sales charge.
- An investor can liquidate a portion of his holdings.
- Tax liabilities for an investor are simplified because each year the fund distributes a 1099 form explaining taxability of distributions.
- A fund may offer various withdrawal plans that allow different payment methods at redemption.

INVESTMENT OBJECTIVES

Once a mutual fund defines its objective, its portfolio is invested to match it. The objective must be clearly stated in the mutual fund's prospectus and can be changed only by a majority vote of the fund's outstanding shares.

Stock Funds

Common stocks normally provide the growth component of any mutual fund that has growth as a primary objective. Preferred, utility, and large-cap stocks are typically used to provide the income component of any stock mutual fund that has income as a primary objective.

Growth Funds. Growth funds invest in stocks of rapidly growing corporations. Growth companies tend to reinvest all or most of their profits for research and development rather than pay dividends. Growth funds are focused on generating capital gains rather than income.

Income Funds. An income fund stresses current income over growth. The fund's objective may be accomplished by investing in the stocks of companies with long histories of dividend payments, such as utility company stocks, large-cap stocks, and preferred stocks.

Combination Funds. A combination fund (also called a growth and income fund) may attempt to combine the objectives of growth and current income by diversifying its portfolio among companies showing long-term growth potential and companies paying high dividends.

Specialized (Sector) Funds. Many funds specialize in particular economic sectors or industries. The funds have 25–100% of their assets invested in their specialties.

EXAMPLE   Gold funds (gold mining stocks), technology funds, and utility funds are examples of sector funds. Sector funds offer high appreciation potential but may also pose higher risks to the investor.

Special Situation Funds. Special situation funds buy securities of companies that may benefit from a change within the corporations or in the economy. Takeover candidates and turnaround situations are common investments.

Index Funds. Index funds invest in securities to mirror a market index, such as the S&P 500. An index fund buys and sells securities in a manner that mirrors the composition of the selected index. The fund's performance tracks the underlying index's performance. This approach reflects the passive style of portfolio management, as opposed to active portfolio management.

Turnover of securities in an index fund's portfolio is minimal. As a result, an index fund generally has lower management costs than other types of funds. Furthermore, because index funds have little turnover, they frequently appeal to investors seeking minimal taxable capital gains.

Foreign Stock Funds. Foreign stock funds invest mostly in the securities of companies that have their principal business activities outside the United States. Long-term capital appreciation is their primary objective, although some funds also seek current income. Foreign investments involve foreign currency risks, as well as the usual risks associated with stock investments.

Bond Funds

Bond funds have income as their primary investment objective. Some funds invest solely in investment-grade corporate bonds. Others, for enhanced safety, invest only in government issues. Others seek capital appreciation by investing in lower-rated issues that may be upgraded in the future.

Tax-Free (Tax-Exempt) Bond Funds. Tax-exempt funds invest in municipal bonds or notes that produce income exempt from federal income tax. Tax-free funds can invest in municipal bonds and tax-exempt money market instruments.

US Government and Agency Securities Funds. US government funds purchase securities issued by the US Treasury or an agency of the US government, such as Ginnie Mae. Investors in these funds seek current income and maximum safety.

Balanced Funds

Balanced funds invest in stocks for appreciation and bonds for income, and different types of securities are purchased according to a formula.

EXAMPLE   A balanced fund's portfolio might contain 60% stocks and 40% bonds.

Asset Allocation Funds

Asset allocation funds split investments between stocks for growth, bonds for income, and money market instruments (or cash) for stability. The fund adviser switches the percentage of holdings in each asset category according to the performance, or expected performance, of that group.

EXAMPLE   A fund may have 60% of its investments in stock, 20% in bonds, and the remaining 20% in cash. If the stock market is expected to do well, the adviser may switch from cash and bonds into stock. The result may be a portfolio of 80% in stock, 10% in bonds, and 10% in cash. Conversely, if the stock market is expected to decline, the fund may invest heavily in cash and sell stocks.

Money Market Funds

Money market funds are no-load, open-end mutual funds that serve as temporary holding accounts for investors' money. The term *no-load* means that investors pay no sales or liquidation fees. Money market mutual funds are most suitable for investors whose financial goals require liquidity above all.

Dividend rates on money market funds are neither fixed nor guaranteed and change often. The interest these funds earn and distribute as dividends is computed daily and credited to customer accounts monthly. Many money market funds offer limited check-writing privileges; however, checks normally must be written for amounts of $500 or more.

The NAV of money market funds is fixed at $1 per share. Although this price is not guaranteed, a fund is managed in order not to "break the buck" regardless of market changes. Thus, the price of money market shares does not fluctuate in response to changing interest rates.

Restrictions on Money Market Funds

SEC rules limit the investments available to money market funds and require certain disclosures to investors.

Restrictions include the following.

- The front cover of every prospectus must prominently disclose that an investment in a money market fund is neither insured nor guaranteed by the US government and that an investor has no assurance the fund will be able to maintain a stable NAV. This statement must also appear in all literature used to market the fund.

- No more than 5% of a fund's assets may be invested in any one issuer's securities.

- Investments are limited to securities with remaining maturities of 397 days or less, with average portfolio maturity not exceeding 90 days.

- Investments are limited to securities that have received a rating from a recognized rating agency in one of the two highest short-tem rating categories.

COMPARING MUTUAL FUNDS

Investors should select funds that match their personal and financial objectives. When comparing funds with similar objectives, the investor should review information regarding funds':

- performance;

- costs;

- taxation;

- portfolio turnover; and

- services offered.

The suitability of a mutual fund must also be considered once the above information has been determined.

Performance

Securities law requires that each fund disclose the average annual total returns for 1, 5, and 10 years or since inception. The manager's track record in keeping with the fund's objectives, as stated in the prospectus, is important as well. Returns must be expressed assuming maximum sales loads applied.

EXAMPLE

A growth fund with a high dividend payout has not followed its investment objective.

Costs

Sales loads, management fees, and operating expenses reduce an investor's returns because they diminish the amount of money invested in a fund. Historically, mutual funds have charged front-end loads of up to 8.5% of the money invested (public offering price). This percentage serves as a sales commission to a sales force and other expenses associated with selling the shares.

Many low-load funds charge between 2% and 5%. Additionally, funds may charge a back-end load when funds are withdrawn. Some funds charge ongoing fees under section 12b-1 of the Investment Company Act of 1940. These funds deduct annual fees to pay for marketing and distribution costs.

A fund's **expense ratio** expresses the management fees and operating expenses as a percentage of the fund's net assets. All mutual funds, load and no-load, have expense ratios. The expense ratio is calculated by dividing a fund's expenses by its average net assets. The sales charge is not generally considered an expense when calculating a fund's expense ratio.

EXAMPLE

An expense ratio of 1.72% means that the fund spends $1.72 per year for every $100 invested.

Typically, more aggressive funds have higher expense ratios.

EXAMPLE

An aggressive growth fund's expense ratio is usually higher than that of a AAA bond fund because more trading occurs in the growth fund's portfolio.

Stock funds generally have expense ratios between 1% and 1.5% of a fund's average net assets. For bond funds, the ratio is typically between .5% and 1%.

Taxation

Mutual fund investors pay taxes on income and capital gains distributed by the fund. Dividends that qualify are taxed at 15%; for test purposes, all capital gains distributions are from the fund's long term gains, so they are taxed at 15% to the investor.

TAKE NOTE

Dividends and capital gains distributions are currently taxable to the shareholder, whether they are taken in cash or reinvested to purchase additional shares. Dividends must be reported as dividend income and will be taxed either as ordinary income or as a qualifying dividend with a maximum rate of 15%; capital gains distributions must be reported as a long-term capital gain.

Portfolio Turnover

The **portfolio turnover rate** reflects a fund's holding period. If a fund has a turnover rate of 100%, it holds its securities, on average, for less than one year. Therefore, all gains are likely to be short term and subject to the maximum tax rate.

On the other hand, a portfolio with a turnover rate of 25% has an average holding period of four years, and most gains are taxed at the long-term rate. It is not uncommon for an aggressive growth fund to reflect an annual turnover rate of 100% or more. High portfolio turnover generally increases a fund's expense ratio.

Services Offered

The services mutual funds offer include retirement accounts, investment plans, check-writing privileges, phone transfers, conversion privileges, combination investment plans, withdrawal plans, and others.

SUITABILITY

In determining suitability of mutual funds, the first step is to determine the customer's primary objective. In general, the following basic rules apply.

- Investors seeking growth should invest in stock funds.

- Investors seeking income should invest in bond funds.

- Investors who are concerned about safety of principal should invest in government bond funds.

- Investors who are concerned with immediate liquidity should invest in money market funds.

Additional objectives of the investor must also be taken into consideration. Some possibilities are listed below.

■ Investors seeking aggressive growth should invest in technology stock funds or stock funds invested in new companies. Aggressive funds or small-cap funds are usually most suitable for younger investors who have high risk tolerance.

■ Investors who are seeking growth but are more conservative should consider balanced funds, which are likely to be large-cap funds. These funds are not as speculative as smaller-cap and aggressive funds.

■ Investors seeking both income and safety of principal should invest in a government bond fund.

■ Investors seeking the highest possible income who can assume moderate risk should invest in a corporate bond fund.

■ High tax bracket investors seeking income should invest in a municipal bond fund.

■ Investors seeking income-producing stock should select a large-cap stock fund (a large-cap stock is a large company stock that has a consistently strong performance history and regularly pays dividends), a preferred stock fund, or a utility stock fund (utility stocks historically pay high, consistent dividends).

■ Investors seeking safety of principal with high liquidity should consider a money market fund.

■ Investors who wish to invest in a portfolio that mirrors the performance of the stock market should consider an index fund.

■ Asset allocation funds provide a combination of stocks and cash bonds (as well as other asset classes) and allow the portfolio manager the flexibility to change the portfolio mix to react to market conditions.

Hedge funds are for the speculative investor. They are not true mutual funds but do provide investors with an undivided interest in a portfolio. They are considered suitable for investors with high risk tolerance.

QUICK QUIZ 5.2

Match the objective with the type of fund.

A. Balanced fund
B. Aggressive growth fund
C. Specialized fund
D. Large cap stock fund

____ 1. Pursues capital growth with minimal risk

____ 2. Invests to maximize capital gains quickly with high risk tolerance

____ 3. Invests to diversify securities and is conservative

____ 4. Invests in medical technology and is not risk averse

QUICK QUIZ 5.3

Match the objective with the type of fund.

   A.   Conservative growth fund
   B.   Money market fund
   C.   Small-cap fund
   D.   Balanced fund

   ____   1.   Capital gains/income/lower risk

   ____   2.   Capital gains/low risk

   ____   3.   Liquidity/moderate risk

   ____   4.   Capital gains/higher risk

QUICK QUIZ 5.4

Match the objective with the type of fund.

   A.   Government bond fund
   B.   Large-cap fund
   C.   Asset allocation fund

   ____   1.   Capital gains/income/lower risk

   ____   2.   Growth/low risk

   ____   3.   Income/low risk

QUICK QUIZ 5.5

Match the objective with the type of fund.

   A.   Ginnie Mae fund
   B.   Special situation fund
   C.   Asset allocation fund
   D.   Index fund

   ____   1.   Purchase different classes of investments to achieve capital gains, income, and diversification

   ____   2.   Mimic stock market indexes to achieve performance comparable to the market overall

   ____   3.   Achieve safety of principal with yields slightly higher than government bond fund

   ____   4.   Seek investments in companies with unusual opportunities

Advantages to Investing in Mutual Funds

- Diversification: The old saying "don't put all of your eggs in one basket" certainly applies to the benefits of diversifying one's portfolio assets. Mutual funds are probably the easiest way to accomplish this. Although diversification may help to reduce risk, it will never completely eliminate it. It is possible to lose all or part of your investment.

- Professional management: Those individuals in charge of managing a mutual fund's portfolio must be registered as investment advisers with the SEC. The Investment Company Act of 1940 requires that they follow the stated objectives set forth in the prospectus. Taking into consideration prevailing market conditions and other factors, the mutual fund manager will decide when to buy or sell securities. Rare is the individual who has the time, knowledge, or resources to compete with these professionals.

- Convenience: With most mutual funds, buying and liquidating shares, changing reinvestment options, and getting information can be accomplished conveniently by going online at the fund's Website, by calling a toll-free phone number, or by mail.

    Although a fund's shareholder is relieved of the day-to-day tasks involved in researching, buying, and selling securities, an investor will still need to evaluate a mutual fund on the basis of investment goals and risk tolerance before making a purchase decision. Investors should always read the prospectus carefully before investing in any mutual fund.

- Liquidity: The Investment Company Act of 1940 requires that an open-end investment company stand ready to redeem shares at the next computed NAV per share. Payment must be made within 7 days of the redemption request. Although there may be a redemption charge, and, of course, the value of the shares may be less than their cost, liquidity is assured.

- Minimum initial investment: As mentioned previously, it doesn't take a great deal of wealth to get started investing in funds and, generally, once you are a shareholder, most funds permit additional investments of $100 or even less.

Disadvantages to Investing in Mutual Funds

- Risks: Even with the benefits offered by diversification and professional management, market prices do fluctuate. Equity funds have market risk, whereas bond funds may be subject to interest rate risk. Unlike an individual bond that ultimately repays principal at maturity, a bond fund doesn't have a maturity date. The only mutual fund that generally does not fluctuate in price is the money market fund, but there is a trade-off in lack of growth. Not only that, but the income of a money market fund will vary, unlike that of a bank CD, which is fixed and insured by the FDIC.

■ Fees and expenses: One must carefully analyze all of the costs involved. These include sales charges, 12b-1 fees, and possible redemption fees. Management fees are probably the largest expense on an ongoing basis. The investor has no control over the manager's timing of purchases and sales, so tax efficiency could become an issue. Prospectuses will not contain all the costs that affect the net return on the fund. This is why it is important to compare net returns after all expenses, including taxes to the investor.

ANNUITIES

An **annuity** is generally a contract between an individual and an insurance company, usually purchased for retirement income. An investor, the **annuitant**, contributes money to the plan in one lump sum or in periodic payments. At a future date, the annuitant begins receiving regular income distributions.

An annuity combines elements of both retirement accounts and mutual funds. It may be established by individuals looking for tax-deferred income or by corporations to serve as an employee retirement plan.

TYPES OF ANNUITY CONTRACTS

Annuity contracts are classified into three types (depending on the payment the annuity makes):

■ fixed annuities;

■ variable annuities; and

■ combination annuities.

Fixed Annuities

A **fixed annuity** guarantees a minimum rate of return. When the individual elects to begin receiving income, the payout is determined by the account's value and the annuitant's life expectancy based on mortality tables. A fixed annuity payment remains constant throughout the annuitant's life.

TAKE NOTE   Because the insurance company guarantees the return and the annuitant bears no risk, a fixed annuity is an insurance product. A salesperson must have a life insurance license to sell fixed annuities.

Although principal and interest are not at risk, a fixed annuity risks loss of purchasing power because of inflation.

EXAMPLE   An individual who annuitized a contract in 1980 may have been guaranteed monthly payments of $800. Decades later, this amount may prove insufficient to live on.

Variable Annuities

An investor who wants to reduce the inflation risk associated with fixed annuities can buy a variable annuity contract. Money deposited in a variable annuity is most often invested in a stock portfolio, which has a better chance of keeping pace with inflation than fixed-income investments.

The greater potential gain of a variable annuity involves more potential risk because it invests in equity securities rather than bonds. Payouts may vary considerably because an annuity unit's worth fluctuates with the securities' value.

Fixed Annuities	Variable Annuities
Guaranteed fixed payments	Variable payments
Guaranteed interest rate	Variable rate of return
Investment risk assumed by insurance company	Investment risk assumed by annuitant
Portfolio of fixed-income securities	Portfolio of equities, debt, money market instruments
General account	Separate account
Vulnerable to inflation	Resistant to inflation
Insurance regulation	Insurance and securities regulation

Separate Account

The contributions that investors make to a variable annuity are kept in a separate account from the insurance company's general funds.

Because the investor rather than the insurance company bears the risk, a variable annuity is considered to be a security. Variable annuity salespersons must be registered with the SEC and NASD, in addition to state insurance departments.

Principal Features of Mutual Funds vs. Variable Annuities

Mutual Funds	Variable Annuities
Investment company	Insurance company
Shares	Units
Investment objectives: varied	Investment objectives: primarily growth and income
No guarantees	Few guarantees
Redeemed by issuer	Redeemed by issuer
Price based on formula	Price based on formula

Combination Annuities

A **combination annuity** attempts to provide guaranteed payments as well as payments that keep pace with inflation. An investor contributes to both a fixed account and a variable account for a combination annuity. The result is a guaranteed return on the fixed annuity portion and a potentially higher return on the variable annuity portion.

PURCHASING ANNUITIES

Insurance companies offer a number of purchase options to make it easy for annuity owners to accumulate money.

Deferred Annuity

An annuity may be purchased with a single lump-sum investment (with payment of benefits deferred until the annuitant elects to receive them). This type of investment is referred to as a **single-premium deferred annuity**.

Periodic Payment Deferred Annuity

A **periodic payment deferred annuity** allows a person to make periodic payments. The contract holder can invest money on a monthly, quarterly, or annual basis (with payment of benefits deferred until the annuitant elects to receive them).

Immediate Annuity

An investor may purchase an **immediate annuity** contract by depositing a single lump sum. The insurance company begins to pay out the annuity's benefits immediately—usually within 60 days.

Accumulation Stage

The pay-in period for an annuity is known as the **accumulation stage**. During the accumulation stage of an annuity contract, the contract terms are flexible. An investor who misses a periodic payment is in no danger of forfeiting the preceding contributions.

The contract holder can terminate the contract at any time during the accumulation stage, although the contract holder is likely to incur surrender charges on amounts withdrawn in the first five to 10 years after issuance of the contract. To discourage termination of contracts, insurance companies often allow contract holders to borrow from their accounts without having to cancel the contracts.

Accumulation Units

An **accumulation unit** is an accounting measure that represents an investor's share of ownership in the separate account. An accumulation unit's value is determined in the same way as the value of mutual fund shares. The unit value changes with the value of the securities held in the separate account and the total number of accumulation units outstanding.

Sales Charges on Variable Annuities

Unlike mutual funds, NASD has not set a maximum sales charge for the sale of variable annuities. However, the SEC has ruled that charges must be reasonable and not excessive.

Variable Annuity Sales and Redemption Practices

Applications and purchase payments must be promptly transmitted to the issuer of the contract. The insurance company must make prompt payments on any redemption requested by contract holders in accordance with the contract terms.

RECEIVING DISTRIBUTIONS FROM ANNUITIES

The payout period for an annuity is known as the **annuity stage**.

Annuity Payout Options

An annuity offers several payout options for amounts accumulated in the annuity contract. The investor can let the money accumulate in the annuity, withdraw the accumulated funds in a lump sum, or withdraw the accumulated funds periodically by **annuitizing** the contract. Annuitizing occurs when the investor converts from the accumulation (pay-in) stage to the distribution (payout) stage.

The decision to annuitize the contract locks in the specified payment option. The contract holder may not change it. Annuity payout options, in order from largest monthly payout to smallest monthly payout, follow.

Life Annuity/Straight Life/Pure Life

Under this option, the payout is structured so that the annuitant receives periodic payments (usually monthly) over his lifetime. No added options or benefits exist; therefore, for a given amount of funds, this option provides the largest periodic payment.

Life Annuity with Period Certain

Under the life annuity with period certain option, an annuitant receives payments for life, with a certain minimum period guaranteed. If the annuitant dies before the period certain expires, payments continue to the annuitant's named beneficiaries for the period certain. If the annuitant lives beyond the period certain, payments continue until the annuitant's death.

EXAMPLE   A client purchases a life annuity with a 10-year period certain. The insurance company guarantees payments for the life of the annuitant or 10 years, whichever is longer. If the annuitant lives for only one year after payments begin, the company continues to make payments to the annuitant's beneficiaries for nine more years. If the annuitant dies after receiving payments for 13 years, payments cease at death.

Joint Life with Last Survivor Annuity

With this option, the annuity covers two or more people, and payment is conditioned on both (all) lives.

EXAMPLE   A husband and wife own an annuity jointly with a last survivor clause. The contract pays benefits as long as one of the annuitants remains alive. The payment may be the same as when both were alive, or it may be reduced for the surviving annuitant, depending on the contract. If this option includes more than two annuitants, payments cease at the last survivor's death.

Mortality Guarantee

Annuity companies guarantee payments for as long as annuitants live. If a change occurs in life expectancy and annuitants live longer than originally anticipated, the insurance companies assume the increased mortality cost—the **mortality guarantee**.

Operating Expense Guarantee

When calculating the amount an annuity company can pay out to a customer, the insurance company must project its own expenses for administering the plan. If for any reason the costs of operation increase, the company sets a ceiling for expenses charged to the separate account. If the actual costs are greater, the company pays the difference. This is known as the **operating expense guarantee**.

Annuity Units

When a contract is annuitized, accumulation units become annuity units. An **annuity unit** is a measure of value used only during an annuitized contract's payout period. It is an accounting measure that determines the amount of each payment to the annuitant during the payout period.

The number of annuity units is calculated when an owner annuitizes the contract. The number of annuity units does not change, but each unit's value fluctuates with the separate account portfolio's value. The number of units credited to the annuitant's account is based on the value of the contract when the payout period begins and on other variables (such as the payout option selected, accumulated value of the annuitant's account, individual's age and sex, and assumed interest rate).

Assumed Interest Rate (AIR)

The **assumed interest rate (AIR)** is a basis for determining distributions from a variable annuity. The rate, usually estimated conservatively, provides an earnings target for the separate account. An AIR is used to estimate the value of an account through the annuitant's age at death as forecasted by mortality tables.

The higher the AIR, the higher the projected value of units and the greater the initial payment. The reverse also is true.

Effects of Investment Performance on Annuity Payouts

The AIR does not guarantee a rate of return. It is a tool for adjusting an annuity unit's value to reflect changes in the investment performance of the separate account portfolio. As the annuity units change in value, so does the amount of the annuitant's monthly payment. The annuitant always receives a payment equal to the value of one or a specified number of annuity units times the unit value.

Variable Annuity Payments

Variable annuity payments are determined initially by mortality tables and the value of an annuitant's account. Variable annuity plans do not guarantee a payment amount because the insurance company cannot guarantee the separate account's performance. The value of the separate account upon annuitization is used to determine the number of annuity units in the account; future payouts are determined by the annuity units' fluctuating value.

EXAMPLE   An investor who annuitized a variable annuity in 1960 and began with monthly payments of $375 may now be receiving $1,275 per month.

Fluctuating Payments

After the insurance company determines the number of annuity units used in calculating each payment, the amount of each payment equals the number of units multiplied by the annuity units' current value. The number of annuity units used to calculate future payment remains the same; however, because the units' value depends on the separate account performance, the annuitant's payments may fluctuate if the units' value fluctuates.

QUICK QUIZ 5.6

Matching

A. Accumulation unit
B. Joint and last survivor annuity
C. Deferred annuity
D. Variable annuity

____   1. Delays distributions until the owner elects to receive them

____   2. Determines an annuitant's interest in the insurer's separate account before distribution from the annuity begins

____   3. Performance of a separate account determines value

____   4. Annuity payments continue as long as one of the annuitants is alive

---

QUICK QUIZ 5.7

Matching

A. Assumed interest rate
B. Immediate annuity
C. Life income with period certain
D. Separate account

____   1. Contract starts to pay the annuitant approximately one month after its issuance

____   2. The basis for projected annuity payments, but not guaranteed

____   3. Holds funds paid by variable annuity contract holders

____   4. If the annuitant dies before a specified time expires, payments go to the annuitant's named beneficiary

---

TAXATION OF ANNUITIES

Contributions to an annuity that is not part of an employer-sponsored retirement plan are made with after-tax dollars. Because contributions have been taxed already, the total amount contributed is not taxable when the account is annuitized. As with other investments, the money invested in an annuity represents the investor's cost basis.

The primary advantage of an annuity as an investment is that the tax on interest, dividends, and capital gains is deferred until the owner withdraws money from the contract. On withdrawal, the amount exceeding the investor's cost basis is taxed as ordinary income.

Random Withdrawals

Since 1982, random withdrawals from annuity contracts have been taxed under the **last in, first out (LIFO)** method. Earnings are presumed by the IRS to be the last monies to hit the account. The earnings are considered to be withdrawn first from the annuity and are taxable as ordinary income. After the withdrawal of all earnings, contributions representing cost basis may be withdrawn without tax.

Lump-Sum Withdrawals

Lump-sum withdrawals are taken by using the LIFO accounting method. This means that earnings are removed before contributions. If an investor receives a lump-sum withdrawal before age 59½, the earnings portion withdrawn is taxed as ordinary income and is subject to an additional 10% penalty under most circumstances.

The penalty does not apply if the funds are withdrawn after age 59½, are withdrawn because of death or disability, or are part of a life-income option plan with fixed payments.

EXAMPLE   A contract with a $100,000 value consists of $40,000 in contributions and $60,000 in earnings. If the investor withdraws all $100,000 at once, the $60,000 in earnings is taxed as ordinary income and the $40,000 cost basis is returned tax free.

Annuitized Payments

Annuitized payments are typically made monthly and are taxed according to an exclusion ratio. The **exclusion ratio** expresses the percentages of the annuity's value upon annuitization of contribution basis to the total.

EXAMPLE   If $50,000 in after-tax dollars was contributed to an annuity contract worth $100,000 at annuitization, 50% of each payment will be treated as ordinary income, whereas the other 50% of each payment will be treated (for tax purposes) as nontaxable return of basis.

Under certain circumstances, the annuitant's life expectancy may also factor in the exclusion ratio.

TEST TOPIC ALERT   Some additional tax concepts related to annuities are demonstrated below.

1. An annuity contract owner, age 45, surrenders his annuity to buy a home. Which of the following best describes the tax consequences of this action?

    A. Ordinary income taxes and a 10% early withdrawal penalty will apply to all money withdrawn.
    B. Capital gains tax will apply to the amount of the withdrawal that represents earnings; there will be no tax on the cost basis.
    C. Ordinary income taxes and a 10% early withdrawal penalty will apply to the amount of the withdrawal that represents earnings; there will be no tax on the cost basis.
    D. Ordinary income taxes apply to the amount of the withdrawal that represents earnings; the 10% early withdrawal penalty does not apply to surrenders.

    Answer: C. Interest earnings are taxable as ordinary income. They are also subject to the 10% early withdrawal penalty when withdrawn before age 59½. The contract holder recovers his cost basis without tax.

2. After the death of the annuitant, beneficiaries under a life and 15-year period certain option are subject to

    A. capital gains taxation on the total amount of payments received
    B. ordinary income taxation on the total amount of payments received, plus a 10% withdrawal penalty if the annuitant was under age 59½
    C. ordinary income taxation on the amount of the payment that exceeds the cost basis
    D. tax-free payout of all remaining annuity benefits

    Answer: C. Payments from the annuity to the beneficiary through a period certain option are taxed in the same way as other periodic annuity payments; benefits over the amount of the cost basis are taxable as ordinary income. However, no 10% penalty applies in this situation.

Advantages to Investing in Variable Annuities

- Tax-deferred growth: All income and capital gains generated in the portfolio of the separate account are free from income tax until the money is withdrawn. Over time, this tax-deferred compounding can make a significant difference in the value of the account.

- Guaranteed death benefit: Most variable annuities contain a provision stating that if the investor dies during the accumulation period, the beneficiary will receive the greater of the current value of the account or the amount invested. Therefore, the estate is assured of getting back at least the original investment.

- Guaranteed lifetime income: Although a variable annuity can not guaranteed how much will be paid, choosing a payout option with lifetime benefits guarantees that there will be a check every month as long as the annuitant is alive.

■ IRS Section 1035 transfers: If you don't like the annuity you're in, you can transfer to another one without any tax consequences. However, it is possible there will be a surrender charge. This is unlike mutual funds, for which use of the exchange privilege is a taxable event.

■ No age 70½ restrictions or requirements: Unlike traditional retirement plans that have required minimum distributions after the age of 70½, an investor can delay withdrawals as desired and, in fact, can continue to contribute.

■ A choice of separate account objectives with professional management: Some variable annuity companies offer 25–30 different subaccounts, each with a slightly different objective and all managed by professionals

■ No probate: Since the annuity calls for direct designation of a beneficiary, upon death, the asset passes directly without the time and expense of probate.

Disadvantages to Investing in Variable Annuities

■ Earnings are taxed as ordinary income: Even though it is possible that the majority of the increase in value is generated through long-term capital gains, all earnings will be taxed at the higher ordinary income rate.

■ The administrative and insurance-related expense fees are typically much higher than the fees incurred by owning a mutual fund.

■ Withdrawals made before age 59½ will generally incur a 10% penalty, in addition to the ordinary income tax.

■ Most variable annuities carry a conditional deferred sales charge. Therefore, surrender in the early years will usually involve additional costs.

■ These are variable investments and carry the same investment risks as mutual funds.

DIRECT PARTICIPATION PROGRAMS (DPPs)

Direct participation programs (DPPs), many of which are limited partnerships, allow the economic consequences of a business to flow through to investors. Unlike corporations, limited partnerships pay no dividends. Rather, they pass income, gains, losses, deductions, and credits directly to investors.

Limited partnerships offer investors limited liability. Should a limited partnership default on its loans, investors could lose their entire investment, which might include a specific share of partnership debt, but they are not personally liable for other partnership debts. Partnerships usually borrow money in **nonrecourse** loans, meaning the general partners (GPs), not the limited partners (LPs), assume responsibility for repayment of the loan.

Units of ownership in a partnership are called interests, rather than shares.

Investors in a Limited Partnership

A limited partnership must have at least one general partner and one limited partner. A certificate of limited partnership filed with the Secretary of State lists the status of each investor as a limited or general partner.

General Partner (GP)

The GPs are the active investors in a limited partnership and assume responsibility for all aspects of the partnership's operations. A general partner:

- makes decisions that bind the partnership;

- buys and sells property for the partnership;

- manages the partnership property and money;

- supervises all aspects of the partnership's business; and

- maintains a minimum 1% financial interest in the partnership.

Unlike LPs, who have limited liability, GPs assume unlimited liability and are therefore personally liable for all partnership business losses and debts. A partnership's creditors may seek repayment from the GPs and may go after their personal assets.

A general partner has a fiduciary relationship to the LPs in that the GP has been entrusted with the LPs' capital and is legally bound to use that capital in the investors' best interests. The GP must manage the business in the partnership's best interest and avoid the appearance of improper use of assets and conflicts of interest. The GP cannot borrow from the partnership, compete with the partnership, or commingle personal funds with partnership funds.

Limited Partner (LP)

LPs are passive investors with no management or day-to-day decision-making responsibilities; therefore, they usually are not held personally responsible for the partnership's indebtedness. LPs may receive cash distributions and capital gains from partnerships. The total yield of a partnership investment takes into account all potential rewards: tax deductions, cash distributions, and capital gains.

Issuing Partnership Investments

DPPs are either public offerings or private placements. In either case, specific documentation is required to form and invest in the partnership.

Private Placements

In a **private placement limited partnership**, each of a small number of LPs contributes a large amount of money, such as $100,000 or more. Private placements are usually offered to **accredited investors**—wealthy investors with substantial investment experience—not the general public.

Public Offerings

In a **publicly offered limited partnership**, a larger number of investors makes relatively small contributions of capital to the partnership, such as $1,000 to $5,000. These partnerships can be publicly advertised, raise relatively large amounts of capital, and may attract investors with smaller budgets and less investment sophistication. Typically, they are more tightly regulated and subject to more stringent federal registration and prospectus requirements than private placements.

Documentation

Subscription Agreement. An investor who buys a limited partnership unit must complete and sign a subscription agreement, which includes a statement of the investor's net worth and annual income and a power of attorney form appointing the GP as the agent of the partnership. The registered representative is responsible to make certain that the information the potential investor provides in the subscription agreement is complete and accurate.

Certificate of Limited Partnership. To be legally recognized as a limited partnership, a business organization must file a certificate of limited partnership in its home state, usually with the office of the Secretary of State. The purpose of the certificate is to let creditors know which partners are liable for the partnership's debts (the GPs) and which partners have limited liability (the LPs). Unless a certificate is filed, all partners may be treated as GPs; that is, investors may be denied limited liability.

The **partnership agreement** is a contract that provides guidelines for operating the partnership and describes the general and limited partners' roles, including each party's rights and responsibilities. Each partner receives a copy of the partnership agreement.

Advantages and Disadvantages of Limited Partnerships

The DPP investor enjoys several advantages, including:

- an investment managed by others;

- flow-through of income and certain expenses; and

- limited liability.

The exam will probably give more attention to the following disadvantages.

- **Liquidity Risk.** The greatest disadvantage is lack of liquidity. Because the secondary market for DPPs is limited, investors who want to sell their interests frequently cannot locate buyers.

- **Legislative Risk.** When Congress changes tax laws, new rules can cause substantial damage to LPs, who may be locked into illiquid investments that lose previously assumed tax advantages.

■ **Risk of Audit.** Statistics from the IRS indicate that reporting ownership of a DPP results in a significantly higher percentage of returns selected for audit.

Tax Reporting for Partnerships

Partnership losses are apportioned among investors, enabling them to claim those losses as deductions on their personal tax returns. If the partnership's operations result in taxable income, that amount is divided proportionally among the partners. Each investor adds that amount to his personal taxable income. Partners receive reports of the partnership's tax results on IRS Schedule K-1.

Under current tax law, LPs are classified as **passive investors**. Any income they receive from a partnership is **passive income**, and any loss passed through to them is a **passive loss**. Investors can deduct passive losses against passive income only. Unused passive losses can be carried forward to the next year and used to offset future passive income. Dividend and interest income and wages are not passive income.

TAKE NOTE   An investor may only use a tax loss from a partnership to offset income from another passive investment.

Real Estate Limited Partnerships

Limited partnerships can be formed to run any type of business. Real estate partnerships are the most common.

Real estate limited partnerships may provide capital growth potential through the appreciation of property. Partnerships may also distribute cash income, which can be sheltered from taxes by deductions for mortgage interest and depreciation. Depreciation is a tax deduction that accounts for the theoretical wearing out of the building and any capital improvements.

Three types of real estate programs are new construction, existing property, and raw land.

New Construction

A new construction program builds new property. The principal advantage of such a program is the potential for appreciation. The disadvantages of new construction are potential cost overruns, no established track record for the new property, the difficulty of finding permanent financing, and an inability to deduct current expenses during the construction period.

Existing Property

Programs based on existing property with track records are generally less risky than new construction programs. Income and expenses are easier to estimate, and cash flow can begin immediately. Potential disadvantages include greater maintenance or repair expenses than for new construction, expiring leases that may not be renewed, and less than favorable existing rental arrangements.

Raw Land

A limited partnership based on raw land is the most speculative type of real estate limited partnership. Its only advantage is the appreciation potential of the property. During the holding period, the partnership must absorb real estate taxes and, in some cases, interest costs. The benefits of owning raw land are delayed until the sale of the property.

ANALYSIS AND EVALUATION OF DIRECT PARTICIPATION PROGRAMS

The total return of a partnership investment takes into account tax deductions, cash distributions, and capital gains. An investor should choose a limited partnership because:

- it is economically viable;

- the GP(s) has(have) demonstrated management ability and expertise in running similar programs;

- the program's objectives match the investor's objectives and does so within a time frame that meets the investor's needs; and

- the start-up costs and projected revenues are in line with the start-up costs and revenues of similar ventures.

Promoters structure DPPs to meet various objectives. When a promoter's tax stance is too aggressive or is without economic purpose in the view of the IRS, the program is considered an abusive tax shelter. If the IRS judges the program to be abusive, it disallows deductions; assesses back taxes, interest, and penalties; and, in some cases, charges the promoter with criminal intent to defraud.

Investors should try to match their current and future objectives with a program's stated objectives.

EXAMPLE

A person seeking taxable passive income should not invest in an oil and gas exploratory drilling program.

DPPs are illiquid, and investors must commit money for a long period of time.

QUICK QUIZ 5.8

True or False?

____ 1. An investor who purchases a limited partnership is required to provide a statement of net worth.

____ 2. One of the greatest advantages of limited partnership investments is that they are readily available secondary market.

____ 3. DPP investors may deduct passive losses from ordinary income.

_____ 4. The general partner is fully liable for all partnership losses and debts.

_____ 5. Limited partners have limited liability and take an active role in the management of partnerships.

_____ 6. Tax deductions, capital gains, and cash distributions are potential rewards for limited partnership investors.

DERIVATIVE SECURITIES—OPTIONS

Options are **derivative securities**, which means that they derive their value from that of an underlying instrument, such as a stock, stock index, interest rate, or foreign currency. Option contracts offer investors a means to **hedge**, or protect, an investment's value or speculate on the price movement of individual securities, markets, foreign currencies, and other instruments.

An **option** is a contract that establishes a price and time frame for the purchase or sale of a particular security. Two parties are involved in the contract: one party receives the right to exercise the contract to buy or sell the underlying security; the other is obligated to fulfill the terms of the contract.

In theory, options can be created on any item with a fluctuating market value. The most familiar options are those issued on common stocks; they are called **equity options**.

CALLS AND PUTS

There are two types of option contracts: calls and puts.

- A **call** option gives its holder the right to buy a stock for a specific price within a specified time frame. A call buyer buys the right to buy a specific stock, and a call seller takes on the obligation to sell the stock.

- A **put** option gives its holder the right to sell a stock for a specific price within a specified time frame. A put buyer buys the right to sell a specific stock, and a put seller takes on the obligation to buy the stock.

Each stock option contract covers 100 shares (a round lot) of stock. An option's cost is its **premium**. Premiums are quoted in dollars per share.

EXAMPLE   Because a contract covers 100 shares, a premium of $3 means $3 for each share times 100 shares, which equals $300.

Leverage

Because an option's cost is normally much less than the underlying stock's cost, option contracts provide investors with leverage: relatively little money allows an investor to control an investment that would otherwise require a much larger capital outlay.

EXAMPLE   An investor can buy RST for $58, investing $5,800, or buy an RST 55 call for $6, an investment of $600. If RST's price increases to $70, the stock investor will see a 20.7% profit, ($12 profit ÷ $58 investment), whereas the option investor, with the call worth a minimum of $15 ($70 – $55), will have more than doubled his money ($15 ÷ 6 = 250%). The opposite is also true; if RST trades below $55 when the option expires, the stock investor has a modest loss, but the option investor loses his whole investment.

OPTION TRANSACTIONS

Because two types of options (calls and puts) and two types of transactions (purchases and sales) exist, four basic transactions are available to an option investor:

- Buy calls
- Sell calls
- Buy puts
- Sell puts

Option buyers are **long** the positions; option sellers are **short** the positions.

Opening and Closing Transactions

Because an option conveys rights and obligations for a limited time, each transaction has a beginning and an end—an open and a close. For instance, an option position opened by an investor buying a call is closed when the call is exercised, is sold, or expires. An option position opened by an investor selling a call is closed when the call is exercised, is bought, or expires.

The owner of a put or call option contract has three ways to close a position:

- **exercise** the option to buy or sell the security specified in the contract;
- let the option **expire;** or
- **sell** the option contract before the expiration date.

The simplest and most common way to close an option position is entering the transaction opposite of the opening transaction. The following table below summarizes potential opening and closing positions.

Open	To Close
Buy call	Sell call
Sell call	Buy call
Buy put	Sell put
Sell put	Buy put

The test may ask you the difference between American- and European-style exercise. American style means the option can be exercised at any time the holder wishes, up to the expiration date. European-style options may only be exercised on their expiration date.

Value of an Option

Option premiums reflect two types of value:

■ Intrinsic value—amount by which an option is in-the-money

■ Time value—amount by which the premium exceeds intrinsic value

Intrinsic Value

If an option is in-the-money, its premium reflects, at a minimum, the difference between the strike price and the stock's price. This difference is known as *intrinsic value*. Intrinsic value is the amount by which an option is in-the-money. An out-of-the-money option has no intrinsic value.

A call option, whether long or short, is **in-the-money** when the stock's price is above the option's strike price.

E X A M P L E   An RST 50 call is in-the-money by seven points if RST stock is $57 because the call owner can exercise the option to buy the stock for $50 and sell it in the market for $57 for an immediate gain of $7 per share.

A put, whether long or short, is in-the-money when the stock price is below the option's strike price.

Time Value

If an option's premium exceeds its intrinsic value, the option has **time value**. An option expires on a preset date; the further away that date is, the more time remains for a change in the underlying stock's price and, therefore, the greater the time value. Time value diminishes as an option's expiration date approaches. At expiration, when no time remains, the option premium equals its intrinsic value, if any. An option premium equal to its intrinsic value is at parity.

Options are wasting or deteriorating assets because the passage of time depletes their value.

The option buyer, like the buyer of any investment, hopes to profit from his position. An option's price, or premium, changes as the following events occur.

■ The underlying security's market price changes (the more volatile the underlying security, the more volatile the premium tends to be).

■ The option's intrinsic value increases or decreases.

■ The time remaining until the option's expiration date grows nearer.

Although most options carry a maximum life of nine months, long-term equity anticipation securities (LEAPS) can be held as long as three years before expiring.

EXAMPLE   An RST 60 put is in-the-money by three points if RST stock is $57 because the put owner can exercise the put to sell the stock for $60 when the stock's market price is $57.

A call option is **out-of-the-money** when the stock price is below the exercise price. No investor will exercise an RST 60 call to buy RST for $60 if he can buy RST in the market for $57.

A put is out-of-the-money if the stock price is above the exercise price. No investor will exercise an RST 50 put to sell the stock for $50 if he can sell RST in the market for $57.

TAKE NOTE   The terms *in-the-money* and *out-of-the-money* refer to the relationship between an option's strike price and the underlying stock's price. They do not reflect the investor's profit or loss. An option's premium is not relevant when determining whether the option is in-the-money or out-of-the-money.

An option is at-the-money when the underlying stock is trading at the option's strike price. Investors are unlikely to exercise at-the-money options.

The true value of an option is quite complicated. There are many different tools used, the most common of which is known as the Black-Scholes options pricing model. You will not be required to use this model; in fact, it usually appears only as a wrong answer choice on the exam.

OPTIONS STRATEGIES

Options strategies are either bullish or bearish positions on the underlying stock. The primary reason for buying or selling options is to profit from or hedge against price movement in the underlying security.

A bullish investor may buy calls or write puts seeking profit if the price of the underlying assets rises. A bearish investor can write calls or buy puts seeking profit if the price of the underlying assets declines.

Bullish and Bearish Options Positions

	Long	Short
Calls	Right to buy Bullish	Obligation to sell Bearish
Puts	Right to sell Bearish	Obligation to buy Bullish
	(Buyer, Holder, Owner)	(Seller, Writer, Grantor)

Buying Calls

Investors expecting a stock to increase in value speculate on that price increase by buying calls on the stock.

By buying a call, an investor can profit from the increase in the stock's price while investing a relatively small amount of money. The most a call buyer can lose is the money paid for the option. The most a call buyer can gain is unlimited because there is no limit to how high the stock price can go. Owners of options (puts or calls) do not receive dividends on the underlying stock.

Writing Calls

A neutral or bearish investor can write a call and collect the premium. An investor who believes a stock's price will stay the same or decline can write a call to:

■ generate income from the option premium;

■ partially protect (hedge) a long stock position by offsetting any loss on the sale of the stock by the premium amount; or

■ speculate on the decline in the stock price.

If the stock price increases, the call may be exercised. The writer will be paid the strike price for the stock, in addition to the premium he received for writing the call. The call writer can gain the premium received for writing the option. The call writer's exposure is unlimited because there is no limit to how high the stock price can go.

Buying Puts

A **bearish investor**—one who believes a stock will decline in price—can speculate on the price decline by buying puts. A put buyer acquires the right to sell 100 shares of the underlying stock at the strike price before the expiration date.

Puts can be used to speculate on or hedge (fully protect) against a decline in a stock's value in the following ways.

■ An investor who expects a stock he does not own to decline can buy a put to profit from the decline.

■ An investor who expects a stock he owns to decline can buy a put to lock in a minimum sale price.

If a put owner is correct and the stock falls in price, he could exercise the put option to sell the stock at the strike price or sell the put at a profit.

Writing Puts

Generally, investors who write puts believe that the stock's price will rise. A put writer is obligated to buy stock at the exercise price if the put buyer puts it to the put writer. If a stock's price is above the put strike price at expiration, the put expires unexercised, allowing the put writer to keep the premium.

Some investors write puts with the intent of having the options exercised against them. Writing a put is a means to buy stock at a reduced price because the premium received, in effect, reduces the cost of the stock. If the put is not exercised, the writer keeps the premium.

TAKE NOTE

The maximum gain and loss of the four basic options positions are summarized below.

	Maximum Gain	Maximum Loss
Long Call	Unlimited	Premium
Short Call	Premium	Unlimited
Long Put	Strike price – premium	Premium
Short Put	Premium	Strike price – premium

The maximum gains and losses for the long and short sides of each contract are opposites of each other.

QUICK QUIZ 5.9

Matching (each has two answers)

A. Long call
B. Short call
C. Long put
D. Short put

_____ 1. Which options positions are bearish?

_____ 2. Which options positions are bullish?

_____ 3. Which positions buy stock at exercise?

_____ 4. Which positions sell stock at exercise?

_____ 5. Which positions have rights?

_____ 6. Which positions have obligations?

1. Options are best described as

   A. derivatives
   B. substitutes
   C. swaps
   D. futures

2. Your customer is long 10 ABC Jul 50 calls at 4.50. He owns how many options?

   A. 1
   B. 4.50
   C. 10
   D. 100

3. Your customer is long 10 ABC Jul 50 calls at 4.50. What is the name of the underlying instrument?

   A. Call options
   B. Common stock
   C. ABC calls
   D. ABC common stock

4. Your customer is long 10 ABC Jul 50 calls at 4.50. The contract gives him the

   A. right to buy stock
   B. right to sell stock
   C. obligation to buy stock
   D. obligation to sell stock

5. Your customer is long 10 ABC Jul 50 calls at 4.50. How many shares of stock will change hands if he exercises his option?

   A. 10
   B. 100
   C. 1,000
   D. 10,000

6. Which term best describes the following situation: A customer has the right to sell 100 shares of MNO at 60 any time between July and October.

   A. Buying calls
   B. Buying puts
   C. Writing calls
   D. Writing puts

7. A call is in-the-money when the market price of the underlying stock is

   A. equal to the strike price
   B. more than the strike price
   C. less than the strike price
   D. more than it was at the previous day's close

HEDGING WITH OPTIONS

An investor with an established position in a stock can use options to hedge the position's risks. Normally, investors seek either to increase potential reward or to reduce potential loss.

Long Stock and Long Puts

An investor who owns a stock can protect against a decline in market value by buying a put. Doing so allows the investor to sell the stock by exercising the put if the stock price declines before expiration, or selling the put at a profit, which will offset the decline in the stock price. This strategy is called **portfolio insurance**. Any profits in the stock are offset by the cost of the put premiums.

EXAMPLE   An investor buys 100 shares of RST at $53 and buys 1 RST 50 put at 2. The maximum gain is unlimited. Should the stock price fall below the strike price of 50, the investor will exercise the put to sell the stock for 50. The investor loses $3 per share on the stock and has spent $2 per share for the put. The total loss equals $500. The breakeven point (the price at which the investor neither makes nor loses money) is reached when the stock rises by the amount paid for the put; in this case, $53 + $2 = $55.

Long Stock and Short Calls (Covered Call Writing)

A **covered call** is a call written (sold) on a stock an investor owns. The covered call writer reduces the risk of his long stock position and generates income with the dollars he receives in premiums from selling the call. If the call is not exercised, the call writer keeps the premium. If the call is exercised, the covered call writer can deliver the stock he owns. The covered call writer limits potential gain in exchange for the partial protection against a loss.

Partial Protection. By writing a covered call and receiving the premium, an investor, in effect, reduces the stock cost by the premium amount. If the stock price falls below the purchase price minus the premium received, the investor incurs a loss. Should the stock price rise dramatically, the stock will likely be called.

EXAMPLE   An investor buys 100 shares of RST at 53 and writes 1 RST 55 call for 2. The premium offsets the stock price by the $2 premium received. The maximum gain equals $400: if the stock price rises above 55, the call will be exercised; thus, the investor will sell the stock for a gain of $200, in addition to the $200 premium received. The maximum loss is $5,100 should the stock become worthless. The breakeven point is reached when the stock falls by the amount of the premium received. Therefore, $53 − $2 = $51.

TAKE NOTE   A covered call provides partial protection that generates income but reduces the stock's potential gain. Buying puts provides nearly total loss protection that costs money yet does not reduce the stock position's potential gain.

Short Stock and Long Calls

An investor who sells a stock short sells borrowed stock, expecting the price to decline. The short seller must buy stock to repay the stock loan and hopes to do so at a lower price. A short seller can buy calls to protect against a price rise.

EXAMPLE   An investor sells short 100 shares of RST at 58 and buys an RST 60 call for 3. The investor's maximum gain is $5,500: if the stock becomes worthless, the investor gains $5,800 from the short sale minus the $300 paid for the call. The maximum loss is $500: if the stock price rises above $60, the investor will exercise the call to buy the stock for 60, incurring a $200 loss on the short sale, in addition to the $300 paid for the call. The breakeven point is the stock's sale price minus the premium paid—in this case, $58 − $3 = $55.

Short Stock and Short Puts

A short stock position can be partially protected by selling puts, known as **covered put writing**. At a certain point, however, the potential loss can be unlimited. An investor who sells a stock short and then sells a put, also limits the potential profit.

EXAMPLE   A customer sells short 100 RST at 55 and writes an RST 55 put for 2.50 for partial protection. The maximum gain is $250. If the stock declines to zero and the put is exercised against him, the customer is obligated to pay $5,500 to buy the stock, losing $5,500. However, he receives a $5,500 gain from the short sale. Because he received the $250 premium, the stock can increase to 57.50, the breakeven point, before the short stock position generates a loss, which is potentially unlimited.

QUICK QUIZ 5.11   Matching (may have more than one answer)

    A. Long call
    B. Short call
    C. Long put
    D. Short put

_____ 1. Used to fully protect a long stock position

_____ 2. Used to fully protect a short stock position

_____   3.   Obligation to buy stock at the strike price if exercised

_____   4.   Right to sell stock at the strike price if exercised

_____   5.   Used to speculate on the upward movement of a stock's price

_____   6.   Used to speculate on the downward movement of a stock's price

_____   7.   Subjects an investor to unlimited risk

_____   8.   The maximum loss is the premium

_____   9.   Used to generate income when an investor owns the underlying stock

_____   10.   Requires investor to buy stock at a price reduced by the amount of premium received, if exercised

HOTSHEETS

For your convenience, Unit HotSheets summarizing the key points are located at the end of the manual on perforated pages.

UNIT TEST

1. Which of the following is NOT a feature in owning a limited partnership?

   A. An investment managed by others
   B. Flow-through of income and expenses of a business to the individual limited partner
   C. Legislative risk
   D. Tax-free income

2. Which of the following is NOT an investment objective that must be stated in an investment company's prospectus?

   A. Growth
   B. Income
   C. Tax-advantaged income
   D. Retirement

3. Which of the following statements regarding derivative securities is NOT true?

   A. Derivative securities can be sold on listed exchanges or in the over-the-counter market.
   B. An option contract is a derivative security because it has no value independent of the value of an underlying security.
   C. An option contract's price fluctuates in relationship to the time remaining to expiration as well as with the price movement of the underlying security.
   D. An owner of a put has the obligation to purchase securities at a designated price (the strike price) before a specified date (the expiration date).

4. Under the Investment Company Act of 1940, the separate account of a variable annuity is

   I. an open-end investment company if the funds in the account are used to purchase securities directly
   II. a unit investment trust if the funds in the account are used to purchase shares in an existing mutual fund managed by someone other than the variable annuity's issuer
   III. structured so that the investor bears the investment risk and so the annuity is required to be registered under the Investment Company Act of 1940
   IV. only allowed to be sold by salespeople who are registered with NASD, in addition to being insurance licensed

   A. I only
   B. I, II and III
   C. II and III
   D. I, II, III and IV

5. When advising an investor on the purchase of mutual funds, the representative should instruct the client to compare open-end mutual funds with the same objective for all of the following EXCEPT

   A. costs
   B. portfolio turnover
   C. liquidity
   D. services offered

6. Which of the following statements regarding investment companies is NOT true?

   A. The Investment Company Act of 1940 classifies investment companies into three types: face-amount certificate companies, unit investment trusts, and management investment companies.

   B. An investment company can offer investors two ways of participating in the fund under management: through the purchase of closed-end shares, or, if the investor prefers, open-end redeemable shares.

   C. When investors sell or redeem their open-end fund shares, they receive the net asset value (NAV) as of the close of the day the order was issued.

   D. When an open-end investment company, or mutual fund, registers its offering with the SEC, it does not specify the exact number of shares it intends to issue.

7. An owner of an annuitized annuity can do all of the following EXCEPT

   A. receive the benefits on a monthly basis or until the time of death

   B. receive the benefits for life with a certain minimum period of time guaranteed

   C. have a joint life with last survivor clause with payments paid until the death of the last survivor

   D. receive monthly payment for a defined period and then 2 years later change the contract to payment for life

8. All of the following are required by limited partnerships EXCEPT

   A. certificate of limited partnership
   B. subscription agreement
   C. SEC approval
   D. partnership agreement

9. Which of the following is NOT a restriction that the SEC has placed on money market mutual funds?

   A. Investments are limited to securities with remaining maturities of 397 days or less, with the average portfolio maturity not to exceed 90 days.

   B. Investments are limited to eligible securities determined to have minimal risk.

   C. No more than 5% of the fund's assets may be invested in below-investment-grade securities.

   D. The prospectus must prominently indicate that the US government does not guarantee the fund and that there is no guarantee that the NAV will be maintained.

10. An investment company that holds which of the following does NOT meet the definition of a diversified investment company under the 1940 Investment Company Act?

   A. 80% of its assets in securities of 47 health care companies

   B. 8% of a given corporation's voting stock in its portfolio

   C. 33% of a small-cap new issue with excellent prospects

   D. 4% of its assets invested in stock of a major publicly held corporation

11. Annuity companies offer a variety of purchase options to owners. Which of the following definitions regarding these annuity options is NOT true?

   A. Accumulation annuity—an annuity that allows the investor to accumulate funds in a separate account before investment in an annuity

   B. Single premium deferred annuity—an annuity with a lump-sum investment, with payment of benefits deferred until the annuitant elects to receive them

   C. Periodic payment deferred annuity—allows a person to make periodic payments over time. The contract holder can invest money on a monthly, quarterly, or annual basis

   D. Immediate annuity—allows an investor to deposit a lump sum with the insurance company. Payout of the annuitant's benefits starts immediately, usually within 60 days

12. Direct participation programs (DPPs), also called limited partnerships, allow the economic consequences of a business to flow through to investors. Among those are all of the following EXCEPT

   A. limited liability
   B. tax credits and deductions
   C. recourse loans
   D. immunity from market or investment risk

13. Which of the following statements regarding the general partner in a direct participation program (DPP) is NOT true?

   A. The general partner (GP) is the active investor in a limited partnership and assumes responsibility for all aspects of the partnership's operations.
   B. A GP has a fiduciary relationship to the limited partners (LPs).
   C. The GP cannot borrow from the partnership, compete with the partnership, or commingle personal funds with partnership funds.
   D. The GP, as the active manager of the partnership, does not maintain a financial interest in the partnership and only receives income distributions from profits on the business prior to the limited partners.

14. With an annuity

   I. taxes on earned dividends, interest, and capital gains are paid annually, until the owner withdraws money from the contract
   II. random withdrawals are handled under LIFO tax rules today
   III. money invested in a nonqualified annuity represents the investor's cost basis
   IV. upon withdrawal, the amount exceeding the investor's cost basis is taxed as ordinary income

   A. I only
   B. I, II and IV
   C. II, III and IV
   D. IV only

15. Covered call writing is a strategy where an investor

   A. sells a call on a security he owns to reduce the volatility of the stock's returns and to generate income with the premium
   B. buys two calls on the same security he owns to leverage the position
   C. buys a put on a security he has sold short
   D. sells a call on an index that contains some of the securities that he has in his portfolio

ANSWERS AND RATIONALES

1. **D.** The income from limited partnerships is not tax exempt. An investor, however, may use a tax loss from a partnership to offset the income from another passive investment. In limited partnerships, the investor enjoys the advantages and disadvantages of owning a business without having to actually manage one. Limited partnerships are vulnerable to legislative changes that adversely affect ownership of such investments.

2. **D.** Retirement savings and income are objectives of an investor, not of an investment company fund. Growth, income, and tax-advantaged income are investment company objectives.

3. **D.** An owner of a put has the right, not the obligation, to sell, not purchase, a security at a designated price (the strike price) before a specified date (the expiration date).

4. **B.** Choices I, II, and III all correctly describe the separate account of a variable annuity. Choice IV is a correct statement regarding those individuals qualified to sell variable annuities, not separate accounts. The variable annuity is the product for sale; the separate account is what makes the product work.

5. **C.** Shares in an open-end mutual fund are liquid. The issuer of the shares is required to redeem them at their net asset value and, therefore, should not be a consideration in comparing mutual funds with the same objective. Sales loads, management fees, and operating expenses reduce an investor's return. Most of these fees continue throughout the holding period and have a significant impact on performance. Portfolio turnover is significant as gains in the portfolio will likely all be short-term gains, which are usually taxable to the investor at a higher rate than long-term capital gains. Services that mutual funds offer include retirement accounts, investment plans, check-writing privileges, telephone transfers, conversion privileges, withdrawal plans, and others.

6. **B.** An investment company cannot offer investors two ways of participating in the fund under management. The fund must either be a closed-end fund with shares traded in the marketplace or an open-end fund with redeemable shares. The Investment Company Act of 1940 classifies investment companies into three types: FACs, UITs, and management investment companies. When investors sell or redeem their open-end fund shares, they receive the NAV as of the close of the day the order was issued (i.e., based on the next computed NAV after the order arrives). When an open-end investment company or mutual fund, registers its offering with the SEC, it does not specify the exact number of shares it intends to issue. A mutual fund is, in effect, a continuous new issuing of shares.

7. **D.** The contract is annuitized when the investor converts from the accumulation (pay-in) stage to the distribution (payout) stage. An annuity owner can elect to receive the benefits on a monthly basis until the time of death. An annuity owner can elect to receive the benefits for life with a certain minimum period of time guaranteed. In addition, an annuity owner can have a joint life with last survivor clause with payments paid until the death of the last survivor.

8. **C.** The SEC does not approve securities or limited partnerships. In public offerings (as opposed to private placements) of limited partnerships, the federal registration and a prospectus is required. To be legally recognized as a limited partnership, a business organization must file a certificate of limited partnership in its home state. An investor who buys a limited partnership must complete and sign a

subscription agreement provided by the general partner. Each partner must sign a partnership agreement, which is a contract that provides guidelines for operating the partnership and describes the general and limited partners' roles.

9. **C.** The SEC requires that money market mutual funds' investments be limited to securities that are rated in the top two ratings categories by the nationally recognized rating services (e.g., Moody's, Standard & Poor's). Investment in below-investment-grade securities is not allowed.

10. **C.** An investment company that owns 33% of a small-cap new issue with excellent prospects exceeds the limits set in the 75-5-10 test. This test requires that 75% of the assets be invested in securities issued by companies other than the investment company (regardless of the type of companies) so that no more than 5% of total assets can be invested in any one company and no more than 10% of an outside corporation's voting securities are owned by the investment company. There are no restrictions on the other 25%, making it possible to have as much as 30% of the fund's assets in the securities of one issuer, but not 33%.

11. **A.** Accumulation does not refer to a purchase option. The pay-in period for an annuity is known as the accumulation stage. A single premium deferred annuity is an annuity with a lump-sum investment, with payment of benefits deferred until the annuitant elects to receive them. Periodic payment deferred annuities allow a person to make periodic payments over time. Immediate annuities allow an investor to deposit a lump sum with the insurance company payout of the annuitant's benefits starting immediately, usually within 60 days.

12. **D.** An investor in a limited partnership is not immune from investment risk. An investor in a limited partnership could lose his entire investment through a failure of the partnership business. Liquidity is also a risk of investing in limited partnerships.

There is generally no secondary market for interests in such partnerships. Tax credits and deductions of the business itself do flow through to the limited partners. The general partner, not the limited partners, is liable for the full amount of any loan taken out in the name of the partnership that is titled a nonrecourse loan. Investors assume some responsibility for recourse loans.

13. **D.** General partners (GPs) must maintain a financial interest in the partnership and generally do not receive distributions from profits before those paid to the limited partners. The GP is the active investor in a limited partnership and assumes responsibility for all aspects of the partnership's operations and has a fiduciary relationship to the LPs. The GP, as a fiduciary, cannot borrow from the partnership, compete with the partnership, or commingle personal funds with partnership funds.

14. **C.** Money randomly withdrawn (not annuitized) is handled under LIFO tax rules; money invested in an annuity represents the investor's cost basis; and on withdrawal, the amount exceeding the investor's cost basis is taxed as ordinary income. Taxes on earned dividends, interest, and capital gains are not paid annually. They are deferred and paid later, when the owner withdraws money from the contract.

15. **A.** An investor who sells a call on a security he owns to reduce the volatility of the stock's returns and generate income with the premium has written a covered call. An investor who buys a put on a security he has sold short has protected his short position, but he has not written a covered call. An investor who sells a call on an index that contains some of the securities he has in his portfolio may have partially protected his security position, but he has not written a covered call. If an investor were long all of the stocks in the entire index in the exact proportion as each stock is represented in the index, the position would be covered.

QUICK QUIZ ANSWERS

Quick Quiz 5.1

1. **B.**
2. **A.**
3. **B.**
4. **B.**
5. **A.**
6. **B.**
7. **A.**
8. **A.**

Quick Quiz 5.2

1. **D.**
2. **B.**
3. **A.**
4. **C.**

Quick Quiz 5.3

1. **D.**
2. **A.**
3. **B.**
4. **C.**

Quick Quiz 5.4

1. **C.**
2. **B.**
3. **A.**

Quick Quiz 5.5

1. **C.**
2. **D.**
3. **A.**
4. **B.**

Quick Quiz 5.6

1. **C.**
2. **A.**
3. **D.**
4. **B.**

Quick Quiz 5.7

1. **B.**
2. **A.**
3. **D.**
4. **C.**

Quick Quiz 5.8

1. **T.**   An investor who purchases a limited partnership is required to provide a statement of net worth.

2. **F.**   Limited partnerships typically have a very limited secondary market. They are generally not liquid.

3. **F.**   Passive losses can only offset passive income.

4. **T.**   The general partner is fully liable for all partnership losses and debts.

5. **F.**   To maintain limited liability, limited partners must not be involved in the day-to-day management of the partnership.

6. **T.**   Tax deductions, capital gains, and cash distributions are potential rewards for limited partnership investors.

Quick Quiz 5.9

1. **B** and **C.**

2. **A** and **D.**

3. **A** and **D.**

4. **B** and **C.**

5. **A** and **C.**

6. **B** and **D.**

Quick Quiz 5.10

1. **A.** Options are a type of derivative because they derive their values from the values of other investment instruments.

2. **C.** 10 options

3. **D.** ABC common stock

4. **A.** Buy; a call is the right to buy stock

5. **C.** 1,000; 100 shares per contract at 10 contracts

6. **B.** The put buyer has the right to sell stock to a put writer who is obligated to buy that stock.

7. **B.** Options are in-the-money when they are worth exercising. Calls are worth exercising when the strike price is less than the market price of the underlying stock.

Quick Quiz 5.11

1. **C.**

2. **A.**

3. **D.**

4. **C.**

5. **A** and **D.**

6. **B** and **C.**

7. **B.**

8. **A** and **C.**

9. **B.**

10. **D.**

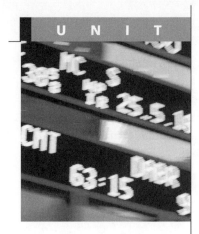

6

Trading Securities

After the initial offering, many stocks and bonds are bought and sold on exchanges in a two-way auction process. The major exchanges include the New York Stock Exchange (NYSE), the American Stock Exchange (AMEX), and Nasdaq. Other trades take place in the nationwide network of broker/dealers known as the **over-the-counter (OTC) market**. This Unit introduces the terminology and language of trading securities.

The Series 65 exam will include approximately four questions on the material presented in this Unit. ■

When you have completed this Unit, you should be able to:

■ **compare** and contrast the exchanges and the over-the-counter market; and

■ **identify** the features and uses of market, stop, and limit orders.

MARKETS AND MARKET PARTICIPANTS

SECURITIES MARKETS

There are two major markets for securities. The **primary market** is the market in which the proceeds of sales go to the issuer of the securities sold. The **secondary market** is where previously issued securities are bought and sold. This Unit will focus on secondary market trading.

Exchange Market

The **exchange market** is composed of the NYSE and other exchanges on which listed securities are traded. *Listed security* refers to any security listed for trading on an exchange. Each stock exchange requires corporations to meet certain criteria before it will allow their stock to be listed for trading on the exchange.

Location. Listed markets, such as the NYSE and AMEX, maintain central marketplaces and trading floors.

Pricing System. Listed markets operate as double-auction markets. Floor brokers compete to execute trades at favorable prices.

Price Dynamics. When a floor broker representing a buyer executes a trade by purchasing stock at a current offer price higher than the last sale, a **plus tick** occurs (market up); when a selling broker accepts a current bid price below the last sale price, a **minus tick** occurs (market down).

Specialist. The specialist maintains an orderly market and provides price continuity. He fills limit and market orders for the public and trades for his own account to either stabilize or facilitate trading when imbalances in supply and demand occur.

The specialist's chief function is to maintain a fair and orderly market in the stocks for which he is responsible. An additional function is to minimize price disparities that may occur at the opening of daily trading. He does this by buying or selling, as a dealer, stock from his own inventory only when a need for such intervention exists. Otherwise, the specialist lets public supply and demand set the stock's price.

Over-the-Counter (OTC) Market

The OTC market functions as an interdealer market in which **unlisted securities**—that is, securities not listed on any exchange—trade.

In the OTC market, securities dealers across the country are connected by computer and telephone. Thousands of securities are traded OTC, including stocks, corporate bonds, and all municipal and US government securities.

Location. No central marketplace facilitates OTC trading. Trading takes place over the phone, over computer networks, and in trading rooms across the country.

Pricing System. The OTC market is an **interdealer network**. Registered market makers compete to post the best bid and ask prices. The OTC market is a negotiated market.

Market Makers. Market makers stand ready to buy and sell at least the minimum trading unit, usually 100 shares (or any larger amount they have indicated), in each stock in which they have published bid and ask quotes. Market makers sell from their inventory at their asking price and buy for their inventory at the bid price.

Price Dynamics. When a market maker raises its bid price to attract sellers, the stock price rises; when a market maker lowers its ask price to attract buyers, the stock price declines.

TAKE NOTE

The differences between the OTC and NYSE markets are summarized below.

OTC	NYSE
Securities prices determined through negotiation	Securities prices determined through auction bidding
Regulated by NASD	Regulated by the NYSE
Broker/dealers must register with both the SEC and NASD	Broker/dealers must be registered with the SEC and Exchange members
Traded at many locations across the country	Traded only on the NYSE floor

Exchange = Listed securities = prices determined by auction

OTC = Unlisted securities = prices determined by negotiation

Government and municipal bonds and unlisted corporate stocks and bonds trade in the OTC market.

THE ROLE OF BROKER/DEALERS

Most securities firms act as both brokers and dealers but not in the same transaction.

Brokers

Brokers are agents that arrange trades for clients and charge commissions. Brokers do not buy shares for inventory but facilitate trades between buyers and sellers.

Dealers

Dealers, or **principals**, buy and sell securities for their own accounts. This practice is often called **position trading**. When selling from their inventories, dealers charge the buying customers a markup rather than a commission. A **markup** is the difference between the current interdealer offering price and the actual price charged the client. When a price to a client includes a dealer's markup, it is called the **net price**.

TAKE NOTE

The term *principal* has several meanings in the securities industry. A broker/dealer acts as a principal in a dealer transaction. A principal of a firm is a person who acts in a supervisory capacity. *Principal* can also mean the face value of a bond or asset in a trust.

A firm cannot act as both a broker and a dealer in the same transaction.

EXAMPLE

A firm cannot make a market in a stock, mark up that stock, and then add an agency commission. If the firm acts as a broker, it may charge a commission. If it acts as a dealer, it may charge a markup or markdown. Violation of this practice is called **making a hidden profit**.

Broker	Dealer
Acts as an agent, transacting orders on the client's behalf	Acts as a principal, dealing in securities for its own account and at its own risk
Charges a commission	Charges a markup or markdown
Is not a market maker	Makes markets and/or takes positions (long or short) in securities
Must disclose its role and the amount of its commission to the client	Must disclose its role to the client, but not necessarily the amount or source of the markup or markdown

TAKE NOTE

An easy way to remember these relationships is to memorize the following letters.

BAC/DPP—**B**rokers act as **A**gents for **C**ommissions/**D**ealers act as **P**rincipals for **P**rofits.

ABCD—**A**gents that are **B**rokers for **C**ommissions that must be **D**isclosed

BIDS, OFFERS, AND QUOTES

A **quote** is a dealer's current bid and offer on a security. The **current bid** is the highest price at which the dealer will buy, and the **current offer** is the lowest price at which the dealer will sell. The difference between the bid and ask is known as the **spread**.

When a customer buys a stock from a firm acting as principal, the dealer marks up the ask price to reach the net price to the customer. Likewise, when a customer sells stock to a firm acting as principal, the dealer marks down from the bid price to reach the net proceeds to the customer.

 EXAMPLE

If WXYZ is quoted as 43.25 to .50, and the dealer wants a half-point for the trade, a customer buying would pay 44 net (43.50 + .50), and a customer selling would receive 42.75 net (43.25 − .50).

TYPES OF ORDERS

Many types of orders are available to customers.

Price

Orders that restrict the price of the transaction include the following:

■ **Market**—executed immediately at the market price

■ **Limit**—limits the amount paid or received for securities

■ **Stop**—becomes a market order if the stock reaches or goes through the stop price

■ **Stop limit**—entered as a stop order and changed to a limit order if the stock hits or goes through the trigger price

Time

Orders based on time considerations include the following:

■ **Day**—expires if not filled by the end of the day

■ **Good till canceled**—does not expire until filled or canceled

■ **Fill or kill**—must be executed immediately in full or be canceled

■ **Immediate or cancel**—must be executed immediately in full or in part; any part of the order that remains unfilled is canceled

■ **All or none**—must be executed in full but not immediately

Effective October 17, 2005, the NYSE eliminated fill-or-kill (FOK) and all-or-none (AON) orders. They are still available on other markets

QUICK QUIZ 6.1

Matching

   A. Fill or kill
   B. All or none
   C. Immediate or cancel

___ 1. Execute immediately in its entirety or cancel

___ 2. Execute in its entirety but not necessarily immediately

___ 3. Execute as much as possible immediately; cancel the rest

Quick Quiz answers can be found at the end of the Unit.

Market Orders

A **market order** is sent immediately to the floor for execution without restrictions or limits. It is executed immediately at the current market price and has priority over all other types of orders. A market order to buy is executed at the lowest offering price available; a market order to sell is executed at the highest bid price available. As long as the security is trading, a market order guarantees execution.

Limit Orders

In a **limit order,** a customer limits the acceptable purchase or selling price. A limit order can be executed only at the specified price or better. *Better* means lower in a buy order and higher in a sell order. If the order cannot be executed at the market, the commission house broker leaves the order with the specialist, who records the trade in the order book and executes the order if and when the market price meets the limit order price.

Risks and Disadvantages of Limit Orders

A customer who enters a limit order risks missing the chance to buy or sell, especially if the market moves away from the limit price. The market may never go as low as the buy limit price or as high as the sell limit price.

Sometimes limit orders are not executed, even if a limit price is met. The most common explanation for this is stock ahead.

■ **Stock ahead.** Limit orders on the specialist's book for the same price are arranged according to when they were received. If a limit order at a specific price was not filled, chances are another order at the same price took precedence; that is, there was stock ahead.

Short Sales

Selling short is a technique to profit from the decline in a stock's price. The short seller initially borrows stock from a broker/dealer to sell at the market. The investor expects the stock price to decline enough to allow him to buy shares at a lower price and replace the borrowed stock at a later date. Unless the stock price declines to zero, the short seller is obligated to buy the stock and replace the borrowed shares to close the short position.

Short sales are risky because if the stock price rises instead of falls, an investor still must buy the shares to replace the borrowed stock—and a stock's price can rise without limit. Therefore, the position has unlimited risk.

Stop Orders

A **stop order**, also known as a **stop loss order**, may be entered to protect a profit or prevent a loss if the stock begins to move in the wrong direction.

The stop order becomes a market order once the stock trades at or moves through a certain price, known as the **stop price**. Stop orders for listed stocks are usually left with and executed by the specialist. No guarantee exists that the executed price will be the stop price, unlike the price on a limit order.

A trade at the stop price **triggers** the order, which then becomes a market order.

A stop order takes two trades to execute:

■ **Trigger**—the trigger transaction at or through the stop price activates the trade

■ **Execution**—the stop order becomes a market order and is executed at the market price, completing the trade

Stop Limit Order

A stop limit order is a stop order that, once triggered, becomes a limit order instead of a market order.

EXAMPLE

An order that reads "sell 100 COD at 52 stop, 51.50 limit" means that the stop will be activated at or below 52. Because a 51.50 limit applies, the order to sell cannot be executed below 51.50.

TAKE NOTE

The uses of buy and sell stop orders are summarized below.

Buy Stop Orders

■ Protect against loss in a short stock position

■ Protect a gain from a short stock position

■ Establish a long position when a breakout occurs above the line of resistance

Sell Stop Orders

■ Protect against loss in a long stock position

■ Protect a gain from a long stock position

■ Establish a short position when a breakout occurs below the line of support (i.e., stock prices decline below low level)

TEST TOPIC ALERT

There is a danger in using stop orders in that once they are triggered, the marketplace receives an increase of sell orders in a falling market and buy orders in a rising market. This can have the tendency to accelerate the direction of the market; sell stops in a bearish market, buy stops in a bullish one.

QUICK QUIZ 6.2

1. Which of the following is appropriate justification for selling a stock short?

   A. To cut losses on a long position
   B. To benefit from a decline in the price of the stock
   C. To benefit from a rise in the price of the stock
   D. To seek a modest potential reward with limited risk

2. When viewing several of your client's trade confirmations, you notice that a recent purchase was made of ABC stock where there was no commission indicated while a sale took place of DEF stock in which the commission listed was $55. From this information you could determine that

   I.   ABC was purchased in an agency transactions
   II. ABC was purchased in a principal transactions
   III. DEF was sold in an agency transaction
   IV. DEF was sold in a principal transactions

   A. I and III
   B. I and IV
   C. II and III
   D. II and V

HOTSHEETS

For your convenience, Unit HotSheets summarizing the key points are located at the end of the manual on perforated pages.

UNIT TEST

1. An exchange specialist is a(n)

   A. trader who makes a market in OTC stocks and ADRs

   B. floor broker on the New York Stock Exchange who only executes trades for other brokers in return for commissions

   C. dealer on the New York Stock Exchange who executes orders for other brokers and who also acts as a market maker charged with the responsibility of keeping an orderly market in designated stocks

   D. electronic brokerage concern that executes trades online and through specialized trading order executing services

2. Which of the following types of orders does NOT restrict the price at which an order is executed?

   A. Limit

   B. Stop

   C. Market

   D. Stop limit

3. A broker/dealer acting as a principal in a trade would

   A. add a markup to the bid price when offering shares to a client

   B. add a markup to the offering price when selling shares to a client

   C. must always disclose the amount of markup on a client's confirmation statement

   D. must disclose to clients the amount of earnings he made on principal transactions in excess of the amount he would have made had he charged a commission

4. Which of the descriptions of time-related orders is NOT true?

   A. A fill-or-kill order must be executed immediately and the remainder of the shares not sold or purchased are canceled.

   B. An immediate or cancel order must be executed immediately and if the entire order is not filled, any remainder is canceled.

   C. A not held order allows the floor broker to use his judgment as to price and timing of the transaction.

   D. An all-or-none order must be filled in full but not immediately.

5. Which of the following orders would be most likely to add fuel to a bullish stock market?

   A. Buy limit

   B. Buy stop

   C. Sell limit

   D. Sell stop

ANSWERS AND RATIONALES

1. **C.** A specialist is a dealer on the NYSE who executes orders for other brokers and who also acts as a market maker charged with the responsibility of keeping an orderly market in designated stocks. A specialist must have sufficient capital to buy and sell from his own account in order to maintain a liquid and orderly market. A trader who makes a market in OTC stocks and ADRs is a market maker in the OTC market and not a specialist on an exchange. A specialist is not limited to floor brokerage on the New York Stock Exchange. This describes a commission house broker (CHB) or a $2 broker. A specialist is not an electronic brokerage concern that executes trades online and through specialized trading order executing services. A specialist executes trades on an exchange.

2. **C.** A market order does not reflect or restrict the price at which a security is executed. A limit order limits the amount to be paid or received for securities. A limit order becomes a market order if the stock reaches or goes through the stop price. A stop limit order becomes a limit order if the stock hits or goes through the trigger price.

3. **B.** When selling a security to a public customer, the broker/dealer adds his markup to the ask/offer (not the bid) price. A broker does not add a markup to the bid price when offering shares to a client. The broker/dealer would mark down the bid price. A broker/dealer does not usually have to disclose to the client the amount of markup on a client's confirmation statement. If a commission were charged, however, it would have to be indicated on the confirmation statement.

4. **A.** A fill-or-kill order must be executed upon presentation for the full amount of the order, or the entire order is canceled; there is no remainder. An immediate or cancel order must be executed immediately, and the remainder of the shares left unsold or not purchased are canceled. A not held order allows the floor broker to use his judgment as to price and timing of the transaction. An all-or-none order must be completed in full but not immediately.

5. **B.** Buy stop orders are placed above the current market price and are usually used by those with short positions. As prices increase, these stop orders are triggered, sending more buy orders to the trading floors.

QUICK QUIZ ANSWERS

Quick Quiz 6.1

1. **A.**

2. **B.**

3. **C.**

Quick Quiz 6.2

1. **B.**   Selling short does not reduce the risk of a long position—the investor is selling borrowed, not owned, stock. The appropriate time to sell short is when one anticipates that the stock price is about to drop. The investor wants to sell at a high price and buy later at a lower price. Both the reward and risk potential of selling short are high. If the stock price moves down dramatically, the investor can reap a large gain. If it moves up dramatically, the investor can lose a great deal of money.

2. **C.**   Whenever a trade is made without a commission indicated on the confirmation, it means that a markup or markdown was charged. That makes it a dealer or principal transaction. Commissions are always disclosed on agency transactions.

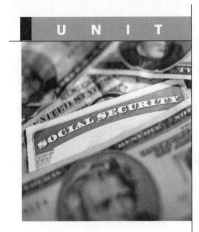

7

Retirement Plans

Retirement plans allow investors to accumulate resources to fund their retirement. Individuals accomplish this through business-sponsored retirement plans, personal plans, or individual and corporate retirement plans. To encourage Americans to save for retirement, Congress has passed legislation that allows investors to invest in certain retirement plans on a tax-deductible and/or tax-deferred basis.

In 2001, the President of the United States signed into law the Economic Growth and Tax Relief Reconciliation Act of 2001. The Series 65 exam will include approximately 4 questions on the material presented in this Unit. ■

When you have completed this Unit, you should be able to:

- **describe** the unique features of traditional, Roth, and simplified employee pension plan individual retirement accounts as well as Coverdell education savings accounts;

- **explain** the purpose of the Employee Retirement Income Security Act of 1974 and its primary features including the fiduciary obligations under the Uniform Prudent Investor Act;

- **define and differentiate** between individual retirement accounts, Keogh plans, 403(b) plans, qualified corporate retirement plans, and nonqualified corporate retirement plans; and

- **understand** distributions from qualified plans and individual retirement accounts.

INDIVIDUAL RETIREMENT ARRANGEMENTS (IRAs)

TAKE NOTE

Although *individual retirement arrangements* is the technical IRS term, (not tested), because everyone refers to these as individual retirement accounts (IRAs), we're going to use the common phrase to avoid confusion

Individual retirement accounts (IRAs) were created to encourage people to save for their retirement. All employed individuals may open and contribute to an IRA. Four types of IRAs are available, with different contribution, tax, and distribution characteristics: traditional IRAs, simplified employee pension plan (SEP) IRAs, Roth IRAs, and Coverdell education savings accounts (Coverdell ESAs).

TRADITIONAL IRAs

A **traditional IRA** allows a maximum **tax-deductible** annual contribution of the lesser of $4,000 per individual or $8,000 per couple, or 100% of earned income for the taxable years 2006–2007. The income and capital gains earned in the account are tax deferred until the funds are withdrawn. For those covered by qualified employer plans, the tax deductibility of contributions to traditional IRAs is phased out as income increases.

TAKE NOTE

The contribution limit for IRAs is scheduled to increase from its current $4,000 level to $5,000 per individual by the year 2008. After 2008, the contribution limit will be adjusted annually for inflation. These limits will also apply to the total combined contribution that might be made to a traditional IRA and a Roth IRA. The yearly increases will be phased in as follows.

Year	IRA Limit Contribution
2006	$4,000
2007	$4,000
2008+	$5,000

ROTH IRAs

The Taxpayer Relief Act of 1997 created the Roth IRA. Contributions to Roth IRAs, unlike those of a traditional IRAs, are not tax deductible. Regular contributions may always be withdrawn tax free because they are made with nondeductible contributions.

Earnings accumulated, however, may be withdrawn tax free after five years, following the initial deposit, provided the:

■ account holder is 59½ or older;

■ money withdrawn is used for the first-time purchase of a principal residence (up to $10,000);

■ account holder has died or become disabled;

■ money is used to pay for authorized higher education expenses; or

■ money is used to pay for certain medical expenses or medical insurance premiums.

Contribution Limits

Contribution limits to Roth IRAs are the same as those for traditional IRAs. For an individual in 2007, the contribution limit is the lesser of $4,000 or 100% of earned income. In addition, a married employee may contribute an additional $4,000 to a nonworking spouse's Roth IRA. Unlike a traditional IRA, contributions may be made past age 70½ as long as the taxpayer has earned income.

An individual may contribute to both a traditional and a Roth IRA. However, the maximum combined contribution is $4,000 (or $5,000, if 50 or older).

Eligibility Requirements

Anyone with earned income is eligible to open a Roth IRA provided the person's AGI falls below specified income levels. The following numbers are effective January 1, 2007. A single person with an AGI of $99,000 or less may contribute the full amount to a Roth IRA. The ability to contribute to a Roth IRA is gradually phased out if the taxpayer's AGI is between $99,000 and $114,000.

For married taxpayers who file joint tax returns, the AGI limit is $156,000, with the deduction phased out for couples whose income is between $156,000 and $166,000.

CATCH-UP CONTRIBUTIONS FOR OLDER IRA OWNERS

The **Economic Growth and Tax Relief Reconciliation Act of 2001, (EGTRRA)**, was the source of the legislation permitting certain individuals to make additional contributions to their IRAs. Individuals aged 50 and older are allowed to make **catch-up contributions** to their IRAs above the scheduled maximum annual contribution limit, which will enable them to save more for retirement. These catch-up payments can go either to a traditional IRA or to a Roth IRA.

Year	Additional Catch-Up Amount Allowed
2006+	$1,000

TEST TOPIC ALERT   The exam will want you to know that EGTRRA is responsible for the catch-up provisions.

SEP IRAs

In 2007, self-employed individuals and corporations may contribute the lesser of 25% of their postcontribution incomes or $45,000 in tax-deductible dollars each year to SEP IRAs established by employees. Other characteristics are the same as those of traditional IRAs.

IRA Withdrawals

Distributions without penalty may begin after age 59½ and must begin by April 1 of the year following the year an individual turns 70½. Distributions before age 59½ may be subject to a tax penalty and withdrawals less than the required minimum distributions (RMDs), after age 70½ may also incur tax penalties.

Withdrawals may be made in lump sums, in varying amounts, or in regular installments and, to the extent withdrawals are from tax-deductible contributions, are taxable as ordinary income. When there are both deductible and nondeductible contributions, a formula is used whereby a portion of the withdrawal represents a nontaxable return of principal. Withdrawals before age 59½ are also subject to a 10% early withdrawal penalty unless they are due to death, disability, first-time purchase of a primary residence ($10,000 maximum), qualified higher education expenses for immediate family members, (including grandchildren, but not nieces or nephews), or certain medical expenses in excess of 7.5% of adjusted gross income (AGI).

Withdrawals must begin by April 1 of the year following the year in which the account owner reaches age 70½, and they must meet minimum Internal Revenue Code (IRC) distribution requirements or incur a 50% penalty on the amounts falling short of the minimum.

One respect in which the Roth IRA differs from other retirement plans is that the age 70½ is irrelevant. There are no required minimum distributions and, as long as the individual has earned income, contributions may be made at any age.

There is one other way to tap your IRA before age 59½ without penalty—through the substantially equal periodic exception. The **substantially equal periodic payment exception** under IRS rule 72t states that if you receive IRA payments at least annually based on your life expectancy (or the joint life expectancies of you and your beneficiary), the withdrawals are not subject to the 10% penalty. The IRS has tables for determining the appropriate amount of each payment at any given age.

EXAMPLE   An IRA owner who reaches age 70½ on January 1, 2007, must begin withdrawals by April 1, 2008.

All distributions are treated as taxable income in the year in which received. Annuitized IRA distributions can be made to the account owner or jointly to the owner and spouse. If the account owner dies, payments are made to a designated beneficiary.

Nondeductible Capital Withdrawals

IRA investors who contribute after-tax dollars to an IRA are not taxed on those funds when they are withdrawn from the account, but taxpayers are taxed at the ordinary income tax rate when they withdraw funds resulting from investment gains or income.

EXAMPLE A client has invested $25,000 in after-tax dollars in an IRA currently worth $75,000. If the client were to withdraw $75,000, only $50,000 would be taxable.

COVERDELL EDUCATION SAVINGS ACCOUNTS

The Taxpayer Relief Act of 1997 also created **Coverdell ESAs,** which allow after-tax contributions for student beneficiaries. Contributions must be made in cash and must be made on or before the date on which the beneficiary attains age 18 unless the beneficiary is a **special needs beneficiary**—an individual who because of a physical, mental, or emotional condition requires additional time to complete their education. Coverdell ESAs fund educational expenses of a designated beneficiary by allowing after-tax (nondeductible) contributions to accumulate on a tax-deferred basis.

When distributions are made from a Coverdell ESA, the earnings portion of the distribution is excluded from income when it is used to pay qualified education expenses. Withdrawn earnings are taxed and subject to a 10% penalty when they are not used to pay qualified education expenses.

TAKE NOTE If the money is not used by a beneficiary's 30th birthday, it must be distributed and is subject to ordinary income taxes and a 10% penalty.

Under EGTRRA, the maximum annual contribution limit to a Coverdell ESA is $2,000 per beneficiary. In addition to qualified higher education expenses (postsecondary education), the account can also be used for elementary and secondary education expenses and for public, private, or religious schools.

The contribution to a Coverdell ESA may be limited depending on the amount of AGI and filing status.

Allowable Contribution	Single Filers	Joint Filers
Full contribution of $2,000 at AGI of and below	$ 95,000	$190,000
Partial phaseout begins at	$ 95,001	$190,001
No contributions may be made at AGI of and above	$110,000	$220,000

TAKE NOTE   There is nothing to prevent more than one individual from contributing to a Coverdell ESA; the annual limit applies to each beneficiary. Parents and grandparents can contribute to a single account, as long as the $2,000 limit per child is not exceeded in any given year.

Other changes made by the EGTRRA of 2001 include:

■ provisions that would allow contributions to continue past age 18 for beneficiaries with special needs;

■ extending the period during which corrective withdrawals can be made to avoid the early distribution and excess contribution penalties; and

■ allowing Coverdell ESA contributions, for any year, to be made up to April 15 of the following year.

TAKE NOTE   The early withdrawal penalties for all IRAs are waived in the event of death or disability.

TEST TOPIC ALERT   Assume questions are about traditional IRAs unless they specifically state otherwise. Below are some key test points about Roth IRAs and Coverdell ESAs.

ROTH IRA

■ Maximum (current) contribution is $4,000 per year per individual.

■ Contributions are not tax deductible.

■ Distributions are tax free if taken after age 59½ and money has been in the account for at least five years.

■ Distributions are not required to begin at age 70½.

■ No 10% early distribution penalty for death, disability, and first-time home purchase.

■ A minor can be named as beneficiary.

COVERDELL ESAs

■ Contribution limit is $2,000 per year per child until the child's 18th birthday.

■ Contributions can be made by parents and other adults; the total for one child is still $2,000.

■ Contributions are not tax deductible.

■ Distributions are tax free if they are taken before age 30 and used for eligible education expenses.

CHARACTERISTICS OF IRAs

Participation in an IRA

Any taxpayer younger than age 70½ who reports earned income for a given tax year may contribute to an IRA. Roth IRA contributions may occur at any age. Passive income from investments is not earned income. Contributions to an IRA may be made up to April 15 of the year following the tax year for which the contribution was made.

IRA Custodians

Taxpayers can appoint IRA custodians of their choice, selecting from securities broker/dealers, banks and savings institutions, insurance carriers, credit unions, and mutual fund distributors.

IRA Contributions

The maximum annual IRA contribution is $4,000 or 100% of earned income, whichever is less, for an employed individual and $4,000 for a spousal IRA, whether or not the spouse is employed.

The deductibility of an individual's contribution is reduced or eliminated if he participates in an employer-sponsored retirement plan and earns more than a specified amount.

 EXAMPLE

A married couple who is ineligible to participate in a qualified plan and whose combined income is $120,000 may contribute and deduct a total of $8,000 ($10,000 if both are 50 or older). No deduction is allowed for a married couple who is eligible to participate in a qualified plan and whose combined income is $100,000 (for 2007) or more. Nevertheless, their contributions are permitted.

IRA contributions for a specific taxable year may be made anytime from January 1st of that year through the required filing date of that year's return, (generally April 15th of the next year, unless the 15th falls on a holiday or weekend). If the individual obtains a filing extension, the deadline is still April 15th.

IRA owners may withdraw any or all funds in their accounts at any time, although the funds attributable to earnings and deductible contributions are subject to income tax and may be subject to early withdrawal penalties.

Excess Contributions

Annual IRA contributions exceeding the maximum allowed are subject to a 6% penalty tax if the excess is not removed by the time the taxpayer files a tax return, but no later than April 15th.

IRA Investments

Funds in an IRA account may be used to buy stocks, bonds, mutual funds, UITs, limited partnerships, government securities, US government-issued gold and silver coins, annuities, and many other investments.

IRA investments should be relatively conservative and should reflect the investor's age and risk tolerance profile. Because an IRA serves as a source of retirement funds, it is important that the account be managed for adequate long-term growth.

Ineligible Investments

Collectibles, including antiques, gems, rare coins, works of art, and stamps, are not acceptable IRA investments. Life insurance contracts (such as cash value and term) may not be purchased in an IRA. Tax-free municipal bonds, municipal bond funds, and UITs are also inappropriate for an IRA because their yields are typically lower than those of other similar investments, and the income generated is taxable on withdrawal from the IRA.

Ineligible Investment Practices

No short sales of stock, speculative option strategies, or margin account trading is permitted in an IRA or any other retirement plan. Covered call writing is allowed.

Ineligible Investments	Ineligible Investment Practices
Collectibles	Short sales of stock
Whole life insurance	Speculative option strategies
Term life Insurance	Margin account trading

Moving IRAs

Individuals may move their funds and investments from one IRA to another IRA through a rollover or transfer.

Rollovers

An IRA account owner may take temporary possession of the account funds to move the retirement account to another custodian. The account owner may do so only once per 12-month period, and the rollover must be completed within 60 calendar days of the funds' withdrawal from the original plan. However, 100% of the withdrawn amount must be rolled into the new account, or the unrolled balance will be subject to income tax and, if applicable, early withdrawal penalty.

A participant in a business-sponsored qualified plan may move his plan assets to a rollover IRA (traditional, not Roth) if he leaves the company. If the rollover transfer is made directly from the qualified plan to an IRA (direct transfer), the participant never takes possession of the funds. If the participant does take possession of the funds, he must complete the rollover within 60 calendar days of withdrawing the funds from the qualified plan.

When the participant takes possession of the funds from a qualified plan to make a rollover, the payor of the distribution must, by law, withhold 20% of the distribution as a withholding tax. The participant must, nonetheless, roll over 100% of the plan distribution, including the funds withheld, or be subject to income tax and, if applicable, early withdrawal penalty.

TAKE NOTE

Rollovers by nonspouse beneficiaries of certain retirement plan distributions. Effective January 1, 2007, the Pension Protection Act of 2006 amends the Internal Revenue Code of 1986 to allow nonspouse beneficiaries to roll over qualified retirement plan distributions to an inherited traditional IRA. Using the term *rollover* may be confusing because these distributions must be made via direct trustee-to-trustee transfer, and any checks made out to the beneficiary are not eligible for rollover. The IRA must be set up as an inherited IRA, with minimum distributions taken under the rules that apply to beneficiaries. It is possible that this will be tested on your exam.

TAKE NOTE

Direct rollovers from retirement plans to Roth IRAs. Effective January 1, 2008, the Pension Protection Act of 2006 amends the Internal Revenue Code of 1986 to allow rollovers from qualified retirement plans directly to Roth IRAs, providing the client meets the requirements for converting a traditional IRA to a Roth IRA. The two main requirements are that the client must report the amount converted as income in the year of the conversion (or rollover) and have modified adjusted gross income of less than $100,000 not counting the amount converted. We do not expect this to be tested until the middle of 2008.

EXAMPLE

A 50-year-old individual with $100,000 in his company retirement plan changes employers. His pension plan may be distributed to him as a rollover in a lump-sum payment, minus the mandatory 20% withholding of $20,000. He must then deposit $100,000 in an IRA rollover account within 60 days. Any portion not rolled over, including the $20,000 withheld, is considered a distribution subject to ordinary income tax and early withdrawal penalty. If he deposits the entire $100,000 into the IRA, he must apply on his next income tax return for a refund of the $20,000 withheld.

Transfers

In a direct transfer of an IRA or a qualified retirement plan, account assets are sent directly from one IRA custodian to another, and the account owner never takes possession of the funds. The number of IRA transfers an account owner may make per year is unlimited. Transfers from qualified plans to IRAs generally make better sense than rollovers because the 20% federal tax withholding does not apply to direct transfers of portfolios.

Simplified Employee Pensions (SEP IRAs)

Simplified employee pension plans (SEPs) offer self-employed persons and small businesses easy-to-administer pension plans. A SEP is a qualified plan that allows an employer to contribute money to SEP IRAs that its employees set up to receive employer contributions.

Eligibility. To be eligible, an employee must be at least 21 years of age, have performed services for the employer during at least three of the last five years, and have received at least $500 (for 2007) in compensation from the employer in the current year (the annual compensation figure is indexed for vinflation).

Participation. SEP rules require the employer allow all eligible employees to participate.

Funding. A SEP allows the employer to contribute up to 25% of an employee's salary to the employee's SEP IRA each year, up to a maximum of $45,000 per employee per year in 2007. The employer determines the level of contributions each year and must contribute the same percentage for each employee, as well as the employer.

Vesting. Participants in a SEP IRA are **fully vested** immediately, meaning that once the money is deposited in an employee's SEP IRA, it belongs to the employee.

Taxation. Employer contributions are tax deductible to the employer. Contributions are not taxable to an employee until withdrawn, and earnings in the account accumulate tax deferred. The same rules for early withdrawal from IRAs apply to SEP IRAs.

Tax Benefits

Traditional and certain SEP IRA participants may deduct contributions to their IRAs from their taxable income. The deductibility limits are lowered for individuals who are eligible for other qualified plans.

These AGI limits increase every year. Individuals who are ineligible to participate in qualified plans may deduct IRA contributions regardless of income level.

The table below outlines the IRA deductibility phaseout range for the years 2005–2007.

Year	Phaseout Range: Single Filers	Phaseout Range: Joint Filers
2005	$50,000–$60,000	$70,000–$80,000
2006	$50,000–$60,000	$75,000–$85,000
2007+	$50,000–$60,000	$80,000–$100,000

Income and capital gains earned from investments in a traditional IRA account are not taxed until the funds are withdrawn.

QUICK QUIZ 7.1

1. An individual younger than age 70½ may contribute to a traditional IRA

   A. if he has earned income
   B. provided he is not covered by a pension plan through an employer
   C. provided he does not own a Keogh plan
   D. provided his adjusted gross income is between $40,000 and $50,000 if married, and $25,000 and $35,000 if single

2. If a 50-year-old individual wants to withdraw funds from her IRA, the withdrawal will be taxed as

   A. ordinary income
   B. ordinary income plus a 10% penalty
   C. capital gains
   D. capital gains plus a 10% penalty

3. Premature distribution from an IRA is generally subject to a

   A. 5% penalty plus tax
   B. 6% penalty plus tax
   C. 10% penalty plus tax
   D. 50% penalty plus tax

4. Who of the following will not incur a penalty on an IRA withdrawal?

   A. Man who has just become totally disabled
   B. Woman who turned 59 a month before the withdrawal
   C. Woman, age 50, who decides on early retirement
   D. Man in his early 40s who uses the money to buy a second home

5. Which of the following statements regarding IRAs is NOT true?

   A. IRA rollovers must be completed within 60 days of receipt of the distribution.
   B. Cash value life insurance is a permissible IRA investment, but term insurance is not.
   C. The investor must be younger than age 70½ to open and contribute to an IRA.
   D. Distributions may begin at age 59½ and must begin by April 1 after the year in which the investor turns 70½.

6. SEP IRAs

   A. are used primarily by large corporations
   B. are used primarily by small businesses
   C. are set up by nonemployees
   D. cannot be set up by self-employed persons

7. Which of the following statements regarding both traditional IRAs and Roth IRAs is TRUE?

   A. Contributions are deductible.
   B. Withdrawals at retirement are tax free.
   C. Contribution limits are identical.
   D. To avoid penalty, distributions must begin April 1 after the year the owner reaches age 70½.

8. The maximum amount that may be invested in a Coverdell ESA in one year is

    A. $500 per parent
    B. $2,000 per child
    C. $500 per couple
    D. $2,000 per couple

Quick Quiz answers can be found at the end of the Unit.

SECTION 529 PLANS

Section 529 plans are state-operated investment plans that give families a federal tax-free way to save money for college.

There are two basic types of 529 plans: prepaid tuition plans and college savings plans. **Prepaid plans** allow donors to lock in current tuition rates by paying now for future education costs. Any adult can open a 529 plan for a future college student. The donor does not have to be related to the student.

With a 529 plan, the donor can invest a small or substantial lump sum or make periodic payments. When the student is ready for college, the donor withdraws the amount needed to pay for qualified education expenses (e.g., tuition, room and board, and books). Contributions are made with after-tax dollars. Since January 2002, qualified withdrawals became exempt from federal taxation. Taxation varies from state to state; if any tax is due on withdrawal, it is the responsibility of the student, not the donor.

A donor (typically a parent or grandparent) may contribute a maximum of $60,000 ($120,000 if married) in a single year for each Section 529 plan beneficiary without gift tax consequences. This represents a five-year advance on the (2007) $12,000 per recipient annual gift tax exclusion.

The donor of the 529 plan assets retains control of most 529 accounts and may take the money back at any time (although a 10% penalty tax may apply).

The other important points about Section 529 plans are as follows.

■   The dollar amount of allowable contribution varies from state to state and may be as high as $300,000.

■   Assets in the account remain under the donor's control even after the student is of legal age.

■   There are no income limitations on donors making contributions to a 529 plan.

■   Plans allow for monthly payments if desired by the account owner.

■   Earnings are exempt from federal taxes (as are withdrawals) if they go toward qualified postsecondary educational expenses.

■   Most states hire experienced investment management companies to manage their accounts.

■   Some states waive state taxes for residents; other states allow deductions on contributions.

■ If funds are withdrawn for purposes other than education, they are subject to a 10% penalty as well as federal income tax. States may assess their own penalties.

KEOGH (HR-10) PLANS

Keogh plans are Employee Retirement Income Security Act (ERISA)-qualified plans intended for self-employed individuals and owner-employees of unincorporated business concerns or professional practices. Included in the self-employed category are independent contractors, consultants, freelancers, and anyone else who files and pays self-employment Social Security taxes. The term *owner-employee* refers to sole proprietors.

Contributions

Contribution limits for a Keogh Plan are significantly higher than those for an IRA. In 2007, as much as $45,000 may be contributed on behalf of a plan participant. Those who are eligible for a Keogh Plan may also maintain an IRA. If the business has employees, they must be covered at the same contribution percentage as the owner in order for the plan to be nondiscriminatory.

Non-Tax-Deductible Contributions

In addition to tax-deductible contributions, a Keogh plan participant may make nondeductible contributions. The income and capital gains accumulate tax free until the owner withdraws them. However, if the voluntary contribution results in a total contribution that exceeds the annual maximum, the excess may be subject to a penalty tax.

Eligibility

Employee participation in a Keogh plan is subject to these eligibility rules.

■ **Full-time employees** are employees who receive compensation for at least 1,000 hours of work per year.

■ **Tenured employees** are employees who have completed one or more years of continuous employment

■ **Adult employees** are employees 21 years and older.

Comparison of IRAs and Keogh Plans

Keogh plans and IRAs are designed to encourage individuals to set aside funds for retirement income. Although both IRAs and Keoghs are tax advantaged, an IRA does not involve employer contributions and, thus, is not a plan qualified by ERISA. The principal similarities between Keoghs and IRAs are listed below.

- **Tax deferral of contributions to plans.** Taxes are deferred on contributions until the individual receives distributions.

- **Tax sheltered.** Investment income and capital gains are not taxed until withdrawn.

- **Contributions.** Only cash may be contributed to a plan. In the event of a rollover or transfer, cash and securities from the transferring account can be deposited.

- **Distributions.** Distributions without penalty can begin as early as age 59½.

- **Penalties for early withdrawal.** The individual pays income tax on the total amount withdrawn, plus a 10% penalty. Early withdrawals without penalty are permitted in the event of death or disability.

- **Payout options.** Distributions may be in a lump sum or periodic payments.

- **Beneficiary.** Upon the planholder's death, payments are made to a designated beneficiary (or beneficiaries).

QUICK QUIZ 7.2

1. Which of the following may participate in a Keogh plan?

    I.   Self-employed doctor
    II. Analyst who makes money giving speeches outside regular working hours
    III. Individual with a full-time job who also has income from freelancing
    IV. Corporate executive who receives $5,000 in stock options from his corporation

    A. I only
    B. I and II
    C. I, II and III
    D. I, II, III and IV

2. Which of the following are characteristics of a Keogh plan?

    I.   Dividends, interest, and capital gains are tax deferred.
    II. Distributions after age 70½ are tax free.
    III. Contributions are allowed for a nonworking spouse.
    IV. Lump-sum distributions are allowed.

    A. I and II
    B. I and III
    C. I and IV
    D. II and III

3. Which would disqualify a person from participation in a Keogh plan?

    A. She turned 70 eight months ago.
    B. She has a salaried position in addition to her self-employment.
    C. Her spouse has company sponsored retirement benefits.
    D. She has an IRA.

403(b) PLANS (TAX-EXEMPT ORGANIZATIONS)

403(b) plans are tax-deferred retirement plans for employees of public school systems, (403(b) employees), and tax-exempt, nonprofit organizations such as churches and charitable institutions, (501(c)(3) employees). Qualified employees may exclude contributions from their taxable incomes provided they do not exceed limits.

Qualified annuity plans offered under Section 403(b) of the IRC, sometimes referred to as **tax-sheltered annuities (TSAs)**, are intended to encourage retirement savings. To ensure this objective, 403(b)s (like IRAs and other retirement plans) are subject to tax penalties if savings are withdrawn before a participant retires.

Tax Advantages

The following tax advantages apply to 403(b)s.

■ Contributions (which generally come from salary reduction) are excluded from a participant's gross income.

■ Participant's earnings accumulate tax free until distribution.

Income Exclusion

If an eligible employee elects to make annual contributions to a 403(b), those contributions are excluded from the employee's gross income for that year. The amount of the contribution is not reported as income, resulting in lower current income taxes.

Tax-Deferred Accumulation

Earnings in a 403(b) accumulate with no current taxation of earnings or gains and do not increase the participant's taxable income until the dollars are withdrawn at retirement, usually when that person is in a lower tax bracket.

Investments

Although, historically, annuities have been the investment vehicle of choice, 403(b) plans offer mutual funds, stocks, bonds, and CDs (but not life insurance policies) as investment vehicles. Because of the range of investments, banks, brokerage houses, savings and loans, and credit unions may offer these plans.

Eligibility Requirements

To be eligible to establish a 403(b), an employer must qualify as a:

■ public educational 403(b) institution;

■ tax-exempt 501(c)3 organization; or

■ church organization.

Tax-Exempt 501(c)3

As stated earlier, 501(c)3 organizations are tax-exempt entities specifically cited in the IRC as eligible to establish 403(b)s for their employees. Typical 501(c)3 organizations include:

■ private colleges and universities;

■ trade schools;

■ parochial schools;

■ zoos and museums;

■ research and scientific foundations;

■ religious and charitable institutions; and

■ private hospitals and medical schools.

Public Educational 403(b)

To qualify as a public educational institution, an organization must be state supported, a political subdivision, or an agency of a state. Private school systems have a separate set of qualifying rules. State-run educational systems include:

■ elementary schools;

■ secondary schools;

■ colleges and universities; and

■ medical schools.

Individuals employed by the above school systems in the following job classifications may enroll in a 403(b) plan. These include:

■ teachers and other faculty members;

■ administrators, managers, principals, supervisors, and other members of the administrative staff;

■ counselors;

■ clerical staff and maintenance workers; and

■ individuals who perform services for the institution, such as doctors or nurses.

Definition of an Employee

Only employees of qualified employers are eligible to participate in a 403(b) plan. Independent contractors are not eligible. It is the employer's responsibility to determine an individual's status or definition.

Eligibility. Similar to other qualified plans, all 403(b)s (whether employer contribution or employee elective deferral) must be made available to each full-time employee who has both reached age 21 and completed one year of service.

Plan Requirements

A 403(b) plan must meet two requirements.

■ The plan must be in writing and must be made through a plan instrument, a trust agreement, or both.

■ The employer must remit plan contributions to an annuity contract, a mutual fund, or another approved investment.

Contribution Limits

An employer can make contributions to a 403(b) solely on behalf of the covered employee or in conjunction with an employee deferral.

Salary Reduction

Year	Amount	Over Age 50 Catch-Up
2005	$14,000	$4,000
2006	$15,000	$5,000
2007	$15,550	$5,000

Employer Contributions

Employer contributions to a 403(b) are generally subject to the same maximums that apply to all defined contribution plans: the lesser of 100% of the participant's compensation or $45,000 per year.

Taxation of Distributions from a 403(b)

Distributions from a 403(b) must follow the same rules as distributions from all qualified plans. Because the employee's 403(b) contributions are made with pretax dollars and all earnings were tax deferred, any distribution is subject to ordinary income tax rates in the year it is received. A normal distribution can start at age 59½. Premature distribution is subject to a 10% penalty tax unless the distribution is made for waiver of the penalty.

Distributions must start by April 1 of the year following the year in which the participant reaches age 70½, or they will be subject to the excess accumulation tax. Once distributions begin, they must be paid annually by December 31 of each tax year following the initial distribution.

QUICK QUIZ 7.3

1. A customer works as a nurse in a public school and wants to know more about participating in the school's TSA plan. Which of the following statements is(are) TRUE?

   I.   Contributions are made with before-tax dollars.
   II. He is not eligible to participate.
   III. Distributions before age 59½ are normally subject to penalty tax.
   IV. Mutual funds and CDs are available investment vehicles.

   A. I, II and III
   B. I and III
   C. I, III and IV
   D. II only

2. The maximum annual employer contribution to a 403(b) for the 2007 plan is

   A. $9,500
   B. $15,500
   C. $25,000
   D. $45,000

3. Minimum distributions from a TSA are required when a covered participant is age

   A. 59½
   B. 70½
   C. 85
   D. There is no minimum distribution rule applicable to TSAs.

CORPORATE-SPONSORED RETIREMENT PLANS

The **Employee Retirement Income Security Act of 1974 (ERISA)** is federal legislation that regulates the establishment and management of corporate pension or retirement plans, also known as private sector plans.

All corporate pension and profit-sharing plans must be established under a trust agreement. A trustee is appointed for each plan and has a fiduciary responsibility for the plan and the beneficial owners (the plan holders).

EMPLOYEE RETIREMENT INCOME SECURITY ACT OF 1974 (ERISA)

ERISA guidelines for the regulation of retirement plans include the following.

- **Participation.** If a company offers a retirement plan, all employees must be covered if they are 21 years old or older, have one year of service, and work 1,000 hours per year.

- **Funding.** Funds contributed to the plan must be segregated from other corporate assets. The plan's trustees have a fiduciary responsibility to invest prudently and manage funds in a way that represents the best interests of all participants.

- **Vesting.** Employees must be entitled to their entire retirement benefit amounts within a certain time, even if they no longer work for the employer.

- **Communication.** The retirement plan must be in writing, and employees must be kept informed of plan benefits, availability, account status, and vesting procedure no less frequently than annually.

- **Nondiscrimination.** A uniformly applied formula determines employee benefits and contributions. Such a method ensures equitable and impartial treatment.

TAKE NOTE   ERISA is often referred to as the Pension Reform Act, but it regulates almost all types of employee benefit plans and personal retirement plans.

ERISA regulations apply to **private sector** (corporate) plans only. Plans for federal or state government workers (**public sector** plans) are not subject to ERISA.

Fiduciary Responsibility Under ERISA

Because most retirement plans were set up under trust agreements, when it came for ERISA to address fiduciary responsibilities of plan trustees, there was a long history of trust law to fall back on.

It all began with the Prudent Man Rule. That legal standard was established in 1830 by a Massachusetts Court decision (*Harvard College v. Amory*, 9 Pick. [26 Mass.] 446, 461 [1830]):

> *All that is required of a trustee to invest is, that he shall conduct himself faithfully and exercise sound discretion. He is to observe how men of prudence, discretion and intelligence manage their own affairs, not in regard to speculation, but in regard to the permanent disposition of their funds, considering the probable income, as well as the probable safety of the capital to be invested.*

Although it was possible to place common stock in a trust portfolio, the emphasis seemed to be on taking defensive positions that while preserving capital, did expose the portfolio to inflation risk. It was clear that some updating was necessary.

Beginning with the dynamic growth of the stock markets in the late 1960s, the investment practices of fiduciaries experienced significant change. As a result, the Uniform Prudent Investor Act (UPIA) was passed in 1994 as an attempt to update trust investment laws in recognition of those many changes. One of the major influences on this legislation was the growing acceptance of modern portfolio theory. The UPIA (now used in almost every state) makes five fundamental alterations in the former criteria for prudent investing. Those changes are as follows.

■ The standard of prudence is applied to any investment as part of the total portfolio, rather than to individual investments. In this context, the term *portfolio* means all of the trust's or estate's assets.

■ The trade-off in all investment between risk and return is identified as the fiduciary's primary consideration.

■ All categorical restrictions on types of investment have been removed; the trustee can invest in anything that plays an appropriate role in achieving the risk/return objectives of the trust and that meets the other requirements of prudent investing.

■ The well-accepted requirement that fiduciaries diversify their investments has been integrated into the definition of prudent investing.

■ The much-criticized former rule forbidding the trustee to delegate investment functions has been reversed. Delegation is now permitted, subject to safeguards.

With greater numbers of trustees delegating investment decisions to investment advisers, NASAA has determined that you must know how the UPIA affects your role. Here are some thoughts that will help you on the exam.

■ A trustee must invest and manage trust assets as a prudent investor would, by considering the purposes, terms, distribution requirements, and other circumstances of the trust. In satisfying this standard, the trustee must exercise reasonable care, skill, and caution.

■ A trustee's investment and management decisions about individual assets must be evaluated not in isolation but in the context of the total portfolio and as a part of an overall investment strategy with risk and return objectives that are reasonably suited to the trust.

■ Among circumstances that a trustee must consider in investing and managing trust assets are any of the following that are relevant to the trust or its beneficiaries:

— General economic conditions

— The possible effect of inflation or deflation

— The expected tax consequences of investment decisions or strategies

— The role that each asset plays within the total portfolio, including financial assets, tangible and intangible personal property, and real property

— The expected total return from income and the appreciation of capital

— Other resources of the beneficiaries

— Needs for liquidity, regularity of income, and preservation or appreciation of capital

— An asset's special relationship or special value, if any, to the purposes of the trust or to one or more of the beneficiaries

■ A trustee who has special skills or expertise, or who is named trustee in reliance upon the trustee's representation that the trustee has special skills or expertise, has a duty to use those special skills or expertise. This particular item led to the most stringent standard, that of the **prudent expert** for one acting as a professional money manager.

■ For those without special skills or expertise, a trustee may delegate investment and management functions as long as the trustee exercises reasonable care, skill, and caution in:

— selecting the adviser,

— establishing the scope and terms of the delegation, consistent with the purposes and terms of the trust, and

— periodically reviewing the adviser's actions, to monitor the adviser's performance and compliance with the terms of the delegation.

■ A trustee who complies with all of the above is not liable to the beneficiaries or the trust for the decisions or actions of the adviser to whom the function was delegated.

■ In performing a delegated function, the adviser owes a duty to the trust to exercise reasonable care to comply with the terms of the delegation.

Specifically, there are a number of regulations that apply directly to retirement plan fiduciaries. The details are spelled out in ERISA Section 404.

Under Section 404 of ERISA, every person who acts as a fiduciary for an employee benefit plan must perform his responsibilities in accordance with the plan document specifications. Under ERISA, trustees cannot delegate fiduciary duties, but they can delegate investment management responsibilities to a qualified investment manager.

Fiduciary responsibilities to the plan are explicit. With respect to the plan, fiduciaries must act:

■ solely in the interest of plan participants and beneficiaries;

■ for the exclusive purpose of providing benefits to participants and their beneficiaries and defraying reasonable plan expenses;

■ with the care, skill, prudence, and diligence under the circumstances then prevailing that a prudent professional would use (known as the **prudent expert rule**);

■ to diversify investments to minimize the risk of large losses, unless doing so is clearly not prudent under the circumstances; and

■ in accordance with the governing plan documents unless they are not consistent with ERISA.

Under ERISA provisions, the fiduciary must be as prudent as the average expert, not the average person. To act with care, skill, prudence, and caution, the fiduciary must also:

■ establish and follow a written investment policy for the plan;

■ diversify plan assets;

■ make investment decisions under the prudent expert standard;

■ monitor investment performance;

■ control investment expenses; and

■ not engage in prohibited transactions.

TAKE NOTE   A plan participant or beneficiary who controls his specific plan account is not a fiduciary.

Investment Policy Statement

Although it is not specifically mandated under ERISA, it is strongly suggested that each employee benefit plan have an investment policy statement, preferably in writing, that serves as a guideline for the plan's fiduciary regarding funding and investment management decisions. Investment policy statements address the specific needs of the plan.

For employee benefit plans that use outside investment managers (such as mutual funds), the fiduciary must ensure that the investment alternatives available to plan members are consistent with the policy statement.

Prohibited Transactions

ERISA allows for a wide range of investments and investment practices, but a plan fiduciary is strictly prohibited from any conflicts of interest, such as:

■ self-dealing, dealing with plan assets in his own interest, or for his own account;

■ acting in a transaction involving the plan on behalf of a party with interests adverse to the plan; and

■ receiving any compensation for his personal account from any party dealing with the plan in connection with plan transactions.

TEST TOPIC ALERT   **Safe Harbor Provisions of Section 404(c)**

Several times, we have mentioned the requirement for the plan fiduciary to diversify the plan's investments. There is a particular part of ERISA, Section 404(c) dealing with 401(k) plans that provides a safe harbor from liability for the trustee if certain conditions are met. Under ERISA Section 404(c), a fiduciary is not liable for losses to the plan resulting from the participant's selection of investment in his own account, provided the participant exercised control over the investment and the plan met the detailed requirements of a Department of Labor regulation—that is, the 404(c) regulation.

There are three basic conditions of this regulation:

- Investment selection
- Investment control
- Communicating required information

Let's look at these individually.

1. Investment selection—A 404(c) plan participant must be able to:

    - materially affect portfolio return potential and risk level;
    - choose between at least three investment alternatives; and
    - diversify his investment to minimize the risk of large losses.

The practical effect of this is that it would be highly unlikely for the plan to meet the requirements by offering highly speculative funds, such as junk bond funds and highly aggressive growth funds.

2. Investment control—control is defined as:

    - allowing employees the opportunity to exercise independent control over the assets in their account by letting them make their own choices among the investment options companies have selected (at least three);
    - informing employees that they can change their investment allocations at least quarterly (a growing number of plans allow employees to make plan changes daily); and
    - even though the employees maintain investment control, the plan fiduciary is not relieved of the responsibility to monitor the performance of the investment alternatives being offered and replace them when necessary.

3. Communicating required information means:

    - making certain information available upon request, such as prospectuses and financial statements or reports relating to the investment options (included must be information such as annual operating expenses and portfolio composition);
    - a statement that the plan is intended to constitute an ERISA Section 404(c) plan and that plan fiduciaries may be relieved of liability for investment losses;
    - a description of the risk and return characteristics of each of the investment alternatives available under the plan;
    - an explanation of how to give investment instructions; and
    - allowing real-time access to employee accounts either by telephone or the Internet.

Defined Contribution and Defined Benefit Plans

All qualified retirement plans fall into one of two categories. Those that shelter contributions of current taxable income are **defined contribution plans**. Those that promise a specific retirement benefit but do not specify the level of current contributions are **defined benefit plans**. It is important to distinguish between these two approaches.

Defined Contribution Plans. Defined contribution plans include profit-sharing plans, money-purchase pension plans, and 401(k) plans.

Defined contribution plan participants' funds accumulate until a future event, generally retirement, when the funds may be withdrawn. The ultimate account value depends on the total amount contributed, along with interest and capital gains from the plan investments. In this type of plan, the plan participant assumes the investment risk.

Defined Benefit Plans. Defined benefit plans are designed to provide specific retirement benefits for participants, such as fixed monthly income. Regardless of investment performance, the promised benefit is paid under the contract terms. A defined benefit plan sponsor assumes the investment risk.

Taxation

Distributions are taxed at the employee's ordinary income rate at the time of distribution.

Profit-Sharing Plans

A **profit-sharing plan** established by an employer allows employees to participate in the business's profits. The benefits may be paid directly to the employee or deferred into an account for future payment, such as retirement, or a combination of both. This discussion concerns profit-sharing plans that defer benefits toward retirement.

Profit-sharing plans need not have a predetermined contribution formula. Plans that do include such a formula generally express contributions as a fixed percentage of profits. In either event, to be qualified, a profit-sharing plan must have substantial and recurring contributions, according to the Internal Revenue Code.

Profit-sharing plans are popular because they offer employers the greatest amount of contribution flexibility. The ability to skip contributions during years of low profits appeals to corporations with unpredictable cash flows. They are also relatively easy to install, administer, and communicate to employees.

401(k) Plans

In a **401(k) plan**, an employee directs an employer to contribute a percentage of his salary to a retirement account. 401(k) plans permit an employer to make matching contributions up to a set percentage of the employee-directed contributions. All contributions are made with pretax dollars. 401(k) plans are permitted to make hardship withdrawals available to participants facing serious and immediate financial difficulty.

For a very high earner, a type of plan known as the solo or uni (k) will generally offer the highest annual contribution limit of any defined contribution plan.

Because all qualified plans must be nondiscriminatory, the IRS has defined a **top-heavy 401(k) plan** as one in which a disproportionate amount of the benefit goes to key employees. The plan must be tested on an annual basis to ensure that it complies with the regulations. On the exam, you may be asked to define a top-heavy plan and will have to choose between key employees and highly compensated employees. The easiest way to remember is to match the (k) in 401(k) with the word *key*.

Several years after the top-heavy rules were written, relief was offered in the form of the safe harbor 401(k). A plan does not have to undergo annual top-heavy testing if all employees, even those who do not elect to participate in the plan, receive a minimum employer-sponsored contribution equal to 3% of earnings with immediate vesting.

QUICK QUIZ 7.4

1. Regulations regarding how contributions are made to tax-qualified plans relate to which of the following ERISA requirements?

   A. Vesting
   B. Funding
   C. Nondiscrimination
   D. Reporting and disclosure

2. Which of the following determines the amount paid into a defined contribution plan?

   A. ERISA-defined contribution requirements
   B. Trust agreement
   C. Employer's age
   D. Employee's retirement age

3. Which of the following would best describe a prudent investor?

   A. A person in a fiduciary capacity who invests in a prudent manner
   B. A trustee who invests with reasonable care, skill, and caution
   C. An investment adviser representative handling a discretionary account
   D. The custodian for a minor under the Uniform Transfers to Minors Act

4. To comply with the safe harbor requirements of Section 404(c) of ERISA, the trustee of a 401(k) plan must

   I. offer plan participants at least 10 different investment alternatives
   II. allow plan participants to exercise control over their investments
   III. allow plan participants to change their investment options no less frequently than monthly
   IV. provide plan participants with information relating to the risks and performance of each investment alternative offered

   A. I and III
   B. I and IV
   C. II and III
   D. II and IV

SUMMARY OF DISTRIBUTION RULES FROM BOTH QUALIFIED PLANS AND IRAs

Distributions from traditional IRAs must generally begin no later than April 1 of the year following the year in which the taxpayer attains age 70½.

In applying distribution rules, all traditional IRAs and SEPs are treated as a single account and must be liquidated at least to the extent of percentages specified on IRS tables. Qualified plans, however, are not aggregated; distributions from one qualified plan are not affected by distributions from another.

LIFETIME DISTRIBUTIONS

Early Withdrawal Penalties

In general, withdrawals from both IRAs and qualified plans are taxed as ordinary income. However, withdrawals from such arrangements occurring before owners turn age 59½ are subject to an additional 10% premature withdrawal penalty. Withdrawals from qualified plans escape the penalty when they are made on account of death or total disability, correcting excess contributions, divorce (under a qualified domestic relations order [QDRO]), or as a series of substantially equal payments over the life of the plan participant and beneficiary, if applicable.

TAKE NOTE

Although pre-59½ withdrawals from IRAs for education and first-time home purchase escape the early withdrawal penalty, withdrawals from qualified plans for those purposes do not.

The 10% tax will not apply before age 59½, however, if the following occurs.

■ The distribution is made to a beneficiary on or after the death of the employee.

■ The distribution is made because the employee acquires a qualifying disability.

The distribution is made as a part of a series of substantially equal periodic payments under IRS Rule 72t, beginning after separation from service and made at least annually for the life or life expectancy of the employee or the joint lives or life expectancies of the employee and his designated beneficiary. (Except in the case of death or disability, the payments under this exception must continue for at least five years or until the employee reaches age 59½, whichever is the longer period.)

Penalty Tax on Failure to Make Required Minimum Distributions

As with IRAs, other than a Roth IRA, failure to distribute the required amount from qualified plans generates a 50% penalty tax on the shortfall in addition to ordinary income taxation.

Withholding on Eligible Rollover Distributions from Qualified Plans

Distributions paid to an employee are subjected to a mandatory federal withholding of 20% if the distribution exceeds $200 for the year and is an eligible rollover distribution. Distributions that are not eligible rollover distributions are not subjected to the mandatory 20% withholding.

TAKE NOTE

An employee may avoid the 20% withholding by having the distribution processed as a direct rollover to an eligible retirement plan. In a direct rollover the distribution check is made payable to the trustee or custodian of the receiving retirement plan.

QUICK QUIZ 7.5

True or False?

_____ 1. A defined contribution plan is a qualified plan that specifies an employer's annual funding.

_____ 2. The movement of funds from one retirement plan to another, generally within a specified period, is called a rollover.

_____ 3. In a defined benefit plan, all employees receive the same benefits at retirement.

_____ 4. In a safe harbor 401(k) plan, all employees are immediately vested.

_____ 5. In a defined benefit plan, high income employees near retirement may receive much larger contributions than younger employees with the same salary.

_____ 6. In a top-heavy 401(k) plan, a disproportionate benefit accrues to eligible highly compensated employees.

NONQUALIFIED CORPORATE RETIREMENT PLANS

A **nonqualified plan** does not allow the employer tax deductibility of contributions. However, earnings may accumulate on a tax-deferred basis. A nonqualified plan need not comply with nondiscrimination rules that apply to qualified plans. The employer can make nonqualified benefits available to key employees and exclude others.

Nonqualified plans are not subject to the same reporting and disclosure requirements as qualified plans. However, nonqualified plans still must be in writing and communicated to the plan participants. Sponsors of nonqualified plans are fiduciaries.

TAXATION

The corporation cannot deduct nonqualified plan contributions made on behalf of participants until paid to the participant. However, if the nonqualified plan is properly designed, contributions are not taxable to the employee until the benefit is received.

Contributions to nonqualified plans that have already been taxed make up the investor's cost base. When the investor withdraws money from the nonqualified plan, the cost base is not taxed. However, earnings are taxed when withdrawn.

TYPES OF PLANS

Two types of nonqualified plans are payroll deduction plans and deferred compensation plans.

Payroll Deduction Plans

A **payroll deduction plan** involves a deduction from an employee's check on a weekly, monthly, or quarterly basis as authorized by the employee. The money is deducted after taxes are paid and may be invested in investment vehicles at the employee's option.

Deferred Compensation Plans

A **nonqualified deferred compensation (NQDC) plan** is a contractual agreement between a firm and an employee in which the employee agrees to defer receipt of current compensation in favor of a payout at retirement. The agreement underlying a deferred compensation plan usually includes the following:

- Conditions and circumstances under which some or all of the benefits may be forfeited, such as if the employee moves to a competing firm

- A statement to the effect that the employee is not entitled to any claim against the employer's assets until retirement, death, or disability

- A disclaimer that the agreement may be void if the firm suffers a business failure or bankruptcy

Company directors are not considered employees for the purpose of establishing eligibility for a deferred compensation plan, and as a result, may not participate in the plan.

Business Failure

Generally, an employee enjoys no benefits from a deferred compensation plan until retirement. If the business fails, the employee is a general creditor of the business with no guarantee that he will receive the deferred payment.

Funding

Deferred compensation plans may be unfunded, in which case the deferred compensation is paid from the firm's operating assets. If the plan is funded, the advantages of tax deferral are lost. Many NQDC plans are informally funded through life insurance or trust arrangements.

Qualified Plans Versus Nonqualified Plans

Qualified Plans	Nonqualified Plans
Contributions tax deductible	Contributions not tax deductible
Plan approved by the IRS	Plan does not need IRS approval
Plan cannot discriminate	Plan can discriminate
Tax on accumulation is deferred	Tax on accumulation may be deferred
All withdrawals taxed	Excess over cost base taxed
Plan is a trust	Plan is not a trust

QUICK QUIZ 7.6   Matching

A. Defined benefit plan
B. Keogh plan
C. Spousal IRA contributions
D. Payroll deduction plan

_____ 1. Nonqualified plan in which an employee authorizes regular reductions from his salary

_____ 2. Specifies the monthly amount an employee will receive at retirement

_____ 3. Qualified retirement plan for self-employed individuals and unincorporated businesses

_____ 4. IRA contributions made for a nonworking husband or wife

HOTSHEETS

For your convenience, Unit HotSheets summarizing the key points are located at the end of the manual on perforated pages.

U N I T   T E S T

1. Under ERISA, a fiduciary must act in all of the following ways EXCEPT
   A. solely in the interest of plan participants and beneficiaries
   B. with care, skill, prudence, and caution under the circumstances then prevailing that a prudent person acting in like capacity and familiar with such matters would use in the conduct of an enterprise of a like character
   C. in accordance with the governing plan documents unless they are not consistent with ERISA
   D. confining investments to only those most likely to achieve growth

2. Which of the following statements regarding a traditional IRA is TRUE?
   A. A traditional IRA allows a maximum tax-deductible annual contribution of $2,500 per individual or $4,000 per couple.
   B. The income and capital gains earned in the account are tax deferred until the funds are withdrawn.
   C. Distributions without penalty may begin after age 59½ and must begin by April 1 of the year preceding the year an individual turns 70½.
   D. Distributions before age 59½ are subject to a 10% penalty in lieu of income taxes.

3. IRAs and Keogh plans are similar in the following ways EXCEPT
   A. deferral of taxes
   B. distributions without penalty can begin as early as age 59½
   C. identical amounts of cash contributions are allowed
   D. there is a 50% tax penalty for insufficient distributions

4. All of the following investments are eligible for a traditional IRA EXCEPT
   A. covered call writing
   B. bank CDs
   C. works of art
   D. growth-oriented securities

5. Which of the following is an allowable early withdrawal from a traditional IRA without penalty?
   A. A wealthy individual withdraws $10,000 from his IRA to purchase his first principal residence.
   B. A single parent withdraws funds from her IRA to pay for the education of a nephew.
   C. A single parent supplements a home equity loan with funds from her IRA to pay for an additional home (a vacation home).
   D. A person withdraws funds from his IRA to buy a principal residence after he sold his first home as a result of medical expenses.

6. All of the following statements regarding qualified corporate retirement plans are true EXCEPT
   A. all corporate pension and profit-sharing plans must be established under a trust agreement
   B. all qualified retirement plans are either defined contribution or defined benefit plans
   C. they are covered under ERISA
   D. with defined benefit plans, the employee bears the investment risk

7. Qualified annuity plans offered under Section 403(b) of the Internal Revenue Code, referred to as tax-sheltered annuities (TSAs), are not available to a
   A. public school custodian
   B. church minister
   C. nurse at a nonprofit hospital
   D. student at a nonprofit college

8. Which of the following would NOT constitute a conflict of interest between the plan and a fiduciary?

    A. A fiduciary sells a real estate investment to the plan at the current market rate.

    B. A fiduciary participates in a transaction on the plan's behalf that involves a party with interests adverse to those of the plan in order to ensure favorable terms for the plan.

    C. A fiduciary offers reduced commissions to the plan for transactions that are executed through his employing financial institution.

    D. The fiduciary receives fees for acting as a trustee to the plan.

9. All of the following are true about college funding plans EXCEPT

    A. proceeds in ESAs may be withdrawn income tax free even if the child is under age 18

    B. proceeds in 529s may be withdrawn income-tax free only if used at an accredited academic institution

    C. Section 529 plans allow a onetime gift tax exclusion equal to five times the annual limit

    D. a beneficiary of an ESA who withdraws the funds for nonqualified expenses will be taxed on the entire amount of the withdrawal plus a 10% penalty.

10. Keogh Plans are qualified plans intended for those with self-employment income and owner-employees of unincorporated businesses or professional practices filing a Form 1040 Schedule C with the IRS. Which of the following statements relating to the Keogh Plan is NOT true?

    A. Owner-employee businesses and professional practices must show a gross profit in order to qualify for a tax-deductible contribution.

    B. A participant in a Keogh Plan may also maintain an IRA.

    C. The maximum allowable contribution to a Keogh Plan is substantially higher than that for an IRA.

    D. A former corporate employee who decides to become self-employed may rollover any distributions from a qualified corporate plan into a newly created Keogh Plan.

ANSWERS AND RATIONALES

1. **D.** Under ERISA, a fiduciary is not limited to confining investments to only those most likely to achieve growth. The fiduciary is required to diversify investments so as to minimize the risk of losses, unless doing so is clearly not prudent under the circumstances.

2. **B.** The income and capital gains earned in the account are tax deferred until the funds are withdrawn. A traditional IRA allows a maximum tax-deductible annual contribution of $4,000 per individual, not $2,500 per individual. Distributions without penalty may begin after age 59½ and must begin by April 1 of the year following the year an individual turns 70½. Distributions before age 59½ are subject to a 10% penalty and subject to taxes.

3. **C.** IRAs and Keogh plans do not have identical contribution amounts; IRAs allow a maximum of $4,000 per individual or $8,000 per couple per year, whereas Keogh plans allow substantially more. Both IRAs and Keoghs allow tax-deferred growth until the individual withdraws the funds. IRAs and Keoghs have premature distribution penalties before age 59½. Once the participant reaches 70½, required minimum distributions must be made or a 50% tax penalty will be assessed.

4. **C.** Gems, intangibles, and works of art are ineligible investments for an IRA. Covered call writing is allowed, but speculative options strategies are not. Bank CDs are permissible investments for an IRA. Growth-oriented securities and securities in general are appropriate investment vehicles for IRAs.

5. **A.** Any individual withdrawing $10,000 from his IRA to purchase his first principal residence would have the penalty waived. The wealth of the individual is not relevant. The purchase must be a first-time purchase as well as the primary residence. A single parent who withdraws funds from her IRA to pay for the education of a nephew will pay a 10% penalty. Educational withdrawals are limited to the taxpayer or a spouse, child, or grandchild. A single parent who supplements a home equity loan with funds from her IRA to pay for an additional home will pay a penalty because only a primary residence can be purchased with early withdrawal funds. A person who withdraws funds from his IRA to buy a principal residence after he sold his first home as a result of medical expenses will pay a penalty because the purchase is not for his first principal residence.

6. **D.** With defined benefit plans, the employer (not the employee) bears the investment risk. The employer must fund the defined benefits, regardless of the investment performance of funds set aside for this purpose. The retiree receives a defined benefit regardless of investment performance. All corporate pension and profit-sharing plans must be established under a trust agreement. All qualified retirement plans are either defined contribution or defined benefit plans.

7. **D.** 403(b) plans are available to employees of nonprofit 501(c)(3) schools, not students. 403(b) plans are also available to employees of public educational institutions such as schools. Church organization employees are allowed 403(b) plans. Employees of tax-exempt institutions such as private colleges, research and scientific foundations, private hospitals, and medical schools are allowed to establish 403(b) plans.

8. **D.** A fiduciary can receive compensation from the sponsor of the plan for acting as a trustee, if fees are reasonable and consistent with duties performed. A fiduciary may not sell a real estate investment to the plan at the going market rate. Such self-dealing presents a conflict of interest regardless of the terms of the transaction. A fiduciary may not participate in a transaction on the plan's behalf that involves a party with interests adverse to those of the plan in order to ensure favorable terms for the plan. The situation is self-dealing and presents a conflict of interest prohibited under ERISA. Offers of reduced commissions to the plan for transactions that are executed through his employing financial institution are prohibited and a conflict of interest.

9. **D.** The tax and 10% penalty is only levied against earnings since the contributions were made with after-tax dollars.

10. **D.** Rollovers are only permitted into an IRA. Tax-deductible contributions are not allowed unless there is potentially taxable income against which to deduct. Anyone with earned income may have an IRA, regardless of participation in another qualified plan, and the Keogh Plan contribution limits are much higher than those for an IRA.

QUICK QUIZ ANSWERS

Quick Quiz 7.1

1. **A.** Any individual with earned income who is under age 70½ may contribute up to $4,000 to a traditional IRA. The deductibility of those contributions will be determined by that person's coverage under qualified plans and by his level of income.

2. **B.** All withdrawals from IRAs are taxed at the individual's ordinary income tax rate at the time of withdrawal. Distributions made before age 59½ will incur an additional 10% penalty.

3. **C.** The penalty for premature withdrawals from an IRA or a Keogh account is 10% plus ordinary income tax. The excess contribution penalty is 6%, whereas the 50% penalty applies after age 70½.

4. **A.** Early withdrawals, without penalty, are permitted only in certain situations (such as death or qualifying disability).

5. **B.** Cash value life insurance, term insurance, and collectibles are not permissible investments in an IRA.

6. **B.** Small businesses and self-employed persons typically establish SEP IRAs because they are easier and less expensive than other plans for an employer to set up and administer.

7. **C.** The common factor for both traditional and Roth IRAs is that the amount that may be contributed is the same for both. Traditional IRAs offer tax-deductible contributions, but withdrawals are generally taxed. Roth IRAs do not offer tax-deductible contributions, but qualified withdrawals are tax free. Traditional IRAs require distributions to begin by April 1 after the year an owner reaches age 70½, but this is not true for Roth IRAs.

8. **B.** Only $2,000 may be invested in each child's ESA per year. If a couple has three children, they may contribute $6,000 in total, or $2,000 per child, per year.

Quick Quiz 7.2

1. **C.** A person with self-employment income may deduct contributions to a Keogh plan. Keogh plans are not available to corporations or their employees.

2. **C.** All interest, dividends, and capital gains accumulated in a Keogh are tax deferred until their withdrawal (which must begin between age 59½ and by April 1 after the year in which the account owner turns 70½). The account owner may choose to take distributions in the form of lifetime income payments or as a single lump sum.

3. **A.** Keogh contributions can only be made before the date on which an individual turns 70½.

Quick Quiz 7.3

1. **C.** Because he is employed by a public school system, the customer is eligible to participate in the tax-sheltered annuity plan. Employee contributions to a TSA plan are excluded from gross income in the year in which they are made. As in other retirement plans, a penalty tax is assessed on distributions received before age 59½. Mutual funds, CDs, and annuity contracts are among the investment choices available for TSA plans.

2. **D.** The maximum annual employer contribution to a 403(b) plan is the same as applied to all defined contribution plans: the lesser of 25% of salary or $45,000.

3. **B.** Minimum distributions from TSAs are required to start by April 1 of the year following the year in which the participant turns 70½.

Quick Quiz 7.4

1. **B.** Funding covers how an employer contributes to or funds a plan.

2. **B.** The retirement plan's trust agreement specifies the formula(s) used to determine the contributions to a defined contribution plan.

3. **B.** Although all of these may have a fiduciary responsibility, the definition, as expressed in the Uniform Prudent Investor Act of 1994, requires reasonable care, skill, and caution.

4. **D.** To comply with the safe harbor provisions of ERISA's Section 404(c), the plan trustee must allow each participant control over their investments and furnish them with full performance and risk information. The rule only mandates a minimum of 3 alternatives and quarterly changes.

Quick Quiz 7.5

1. **T.**

2. **T.**

3. **F.**

4. **T.**

5. **T.** The maximum contributions for defined benefit plans allow a larger contribution in a shorter period for highly paid individuals nearing retirement.

6. **F.** Remember the (k) in 401(k) reminds us that top-heavy plans benefit key employees.

Quick Quiz 7.6

1. **D.**

2. **A.**

3. **B.**

4. **C.**

8

Customer Accounts

I nvestment advisers counsel clients whose securities transactions are made through broker/dealers. The customer account at a brokerage firm serves as a repository for cash and securities as well as the record of all customer investment activity. A customer's investment objectives, approach, and account trading authority determine which of the several types of available accounts an investment adviser representative will open for the customer. Strict requirements apply to all accounts, and each account type has its own requirements, documents, and, in some cases, authorization.

The Series 65 exam will include six questions on the material presented in this Unit. ■

When you have completed this Unit, you should be able to:

■ **discuss** the steps necessary to open new accounts;

■ **describe** required brokerage account documentation;

■ **identify** specific account recordkeeping requirements;

■ **compare** and contrast cash and margin accounts;

■ **define** procedures for opening accounts for employees of other broker/dealers;

■ **list** discretionary account requirements;

■ **explain** procedures at the death or incompetence of an account holder; and

■ **distinguish** the unique features of UGMA and UTMA accounts.

OPENING CUSTOMER ACCOUNTS

When an account is opened, it is registered in the name(s) of one or more persons; they are the account owners and the only individuals allowed access to and control of the investments in the account. Generally, any competent person of majority age can open an account, and anyone declared legally incompetent cannot. Fiduciary or custodial accounts may be opened for minors or legally incompetent individuals.

NEW ACCOUNTS

Filling Out the New Account Form

An investment adviser representative must completely fill out a new account form for each account opened and enter the following information for each account owner:

- Full name

- Date of birth

- Address and telephone numbers (business and residence)

- Social Security or tax identification number

- Occupation, employer, and type of business

- Citizenship

- Estimated income and net worth

- Investment objectives

- Bank and brokerage references

- Whether the customer is an employee of another NASD member

- How the account was acquired

- Whether the customer is an officer, director, or more than 10% shareholder of a publicly traded company

- Name and occupation of each person with authority to make transactions in the account

- Signatures of both the representative opening the account and a principal of the firm (the customer's signature is not required on a new account form)

Customer information should be updated periodically as situations change.

To monitor trading activity associated with insiders, it is required that the new account form identify whether the customer is a director, officer, or a shareholder of more than 10% of a publicly traded company.

Suitability Information

When an account is opened, all SROs require that representatives attempt to collect **suitability information**—that is, the information necessary to make suitable investment recommendations for customers. The representative should know all essential facts about a customer's income, net worth, tax status, number of dependents, current financial situation, present holdings, risk tolerance, needs, and investment objectives.

Incomplete Information

Even if a customer refuses to provide all of the information requested, a firm may open the account if it believes the customer has the financial resources necessary to carry it.

If a customer wants to place a transaction that an investment adviser representative considers unsuitable or that the representative has not recommended, the representative should mark the order ticket "Unsolicited." If the ticket is not marked, the trade is assumed to be solicited.

Aproval of an Account

A partner or a principal of the firm must approve every new account in writing on the account form before or promptly after the completion of the first transaction in the account.

Signature Cards

Many firms ask customers to fill out a signature card. The customer is not legally required to complete one for a cash account, but the card provides protection and convenience by allowing the customer to send written orders to the representative or sponsor, who can then verify an order's accuracy by comparing the signature to the one the firm has on file.

Mailing Instructions

A customer must give specific mailing instructions when opening a new account. Statements and confirmations may be sent to someone who holds power of attorney for the customer if the customer requests it in writing and if the firm sends duplicate confirmations to the customer.

Trading Authorization/Power of Attorney

A **power of attorney**, or a **discretionary power**, allows a party other than the account owner to make investment decisions for the account without consulting the account owner. A signed copy of the document must be kept on file.

Account Records

Investment adviser representatives must maintain records for each customer's account and each securities holding. All customer transactions are posted daily and kept at the branch. Required information includes the following:

- The customer's name, address, and telephone number

- The type of account and account number

- The customer's investment objective

- A list of all securities deposited with the firm

- A list of all transactions

OPENING CASH AND MARGIN ACCOUNTS

Customers can open either cash accounts or margin accounts, depending on how they choose to pay for securities. In cash accounts, customers pay the full purchase price of securities by the transaction settlement date, whereas in margin accounts, customers may borrow part of a security's purchase price from the broker/dealer.

Cash Accounts

A **cash account** is the basic investment account, and anyone eligible to open an investment account can open one. In a cash account, a customer must pay in full for any securities purchased. Certain accounts may only be opened as cash accounts, including:

- personal retirement accounts, such as IRAs, Keoghs, and TSAs;

- corporate retirement accounts; and

- custodial accounts, such as Uniform Gift to Minors Act accounts (UGMAs).

Margin Accounts

Margin accounts allow customers to control investments for less money than they would need if they were to buy the securities outright because a margin account allows a customer to borrow money for investing. The term *margin* refers to the minimum amount of cash or marginable securities a customer must deposit to buy securities.

Margin also is a potential source of cash. If a customer has fully paid securities in an account and needs cash, a firm normally lends money against those securities up to the margin limit that the Federal Reserve Board (FRB) has set.

Customers who open margin accounts must meet certain minimal financial requirements. The customer may then buy securities on margin and pay interest on the borrowed funds. The securities purchased are held in street name as collateral for the margin loan.

Documenting a Margin Account

Opening a margin account requires more documentation than opening a regular cash account. The customer signs a margin agreement, which includes the required credit agreement, hypothecation agreement, and an optional loan consent.

Margin Account Agreements

Credit Agreement	Discloses the terms under which credit is extended. SEC Rule 10b-16 requires firms to disclose the method of computing interest and the conditions under which interest rates and charges will be changed. Firms must send customers an assurance that statements accounting for interest charges will be sent at least quarterly.
Hypothecation Agreement	Gives the firm permission to pledge (hypothecate) securities held on margin; a mandatory part of a margin agreement.
Loan Consent (optional)	Gives the firm permission to lend securities held in the margin account to other brokers, usually for short sales. It is not mandatory for customers to sign the loan consent agreement.

TEST TOPIC ALERT

■ A principal must approve every new account opened for the firm.

■ Only two signatures are required on a new account form—the principal approving the account and the representative introducing the account.

QUICK QUIZ 8.1

1. All of the following customer information is required on a new account form EXCEPT

   A. name
   B. degrees earned
   C. Social Security number
   D. date of birth

2. If a customer opens a margin account with ABC Discount Securities and signs a loan consent agreement, the firm is permitted to

   A. hypothecate securities in the customer's account
   B. loan out the customer's margin securities
   C. commingle the customer's securities with securities owned by the firm
   D. lend the customer money and charge interest

3. An investment adviser representative is permitted to open all of the following customer accounts EXCEPT

   A. individual account opened by the individual's spouse
   B. minor's account opened by a custodian
   C. corporate account opened by the designated officer
   D. partnership account opened by the designated partner

Quick Quiz answers can be found at the end of the Unit.

TYPES OF ACCOUNTS

Procedures and regulations vary according to account ownership. The principal types of ownership are:

- individual;
- joint;
- partnership;
- corporate; and
- fiduciary/custodial.

INDIVIDUAL ACCOUNTS

An **individual account** has one beneficial owner. The account holder is the only person who can:

- control the investments within the account; or
- request distributions of cash or securities from the account.

JOINT ACCOUNTS

A **joint account** is owned by two or more adults, and each is allowed some form of control over the account.

In addition to the new account form, a **joint account agreement** must be signed, and the account must be designated as either tenants in common (TIC) or joint tenants with right of survivorship (JTWROS). Account forms for joint accounts require the signatures of all owners. Joint account agreements provide that any or all tenants may transact business in the accounts. Checks must be made payable to the names in which the account is registered and must be endorsed for deposit by all tenants, although mail need only be sent to a single address. To be in **good delivery form**, securities sold from a joint account must be signed by all tenants.

Tenants in Common (TIC)

TIC ownership provides that a deceased tenant's fractional interest in the account is retained by that tenant's estate and is not passed to the surviving tenant(s). Ownership of a TIC account may be divided unequally. At the death of an account owner, that person's proportionate share of the cash and securities in the account is distributed according to the instructions in the decedent's will. If one account owner dies or is declared incompetent, all pending transactions and outstanding orders must be canceled immediately.

EXAMPLE

If a TIC agreement provides for 60% ownership interest by one owner and 40% ownership interest by the other, that fraction of the account would pass into the deceased owner's estate if he died. The TIC agreement may be used by more than two individuals.

Joint Tenants with Right of Survivorship (JTWROS)

JTWROS ownership stipulates that a deceased tenant's interest in the account passes to the surviving tenant(s). Regardless of contributions, each JTWROS account owner has an equal and undivided interest in the cash and securities in the account. Upon the death or declaration of incompetency of any or all of the account owners, account ownership passes to the survivor(s); a right of succession occurs and the other party becomes sole owner of the account.

Transfer-on-Death Accounts (TOD)

Using a transfer-on-death (TOD) account is the simplest way to keep assets held in brokerage accounts from becoming subject to probate upon a client's death. However, the TOD account does not avoid estate taxes if applicable. TOD accounts are available for most types of paper assets, such as savings and checking accounts in banks and credit unions, certificates of deposit, stocks, bonds, and other securities.

The owner, while alive, is the only person with any rights to the property. Upon the owner's death, the property is immediately transferred to the named beneficiaries, usually without any added cost. The owner has the right to change beneficiaries at any time.

A cautionary note regarding TOD accounts: the client's will does not control who inherits the assets so without proper coordination, it could be very difficult to predict who would receive what share of the estate.

The only types of accounts that may be opened with a TOD designation are individual accounts and JTWROS accounts.

TEST TOPIC ALERT

Tenants in common can own unequal interests in the account, unlike joint tenants with right of survivorship, who always share equally.

- TIC: interest can be unequal.
- JTWROS: all parties must have equal interests.

Checks or distributions must be made payable in the account name and endorsed by all parties.

PARTNERSHIP ACCOUNTS

A **partnership** is an unincorporated association of two or more individuals. Partnerships frequently open cash, margin, retirement, and other accounts necessary to conduct business. A partnership must fill out the new account form and provide a partnership agreement stating which of the partners can trade in the account. If the partnership opens a margin account, the partnership must disclose any investment limitations.

TAKE NOTE

Margin account trading is only permissible in partnership and corporate accounts if such trading is expressly stated in the partnership agreement or corporate charter.

CORPORATE ACCOUNTS

A corporate resolution is needed to open a corporate account. If a company wants to trade on margin, the corporate charter must state that margin account trading is permissible. A member must obtain a copy of the corporate charter and a corporate resolution (with the corporate seal) signed by the secretary of the corporation, identifying which officers may trade in the account.

The charter is proof that the corporation exists, and the resolution authorizes both the opening of the account and the officers designated to enter orders.

WRAP ACCOUNTS

In a **wrap account**, a firm charges a fixed fee expressed as an annual percentage for portfolio management and related services. Because a portion of the fee is specifically for investment advice, firms offering wrap accounts must register as investment advisers. Furthermore, registered representatives handling these accounts must have either a Series 65 or 66 registration/license as an investment adviser representative.

FIDUCIARY AND CUSTODIAL ACCOUNTS

Third-Party Accounts

Accounts cannot be opened for third parties; however, a person can open an account for himself and grant power of attorney (trading authorization) to someone else. Although an adult can open an account for a minor with the minor as beneficial owner, an adult cannot open an account for another adult or trade for the account of another (even a spouse) without a power of attorney.

Persons other than an account owner can be authorized to buy and sell securities on behalf of the owner. The primary types of trading authorization occur in fiduciary and custodial accounts. When securities are placed in fiduciary or custodial accounts, someone other than the owner initiates trades.

Fiduciary Accounts

In a **fiduciary account**, the individual granted fiduciary responsibility enters trades for the account, makes all of the investment, management, and distribution decisions, and must manage the account in the owner's best interests.

Examples of fiduciaries include the following:

■ Trustee designated to administer a trust

■ Executor designated in a decedent's will to manage the estate's affairs

■ Administrator appointed by the courts to liquidate the estate of a person who died intestate (without a will)

■ Guardian (conservator) designated by the courts to handle a minor's affairs

■ Custodian of an UGMA account

■ Receiver in a bankruptcy

■ Conservator for an incompetent person

E X A M P L E   The most familiar fiduciary account is a **trust account**, in which money or securities are placed in trust, and someone else manages the account. The manager, or **trustee**, is a fiduciary.

A **fiduciary** is anyone legally appointed and authorized to represent another person, act on that person's behalf, and make decisions necessary to the prudent management of that person's account. A fiduciary cannot use account contents for personal benefit but may be reimbursed for reasonable expenses incurred in managing the account.

T A K E   N O T E

Any trades the fiduciary enters must be consistent with the trust's investment objectives.

State law often places limits on the actions of a fiduciary. Most states are **prudent investor** states, which means the fiduciary must act prudently. Other states are **legal list** states, which means that the only securities a fiduciary can purchase are those on the state's legal list. Generally, legal list securities must be of investment grade.

The prudent investor rule is an update to the prudent man rule, and it allows fiduciaries to designate a third party to manage the affairs of the portfolio. Previously, all portfolio management was the responsibility of the named fiduciary. Now, if that person does not feel qualified, the duties of portfolio selection may be delegated to someone else.

Any trades into which the fiduciary enters must be compatible with the trust's investment objectives.

Opening a Fiduciary Account

Opening a fiduciary account may require a court certification of the individual's appointment and authority. An account for a trustee must include a trust agreement detailing the limitations placed on the fiduciary. No documentation of custodial rights or court certification is required for an individual to open an UGMA or UTMA account.

Specific requirements for the two most common fiduciary accounts follow.

- **Trust accounts.** A copy of the trust agreement is required; such agreements are usually precise about how the account must be operated. Unless specifically authorized in the agreement, margin accounts may not be opened for trust accounts; only cash accounts are permitted.

- **Guardian/conservator accounts.** A copy of the court order appointing the guardian must be obtained. A guardian is often appointed to oversee and protect the assets of an orphaned child or an incompetent person.

T E S T   T O P I C   A L E R T

The principal and representative for a fiduciary account must know the following.

- Proper authorization must be given (i.e., the necessary court documents must be filed with and verified by the broker/dealer).
- Speculative transactions are generally not permitted.
- Margin accounts are permitted only if the legal documents establishing the fiduciary accounts authorize them.
- The prudent investor rule requires fiduciaries to make wise and safe investments.
- A fiduciary may not share in an account's profits but may charge a reasonable fee for services.

Power of Attorney

If a person who is not named on an account will have trading authority, the customer must file written authorization with the broker/dealer giving that person access to the account. Trading authorization usually takes the form of a power of attorney. Two basic types of trading authorizations are full and limited powers of attorney.

Full Power of Attorney. A full power of attorney allows an individual who is not the owner of an account to:

■ deposit or withdraw cash or securities; and/or

■ make investment decisions for the account owner.

Limited Power of Attorney. A limited power of attorney allows an individual to have some, but not total, control over an account. The document specifies the level of access the person may exercise.

TEST TOPIC ALERT   Limited power of attorney, also called limited trading authorization, allows entering of buy and sell orders but not the withdrawal of funds. Entry of orders and withdrawal of funds is allowed if full power of attorney is granted.

Custodial Accounts

In a **custodial account**, the custodian for the beneficial owner enters all trades. UGMA and UTMA accounts require an adult or a trustee to act as custodian for a minor (the beneficial owner). Any kind of security or cash may be gifted to the account without limitation.

The Uniform Law Commissioners adopted the Uniform Gift to Minors Act (UGMA) in 1956 (the same year as the Uniform Securities Act). The primary focus then was to provide a convenient way to make gifts of money and securities to minors. Later, it became clear that a more flexible law was desirable. The Uniform Law Commissioners adopted the Uniform Transfers to Minors Act (UTMA) in 1986. UTMA expands the types of property you can transfer to a minor and provides that you can make other types of transfers besides gifts.

Nearly all states have adopted UTMA, but people still tend to refer to UGMA out of habit. For exam purposes, it doesn't matter which law is in effect in your state because the essential principles of both acts are the same.

Custodian

Securities in an UGMA/UTMA account are managed by a custodian until the minor reaches the age of majority. The custodian has full control over the minor's account and can:

■ buy or sell securities;

■ exercise rights or warrants; and

■ liquidate, trade, or hold securities.

The custodian also may use the property in the account in any way the custodian deems proper for the minor's support, education, maintenance, general use, or benefit. However, the account is not normally used to pay expenses associated with raising a child.

Opening an UGMA/UTMA Account

UGMA/UTMA account applications must contain the custodian's name, minor's name and Social Security number, and the state in which the UGMA/UTMA is registered.

TEST TOPIC ALERT

The minor's Social Security number is used on the account.

Fiduciary Responsibility. An UGMA/UTMA custodian assumes fiduciary responsibilities in managing a minor's account. Restrictions are placed on improper handling of investments in an UGMA/UTMA. The most important limitations follow.

- UGMAs/UTMAs may be opened and managed as cash accounts only.

- A custodian may never purchase securities on margin or pledge them as collateral for a loan.

- A custodian must reinvest all cash proceeds, dividends, and interest within a reasonable period of time. Cash proceeds may be held in an interest-bearing custodial account for a reasonable period.

- Investment decisions must consider a minor's age and the custodial relationship; examples of inappropriate investments are commodity futures, naked options, and high-risk securities.

- Options may not be bought in a custodial account because no evidence of ownership is issued to an options buyer.

- Covered call writing is normally allowed.

- Stock subscription rights or warrants must be either exercised or sold.

A custodian may be reimbursed for any reasonable expenses incurred in managing the account. Compensation may be paid to the custodian unless the custodian is also the donor.

Donating Securities. When a person makes a gift of securities to a minor under the UGMA/UTMA laws, that person is the securities' **donor**. A gift under UGMA/UTMA conveys an **indefeasible title**—that is, the donor may not take back the gift, nor may the minor return the gift until the minor has reached the age of majority. Once a gift is donated, the donor gives up all rights to the property. When the minor reaches the specified age, the property in the account is transferred into the minor's name.

UGMA/UTMA Rules. Registered investment advisers should know the following UGMA/UTMA custodial account rules.

■ All gifts are irrevocable. Gifts may be in the form of cash or fully paid securities.

■ An account may have only one custodian and one minor or beneficial owner.

■ A donor of securities can act as custodian or appoint someone to do so.

■ Unless they are acting as custodians, parents have no legal control over an UGMA/UTMA account or the securities in it.

■ A minor can be the beneficiary of more than one account, and a person may serve as custodian for more than one UGMA/UTMA, provided each account benefits only one minor.

■ The minor has the right to sue the custodian for improper actions.

TAKE NOTE

Although an investment adviser representative is not responsible for determining whether an appointment is valid or a custodian's activities are appropriate, he should always be sensitive to the appearance of unethical behavior.

Registration of UGMA/UTMA Securities. Any securities in an UGMA/UTMA account are registered in the custodian's name for the benefit of the minor and cannot be registered in street name. Securities bought in a custodial account must be registered so that the custodial relationship is evident.

EXAMPLE

In an account where Marilyn Johns, the donor, has appointed her daughter's aunt, Barbara Wood, as custodian for the account of her minor daughter, Alexis, the account and the certificates would read "Barbara Wood as custodian for Alexis Johns" (or a variation of this form).

When the minor reaches the age of majority, all of the securities in the account are registered in her name.

Taxation. The minor's Social Security number appears on an UGMA/UTMA account, and the minor must file an annual income tax return and pay taxes on any income exceeding $1,700 (2007) produced by the UGMA/UTMA at the parent's top marginal tax rate, regardless of the source of the gift, until the minor reaches age 18 (commonly referred to as the **kiddie tax**). Lower amounts of annual unearned income are not subject to the kiddie tax.

When the minor reaches age 18, the account will be taxed at the minor's tax rate. Although the minor is the account's beneficiary and is responsible for any and all taxes on the account, in most states it is the custodian's responsibility to see that the taxes are paid.

EXAMPLE

In 2007, the first $850 of a minor's earnings are tax free, and the next $850 are taxed at the minor's rate, usually 15%. Earnings exceeding $1,700 are taxed at the parents' top rate if the child is under 18.

Death of the Minor or Custodian. If the beneficiary of an UGMA/UTMA dies, the securities in the account pass to the minor's estate, not to the parents or the custodian. If the custodian dies or resigns, either a court of law or the donor must appoint a new custodian.

Uniform Transfers to Minors (UTMA)

Although UTMA and UGMA share many characteristics, there are a few important differences. First, although UGMA accounts may not hold real estate (real property), certain partnership interests, and other types of intangible property, UTMA accounts may. Thus, UTMA accounts offer greater investment choice.

In many states, UTMA account assets are not required to be transferred upon the age of majority of the beneficial owner (the child). In many UTMA states, the custodian may delay transferring the UTMA assets to the beneficial owner until he becomes age 21 or 25 (depending on the particular state statute).

TAKE NOTE

A potential estate tax trap is present with custodial accounts such as UGMAs and UTMAs. Under certain circumstances, the assets in the minor's custodial account may be includable, for federal estate tax purposes, in the estate of the custodian when the custodian dies. This could be a problem for the parent or grandparent who incorrectly assumes that the gift made to the minor is no longer in his estate.

DISCRETIONARY ACCOUNTS

A **discretionary account** is an account set up with preapproved authority for an agent or investment adviser representative to make transactions without having to ask for specific approval.

Discretion is defined as the authority to decide:

- which security;
- the number of shares or units; or
- whether to buy or sell.

TAKE NOTE

Discretion does not apply to decisions regarding the timing of an investment or the price at which it is acquired.

EXAMPLE

An order from a customer worded "Buy 100 shares of ABC for my account whenever you think the price is right" is not a discretionary order (it is a **market not held order**).

Discretionary Authority

Customers can give discretionary power over their account(s) only by filing a written trading authorization or a limited power of attorney with the broker/dealer or investment adviser. No discretionary transactions can take place without this document on file. Once authorization is given, the customer is legally bound to accept the representative's decisions, although the customer may continue to enter orders.

The customer may only give discretion to a specific individual. If that person leaves the firm or stops working with the account, discretionary authority ends immediately.

In addition to requiring the proper documentation, discretionary accounts are subject to the following rules.

■ Each discretionary order must be identified as such when it is entered for execution.

■ An officer or a partner of the firm must approve each order promptly and in writing, not necessarily before order entry.

■ A record must be kept of all transactions.

■ No excessive trading may occur in the account, relative to the size of the account and the customer's investment objectives.

■ To safeguard against the possibility of churning, a designated supervisor or manager must review all trading activity frequently and systematically.

TEST TOPIC ALERT

To identify a discretionary order, try this method: an order is discretionary if any one of the **three As** is missing. The three As are:

■ **A**ctivity;

■ **A**mount; and

■ **A**sset.

EXAMPLE

If a customer asks an agent to sell 1,000 shares of XYZ stock, the order is not discretionary even though the customer did not specifically say when or at what price.

Activity = sell; **A**mount = 1,000 shares; **A**sset = XYZ stock. All three As are defined.

However, if a customer asks an agent to buy 1,000 shares of the best computer company stock available, the order is discretionary. The **A**sset is missing because the company was not defined.

EXAMPLE

A customer wishes to buy 1,000 shares of XYZ whenever a representative thinks he can get the best price. The order is nondiscretionary. The three As were all defined. Omitting the time or price does not make an order discretionary.

TEST TOPIC ALERT

Remember that time and/or price are not discretion. Although there are special requirements for advisers who exercise discretion, do not confuse those rules as applicable when the adviser is given the power to decide time or price.

QUICK QUIZ 8.2

Match each of the following terms with the appropriate description below.

A. Hypothecation agreement
B. Tenants in common
C. Limited power of attorney
D. Discretionary authorization

_____ 1. Specifies conditions for pledging securities to a broker/dealer as collateral for the margin loan

_____ 2. Enables the investment adviser representative to make investment decisions in a client's account

_____ 3. A deceased's fractional interest in an account is retained by his estate

_____ 4. Legal document that authorizes someone other than the customer to have trading privileges in an account

QUICK QUIZ 8.3

True or False?

_____ 1. A discretionary trade is one in which the member chooses either the action, the security, or the price.

_____ 2. A principal must approve all discretionary order tickets before execution.

_____ 3. The custodian in an UGMA account must be an immediate family member of the minor.

QUICK QUIZ 8.4

Match each of the following items with the appropriate description below.

A. Executor
B. Credit agreement
C. Fiduciary
D. Cash account

_____ 1. Person legally appointed to manage and/or hold assets for the benefit of another person

_____ 2. Outlines conditions for loans between broker and customer

_____ 3. Customer is required to pay in full for securities purchased

_____ 4. Person authorized by law to liquidate the estate of a decedent

QUICK QUIZ 8.5   Match each type of account with the appropriate description below.

    A. Partnership account
    B. TOD
    C. TIC
    D. JTWROS

_____   1. Each party specifies a percentage interest in the account. If one party dies, her interest in the account passes to her estate.

_____   2. Parties share an undivided interest in the account. If one party dies, his interest passes to the other owner(s) of the account.

_____   3. The assets in the account become the property of the beneficiary on the death of the account owner without passing through probate.

_____   4. An unincorporated interest of two or more individuals. An annual agreement specifies which individuals can trade the account.

QUICK QUIZ 8.6   1. Which of the following persons are considered fiduciaries?

    I. Executor of an estate
    II. Administrator of a trust
    III. Custodian of an UGMA/UTMA account
    IV. Conservator for a legally incompetent person

    A. I and II
    B. I, II and III
    C. III and IV
    D. I, II, III and IV

2. If a customer would like to open a custodial UGMA or UTMA account for his nephew, a minor, the uncle can

    A. open the account provided the proper trust arrangements are filed first
    B. open the account and name himself custodian
    C. open the account, but he needs a legal document evidencing the nephew's parents' prior approval of the account
    D. be custodian for the account only if he is also the minor's legal guardian

3. Which of the following regarding customer accounts is NOT true?

    A. Stock held in a custodial account may not be held in street name.
    B. The customer who opens a numbered account must sign a statement attesting to ownership.
    C. Stock held under JTWROS goes to the survivor(s) in the event of the death of one of the tenants.
    D. Margin trading in a fiduciary account does not require any special consideration.

4. An investor wants to provide for his 3 nephews after his brother dies. Under the UGMA, the investor may open

    A. 1 account for all 3 nephews
    B. 3 separate accounts and deposit cash and securities
    C. 3 separate accounts and deposit insurance policies
    D. 3 separate accounts and deposit fixed annuities

5. An individual who has been declared legally incompetent wants to open an account. Which of the following actions must the firm take?

    A. Obtain a power of attorney
    B. Obtain a copy of a guardianship document
    C. Open the account as a cash account
    D. Request to talk to a relative

6. Which of the following individuals may NOT open a joint account?

    A. 2 spouses
    B. 3 sisters
    C. 2 strangers
    D. Parent and a minor

HOTSHEETS

For your convenience, Unit HotSheets summarizing the key points are located at the end of the manual on perforated pages.

UNIT TEST

1. A new account is opened for joint tenants with rights of survivorship. All of the following statements are true EXCEPT

   A. orders may be given by either party
   B. mail can be sent to either party with the permission of the other party
   C. checks can be drawn in the name of either party
   D. in the event of death, the decedent's interest in the account goes to the other party

2. If 3 individuals have a tenants in common account with a firm and one individual dies, then

   A. the account must be liquidated and the proceeds split evenly among the 2 survivors and the decedent's estate
   B. the 2 survivors continue as cotenants with the decedent's estate
   C. trading is discontinued until the executor names a replacement for the deceased
   D. the account is converted to joint with rights of survivorship

3. Which of the following accounts is(are) prohibited from using margin?

   I. Joint account for a husband and wife
   II. Discretionary account
   III. Corporation account
   IV. Custodian account under the Uniform Gift to Minors Act

   A. I and II
   B. I, II and III
   C. II and IV
   D. IV only

4. All of the following information must be obtained from new customers EXCEPT

   A. employer name and address
   B. tax identification number
   C. educational background
   D. date of birth

5. Over which of the following would the investment adviser representative have discretionary authority?

   A. Order that specifies the size of the trade and name of the security but leaves the choice of price and time up to the investment adviser representative
   B. Account in which the investment adviser representative chooses portfolio securities on behalf of the client
   C. Account in which a customer has power of attorney over another individual's account
   D. Account in which a trustee has power of attorney over another individual's account

6. Which of the following are fiduciaries?

   I. Executor of an estate
   II. Administrator of a trust
   III. Custodian of an UGMA account
   IV. Investment adviser representative granted with discretionary authority over the account

   A. I and II
   B. I, II and III
   C. II, III and IV
   D. I, II, III and IV

7. Under the UGMA, which of the following statements is NOT true?

   A. An UGMA account may have only one custodian for only one minor.
   B. Only an adult can make a gift to a minor.
   C. The maximum amount of money an adult can give to a minor in any one year is $12,000.
   D. Once a gift is given to a minor, it cannot be reclaimed.

8. A client of a brokerage firm purchases 100 shares of ABC common stock at a price of $50 per share. On settlement date, the firm journals $2,500 from the client's money market account to pay for the trade. No further call for money is made. This trade must have taken place in a

A. cash account
B. depository account
C. margin account
D. wrap fee account

9. A trade order must be marked discretionary if the agent or investment adviser representative has the ability to determine any one of the following EXCEPT

A. acquisition cost
B. action to be taken
C. amount to acquire
D. asset to trade

10. Which of the following accounts could be opened with a TOD designation?

I. Individual
II. Joint tenants in common
III. Joint tenants with rights of survivorship
IV. UTMA

A. I and II
B. I and III
C. I, III and IV
D. II and IV

ANSWERS AND RATIONALES

1. **C.** Although either party may enter an order, any money or securities delivered out of the account must be in the names of both owners.

2. **B.** The decedent's estate becomes a tenant in common with the survivors.

3. **D.** Although no legal papers are required to open a custodial account, the account must be kept in accordance with state law under UGMA. This act prohibits securities in a custodial account from being bought on margin.

4. **C.** A customer's educational background need not be ascertained when opening an account.

5. **B.** An order is discretionary when it is placed by the member firm or its representative for a customer's account without the customer's express authorization for that order. Also, for the order to be considered discretionary, the firm must choose more than just the price or time of execution—that is, the size of the trade, whether to buy or sell, and/or the security must be chosen by the firm.

6. **D.** Each of these persons is in a relationship of trust to the customer and is therefore a fiduciary.

7. **C.** Any adult can give a gift to a minor in a custodial account. There is no limitation on the size of the gift. However, any gift in excess of $12,000 (or such higher number as indexing provides for) will possibly subject the donor to a gift tax liability.

8. **C** When a purchase is made and only 50% of the cost of the transaction is required, the trade is being made on margin.

9. **A** The ability to decide the timing or price of a securities transaction does not constitute discretion.

10. **B.** The only types of accounts that may have the Transfer on Death (TOD) designation are individual and JTWROS. Minors can not designate a beneficiary. Upon the death of a minor, any assets belong in the deceased's estate.

QUICK QUIZ ANSWERS

Quick Quiz 8.1

1. **B.** The investment adviser representative must ascertain the customer's name, date of birth, and Social Seucirity number. Ascertaining degrees earned is not a requirement.

2. **B.** A signed loan consent agreement permits the firm to lend the customer's margin securities. Firms must keep customer margin securities segregated from firm securities—commingling is prohibited.

3. **A.** A representative is not permitted to open an individual account in the name of an individual (other than the beneficial owner), even in the name of a spouse.

Quick Quiz 8.2

1. **A.**

2. **D.**

3. **B.**

4. **C.**

Quick Quiz 8.3

1. **F.** Deciding the price at which to buy or sell a security does not require discretionary authority. Discretionary authority is required if the representative chooses the action (buy or sell), the security, or the number of shares being bought or sold.

2. **F.** Discretionary order tickets must be reviewed by a principal promptly after execution, and a principal must frequently review all discretionary accounts to detect potential abuses.

3. **F.** The custodian must be an adult but need not be a relative of the minor child.

Quick Quiz 8.4

1. **C.**

3. **B.**

4. **D.**

5. **A.**

Quick Quiz 8.5

1. **C.**

2. **D.**

3. **B.**

4. **A.**

Quick Quiz 8.6

1. **D.** All of the persons listed have fiduciary responsibilities because of the authority with which they are entrusted.

2. **B.** The donor may name himself the custodian of an UGMA or UTMA account. No documentation of custodial status is required to open an UGMA account, and the custodian is not required to be the minor's legal guardian.

3. **D.** Trading on margin is prohibited in fiduciary accounts except under special circumstances and with the appropriate documentation.

4. **B.** UGMA rules require that any UGMA account have only one beneficial owner and one custodian. Cash and securities may be donated into the account, but insurance contracts and fixed annuities may not.

5. **B.** Court documents appointing a guardian must be on file before an account can be opened for a person declared legally incompetent. The guardian will be the nominal owner of the account.

6. **D.** A minor may not be a party in a joint account because minors cannot legally exercise control over an account. A custodial account should be set up for the minor.

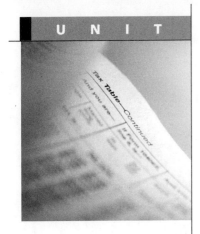

9

Clients, Risks, Strategies, Portfolios, and Taxation

Each investment advisory client is unique. The investment adviser's role is to formulate investment recommendations suitable to the client's needs and objectives in light of the client's resources and circumstances.

The Series 65 exam will include approximately 23 questions on the material presented in this Unit. ■

When you have completed this Unit, you should be able to:

■ **identify** the financial and personal client issues that affect investment adviser recommendations;

■ **compare and contrast** the various portfolio management styles and strategies; and

■ **list** critical taxation issues and their impact on investment decisions.

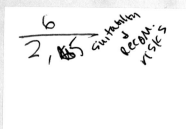

TYPES OF CLIENTS

Because an investment adviser serves in a fiduciary capacity, an adviser needs to develop a comprehensive understanding of a client's financial and personal circumstances before developing suitable investment recommendations.

A **client** of an investment adviser may be an individual, a company, a trust, or an estate. The type of client account can affect the investment recommendations an adviser makes.

Individual Account

An **individual account** may be for a person, a trust, or a deceased person through an estate account. Normally, an individual client is a person who has his investments managed by an adviser for a fee. The adviser must establish, in consultation with the client, a written statement of objectives and investment strategy before executing trades on the client's behalf.

The adviser must periodically review the client's investment profile to determine whether any changes in circumstances could alter the client's objectives.

TAKE NOTE

It is highly recommended that advisers perform annual reviews with their clients to ensure that all recommendations remain suitable.

As a fiduciary, the adviser must ensure that the client's portfolio is suitable for the client and is developed in the client's best interest.

Trusts Accounts

A **trust** is a legal entity that offers flexibility to an individual who wishes to transfer property. Trusts may be established for a variety of personal and charitable property transfers. Trusts are also established as the legal entity for a corporate retirement plan.

The subject of trust law is very complicated and should only be addressed by one who is competent in the subject, usually an attorney. As described in the Retirement Plans Unit, the prudent investor rule is an outgrowth of defining trustee responsibilities.

This exam will require you to know the basics of trusts, how trusts are taxed, trustee responsibility, and your obligations when acting as an adviser to the account.

Trust Parties

For a trust to be valid, three parties must be specified in the trust document (trust agreement). These parties are a settlor, a trustee, and a beneficiary. Under certain circumstances, the settlor, trustee, and beneficiary may be the same individual. For a trust to be valid, both the settlor and the trustee must be competent parties. However, the beneficiary may be a minor or a legally incompetent adult.

The Settlor

The **settlor** is the person who supplies the property for the trust. Trust property is also referred to as its principal or corpus. This party is also known as the maker, grantor, trustor, or donor.

Trustee

A **trustee** is an individual or other party holding legal title to property held for the benefit of another person (or persons). The trustee must administer the trust by following directions in a trust agreement or in a will. A trustee must perform certain duties relative to the trust property.

A trustee is a fiduciary and is obliged to perform in the interest of the beneficiaries. The trustee may be one or more adult individuals or an entity in the business of trusteeship that is responsible for investing, administering, and distributing trust assets for benefit of the beneficiary (or beneficiaries).

In many ways, a trustee's duties are like those of an **executor** (for an estate). However, a trustee's duties generally continue for more time than a typical estate settlement, and the trustee is charged with the greater duty of investing trust assets.

Beneficiary

A **beneficiary** is a person for whose benefit property is held in trust. A beneficiary is one who receives or who is designated to receive benefits from property transferred by a trustor. Beneficiaries to a trust include only those persons upon whom the settlor intended to benefit from the trust property or those who would succeed their interests.

EXAMPLE

Jill establishes a trust under which her husband, Julian, is to receive all income produced by the trust property for as long as he lives. Upon Julian's death, their daughter, Janet, will receive the trust principal. Julian is a primary beneficiary. However, until Julian's death, Janet is a contingent beneficiary because her benefit depends on the occurrence of an event, in this case, Julian's death.

There is no requirement that the beneficiary hold legal capacity. Thus, the beneficiary of a trust may be one or more minors or an adult individual declared legally incompetent.

Simple Trusts Versus Complex

Simple Trusts

All income earned on assets placed into a **simple trust** must be distributed during the year it is received. If the trust does not distribute all of its net income at least annually, the trust is a complex trust. The trustee is not empowered to distribute the trust principal from a simple trust.

Complex Trust

On the other hand, a **complex trust** may accumulate income. A complex trust is permitted deductions for distributions of net income or principal. Capital gains are deemed part of the distributable net income of a complex trust unless reinvested. Furthermore, the trustee may distribute trust principal according to trust terms.

TEST TOPIC ALERT   The key difference between a simple and a complex trust is that the simple trust must distribute all of its annual income, whereas a complex trust is not obligated to do so.

Living Versus Testamentary Trusts

Living Trust

A **living trust**, also known as an **inter vivos trust**, is established during the maker's lifetime. A testamentary trust is established according to the instructions of a will—that is, not with the death of the maker.

Testamentary Trust

With a **testamentary trust**, the settlor retains control over assets until he dies. The individual's will specifies that, at death, the testator's property is to be placed in trust for the benefit or one or more beneficiaries.

The testamentary trust does not reduce the grantor's income or estate tax exposure. Furthermore, assets that pass to a testamentary trust do not avoid probate, because the validity of the will's instructions to pass property to the trust must be substantiated in probate court.

Revocable Versus Irrevocable Trusts

Trusts can be revocable or irrevocable. Terms of a revocable trust may be changed during the maker's lifetime. Terms of an irrevocable trust generally cannot be changed.

Revocable Trust

A revocable trust must be a living trust because only the living grantor has the power to change or revoke (undo) the trust. At the grantor's death, the trust becomes irrevocable because the individual with the power to change or revoke the trust no longer lives.

No estate tax benefit is available for a revocable living trust. The value of any trust assets in which the grantor retains power to revoke the trust and again own the trust property outright is includable in the grantor's gross estate.

Irrevocable Trust

For a trust to be considered irrevocable, the settlor must give up all ownership in property transferred into the trust. Property placed in an irrevocable trust is usually not includable in the trustor's estate for federal estate tax purposes. Certain exceptions to the general rule can jeopardize the effectiveness of an irrevocable trust to reduce estate taxes. The exceptions follow.

- The grantor retains a life interest, or life income.

- The grantor retains a reversionary interest in the trust that is considered more than incidental. Reversionary interest means, without getting overly complicated, that the grantor may receive property back from the trust. Under tax law, the grantor is treated as the owner of any portion of a trust in which he has a reversionary interest in either the corpus or the income if the value of the interest exceeds 5% of the value of that portion.

- The grantor retains general power to direct to whom trust property will pass.

- The grantor transfers one or more life insurance policies into an irrevocable trust while retaining certain incidents of ownership, including the ability to make loans from policy cash values and/or change beneficiaries.

Taxation of Trusts

Taxation of trusts and estates is based on what is distributed and what is retained. In the case of nondistributed income, the tax consequences can be quite severe. For example, although a joint return in 2006 would have to report income in excess of $336,550 to be subject to the highest tax bracket of 35%, that rate is reached once a trust or estate has nondistributed income in excess of $10,050. Obviously, this can have a major impact on investment planning.

Distributable Net Income (DNI)

Because of the onerous tax implications described above, most trusts and estates distribute their income. In the context of a trust or an estate, the taxable income is known as distributable net income (DNI). DNI determines the amount of income that may be taxable to beneficiaries (or the grantor in the case of a living trust), whereas the balance may be taxed to the trust as indicated above. Commissions and other fees charged for buying and selling securities held in a trust are subtracted from the trust's DNI. Realized capital gains that are reinvested in the corpus of the trust are not considered part of DNI.

 EXAMPLE   The Gordon Clark Trust had dividend income of $10,000 and interest income of $7,000. In addition, the trust realized capital gains of $3,000, half of which were reinvested in the corpus of the trust. Transaction costs for the year were $2,000. The Gordon Clark Trust has DNI for the year of $16,500 ($10,000 + $7,000 + $1,500 − $2,000). The $1,500 of realized gains reinvested is not part of DNI.

Tax-exempt interest from municipal bonds remains tax exempt to trust beneficiaries.

Regardless of whether trust income is actually distributed to beneficiaries, each beneficiary is considered to be in receipt of taxable income, even if the beneficiary does not actually receive the income.

Estate

An **estate account** is a custodial account that, like a trust account, is directed by an executor on behalf of the beneficiary or beneficiaries of an estate. The executor makes the investment, management, and distribution decisions for the account. The taxation on undistributed income of an estate is the same as that of trusts just described.

Suitability Issues

Just as with any other account, recommendations must be suitable when considering all of the relevant information. In the case of a trust or estate, however, there are several considerations that do not arise in other individual accounts. Some of these are as follows.

- The trust document will usually spell out the trust's objectives, and these must be followed.

- In the case of an estate, the will must be followed.

- If the investment adviser is actually managing the portfolio, in addition to the normal fiduciary responsibility assumed by all investment advisers, there are the formal requirements of the prudent investor rule.

- There are tax considerations, as mentioned above.

- Conflicts between the grantor and the beneficiary may exist.

 E X A M P L E

A widow was left a trust with her children as contingent beneficiaries. She is to receive income from the trust, and her two children will receive the principal upon her death. To maximize their value, the children ask you to allocate half of the corpus to growth stocks while leaving the balance in bonds for their mother. Because the trust document called for the widow to receive income, the adviser must pursue that objective and cannot follow the wishes of the children until the trust becomes theirs.

BUSINESS ACCOUNTS

A business may open an investment account with an adviser. Each type of business account requires specific documentation.

Sole Proprietorship

A **sole proprietorship** is the business of an individual businessowner and is treated like an individual account. Therefore, the same issues of suitability that apply to individual accounts apply to the management of sole proprietorship accounts.

Partnerships

A **partnership** is a business formed under a partnership agreement that identifies the goals and purpose of the partnership. Partnerships allow the business' profits and losses to flow directly through to the investors for tax purposes, thus avoiding double taxation of profits at the business and individual levels.

Because the income and losses flow through to the individual partners, the objectives and financial constraints of the individual partners must be considered from a suitability standpoint.

Limited Liability Company (LLC)

A **limited liability company (LLC)** is a business structure that combines benefits of incorporation (limited liability) with the tax advantages of a partnership (flow-through of taxable earnings). The LLC owners are members (not shareholders) and are not personally liable for the debts of the LLC.

Just as with the partnership client described above, the objectives and financial constraints of the individual members must be considered from a suitability standpoint.

S Corporations

An **S corporation**, although taxed like a partnership, offers investors the limited liability associated with corporations in general. The profits and losses are passed through directly to the shareholders in proportion to their ownership in the S corporation. Unlike an LLC, which can have an unlimited number of members, an S corporation may not have more than 100 shareholders, none of whom may be a nonresident alien, or more than one class of stock (presumably common).

Losses on S corporation stock may be claimed only to the extent of an investor's basis in the shares. The basis includes money contributed or lent to the corporation.

Any business organization client where the entity itself has no liability and is not subject to tax, such as the partnership, LLC, and S corporation, requires the adviser to look through the entity to the owners in order to properly meet the suitability standards.

TAKE NOTE

Geraldine invested $25,000 in an S corporation, along with nine other investors who invested the same amount. Within a year, the corporation needed additional candy-making equipment, so Geraldine lent $10,000 to the business from her own funds. Her basis is now $35,000. If the corporation experiences a $400,000 loss, Geraldine's portion is $40,000. However, she may deduct only $35,000 of the loss because that is the amount of her basis.

C Corporations

A **C corporation** is a business structure that distinguishes the company as a separate entity from its owners. The corporation's officers and directors are shielded from personal liability for the corporation's debts and losses in most circumstances. A corporation's creditors cannot reach the shareholder's assets to satisfy the corporation's debts. Corporate income tax applies to the corporation as an entity rather than being passed through to the shareholder.

TAKE NOTE   C corporation dividends are subject to double taxation. Before distribution, the earnings are taxable to the corporation and then are taxed again to the shareholder. Distributions from LLCs and S corporations are taxed only once because there is no taxation at the business entity level.

CLIENT PERSONAL PROFILE

An adviser must be familiar with each client's circumstances, financial goals, and needs to formulate suitable investment recommendations.

Financial Status

A **financial profile** should include an assessment of the client's:

■ current expenditures;

■ debt obligations;

■ tax status;

■ income sources; and

■ assets, including

— cash, CDs, and savings accounts,

— real estate holdings,

— value and composition of securities holdings,

— pension and retirement accounts,

— life insurance policies, and

— personal items such as jewelry and automobiles.

Using this information, the adviser will prepare a family balance sheet. This balance sheet reflects all of the client's assets and liabilities in order to determine the overall net worth and liquidity of that client.

Nonfinancial Considerations

A client's nonfinancial considerations can be more important than the financial information. Relevant nonfinancial information includes the following:

- Age
- Marital status
- Investment experience
- Attitudes and values
- Number and age of dependents
- Employment stability
- Employment of family members
- Current and future family educational needs
- Current and future family health care needs

Risk Tolerance

Investor **risk tolerance**—the attitude toward risk and safety—is an important part of a client's profile. Regardless of a person's financial status, the customer's motivation to invest and risk tolerance should shape the portfolio. To understand a customer's risk tolerance, an adviser should know information such as the following:

- How much of a loss the investor can tolerate (e.g., 5%, 50%, or 100%)
- The liquidity requirements for investments
- The importance of tax considerations
- Investment time horizon, either long-term or short-term
- Investment experience
- Current investment holdings
- Expectations regarding investment returns
- Investment temperament (i.e., is the client bored with stable investments or anxious with volatile ones?)
- Level of tolerance for market fluctuations

A person's risk tolerance is often characterized as either aggressive or conservative.

Aggressive investors are willing to risk greater amounts and withstand market volatility in exchange for the chance to realize substantial returns. An aggressive investor may be willing to sustain losses of 10%, 25%, or even 50% on an investment. **Conservative investors** normally want the relative safety of guaranteed interest income. Very conservative investors are unwilling to sustain even modest losses on their investments. There is a full spectrum of risk profiles between these two extremes.

TAKE NOTE   An investor who claims to be aggressive but is unwilling to sustain losses is actually conservative.

A client's tolerance for volatility and risk will often narrow the field of potential investments.

FINANCIAL GOALS/OBJECTIVES

Within the parameters determined by a client's circumstances and financial resources, the adviser and client should establish financial goals. The most commonly specified goals include capital preservation, current income, capital growth, and speculation. The objectives behind these goals may be planning for college education, retirement, death, or disability.

Preservation of Capital

Many people are averse to any decline in value of their investments. For such investors, CDs, savings accounts, and money market funds offer the safety they seek. However, the relatively low income earned from such investments subjects the investor to a loss of purchasing power due to inflation.

Current Income

Investors seeking current income will normally focus on individual securities or mutual funds that invest in fixed-income investments such as:

- government bonds and notes and agency bonds;
- corporate bonds and notes;
- preferred stock; and
- utility company stock.

Not all income-producing investments are the same. Money market mutual funds invest in very safe, very short-term instruments. As a result, they can be structured so that the principal will not fluctuate; the value of each share will remain $1. All this safety comes at a cost. Money market funds tend to have relatively low yields. On the other end of the spectrum are bonds of corporations with very low credit ratings. These bonds tend to yield high, if somewhat uneven, income, with principal subject to credit risk.

In choosing between income-producing investments, the time the investor expects to remain in the holding is a primary consideration. If the client will likely need to use the money invested in less than two years, a money market mutual fund would ensure a positive return on investment with no fluctuation of principal. If the client can afford to remain in the investment for 5–10 years, a corporate bond would produce much greater returns. In the three- to five-year range, an intermediate-term government bond can provide relative safety of principal and a competitive interest rate.

Capital Growth

Stock investments generally provide a means to preserve and increase the buying power of an investor's money over and above the inflation rate. Although subject to short-term volatility, the equity market tends to provide higher investment returns over time.

As with income, the term *growth* refers to a broad spectrum of investments. Aggressive growth stocks may be very appropriate for a person with a very high tolerance for risk and the ability to remain invested for many years. At the other end of the spectrum are large capitalization stock funds that invest in some of the largest and most respected companies. These funds may be a better choice for older investors, who may need to liquidate the investment in three to five years, or investors who are more comfortable knowing they have invested in a fund that is less risky.

Speculation

A customer may want to speculate with a portion of their investments. Speculative investments offer the opportunity to earn substantial returns but carry a commensurate amount of risk. Speculative investments may include:

- highly volatile stocks;
- high-yield (junk) bonds;
- options on stocks or stock indexes; and
- futures.

College Tuition

In addition to other types of investments, investors planning for college tuition often invest in zero-coupon bonds that mature when the tuition expenses are due. It may be advisable to establish college tuition investment programs such as Coverdell ESAs (formerly known as Education IRAs) and Section 529 plans because of their tax advantages.

Retirement

In determining a client's retirement needs, Social Security, company pensions, retirement savings accounts, and insurance (as well as investments outside of a retirement planning framework) should all be considered.

The earlier an individual begins to save for retirement, the more time the investment assets are able to grow. A long-term retirement planning time horizon may enable an investor to assume additional risk in the portfolio, generally through equities. This helps a client accumulate significant funds to support a long retirement period.

Death Benefits

Because death can eliminate a family's primary income earner and cause a possible substantial estate tax liability, life insurance is an important component of customer portfolios. Family businesses are often lost as a result of estate taxes insufficiently covered by insurance. At minimum, life insurance coverage should provide for:

- payoff of the client's mortgage and other debts;

- income for the survivor(s) for a reasonable time;

- college tuition; and

- estate taxes for investment and other assets that may exceed $2 million in 2006 (gradually rising to $3.5 million in 2009).

TEST TOPIC ALERT   For test purposes, younger people with children are better off purchasing term insurance because the lower premiums allow significantly more protection. For those age 60 and older, the rates are generally prohibitive.

Income Tax Implications of Life Insurance

Premiums for individually purchased life insurance are generally nondeductible for income tax purposes. Generally, proceeds from life insurance policies made to a beneficiary are exempt from federal income tax.

Estate Tax Implications to Owning Life Insurance

If someone named as the insured individual on a life insurance policy holds incidents of ownership in that policy, the entire death benefit payable under that policy is included for federal estate tax purposes in the insured individual's estate.

If a person retains the right to designate a beneficiary, transfer ownership of an insurance policy (assign), choose how dividends or policy proceeds will be paid out, borrow money from the accumulated cash value of the policy, or perform any other functions that are rights of ownership, then that person has incidents of ownership in the policy.

Irrevocable Life Insurance Trust

In light of the estate tax implications, it is best that a party other than the insured own the life insurance policy. An effective alternative to ownership of a policy on one's own life is to have the life insurance acquired by or transferred to an irrevocable life insurance trust (ILIT). If certain provisions, known as Crummey powers, are included in the ILIT document, premiums paid by the insured may qualify for the annual gift tax exclusion (currently $12,000 per year, per beneficiary).

Disability

Should a client become disabled, there are three possible sources of replacement income: workers' compensation, Social Security, and disability insurance.

Workers' Compensation. If an employee is injured on the job, workers' compensation can provide protection to cover medical expenses, replace lost income, and provide death benefits to the family.

Social Security. Like other Social Security benefits, a worker's disability benefit will depend on a number of factors, such as age and income.

Disability Insurance. In addition to the limited disability benefits provided by the employee's workers' compensation and Social Security, a client can purchase private disability income insurance. The amount of insurance can be determined by the information derived from the client's income, needs, and occupation. Many clients are covered under group medical, disability, and life insurance programs supported fully or in part by employers.

Tax Planning

A client's tax situation is often an important factor in determining suitable investments. Taxes may be reduced by using the following three strategies: asset and income shifting, tax deferral, or tax-free income.

Asset and Income Shifting. A client can shift investment assets and income to a person in a lower tax bracket. Until early 2006, it was common to place income-producing assets in the name of a child aged 14 or older to avoid the "kiddie" tax, but since that age has been raised to 18, we don't expect many will be using that tool in the future. However, with many of today's baby boomers supporting elderly parents, placing those assets in the parent's name will remove the income from your client and let the parent receive the income directly with little or no tax liability. As mentioned previously, trusts may also be used to shift assets and income.

Tax Deferral. Contributions to a qualified retirement plan or tax-sheltered annuity are not taxed until withdrawn. Investing funds that have not been taxed allows a substantially larger portion of the investor's money to earn income or capital gains, also not taxed until withdrawn.

Tax-Free Income. Most municipal bonds pay interest that is free from federal taxation. Municipal bonds pay a lower interest rate than taxable bonds but, depending on the investor's tax bracket, may result in higher returns on an after-tax basis.

TAKE NOTE   Although interest income from municipal bonds is tax free, capital gains are fully taxable. Capital gains occur when the bond is sold for a price that is greater than the investor's cost basis (investment) in the bond. Additionally, Section 529 plans, Roth IRAs, and Coverdell ESAs may provide tax-free earnings.

Time Horizon

An investor's time horizon and liquidity needs will determine the level of volatility the client should assume. Over a 20- or 30-year time frame, dramatic short-term volatility is acceptable, even to those who are risk averse. Money that will be needed within three to five years should be invested for safety and liquidity.

QUICK QUIZ 9.1

1. A husband and wife are 55 and 57 years old, respectively. The husband plans to retire at 62 and the wife at 65, and both are healthy. What is the most appropriate estimate of the time horizon for their retirement portfolio?

    A. 5 years
    B. 7 years
    C. 8 years
    D. More than 20 years

Quick Quiz answers can be found at the end of the Unit.

Life Cycle Considerations

An investor's goals may change over time. This is especially true as investors move from one phase of life to another. For example, a young couple may have a primary goal of funding a child's education. Later, the same family, having provided for their children's education, may turn their attention to the aggressive accumulation of wealth, perhaps to provide for an early retirement or a dream home. Upon retirement, this couple may need to move toward income-producing investments. Income and net worth change over time, as do investment goals and life cycle considerations. Because the adviser's responsibility to know his client is ongoing, the account form should be updated regularly to reflect the client's new goals and financial considerations.

TEST TOPIC ALERT   The following chart summarizes common investor objectives and appropriate recommendations. Be ready for a significant number of situational questions that require determining the best solution for the investor.

Investor Objective	Suitable Recommendation
Preservation of capital; safety	Government securities or Ginnie Maes
Growth — Balanced/moderate growth — Aggressive growth	Common stock or common stock mutual funds — Large-cap stocks, defensive stocks — Technology stocks, sector funds, or cyclical stocks
Income — Tax-free income — High-yield income — From a stock portfolio	Bonds (but not zero-coupons) — Municipal bonds or municipal bond funds — Corporate bonds or corporate bond funds — Preferred stock and utility stocks
Liquidity	Money market funds — (DPPs, CDs, real estate, and annuities are not considered liquid)
Speculation	Volatile stocks, high-yield bonds, stock/index options

PORTFOLIO MANAGEMENT STYLES AND STRATEGIES

Portfolio managers use a range of investment styles. Although each style attempts to generate superior investment returns and reduce investment risks, no single style is suited to every investor. Often, an investment adviser's role is to guide clients toward a mutual fund or private money manager that is consistent with the client's objectives and temperament.

ASSET ALLOCATION

Asset allocation refers to the spreading of portfolio funds among different asset classes. Proponents of asset allocation feel that the mix of assets within a portfolio, rather than individual stock selection, is the primary factor underlying portfolio performance. There are three major types (each with subclasses) of asset classes:

■ Stock, with subclasses based on market capitalization, value versus growth, and foreign equity

■ Bonds, with subclasses based on maturity (intermediate versus long-term), and issuer (Treasury versus corporate versus non-US issuers)

■ Cash, focusing mainly on the standard risk-free investment, the 90-day Treasury bill, but also including other short-term money market instruments

In some instances, tangible assets, such as real estate or precious metals, are part of the asset allocation because these types of assets tend to reduce inflation risk. Increasingly, institutional investors (and some very high net worth individuals) are using such alternative investment asset classes as hedge funds, private equity, and venture capital.

Strategic Asset Allocation

Strategic asset allocation refers to the proportion of various types of investments composing a long-term investment portfolio.

EXAMPLE

A standard asset allocation model suggests subtracting a person's age from 100 to determine the percentage of the portfolio to be invested in stocks. According to this method, a 30-year-old would be 70% invested in stocks and 30% in bonds and cash; a 70-year-old would be invested 30% in stocks with the remainder in bonds and cash.

Rebalancing is a term often used for this process. If the stock market should perform better than expected, the client's proportion of stocks to bonds would be out of balance. So, on some timely basis (perhaps quarterly), stocks would be sold and bonds would be purchased (or funds would be placed in cash) to bring the proportions back to the desired levels.

EXAMPLE

Using the 70% equity/30% debt model described above, the investor's initial investment of $100,000 is split $70,000 into equity securities and $30,000 into debt securities. Let's say the account is to be rebalanced semiannually. Because of a bull market in stocks, six months later, the account value is $120,000. Analysis of the account indicates that the value of the equities is now $90,000, whereas the bonds have remained stable at $30,000. To rebalance—that is, to bring the account back to the 70/30 ratio—it will be necessary to sell $6,000 of the equity and invest those funds into debt. That will make the account $84,000 equity and $36,000 debt, our desired 70/30 ratio. The effect of this is that stocks are sold in a rising market and purchased in a falling market, following the old adage of "buy low and sell high."

Tactical Asset Allocation

Tactical asset allocation refers to short-term portfolio adjustments that adjust the portfolio mix between asset classes in consideration of current market conditions.

EXAMPLE

If the stock market is expected to do well over the near term, a portfolio manager may allocate greater portions of a portfolio to stocks. If the market is expected to decline, the portfolio manager may allocate greater portions of the portfolio entirely to bonds and cash.

ACTIVE AND PASSIVE MANAGEMENT

An active portfolio manager, using a particular stock selection approach, buys and sells individual stocks. **Active management** relies on the manager's stock picking and market timing ability to outperform market indexes.

EXAMPLE

An active portfolio manager may position the portfolio in stocks within a few market sectors (such as pharmaceuticals and technology) frequently trading in and out of the stocks. An active manager may change the sector focus to capitalize on relative performance of different sectors during different stages of the business cycle.

A _passive portfolio manager_ believes that no particular management style will consistently outperform market averages and therefore constructs a portfolio that mirrors a market index, such as the S&P 500. Passive portfolio management seeks low-cost means of generating consistent, long-term returns with minimal turnover.

TEST TOPIC ALERT

For purposes of the examination, passive portfolio management is very similar to strategic asset allocation. The same could be said about the relationship between active management and tactical asset allocation.

Growth

Growth portfolio managers focus on stocks of companies whose earnings are growing faster than most other stocks and are expected to continue to do so. Because rapid growth in earnings is often priced into the stocks, growth investment managers are likely to buy stocks that are at the high end of their 52-week price range. Therefore, in the eyes of some, they might be buying stocks that are overvalued.

Value

Value portfolio managers concentrate on undervalued or out-of-favor securities whose price is low relative to the company's earnings or book value and whose earnings prospects are believed to be unattractive by investors and securities analysts. Value investment managers seek to buy undervalued securities before the company reports positive earnings surprises. Value investment managers are more likely to buy stocks that are at the bottom of their 52-week price range.

EXAMPLE

ABC Co. is a metal processor for parts used in the automotive industry. The company has grown by 10% per year for the past 15 years but is somewhat susceptible to downturns in the economy. The stock has paid a quarterly dividend that has increased five times in the past 10 years. Conservatively managed, the company owns assets and cash that exceed the market value of its common stock. ABC would be attractive to investors because its intrinsic value is lower than its market value.

Market Capitalization

Although the boundaries are imprecise, micro-cap companies are generally those with a market capitalization of less than $300 million; small-cap companies are generally those with a market capitalization of between $300 and $2 billion; mid-cap companies are those with $2 billion to $10 billion; and large-cap companies are those with more than $10 billion.

It is generally assumed that small companies with a short history, small product line, and limited financial resources represent a larger degree of risk in an economic downturn. As revenues, product diversification, and financial worth increase, the relative risk the company carries in a weak economy diminishes.

TAKE NOTE   In a strong economy, small, fast-moving companies with a concentrated product line in a fast-growing sector can dramatically outperform larger, more bureaucratic companies.

Buy/Hold

The **buy and hold technique** can be used with any investment style. A buy and hold manager rarely trades in the portfolio, which results in lower transaction costs and long-term capital gains taxes. A low expense ratio in a mutual fund often may reflect a buy and hold approach.

Indexing

Investment portfolios constructed to mirror the components of a particular stock index, such as the S&P 500, will normally perform in line with the index. Because such portfolios are not actively managed, the costs of managing the portfolio are relatively low. Because most professional money managers are unable to consistently outperform market indexes, indexed mutual fund portfolios are a popular investment vehicle for investors.

Diversification

Portfolio diversification (i.e., committing to an array of separate investments) reduces risk and enhances returns. The securities in a diversified portfolio are selected, in part, because they do not tend to move up or down in relation to each other.

QUICK QUIZ 9.2   True or False?

_____ 1. Workers' compensation generally provides a larger disability income benefit than private disability insurance.

_____ 2. Utility company stock is generally considered suitable for satisfying a current income objective.

_____ 3. An investor's temperament and level of tolerance for market fluctuation should be considered in preparing investment recommendations.

_____ 4. Both LLCs and S corporations are taxed like partnerships.

_____ 5. As a fiduciary, an investment adviser has the responsibility to ensure that a client's portfolio is suitable and developed in the best interest of the client.

_____ 6. Conservative investors are generally interested in guaranteed interest income with little chance for loss of principal.

_____ 7. Government instruments are guaranteed to preserve investor capital.

_____ 8. Zero-coupon bonds are typically considered suitable for funding college educations.

QUICK QUIZ 9.3   Matching

A. Indexing
B. Growth investing
C. Value investing
D. Tactical asset allocation
E. Strategic asset allocation

_____ 1. Balancing portfolio assets for the long term

_____ 2. Selecting companies currently out of favor on the basis of earnings prospects

_____ 3. Constructing a portfolio to mirror the performance of the S&P 500

_____ 4. Constructing a portfolio of companies that are outperforming most other stocks in that industry

_____ 5. Involves short-term adjustments to portfolio asset class mix

---

FUNDING TECHNIQUES

A client can commit a large sum of money at one time to an investment or fund an investment program over time. Popular time-based investment programs used by investors include dollar cost averaging and income reinvestment.

Dollar Cost Averaging

Investors use **dollar cost averaging** as a means to invest consistent amounts of money in a mutual fund or stock at regular periodic intervals, such as monthly or quarterly. This form of investing allows the individual to purchase more shares when prices are low and fewer shares when prices are high. In a fluctuating market, the average cost per share is lower than the average price per share.

EXAMPLE   The following table illustrates how average price and average cost may vary with dollar cost averaging.

Month	Amount Invested	Price per Share	No. of Shares
January	$600	$20	30
February	$600	$24	25
March	$600	$30	20
April	$600	$40	15
Total	$2,400	$114	90

The average cost per share equals $2,400 (the total investment) divided by 90 (the total number of shares purchased), or $26.67 per share, whereas the average price per share is $28.50 ($114 ÷ 4). With any market fluctuations, this strategy will produce a lower cost ($26.67) than average price ($28.50). This average cost of $26.67, not the average price paid of $28.50, is the investor's cost basis when the shares are subsequently sold.

TEST TOPIC ALERT   Although it is unlikely that you will have to compute the average price or average cost per share, a question may ask the purpose of dollar cost averaging. The purpose of dollar cost averaging is to reduce the investor's average cost to acquire a security over the buying period relative to its average price.

Income Reinvestment

Stocks and bonds normally pay dividends and interest in cash, and the investor only realizes a capital gain or loss when the investment is sold. Mutual funds normally allow dividends, interest, and capital gains to be automatically reinvested in the fund shares at the net asset value (NAV) per share.

Dividend Reinvestment Plans

Some corporations offer their shareholders the opportunity to purchase additional stock using their cash dividend. Under most **dividend reinvestment plans (DRIPs)**, the shareholder is entitled to purchase the additional shares directly from the issuer without paying a commission and often at a discount to market price.

Taxation of Reinvested Distributions

Distributions are taxable to shareholders whether the distributions are taken in cash or reinvested. The issuer must disclose whether each distribution comes from income or realized capital gains. **Form 1099**, which is sent to shareholders after the close of the year, details tax information related to distributions for the year.

TAXATION

Taxes on income and capital gains diminish the amount of money available to the person who earns it. As a result, personal and business investment decisions are often influenced by the tax implications.

CORPORATE TAXES

Corporations are major investors in securities. Some Internal Revenue Code (IRC) provisions affecting corporations as investors include the following.

- **Dividend exclusion rule:** Dividends paid from one corporation to another are 70% exempt from taxation. A corporation that receives dividends on stocks of other domestic corporations, therefore, pays taxes on only 30% of the dividends received. This encourages corporations to invest in common and preferred stock of other US corporations.

- **Municipal securities:** Like individual taxpayers, corporations do not pay federal taxes on interest received from municipal bonds.

INDIVIDUAL INCOME TAXES

Taxes function as either regressive or progressive costs. **Regressive taxes** (e.g., sales, excise, payroll, property, and gasoline taxes) are levied equally regardless of income and thus represent a smaller percentage of income for wealthy taxpayers than for taxpayers with lower incomes. Because low-income families spend a larger percentage of their incomes than they save or invest, regressive taxes consume a larger fraction of the income of the poor than of the wealthy. **Progressive taxes** (e.g., estate and income taxes) increase the tax rate as income increases. Progressive taxes are costlier to people with high incomes than to people with low incomes.

Earned Income

Earned income includes salary, bonuses, and income derived from active participation in a trade or business.

Alimony and Child Support

Alimony is payment made under a (divorce) court order (or under a legal separation agreement) to an ex-spouse. Alimony may be paid directly to the ex-spouse or to a third party on the ex-spouse's behalf (e.g., to pay premiums on the ex-spouse's life insurance or contribute to the ex-spouse's IRA). Alimony payments, within limits, are generally deductible to the spouse making the payments and includable in income for tax purposes by the spouse receiving them.

Child Support

Alimony should not be confused with child support. **Child support** is a legal obligation of a parent to provide financial support for a child (typically occurring when the parent providing the support is not the parent with whom the child or children lives). Child support is not deductible by the parent who pays it, nor is it includable in income by the recipient, who is often the other parent receiving the support on behalf of the child of the dissolved marriage.

EXAMPLE

Chuck and Alice divorced after a 10-year marriage that produced two children, Tim, age 6, and Kim, age 8. Under a court order, it is decided that Chuck will pay Alice $1,000 per month in alimony and $600 per child per month ($1,200 in total child support). Chuck may deduct $12,000 for the tax year ($1,000 × 12 months) on his federal income tax return. Alice must report $12,000 for the tax year on her federal income tax return. Chuck cannot deduct any of the child support, nor is any of it reportable for income tax by Alice or their children.

Passive Income

Passive income and losses come from rental property, limited partnerships, and enterprises (regardless of business structure) in which an individual does not actively participate. For the general partner, income from a limited partnership is earned income; for the limited partner, the income is passive. Passive income is netted against passive losses to determine net taxable income. Passive losses may be used to offset only passive income.

Portfolio Income

Portfolio income includes dividends, interest, and net capital gains derived from the sale of securities. No matter what the source of the income, it is taxed in the year in which it is received.

Retirement Plan Distributions

Qualified retirement plan distributions are, with few exceptions, taxed at the investor's ordinary income tax rate when funds are withdrawn from the plan. Distributions from a qualified plan before the investor reaches age 59½ are also subject to a 10% early withdrawal penalty. Distributions from a qualified plan must begin by April 1 following the year the participant reaches 70½.

Alternative Minimum Tax

Congress enacted the **alternative minimum tax (AMT)** to ensure that high-income taxpayers do not escape federal income taxes. Certain items that receive favorable tax treatment must be added back into taxable income for the AMT and include the following:

■ Accelerated depreciation on property placed in service after 1986

- Certain costs associated with limited partnership programs, such as research and development costs and excess intangible drilling costs

- Local tax and interest on investments that do not generate income

- Tax-exempt interest on private purpose municipal bonds issued after August 7, 1986

- Incentive stock options to the extent that the fair market value of the employer's stock is in excess the strike price of the option

TAKE NOTE   Items that must be added back in for the purpose of the AMT computation are sometimes called **tax-preferenced items**. If the tax liability computed under the AMT computation is greater than the taxpayer's regular tax computation, the taxpayer must pay the AMT amount.

CAPITAL GAINS AND LOSSES

The sale of a security can result in a capital gain or a capital loss. A **capital gain** occurs when a security is sold for a price higher than its cost basis; if the selling price is lower than the cost basis, a **capital loss** occurs.

Adjusting Cost Basis

An investment's **cost basis** (total cost of the investment) is used to determine whether a capital gain or a capital loss occurs when an asset is sold. Because many factors affect an asset's cost basis, the IRS requires the cost basis to be adjusted for such occurrences as stock splits and stock dividends.

EXAMPLE   An investor buys 100 shares of RST at $55. Later, the company declares a stock dividend and the investor receives 10 more shares. His total investment remains $5,500, but he now owns 110 shares of RST. The investor's adjusted cost basis per share is now $50 ($5,500 ÷ 110).

Capital Gains

A capital gain occurs when capital assets (securities, real estate, and tangible property) are sold at prices that exceed the adjusted cost basis. Usually, computing the capital gain or loss on an asset is a matter of comparing the purchase price with the selling price less commissions.

TAKE NOTE   A lower cost basis results in a larger capital gain. The gain is determined by comparing the sales proceeds with the cost basis.

EXAMPLE   If the investor's cost basis in stock is $50 per share and shares are sold for $60, the investor has a capital gain of $10. However, if the investor's cost basis is $55 and the shares are sold for $60, the investor's capital gain is only $5.

Capital Losses

A **capital loss** occurs when capital assets are sold at prices that are lower than the adjusted cost basis.

Net Capital Gains and Losses

To calculate tax liability, a taxpayer must first add all short-term capital gains and losses for the year. (Short-term gains are investments held 12 months or less and are taxed at the investor's ordinary income tax rate.) Then all long-term capital gains and losses are added. (A long-term capital gain or loss only occurs after the investor has held the investment at risk for a period exceeding one year.) Finally, the taxpayer offsets the totals to determine his net capital gain or loss for the year. If the result is a net long-term capital gain, it is taxed at the capital gains rate, currently at 15% for most taxpayers.

Capital losses that exceed capital gains are deductible against earned income up to a maximum of $3,000 per year. Any capital losses not deducted in a taxable year may be carried forward indefinitely as a deduction to offset capital gains in future years.

Determining Which Shares to Sell

An investor holding identical securities with different acquisition dates and cost bases may determine which shares to sell by electing one of three accounting methods: first in, first out (FIFO); share identification; or average cost basis. If the investor fails to choose, the IRS assumes the investor liquidates shares on a FIFO basis.

When FIFO shares are sold, the cost of the shares held the longest is used to calculate the gain or loss. In a rising market, this method normally creates adverse tax consequences.

When using the **share identification** accounting method, the investor keeps track of the cost of each share purchased and uses this information to liquidate the shares that would provide the lowest capital gain. Share identification is used to identify the specific per-share cost basis when shares are sold. The investor keeps track of the cost of each share purchased and specifies which shares to sell on the basis of his tax needs.

A shareholder may elect to use an **average cost basis** when redeeming mutual fund shares (but not shares of specific stocks). The investor would calculate average basis by dividing the total cost of all shares owned by the total number of shares. The shareholder may not change the decision to use the average basis method without IRS permission.

TAKE NOTE   Share identification may result in more advantageous tax treatment, but most accountants prefer the convenience of the averaging method for mutual fund shares. Share identification is most commonly used with stock sales.

Wash Sales

An investor may not use capital losses to offset gains or income if the taxpayer sells a security at a loss and purchases the same or a substantially identical security within 30 days before or after the trade date establishing the loss. The sale at a loss and the repurchase within this period is a **wash sale**. The loss that was disallowed, however, is added to the repurchased shares' cost basis.

EXAMPLE   An investor buys 100 shares for $50. One year later, the investor sells the shares for $40. Fifteen days after the sale, he repurchases 100 shares of the same stock for $42. His new cost basis is $52 because the $10 loss that was disallowed is added to the repurchase price of $42.

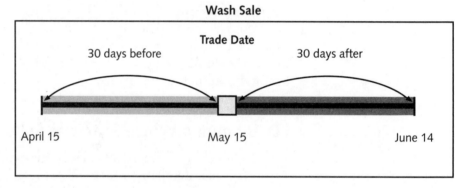

Wash Sale

Substantially identical securities include stock rights, call options, warrants, and convertible securities of the same issue.

The IRS compares three qualities of debt securities in determining whether they are substantially identical: the maturity, coupon, and issuer. A bond is substantially identical if all three qualities of the bond sold at a loss and the newly purchased bond are the same.

After selling a bond, an investor can buy another bond with either a different maturity, coupon, or issuer without violating the wash sale rule.

EXAMPLE   An investor could sell an ABC 8% bond that matures in 2010 at a loss and buy back an ABC 8% bond that matures in 2011 and claim the loss. This is commonly called tax-swapping.

TAKE NOTE   The wash sale rule applies only to realized losses—not to realized gains.

Donated (Gifted) and Inherited Securities

Gifts. When a donor makes a gift of securities, the cost basis to the recipient (the donee) is the donor's cost basis. This describes **carryover basis**.

EXAMPLE

In 1995, Joe Smith bought 1,000 shares of COD at $24 per share, for a total cost of $24,000. In 2002, when COD was trading at $32.50, Joe gave those 1,000 shares to his daughter, Sally. When Sally sells the shares, her cost basis is Joe's cost basis on the date of his original purchase—$24 per share—not the market value on the date of the gift. So, if Sally were to sell those shares for $33 per share one month after receiving the gift, she would be replacing a long-term capital gain of $9,000.

TAKE NOTE

If a charitable gift of securities held for more than one year is made, the tax treatment is more favorable. Under these circumstances, Joe's deduction is based on the fair market value on the date of the gift, not his cost basis. He would have received a $32,500 tax deduction and avoided capital gains taxes on the $8,500 profit.

Inherited Securities. When a person dies and leaves securities to heirs, the cost basis to the recipients is usually the **fair market value** on the date of the owner's death. In other words, the cost basis steps up to the date of death value.

EXAMPLE

In 1995, Joe Smith bought 1,000 shares of COD at $24 per share for a total cost of $24,000. In 2003, when COD was trading at $32.50, Joe died. His daughter, Sally, is Joe's sole heir and inherits the 1,000 shares upon his death. When Sally sells the shares, her cost basis is the fair market value on the date of Joe's death—$32.50 per share—not Joe's original purchase cost.

TEST TOPIC ALERT

The step up provision does not apply when inheriting an annuity.

Margin Expenses

Margin interest is a tax-deductible expense. The one exception is interest expenses incurred in the purchase of municipal securities. Because municipal interest income is federally tax exempt, the IRS does not allow taxpayers to deduct the margin interest expenses for municipal securities. Investors can deduct interest expenses for other securities, including margin account interest, to the extent they do not exceed their net investment incomes, which includes interest income, dividends, and all capital gains.

ESTATE AND GIFT TAXES

The federal government imposes a tax on a decedent's estate based on the value of the estate, as well as on gifts conveyed to heirs, before a person dies.

Estate Tax

Estate tax is imposed on the transfer of substantial amounts of property at death. An individual may transfer an unlimited amount to a spouse who is a US citizen without the imposition of federal estate tax. In addition, an individual may transfer unlimited amounts of money and other property to an eligible charity with no federal estate tax. For heirs other than spouses, an estate tax credit will offset estate tax on transfers of up to $2 million (in 2006 and scheduled to increase through 2009) of property.

The Gross Estate Versus the Taxable Estate

Federal estate tax is calculated using a formula that begins with the gross estate. The **gross estate** includes all interests in property held by an individual at the time of death. Although amounts of property transferred to a spouse or a charity will generally not be subject to federal estate tax, such amounts are includable in calculating the gross estate.

Certain expenses are then deducted from the gross estate to arrive at the **adjusted gross estate (AGE)**. Examples of deductions for the AGE include funeral expenses and debts of the decedent.

Once the amount of the AGE is determined, the unlimited marital and charitable deductions are subtracted to arrive at the **taxable estate**.

TAKE NOTE   Caroline, who is unmarried, dies in 2006 owning $2.5 million in property. The amount of her gross estate is $2.5 million. However, her estate incurred $20,000 in funeral expenses and $30,000 in Caroline's credit card balances. Thus, her AGE is $2,450,000. In 2006, because of an estate tax credit that exempts the first $2 million in property transferred after death, Caroline's estate will be taxed on the remaining $450,000 in transferred property.

Gift Tax

Gift tax is a federal tax imposed on the transfer of property during the lifetime of the donor; up to $1 million in lifetime gifts may be made without incurring gift tax. Additionally, an individual may give up to $12,000 per year (indexed for inflation in $1,000 increments) to any number of individuals without generating the federal gift tax.

When a gift is made between spouses, the rule is somewhat different. Generally, there is an unlimited exclusion for these gifts. However, there are limits if your spouse is not a citizen of the United States. In 2007, a spouse may gift up to $125,000 to a noncitizen spouse. The number won't be tested because it changes each year, but the concept might be on your exam.

TAKE NOTE
Gift tax is the responsibility of the giver of the gift (donor), not the receiver of the gift (donee).

Taxation of Foreign Securities

Dividend and interest income received from foreign securities is normally subject to 15% withholding tax by the investor's country of citizenship. A foreign tax credit allows many investors to reclaim the withheld income on their tax returns.

QUICK QUIZ 9.4
True or False?

_____ 1. Straight line depreciation is considered a tax preference item for the AMT computation.

_____ 2. Dividend income from stock ownership is considered passive income by the IRS.

_____ 3. If an investor does not choose an acceptable basis when shares are sold, the IRS will assign LIFO.

_____ 4. Investors are not subject to capital gains tax when they receive stock dividends. Instead, the cost basis of shares is adjusted downward.

_____ 5. If an investor sells stock at a loss and within 20 days purchases a call option on that stock, the investor's loss on the stock is disallowed.

_____ 6. The cost basis of inherited securities is the original purchase price of the securities.

_____ 7. Although interest income on municipal bonds is exempt from federal taxation to individual investors, corporate investors are taxed.

_____ 8. A corporation is required to pay taxes on 70% of its dividend income.

_____ 9. The limit on the marital deduction is currently $1 million.

HOTSHEETS

For your convenience, Unit HotSheets summarizing the key points are located at the end of the manual on perforated pages.

UNIT TEST

1. In making suitable investment recommendations, the least significant element would be the client's

    A. retirement needs
    B. death and disability needs
    C. educational level
    D. current income

2. An estate account with an investment adviser must be managed at the direction of the

    A. investment adviser
    B. estate creditors
    C. estate's executor or administrator
    D. attorney with guardianship over the surviving children

3. Since a trust account is managed for the beneficial interest of the beneficiary, the investment adviser representative can

    A. have funds withdrawn from the account at the direction of the beneficiary
    B. arrange to have the trust's funds pledged to support a loan for the trustee
    C. have a check drawn on the account, and payable to the trustee for trustee expenses
    D. place the securities in the trust fund in a non-custodial brokerage account

4. Which of the following is an example of a passive investment management style?

    A. Use of index funds in conjunction with selecting specific securities in the index to overweight certain sectors
    B. Investment in small capitalization technology securities
    C. Exclusive use of index funds
    D. Value investing

5. In determining an investor's risk tolerance, an investment adviser representative must consider

    I. level of tolerance toward market volatility
    II. investment time horizon, long term or short term
    III. liquidity requirements
    IV. investment temperament

    A. I only
    B. I and II
    C. I, II and III
    D. I, II, III and IV

6. With respect to taxation, the investment adviser representative should NOT

    A. draft tax and estate documents to ensure compliance with current law in order to provide substantial after-tax returns
    B. discuss the tax implications of investments
    C. explain the taxable status of particular investments
    D. consider tax implications as a way of improving a client's after-tax returns

7. Which of the following statements is an accurate description of dollar cost averaging?

    A. An investor buys the same number of shares each interval, averaging out his purchase prices over time.
    B. An investor sells shares when the market rises and buys shares when the market declines in order to average his costs.
    C. An investor invests a set amount of money each interval to buy more shares when the prices are low and fewer shares when prices are high.
    D. An investor averages the costs of his shares purchased and then enters limit orders to purchase additional shares at the average price.

8. Which of the following statements regarding taxation is NOT true?

   A. Earned income includes salary, bonus, and income as an owner of a limited partnership.

   B. Passive income is derived from rental property, limited partnerships, and enterprises in which an individual is not actively involved.

   C. Portfolio income includes dividends, interest, and net capital gains derived from the sale of securities.

   D. Items that must be added back into taxable income for calculation of the alternative minimum tax (AMT) include: accelerated depreciation on property placed in service after 1986; local taxes and interest on investments that do not generate income; and incentive stock options exceeding the fair market value of the employer's stock.

9. As part of its suitability determination, an IA firm requires that all potential nonbusiness clients complete a family balance sheet. Items that would be included are

   I. gold jewelry

   II. loan secured by the family automobile

   III. the amount paid thus far this year for Botox injections

   IV. the balance owed to the dentist for new crowns

   A. I, II and IV

   B. I and IV

   C. II and III

   D. I, II, III and IV

10. During the previous fiscal year, The Kaplan Family Trust received $24,000 in dividends and $35,000 in interest from corporate bonds. Securities transactions during the year resulted in long-term capital gains of $48,000, $20,000 of which were reinvested in the corpus. The DNI for the Kaplan Family Trust is

   A. $11,000

   B. $79,000

   C. $87,000

   D. $107,000

ANSWERS AND RATIONALES

1. **C.** A client's educational level is not as important as retirement, death and disability, and current income. However, the adviser should take note of the client's educational level to ensure that the client fully understands the investments recommended. Also, a person with a professional educational background may have more employment opportunities and be able to take more risk as a result.

2. **C.** Only the estate administrator or executor can make investment management and distribution decisions. This does not mean that the executor must manage the account, only that decisions as to who will do the management are within his purview. A guardian with authority over the children does not necessarily have power over the estate unless the guardian is also the administrator or the executor of the estate.

3. **C.** The trustee can be reimbursed for trustee expenses that are reasonable. A trust account must be managed by the trustee and not by the beneficiary. Only the trustee can withdraw funds, provided the withdrawal is done in a manner consistent with the trust document. Trust funds must be placed in custodial accounts, not in noncustodial accounts.

4. **C.** A passive investment style uses index funds because the manager does not believe that returns above the averages can be sustained for any length of time because the market is efficiently priced. Use of index funds in conjunction with specific securities in order to overweight sectors is an active style. Investment in small capitalization technology securities involves actively selecting securities that the manager believes will perform well or better than the market. Value investing involves the active search for securities that are undervalued by the market.

5. **D.** The investment adviser representative must consider a client's volatility tolerance, investment time frame, liquidity needs, and comfort with different types of investments. These are all elements in the understanding of a customer's attitude toward risk.

6. **A.** An investment adviser representative must not draft estate documents. This should only be drafted by an attorney because it constitutes practicing law. An investment adviser representative should, however, discuss tax implications of investments as a way of improving a client's after-tax returns.

7. **C.** Dollar cost averaging involves investing a set amount of money each interval. If the market fluctuates, this will cause the client to buy more shares when the prices are low and fewer shares when prices are high. The result of this is a lower average cost per share than average price paid. An investor who sells shares when the market rises and buys shares when the market declines is not dollar cost averaging, but is attempting to time the market. An investor who averages the cost of the shares purchased and then enters limit orders to purchase additional shares at the average price is not engaged in a dollar cost averaging program. In dollar cost averaging, the same dollar amount is invested each interval.

8. **A.** Earned income includes salary and bonus but not income as an owner of a limited partnership. Passive income is derived from rental property, limited partnerships, and enterprises in which an individual is not actively involved.

9. **A.** The balance sheet contains assets and liabilities as of a specific point in time. Personal property currently owned, such as jewelry, is an asset. A loan still outstanding, such as the car loan and the debt to the dentist, are liabilities. The amount already paid for the Botox injections is no longer on the balance sheet.

10. **C.** Distributable Net Income (DNI) is dividends and interest plus capital gains that have not been reinvested back into the trust. In this case, $24,000 + $35,000 + $28,000 = $87,000.

QUICK QUIZ ANSWERS

Quick Quiz 9.1

1. **D.** Time horizon does not end at retirement age. The portfolio will have to last them throughout their retirement until their death. On the basis of current life expectancy tables, the money will have to last them at least 20 years.

Quick Quiz 9.2

1. **F.** Workers' compensation and Social Security insurance provide relatively modest disability income benefits.

2. **T.**

3. **T.**

4. **T.**

5. **T.**

6. **T.**

7. **F.** CDs and savings accounts offer guaranteed principal. Government debt instruments are subject to price fluctuation as interest rates fluctuate.

8. **T.**

Quick Quiz 9.3

1. **E.**

2. **C.**

3. **A.**

4. **B.**

5. **D.**

Quick Quiz 9.4

1. **F.** Only accelerated depreciation is a tax preference item for computing AMT.

2. **F.** Dividend income is considered portfolio, or investment, income. Passive income results from limited partnerships and real estate.

3. **F.** The IRS assigns FIFO when an acceptable basis has not been selected. FIFO generally results in the largest capital gain.

4. **T.**

5. **T.**

6. **F.** The cost basis of inherited securities is the market value of the securities on the date of the owner's death.

7. **F.** Interest income from municipal bonds is exempt from taxation when paid to corporations or individuals.

8. **F.** A corporation is taxed on 30% of its dividend income; 70% is excluded.

9. **F.** Marital deduction on transfer of property between spouses is unlimited.

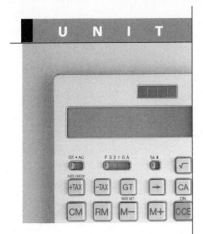

10

Economics and Analysis

Investment decisions are made within the context of the general economic climate and are based on the specific merits of the selected investments. There are two broad categories of investment analysis: fundamental and technical analysis.

Fundamental analysis takes into consideration the financial statements and historical performance of the investment, as well as economic conditions (such as the phases of the business cycle). **Technical analysis** of an investment focuses on pricing patterns as revealed in the market rather than on fundamental economic and financial data.

The Series 65 exam will include approximately 25 questions on the material presented in this unit. ■

WHEN YOU HAVE COMPLETED THIS UNIT, YOU SHOULD BE ABLE TO:

■ **identify** fundamental economic principles and the four stages of the business cycle;

■ **compare** and contrast balance sheet and income statement items and various ratios that are computed to measure corporate performance;

■ **differentiate** between fundamental and technical analysis;

■ **list** several investment-related risks; and

■ **describe** how investment advisers apply the following quantitative measurements.

— Time value of money concepts

— Investment return measurements

— Risk measurements

20 questions

GT • AC   F 3 2 1 0 A   5/4

RATE CHECK

RATE SET

BASIC ECONOMICS

Economics is the social science concerned chiefly with the description and analysis of production, distribution, and consumption of goods and services.

TAKE NOTE

Economics is about how people choose. From the most important to the most mundane, any decision is economic in nature. Every choice made in terms of the decision maker's utility can be thought of as satisfaction. In every choice we make, we try to find the combination of cost and benefit that maximizes our utility (satisfaction).

There are two major branches of economics: microeconomics and macroeconomics. **Microeconomics** focuses on the economic behavior of narrowly defined units, such as households or business firms.

Macroeconomics is the branch of economics that analyzes aggregates, such as the rate of growth in national economic output as measured by the gross domestic product (GDP), the rate of inflation, and unemployment. Though the two areas overlap in many ways, the Series 65 exam focuses primarily on macroeconomic concepts.

TAKE NOTE

It is important for you to know that the fiscal policy of the United States is determined by the President and Congress through the process of budgeting and taxation. Monetary policy is determined by the Board of Governors of the Federal Reserve System.

MAJOR SCHOOLS OF ECONOMICS

Keynesian Economics

Named after the economist John Maynard Keynes, Keynesian economists recognize the importance of government intervention. In 1936, Keynes published *The General Theory of Employment, Interest, and Money* in which he revolutionized the way economists think about macroeconomics. He laid out how and why recessions happen and what must be done to recover from them. His strategy for recovery from a recession was for government to run deficits to stimulate demand and employment. In this approach, Keynes varied widely from classical economists, such as Adam Smith, who advocated a strict hands-off approach to government. Classical economists argue that market wages and prices will decline quickly enough during a recession to bring about an economic recovery.

Classical and Supply-Side Economics

Classical economists favor a school of thought referred to as supply-side economics. **Supply-side economics** holds that supply creates demand by providing jobs and wages. The prices of goods of which there is excess supply will fall, and the prices of goods in demand will rise. Deficient demand can never be a problem because the production of goods will always generate (through employment) sufficient demand to purchase the goods produced.

Markets will always adjust quickly to direct the economy to full employment. It is argued that if unemployment is temporarily high, wages will fall, which will reduce costs and prices. Reduced prices will increase product demand, which will increase the demand for labor until the excess supply of labor is eliminated.

Monetarist Theory

Monetarists, such as the late Milton Friedman, believe that the quantity of money, or money supply, determines overall price levels and economic activity. Too many dollars chasing too few goods leads to inflation, and too few dollars chasing too many goods leads to deflation.

Monetarists believe a well-controlled, moderately increasing money supply leads to price stability. Price stability allows business managers, who are more efficient allocators of resources than the government, to plan and invest, which in turn keeps the economy from experiencing extremes in the business cycle.

IMPORTANT TERMS AND CONCEPTS IN ECONOMICS

Business Cycles

Business cycles reflect fluctuations in economic activity as measured by the level of activity in such macroeconomic variables as the rate of unemployment and the GDP. Periods of economic expansion have been followed by periods of contraction in a pattern called the **business cycle**. Business cycles go through four stages:

- Expansion

- Peak

- Contraction

- Trough

Expansion

Expansion is characterized by increasing business activity—in sales, manufacturing, and wages—throughout the economy. When GDP increases rapidly and businesses reach their productive capacity, the nation's economy cannot expand further. At this point, the economy is said to have reached its peak. When business activity declines from its peak, the economy is contracting.

Economists call mild short-term contractions **recessions**. Longer, more severe contractions are **depressions**. When business activity stops declining and levels off, the cycle makes a **trough**.

According to the US Department of Commerce, the economy is in a recession when a decline in real output of goods and services—the GDP—continues for two or more consecutive quarters. It defines a depression as a decrease in GDP for six consecutive quarters.

The Four Stages of the Business Cycle

To determine the economy's overall direction, economists consider many trends in business activity.

Expansions are characterized by:

- increasing consumer demand for goods and services;

- increasing industrial production;

- falling inventories;

- rising stock markets;

- rising property values; and

- increasing GDP.

Contractions in the business cycle tend to be characterized by:

- rising numbers of bankruptcies and bond defaults;

- falling stock markets;

- rising inventories (a sign of slackening consumer demand); and

- decreasing GDP.

Inflation

Inflation is a general increase in prices as measured by an index such as the consumer price index (CPI). The **CPI** reflects the average cost of goods and services (a **market basket**) purchased by consumers, compared with those same goods and services purchased during a base period. Mild inflation can encourage economic growth because gradually increasing prices tend to stimulate business investments. High inflation reduces a dollar's buying power, which can reduce demand for goods and services.

Causes of Inflation

Excessive demand occurs when aggregate demand exceeds the aggregate supply and prices rise.

Monetary expansion is a rapid increase in a nation's money stock in excess of the nation's growth rate.

Increased inflation drives interest rates higher and drives bond prices lower. Decreases in the inflation rate have the opposite effect: bond yields decline and bond prices rise.

TAKE NOTE   An increase in real income means the percentage increase in income is greater than the rate of inflation. Buying power has increased.

Deflation

Though rare, **deflation** is a general decline in prices. Deflation usually occurs during severe recessions when unemployment is on the rise.

Causes of Deflation

Deflation is caused by conditions opposite those that cause inflation. Basically, when demand for goods and services are substantially below the supply of those goods or services, prices must spiral downward to encourage an increased demand. One other possible cause of deflation is a severe shrinkage in the money supply.

QUICK QUIZ 10.1   True or False?

___ 1. Monetarists believe that the government should take an active role in managing the economy through fiscal policy.

___ 2. A depression is defined as a decrease in the GDP for 6 or more consecutive months.

___ 3. Rising inventories are characteristic of an economic expansion.

___ 4. The CPI is a measurement of inflation.

___ 5. High consumer debt is characteristic of a downturn in the business cycle.

Quick Quiz answers can be found at the end of the unit.

INTEREST RATES AND YIELD CURVES

Although interest rates in general reflect investor expectations about inflation, short-term rates reflect the policy decisions of the Federal Reserve Board (FRB) as it implements the nation's monetary policy.

INTEREST RATES

An **interest rate** is the cost of borrowing money. The rate a borrower pays for funds is determined by the supply and demand for loanable funds, the credit quality of the borrower, and the length of time for which money is borrowed. In addition, the cost of funds is influenced by factors not related to the borrower, such as current and expected inflation and the overall supply and demand for funds in the economy.

When a company borrows money by issuing bonds, the bonds have a fixed interest rate, or coupon payment. As interest rates fluctuate, the price of the bonds in the secondary market also fluctuates. When interest rates increase, the bond prices decrease; when interest rates decrease, bond prices increase. Thus, there is an inverse relationship between interest rates and bond prices.

Nominal and Real Interest Rates

The **nominal rate of interest** is the money rate of interest or the actual amount a borrower pays for loanable funds. If inflation is expected, the nominal rate of interest will exceed the real rate of interest on a loan to compensate the lender for the decline in purchasing power. The **real rate of interest** is the nominal rate of interest minus the expected rate of inflation.

TAKE NOTE

If a corporation pays 8% for a 1-year loan and the rate of inflation for the year is 2%, the real rate of interest is 8% − 2% = 6%.

Federal Funds Rate

The **federal funds rate** is the rate banks that are members of the Federal Reserve System charge each other for overnight loans of $1 million or more. The rate is considered a barometer of the direction of short-term interest rates. The federal funds rate is listed in daily newspapers and is the most volatile rate; it can fluctuate drastically under certain market conditions.

Prime Rate

The **prime rate** is the interest rate that large US money center commercial banks charge their most creditworthy corporate borrowers for unsecured loans. Each bank sets its own prime rate, with larger banks generally setting the rate that other banks follow. Banks lower their prime rates when the Fed eases the money supply and raise rates when the Fed contracts the money supply.

Discount Rate

The **discount rate** is the rate the New York Federal Reserve Bank charges for short-term loans to member banks.

TAKE NOTE

The Federal Reserve Board establishes the discount rate. The discount rate, unlike the federal funds rate, is a managed rate. It is one of the tools of monetary policy. In contrast, the **federal funds rate** is a market rate determined by the demand for bank reserves on the part of deposit-based financial institutions.

Broker Call Loan Rate

The **broker call loan rate** is the interest rate banks charge broker/dealers on money they borrow to lend to margin account customers. The broker call loan rate is also known as the *call loan rate* or *call money rate*. The broker call loan rate usually is slightly higher than other short-term rates. Broker call loans are callable on 24-hour notice.

Yield Curve

Plotted on a graph, the difference between short- and long-term interest rates normally reflects an upward sloping line known as the **yield curve**. When it is an upward sloping curve it is a positive, or normal, yield curve. Long-term interest rates are normally higher than short-term rates for a number of reasons. Lenders must be compensated for the:

■ time value of money;

■ reduced buying power of money resulting from inflation;

■ increased risk of default over long periods; and

■ loss of liquidity associated with long-term investments.

The yield curve is also a reflection of investor expectations about inflation. If investors expect high inflation rates, they will require higher rates of interest to compensate for the reduction in purchasing power over time.

TAKE NOTE   When the yield curve is normal, long-term interest rates are higher than short-term interest rates. On a graph, the normal yield curve is upward sloping.

In unusual circumstances, the yield curve can be inverted, or downward sloping. An inverted yield curve can be the result of high current demand for money relative to the available supply. Short-term interest rates tend to be more sensitive to Fed policy than long-term rates. An inverted yield curve may occur because of a sharp increase in short-term rates.

TAKE NOTE   Although short-term interest rates are more sensitive to Fed monetary policies, the prices of long-term bonds are more volatile than those of short-term bond.

ECONOMIC INDICATORS

Certain statistical indicators are used to measure the economic health of a country at a given time. Some of the primary indicators used are discussed below.

Gross Domestic Product (GDP)

Gross domestic product (GDP) expresses the total value of all final goods and services produced within the United States during the year. GDP includes personal consumption, government spending, gross private investment, foreign investment, and the total value of exports. The GDP measures a country's output produced within its borders regardless of who generated it.

The **gross national product (GNP)** is another measure of economic activity. In addition to GDP, GNP includes the income a country's citizens earned abroad and excludes the income foreigners earned domestically. GNP measures the output generated by the country's citizens regardless of where they did so. Today, virtually all measurements are in GDP rather than GNP.

EXAMPLE

A US-based firm assembles electronic equipment using parts imported from Singapore. Its income statement looks like this:

Sales:	$60 million
Wages:	30 million
Parts:	16 million
Expenses:	46 million
Net Income:	14 million

What is this firm's contribution to the US GDP?

A. $14 million
B. $30 million
C. $44 million ←
D. $60 million

Answer: C. The question is how we measure this firm's contribution to US output. At first glance, the answer would seem to be $60 million, the total value of its sales. However, $16 million of this was produced somewhere else, so it shouldn't be counted as part of the firm's—or the United States'—output. Thus, the correct answer is $44 million, the amount of value the firm has added to the imported parts.

Employment Indicators

The unemployment level is a key indicator of a country's economic health and bears a relationship to inflation. The two most common employment indicators are the average weekly initial claims for unemployment compensation and the average workweek in manufacturing. Both measures serve to predict the direction of economic activity. Many economists believe an unemployment level of about 4% reflects full employment, the point at which wage pressures do not create undue inflation.

Consumer Price Index (CPI)

The **consumer price index (CPI)** is a measure of the general retail price level. The index compares the current cost of buying a basket of goods with the cost of buying the same basket a year ago. In doing so, the CPI figure attempts to measure the rate of increase or decrease in a broad range of prices, such as food, housing, transportation, medical care, clothing, electricity, entertainment, and services. The CPI is computed monthly.

Balance of Payments

The **balance of payments** measures all the nation's import and export transactions with those of other countries for the year. The balance of payments account contains all payments and liabilities to foreigners (debits) and all payments and obligations (credits) received from foreigners.

If the US dollar weakens, meaning it buys less of a foreign currency such as Japanese yen, it makes US exports more competitive in foreign markets. Conversely, if the US dollar strengthens and buys more yen per dollar, it makes US exports less competitive in foreign markets.

Trade Deficit

A **trade deficit** is an excess of one country's imports over its exports and is reported as part of the balance of payments figures. Over time, an excessive trade deficit can lead to the devaluation of a country's currency because the country will be converting, or selling, its currency to obtain foreign currency to pay for its increasing imports.

Barometers of Economic Activity

Certain aspects of economic activity serve as barometers, or indicators, of business cycle phases. There are three broad categories of economic indicators: leading, coincident, and lagging.

Leading Indicators

Leading indicators are economic activities that tend to turn down before the beginning of a recession or turn up before the beginning of a business expansion. These indicators are used by economists to predict the future direction of economic activity four to six months hence. The leading economic indicators include the following:

- Money supply

- Building permits (housing starts)

- Average weekly initial claims for state unemployment compensation

- Average length of workweek in manufacturing

- New orders for consumer goods

- Contracts and orders for plants and equipment

- Changes in inventories of durable goods

- Changes in sensitive materials prices

- Stock prices (e.g., S&P 500)

- Changes in business and consumer borrowing

Not all leading indicators move in tandem. Positive changes in a majority of leading indicators point to increased spending, production, and employment. Negative changes in a majority of indicators can forecast a recession.

Coincident (or Current) Indicators

Coincident, or **current, indicators** are economic measurements that change directly and simultaneously with the business cycle. Widely used coincident indicators include the following:

- Nonagricultural employment

- Personal income, minus Social Security, veteran benefits, and welfare payments

- Industrial production

- Manufacturing and trade sales in constant dollars

Lagging Indicators

Lagging indicators are measurements that change four to six months after the economy has begun a new trend and serve to confirm the new trend. Lagging indicators help analysts differentiate long-term trends from short-term reversals that occur in any trend. Lagging indicators include the following:

- Average duration of unemployment

- Ratio of consumer installment credit to personal income

- Ratio of manufacturing and trade inventories to sales

- Average prime rate

- Change in the CPI for services

- Total amount of commercial and industrial loans outstanding

- Change in the index of labor cost per unit of output (manufacturing)

QUICK QUIZ 10.2

Matching

A. Prime rate
B. Lagging indicator
C. Leading indicator
D. Coincident indicator
E. Trade deficit
F. Call money rate

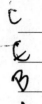

C ___ 1. New orders for consumer goods

C ___ 2. An excess of a country's imports over exports

B ___ 3. Manufacturing inventories

A ___ 4. Rate charged by banks to corporate customers

D ___ 5. GDP

E ___ 6. Rate charged by banks on loans to broker/dealers with securities as collateral

INVESTMENT ANALYSIS

The two approaches most commonly used to select investments are fundamental and technical analysis. Both fundamental and technical analysts attempt to forecast prices or values of securities and markets.

Fundamental analysts evaluate broad-based economic trends, current business conditions within an industry, and the quality of a particular corporation's business, finances, and management. **Technical analysts** attempt to predict the direction of prices on the basis of historic price and trading volume patterns.

Investment Analysis Terminology

Alpha is the extent to which an asset's or portfolio's actual return exceeds or falls short of its expected returns. A positive alpha rather than a negative one is desirable.

Arbitrage is a strategy that generates a guaranteed profit from a transaction. A common form of arbitrage is the simultaneous purchase and sale of the same security in different markets at different prices to lock in a profit.

A benchmark portfolio is a model portfolio of a large number of assets, such as the S&P 500, against which the performance of a fund or portfolio is measured.

Beta Coefficient

Beta and *beta coefficient* mean the same thing. In the securities industry, *coefficient* is ordinarily dropped for purposes of convenience. A stock or portfolio's **beta** is a measure of its volatility in relation to the overall market. A security that has a beta of 1 moves in line with the market. A security with a beta of greater than 1 is more volatile than the overall market. A stock with a beta less than 1 is less volatile than the market.

TAKE NOTE   If the S&P 500 rises or falls by 10%, a stock with a beta of 1 rises or falls by about 10%, a stock with a beta of 1.5 rises or falls by about 15%, and a stock with a beta of .75 rises or falls by about 7.5%.

Capital asset pricing model (CAPM) is a securities market investment theory that attempts to derive the expected return on an asset on the basis of the asset's systematic risk.

Completely diversified portfolio is a portfolio in which the specific risk of each asset in the portfolio has been diversified away.

Earnings multiplier is another term for the *price-to-earning (PE) ratio*. The **earnings multiplier** is the price of the stock divided by its earnings per share.

Efficient market theory believes that prices of securities rapidly reflect simultaneous access to all information.

A **eurobond** is a bond denominated in a currency other than the currency of the country in which it is issued.

TAKE NOTE

A bond issued in France denominated in British pounds is a **eurobond**.

Monte Carlo simulation is a statistical method to determine the return profile of a security or portfolio that recreates potential outcomes by generating random values on the basis of the risk and return characteristics of the securities themselves.

Optimal portfolio is a portfolio that provides the highest expected returns for a given level of risk.

Risk-free rate generally refers to the interest rate of 90-day US Treasury bills.

Sharpe ratio is a measure of a portfolio's risk in comparison to its expected return. The **Sharpe ratio** of a portfolio is calculated as the portfolio's average return that is in excess of the risk-free rate divided by the standard deviation in returns of the portfolio.

TAKE NOTE

The higher the Sharpe ratio, the more attractive an investment becomes.

Systematic risk is the risk in the return of an investment that is associated with the macroeconomic factors that affect all risky assets. Systematic plus unsystematic risk equals the total risk of an investment.

Unsystematic risk is the specific risk associated with an investment. It is not related to macroeconomic factors.

FUNDAMENTAL INVESTMENT ANALYSIS

Fundamental analysis is the study of the business prospects of an individual company within the context of its industry and the overall economy. Because business cycle phases have different effects on different industries, fundamental analysts look for companies in industries that offer better-than-average opportunities within the current business cycle. It is useful to distinguish between the four types of industries: defensive, cyclical, growth, and special situation.

Defensive Industries

Defensive industries are least affected by normal business cycles. Companies in defensive industries generally produce nondurable consumer goods, such as food, pharmaceuticals, tobacco, and energy. Public consumption of such goods remains fairly steady throughout the business cycle.

During recessions and bear markets, stocks in defensive industries generally decline less than stocks in other industries. During expansions and bull markets, defensive stocks may advance less. Investments in defensive industries tend to involve less risk and, consequently, lower investment returns.

Cyclical Industries

Cyclical industries are highly sensitive to business cycles and inflation trends. Most cyclical industries produce durable goods, such as heavy machinery and automobiles, as well as raw materials such as steel.

During recessions, the demand for durable goods declines as manufacturers postpone investments in new capital goods and consumers postpone purchases of automobiles. **Countercyclical industries,** on the other hand, tend to turn down as the economy heats up and to rise when the economy turns down. Gold mining has historically been a countercyclical industry.

Growth Industries

Every industry passes through four phases during its existence: introduction, growth, maturity, and decline. An industry is considered in its growth phase if the industry is growing faster than the economy as a whole because of technological changes, new products, or changing consumer tastes. Computers and bioengineering are current growth industries. Because many growth companies retain nearly all of their earnings to finance their business expansion, growth stocks usually pay little or no dividends.

Special Situation Stocks

Special situation stocks are stocks of a company with unusual profit potential resulting from nonrecurring circumstances, such as new management, the discovery of a valuable natural resource on corporate property, or the introduction of a new product.

THE TOOLS OF FUNDAMENTAL ANALYSIS: FINANCIAL STATEMENTS

A corporation's **financial statements** provide a fundamental analyst with the information needed to assess that corporation's profitability, financial strength, and operating efficiency. By examining how certain numbers from one statement relate to prior statements and how the resulting ratios relate to the company's competitors, the analyst can determine how financially viable the company is.

Companies issue quarterly and annual financial reports to the SEC. A company's balance sheet and income statement are included in these reports.

Balance Sheet

The **balance sheet** provides a snapshot of a company's financial position at a specific point in time. It identifies the value of the company's **assets** (what it owns) and its **liabilities** (what it owes). The difference between these two figures is the corporation's **equity**, or **net worth**.

The **balance sheet equation** is:

Assets = liabilities + owner's equity; or
Assets − liabilities = owner's equity.

TAKE NOTE

A corporation can be compared to a homeowner who borrows money to buy a home. The homeowner's equity is the difference between mortgage balance (liability) and home market value (asset value).

A corporation can buy assets by using borrowed money (liabilities) and equity capital raised by selling stock. The value of its assets must equal (balance with) the value of its liabilities and equity.

Although it is useful in determining a company's current value, the balance sheet does not indicate whether the company's business is improving or deteriorating. The balance sheet gets its name from the fact that its two sides must balance. The balance sheet equation mathematically expresses the relationship between the two sides of the balance sheet.

Assets

Assets appear on the balance sheet in order of liquidity, which is the ease with which they can be turned into cash. Assets that are most readily convertible into cash are listed first, followed by less liquid assets. Balance sheets commonly identify three types of assets: current assets (cash and assets easily convertible into cash), fixed assets (physical assets that could eventually be sold), and other assets (usually intangible and only of value to the corporation that owns them).

Current Assets

Current assets include all cash and other items expected to be converted into cash within the next 12 months, including the following.

- **Cash and equivalents** include cash and short-term safe investments, such as money market instruments that can be readily sold, as well as other marketable securities.

- **Accounts receivable** include amounts due from customers for goods delivered or services rendered, reduced by the allowance for bad debts.

■ **Inventory** is the cost of raw materials, work in process, and finished goods ready for sale.

■ **Prepaid expenses** are items a company has already paid for but has not yet benefited from, such as prepaid advertising, rents, taxes, and operating supplies.

Fixed Assets

Fixed assets are property, plant, and equipment. Unlike current assets, they are not easily converted into cash. Fixed assets, such as factories, have limited useful lives because wear and tear eventually reduce their value. For this reason, their cost can be depreciated over time or deducted from taxable income in annual installments to compensate for loss in value.

Other Assets

Intangible assets are nonphysical properties, such as formulas, brand names, contract rights, and trademarks. Goodwill, also an intangible asset, reflects the corporation's reputation and relationship with its clients.

TAKE NOTE   Although intangible assets may have great value to the corporation owning them, they generally carry little value to other entities.

Liabilities

Total liabilities on a balance sheet represent all financial claims by creditors against the corporation's assets. Balance sheets usually include two main types of liabilities: current liabilities and long-term liabilities.

Current Liabilities

Current liabilities are corporate debt obligations due for payment within the next 12 months. These include the following:

■ **Accounts payable**—amounts owed to suppliers of materials and other business costs

■ **Accrued wages payable**—unpaid wages, salaries, commissions, and interest

■ **Current long-term debt**—any portion of long-term debt due within 12 months

■ **Notes payable**—the balance due on equipment purchased on credit or cash borrowed

■ **Accrued taxes**—unpaid federal, state, and local taxes

Long-Term Liabilities

Long-term debts are financial obligations due for payment after 12 months.

TAKE NOTE   Long-term debts include mortgages on real property, long-term promissory notes, and outstanding corporate bonds.

Sample Balance Sheet

Balance Sheet
Amalgamated Widget
as of Dec. 31, 2007

ASSETS

Current assets	Cash and equivalents	$ 5,000,000	
	Accounts receivable	15,000,000	
	Inventory	19,000,000	
	Prepaid expenses	1,000,000	
	Total current assets		$ 40,000,000
Fixed assets	Buildings, furniture, and fixtures (including $10 million depreciation)	$40,000,000	
	Land	15,000,000	
	Total fixed assets		$ 55,000,000
Other (intangibles, goodwill)		$5,000,000	
Total assets			$100,000,000

LIABILITIES AND NET WORTH

Current liabilities	Accounts payable	$5,000,000	
	Accrued wages payable	4,000,000	
	Current portion of long-term debt	1,000,000	
	Total current liabilities		$ 10,000,000
Long-term liabilities	8% 20-year convertible debentures		$ 60,000,000
Total liabilities			
Net worth	Preferred stock $100 par ($5 noncumulative convertible 200,000 shares issued)	$20,000,000	
	Common stock $1 par (1 million shares)	1,000,000	
	Capital in excess of par	4,000,000	
	Retained earnings	15,000,000	
Total net worth			$ 40,000,000
Total liabilities and net worth			$100,000,000

Shareholder Equity

Shareholder equity, also called **net worth** or **owners' equity**, is the stockholder claims on a company's assets after all of its creditors have been paid. Shareholder equity equals total assets less total liabilities. On a balance sheet, three types of shareholder equity are identified: capital stock at par, capital in excess of par, and retained earnings.

T A K E N O T E   Net worth = assets – liabilities.

Capital Stock at Par

Capital stock includes preferred and common stock, listed at par value. **Par value** is the total dollar value assigned to stock certificates when a corporation's owners (the stockholders) first contributed capital. Par value of common stock is an arbitrary value with no relationship to market price.

Capital in Excess of Par

Capital in excess of par, often called **additional paid-in capital** or **paid-in surplus**, is the amount of money over par value that a company received for selling stock.

Retained Earnings

Retained earnings, sometimes called **earned surplus**, are profits that have not been paid out in dividends. Retained earnings represent the total of all earnings held since the corporation was formed less dividends paid to stockholders. Operating losses in any year reduce the retained earnings from prior years.

Capitalization

A company's **capitalization** is the combined sum of its long-term debt and equity accounts. The **capital structure** is the relative amounts of debt and equity that compose a company's capitalization. Some companies finance their business with a large proportion of borrowed funds; others finance growth with retained earnings from normal operations and little or no debt.

Working Capital

Working capital is the amount of capital or cash a company has available. Working capital is a measure of a firm's liquidity, which is its ability to quickly turn assets into cash to meet its short-term obligations.

The formula for working capital is:

Current assets – current liabilities = working capital.

Factors that affect working capital include:

- increases in working capital, such as profits, sale of securities (long-term debt or equity), and sale of noncurrent assets; and

- decreases in working capital, such as dividends declared, paying off long-term debt, and net loss.

Liquidity measures a company's ability to pay the expenses associated with running the business.

Changes That Affect the Balance Sheet

Balancing the Balance Sheet

Balance sheets, by definition, must balance. Every financial change in a business requires two offsetting changes on the company books, known as **double-entry bookkeeping**.

Depreciating Assets

Because fixed assets (e.g., buildings, equipment, and machinery) wear out as they are used, they decline in value over time. This decline in value is called **depreciation**. A company's tax bills are reduced each year the company depreciates fixed assets used in the businesses.

Depreciation affects the company in two ways: accumulated depreciation reduces the value of fixed assets on the balance sheet, and the depreciation deduction reduces taxable income on the income statement.

Companies may elect either straight line or accelerated depreciation. By use of the straight-line method, a company depreciates fixed assets by an equal amount each year over the asset's useful life. A piece of equipment costing $1 million with a 10-year useful life will generate a depreciation deduction of $100,000 per year.

Accelerated depreciation is a method that depreciates fixed assets more during the earlier years of their useful life and less during the later years.

Compared with straight line, accelerated depreciation generates larger deductions (lower taxable income) during the early years and smaller deductions (higher taxable income) during the later years.

CAPITAL STRUCTURE

A corporation builds its capital structure with the following four elements:

- Long-term debt
- Capital stock (common and preferred)
- Capital in excess of par
- Retained earnings (earned surplus)

EXAMPLE

(See the table below for reference and explanation of the following terms.) The total capitalization on the sample balance is $90 million ($50 million in long-term debt, $20 million in preferred stock, and $20 million in common shareholders' equity). Remember, capital stock + capital in excess of par + retained earnings = shareholders' equity (net worth).

Total capitalization	$90 million
LT debt	$50 million
+ Pfd.	$20 million
+ Common	$ 1 million
+ Cap. surplus	$ 4 million
+ Ret. earnings	$15 million

If a company changes its capitalization by issuing stock or bonds, the effects will show up on the balance sheet.

Issuing Securities

The example balance sheet indicates the company issued 1 million shares of $1 par common stock. If it issues another 1 million shares, the net worth (shareholders' equity) will increase by the additional capital raised, and the amount of cash on the asset side of the balance sheet will increase.

Convertible Securities

When an investor converts a convertible bond into shares of common stock, the amount of liabilities decreases, and the owners' equity increases. The changes are on the same side of the balance sheet, so there is no change to the assets.

Bond Redemption

When bonds are redeemed, liabilities on the balance sheet are reduced. The offsetting change would be a decrease in cash on the asset side of the balance sheet. The company would have less debt outstanding, but it would also have less cash. The balance sheet balances.

Dividends

When a cash dividend is declared, retained earnings are lowered and current liabilities are increased. The declaration of a cash dividend establishes a current liability until it is paid. Once paid, it reduces cash in current assets and also reduces current liabilities.

Distribution of stock dividends has no effect on corporate assets or liabilities, nor does it change the stockholders' proportionate equity in the corporation. The number of shares each stockholder owns increases, but each single share represents a smaller slice of ownership in the corporation.

Stock Splits

Like a stock dividend, a stock split does not affect shareholders' equity. On the balance sheet, only the par value per share and number of shares outstanding change.

Financial Leverage

Financial leverage is a company's ability to use long-term debt to increase its return on equity. A company with a high ratio of long-term debt to equity is said to be highly leveraged.

Stockholders benefit from leverage if the return on borrowed money exceeds the debt service costs. But leverage is risky because excessive increases in debt raise the possibility of default in a business downturn.

In general, industrial companies with debt-to-equity ratios of 50% or higher are considered highly leveraged. However, utilities, with their relatively stable earnings and cash flows, can be more highly leveraged without subjecting stockholders to undue risk. If a company is highly leveraged, it is also affected more by changes in interest rates.

Book Value Per Share

In a **liquidation**, a company sells its tangible assets and uses the proceeds to pay creditors and stockholders. Potential investors want to know how the value of **tangible assets**, also known as **net tangible asset value**, compares to the size of the company's debt and equity.

The **book value** of a company's assets (the amount at which they are carried on the books) is determined by deducting all liabilities and preferred stock from the company's total tangible assets. Dividing this figure by the number of shares of common stock shows how much a company's assets are worth (assuming they are sold for their book value) per share, as shown below:

$$\frac{\text{assets} - \text{liabilities} - \text{par value of preferred}}{\text{shares of common stock outstanding}} = \text{book value per share.}$$

TEST TOPIC ALERT The Series 65 exam does not generally ask for calculations with balance sheet or income statement items. Make sure to recognize the main components of each of these financial statements. You may be asked about the impact of a certain transaction on the balance sheet.

1. Which of the following choices are affected when a corporation purchases a printing press for cash?

    A. Current assets
    B. Current liabilities
    C. Working capital
    D. Total assets
    E. Total liabilities
    F. Net worth

Answer: A and C. A payment of cash reduces current assets. Whenever either current assets or current liabilities change, working capital is also affected. The new printing press increases the value of the fixed assets. Total assets, however, are unchanged because the decrease in current assets is offset by the increase in fixed assets.

2. Which are affected when a corporation declares a cash dividend?

Answer: B, C, E, and F. The declaration (not payment) of a dividend creates a current liability on the books of the corporation. Because current liabilities are affected, working capital and total liabilities also change. The declaration of a dividend reduces the net worth because the dividend will be paid from retained earnings. When the dividend is paid, current assets will decrease and current liabilities will decrease (this also decreases both total assets and total liabilities). Working capital does not change because both current assets and current liabilities decrease by the same amount.

If a corporation has a stock split, the balance sheet categories above are not affected. A stock split will increase the number of shares and reduce the value of each share, but the total par value as shown in the equity section of the balance sheet is not affected.

QUICK QUIZ 10.3

1. The difference between current assets and current liabilities is called
   A. net worth
   B. working capital
   C. cash flow
   D. quick assets

2. As a result of corporate transactions, a company's assets remain the same and its equity decreases. Which of the following statements is TRUE?
   A. Prepaid expenses decrease.
   B. Total liabilities increase.
   C. Accrued expenses decrease.
   D. Net worth increases.

3. Which of the following is NOT affected by the issuance of a bond?
   A. Assets
   B. Total liabilities
   C. Working capital
   D. Shareholders' equity

4. A company has been experiencing increased earnings but has kept its dividend payments constant. As a result solely of this, the company's balance sheet would reflect
   A. decreased net working capital
   B. decreased net worth
   C. decreased retained earnings
   D. increased shareholders' equity

Footnotes

Footnotes to the financial statements identify significant financial and management issues that may affect the company's overall performance, such as accounting methods used, pending lawsuits, and management philosophy.

The balance sheet reports what resources (assets) a company owns and how it has funded them. How the firm has financed the assets is revealed by the capital structure—for example, long-term debt and owners' equity (preferred stock, common stock, and retained earnings).

INCOME STATEMENT

The **income statement,** sometimes referred to as the profit and loss or P&L statement, summarizes a company's revenues (sales) and expenses for a fiscal period, usually quarterly, year to date, or the full year. It compares revenue against costs and expenses during the period. Fundamental analysts use the income statement to judge the efficiency and profitability of a company's operation.

Components of the Income Statement

The various operating and nonoperating expenses on the income statement are discussed below.

Revenues indicate the firm's total sales during the period.

The **cost of goods sold** is the costs of labor, material, and production used to create finished goods. The two major methods of accounting for material costs are the first in, first out method (FIFO) and last in, first out method (LIFO). Under LIFO accounting, COGS normally will reflect higher costs of more recently purchased inventory (last items in). As a result of higher reported production costs under LIFO, reported income is reduced. The opposite is true if the FIFO method is used.

Pretax margin is determined by subtracting COGS and other operating costs (such as depreciation) from sales to arrive at gross operating profit. Income from nonoperating activities is added to this figure to arrive at total pretax earnings, or earnings before interest and taxes (EBIT).

Interest payments on a corporation's debt is not considered an operating expense. However, interest payments reduce the corporation's taxable income. **Pretax income,** the amount of taxable income, is operating income less interest payment expenses.

If dividends are paid to stockholders, they are paid out of net income after taxes have been paid. After dividends have been paid, the remaining income (earnings) is available to invest in the business.

Interest payments reduce a corporation's taxable income, whereas dividend payments to stockholders are paid from after-tax dollars. Because they are taxable as income to stockholders, dividends are taxed twice, whereas interest payments are taxed once as income to the recipient.

Earnings per share indicates what remains after payment of interest, taxes, and preferred dividends. Dividing net income after taxes, interest, and payment of preferred dividends by the number of common shares outstanding determines earnings per share.

Simplified Income Statement

Total Revenues (Sales)	$10,000,000
− Cost of Goods Sold	6,000,000
= Operating or Gross Profit	4,000,000
− Interest Expense	750,000
= Income after Interest Expense	3,250,000
− Income Tax	1,000,000
= Net Income	2,250,000
or Income per Share (1,000,000 shares outstanding)	$2.25

Accounting for Depreciation

On the balance sheet, tangible assets (e.g., plant and equipment) are valued at their cost as of the date of their acquisition. To account for the wasting or using up of an asset, generally accepted accounting principles allow for depreciating those assets to their net depreciated cost on the balance sheet. There are two general depreciation methods: straight line and accelerated depreciation.

Straight line depreciation writes off the value of an asset evenly over its useful life. The accumulated depreciation is charged against the asset value on the balance sheet to reflect the net depreciated value.

Accelerated depreciation allows for depreciating the value of an asset at a higher rate in the earlier years of the asset's life and at a lower rate in later years.

TEST TOPIC ALERT

One other important use of depreciation is in the company's cash flow statement. Most financial professionals add the year's charge for depreciation back to the company's net income to determine the cash flow

---

QUICK QUIZ 10.4

Matching: Are the following items found on the balance sheet or the income statement?

A. Balance sheet
B. Income statement

_A_ 1. Current liabilities

_B_ 2. Revenues

A____   3.   Net worth

A____   4.   Retained earnings

B____   5.   Cost of goods sold

B____   6.   Net income

VALUATION RATIOS

Valuation ratios are used by analysts to compare companies within an industry as well as in different industries.

Earnings Per Share (EPS)

Among the most widely used statistics, EPS measures the value of a company's earnings for each common share:

$$EPS = \frac{\text{earnings available to common}}{\text{number of shares outstanding}}.$$

Earnings available to common are the remaining earnings after the preferred dividend has been paid. Earnings per share relates to common stock only. Preferred stockholders have no claims to earnings beyond the stipulated preferred stock dividends.

Earnings Per Share After Dilution

If a corporation has rights, warrants, convertible preferred stock, or convertible bonds outstanding, the EPS could be diluted by an increase in the number of shares of common outstanding. That is, if the same amount of earnings available to common stockholders were allocated to more shares of stock, earnings would be less for each share. EPS is sometimes called *primary earnings per share* or *basic earnings per share* to differentiate it from earnings after dilution.

EPS after dilution assumes that all convertible securities have been converted into the common. Because of tax adjustments, the calculations for figuring EPS after dilution can be complicated.

Dividends Per Share

The **dividends per share** is simply the dollar amount of cash dividends paid on each common share during the year:

$$\text{dividends per share} = \frac{\text{annual cash dividends}}{\text{number of common shares outstanding}}.$$

Current Yield (Dividend Yield)

A common stock's **current yield**, like the current yield on bonds, expresses the annual dividend payout as a percentage of the current stock price:

$$\text{current yield} = \frac{\text{annual dividends per common share}}{\text{market value per common share}}.$$

Dividend Payout Ratio

The **dividend payout ratio** measures the proportion of earnings paid to stockholders as dividends:

$$\text{dividend payout ratio} = \frac{\text{annual dividends per common share}}{\text{earnings per share (EPS)}}.$$

In general, older companies pay out larger percentages of earnings as dividends. Utilities as a group have an especially high payout ratio. Growth companies normally have the lowest ratios because they reinvest their earnings in the businesses. Companies on the way up hope to reward stockholders with gains in the stock value rather than with high dividend income.

Price-to-Earnings Ratio

The widely used **price-to-earnings (PE) ratio** provides investors with a rough idea of the relationship between the prices of different common stocks compared with the earnings that accrue to one share of stock:

$$\text{PE ratio} = \frac{\text{current market price of common share}}{\text{earnings per share (EPS)}}.$$

Growth companies usually have higher PE ratios than do cyclical companies. Investors are willing to pay more per dollar of current earnings if a company's future earnings are expected to be dramatically higher than earnings for stocks that rise and fall with business cycles. Companies subject to cyclical fluctuations generally sell at lower PEs; declining industries sell at still lower PEs. Investors should beware of extremely high or extremely low PEs. Speculative stocks often sell at one extreme or the other.

If a stock's market price and PE ratio are known, the earnings per share can be calculated as follows:

$$\text{EPS} = \frac{\text{current market price of common stock}}{\text{PE ratio}}.$$

TAKE NOTE   A company's stock trades for $30 per share and has earnings of $1.50 per share. It has a PE (multiple) of 20 ($30 ÷ 1.5 = 20). If the average PE of the company's industry is 11, this stock is high priced. If the average PE is 35, this company is low priced.

Some analysts feel that the company's sales to earnings ratio is more valuable than the PE ratio

Price-to-Book Ratio

The **price-to-book ratio** reflects the market price of the stock relative to its book value per share. **Book value** is the theoretical value of a company (stated in dollars per share) in the event of liquidation.

A company whose stock sells for $50 per share has a book value of $5 per share. Its price-to-book ratio is 10 ($50 ÷ 5 = 10).

A quick rundown of the most testable points about ratios follows.

- Book value is the company's theoretical liquidation value expressed on a per share basis.
- Speculative companies typically have very high or very low PE ratios.
- Growth companies have higher PE ratios than do cyclical companies.
- Earnings per share relates only to common stock; it assumes preferred dividends were paid.

TECHNICAL INVESTMENT ANALYSIS

Although fundamental analysis looks at the company, technical analysis looks at the market. A fundamental analyst attempts to measure the business or financial risk inherent in investing in a particular security, whereas technical analysis is used by an analyst to measure the market risk assumed when investing in a particular security. You have to know the goal of technical analysis and several of the more popular technical systems.

Technical analysis is a method of attempting to predict stock price trends over the near term, generally four to six weeks. The prediction is based on current stock price trends and the relationship of the present trend to prior trends. These trends are measured through charts of price movements; therefore, it would be correct to say that a technician uses charts to attempt to predict future price movements. In using these charts of price movements, a technician also uses the trading volume of the stock in an attempt to validate the trends. Before looking further at chart patterns, let's define some key terms.

OVERBOUGHT

When a technician says that the market is overbought, it means that there has been an extended period of vigorous buying in the market. With no more buyers to provide the demand for the security, it is likely that future prices will head downward or remain on a horizontal level until more buyers enter the market.

OVERSOLD

This is the opposite of overbought—that is, there has been so much selling that the sellers have run out of securities to sell, and hence the prices will stabilize or perhaps begin to increase.

CONSOLIDATION

In Military Tactics 101, soldiers are taught the importance of consolidating one's gains. Simply stated, when an army overruns the enemy's position, before they continue to advance, they should make sure they do not become overextended. The same is true during a period of rapidly rising stock prices. If the market does not pause to consolidate the gains, it may become overbought.

TRENDLINES

In an effort to see where the price of stock may be going, the technician charts where it has been. He attempts to determine from his chart what the trend has been by drawing a trendline (as shown on the following page).

HEAD AND SHOULDERS

When a stock is rising, it rarely does so in a straight line. It will generally rise in a pattern somewhat similar to that shown in Figure A1. The same is true when a stock is declining; it does not go straight down (Figure B1). In a rising market, the trendline is a straight line connecting the bottoms, whereas in a declining market, the trendline attempts to connect the tops. This is because if the price should penetrate the trendline, as in Figure A1-P, it is probably a warning of a reversal in the trend. One of the patterns found in a trendline is called head and shoulders. Figures A2 and B2 show a head and shoulders, bottom and top, respectively. A head and shoulders top indicates the likelihood that the market has topped and the future trend of the price will be downward. A head and shoulders bottom indicates that the market has likely bottomed and the future trend is up. Sometimes the pattern is that of a saucer, a smooth curve coming down and rising up on the other side (Figure A3). The standard saucer pattern indicates that a bottom has been reached and is therefore bullish. An inverted saucer pattern is sometimes referred to as an umbrella pattern because it looks somewhat like an open umbrella (Figure B3). Looking at the example of the inverted or umbrella pattern, it is easy to see why this is considered bearish.

If you should be asked on the exam what the most important factor giving authority to the trendline is, the answer would be the number of times the trendline has been touched (i.e., the more times it has been touched, the greater the validity). Almost as important as the number of times the trendline is touched is the length of the trendline. The longer the trend exists, the more significant is a penetration of the line. Figures A4 and B4 show how a typical oversold and overbought condition might look on a chart.

A. Examples rated bullish and reflecting accumulation.

1) Ascending Support Levels

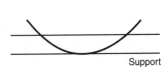

3) Saucer Pattern

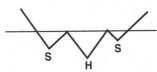

2) Head (H) and Shoulders (S) Bottom

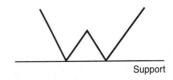

4) Double (or Triple) Bottom

Technical Explanation: (1) ascending tops and bottoms; (2) a decisive upside breakout from a previously established trading range; (3) holding above an indicated support level; (4) sharp recoveries from temporarily oversold positions.

B. Examples rated bearish and reflecting distribution.

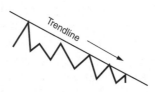

1) Descending Resistance Levels

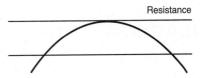

3) Umbrella Pattern

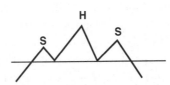

2) Head (H) and Shoulders (S) Top

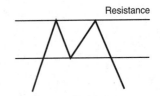

4) Double (or Triple) Top

Technical Explanation: (1) descending tops and bottoms; (2) a decisive downside breakout from established trading range; (3) turning down at a resistance level; (4) sharp declines from overbought position.

C. Examples of Resistance and Support

Technical Explanation: Line A represents the price level at which resistance occurs and the price goes no higher. Line B represents the price level at which support is found, and the price goes no lower. Finally, a breakout appears, and the price goes below the support level. If it penetrates by more than 3%, the breakout is confirmed, and the price should drop several more points until a new support level is established.

SUPPORT AND RESISTANCE

Chartists believe that one can understand more about a stock by studying its chart. Two of the most important conclusions drawn from a chart are the support levels and resistance levels. An example of support and resistance is illustrated in Figure C. This figure represents the price action at the end of a long rising trend. See what happens each time the price rises to line A-A, which is technically called the resistance level because, at this point, the price of the stock shows a resistance to a further price rise. Because prices are based on supply and demand, at price A-A there will be more sellers than buyers, probably because there are no longer any buyers who think the price will go higher. Possibly, potential sellers are attracted to the high price. Maybe it is a combination of both. The prices head downward until they reach the price indicated by line B-B. This is called a **support level**, a level below which the price does not seem to want to go. At the support level, the supply of sellers seems to disappear, and buyers who feel they missed the boat on the way up jump in again. The price continues to move between support and resistance until the price penetrates one of the lines. In the example, the price fell through B-B and a new downtrend was signaled.

BREAKOUT

When the price movement penetrates the support or the resistance level, it is known as a **breakout**. To avoid misreading an insignificant change, most analysts agree that the breakout is confirmed as valid when the movement is at least 3% penetration. For example, if a stock had a support level of 25, analysts would not confirm a breakout until the price had fallen at least 75 cents of a point (3% × 25) to 24.25. A second factor confirming the breakout is that the volume during a breakout is higher than normal during the charted period. The analyst believes that once a breakout has been confirmed, there will be rapid price movement in the direction of the break until a new support or resistance level is established. A technician believes that stock should be accumulated (bought) as the trendline is moving up from support to resistance and should be distributed (sold) as the trendline begins moving down from resistance toward support. It is just a strange way of saying buy low and sell high. The technician believes that if a breakout through resistance can be spotted, it represents a good buying opportunity for those quick enough to take advantage. Conversely, a breakout through the support level would represent a good opportunity for short sellers able to move quickly.

MOVING AVERAGES

To avoid the volatility frequently present in stock price trends, analysts will frequently use the moving average. A **moving average** attempts to modify the fluctuations of stock prices into a smoothed trend; the distortions are reduced to a minimum. For example, to plot a 13-week moving average on a particular stock, take the Friday closing price for each of the previous 13 weeks, add them together, and divide by 13. That number will be the average closing price for the last 13 weeks and that number is plotted. The next week you would add the new closing price for that week and delete the closing price for the first week used, 14 weeks ago. Unless the two prices were exactly the same, this would be a new total and, when divided by 13, a new average would be plotted for this week. One would continue to add a price and drop a price each week—hence, the term *moving average*. This average would be plotted on the same chart as the actual current price movement of the stock. Changes in the trend of the stock being plotted are identified, not by a change in the direction of the moving average, but by the price of the security crossing over the moving average. If the stock price moved below the moving average, it is usually a signal of a change from a rising to declining market. The reverse is also true.

Generally speaking, fundamental analysis is concerned more with what stocks to buy or sell, and the technical approach with when to buy or sell (although there are certainly technicians who claim to have effective techniques for stock selection as well as timing).

INDEXES AND AVERAGES

Before leaving the subject of technical analysis, it is important to mention that many technicians plot market indexes or averages instead of or in addition to plotting individual stocks. They feel that if one can identify the future price movement of an index, which measures the market as a whole, then one will be able to make profits trading those securities whose performance tends to mirror that of the index.

Beta, mentioned earlier in this unit, is used to measure the correlation between a particular stock movement and that of the market in general. A stock with a beta of 1.00 will tend to have a market risk similar to that of the market as a whole. Most frequently, beta is measured against the Standard & Poor's 500 composite index. A stock with a beta of 1.50 will be considerably more volatile than the market; a stock with a beta of 0.70 will be much less than volatile the market. Although most assets have a positive beta, it is possible to find some with a negative beta. Assets with a negative beta can be an important component when diversifying a portfolio because a proper mix would create a portfolio with zero beta (i.e., without systematic risk). For example, if beta is −1.2, a 10% up move in the market's return will cause the stock return to decline by 12%. Know that conservative clients need securities with low betas, whereas aggressive clients will find betas in excess of 1.00 to be quite suitable.

STANDARD & POOR'S 500

The composition of the Standard & Poor's 500 (S&P 500) Composite Index includes four main groups of securities: 400 industrials, 20 transportation companies, 40 public utilities, and 40 financial institutions. The S&P

500 is a cap-weighted index using a base period of 1941–1943 equal to 10. Although most of the stocks in the S&P 500 are listed on the NYSE, some are found on the AMEX and Nasdaq.

NEW YORK STOCK EXCHANGE (NYSE) INDEX

The NYSE publishes a composite index that covers all of the common stocks listed on the NYSE, more than 3,000 different companies. This index provides the most comprehensive measure of market activity on the NYSE. The NYSE index is cap weighted, similar to the S&P 500, but the base is December 31, 1965, and the index for the base is 50.

DOW JONES INDUSTRIAL AVERAGE

The best known of all of the market indexes are those published by Dow Jones & Company. There are probably two reasons why the Dow Jones Industrial Average (DJIA) is so well known: first, because the 30 industrial stocks are among the 30 best-known corporations in the world and second (and some would say more important) the Dow Jones & Company also publishes *The Wall Street Journal,* the nation's leading financial newspaper. Because it is price weighted, the Dow Jones is truly an average. Originally it was computed by adding together the prices of one share for each of the 30 different companies and then dividing by 30. That had to be changed as soon as the first one of those 30 companies had a 2:1 stock split. Because a stock split will cause the market price of the stock to drop—that is, the average would be distorted by continuing to divide the 30 current market prices by 30—an adjustment had to be made to the 30 (called the divisor). Over the years, stock splits and other distributions have caused that original divisor of 30 to be adjusted. There are three other Dow Jones Averages: the 20 transportations, the 15 utilities, and the composite of all 65. On November 1, 1999, history was made when non-NYSE stocks were included in the DJIA for the first time. Added to the average were Microsoft and Intel, which are both listed on Nasdaq.

NASDAQ COMPOSITE INDEX

The over-the-counter market is represented by the Nasdaq Composite Index, which covers more than 3,000 over-the-counter companies. The Nasdaq Composite Index is calculated in a manner similar to those used for the S&P and NYSE indexes, with a base period of February 5, 1971, and an index number of 100. These indexes, their subgroups, and several other popular indexes are quoted daily in *The Wall Street Journal.* As with the others (except for the Dow Jones), this is also a cap-weighted index.

QUICK QUIZ 10.5

Match the following items with technical or fundamental analysis.

    A. Technical analysis
    B. Fundamental analysis

  A   1. Market timing

  B   2. PE ratios

  A   3. Support and resistance

  A   4. Industry performance

        5. Breadth of the market

  B   6. Financial statements

TECHNICAL MARKET THEORIES

Technical analysts follow various theories regarding market trends.

Short Interest Theory

Short interest refers to the number of shares that have been sold short. Because short positions must be repurchased eventually, some analysts believe that short interest reflects mandatory demand that creates a support level for stock prices. High short interest is a bullish indicator, and low short interest is a bearish indicator.

Odd-Lot Theory

Typically, small investors engage in **odd-lot trading**, which is transactions of fewer than 100 shares.

Odd-lot theorists believe that small investors invariably buy and sell at the wrong times. When odd-lot traders buy, odd-lot analysts are bearish. When odd-lot traders sell, odd-lot analysts are bullish.

OTHER MARKET THEORIES

Efficient Market Hypothesis

The **efficient market hypothesis** maintains that security prices adjust rapidly to new information with security prices fully reflecting all available information. In other words, markets are efficiently priced as a result. This is sometimes referred to as the **random walk theory**. The random walk theory would suggest that throwing darts at the stock listings is as good a method as any for selecting stocks for investment.

Modern Portfolio Theory

Instead of emphasizing particular stocks, **modern portfolio theory (MPT)** focuses on the relationships among all the investments in a portfolio. This theory holds that specific risk can be diversified away by building portfolios of assets whose returns are not correlated.

MPT diversification allows investors to reduce the risk in a portfolio while simultaneously increasing expected returns.

Holding securities that tend to move in the same direction as one another does not lower an investor's risk. Diversification reduces risk only when assets whose prices move inversely, or at different times, in relation to each other are combined.

Harry Markowitz, founder of MPT, explained how to best assemble a diversified portfolio and proved that such a portfolio would likely do well. He proved that, all factors being equal, the portfolio with the least amount of volatility would do better than one with a greater amount of volatility.

QUANTITATIVE EVALUATION MEASUREMENTS

Quantitative evaluation refers to statistical concepts used to analyze investments.

TAKE NOTE   Expect to see questions that ask for recognition of the quantitative measures described here, and look for questions that require calculations.

TIME VALUE OF MONEY

The **time value of money** is the difference between the value of money today (its **present value**) and its value sometime in the future (its **future value**).

We've all heard the famous saying "time is money." The concept applies to investments. For example, if a person promises to pay a certain sum 10 years from now, what is it worth to have the money today so that the investor will have use of it over the next 10 years instead of having to wait? If the investor could earn 10% on the money, compounded annually, having about $38.55 today would be equivalent in value to receiving $100 in 10 years. The second view of time value relates to computing the amount necessary to be invested today, using an assumed rate of return, so that it will have a defined amount in the future. Using the above case, if the investor were to invest $38.55 today and earn 10% compounded annually, he would have $100 in 10 years.

PRESENT VALUE

Present value is the formal term for value today of the future cash flows of an investment discounted at a specified interest rate to determine the present worth of those future cash flows.

Intuitively, investors recognize that a dollar in hand is worth more than a dollar in the future. The difference between the value today and some time in the future is a function of the time elapsed and the rate of interest earned.

The formula used to calculate present value is as follows:

$$PV = FV \div (1 + r)^t.$$

In the formula above, **PV** stands for the present value, **FV** stands for the future value, r is the interest rate, and t is the number of time periods the money is compounded.

This formula says that the present value (PV) of an investment equals the investment's future value (FV) discounted at (divided by) an interest rate over a time period specified by t. The factor $(1 + r)^t$ is known as the **discount factor**.

 E X A M P L E

What is the present value of $20,000 that will be received 5 years (t) from today? If the investor requires a 12% return (r) for the $20,000, the value of that $20,000 today (PV) to be received in 5 years is calculated as follows:

$$PV = \frac{FV}{(1 + .12)^5} = \frac{\$20,000}{1.7623} = (\$11,348.81).$$

The $20,000 to be received in 5 years discounted by the required 12% interest rate is worth $11,348.54 today.

FUTURE VALUE

Future value is the formal term that indicates what an amount invested today at a given rate will be worth at some period in the future. The future value of a dollar invested today depends on the:

- rate of return it earns (r); and

- time period over which it is invested (t).

The equation to calculate the FV of an investment is expressed as:

$$FV = PV \times (1 + r)^t.$$

EXAMPLE

The value of $11,348.54 five years from today, its future value, is calculated using the above formula as follows:

$$FV = \$11{,}348.81 \text{ (the PV)} \times 1.12^5 = \$20{,}000.$$

The future value expressed here reflects a **compound rate of return** on the original $11,348.54 invested. The compound return assumes that the interest earned (12% in this case) in a given period (five years) is reinvested at the identical rate for the number of periods in which it is invested.

TAKE NOTE

To find PV, you must already know the FV.
To find FV, you must already know the PV.

RULE OF 72

The **rule of 72** is a shortcut method for determining the number of years it takes for an investment to double in value. To find the number of years for an investment to double, simply divide the number 72 by the interest rate the investment pays. For example, an investment of $2,000 earning 6% will double in 12 years ($72 \div 6 = 12$).

Here is another example of the rule of 72. A savings account with $1,000 in it bearing 4% per year in interest would double (i.e., the account would be worth $1,000) in 18 years; $72 \div 4 = 18$.

INVESTMENT RETURN MEASUREMENTS

When investing money, investors expect some form of return or income from their investment. There are several different measurements used to evaluate the returns from an investment; the most commonly used measurements are discussed below.

BOND YIELDS

Because bonds most frequently trade for prices other than par value, the price difference (discount or premium) from par is considered when calculating a bond's overall return. A bond's yield can be analyzed several ways.

Nominal Yield

A bond's coupon yield, or nominal yield, is set at issuance and printed on the face of the bond. The **nominal yield** is a fixed percentage of the bond's par value.

A coupon of 6% indicates the bondholder is paid $60 in interest annually until the bond matures.

Current Yield (CY)

Current yield (CY) is determined by dividing the coupon yield by the current price of the investment. It measures current income as a measure of price much like dividend yield measures the current income of common stock. CY excludes capital gains or losses on the principal and hence is not a measure of total return.

A bond's CY measures the bond's coupon payment relative to its market price, as shown in the following equation:

$$\text{coupon payment} \div \text{market price} = \text{current yield.}$$

Relationship Between Bond Prices and Current Yields

Bond prices and yields move in opposite directions: as a bond's price rises, its yield declines, and vice versa. When a bond trades at a discount, its current yield increases; when it trades at a premium, its CY decreases.

A 6% coupon bond trading for $750 has a CY of 8% ($60 ÷ $750 = 8%). Conversely, the CY of a bond bought at a premium is lower than its nominal yield. An investor who buys a 6% bond for $1,200 receives a CY of 5% ($60 ÷ $1,200 = 5%).

Know how to calculate the CY of a bond or a stock. Expect to see one question on the calculation of CY.

The CY of common stock is calculated by dividing the current dividend by the current price of the stock. For instance, a stock with a $2 dividend trading on the market for $40 has a 5% CY ($2 ÷ $40 = 5%).

Yield to Maturity (YTM)

A bond's **yield to maturity (YTM)** reflects the annualized return of the bond if held to maturity. In calculating YTM, the bondholder takes into account the difference between the price paid for a bond and par value. If the bond's price is less than par, the discount amount is **accreted**. If the bond's price is greater than par, the premium is **amortized**.

An investor who buys a 10% coupon bond at 105 ($1,050 per bond) with 10 years remaining to maturity can expect $100 in interest per year. If he holds the bond to maturity, the bondholder loses $50 ($1,050 − $1,000 = $50; $50 ÷ 10 years = $5 per year). This loss is included in the YTM approximation.

The YTM of a bond bought at a discount is always higher than both the coupon yield and the CY because the investor has a gain when the bond matures at par. The YTM of a bond bought at a premium is always lower than both the coupon yield and the CY because the investor has a loss when the bond matures at par.

TAKE NOTE

If an investor buys a bond with a 10% coupon for 95 ($950 per bond), he receives $100 a year in coupon interest payments and a gain of $50 ($1,000 − $950) per bond at maturity. This gain is included in the YTM approximation.

TAKE NOTE

YTM is also called the **market-driven yield** because it reflects the internal rate of return (IRR) from the bond investment.

Because the YTM reflects the gain or loss from a discount or premium purchase price, it differs from the CY if the bondholder pays a price other than par.

Yield to Call (YTC)

A bond with a call feature may be redeemed before maturity at the issuer's option. Unless the bond was bought at par and is callable at par, yield to call (YTC) calculations reflect the early redemption date and consequent acceleration of the premium loss from the purchase price.

A bond's **yield to call**, similar to YTM, is the rate of return the bond provides from the purchase date to the call date and price. This calculation generates a lower return than does the YTM and should be considered by investors when evaluating a callable bond trading at a premium.

TOTAL RETURN

Total return comprises the yield and growth from an investment.

EXAMPLE

A common stock purchased for $20 with an annual dividend of $1 is sold after one year for $24. The total return on the investment is $5: $1 in dividends plus $4 in capital appreciation. The total return, then, is 25% ($5 ÷ $20 = 25%).

TEST TOPIC ALERT

The exam will require you to know how to calculate total return. Keep in mind that the total annual return on an investment includes income and capital appreciation. In the case of bonds held to maturity, this is the YTM. Otherwise, it is the coupon income plus any appreciation or less any price depreciation. In the case of stocks, one would use the dividend income plus or minus the appreciation or depreciation.

HOLDING PERIOD RETURN

The length of time an investor owns an investment is called the **holding period**. The return for that period is called the **holding period return (HPR)**. HPR is the total return, income plus capital appreciation, of an investment over a specified period, the holding period.

EXAMPLE

An investment purchased for $100 and sold 3 years later for $120 ($20 capital appreciation) after paying a total of $30 ($10 per year) in dividends has a holding period return of 50% ($120 + $30 = $150). The total gain is $150 − $100 = $50. A $50 return on a $100 investment is 50% ($50 ÷ $100 = 50%).

TAKE NOTE

Holding period return is not an annualized return. It is the percentage return over a defined period.

ANNUALIZED RETURN

Annualized return is the return an investor would have received had he held an investment for one year. Annualized return is determined by multiplying the actual return by an annualization factor. The **annualization factor** is the number of days in the year divided by the number of days an investment is held.

TAKE NOTE

An investor receives $5 on a $100 investment held for 6 months. The annualized return is determined by multiplying the 5% return by the annualization factor of 2 (360 days ÷ 180 days = 2) for an annualized return of 10%. Another investor has a capital gain of 30% from an investment held for 18 months. The annualized return is 20%, calculated as follows: 30 × (12 ÷ 18) = 20.

AFTER-TAX RETURN/YIELD

Capital gains and income are generally taxable; thus, taxes reduce the return of an investment. The **adjusted**, or **after-tax**, **return** is determined by reducing the investment's return by the client's tax rate.

TAKE NOTE   The after-tax return of an investment that yields 10% for an investor in the 25% tax bracket is calculated by multiplying the return by (1 − .25), or .75. The investor retains 75% of the 10% yield, for a 7.5% after-tax return. Likewise, an investment that returns 45% over 3 years provides an after-tax return of 33.75% (.75 x 45%).

INFLATION-ADJUSTED RETURN (REAL RETURN)

Because inflation reduces the buying power of a dollar, investment performance measurements are often adjusted to provide a measure of the buying power earned from a given investment. Returns that have been adjusted for inflation are called **real rates of return**.

To determine the inflation-adjusted rate of return of an investment, reduce its nominal return by the inflation rate as reflected in a benchmark index such as the consumer price index (CPI).

TAKE NOTE   A bond with an 8% coupon has a nominal return of 8%. If inflation (as measured by the CPI) is 3%, then the inflation-adjusted return of the bond investment is 8% − 3%, or 5%.

TAKE NOTE   For fixed income investors, inflation and taxes reduce the buying power of their dollars. For an investor in the 25% tax bracket in a 2.5% inflationary environment, an investment that yields 10% before taxes provides the investor with a 5% inflation-adjusted, after-tax return. To calculate the 5% after-tax inflation adjusted return, first determine the after-tax return. In this case, 10% less 25% for taxes results in a 7.5% after-tax return. The formal mathematical way to calculate inflation adjusted returns is to divide (1 + the return) by (1 + the inflation rate) − 1. In this case, divide 1.075 by 1.025 and then subtract 1, or 1.049 − 1 = 4.9%.

A shorthand way to approximate the real rate of return is to reduce the return by the amount of inflation during the period. In this case, 7.5% less 2.5% inflation results in a 5% after-tax inflation adjusted return.

TEST TOPIC ALERT   The exam will require you to know how to calculate the approximate inflation-adjusted return.

EXPECTED RETURN

Unlike historical or actual rates of returns, **expected returns** are estimates of the probable returns an investment may yield. To determine the expected return of an investment, the adviser assigns a probability to each return that the investment is likely to earn and then multiplies that return by the probability of it occurring. The sum of those probable returns is the expected return for that investment. The formula is as follows: expected return = (probability of return #1 × possible return #1) + (probability of return #2 × possible return #2).

TAKE NOTE

The expected return of an investment with a 30% probability of returning 15% and a 70% chance of returning 10% has a total expected return of 11.5%, calculated as follows: (.30 × 15% = 4.5%) + (.70 × 10% = 7.0%), or 4.5% + 7.0% = 11.5%.

Expected return is also a mean return. When one constructs a portfolio, there are usually securities with different grades of risk and, hence, different expectations of reward. Investors view the portfolio as a whole, looking to maximize for return for each level of risk. This overall view, or mean, of the entire portfolio is the expected return of the portfolio.

NET PRESENT VALUE (NPV)

Net present value (NPV) is the difference between an investment's present value and its cost. An NPV of $10 means that an investment that cost $100 must have a discounted present value of $110, for an NPV of $10. Note that the difference between the cost ($100) and the discounted present value of the investment's future returns ($110) equals the NPV ($10).

TAKE NOTE

NPV is expressed in dollar amounts and not as a rate of return.

NPV is an analytical concept used by corporations to determine whether to invest in a capital project (e.g., a new factory). The anticipated income from the factory is discounted to its present value by using the company's required rate of return as the discount rate.

If the discounted PV of the projected income is greater than the cost of the factory, the project has a positive NPV. If this is the case, the project will add value to the company because its return is more than the company's cost of capital. If the NPV is negative, the project will drain value from the firm.

An investment adviser could use the NPV concept to evaluate a client's investment in any investment vehicle with a projected income stream. The adviser would project the cash flows from the investment and then discount them to their present value at the investor's required rate of return. If the NPV is positive, the investment adds value to the investor's portfolio.

INTERNAL RATE OF RETURN (IRR)

The **internal rate of return (IRR)** is the discount rate (r) that makes the future value of an investment equal to its present value. The IRR can be thought of as the r in the present and future value calculations. The IRR is difficult to calculate directly; it must be determined by a trial-and-error process called **iteration**. The YTM of a bond is actually the bond's internal rate of return because it is the interest rate that equates the value of the bond's future cash flows with its current price. IRR takes into consideration the time value of money.

TAKE NOTE   The IRR calculation can be used to determine whether an investment meets the investor's required rate of return. If an investor requires an investment return of 10% and the IRR for a proposed investment is 12%, the investor will view that investment as attractive because it returns a higher rate than the investor's required rate.

TAKE NOTE   As you review these quantitative evaluation measurements, know that the exam is more concerned with the ability to identify what they measure than how to perform the calculation. One or two questions might require a relatively simple calculation on current yield, after-tax return/yield, inflation-adjusted return, or total return.

RISK MEASUREMENTS

In finance, **risk** is defined as the uncertainty that an investment will earn its expected rate of return. There are several types of risk measures. Some measures refer to historical or past risk and some refer to expected or future risk of individual securities or portfolios of securities.

Beta measures a security's **systemic** (or **systematic**) **risk**—that is, the risk that can be associated with the market in general. The higher the beta, the more volatile the stock. High betas imply greater capital gains in a rising market and greater potential losses in declining markets. High beta stocks are usually considered aggressive, and low beta stocks are considered conservative. Risks specific to a stock, such as those resulting from competition, mismanagement, or product deficiencies, are independent of the general market. This is **nonsystematic risk**.

TEST TOPIC ALERT   Beta measures the volatility of a given stock or portfolio relative to the overall stock market.

CORRELATION AND CORRELATION COEFFICIENT

Correlation means that securities move in the same direction. A **strong** or **perfect correlation** means two securities prices move in a perfect positive linear relationship with each other.

EXAMPLE

Two securities are correlated if one security's price rises by 5% and the other security's price then rises by 5%, or if one declines by 4% and the other also declines by 4%.

The correlation coefficient is a number that ranges from −1 to +1. Securities that are perfectly correlated have a correlation coefficient of +1. Securities whose price movements are unrelated to each other have a correlation coefficient of 0. If prices move in perfectly opposite directions, they are negatively correlated or have a correlation coefficient of −1.

TAKE NOTE

Index funds attempt to achieve perfect correlation (+1) with the index they are mirroring (e.g., the Standard & Poor's 500).

STANDARD DEVIATION

Standard deviation is a measure of the volatility of an investment's projected returns. The larger the standard deviation, the larger the security's returns are expected to deviate from its average return, and, hence, the greater the risk.

Standard deviation is expressed in terms of percentage. It is generally accepted that a security will vary within one standard deviation about two-thirds of the time and within two standard deviations about 95% of the time. A standard deviation of 7.5 means that the return of a stock for a given period may vary by 7.5% above or below its predicted return about two-thirds of the time and within 15% about 95% of the time.

EXAMPLE

A security has an expected return of 12% and a standard deviation of 5%. Investing in a security with an expected 12% return, an investor can expect returns to range within 7% to 17% about 67% of the time and within 2% to 22% about 95% of the time.

TAKE NOTE

An investor can use standard deviation to compare the risk/reward between investments.

EXAMPLE

If an investor had a choice between an investment that returned 12% with a standard deviation of 6% and another investment that also returned 12% but had a standard deviation of 10%, the investor would choose the first one. In effect, he would receive that same return for less risk.

BETA VERSUS STANDARD DEVIATION

Beta is a volatility measure of a security compared with the overall market; standard deviation is a volatility measure of a security compared with its expected performance.

SHARPE RATIO

Securities practitioners have developed many measures to quantify the risk characteristics of a portfolio. One such measure that may show up on the exam is called the **Sharpe ratio**. The ratio is calculated by subtracting the risk-free rate (e.g., the 90-day Treasury bill rate) from the overall return of the portfolio. This result, which is the portfolio's risk premium, is then divided by the standard deviation of the portfolio. This ratio measures the amount of return per unit of risk taken. The higher the ratio, the better or more return per unit of risk taken.

TAKE NOTE

The Sharpe ratio is a risk-adjusted return as a measure of an investment's standard deviation.

DURATION

Duration measures the time in years it takes for a bond to pay for itself.

TAKE NOTE

If a bond has a duration of nine, the owner of the bond will receive his investment back in nine years.

Duration can also be used to measure the percentage change in the price of a bond (or bond portfolio) as a result of a small change in interest rates. The formula is as follows:

percentage change in price = +/– duration × the change in interest rate.

TAKE NOTE

If an investor owns a bond with a duration of nine years, the investor could estimate the price change the bond would experience if there were a 1% increase in interest rates.

To calculate the increase in the price of the bond, the investor would apply the formula as follows: –9 (duration) x 1% increase in interest rates = a 9% price decline in the bond.

The minus (–) sign is used before the duration measure because an increase in interest rates results in a decline in price. Had interest rates declined, a plus (+) sign would be used because declining rates mean higher bond prices.

TAKE NOTE

The general characteristics of duration follow.

- The lower the coupon rate, the greater a bond's duration; the higher the coupon rate, the lower the duration.
- The longer a bond's maturity, the greater the bond's duration.
- For coupon bonds, duration is less than the bond's maturity.
- Duration for a zero-coupon bond is equal to its maturity.
- The higher a bond's duration, the more its value will change for a 1% change in interest rates; the lower the duration, the less it will change.

TAKE NOTE

The duration of a bond with coupon payments is always shorter than the maturity of the bond. By the same token, the duration of a zero-coupon bond is equal to its maturity.

TAKE NOTE

A five-year zero-coupon bond has a duration of five because it takes five years to make the money back; the buyer gets a single payment (par) at maturity five years after purchase.

MONTE CARLO SIMULATIONS

Monte Carlo simulation (MCS) is a risk analysis technique in which probable future events are simulated on a computer, generating estimated rates of return.

MCSs, for example, can be used to randomly generate the behaviors of various asset classes to obtain the range of possible outcomes for a portfolio.

MCSs are well suited to addressing:

- situations where no real-world data exist;

- problems with unknown variables; and

- problems for which no analytical solution exists.

MCSs are commonly used in personal financial planning for wealth forecasting with estimated cash flows.

EXAMPLE

A client might want to know how long a portfolio will last in retirement, or what the odds are that a portfolio will be depleted before he dies.

If there were no cash flows into or out of the portfolio, the time frame was long enough, and we could be assured of receiving the historical average returns for each asset class, it would be fairly easy to forecast the future value of a portfolio without resorting to MCSs. In such an example, we are only solving for the terminal value of the portfolio, so the sequence of returns does not matter.

For an individual entering retirement, the timing of the cash flows out of the portfolio and the sequence of returns are critical.

EXAMPLE

Consider two clients, Mr. Jones and Ms. Smith. Both enter retirement with $1 million, both withdraw $50,000 per year from their portfolios, and both portfolios generate an average return of 10% over the life of the portfolios. Their yearly results are the same, but they come in different sequences. Mr. Jones experiences 15 up years followed by 5 down years. Ms. Smith experiences 5 down years followed by 15 up years. Mr. Jones will be better off than Ms. Smith, because Ms. Smith will deplete her portfolio in the early years, and hence her portfolio will not benefit fully from the positive return years down the line.

The concept of ill-timed cash flows may be easy for experienced advisers to grasp, but it is not one that clients readily understand. Through the use of MCSs, advisers can easily generate charts and graphs to educate clients about sequential return issues.

QUICK QUIZ 10.6

Matching

A. Future value
B. Present value
C. Current yield
D. Yield to maturity
E. Total return
F. Holding period return
G. Risk-adjusted rate of return
H. Expected return
I. Real return
J. Internal rate of return

H___ 1. Used to calculate the estimated return of an investment

I___ 2. Return that has been adjusted for inflation

F___ 3. Rate of return calculated over the period an investor owns the security

C___ 4. Annual interest divided by the current market price

E___ 5. Return that includes an investment's income and capital appreciation over a 1-year period

D___ 6. A bond's return if held until the principal is repaid

___ 7. Used to calculate what $1,000 would be worth if held for 10 years at 8%

8. Determined by dividing the difference between a security's actual return and the risk-free rate by its standard deviation

  9. Calculated from cash flows of a specific investment

10. How much an investor must invest today to result in a retirement fund of $1 million in 20 years

SOURCES OF INVESTMENT RISKS

The quantitative concepts discussed thus far are measures of risk and the performance of a security or portfolio. The following concepts are sources of risk that both businesses and investors bear. Though not a comprehensive list, they are among the most common.

Although we routinely use the term *risk*, we often have difficulty defining it precisely. In finance, **risk** is defined as the uncertainty that an investment will earn its expected rate of return.

MARKET RISK

Market risk, sometimes called **systemic** or **systematic risk**, is the risk that changes in the overall market will have an adverse effect on individual securities regardless of the company's circumstances.

TAKE NOTE   Systematic risk is measured by a security's beta. A security's unsystematic risk is its standard deviation.

BUSINESS RISK (UNSYSTEMATIC RISK)

Whether because of bad management or unfortunate circumstances, some businesses will inevitably fail, even more so during economic recessions. Typically, when a business fails, it liquidates (sells off all of its assets) in a bankruptcy, pays its creditors from the proceeds, and pays whatever is left, if anything, to its shareholders.

When a business is liquidated in a bankruptcy proceeding, the value of the company's stock often becomes worthless, resulting in a capital loss to investors.

TAKE NOTE   Unsystematic risk can be minimized through portfolio diversification.

EXAMPLE

Should a war break out between two major oil-producing countries, the stock market could decline dramatically. The stocks of individual companies would likely decline as well, regardless of whether the war directly affected their businesses.

TAKE NOTE

Systematic risk cannot be diversified away.

INTEREST RATE RISK

Interest rates fluctuate in the market all the time. If market conditions or the Federal Reserve push interest rates higher, the market price of all bonds will be affected. When interest rates rise, the market price of bonds falls.

EXAMPLE

If the Federal Reserve increases interest rates dramatically, the market price of all bonds, regardless of credit quality, will decline. Likewise, the stock market could decline as a result of portfolio managers adjusting their valuation models to reflect the revised interest rate environment.

INFLATION RISK

Inflation reduces the buying power of a dollar. A modest amount of inflation is inherent in a healthy, growing economy, but uncontrolled inflation causes uncertainty among individual investors as well as corporate managers attempting to evaluate potential returns from projects.

REGULATORY RISK (LEGISLATIVE RISK)

A sudden change in the regulatory climate can have a dramatic effect on the performance or risk of a business and entire business sectors. Overreaching bureaucrats, tax policies, and court judgments that change the rues a business must comply with can devastate individual companies and industries almost overnight. Changes in tax or other laws can make certain types of investments more or less beneficial.

EXAMPLE

Investments that could be affected by regulatory changes include real estate, municipal bonds, airlines, and pharmaceutical manufacturers. The most common regulatory risk comes from government attempts to control or influence product prices or the competitive structure of a particular industry.

EXAMPLE

The domestic boat-building business in the United States was nearly wiped out in the early 1990s after the government instituted a luxury tax for yacht purchases.

LIQUIDITY RISK

Liquidity measures the speed or ease of converting an investment into cash. **Liquidity risk** is the risk that when an investor wishes to dispose of an investment, no one will be willing to buy it, or that a very large purchase or sale would not be possible at the current price.

EXAMPLE

The Treasury bill market is a highly liquid market because investors can sell a Treasury bill within seconds. Real estate investments, however, can take months or years to sell. The longer it takes to convert an investment into cash, the greater the liquidity risk.

TAKE NOTE

Listed stocks and mutual funds have virtually no liquidity risk. Thinly traded stocks, many municipal bonds, and most tangible assets have a greater degree of inability to liquidate rapidly at your price.

OPPORTUNITY COST

Opportunity cost is the foregone return, or the return given up, on an alternative investment. In economic terms, opportunity cost is defined as the highest valued alternative that must be sacrificed as a result of choosing among alternatives. More simply, one can invest in short-term Treasury bills incurring virtually no risk. That is the risk-free alternative that can be earned by basically doing nothing. Any return that deviates from the risk-free return represents your opportunity gained or lost.

EXAMPLE

The 90-day Treasury bill is currently yielding 6%. An investor decides to purchase a stock with an expected return of 11%. If that stock actually returns 2%, the opportunity cost is 4% (6% − 2%) because that is the rate that the investor gave up, risk free, to assume the risk of investing in the alternative choice.

QUICK QUIZ 10.7

True or False?

 1. Market risk (systematic risk) is the risk associated with the specific business decisions of a company's manager.

 2. The term *risk* refers to the uncertainty that an investment will earn less than its historical return.

 3. Regulatory risk is the risk that the legal or regulatory environment in which a company operates will change as a result of legislation.

4. Standard deviation is a measure of inflationary pressures on the performance of a company.

PORTFOLIOS

Tens of thousands of stocks trade in the stock markets. Stock indexes, such as the S&P 500 or the Utility Index, are smaller groups of stocks that serve as a benchmark for measuring the performance of the overall market or sectors of the market.

Indexes are generally weighted for the capitalization (number of outstanding shares) of the companies included. Therefore, a large company's stock price changes will have a greater effect on the index. Indexes are often used as benchmark portfolios against which managed portfolios are measured in order to gauge the performance, or added value, of the fund manager. In addition, index mutual funds will invest in the securities that compose an index to specifically mirror the index's performance.

The exam will want you to know which index serves as the benchmark for which type of portfolio:

- Large Cap—S&P 500

- Mid Cap—S&P 400

- Small Cap—Russell 2000

OPTIMAL PORTFOLIO

An **optimal portfolio** is one that returns the highest rate of return consistent with the amount of risk an investor is willing to take. In other words, an optimal portfolio is the portfolio that makes the best trade-off between risk and reward for a given investor's investment profile.

QUICK QUIZ 10.8   True or False?

_F_   1. A stock with a beta of 1.25 is less volatile than the overall market.

_F_   2. If the average PE ratio of an industry is 15, a stock in that industry with a PE of 20 is high priced.

_T_   3. A benchmark portfolio attempts to mimic the performance of an index such as the S&P 500.

_T_   4. Treasury bills have a relatively high amount of liquidity risk.

_F_   5. Systematic risk is another name for business risk.

_F_   6. Interest rate risk has no great impact on stock prices.

HOTSHEETS

For your convenience, Unit HotSheets summarizing the key points are located at the end of the manual on perforated pages.

UNIT TEST

1. John purchased securities in the yacht-building business. Two years ago, his securities had lost most of their value as a result of a congressionally imposed luxury tax on purchases of more than $30,000. John's purchase of an investment in the yacht-building business suffered

   A. interest rate risk
   B. business risk
   C. regulatory (legislative) risk
   D. volatility

2. Balance sheets contain

   A. gross revenues for the year
   B. the amount of cash and cash equivalents expended during the first half of the fiscal year as opposed to the second half
   C. the net worth of the firm at the end of the reporting period
   D. no reference to the accounting methods used to construct the balance sheet

3. An investor owns 2 corporate bonds, X and Y, of equal quality. If Bond X has a duration of 5.79 years, which of the following statements about the effect of a 1% decline in interest rates is CORRECT?

   A. Bond Y, which has a longer duration than Bond X, would have a greater percentage increase in price than Bond X.
   B. Bond X would have a greater percentage change in price than Bond Y because it has a shorter duration.
   C. It is not possible to determine the percentage change in price of Bond X versus Bond Y because the duration of Bond Y is not given.
   D. Bond Y, which has a longer duration than Bond X, would have a greater percentage decrease in price than Bond X.

4. Which of the following is a coincident economic indicator?

   A. Stock market prices as measured by the S&P 500
   B. Machine tool orders
   C. Industrial production
   D. Agricultural employment

5. Risk-adjusted return is calculated by

   A. multiplying the return of an investment by its standard deviation
   B. dividing the price of the stock by its standard deviation
   C. dividing the remainder of the risk-free rate subtracted from the security's actual return by its standard deviation
   D. dividing the security's price by its beta

6. Which of the following statements about the consumer price index (CPI) is NOT true?

   A. The CPI measures the increase in the general price level of a basket of consumer goods.
   B. The CPI measures the increase or decrease in the level of consumer prices with respect to the level of wholesale prices upon which consumer prices depend.
   C. The CPI is computed monthly.
   D. The CPI measures the rate of increase or decrease in a broad range of prices, such as food, housing, medical care, and clothing.

7. What is the total return on a 1-year, newly issued (365 days to maturity) zero-coupon bond priced at 5?

   A. The return cannot be determined without knowing current interest rates.
   B. 5%
   C. 5.26% plus the implied coupon rate
   D. 5.26%

8. Duration is

   A. equivalent to the yield to maturity
   B. a measure of a bond's volatility with respect to a change in interest rates
   C. the deviation of a bond's returns from its average returns
   D. identical to a bond's maturity

9. The future value of an invested dollar is dependent on

   I. the exchange rate of the dollar at the beginning and end of the period
   II. the interest rate at maturity
   III. the rate of return it earns
   IV. the time period over which it is invested

   A. I only
   B. II only
   C. II and III
   D. III and IV

10. Which of the following statements reflects the monetarist economic position?

   A. The amount of money in the economy is not significant because economic activity reflects the value of real goods and services and, therefore, the Federal Reserve should not attempt to manage the money supply.
   B. The total amount of money in the economy is the result of the level of interest rates.
   C. The amount of money in the economy determines the overall price level over time and, therefore, the Federal Reserve should control the growth in the amount of money in the economy in a gradual and predictable way.
   D. The best way to control the money supply is to raise taxes, which, in turn, will reduce the amount of money in the economy and lower prices.

11. If the US dollar has fallen relative to foreign currencies, which of the following statements are TRUE?

   I. US exports are likely to rise.
   II. exports are likely to fall.
   III. Foreign currencies buy fewer US dollars.
   IV. Foreign currencies buy more US dollars.

   A. I and III
   B. I and IV
   C. II and III
   D. II and IV

12. The yield to maturity is

   A. set at issuance and printed on the face of the bond
   B. determined by dividing the coupon rate by the current market price of the bond
   C. the annualized return of a bond if it is held to maturity
   D. the annualized return of a bond if it is held to call date

13. An upward sloping yield curve represents all of the following EXCEPT

   A. time value of money
   B. increased risk of default over time
   C. inflation expectations
   D. foreign interest rate differentials

14. "Stock prices adjust rapidly to the release of all new public information." This statement is an expression of which of the following ideas?

   A. Arbitrage pricing theory
   B. Efficient market hypothesis
   C. Odd-lot theory
   D. Tactical allocation

15. When discussing employment and production, which of the following industries are typically more affected by a recession?

   I. Capital goods
   II. Consumer durable goods
   III. Consumer nondurable goods
   IV. Services

   A. I and II
   B. I and III
   C. II and IV
   D. III and IV

16. The present value of a dollar

   A. is the amount of goods and services the dollar will buy in the future at today's rate price level
   B. indicates how much needs to be invested today at a given interest rate to equal a specific cash value in the future
   C. is equal to its future value if the level of interest rates stays the same
   D. cannot be calculated without knowing the level of inflation

17. Which of the following statements regarding significant interest rates in the US economy is NOT true?

   A. Federal funds rate is the rate the Federal Reserve charges for overnight loans to member commercial banks.

   B. The prime rate is the interest rate that large US money center commercial banks charge their most creditworthy corporate borrowers.

   C. The discount rate is the rate the New York Federal Reserve Bank charges for short-term loans to member banks.

   D. Broker loan rate is the interest rate banks charge broker/dealers on money they borrow to lend to margin account customers.

18. If the dollar weakens, which of the following statements is TRUE?

   A. The dollar buys more foreign currency.

   B. US exports become less competitive.

   C. Foreign securities denominated in their domestic currency decrease in value to the US investor.

   D. An increase in US interest rates might strengthen the dollar.

19. Expected return is

   A. the difference between an investment's present value and its cost

   B. the current worth of future income discounted to reflect what that income is worth today

   C. an estimate of probable returns an investment may yield

   D. the one discount rate that equates the future value of an investment with its net present value

20. Dan is the owner of a mutual fund that returned him a before-tax return of 15% last year. Inflation is running at an annual rate of 3%, and Dan is in a 27% marginal income tax bracket. What has been Dan's approximate inflation-adjusted after-tax return on the fund over the course of the last year (rounded to the nearest 2 decimal points)?

   A. 7.95%

   B. 8.76%

   C. 10.95%

   D. 12.00%

ANSWERS AND RATIONALES

1. **C.** John's investment in the yacht-building business suffered a loss as a result of regulatory (legislative) risk. In other words, the rules of the game (i.e., tax treatment) changed after John purchased the security.

2. **C.** The balance sheet provides a snapshot view of the financial condition of the firm at the end of the reporting period. It does not provide information on the flow of expenses, revenues, and cash during the reporting period. Gross revenues are reflected on the income statement, not on the balance sheet. The balance sheet provides a description of the assets, liabilities, and owner's equity at the end of the reporting period. References to accounting methods used are contained in the footnotes of the balance sheet.

3. **A.** The bond with the longest duration has the greatest interest rate risk. Reducing the duration of a portfolio of bonds is one method of reducing that risk. Even though Bond Y's duration is not given, the correct choice makes an accurate statement. Remember that if interest rates decline, bond prices go up.

4. **C.** Industrial production is a coincident indicator. The stock indexes and manufacturing orders are leading indicators. Economists do not use agricultural employment as an indicator.

5. **C.** The return from a security can be adjusted for the risk associated with it by subtracting the risk-free rate from the security's actual return and then dividing that by its standard deviation, the basic measure of unsystematic risk. This is commonly known as the Sharpe ratio.

6. **B.** The CPI does not measure the increase or decrease in the level of consumer prices with respect to the level of wholesale prices. The CPI only measures retail prices whether or not wholesale prices are passed through to the consumer.

7. **D.** To determine the total return on this zero-coupon bond, the $5 capital appreciation is divided by the cost of the bond, in this case $95, for a total return of 5.26%. Total return of a zero-coupon bond is made up entirely of the difference between the cost of the bond and the sale or maturity price of the bond. The market price of the bond, not current interest rates, is used in the calculation of total return. Five percent would be the return had the bond cost 100, or par. There is no coupon rate to be added to the calculation.

8. **B.** Duration measures a bond's volatility with respect to a change in interest rates. The higher the duration, the greater the change in a bond's price with respect to interest rate changes.

9. **D.** The future value of a dollar reflects the interest rate it earns over time. The rate of foreign exchange is not related to or used in the calculation of the future value of a dollar. The foreign exchange rate is not relevant.

10. **C.** Monetarists believe that the economy and inflation are best controlled through the management of the money supply rather than through fiscal policy stimulation.

11. **B.** When the US dollar loses value, compared with a foreign currency, the same amount of the foreign currency now buys more dollars. As a result, US goods are cheaper in terms of that foreign currency, which means that the foreign country tends to buy more US products and US exports rise.

12. **C.** The yield to maturity reflects the annualized return of a bond if it is held to its maturity. The computation reflects internal rate of return and is frequently referred to as the market required rate of return for a debt security. The rate set at issuance and printed on the face of the bond is the nominal or coupon rate. Dividing the coupon rate by the current market price of the bond provides the current yield. The return of a bond if it is held to the call date is the yield to call.

13. **D.** Foreign interest rate differentials are not reflected in an upward sloping yield curve. Interest rate differentials between countries reflect differences in domestic monetary and fiscal conditions. The time value of money is reflected in the upward sloping yield curve. Longer-term rates require higher rates to compensate for loss of current buying power and liquidity. Longer-term funds bear a higher risk of default than do shorter-term funds and, as a result, command higher rates. Increasing inflation expectations cause the yield curve to slope upward to compensate lenders for the loss of future buying power.

14. **B.** In an efficient market, all participants have equal access to information and, therefore, stock prices reflect that equality almost immediately.

15. **A.** Durable goods and capital goods are more affected by a recession than are nondurable goods and services. This is primarily because they are larger items, last for a longer period, and are somewhat discretionary.

16. **B.** The present value of a dollar will indicate how much needs to be invested today at a given interest rate to equal a cash amount required in the future.

17. **A.** The federal funds rate is the rate that member banks charge each other for overnight loans of $1 million or more; it is not the rate that the Federal Reserve charges member banks for overnight loans.

18. **D.** When US interest rates rise, foreign investors invest in US dollar-denominated securities, thereby increasing the demand for dollars and causing the dollar to strengthen.

19. **C.** The expected return is the estimate of probable returns that an investment may yield when added up.

20. **A.** First, compute Dan's after-tax rate of return of 10.95% as follows: .15 × (1 − .27), or .73 = .1095. Then, compute Dan's inflation-adjusted, or real, rate of return by subtracting the 3% inflation rate from his 10.95% after-tax return.

Q U I C K   Q U I Z   A N S W E R S

Quick Quiz 10.1

1. **F.** Monetarists prefer less government intervention. Keynesian economists believe that the federal government should manage inflation through taxation and spending.

2. **F.** A depression is a decrease in the GDP for at least six consecutive quarters.

3. **F.** Rising inventories are characteristic of a downturn in the business cycle. Inventories accumulate when consumers buy less.

4. **T.** The CPI is a measurement of inflation.

5. **T.** High consumer debt is characteristic of a downturn in the business cycle.

Quick Quiz 10.2

1. **C.**
2. **E.**
3. **B.**
4. **A.**
5. **D.**
6. **F.**

Quick Quiz 10.3

1. **B.** Working capital (or net working capital) is, by definition, the difference between current assets and current liabilities.

2. **B.** The formula for the balance sheet is as follows: assets = liabilities + shareholders' equity. If assets stay the same and equity (net worth) decreases, liabilities must increase. Prepaid expenses are assets; accrued expenses are liabilities.

3. **D.** On the issuance of a bond, cash is received (thus increasing current assets) and long-term debt increases (increasing total liabilities). Because there is no corresponding increase in current liabilities, working capital will increase; it would have no effect on shareholders' equity.

4. **D.** If earnings increase, retained earnings also increase. If the increased retained earnings are not paid out as dividends, shareholders' equity increases.

Quick Quiz 10.4

1. **A.**
2. **B.**
3. **A.**
4. **A.**
5. **B.**
6. **B.**

Quick Quiz 10.5

1. **A.**
2. **B.**
3. **A.**
4. **B.**
5. **A.**
6. **B.**

Quick Quiz 10.6

1. **H.**
2. **I.**
3. **F.**
4. **C.**
5. **E.**
6. **D.**
7. **A.**
8. **G.**
9. **J.**
10. **B.**

Quick Quiz 10.7

1. **F.** Market risk is systematic risk, or the risk that the overall market will have an adverse effect on a security independent of the company's circumstances.

2. **F.** In finance, the term *risk* is defined as the uncertainty that an investment will earn its expected rate of return.

3. **T.** Regulatory, or legislative, risk is the risk a company faces that the legal rules of the game will change as a result of legislative action.

4. **F.** Standard deviation is a measure of an investment's volatility. It measures the amount of variance in price or returns from the investment's mean return during an expected period.

Quick Quiz 10.8

1. **F.** The overall market has a beta of 1. A stock with a beta of 1.25 experiences 25% more price movement than the overall market.

2. **T.** If the average PE ratio of an industry is 15, a stock in that industry with a PE of 20 is high priced.

3. **T.** A benchmark portfolio attempts to mimic the performance of an index such as the S&P 500.

4. **F.** Securities with a high amount of liquidity risk are not easily convertible into cash. Treasury bills can be sold easily, and as such have little liquidity risk.

5. **F.** Systematic risk is the same as market risk. Generally, stock prices move together as the overall market changes. Diversification cannot offset systematic risk.

6. **F.** Because bond prices are sensitive to changing interest rates, they carry interest rate risk. Common stock prices are also sensitive to changes in interest rates. The stock market generally reacts negatively to increases in interest rates.

Glossary

A

accrued interest The interest that has accumulated since the last interest payment, up to but not including the settlement date, and that is added to a bond transaction's contract price.

accumulation stage The period during which contributions are made to an annuity account. *See* accumulation unit; distribution stage.

accumulation unit An accounting measure used to determine an annuitant's proportionate interest in the insurer's separate account during an annuity's accumulation (deposit) stage. *See* accumulation stage; separate account.

Act of 1933 *See* Securities Act of 1933.

Act of 1934 *See* Securities Exchange Act of 1934.

adjusted basis The value attributed to an asset or security that reflects any deductions taken on, or capital improvements to, the asset or security. Adjusted basis is used to compute the gain or loss on the sale or other disposition of the asset or security.

adjusted gross income (AGI) Earned income plus net passive income, portfolio income, and capital gains. *See* tax liability.

administrator (1) A person authorized by a court of law to liquidate an intestate decedent's estate. (2) An official or agency that administers a state's securities laws.

ADR *See* American depositary receipt.

ADS *See* American depositary receipt.

advertisement Any notice, circular, letter, or other written communication addressed to more than one person, or any notice or other announcement in any publication or by radio or television, that offers (1) any analysis, report, or publication concerning securities, or that is to be used in making any determination as to when to buy or sell any security, or which security to buy or sell; or (2) any graph, chart, formula, or other device to be used in making any determination as to when to buy or sell any security, or which security to buy or sell; or (3) any other investment advisory service with regard to securities.

agency basis *See* agency transaction.

agency cross-transaction For an advisory client, a transaction in which a person acts as an investment adviser in relation to a transaction in which that investment adviser, or any person controlling, controlled by, or under common control with that investment adviser, acts as broker for both an advisory client and for another person on the other side of the transaction.

agency issue A debt security issued by an authorized agency of the federal government. Such an issue is backed by the issuing agency itself, not by the full faith and credit of the US government (except GNMA issues). *See* government security.

agency transaction A transaction in which a broker/dealer acts for the accounts of others by buying or selling securities on behalf of customers. *Syn.* agency basis. *See* agent; broker; principal transaction.

agent (1) An individual or a firm that effects securities transactions for the accounts of others. (2) A securities salesperson who represents a broker/dealer or an issuer when selling or trying to sell securities to the investing public; this individual is considered an agent whether he actually receives or simply solicits orders. *See* broker; broker/dealer; dealer; principal.

aggressive investment strategy A method of portfolio allocation and management aimed at achieving maximum return. Aggressive investors place a high percentage of their investable assets in equity securities and a far lower percentage in safer debt securities and cash equivalents, and they pursue aggressive policies including margin trading, arbitrage, and option trading. *See* balanced investment strategy; defensive investment strategy.

AGI *See* adjusted gross income.

all or none order (AON) An order that instructs the floor broker to execute the entire order in one transaction; if the order cannot be executed in its entirety, it is allowed to expire.

alpha   The risk-adjusted returns that a portfolio manager generates in excess of the risk-adjusted returns expected by the capital asset pricing model (CAPM). Suppose an index return is 10%, the portfolio beta is 1.5, and the actual return is 25%. According to the CAPM, the portfolio should be expected to return 15% (1.5 times 10%). This is because the portfolio is 1.5 times riskier than the market. If the risk-free rate is 5%, the risk-adjusted CAPM return should be 10%. Now, the actual risk-adjusted return is 20% (actual return less risk-free rate). This means that the portfolio manager demonstrated superior stock picking or market timing skills. The difference between the risk-adjusted CAPM return and the actual risk-adjusted return is the alpha. In the above example, it is 10%.

alternative minimum tax (AMT)   An alternative tax computation that adds certain tax preference items back into adjusted gross income. If the AMT is higher than the regular tax liability for the year, the regular tax and the amount by which the AMT exceeds the regular tax are paid. *See* tax preference item.

American depositary receipt (ADR)   A negotiable certificate representing a given number of shares in a foreign corporation. It is issued by a domestic bank. ADRs are bought and sold in the American securities markets, and are traded in English and US dollars. *Syn.* American depositary share (ADS).

American Stock Exchange (AMEX)   A private, not-for-profit corporation located in New York City that handles approximately 5% of all securities trades within the United States.

AMEX   *See* American Stock Exchange.

appreciation   The increase in an asset's value.

arbitrage   The simultaneous buying and selling of the same security in two different markets to take advantage of a temporary price disparity. This is not considered market manipulation.

ask   An indication by a trader or a dealer of a willingness to sell a security or a commodity; the price at which an investor can buy from a broker/dealer. *Syn.* offer. *See* bid; public offering price; quotation.

assessable stock   A stock that is issued below its par or stated value. The issuer and/or creditors have the right to assess the shareholder for the deficiency. All stock issued today is nonassessable.

asset   (1) Anything that an individual or a corporation owns. (2) A balance sheet item expressing what a corporation owns.

auction market   A market in which buyers enter competitive bids and sellers enter competitive offers simultaneously. The NYSE is an auction market. *Syn.* double auction market.

audited financial statement   A financial statement of a program, a corporation, or an issuer (including the profit and loss statement, cash flow and source and application of revenues statement, and balance sheet) that has been examined and verified by an independent certified public accountant.

average basis   An accounting method used when an investor has made multiple purchases at different prices of the same security; the method averages the purchase prices to calculate an investor's cost basis in shares being liquidated. The difference between the average cost basis and the selling price determines the investor's tax liability. *See* first in, first out; last in, first out.

B

balanced fund   A mutual fund whose stated investment policy is to have at all times some portion of its investment assets in bonds and preferred stock, as well as in common stock, in an attempt to provide both growth and income. *See* mutual fund.

balanced investment strategy   A method of portfolio allocation and management aimed at balancing risk and return. A balanced portfolio may combine stocks, bonds, packaged products, and cash equivalents.

balance of payments (BOP)   An international accounting record of all transactions made by one particular country with others during a certain period; it compares the amount of foreign currency the country has taken in with the amount of its own currency it has paid out. *See* balance of trade.

balance of trade   The largest component of a country's balance of payments; it concerns the export and import of merchandise (not services). Debit items include imports, foreign aid, domestic spending abroad, and domestic investments abroad. Credit items include exports, foreign spending in the domestic economy, and foreign investments in the domestic economy. *See* balance of payments.

balance sheet   A report of a corporation's financial condition at a specific time.

balance sheet equation   A formula stating that a corporation's assets equal the sum of its liabilities plus shareholders' equity.

basis point   A measure of a bond's yield, equal to $\frac{1}{100}$ of 1% of yield. A bond whose yield increases from 5.0% to 5.5% is said to increase by 50 basis points. *See* point.

BD *See* broker/dealer.

bear An investor who acts on the belief that a security or the market is falling or will fall. *See* bull.

bear market A market in which prices of a certain group of securities are falling or are expected to fall. *See* bull market.

beta A means of measuring the volatility of a security or a portfolio of securities in comparison with the market as a whole. A beta of 1 indicates that the security's price will move with the market. A beta greater than 1 indicates that the security's price will be more volatile than the market. A beta less than 1 means that it will be less volatile than the market.

bid An indication by an investor, a trader, or a dealer of a willingness to buy a security; the price at which an investor can sell to a broker/dealer. *See* offer; public offering price; quotation.

board of directors Individuals elected by stockholders to establish corporate management policies. A board of directors decides, among other issues, if and when dividends will be paid to stockholders.

bond An issuing company's or government's legal obligation to repay the principal of a loan to bond investors at a specified future date. Bonds are usually issued with par or face values of $1,000, representing the amount of money borrowed. The issuer promises to pay a percentage of the par value as interest on the borrowed funds. The interest payment is stated on the face of the bond at issue.

bond fund A mutual fund whose investment objective is to provide stable income with minimal capital risk. It invests in income-producing instruments, which may include corporate, government, or municipal bonds. *See* mutual fund.

bond quote One of a number of quotations listed in the financial press and most daily newspapers that provide representative bid prices from the previous day's bond market. Quotes for corporate and government bonds are percentages of the bonds' face values (usually $1,000). Corporate bonds are quoted in increments of ⅛. Government bonds are quoted in increments of 1/32. Municipal bonds may be quoted on a dollar basis or on a yield-to-maturity basis. *See* quotation; stock quote.

bond rating An evaluation of the possibility of a bond issuer's default, based on an analysis of the issuer's financial condition and profit potential. Standard & Poor's, Moody's Investors Service, and Fitch Investors Service, among others, provide bond rating services.

bond ratio One of several tools used by bond analysts to assess the degree of safety offered by a corporation's bonds. It measures the percentage of the corporation's capitalization that is provided by long-term debt financing, calculated by dividing the total face value of the outstanding bonds by the total capitalization. *Syn.* debt ratio.

bond yield The annual rate of return on a bond investment. Types of yield include nominal yield, current yield, yield to maturity, and yield to call. Their relationships vary according to whether the bond in question is at a discount, at a premium, or at par. *See* current yield; nominal yield.

book-entry security A security sold without delivery of a certificate. Evidence of ownership is maintained on records kept by a central agency; for example, the Treasury keeps records of Treasury bill purchasers. Transfer of ownership is recorded by entering the change on the books or electronic files. *See* coupon bond.

book value per share A measure of the net worth of each share of common stock is calculated by subtracting intangible assets and preferred stock from total net worth, then dividing the result by the number of shares of common outstanding. *Syn.* net tangible assets per share.

BOP *See* balance of payments.

breadth-of-market theory A technical analysis theory that predicts the strength of the market according to the number of issues that advance or decline in a particular trading day.

broad-based index An index designed to reflect the movement of the market as a whole. Examples include the S&P 100, the S&P 500, the AMEX Major Market Index, and the Value Line Composite Index. *See* index.

broker (1) An individual or a firm that charges a fee or commission for executing buy and sell orders submitted by another individual or firm. (2) The role of a firm when it acts as an agent for a customer and charges the customer a commission for its services. *See* agent; broker/dealer; dealer.

broker/dealer (BD) A person or firm in the business of buying and selling securities. A firm may act as both broker (agent) and dealer (principal), but not in the same transaction. Broker/dealers normally must register with the SEC, the appropriate SROs, and any state in which they do business. *See* agent; broker; dealer; principal.

bull An investor who acts on the belief that a security or the market is rising or will rise. *See* bear.

bulletin board *See* OTC Bulletin Board.

bull market A market in which prices of a certain group of securities are rising or will rise. *See* bear market.

business cycle A predictable long-term pattern of alternating periods of economic growth and decline. The cycle passes through four stages: expansion, peak, contraction, and trough.

buy stop order An order to buy a security that is entered at a price above the current offering price and that is triggered when the market price touches or goes through the buy stop price.

bypass trust A trust that is funded with property in an amount equal to the exemption equivalent of the transfer tax credit amount applicable to the decedent ($2 million in 2006); thus, the property is not subject to federal estate tax.

C

call (1) An option contract giving the owner the right to buy a specified amount of an underlying security at a specified price within a specified time. (2) The act of exercising a call option. *See* put.

callable bond A type of bond issued with a provision allowing the issuer to redeem the bond before maturity at a predetermined price.

callable preferred stock A type of preferred stock issued with a provision allowing the corporation to call in the stock at a certain price and retire it. *See* call price; preferred stock.

call buyer An investor who pays a premium for an option contract and receives, for a specified time, the right to buy the underlying security at a specified price. *See* call writer; put.

call date The date, specified in the prospectus of every callable security, after which the security's issuer has the option to redeem the issue at par or at par plus a premium.

call feature *See* call provision.

call protection A provision in a bond indenture stating that the issue is noncallable for a certain period (e.g., 5 years or 10 years) after the original issue date. *See* call provision.

call provision The written agreement between an issuing corporation and its bondholders or preferred stockholders giving the corporation the option to redeem its senior securities at a specified price before maturity and under certain conditions. *Syn.* call feature.

call risk The potential for a bond to be called before maturity, leaving the investor without the bond's current income. Because this is more likely to occur during times of falling interest rates, the investor may not be able to reinvest his principal at a comparable rate of return.

call writer An investor who receives a premium and takes on, for a specified time, the obligation to sell the underlying security at a specified price at the call buyer's discretion. *See* call buyer; put.

capital Accumulated money or goods available for use in producing more money or goods.

capital appreciation An increase in an asset's market price.

capital asset All tangible property, including securities, real estate, and other property, held for the long term.

capital gain The profit realized when a capital asset is sold for a higher price than the purchase price. *See* capital loss; long-term gain.

capitalization The sum of a corporation's long-term debt, stock, and surpluses. *Syn.* invested capital. *See* capital structure.

capitalization ratio A measure of an issuer's financial status that calculates the value of its bonds, preferred stock, or common stock as a percentage of its total capitalization.

capital loss The loss incurred when a capital asset is sold for a price lower than the purchase price. *See* capital gain; long-term loss.

capital market The segment of the securities market that deals in instruments with more than one year to maturity—that is, long-term debt and equity securities.

capital stock All of a corporation's outstanding preferred stock and common stock, listed at par value.

capital structure The composition of long-term funds (equity and debt) a corporation has as a source for financing. *See* capitalization.

capital surplus The money a corporation receives in excess of the stated value of stock at the time of first sale. *Syn.* paid-in capital; paid-in surplus. *See* par.

capping An illegal form of market manipulation that attempts to keep the price of a subject security from rising. It is used by those with a short position. *See* pegging.

cash account An account in which the customer is required by the SEC's Regulation T to pay in full for securities purchased not later than two days after the standard payment period set by NASD's Uniform Practice Code. *Syn.* special cash account.

cash dividend Money paid to a corporation's stockholders out of the corporation's current earnings or accumulated profits. The board of directors must declare all dividends.

cash equivalent A security that can be readily converted into cash. Examples include Treasury bills, certificates of deposit, and money market instruments and funds.

cash flow The money received by a business minus the money paid out. Cash flow is also equal to net income plus depreciation or depletion.

CBOE *See* Chicago Board Options Exchange.

CD *See* negotiable certificate of deposit.

certificate of deposit (CD) *See* negotiable certificate of deposit.

chartist A securities analyst who uses charts and graphs of the past price movements of a security to predict its future movements. *Syn.* technician. *See* technical analysis.

Chicago Board Options Exchange (CBOE) The self-regulatory organization with jurisdiction over all writing and trading of standardized options and related contracts listed on that exchange. Also, the first national securities exchange for the trading of listed options.

Chinese wall A descriptive name for the division within a brokerage firm that prevents insider information from passing from corporate advisers to investment traders, who could make use of the information to reap illicit profits. *See* Insider Trading and Securities Fraud Enforcement Act of 1988.

churning Excessive trading in a customer's account by a registered representative who ignores the customer's interests and seeks only to increase commissions; violates NASAA's policies on unethical business practices. *Syn.* overtrading.

closed-end investment company An investment company that issues a fixed number of shares in an actively managed portfolio of securities. The shares may be of several classes; they are traded in the secondary marketplace, either on an exchange or over the counter. The market price of the shares is determined by supply and demand and not by net asset value. *Syn.* publicly traded fund. *See* mutual fund.

closed-end management company An investment company that issues a fixed number of shares in an actively managed portfolio of securities. The shares may be of several classes; they are traded in the secondary marketplace, either on an exchange or over the counter. The shares' market price is determined by supply and demand, not by net asset value. *Syn.* publicly traded fund.

closing purchase An options transaction in which the seller buys back an option in the same series; the two transactions effectively cancel each other out and the position is liquidated. *See* opening purchase.

CMO *See* collateralized mortgage obligation.

coincident indicator A measurable economic factor that varies directly and simultaneously with the business cycle, thus indicating the current state of the economy. Examples include nonagricultural employment, personal income, and industrial production. *See* lagging indicator; leading indicator.

collateral Certain assets set aside and pledged to a lender for the duration of a loan. If the borrower fails to meet obligations to pay principal or interest, the lender has claim to the assets.

collateralized mortgage obligation (CMO) A mortgage-backed corporate security. These issues attempt to return interest and principal at a predetermined rate.

collateral trust bond A secured bond backed by stocks or bonds of another issuer. The collateral is held by a trustee for safekeeping. *Syn.* collateral trust certificate.

collateral trust certificate *See* collateral trust bond.

combination fund An equity mutual fund that attempts to combine the objectives of growth and current yield by dividing its portfolio between companies that show long-term growth potential and companies that pay high dividends. *See* mutual fund.

combination privilege A benefit offered by a mutual fund whereby the investor may qualify for a sales charge breakpoint by combining separate investments in two or more mutual funds under the same management.

commercial paper An unsecured, short-term promissory note issued by a corporation for financing accounts receivable and inventories. It is usually issued at a discount reflecting prevailing market interest rates. Maturities range up to 270 days.

commingling The combining by a brokerage firm of one customer's securities with another customer's securities and pledging them as joint collateral for a bank loan; unless authorized by the customers, this violates SEC Rule 15c2-1.

commission A service charge an agent assesses in return for arranging a security's purchase or sale. A commission must be fair and reasonable, considering all the relevant factors of the transaction. *Syn.* sales charge. *See* markup.

common stock A security that represents ownership in a corporation. Holders of common stock exercise control by electing a board of directors and voting on corporate policy. *See* equity; preferred stock.

complex trust A trust that accumulates income over time and is not required to make scheduled distributions to its beneficiaries.

Composite Average *See* Dow Jones Composite Average.

conduit theory A means for an investment company to avoid taxation on net investment income distributed to shareholders. If a mutual fund acts as a conduit for the distribution of net investment income, it may qualify as a regulated investment company and be taxed only on the income the fund retains. *Syn.* pipeline theory.

confirmation A printed document that states the trade date, settlement date, and money due from or owed to a customer. It is sent or given to the customer on or before the settlement date.

Consumer Price Index (CPI) A measure of price changes in consumer goods and services used to identify periods of inflation or deflation.

consumption A term used by economists to refer to the purchase by household units of newly produced goods and services.

contraction A period of general economic decline, one of the business cycle's four stages. *See* business cycle.

control person (1) A director, an officer, or another affiliate of an issuer. (2) A stockholder who owns more than 10% of any class of a corporation's outstanding securities. (3) Spouse or other immediate family of any of the previous. *See* affiliate; insider.

control security Any security owned by a director, an officer, or another affiliate of the issuer or by a stockholder who owns more than 10% of any class of a corporation's outstanding securities. Who owns a security, not the security itself, determines whether it is a control security.

conversion parity Two securities, one of which can be converted into the other, of equal dollar value. A convertible security holder can calculate parity to help decide whether converting would lead to gain or loss.

conversion price The dollar amount of a convertible security's par value that is exchangeable for one share of common stock.

conversion privilege A feature the issuer adds to a security that allows the holder to change the security into shares of common stock. This makes the security attractive to investors and, therefore, more marketable. *See* convertible bond; convertible preferred stock.

conversion rate *See* conversion ratio.

conversion ratio The number of shares of common stock per par value amount that the holder would receive for converting a convertible bond or preferred share. *Syn.* conversion rate.

convertible bond A debt security, usually in the form of a debenture, that can be exchanged for equity securities of the issuing corporation at specified prices or rates. *See* debenture.

convertible preferred stock An equity security that can be exchanged for common stock at specified prices or rates. Dividends may be cumulative or noncumulative. *See* cumulative preferred stock; noncumulative preferred stock; preferred stock.

cooling-off period The period (a minimum of 20 days) between a registration statement's filing date and the registration's effective date. In practice, the period varies in length.

corporate account An account held in a corporation's name. The corporate agreement, signed when the account is opened, specifies which officers are authorized to trade in the account. In addition to standard margin account documents, a corporation must provide a copy of its charter and bylaws authorizing a margin account.

corporate bond A debt security issued by a corporation. A corporate bond typically has a par value of $1,000, is taxable, has a term maturity, and is traded on a major exchange.

corporation The most common form of business organization, in which the organization's total worth is divided into shares of stock, each share representing a unit of ownership. A corporation is characterized by a continuous life span and its owners' limited liability.

correlation The extent to which two or more securities or portfolios move together. The correlation coefficient is a number that ranges from –1 to +1. A perfect correlation would have a coefficient of +1, whereas two securities that move in total opposite directions would have a –1. A coefficient of 0 would reflect a totally random correlation between the two securities.

cost basis The price paid for an asset, including any commissions or fees, used to calculate capital gains or losses when the asset is sold.

coupon yield *See* nominal yield.

covered call writer An investor who sells a call option while owning the underlying security or some other asset that guarantees the ability to deliver if the call is exercised.

covered put writer An investor who sells a put option while owning an asset that guarantees the ability to pay if the put is exercised.

CPI *See* Consumer Price Index.

credit risk The degree of probability that a bond's issuer will default in the payment of either principal or interest. Securities issued by the US government are considered to have no credit risk. *Syn.* default risk; financial risk.

C trust *See* QTIP trust

cumulative preferred stock An equity security that offers the holder any unpaid dividends in arrears. These dividends accumulate and must be paid to the cumulative preferred stockholder before any dividends can be paid to the common stockholders. *See* noncumulative preferred stock; preferred stock.

cumulative voting A voting procedure that permits stockholders either to cast all of their votes for any one candidate or to cast their total number of votes in any proportion they choose. This results in greater representation for minority stockholders. *See* statutory voting.

current assets Cash and other assets that are expected to be converted into cash within the next 12 months. Examples include such liquid items as cash and equivalents, accounts receivable, inventory, and prepaid expenses.

current liabilities A corporation's debt obligations due for payment within the next 12 months. Examples include accounts payable, accrued wages payable, and current long-term debt.

current market value (CMV) The worth of the securities in an account. The market value of listed securities is based on the closing prices on the previous business day. *Syn.* long market value. *See* market value.

current ratio A measure of a corporation's liquidity; that is, its ability to transfer assets into cash to meet current short-term obligations. It is calculated by dividing total current assets by total current liabilities. *Syn.* working capital ratio.

current yield The annual rate of return on a security, calculated by dividing the interest or dividends paid by the security's current market price. *See* bond yield.

custodial account An account in which a custodian enters trades on behalf of the beneficial owner, often a minor. *See* custodian.

custodian An institution or a person responsible for making all investment, management, and distribution decisions in an account maintained in the best interests of another. Mutual funds have custodian banks responsible for safeguarding certificates and performing clerical duties.

customer Any person who opens a trading account with a broker/dealer. A customer may be classified in terms of account ownership, trading authorization, payment method, or types of securities traded.

customer statement A document showing a customer's trading activity, positions, and account balance. The SEC requires that customer statements be sent quarterly, but customers generally receive them monthly.

cyclical industry A fundamental analysis term for an industry that is sensitive to the business cycle and price changes. Most cyclical industries produce durable goods, raw materials, and heavy equipment.

D

day order An order that is valid only until the close of trading on the day it is entered; if it is not executed by the close of trading, it is canceled.

dealer (1) An individual or a firm engaged in the business of buying and selling securities for its own account, either directly or through a broker. (2) The role of a firm when it acts as a principal and charges the customer a markup or markdown. *Syn.* principal. *See* broker; broker/dealer.

debenture A debt obligation backed by the issuing corporation's general credit. *Syn.* unsecured bond.

debt security A security representing an investor's loan to an issuer, such as a corporation, a municipality, the federal government, or a federal agency. In return for the loan, the issuer promises to repay the debt on a specified date and to pay interest. *See* equity security.

debt-to-equity ratio The ratio of total long-term debt to total stockholders' equity; it is used to measure leverage.

deduction An item or expenditure subtracted from adjusted gross income to reduce the amount of income subject to tax.

default The failure to pay interest or principal promptly when due.

default risk *See* credit risk.

defensive industry A fundamental analysis term for an industry that is relatively unaffected by the business cycle. Most defensive industries produce nondurable goods for which demand remains steady throughout the business cycle; examples include the food industry and utilities.

defensive investment strategy A method of portfolio allocation and management aimed at minimizing the risk of losing principal. Defensive investors place a high percentage of their investable assets in bonds, cash equivalents, and stocks that are less volatile than average.

deferred annuity An annuity contract that delays payment of income, installments, or a lump sum until the investor elects to receive it.

deferred compensation plan A nonqualified retirement plan whereby the employee defers receiving current compensation in favor of a larger payout at retirement (or in the case of disability or death).

deficiency letter The SEC's notification of additions or corrections that a prospective issuer must make to a registration statement before the SEC will clear the offering for distribution.

defined benefit plan A qualified retirement plan that specifies the total amount of money that the employee will receive at retirement.

defined contribution plan A qualified retirement plan that specifies the amount of money that the employer will contribute annually to the plan.

deflation A persistent and measurable fall in the general level of prices. *See* inflation.

demand A consumer's desire and willingness to pay for a good or service. *See* supply.

depreciation (1) A tax deduction that compensates a business for the cost of certain tangible assets. (2) A decrease in the value of a particular currency relative to other currencies.

depreciation expense A bookkeeping entry of a non-cash expense charged against earnings to recover the cost of an asset over its useful life.

depression A prolonged period of general economic decline.

derivative An investment vehicle, the value of which is based on another security's value. Futures contracts, forward contracts, and options are among the most common types of derivatives. Institutional investors generally use derivatives to increase overall portfolio return or to hedge portfolio risk.

dilution A reduction in earnings per share of common stock. Dilution occurs through the issuance of additional shares of common stock and the conversion of convertible securities.

directed brokerage The ability of an investment adviser to determine broker/dealers to be used in the execution of transactions on behalf of their advisory clients. *See* soft dollar compensation.

direct participation program (DPP) A business organized so as to pass all income, gains, losses, and tax benefits to its owners, the investors; the business is usually structured as a limited partnership. Examples include oil and gas programs, real estate programs, agricultural programs, cattle programs, condominium securities, and Subchapter S corporate offerings. *Syn.* program.

discount The difference between the lower price paid for a security and the security's face amount at issue.

discount bond A bond that sells at a lower price than its face value. *See* par.

discount rate The interest rate charged by the 12 Federal Reserve Banks for short-term loans made to member banks.

discretion The authority given to someone other than an account's beneficial owner to make investment decisions for the account concerning the security, the number of shares or units, and whether to buy or sell. The authority to decide only timing or price does not constitute discretion. *See* limited power of attorney.

discretionary account An account in which the customer has given the registered representative authority to enter transactions at the representative's discretion.

disposable income (DI) The sum that people divide between spending and personal savings. *See* personal income.

distributable net income (DNI) Taxable income from a trust that determines the amount of income that may be taxable to beneficiaries.

diversification A risk management technique that mixes a wide variety of investments within a portfolio, thus minimizing the impact of any one security on overall portfolio performance.

diversified common stock fund A mutual fund that invests its assets in a wide range of common stocks. The fund's objectives may be growth, income, or a combination of both. *See* growth fund; mutual fund.

diversified investment company As defined by the Investment Company Act of 1940, an investment company that meets certain standards as to the percentage of assets invested. These companies use diversification to manage risk. *See* management company; nondiversified investment company; 75-5-10 test.

dividend A distribution of a corporation's earnings. Dividends may be in the form of cash, stock, or property. The board of directors must declare all dividends. *Syn.* stock dividend. *See* cash dividend; dividend yield; property dividend.

dividend exclusion rule An IRS provision that permits a corporation to exclude from its taxable income 70% of dividends received from domestic preferred and common stocks. The Tax Reform Act of 1986 repealed the dividend exclusion for individual investors.

dividend payout ratio A measure of a corporation's policy of paying cash dividends, calculated by dividing the dividends paid on common stock by the net income available for common stockholders. The ratio is the complement of the retained earnings ratio.

dividends per share The dollar amount of cash dividends paid on each common share during one year.

dividend yield The annual rate of return on a common or preferred stock investment. The yield is calculated by dividing the annual dividend by the stock's purchase price. *See* current yield; dividend.

DNI *See* distributable net income.

dollar cost averaging A system of buying mutual fund shares in fixed dollar amounts at regular fixed intervals, regardless of the share's price. The investor purchases more shares when prices are low and fewer shares when prices are high, thus lowering the average cost per share over time.

donor A person who makes a gift of money or securities to another. Once the gift is donated, the donor gives up all rights to it. Gifts of securities to minors under the Uniform Gift to Minors Act provide tax advantages to the donor. *See* Uniform Gift to Minors Act.

Dow Jones averages The most widely quoted and oldest measures of change in stock prices. Each of the four averages is based on the prices of a limited number of stocks in a particular category. *See* average; Dow Jones Industrial Average.

Dow Jones Composite Average (DJCA) A market indicator composed of the 65 stocks that make up the Dow Jones Industrial, Transportation, and Utilities Averages. *See* average; Dow Jones Industrial Average; Dow Jones Transportation Average; Dow Jones Utilities Average.

Dow Jones Industrial Average (DJIA) The most widely used market indicator, composed of 30 large, actively traded issues of industrial stocks.

Dow Jones Transportation Average (DJTA) A market indicator composed of 20 transportation stocks. *See* average; Dow Jones Composite Average; Dow Jones Industrial Average; Dow Jones Utilities Average.

Dow Jones Utilities Average (DJUA) A market indicator composed of 15 utilities stocks. *See* average; Dow Jones Composite Average; Dow Jones Industrial Average; Dow Jones Transportation Average.

E

earned income Income derived from active participation in a trade or business, including wages, salary, tips, commissions, and bonuses. Also included is alimony received. One must have earned income in order to make contributions to an IRA. *See* portfolio income; unearned income.

earned surplus *See* retained earnings.

earnings per share (EPS) A corporation's net income available for common stock divided by its number of shares of common stock outstanding. *Syn.* primary earnings per share.

effective date The date the registration of an issue of securities becomes effective, allowing the underwriters to sell the newly issued securities to the public and confirm sales to investors who have given indications of interest.

efficient market theory A theory based on the premise that the stock market processes information efficiently. The theory postulates that, as new information becomes known, it is reflected immediately in the price of stock and therefore stock prices represent fair prices. *Syn.* Efficient market hypothesis.

elasticity The responsiveness of consumers and producers to a change in prices. A large change in demand or production resulting from a small change in price for a good is considered an indication of elasticity.

equity (EQ) Common and preferred stockholders' ownership interests in a corporation. *See* common stock; preferred stock.

equity financing Raising money for working capital or for capital expenditures by selling common or preferred stock to individual or institutional investors. In return for the money paid, the investors receive ownership interests in the corporation. *See* debt financing.

equity security A security representing ownership in a corporation or another enterprise. Examples of equity securities include:

- common and preferred stock;
- interests in a limited partnership or joint venture;
- securities that carry the right to be traded for equity securities, such as convertible bonds, rights, and warrants; and
- put and call options on equity securities.

eurobond A long-term debt instrument of a government or corporation that is denominated in the currency of the issuer's country but is issued and sold in a different country.

eurodollar US currency held in banks outside the United States.

exchange Any organization, association, or group of persons that maintains or provides a marketplace in which securities can be bought and sold. An exchange need not be a physical place, and several strictly electronic exchanges do business around the world.

exchange-listed security A security that has met certain requirements and has been admitted to full trading privileges on an exchange. The NYSE, the AMEX, and regional exchanges set listing requirements for volume of shares outstanding, corporate earnings, and other characteristics.

exchange privilege A feature offered by a mutual fund allowing an individual to transfer an investment in one fund to another fund under the same sponsor without incurring an additional sales charge.

exempt security A security exempt from the registration requirements (although not from the antifraud requirements) of the Securities Act of 1933 or the Uniform Securities Act. Examples include US government securities and municipal securities.

exempt transaction A transaction that does not trigger a state's registration and advertising requirements under the Uniform Securities Act. Examples of exempt transactions include:

- nonissuer transactions in outstanding securities (normal market trading);

- transactions with financial institutions;

- unsolicited transactions; and

- private placement transactions.

No transaction is exempt from the Uniform Securities Act's antifraud provisions.

exercise price The cost per share at which an option or a warrant holder may buy or sell the underlying security. *Syn.* strike price.

expansion A period of increased business activity throughout an economy; one of the four stages of the business cycle. *Syn.* recovery. *See* business cycle.

expansionary policy A monetary policy that increases the money supply, usually with the intention of lowering interest rates and combating deflation.

expense ratio A ratio for comparing a mutual fund's efficiency by dividing the fund's expenses by its net assets.

F

face value *See* par.

Fannie Mae *See* Federal National Mortgage Association.

Farm Credit Administration (FCA) The government agency that coordinates the activities of the banks in the Farm Credit System. *See* Farm Credit System.

Farm Credit System (FCS) An organization of 37 privately owned banks that provide credit services to farmers and mortgages on farm property. Included in the system are the Federal Land Banks, Federal Intermediate Credit Banks, and Banks for Cooperatives. *See* Federal Intermediate Credit Bank.

Federal Deposit Insurance Corporation (FDIC) The government agency that provides deposit insurance for member banks and prevents bank and thrift failures.

federal funds The reserves of banks and certain other institutions greater than the reserve requirements or excess reserves. These funds are available immediately.

federal funds rate The interest rate charged by one institution lending federal funds to another.

Federal Home Loan Bank (FHLB) A government-regulated organization that operates a credit reserve system for the nation's savings and loan institutions.

Federal Home Loan Mortgage Corporation (FHLMC) A publicly traded corporation that promotes the nationwide secondary market in mortgages by issuing mortgage-backed pass-through debt certificates. *Syn.* Freddie Mac.

Federal Intermediate Credit Bank (FICB) One of 12 banks that provide short-term financing to farmers as part of the Farm Credit System.

Federal National Mortgage Association (FNMA) A publicly held corporation that purchases conventional mortgages and mortgages from government agencies, including the Federal Housing Administration, Department of Veterans Affairs, and Farmers Home Administration. *Syn.* Fannie Mae.

Federal Open Market Committee (FOMC) A committee that makes decisions concerning the Fed's operations to control the money supply.

Federal Reserve Board (FRB) A seven-member group that directs the operations of the Federal Reserve System. The President appoints board members, subject to Congressional approval.

Federal Reserve System The central bank system of the United States. Its primary responsibility is to regulate the flow of money and credit. The system includes 12 regional banks, 24 branch banks, and hundreds of national and state banks. *Syn.* Fed.

fiduciary A person legally appointed and authorized to hold assets in trust for another person and manage those assets for that person's benefit.

filing date The day on which an issuer submits to the SEC the registration statement for a new securities issue.

fill-or-kill order (FOK) An order that instructs the floor broker to fill the entire order immediately; if the entire order cannot be executed immediately, it is canceled.

final prospectus The legal document that states a new issue security's price, delivery date, and underwriting spread, as well as other material information. It must be given to every investor who purchases a new issue of registered securities. *Syn.* prospectus.

Financial Industry Regulatory Authority (FINRA) Organized in July 2007 as a joint effort of NASD and the NYSE to harmonize regulation in the securities industry.

financial risk *See* credit risk.

FINRA The acronym for the Financial Industry Regulatory Authority, the result of the cooperative effort of NASD and the NYSE to harmonize regulation in the securities industry.

firm quote The actual price at which a trading unit of a security (such as 100 shares of stock or five bonds) may be bought or sold. All quotes are firm quotes unless otherwise indicated.

first in, first out (FIFO) An accounting method used to assess a company's inventory, in which it is assumed that the first goods acquired are the first to be sold. The same method is used by the IRS to determine cost basis for tax purposes. *See* average basis; last in, first out.

fiscal policy The federal tax and spending policies set by Congress or the President. These policies affect tax rates, interest rates, and government spending in an effort to control the economy. *See* monetary policy.

fixed annuity An insurance contract in which the insurance company makes fixed dollar payments to the annuitant for the term of the contract, usually until the annuitant dies. The insurance company guarantees both earnings and principal. *Syn.* fixed dollar annuity; guaranteed dollar annuity.

fixed asset A tangible, physical property used in the course of a corporation's everyday operations, including buildings, equipment, and land.

flat yield curve A chart showing the yields of bonds with short maturities as equal to the yields of bonds with long maturities. *Syn.* even yield curve. *See* inverted yield curve; normal yield curve; yield curve.

flow-through A term that describes the way income, deductions, and credits resulting from the activities of a business are applied to individual taxes and expenses as though each incurred the income and deductions directly. *See* limited partnership.

FNMA *See* Federal National Mortgage Association.

FOK *See* fill-or-kill order.

FOMC *See* Federal Open Market Committee.

foreign currency Money issued by a country other than the one in which the investor resides. Options and futures contracts on numerous foreign currencies are traded on US exchanges.

foreign exchange rate The price of one country's currency in terms of another currency. *Syn.* exchange rate.

forward pricing The valuation process for mutual fund shares, whereby an order to purchase or redeem shares is executed at the price determined by the portfolio valuation calculated after the order is received. Portfolio valuations occur at least once per business day.

fractional share A portion of a whole share of stock. Mutual fund shares are frequently issued in fractional amounts. Fractional shares used to be generated when corporations declared stock dividends, merged, or voted to split stock, but today it is more common for corporations to issue the cash equivalent of fractional shares.

fraud The deliberate concealment, misrepresentation, or omission of material information or the truth, so as to deceive or manipulate another party for unlawful or unfair gain.

FRB *See* Federal Reserve Board.

Freddie Mac *See* Federal Home Loan Mortgage Corporation.

front-end load A mutual fund commission or sales fee that is charged at the time shares are purchased. The load is added to the share's net asset value when calculating the public offering price.

Full Disclosure Act *See* Securities Act of 1933.

full power of attorney A written authorization for someone other than an account's beneficial owner to make deposits and withdrawals and to execute trades in the account. *See* limited power of attorney.

full trading authorization An authorization, usually provided by a full power of attorney, for someone other than the customer to have full trading privileges in an account. *See* limited trading authorization.

fundamental analysis A method of evaluating securities by attempting to measure the intrinsic value of a particular stock. Fundamental analysts study the overall economy, industry conditions, and the financial condition and management of particular companies. *See* technical analysis.

fund manager *See* portfolio manager.

G

GDP *See* gross domestic product.

general obligation bond (GO) A municipal debt issue backed by the full faith, credit, and taxing power of the issuer for payment of interest and principal. *Syn.* full faith and credit bond. *See* revenue bond.

general partnership (GP) An association of two or more entities formed to conduct a business jointly. The partnership does not require documents for formation, and the general partners are jointly and severally liable for the partnership's liabilities. *See* limited partnership.

good-til-canceled order (GTC) An order that is left on the specialist's book until it is either executed or canceled. *Syn.* open order.

goodwill An intangible asset that represents the value that a firm's business reputation adds to its book value.

Government National Mortgage Association (GNMA) A wholly government-owned corporation that issues pass-through mortgage debt certificates backed by the full faith and credit of the US government. *Syn.* Ginnie Mae.

grantor An individual or organization that gives assets to a beneficiary by transferring fiduciary duty to a third-party trustee that will maintain the assets for the benefit of the beneficiaries. *Syn.* settlor, trustor

grantor trust A trust that requires that the grantor be taxed on income produced by trust property if trust income is distributed to the grantor or to the grantor's spouse; trust income discharges a legal obligation of the grantor or grantor's family; and the grantor retains power to revoke or amend the trust.

gross domestic product (GDP) The market value of all final goods and services produced within a country in a given period of time. GDP = consumption + investment + government spending + (exports – imports) investment

gross income All income of a taxpayer, from whatever source derived.

gross revenues All money received by a business from its operations. The term typically does not include interest income or income from the sale, refinancing, or other disposition of properties.

growth fund A diversified common stock fund that has capital appreciation as its primary goal. It invests in companies that reinvest most of their earnings for expansion, research, or development. *See* diversified common stock fund; mutual fund.

growth industry An industry that is growing faster than the economy as a whole as a result of technological changes, new products, or changing consumer tastes.

growth stock A relatively speculative issue that is believed to offer significant potential for capital gains. It often pays low dividends and sells at a high price-earnings ratio.

guaranteed bond A debt obligation issued with a promise from a corporation other than the issuing corporation to maintain payments of principal and interest.

guaranteed stock An equity security, generally a preferred stock, issued with a promise from a corporation other than the issuing corporation to maintain dividend payments. The stock still represents ownership in the issuing corporation, but it is considered a dual security.

guardian A fiduciary who manages the assets of a minor or an incompetent for that person's benefit. *See* fiduciary.

H

head and shoulders On a technical analyst's trading chart, a pattern that has three peaks resembling a head and two shoulders. The stock price moves up to its first peak (the left shoulder), drops back, then moves to a higher peak (the top of the head), drops again but recovers to another, lower peak (the right shoulder). A head and shoulders top typically forms after a substantial rise and indicates a market reversal. A head and shoulders bottom (an inverted head and shoulders) indicates a market advance.

hedge An investment made to reduce the risk of adverse price movements in a security. Normally, a hedge consists of a protecting position in a related security. *See* long hedge; selling a hedge; short hedge.

hedge clause Any legend, clause, or other provision that is likely to lead an investor to believe that he has in any way waived any right of action he may have.

hedge fund A fund that can use one or more alternative investment strategies, including hedging against market downturns, investing in asset classes such as currencies or distressed securities, and utilizing return-enhancing tools such as leverage, derivatives, and arbitrage. These funds tend to have very high minimum investment requirements.

holder The owner of a security. *See* long.

holding company A company organized to invest in and manage other corporations.

holding period A time period signifying how long the owner possesses a security. It starts the day after a purchase and ends on the day of the sale.

HR-10 plan *See* Keogh plan.

hypothecation Pledging to a broker/dealer securities bought on margin as collateral for the margin loan. *See* rehypothecation.

I

immediate-or-cancel order (IRC) An order that instructs the floor broker to execute it immediately, in full or in part. Any portion of the order that remains unexecuted is canceled.

income fund A mutual fund that seeks to provide stable current income by investing in securities that pay interest or dividends. *See* mutual fund.

income statement The summary of a corporation's revenues and expenses for a specific fiscal period.

index A comparison of current prices to some baseline, such as prices on a particular date. Indexes are frequently used in technical analysis.

indication of interest (IOI) An investor's expression of conditional interest in buying an upcoming securities issue after the investor has reviewed a preliminary prospectus. An indication of interest is not a commitment to buy.

industrial development bond (IDB) A debt security issued by a municipal authority, which uses the proceeds to finance the construction or purchase of facilities to be leased or purchased by a private company. The bonds are backed by the credit of the private company, which is ultimately responsible for principal and interest payments. *Syn.* industrial revenue bond.

industrial revenue bond (IRB) *See* industrial development bond.

industry fund *See* sector fund.

inelasticity A lack of responsiveness on the part of consumers and producers to a change in prices. *See* elasticity.

inflation A persistent and measurable increase in the general level of prices. *See* deflation.

inflation risk *See* purchasing power risk.

initial public offering (IPO) A corporation's first sale of common stock to the public. *See* new issue market; public offering.

inside information Material information that has not been disseminated to or is not readily available to the general public.

insider Any person who possesses or has access to material nonpublic information about a corporation. Insiders include directors, officers, and stockholders who own more than 10% of any class of equity security of a corporation.

Insider Trading Act *See* Insider Trading and Securities Fraud Enforcement Act of 1988.

Insider Trading and Securities Fraud Enforcement Act of 1988 Legislation that defines what constitutes the illicit use of nonpublic information in making securities trades and the liabilities and penalties that apply. *Syn.* Insider Trading Act. *See* Chinese wall; insider.

institutional account An account held for the benefit of others. Examples of institutional accounts include banks, trusts, pension and profit-sharing plans, mutual funds, and insurance companies.

institutional investor A person or an organization that trades securities in large enough share quantities or dollar amounts that it qualifies for preferential treatment and lower commissions. An institutional order can be of any size. Institutional investors are covered by fewer protective regulations because it is assumed that they are more knowledgeable and better able to protect themselves.

intangible asset A property owned that is not physical, such as a formula, a copyright, or goodwill. *See* goodwill.

interest The charge for the privilege of borrowing money, usually expressed as an annual percentage rate.

interest rate risk The risk associated with investments relating to the sensitivity of price or value to fluctuation in the current level of interest rates; also, the risk that involves the competitive cost of money. This term is generally associated with bond prices, but it applies to all investments. In bonds, prices carry interest risk because if bond prices rise, outstanding bonds will not remain competitive unless their yields and prices adjust to reflect the current market.

Internal Revenue Code (IRC) The legislation that defines tax liabilities and deductions for US taxpayers.

Internal Revenue Service (IRS) The US government agency responsible for collecting most federal taxes and for administering tax rules and regulations.

interstate offering An issue of securities registered with the SEC sold to residents of states other than the state in which the issuer does business.

in-the-money The term used to describe an option that has intrinsic value, such as a call option when the stock is selling above the exercise price or a put option when the stock is selling below the exercise price. *See* at-the-money; intrinsic value; out-of-the-money.

intrastate offering An issue of securities exempt from SEC registration, available to companies that do business in one state and sell their securities only to residents of that same state. *See* Rule 147.

intrinsic value The potential profit to be made from exercising an option. A call option is said to have intrinsic value when the underlying stock is trading above the exercise price. *See* time value.

inverted yield curve A chart showing long-term debt instruments that have lower yields than short-term debt instruments. *Syn.* negative yield curve. *See* flat yield curve; normal yield curve.

investment adviser (1) Any person who makes investment recommendations in return for a flat fee or a percentage of assets managed. (2) For an investment company, the individual who bears the day-to-day responsibility of investing the cash and securities held in the fund's portfolio in accordance with objectives stated in the fund's prospectus.

Investment Advisers Act of 1940 Legislation governing who must register with the SEC as an investment adviser. *See* investment adviser.

investment banker An institution in the business of raising capital for corporations and municipalities. An investment banker may not accept deposits or make commercial loans. *Syn.* investment bank.

investment banking business A broker, dealer, or municipal or government securities dealer that underwrites or distributes new issues of securities as a dealer or that buys and sells securities for the accounts of others as a broker. *Syn.* investment securities business.

investment company A company engaged in the business of pooling investors' money and trading in securities for them. Examples include face-amount certificate companies, unit investment trusts, and management companies.

Investment Company Act Amendments of 1970 Amendments to the Investment Company Act of 1940 requiring, in particular, that sales charges relate to the services a fund provides its shareholders. *See* Investment Company Act of 1940.

Investment Company Act of 1940 Congressional legislation regulating companies that invest and reinvest in securities. The act requires an investment company engaged in interstate commerce to register with the SEC.

investment-grade security A security to which the rating services (e.g., Standard & Poor's and Moody's) have assigned a rating of BBB/Baa or above.

investment objective Any goal a client hopes to achieve through investing. Examples include current income, capital growth, and preservation of capital.

investor The purchaser of an asset or security with the intent of profiting from the transaction.

IPO *See* initial public offering.

irrevocable trust A trust that cannot be altered or canceled by the grantor at any time.

issuer The entity, such as a corporation or municipality, that offers or proposes to offer its securities for sale.

J

joint account An account in which two or more individuals possess some form of control over the account and may transact business in the account. The account must be designated as either joint tenants in common or joint tenants with right of survivorship. *See* tenants in common; joint tenants with right of survivorship.

joint life with last survivor An annuity payout option that covers two or more people, with annuity payments continuing as long as one of the annuitants remains alive.

joint tenants with right of survivorship (JTWROS) A form of joint ownership of an account whereby a deceased tenant's fractional interest in the account passes to the surviving tenant(s). Used almost exclusively by husbands and wives. *See* tenants in common.

K

Keogh plan A qualified tax-deferred retirement plan for persons who are self-employed and unincorporated or who earn extra income through personal services aside from their regular employment. *Syn.* HR-10 plan. *See* individual retirement account.

Keynesian economics The theory that active government intervention in the marketplace is the best method of ensuring economic growth and stability.

L

lagging indicator A measurable economic factor that changes after the economy has started to follow a particular pattern or trend. Lagging indicators are believed to confirm long-term trends. Examples include average duration of unemployment, corporate profits, and labor cost per unit of output. *See* coincident indicator; leading indicator.

last in, first out (LIFO) An accounting method used to assess a corporation's inventory in which it is assumed that the last goods acquired are the first to be sold. The method is used to determine cost basis for tax purposes; the IRS designates last in, first out as the order in which sales or withdrawals from an investment are made. *See* average basis; first in, first out.

leading indicator A measurable economic factor that changes before the economy starts to follow a particular pattern or trend. Leading indicators are believed to predict changes in the economy. Examples include new orders for durable goods, slowdowns in deliveries by vendors, and numbers of building permits issued. *See* coincident indicator; lagging indicator.

legal list The selection of securities a state agency (usually a state banking or insurance commission) determines to be appropriate investments for fiduciary accounts such as mutual savings banks, pension funds, and insurance companies. This is used in states that do not have the prudent investor rule.

legislative risk The potential for an investor to be adversely affected by changes in investment or tax laws.

letter of intent (LOI) A signed agreement allowing an investor to buy mutual fund shares at a lower overall sales charge based on the total dollar amount of the intended investment. A letter of intent is valid only if the investor completes the terms of the agreement within 13 months of signing the agreement. A letter of intent may be backdated 90 days. *Syn.* statement of intention.

level load A mutual fund sales fee charged annually and based on the net asset value of a share. *See* back-end load; Class C share; front-end load.

leverage Using borrowed capital to increase investment return. *Syn.* trading on the equity.

liability A legal obligation to pay a debt owed. Current liabilities are debts payable within 12 months. Long-term liabilities are debts payable over a period of more than 12 months.

limited liability An investor's right to limit potential losses to no more than the amount invested. Equity shareholders, such as corporate stockholders and limited partners, have limited liability.

limited liability company (LLC) A hybrid between a partnership and a corporation in that it combines the pass-through treatment of a partnership with the limited liability accorded to corporate shareholders.

limited partnership (LP) An association of two or more partners formed to conduct a business jointly and in which one or more of the partners is liable only to the extent of the amount of money they have invested. Limited partners do not receive dividends but enjoy direct flow-through of income and expenses. *See* flow-through; general partnership.

limited power of attorney A written authorization for someone other than an account's beneficial owner to make certain investment decisions regarding transactions in the account. *See* discretion; full power of attorney.

limited trading authorization An authorization, usually provided by a limited power of attorney, for someone other than the customer to have trading privileges in an account. These privileges are limited to purchases and sales; withdrawal of assets is not authorized. *See* full trading authorization.

limit order An order that instructs the floor broker to buy a specified security below a certain price or to sell a specified security above a certain price. *Syn.* or better order. *See* stop limit order; stop order.

liquidation priority In the case of a corporation's liquidation, the order that is strictly followed for paying off creditors and stockholders: 1, unpaid wages; 2, taxes; 3, secured claims (mortgages); 4, secured liabilities (bonds); 5, unsecured liabilities (debentures) and general creditors; 6, subordinated debt; 7, preferred stockholders; and 8, common stockholders.

liquidity The ease with which an asset can be converted to cash in the marketplace. A large number of buyers and sellers and a high volume of trading activity provide high liquidity.

lliquidity risk The potential that an investor might not be able to sell an investment as and when desired. *Syn.* marketability risk.

listed option An option contract that can be bought and sold on a national securities exchange in a continuous secondary market. Listed options carry standardized strike prices and expiration dates. *Syn.* standardized option. *See* OTC option.

listed security A stock, a bond, or another security that satisfies certain minimum requirements and is traded on a regional or national securities exchange such as the New York Stock Exchange. *See* over the counter.

living trust A trust created during the lifetime of the grantor; also known as an inter vivos trust.

LLC *See* limited liability company.

long The term used to describe the owning of a security, contract, or commodity. For example, a common stock owner is said to have a long position in the stock. *See* short.

long-term gain The profit earned on the sale of a capital asset that has been owned for more than 12 months. *See* capital gain; capital loss; long-term loss.

long-term loss The loss realized on the sale of a capital asset that has been owned for more than 12 months. *See* capital gain; capital loss; long-term gain.

loss carryover A capital loss incurred in one tax year that is carried over to the next year or later years for use as a capital loss deduction. *See* capital loss.

M

make a market To stand ready to buy or sell a particular security as a dealer for its own account. A market maker accepts the risk of holding the position in the security. *See* market maker.

Maloney Act An amendment enacted in 1938 to broaden Section 15 of the Securities Exchange Act of 1934. Named for its sponsor, the late Sen. Francis Maloney of Connecticut, the amendment provided for the creation of a self-regulatory organization for the specific purpose of supervising the over-the-counter securities market. *See* National Association of Securities Dealers, Inc.

management company An investment company that trades various types of securities in a portfolio in accordance with specific objectives stated in the prospectus. *See* closed-end management company; diversified management company; mutual fund; nondiversified management company.

margin The amount of equity contributed by a customer as a percentage of the current market value of the securities held in a margin account. *See* equity; initial margin requirement; Regulation T.

margin of profit ratio A measure of a corporation's relative profitability. It is calculated by dividing the operating profit by the net sales. *Syn.* operating profit ratio; profit margin.

marital trust A trust that seeks to pass property to a survivor spouse while taking advantage of the marital deduction; also known as an A trust.

market letter A publication that comments on securities, investing, the economy, or other related topics and is distributed to an organization's clients or to the public. *See* sales literature.

market maker A dealer willing to accept the risk of holding a particular security in its own account to facilitate trading in that security. *See* make a market.

market order An order to be executed immediately at the best available price. A market order is the only order that guarantees execution. *Syn.* unrestricted order.

market risk The potential for an investor to experience losses owing to day-to-day fluctuations in the prices at which securities can be bought or sold. *See* systematic risk.

market value The price at which investors buy or sell a share of common stock or a bond at a given time. Market value is determined by buyers' and sellers' interaction. *See* current market value.

markup The difference between the lowest current offering price among dealers and the higher price a dealer charges a customer.

material information Any fact that could affect an investor's decision to trade a security.

maturity date The date on which a bond's principal is repaid to the investor and interest payments cease. *See* par; principal.

modern portfolio theory (MPT) A method of choosing investments that focuses on the importance of the relationships among all of the investments in a portfolio rather than the individual merits of each investment. The method allows investors to quantify and control the amount of risk they accept and return they achieve.

monetarist theory An economic theory holding that the money supply is the major determinant of price levels and that therefore a well-controlled money supply will have the most beneficial impact on the economy.

monetary policy The Federal Reserve Board's actions that determine the size and rate of the money supply's growth, which in turn affect interest rates. *See* fiscal policy.

money market The securities market that deals in short-term debt. Money market instruments are very liquid forms of debt that mature in less than one year. Treasury bills make up the bulk of money market instruments.

money market fund A mutual fund that invests in short-term debt instruments. The fund's objective is to earn interest while maintaining a stable net asset value of $1 per share. Generally sold with no load, the fund may also offer draft-writing privileges and low opening investments. *See* mutual fund.

money supply The total stock of bills, coins, loans, credit, and other liquid instruments in the economy. It is divided into four categories—L, M1, M2, and M3—according to the type of account in which the instrument is kept.

Moody's Investors Service One of the best known investment rating agencies in the United States. A subsidiary of Dun & Bradstreet, Moody's rates bonds, commercial paper, preferred and common stocks, and municipal short-term issues. *See* bond rating; Standard & Poor's Corporation.

mortgage bond A debt obligation secured by a property pledge. It represents a lien or mortgage against the issuing corporation's properties and real estate assets.

moving average chart A tool used by technical analysts to track the price movements of a commodity. It plots average daily settlement prices over a defined period of time (for example, over three days for a three-day moving average).

municipal bond A debt security issued by a state, a municipality, or another subdivision (such as a school, a park, a sanitation, or another local taxing district) to finance its capital expenditures. Such expenditures might include the construction of highways, public works, or school buildings. *Syn.* municipal security.

municipal bond fund A mutual fund that invests in municipal bonds and operates either as a unit investment trust or as an open-end fund. The fund's objective is to maximize federally tax-exempt income. *See* mutual fund; unit investment trust.

municipal note A short-term municipal security issued in anticipation of funds from another source.

Municipal Securities Rulemaking Board (MSRB) A self-regulatory organization that regulates the issuance and trading of municipal securities. The Board functions under the Securities and Exchange Commission's supervision; it has no enforcement powers. *See* Securities Acts Amendments of 1975.

mutual fund An investment company that continuously offers new equity shares in an actively managed portfolio of securities. All shareholders participate in the fund's gains or losses. The shares are redeemable on any business day at the net asset value. Each mutual fund's portfolio is invested to match the objective stated in the prospectus. *Syn.* open-end investment company; open-end management company. *See* balanced fund; contractual plan; net asset value.

N

NASAA *See* North American Securities Administrators Association.

NASD *See* National Association of Securities Dealers, Inc.

Nasdaq *See* National Association of Securities Dealers Automated Quotation System.

Nasdaq Capital Market Effective September 2005, the new name for the Nasdaq SmallCap Market listings. Effective May 24, 2007, these are federal covered securities.

Nasdaq Global Market Effective July 2006, the new name for Nasdaq National Market listings. This is the second highest tier of companies traded on the Nasdaq Stock Exchange. These are federal covered securities.

Nasdaq Global Select Market Effective July 2006, a select group of securities traded on the Nasdaq Stock Exchange meeting the highest listing standards in the world. Effective May 24, 2007, these are federal covered securities.

NASD 5% markup policy A guideline for reasonable markups, markdowns, and commissions for secondary over-the-counter transactions. According to the policy, all commissions on broker transactions and all markups or markdowns on principal transactions should equal 5% or should be fair and reasonable for a particular transaction. *Syn.* markup policy.

National Association of Securities Dealers, Inc. (NASD) The self-regulatory organization for the over-the-counter market. NASD was organized under the provisions of the 1938 Maloney Act. *See* Maloney Act, FINRA.

National Association of Securities Dealers Automated Quotation System (Nasdaq) The nationwide electronic quotation system for up-to-the-second on approximately 3,500 over-the-counter stocks trade information.

NAV per share The value of a mutual fund share, calculated by dividing the fund's total net asset value by the number of shares outstanding.

negotiability A characteristic of a security that permits the owner to assign, give, transfer, or sell it to another person without a third party's permission.

negotiable certificate of deposit (CD) An unsecured promissory note issued with a minimum face value of $100,000. It evidences a time deposit of funds with the issuing bank and is guaranteed by the bank.

net asset value (NAV) A mutual fund share's value, as calculated once a day on the basis of the closing market price for each security in the fund's portfolio. It is computed by deducting the fund's liabilities from the portfolio's total assets and dividing this amount by the number of shares outstanding. *See* mutual fund.

net investment income The source of an investment company's dividend payments. It is calculated by subtracting the company's operating expenses from the total dividends and interest the company receives from the securities in its portfolio.

net worth The amount by which assets exceed liabilities.

new account form The form that must be filled out for each new account opened with a brokerage firm. The form specifies, at a minimum, the account owner, trading authorization, payment method, and types of securities appropriate for the customer.

new issue market The securities market for shares in privately owned businesses that are raising capital by selling common stock to the public for the first time. *Syn.* primary market. *See* initial public offering; secondary market.

New York Stock Exchange (NYSE) The largest stock exchange in the United States. It is a corporation, operated by a board of directors, responsible for setting policy, supervising Exchange and member activities, listing securities, overseeing the transfer of members' seats on the Exchange, and judging whether an applicant is qualified to be a specialist.

no-load fund A mutual fund whose shares are sold without a commission or sales charge. The investment company distributes the shares directly. *See* mutual fund; net asset value; sales load.

nominal yield The interest rate stated on the face of a bond that represents the percentage of interest the issuer pays on the bond's face value. *Syn.* coupon rate; stated yield. *See* bond yield.

nonaccredited investor An investor not meeting the net worth requirements of Regulation D. Nonaccredited investors are counted for purposes of the 35-investor limitation for Regulation D private placements. *See* accredited investor; private placement; Regulation D.

noncumulative preferred stock An equity security that does not have to pay any dividends in arrears to the holder. *See* cumulative preferred stock; preferred stock.

nondiversification A portfolio management strategy that seeks to concentrate investments in a particular industry or geographic area in hopes of achieving higher returns. *See* diversification.

nondiversified investment company A management company that does not meet the diversification requirements of the Investment Company Act of 1940. These companies are not restricted in the choice of securities or by the concentration of interest they have in those securities. *See* diversified investment company; management company; mutual fund.

nonrecourse financing Debt incurred for the purchase of an asset that pledges the asset as security for the debt but that does not hold the borrower personally liable.

nonsystematic risk The potential for an unforeseen event to affect the value of a specific investment. Examples of such events include strikes, natural disasters, introductions of new product lines, and attempted takeovers. *See* systematic risk.

no-par stock An equity security issued without a stated value.

normal yield curve A chart showing long-term debt instruments having higher yields than short-term debt instruments. *Syn.* positive yield curve. *See* flat yield curve; inverted yield curve; yield curve.

North American Securities Administrators Association Organized in 1919, the North American Securities Administrators Association (NASAA) is the oldest international organization devoted to investor protection. NASAA is a voluntary association whose membership consists of 67 state, provincial, and territorial securities administrators in the 50 states, the District of Columbia, Puerto Rico, the US Virgin Islands, Canada, and Mexico.

note A short-term debt security, usually maturing in five years or less. *See* Treasury note.

notice filing Method by which a registered investment company and certain other federal covered securities file records with state securities Administrators.

O

offering circular An abbreviated prospectus used by corporations issuing less than $5 million of stock. The SEC's Regulation A allows these offerings an exemption from the full registration requirements of the 1933 Act. *See* Regulation A.

open-end investment company *See* mutual fund.

opening purchase Entering the options market by buying calls or puts. *See* opening sale.

opening sale Entering the options market by selling calls or puts. *See* closing purchase; opening purchase.

open-market operations The buying and selling of securities (primarily government or agency debt) by the Federal Open Market Committee to effect control of the money supply. These transactions increase or decrease the level of bank reserves available for lending.

operating income The profit realized from one year of operation of a business.

operating ratio The ratio of operating expenses to net sales; the complement to the margin of profit ratio.

ordinary income Earnings other than capital gain.

OTC Bulletin Board An electronic quotation system for equity securities that are not listed on a national exchange or included in the Nasdaq system.

OTC market The security exchange system in which broker/dealers negotiate directly with one another rather than through an auction on an exchange floor. The trading takes place over computer and telephone networks that link brokers and dealers around the world. Both listed and OTC securities, as well as municipal and US government securities, trade in the OTC market.

over the counter (OTC) The term used to describe a security traded through the telephone-linked and computer-connected OTC market rather than through an exchange. *See* OTC market.

P

par The dollar amount the issuer assigns to a security. For an equity security, par is usually a small dollar amount that bears no relationship to the security's market price. For a debt security, par is the amount repaid to the investor when the bond matures, usually $1,000. *Syn.* face value; principal; stated value. *See* capital surplus; maturity date.

parity price of common The dollar amount at which a common stock is equal in value to its corresponding convertible security. It is calculated by dividing the convertible security's market value by its conversion ratio.

parity price of convertible The dollar amount at which a convertible security is equal in value to its corresponding common stock. It is calculated by multiplying the market price of the common stock by its conversion ratio.

participation The provision of the Employee Retirement Income Security Act of 1974 requiring that all employees in a qualified retirement plan be covered within a reasonable time of their dates of hire.

partnership A form of business organization in which two or more individuals manage the business and are equally and personally liable for its debts.

partnership account An account that empowers the individual members of a partnership to act on the behalf of the partnership as a whole.

partnership management fee The amount payable to the general partners of a limited partnership, or to other persons, for managing the day-to-day partnership operations. *Syn.* program management fee; property management fee.

par value The dollar amount assigned to a security by the issuer. For an equity security, par value is usually a small dollar amount that bears no relationship to the security's market price. For a debt security, par value is the amount repaid to the investor when the bond matures, usually $1,000. *Syn.* face value; principal; stated value. *See* capital surplus; discount bond; premium bond.

passive income Earnings derived from a rental property, limited partnership, or other enterprise in which the individual is not actively involved. Passive income therefore does not include earnings from wages or active business participation, nor does it include income from dividends, interest, and capital gains. *See* passive loss; unearned income.

passive loss A loss incurred through a rental property, limited partnership, or other enterprise in which the individual is not actively involved. Passive losses can be used to offset passive income only, not wage or portfolio income. *See* passive income.

pass-through certificate A security representing an interest in a pool of conventional, Veterans Administration, Farmers Home Administration, or other agency mortgages. The pool receives the principal and interest payments, which it passes through to each certificate holder. Payments may or may not be guaranteed. *See* Federal National Mortgage Association; Government National Mortgage Association.

pattern A repetitive series of price movements on a chart used by a technical analyst to predict future movements of the market.

payment date The day on which a declared dividend is paid to all stockholders owning shares on the record date.

PE *See* price-earnings ratio.

peak The end of a period of increasing business activity throughout the economy, one of the four stages of the business cycle. *Syn.* prosperity. *See* business cycle.

pegging An illegal form of market manipulation that attempts to keep the price of a subject security from falling. It is used by those with a long position. *See* capping.

pension plan A contract between an individual and an employer, a labor union, a government entity, or another institution that provides for the distribution of pension benefits at retirement.

Pension Reform Act *See* Employee Retirement Income Security Act of 1974.

PE ratio *See* price-earnings ratio.

person As defined in securities law, an individual, corporation, partnership, association, fund, joint stock company, unincorporated organization, trust, government, or political subdivision of a government.

personal income (PI) An individual's total earnings derived from wages, passive business enterprises, and investments. *See* disposable income.

point A measure of a bond's price; $10 or 1% of the par value of $1,000. *See* basis point.

portfolio income Earnings from interest, dividends, and all nonbusiness investments. *See* earned income; passive income; unearned income.

portfolio manager The entity responsible for investing a mutual fund's assets, implementing its investment strategy, and managing day-to-day portfolio trading. *Syn.* fund manager.

position The amount of a security either owned (a long position) or owed (a short position) by an individual or a dealer. Dealers take long positions in specific securities to maintain inventories and thereby facilitate trading.

preferred stock An equity security that represents ownership in a corporation. It is issued with a stated dividend, which must be paid before dividends are paid to common stockholders. It generally carries no voting rights. *See* callable preferred stock; cumulative preferred stock.

preferred stock fund A mutual fund whose investment objective is to provide stable income with minimal capital risk. It invests in income-producing instruments such as preferred stock. *See* bond fund.

preliminary prospectus An abbreviated prospectus that is distributed while the SEC is reviewing an issuer's registration statement. It contains all of the essential facts about the forthcoming offering except the underwriting spread, final public offering price, and date on which the shares will be delivered. *Syn.* red herring.

premium (1) The amount of cash that an option buyer pays to an option seller. (2) The difference between the higher price paid for a security and the security's face amount at issue. *See* discount.

premium bond A bond that sells at a higher price than its face value. *See* discount bond; par value.

price-earnings ratio (PE) A tool for comparing the prices of different common stocks by assessing how much the market is willing to pay for a share of each corporation's earnings. It is calculated by dividing the current market price of a stock by the earnings per share.

primary offering An offering in which the proceeds of the underwriting go to the issuing corporation, agency, or municipality. The issuer seeks to increase its capitalization either by selling shares of stock, representing ownership, or by selling bonds, representing loans to the issuer. *Syn.* primary distribution.

prime rate The interest rate that commercial banks charge their prime or most creditworthy customers, generally large corporations.

principal (1) A person who trades for his own account in the primary or secondary market. (2) *See* dealer. (3) *See* par.

principal transaction A transaction in which a broker/dealer either buys securities from customers and takes them into its own inventory or sells securities to customers from its inventory. *See* agency transaction; agent; broker; dealer; principal.

private placement An offering of new issue securities that complies with Regulation D of the Securities Act of 1933. According to Regulation D, a security generally is not required to be registered with the SEC if it is offered to no more than 35 nonaccredited investors or to an unlimited number of accredited investors. *See* Regulation D.

profitability The ability to generate a level of income and gain in excess of expenses.

profitability ratio One of several measures of a corporation's relative profit or income in relation to its sales. *See* margin of profit ratio; return on equity.

profit-sharing plan An employee benefit plan established and maintained by an employer whereby the employees receive a share of the business's profits. The money may be paid directly to the employees or deferred until retirement. A combination of both approaches is also possible.

progressive tax A tax that takes a larger percentage of the income of high-income earners than that of low-income earners. An example is the graduated income tax. *See* regressive tax.

proxy A limited power of attorney from a stockholder authorizing another person to vote on stockholder issues according to the first stockholder's instructions. To vote on corporate matters, a stockholder must either attend the annual meeting or vote by proxy.

prudent expert rule A modern application of the prudent man rule to those with a fiduciary responsibility over qualified plans coming under the jurisdiction of ERISA.

prudent investor rule A legal maxim that restricts discretion in a fiduciary account to only those investments that a reasonable and prudent person might make.

publicly traded fund *See* closed-end investment company.

public offering The sale of an issue of common stock, either by a corporation going public or by an offering of additional shares. *See* initial public offering.

public offering price (POP) (1) The price of new shares that is established in the issuing corporation's prospectus. (2) The price to investors for mutual fund shares, equal to the net asset value plus the sales charge. *See* ask; bid; mutual fund; net asset value.

purchasing power risk The potential that, because of inflation, a certain amount of money will not purchase as much in the future as it does today. *Syn.* inflation risk.

put (1) An option contract giving the owner the right to sell a certain amount of an underlying security at a specified price within a specified time. (2) The act of exercising a put option. *See* call.

Q

QTIP trust A trust that is funded with qualified terminable interest property, meaning that the spouse's interest in the property terminates upon his death; also knows as a Q trust, C trust, or current income trust.

Q trust *See* QTIP trust.

quotation The price or bid a market maker or broker/dealer offers for a particular security. *Syn.* quote. *See* ask; bid; bond quote; stock quote.

quote machine A computer that provides representatives and market makers with the information that appears on the Consolidated Tape. The information on the screen is condensed into symbols and numbers.

R

rating An evaluation of a corporate or municipal bond's relative safety, according to the issuer's ability to repay principal and make interest payments. Bonds are rated by various organizations, such as Standard & Poor's and Moody's. Ratings range from AAA or Aaa (the highest) to C or D, which represents a company in default.

rating service A company, such as Moody's or Standard & Poor's, that rates various debt and preferred stock issues for safety of payment of principal, interest, or dividends. The issuing company or municipality pays a fee for the rating. *See* bond rating; rating.

real estate investment trust (REIT) A corporation or trust that uses the pooled capital of many investors to invest in direct ownership of either income property or mortgage loans. These investments offer tax benefits in addition to interest and capital gains distributions.

realized gain The amount a taxpayer earns when he sells an asset. *See* unrealized gain.

recession A general economic decline lasting from six to 18 months.

redeemable security A security that the issuer redeems upon the holder's request. Examples include shares in an open-end investment company and Treasury notes.

redemption The return of an investor's principal in a security, such as a bond, preferred stock, or mutual fund shares. By law, redemption of mutual fund shares must occur within seven days of receiving the investor's request for redemption.

refunding Retiring an outstanding bond issue before maturity by using money from the sale of a new debt offering.

regional exchange A stock exchange that serves the financial community in a particular region of the country. These exchanges tend to focus on securities issued within their regions, but also offer trading in NYSE- and AMEX-listed securities.

registration by coordination A process that allows a security to be sold in a state. It is available to an issuer that files for the security's registration under the Securities Act of 1933 and files duplicates of the registration documents with the state Administrator. The state registration becomes effective at the same time the federal registration statement becomes effective as long as paperwork is on file with the Administrator for the required period, which ranges from 10 to 20 days depending on the state.

registration by qualification A process that allows a security to be sold in a state. It is available to an issuer who files for the security's registration with the state Administrator, meets minimum net worth, disclosure, and other requirements, and files appropriate registration fees. The state registration becomes effective when the Administrator so orders.

registration statement The legal document that discloses all pertinent information concerning an offering of a security and its issuer. It is submitted to the SEC in accordance with the requirements of the Securities Act of 1933, and it forms the basis of the final prospectus distributed to investors.

regressive tax A tax that takes a larger percentage of the income of low-income earners than that of high-income earners. Examples include gasoline tax and cigarette tax. *See* progressive tax.

regulated investment company An investment company to which Subchapter M of the Internal Revenue Code grants special status that allows the flow-through of tax consequences on a distribution to shareholders. If 90% of its income is passed through to the shareholders, the company is not subject to tax on this income.

Regulation A The provision of the Securities Act of 1933 that exempts from registration small public offerings valued at no more than $5 million worth of securities issued during a 12-month period.

Regulation D The provision of the Securities Act of 1933 that exempts from registration offerings sold to a maximum of 35 nonaccredited investors during a 12-month period. *See* private placement.

Regulation T The Federal Reserve Board regulation that governs customer cash accounts and the amount of credit that brokerage firms and dealers may extend to customers for the purchase of securities. Regulation T currently sets the loan value of marginable securities at 50% and the payment deadline at two days beyond regular way settlement. *Syn.* Reg. T.

reinstatement privilege A benefit offered by some mutual funds, allowing an investor to withdraw money from a fund account and then redeposit the money without paying a second sales charge.

required minimum distribution (RMD) The amount that traditional and SEP IRA owners and qualified plan participants must begin withdrawing from their retirement accounts by April 1 following the year they reach age 70½. RMD amounts must then be distributed each subsequent year.

reserve requirement The percentage of depositors' money that the Federal Reserve Board requires a commercial bank to keep on deposit in the form of cash or in its vault. *Syn.* reserves.

residual claim The right of a common stockholder to corporate assets in the event that the corporation ceases to exist. A common stockholder may claim assets only after the claims of all creditors and other security holders have been satisfied.

resistance level A technical analysis term describing the top of a stock's historical trading range. *See* support level.

restricted security An unregistered, nonexempt security acquired either directly or indirectly from the issuer, or an affiliate of the issuer, in a transaction that does not involve a public offering. *See* holding period; Rule 144.

retained earnings The amount of a corporation's net income that remains after all dividends have been paid to preferred and common stockholders. *Syn.* earned surplus; reinvested earnings.

retiring bonds Ending an issuer's debt obligation by calling the outstanding bonds, by purchasing bonds in the open market, or by repaying bondholders the principal amount at maturity.

return on common equity A measure of a corporation's profitability, calculated by dividing after-tax income by common shareholders' equity.

return on equity A measure of a corporation's profitability, specifically its return on assets, calculated by dividing after-tax income by tangible assets.

return on investment (ROI) The profit or loss resulting from a security transaction, often expressed as an annual percentage rate.

revenue bond A municipal debt issue whose interest and principal are payable only from the specific earnings of an income-producing public project.

reverse split A reduction in the number of a corporation's shares outstanding that increases the par value of its stock or its earnings per share. The market value of the total number of shares remains the same. *See* stock split.

revocable trust A trust that can be altered or canceled by the grantor. During the life of the trust, income earned is distributed to the grantor, and only after death does property transfer to the beneficiaries.

right A security representing a stockholder's entitlement to the first opportunity to purchase new shares issued by the corporation at a predetermined price (normally less than the current market price) in proportion to the number of shares already owned. Rights are issued for a short time only, after which they expire. *Syn.* subscription right; subscription right certificate.

right of accumulation A benefit offered by a mutual fund that allows the investor to qualify or reduced sales loads on additional purchases according to the fund account's total dollar value.

RMD *See* required minimum distribution.

Rule 144 SEC rule requiring that persons who hold control or restricted securities may sell them only in limited quantities, and that all sales of restricted stock by control persons must be reported to the SEC by filing a Form 144, Notice of Proposed Sale of Securities. *See* control security; restricted security.

Rule 147 SEC rule that provides exemption from the registration statement and prospectus requirements of the 1933 Act for securities offered and sold exclusively intrastate.

S

safe harbor A provision in a regulatory scheme that provides protection against legal action if stated procedures are followed. In this exam, it may apply in three different cases: (1) Section 28(e) of the Securities Exchange Act of 1934 describes those research and brokerage activities that may be received by an investment adviser in exchange for directed brokerage transactions; (2) Section 404c of ERISA describes what a fiduciary of a qualified plan must do to minimize personal responsibility; and (3) top-heavy 401(k) concerns are minimized if the employer covers all employees with immediate vesting. See soft dollar compensation; top heavy.

sales load The amount added to a mutual fund share's net asset value to arrive at the offering price. *See* mutual fund; net asset value; no-load fund.

S corporation A small business corporation that meets certain requirements and is taxed as a partnership while retaining limited liability.

secondary distribution A distribution, with a prospectus, that involves securities owned by major stockholders (typically founders or principal owners of a corporation). The sale proceeds go to the sellers of the stock, not to the issuer.

secondary market The market in which securities are bought and sold subsequent to their being sold to the public for the first time. *See* new issue market.

secondary offering A sale of securities in which one or more major stockholders in a company sell all or a large portion of their holdings; the underwriting proceeds are paid to the stockholders rather than to the corporation. Typically, such an offering occurs when the founder of a business (and perhaps some of the original financial backers) determine that there is more to be gained by going public than by staying private. The offering does not increase the number of shares of stock outstanding. *See* secondary distribution.

Section 28(e) A code section of the Securities Exchange Act of 1934 hat deals with soft dollar compensation. *See* soft dollar compensation; state harbor.

sector fund A mutual fund whose investment objective is to capitalize on the return potential provided by investing primarily in a particular industry or sector of the economy. *Syn.* industry fund; specialized fund.

secured bond A debt security backed by identifiable assets set aside as collateral. In the event that the issuer defaults on payment, the bondholders may lay claim to the collateral. *See* debenture.

Securities Act of 1933 Federal legislation requiring the full and fair disclosure of all material information about the issuance of new securities. *Syn.* Act of 1933; Full Disclosure Act; New Issues Act; Prospectus Act; Trust in Securities Act; Truth in Securities Act.

Securities Acts Amendments of 1975 Federal legislation that established the Municipal Securities Rulemaking Board.

Securities and Exchange Commission (SEC) Commission created by Congress to regulate the securities markets and protect investors. It is composed of five commissioners appointed by the President of the United States with the advice and consent of the Senate. The SEC enforces, among other acts, the Securities Act of 1933, the Securities Exchange Act of 1934, the Trust Indenture Act of 1939, the Investment Company Act of 1940, and the Investment Advisers Act of 1940.

Securities Exchange Act of 1934 Federal legislation that established the Securities and Exchange Commission. The act aims to protect investors by regulating the exchanges, the OTC market, the extension of credit by the Federal Reserve Board, broker/dealers, insider transactions, trading activities, client accounts, and net capital. *Syn.* Act of 1934; Exchange Act.

Securities Investor Protection Corporation (SIPC) A nonprofit membership corporation created by an act of Congress to protect clients of brokerage firms that are forced into bankruptcy. Membership is composed of all brokers and dealers registered under the Securities Exchange Act of 1934, all members of national securities exchanges, and most NASD members. SIPC provides brokerage firm customers up to $500,000 coverage for cash and securities held by the firms (although cash coverage is limited to $100,000).

security Other than an insurance policy or a fixed annuity, any piece of securitized paper that can be traded for value. Under the Act of 1934, this includes any note, stock, bond, investment contract, debenture, certificate of interest in a profit-sharing or partnership agreement, certificate of deposit, collateral trust certificate, preorganization certificate, option on a security, or other instrument of investment commonly known as a security.

self-regulatory organization (SRO) One of eight organizations accountable to the SEC for the enforcement of federal securities laws and the supervision of securities practices within an assigned field of jurisdiction. For example, the National Association of Securities Dealers regulates the over-the-counter market; the Municipal Securities Rulemaking Board supervises state and municipal securities; and certain exchanges, such as the New York Stock Exchange and the Chicago Board Options Exchange, act as self-regulatory bodies to promote ethical conduct and standard trading practices.

sell To convey ownership of a security or another asset for money or value. This includes giving or delivering a security with or as a bonus for a purchase of securities, a gift of assessable stock, and selling or offering a warrant or right to purchase or subscribe to another security. Not included in the definition is a bona fide pledge or loan or a stock dividend if nothing of value is given by the stockholders for the dividend. *Syn.* sale.

selling away An associated person engaging in private securities transactions without the employing broker/dealer's knowledge and consent. This violates the NASD Conduct Rules.

selling dividends (1) Inducing customers to buy mutual fund shares by implying that an upcoming distribution will benefit them. This practice is illegal. (2) Combining dividend and gains distributions when calculating current yield.

sell stop order An order to sell a security that is entered at a price below the current market price and that is triggered when the market price touches or goes through the sell stop price.

senior security A security that grants its holder a prior claim to the issuer's assets over the claims of another security's holders. For example, a bond is a senior security over common stock.

separate account The account that holds funds paid by variable annuity contract holders. The funds are kept separate from the insurer's general account and are invested in a portfolio of securities that match the contract holders' objectives. *See* accumulation unit; annuity.

settlor An individual or organization that gifts assets to a beneficiary by transferring fiduciary duty to a third-party trustee that will maintain the assets for the benefit of the beneficiaries. *Syn.* grantor, trustor

75-5-10 test The standard for judging whether an investment company qualifies as diversified under the Investment Company Act of 1940. Under this act, a diversified investment company must invest at least 75% of its total assets in cash, receivables, or invested securities, of which no more than 5% of its total assets can be invested in any one company's voting securities. In addition, of that 75% no single investment may represent ownership of more than 10% of any one company's outstanding voting securities. *See* diversified management company.

short The term used to describe the selling of a security, contract, or commodity that the seller does not own. For example, an investor who borrows shares of stock from a broker/dealer and sells them on the open market is said to have a short position in the stock. *See* long.

short sale The sale of a security that the seller does not own, or any sale consummated by the delivery of a security borrowed by or for the account of the seller.

short-term capital gain The profit realized on the sale of an asset that has been owned for 12 months or less. *See* capital gain; capital loss; short-term capital loss.

short-term capital loss The loss incurred on the sale of a capital asset that has been owned for 12 months or less. *See* capital gain; capital loss; short-term capital gain.

simple trust A trust that accumulates income and distributes them to its beneficiaries on an annual basis.

soft dollar compensation Noncash compensation received by an investment adviser from a broker/dealer, generally in exchange for directed brokerage transactions. Must always be disclosed and should come under the safe harbor provisions of Section 28(e). *See* safe harbor.

solvency The ability of a corporation both to meet its long-term fixed expenses and to have adequate money for long-term expansion and growth.

specialist Stock exchange member who stands ready to quote and trade certain securities either for his own account or for customer accounts. The specialist's role is to maintain a fair and orderly market in the stocks for which he is responsible. *See* specialist's book.

special situation fund A mutual fund whose objective is to capitalize on the profit potential of corporations in nonrecurring circumstances, such as those undergoing reorganizations or being considered as takeover candidates.

speculation Trading a security with a higher than average risk in return for a higher than average profit potential. The trade is effected solely for the purpose of profiting from it and not as a means of hedging or protecting other positions.

spousal account A separate individual retirement account established for a nonworking spouse. Contributions to the account made by the working spouse grow tax deferred until withdrawal.

spread In a quotation, the difference between a security's bid and ask prices.

Standard & Poor's Composite Index of 500 Stocks (S&P 500) A value-weighted index that offers broad coverage of the securities market. It is composed of 400 industrial stocks, 40 financial stocks, 40 public utility stocks, and 20 transportation stocks. The index is owned and compiled by Standard & Poor's Corporation. *See* index; Standard & Poor's Corporation; Standard & Poor's 100 Stock Index.

Standard & Poor's Corporation (S&P) A company that rates stocks and corporate and municipal bonds according to risk profiles and that produces and tracks the S&P indexes. The company also publishes a variety of financial and investment reports. *See* bond rating; Moody's Investors Service; rating; Standard & Poor's 100 Stock Index; Standard & Poor's Composite Index of 500 Stocks.

standardized contract A futures contract in which all the contract terms are set by the exchange except for price.

stock certificate Written evidence of ownership in a corporation.

stock split An increase in the number of a corporation's outstanding shares, which decreases its stock's par value. The market value of the total number of shares remains the same. The proportional reductions in orders held on the books for a split stock are calculated by dividing the stock's market price by the fraction that represents the split.

stop limit order A customer order that becomes a limit order when the market price of the security reaches or passes a specific price. *See* limit order; stop order.

stop order (1) A directive from the SEC that suspends the sale of new issue securities to the public when fraud is suspected or filing materials are deficient. (2) A customer order that becomes a market order when the market price of the security reaches or passes a specific price. *See* limit order; market order; stop limit order.

subordinated debenture A debt obligation, backed by the general credit of the issuing corporation, that has claims to interest and principal subordinated to ordinary debentures and all other liabilities. *See* debenture.

suitability A determination made by a registered representative as to whether a particular security matches a customer's objectives and financial capability. The representative must have enough information about the customer to make this judgment.

supervision A system implemented by a broker/dealer to ensure that its employees and associated persons comply with the applicable rules and regulations of the SEC, the exchanges, and the SROs.

supply The total amount of a good or service available for purchase by consumers. *See* demand.

supply-side theory An economic theory holding that bolstering an economy's ability to supply more goods is the most effective way to stimulate economic growth. Supply-side theorists advocate income tax reduction insofar as this increases private investment in corporations, facilities, and equipment.

support level A technical analysis term describing the bottom of a stock's historical trading range. *See* resistance level.

systematic risk The potential for a security to decrease in value owing to its inherent tendency to move together with all securities of the same type. Neither diversification nor any other investment strategy can eliminate this risk. *See* market risk, systematic risk.

T

taxable gain The portion of a sale or distribution of mutual fund shares subject to taxation.

tax credit An amount that can be subtracted from a tax liability, often in connection with real estate development, energy conservation, and research and development programs. Every dollar of tax credit reduces the amount of tax due, dollar for dollar. *See* deduction.

tax-equivalent yield The rate of return a taxable bond must earn before taxes in order to equal the tax-exempt earnings on a municipal bond. This number varies with the investor's tax bracket.

tax-exempt bond fund A mutual fund whose investment objective is to provide maximum tax-free income. It invests primarily in municipal bonds and short-term debt. *Syn.* tax-free bond fund.

tax liability The amount of tax payable on earnings, usually calculated by subtracting standard and itemized deductions and personal exemptions from adjusted gross income, then multiplying by the tax rate. *See* adjusted gross income.

tax preference item An element of income that receives favorable tax treatment. The item must be added to taxable income when computing alternative minimum tax. Tax preference items include accelerated depreciation on property, research and development costs, intangible drilling costs, tax-exempt interest on municipal private purpose bonds, and certain incentive stock options. *See* alternative minimum tax.

technical analysis A method of evaluating securities by analyzing statistics generated by market activity, such as past prices and volume. Technical analysts do not attempt to measure a security's intrinsic value. *See* chartist; fundamental analysis.

Telephone Consumer Protection Act of 1991 (TCPA) Federal legislation restricting the use of telephone lines for solicitation purposes. A company soliciting sales via telephone, facsimile, or email must disclose its name and address to the called party and must not call any person who has requested not to be called.

tenants in common (TIC) A form of joint ownership of an account whereby a deceased tenant's fractional interest in the account is retained by his estate. *Syn.* tenants in common. *See* joint tenants with right of survivorship.

testamentary trust A trust created as a result of instructions from a deceased's last will and testament.

testimonial An endorsement of an investment or service by a celebrity or public opinion influencer. The use of testimonials by investment advisers is prohibited.

time value The amount an investor pays for an option above its intrinsic value; it reflects the amount of time left until expiration. The amount is calculated by subtracting the intrinsic value from the premium paid. *See* intrinsic value.

tombstone advertisement A printed advertisement that solicits indications of interest in a securities offering. The text is limited to basic information about the offering, such as the name of the issuer, type of security, names of the underwriters, and where a prospectus is available.

top heavy The term used to describe a 401(k) plan that offers a disproportionate benefit to key employees. Top-heavy testing must be done on an annual basis unless the plan qualifies as a safe harbor 401(k). *See* safe harbor.

total capitalization The sum of a corporation's long-term debt, stock accounts, and capital in excess of par.

trading authorization *See* full trading authorization; limited trading authorization.

tranche One of the classes of securities that form an issue of collateralized mortgage obligations. Each tranche is characterized by its interest rate, average maturity, risk level, and sensitivity to mortgage prepayments. Neither the rate of return nor the maturity date of a collateralized mortgage obligation tranche is guaranteed. *See* collateralized mortgage obligation.

transfer agent A person or corporation responsible for recording the names and holdings of registered security owners, seeing that certificates are signed by the appropriate corporate officers, affixing the corporate seal, and delivering securities to the new owners.

Treasury bill A marketable US government debt security with a maturity of less than one year. Treasury bills are issued through a competitive bidding process at a discount from par; they have no fixed interest rate. *Syn.* T-bill.

Treasury bond A marketable, fixed-interest US government debt security with a maturity of more than 10 years. *Syn.* T-bond.

Treasury note A marketable, fixed-interest US government debt security with a maturity of between 2 and 10 years. *Syn.* T-note.

trendline A tool used by technical analysts to trace a security's movement by connecting the reaction lows in an upward trend or the rally highs in a downward trend.

trough The end of a period of declining business activity throughout the economy, one of the four stages of the business cycle. *See* business cycle.

trustee A person legally appointed to act on a beneficiary's behalf.

trustor An individual or organization that gifts assets to a beneficiary by transferring fiduciary duty to a third-party trustee that will maintain the assets for the benefit of the beneficiaries. *Syn.* settlor, grantor

12b-1 asset-based fees Investment Company Act of 1940 provision that allows a mutual fund to collect a fee for the promotion or sale of or another activity connected with the distribution of its shares. This fee will not exceed .75%.

U

underlying securities The securities that are bought or sold when an option, right, or warrant is exercised.

underwriter An investment banker that works with an issuer to help bring a security to the market and sell it to the public.

underwriting The procedure by which investment bankers channel investment capital from investors to corporations and municipalities that are issuing securities.

unearned income Income derived from investments and other sources not related to employment services. Examples of unearned income include interest from a savings account, bond interest, and dividends from stock. *See* earned income; passive income; portfolio income.

Uniform Gift to Minors Act (UGMA) Legislation that permits a gift of money or securities to be given to a minor and held in a custodial account that an adult manages for the minor's benefit. Income and capital gains transferred to a minor's name are usually taxed at the minor's rate. However, if the child is under 18 and has unearned income above a certain level, those earnings are taxed at the parent's rate. *See* Uniform Transfers to Minors Act.

Uniform Securities Act (USA) Model legislation for securities industry regulation at the state level. Each state may adopt the legislation in its entirety or it may adapt it (within limits) to suit its needs.

Uniform Transfers to Minors Act (UTMA) Legislation adopted in most states that permits a gift of money or securities to be given to a minor and held in a custodial account that an adult manages for the minor's benefit until the minor reaches a certain age (not necessarily the age of majority). *See* Uniform Gift to Minors Act.

unit A share in the ownership of a direct participation program that entitles the investor to an interest in the program's net income, net loss, and distributions.

unit investment trust (UIT) An investment company that sells redeemable shares in a professionally selected portfolio of securities. It is organized under a trust indenture, not a corporate charter.

unit of beneficial interest A redeemable share in a unit investment trust, representing ownership of an undivided interest in the underlying portfolio. *Syn.* share of beneficial interest. *See* unit investment trust.

unrealized gain The amount by which a security appreciates in value before it is sold. Until it is sold, the investor does not actually possess the sale proceeds. *See* realized gain.

US government and agency bond fund A mutual fund whose investment objective is to provide current income while preserving safety of capital through investing in securities backed by the US Treasury or issued by a government agency.

V

volatility The magnitude and frequency of changes in the price of a security or commodity within a given period.

volume of trading theory A technical analysis theory holding that the ratio of the number of shares traded to total outstanding shares indicates whether a market is strong or weak.

W

warrant A security that gives the holder the right to purchase securities from the warrant issuer at a stipulated subscription price. Warrants are usually long-term instruments, with expiration dates years in the future.

wash sale Selling a security at a loss for tax purposes and, within 30 days before or after, purchasing the same or a substantially identical security. The IRS disallows the claimed loss.

withdrawal plan A benefit offered by a mutual fund whereby a customer receives the proceeds of periodic systematic liquidation of shares in the account. The amounts received may be based on a fixed dollar amount, a fixed number of shares, a fixed percentage, or a fixed period.

working capital A measure of a corporation's liquidity—that is, its ability to transfer assets into cash to meet current short-term obligations. It is calculated by subtracting total current liabilities from total current assets.

Y

yield The rate of return on an investment, usually expressed as an annual percentage rate. *See* current yield; dividend yield; nominal yield.

yield curve A graphic representation of the actual or projected yields of fixed-income securities in relation to their maturities. *See* flat yield curve; inverted yield curve.

yield to call (YTC) The rate of return on a bond that accounts for the difference between the bond's acquisition cost and its proceeds, including interest income, calculated to the earliest date that the bond may be called by the issuing corporation. *See* bond yield.

yield to maturity (YTM) The rate of return on a bond that accounts for the difference between the bond's acquisition cost and its maturity proceeds, including interest income. *See* bond yield.

Z

zero-coupon bond A corporate or municipal debt security traded at a deep discount from face value. The bond pays no interest; rather, it may be redeemed at maturity for its full face value. It may be issued at a discount, or it may be stripped of its coupons and repackaged.

Appendix A

FEDERAL VERSUS STATE LAW

Definition of Investment Adviser	
Any person who, for compensation, engages in the business of advising others as to the value of securities or the advisability of investing in securities or, as part of a regular business, issues analyses or reports concerning securities.	Same as federal.
Exclusions from Above Definition	
1. Banks	1. Banks
2. Attorneys, accountants, engineers, teachers	2. Attorneys, accountants, engineers, teachers
3. Broker/dealers	3. Broker/dealers
4. Publisher of any bona fide newspaper, news magazine, or other publication of general circulation	4. Publishers of any bona fide newspaper, news magazine, newsletter, or other publication that does not consist of the rendering of advice on the basis of the specific investment situation of each client
5. Any person whose advice relates solely to US government securities	5. Investment adviser representatives
Exemptions	
1. De minimis: fewer than 15 clients during the previous 12 months, none of whom is a registered investment company and does not hold himself out to the public as an investment adviser.	1. He has no place of business within that state and
2. His only clients are insurance companies.	a. his only clients are institutions such as investment companies, banks and trust companies, insurance companies, broker/dealers and other investment advisers, $1 million or larger employee benefit plans, governmental agency, or instrumentalities; or
3. Intrastate business only and does not furnish advice with respect to securities listed on any national securities exchange.	b. he does not direct communications to more than five clients in the state (other than above) during the previous 12 months (de minimis).
Registration	
File Form ADV with the SEC. Effective within 45 days. No net worth requirements. No surety bonds. Annual updating report is filed on ADV Schedule I. Withdrawal of registration is on ADV-W. ADV must be amended promptly for key changes, 90 days after fiscal year-end for others.	File application with the Administrator and pay initial and renewal (12/31) fees. There are net worth and/or surety bonds required (custody or discretion). Effective on noon of the 30th day. Successor firm pays no fee until renewal. Registration automatically registers any adviser representative who is a partner, officer, director, or similar in status.
Recordkeeping	
Records must be kept easily accessible for five years.	Generally three years for broker/dealers and five years for investment advisers.
Fines/Penalties	
$10,000 and five years in jail	$5,000 and three years in jail
Custody of Customer Funds/Securities	
Annual filing of audited balance sheet is SEC required. If custody held by broker/dealer subsidiary, investment adviser balance sheet is still required. Automatic draft for fee is considered custody. Balance sheet would also be required if adviser takes advance fees of more than $500, six months or more in advance.	If not prohibited, with written notice to the Administrator. Requires minimum net worth or surety bond of $35,000.

Performance Fees	
Prohibited unless: 1. contract with investment company 2. certain institutions with more than $1 million in managed assets 3. certain clients with $750,000 under management or net worth over $1.5 million.	Not allowable, but compensation can be based on the total value of the account averaged over a definite period. An exception may be made to coordinate with federal law.
Statute of Limitations for Civil Action	
Sooner of three years after the sale or one year after discovery.	Sooner of three years after the sale or two years after discovery.
A "Person"	
A natural person or company (includes a corporation, a partnership, an association, a joint stock company, a trust, or any organized group of persons, whether incorporated or not).	An individual, a corporation, an association, a joint stock company, a trust where the interests of the beneficiaries are evidenced by a security, an unincorporated organization, a government, or a political subdivision of a government.
Filing of Advertisements	
No filing with the SEC ever.	No filing for exempt securities or exempt transactions, otherwise filed with the Administrator.
Private Placement Exemption	
Up to 35 nonaccredited investors.	Up to 10 offers within the state over a 12-month period. The term *accredited investor* is meaningless.
Miscellaneous	
No assignment of the contract may be made without the client's comment.	No assignment of the contract may be made without the client's consent.
The adviser, if a partnership, must notify the client of any charge in the membership of the partnership.	The adviser, if a partnership, must notify the client of any change in the membership of the partnership.
The Brochure Rule.	States don't have a brochure rule, but most administrators accept the ADV Part II.
The term *investment counsel* may not be used unless: 1. principal business is investment advice; and 2. substantial portion of his service is providing investment supervisory services (the giving of continuous advice on the investment of funds on the basis of the individual needs of each client).	An investment adviser representative is an associated person of an adviser firm (not clerical) who: 1. makes recommendations or otherwise gives advice; 2. manages accounts of clients; 3. solicits or negotiates for the sale of advisory service; and 4. supervises any of the above.
Withdrawal takes effect 60 days after filing the ADV-W.	Withdrawal of registration takes effect 30 days after filing.
May not use initials R.I.A. on business card or letterhead.	
Insolvency is *not* a cause for revocation.	Insolvency is a cause for revocation.
$30 million or more under management registers with the SEC.	Less than $25 million under management registers with the state.

NASAA's Statement of Policy—Unethical Business Practices of Investment Advisers [with review annotation notes]

The North American Securities Administrators Association has adopted a statement of policy on "Unethical Business Practices of Investment Advisers." This statement of policy is reproduced here, with review notes included. ∎

An investment adviser is a fiduciary and has a duty to act primarily for the benefit of its clients. While the extent and nature of this duty varies according to the nature of the relationship between an investment adviser and its clients and the circumstances of each case, an investment adviser shall not engage in unethical business practices, including the following:

1. Recommending to a client to whom investment supervisory, management or consulting services are provided the purchase, sale or exchange of any security without reasonable grounds to believe that the recommendation is suitable for the client on the basis of information furnished by the client after reasonable inquiry concerning the client's investment objectives, financial situation and needs, and any other information known by the investment adviser.

    Review Note: *An investment adviser providing investment supervisory, management, or consulting services has a fundamental obligation to analyze a client's financial situation and needs before making any recommendation to the client. Recommendations made to a client must be reasonable in relation to the information that is obtained concerning the client's investment objective, financial situation and needs, and other information known by the investment adviser. By failing to make reasonable inquiry or by failing to make recommendations that are in line with the financial situation, investment objectives, and character of a client's account, an investment adviser has not met its primary responsibility.*

2. Exercising any discretionary power in placing an order for the purchase or sale of securities for a client without obtaining prior written discretionary authority from the client, unless the discretionary power relates solely to the price at which, or the time when, an order involving a definite amount of a specified security shall be executed, or both.

    Review Note: *This rule pertains only to investment advisers that place orders for client accounts. Before placing an order for an account, an investment adviser exercising discretion should have written discretionary authority from the client. In most cases, discretionary authority is granted in an advisory contract or in a separate document executed at the time the contract is executed. The rule permits oral discretionary authority to be used for the initial transactions in a customer's account within the first 10 business days after the date of the first transaction. An investment adviser is not precluded from exercising discretionary power that relates solely to the price or time at which an order involving a specific amount of a security is authorized by a customer because time and price do not constitute discretion.*

3. Inducing trading in a client's account that is excessive in size or frequency in view of the financial resources, investment objectives, and character of the account.

    Review Note: *This rule is intended to prevent an excessive number of securities transactions from being induced by an investment adviser. There are many situations where an investment adviser may receive commissions or be affiliated with a person that receives commissions from the securities transactions that are placed by the investment adviser. Because an adviser in such situations can directly benefit from the number of securities transactions effected in a client's account, the rule appropriately forbids an excessive number of transaction orders to be induced by an adviser for a customer's account.*

4. Placing an order to purchase or sell a security for the account of a client without authority to do so.

   Review Note: *This rule is not new to either the securities or investment advisory professions. An investment adviser must have authority to place any order for the account of a client. The authority may be obtained from a client orally or in an agreement executed by the client giving the adviser blanket authority.*

5. Placing an order to purchase or sell a security for the account of a client upon instruction of a third party without first having obtained a written third-party trading authorization from the client.

   Review Note: *It is sound business practice for an investment adviser not to place an order for the account of a customer at the instruction of a third party without first knowing that the third party has obtained authority from the client for the order. For example, it would be important for an investment adviser to know that an attorney had power-of-attorney over an estate whose securities the adviser was managing before placing any order at the instruction of the attorney. Placing orders under such circumstances could result in substantial civil liability, besides being an unethical practice.*

6. Borrowing money or securities from a client unless the client is a broker/dealer, an affiliate of the investment adviser, or financial institution engaged in the business of loaning funds.

   Review Note: *Unless a client of an investment adviser is engaged in the business of loaning money, is an affiliate of the investment adviser, or is an institution that would engage in this type of activity, an investment adviser must not take advantage of its advisory role by borrowing funds from a client. A client provides a substantial amount of confidential information to an investment adviser regarding the client's financial situation and needs. Using that information to an investment adviser's own advantage by borrowing funds is a breach of confidentiality and may create a material conflict of interest that could influence the advice rendered by the adviser to the client.*

7. Loaning money to a client unless the investment adviser is a financial institution engaged in the business of loaning funds or the client is an affiliate of the investment adviser.

   Review Note: *Like borrowing money from a client, loaning funds to a client by an investment adviser should not be an allowable practice unless the investment adviser is a financial institution normally engaged in the business of loaning funds or unless the client is affiliated with the adviser. Loaning funds may influence decisions made for a client's account and puts the investment adviser in a conflict of interest position because the client becomes a debtor of the adviser after a loan is made.*

8. To misrepresent to any advisory client, or prospective advisory client, the qualifications of the investment adviser or any employee of the investment adviser, or to misrepresent the nature of the advisory services being offered or fees to be charged for such service, or to omit to state a material fact necessary to make the statements made regarding qualifications, services or fees, in light of the circumstances under which they are made, not misleading.

Review Note: *When an investment adviser offers its services to a prospective client or when it provides services to an existing client, the qualifications of the investment adviser or any employee of the investment adviser and the nature of the advisory services and the fees to be charged must be disclosed in such a way as to not mislead. Overstating the qualifications of the investment adviser or disclosing inaccurately the nature of the advisory services to be provided or fees to be charged are not ethical ways to either acquire or retain clients.*

9. Providing a report or recommendation to any advisory client prepared by someone other than the adviser without disclosing the fact. (This prohibition does not apply to a situation where the adviser uses published research reports or statistical analyses to render advice or where an adviser orders such a report in the normal course of providing service.)

   Review Note: *If an investment adviser provides a report to a client that is prepared by a third party, the adviser has a responsibility to disclose the fact to the client. By entering into an investment advisory agreement, the client relies on the expertise of the adviser to provide the advisory service. Thus, if the advice is provided by a third party, it is imperative that the adviser disclose this fact to the client so the client is not misled. The prohibition does not apply when an investment adviser gathers and uses research materials before making its recommendation to a client.*

10. Charging a client an unreasonable advisory fee.

    Review Note: *This rule is intended to prohibit an investment adviser from charging an excessively high advisory fee. Unreasonable as used in this rule means unreasonable in relation to fees charged by other advisers for similar services. Although no two advisory services are exactly alike, comparisons can be drawn. In those instances where an advisory fee is out of line with fees charged by other advisers providing essentially the same services, an investment adviser should justify the charge. It would be very difficult for a client to compare various advisory services to evaluate those services and the fees charged. This rule will allow state Administrators to research the competitiveness of an adviser's services and fees, and to determine whether the fees being charged are unreasonably high.*

11. Failing to disclose to clients in writing, before any advice is rendered, any material conflict of interest relating to the adviser or any of its employees which could reasonably be expected to impair the rendering of unbiased and objective advice including:

    a. Compensation arrangements connected with advisory services to clients which are in addition to compensation from such clients for such services, and

    b. Charging a client an advisory fee for rendering advice when a commission for executing securities transactions pursuant to such advice will be received by the adviser or its employees.

    Review Note: *This rule is designed to require disclosure of all material conflicts of interest relating to the adviser or any of its employees that could affect the advice that is rendered. The two examples cited in the rule pertain to compensation arrangements that benefit the adviser and that are connected with advisory* *services being provided. However, full disclosure of all other material conflicts of interest, such as affiliations between the investment adviser and product suppliers, are also required to be made under the rule.*

12. Guaranteeing a client that a specific result will be achieved (gain or no loss) with advice which will be rendered.

    Review Note: *An investment adviser should not guarantee any gain or against loss in connection with advice that is rendered. By doing so, the adviser fails to maintain an arms-length relationship with a client and puts himself in a conflict of interest position by having a direct interest in the outcome of the advice rendered by the adviser.*

13. Publishing, circulating, or distributing any advertisement which does not comply with the Investment Advisers Act of 1940.

    Review Note: *An investment adviser should not publish, circulate, or distribute any advertisement that is inconsistent with federal rules governing the use of advertisements. Rule 206(4)-1 of the Investment Advisers Act of 1940 contains prohibitions against advertisements that contain untrue statements of material fact, that refer directly or indirectly to any testimonial of any kind, that refer to past specific recommendations of the investment adviser unless certain conditions are met, that represent that a chart or formula or other device being offered can, by itself, be used to determine which securities are to be bought or sold, or that contain a statement indicating that any analysis, report, or service will be furnished free when such is not the case. These prohibitions are fundamental and sound standards that all investment advisers should follow.*

14. Disclosing the identity, affairs, or investments of any client unless required by law to do so, or unless consented to by the client.

    Review Note: *An investment advisory firm has a responsibility to ensure that all information collected from a client be kept confidential. The only exception to the rule should be in those instances where the client authorized the release of such information, or when the investment advisory firm is required by law to disclose such information.*

15. Taking any action, directly or indirectly, with respect to those securities or funds in which any client has any beneficial interest, where the investment adviser has custody or possession of such securities or funds when the adviser's action is subject to and does not comply with the requirements of the Investment Advisers Act of 1940.

    Review Note: *In instances where an investment adviser has custody or possession of client's funds or securities, it should comply with the regulations under the Investment Advisers Act of 1940 designed to ensure the safekeeping of those securities and funds. The rules under the act specifically provide that securities of clients be segregated and properly marked, that the funds of the clients be deposited in separate bank accounts, that the investment adviser notify each client as to the place and manner in which such funds and securities are being maintained, that an itemized list of all securities and funds in the adviser's possession be sent to the client not less frequently than every three months, and that all such funds and securities be verified annually by actual examination by an independent CPA on a surprise basis. The rule establishes very conservative measures to safeguard each client's funds and securities held by an investment adviser.*

16. Entering into, extending or renewing any investment advisory contract unless such contract is in **_writing_** and discloses, in substance, the services to be provided, the term of the contract, the advisory fee, the formula for computing the fee, the amount of prepaid fee to be returned in the event of contract termination or non-performance, whether the contract grants discretionary power to the adviser and that no assignment of such contract shall be made by the investment adviser without the consent of the other party to the contract.

Review Note: _The purpose of this rule is to ensure that clients have a document to refer to that describes the basic terms of the agreement the client has entered into with an adviser._

The conduct set forth above is not inclusive. Engaging in other conduct such as non-disclosure, incomplete disclosure, or deceptive practices shall be deemed an unethical business practice.

Appendix C

Adopted May 23, 1983

HIGH STANDARDS AND JUST PRINCIPLES. Each broker/dealer and agent shall observe high standards of commercial honor and just and equitable principles of trade in the conduct of their business. Acts and practices, including but not limited to the following, are considered contrary to such standards and may constitute grounds for denial, suspension or revocation of registration or such other action authorized by statute.

1. Broker/Dealers

a. Engaging in a pattern of unreasonable and unjustifiable delays in the delivery of securities purchased by any of its customers and/or in the payment upon request of free credit balances reflecting completed transactions of any of its customers.

b. Inducing trading in a customer's account which is excessive in size or frequency in view of the financial resources and character of the account.

c. Recommending to a customer the purchase, sale or exchange of any security without reasonable grounds to believe that such transaction or recommendation is suitable for the customer based upon reasonable inquiry concerning the customer's investment objectives, financial situation and needs, and any other relevant information known by the broker/dealer.

d. Executing a transaction on behalf of a customer without authorization to do so.

e. Exercising any discretionary power in effecting a transaction for a customer's account without first obtaining written discretionary authority from the customer, unless the discretionary power relates solely to the time and/or price for the executing of orders.

f. Executing any transaction in a margin account without securing from the customer a properly executed written margin agreement promptly after the initial transaction in the account.

g. Failing to segregate customers' free securities or securities held in safekeeping.

h. Hypothecating a customer's securities without having a lien thereon unless the broker/dealer secures from the customer a properly executed written consent promptly after the initial transaction, except as permitted by Rules of the Securities and Exchange Commission.

i. Entering into a transaction with or for a customer at a price not reasonably related to the current market price of the security or receiving an unreasonable commission or profit.

j. Failing to furnish to a customer purchasing securities in an offering, no later than the due date of confirmation of the transaction, either a final prospectus or a preliminary prospectus and an additional document, which together include all information set forth in the final prospectus.

k. Charging unreasonable and inequitable fees for services performed, including miscellaneous services such as collection of monies due for principal, dividends or interest, exchange or transfer of securities, appraisals, safekeeping, or custody of securities and other services related to its securities business.

l. Offering to buy from or sell to any person any security at a stated price unless such broker/dealer is prepared to purchase or sell, as the case may be, at such price and under such conditions as are stated at the time of such offer to buy or sell.

m. Representing that a security is being offered to a customer "at the market" or a price relevant to the market price unless such broker/dealer knows or has reasonable grounds to believe that a market for such security exists other than that made, created or controlled by such broker/dealer, or by any such person for whom he is acting or with whom he is associated in such distribution, or any person controlled by, controlling or under common control with such broker/dealer.

n. Effecting any transaction in, or inducing the purchase or sale of, any security by means of any manipulative, deceptive or fraudulent device, practice, plan, program, design or contrivance, which may include but not be limited to:

(1) Effecting any transaction in a security which involves no change in the beneficial ownership thereof;

(2) Entering an order or orders for the purchase or sale of any security with the knowledge that an order or orders of substantially the same size, at substantially the same time and substantially the same price, for the sale of any such security, has been or will be entered by or for the same or different parties for the purpose of creating a false or misleading appearance of active trading in the security or a false or misleading appearance with respect to the market for the security; provided, however, nothing in this subsection shall prohibit a broker/dealer from entering bona fide agency cross transactions for its customers; or

(3) Effecting, alone or with one or more other persons, a series of transactions in any security creating actual or apparent active trading in such security or raising or depressing the price of such security, for the purpose of inducing the purchase or sale of such security by others.

o. Guaranteeing a customer against loss in any securities account of such customer carried by the broker/dealer or in any securities transaction effected by the broker/dealer or in any securities transaction effected by the broker/dealer with or for such customer.

p. Publishing or circulating, or causing to be published or circulated, any notice, circular, advertisement, newspaper article, investment service, or communication of any kind which purports to report any transaction as a purchase or sale of any security unless such broker/dealer believes that such transaction was a bona fide purchase or sale or such security; or which purports to quote the bid price or asked price for any security, unless such broker/dealer believes that such quotation represents a bona fide bid for, or offer of, such security.

q. Using any advertising or sales presentation in such a fashion as to be deceptive or misleading. An example of such practice would be a distribution of any nonfactual data, material or presentation based on conjecture, unfounded or unrealistic claims or assertions in any brochure, flyer, or display by words, pictures, graphs or otherwise designed to supplement, detract from, supersede or defeat the purpose or effect of any prospectus or disclosure.

r. Failing to disclose that the broker/dealer is controlled by, controlling, affiliated with or under common control with the issuer of any security before entering into any contract with or for a customer for the purchase or sale of such security, the existence of such control to such customer, and if such disclosure is not made in writing, it shall be supplemented by the giving or sending of written disclosure at or before the completion of the transaction.

s. Failing to make a bona fide public offering of all of the securities allotted to a broker/dealer for distribution, whether acquired as an underwriter, a selling group member, or from a member participating in the distribution as an underwriter or selling group member.

t. Failure or refusal to furnish a customer, upon reasonable request, information to which he is entitled, or to respond to a formal written request or complaint.

2. Agents

a. Engaging in the practice of lending or borrowing money or securities from a customer, or acting as a custodian for money, securities or an executed stock power of a customer.

b. Effecting securities transactions not recorded on the regular books or records of the broker/dealer which the agent represents, unless the transactions are authorized in writing by the broker/dealer prior to execution of the transaction.

c. Establishing or maintaining an account containing fictitious information in order to execute transactions which would otherwise be prohibited.

d. Sharing directly or indirectly in profits or losses in the account of any customer without the written authorization of the customer and the broker/dealer which the agent represents.

e. Dividing or otherwise splitting the agent's commissions, profits or other compensation from the purchase or sale of securities with any person not also registered as an agent for the same broker/dealer, or for a broker/dealer under direct or indirect common control.

f. Engaging in conduct specified in Subsection 1.b, c, d, e, f, i, j, n, o, p, or q.

CONDUCT NOT INCLUSIVE. The conduct set forth above is not inclusive. Engaging in other conduct such as forgery, embezzlement, nondisclosure, incomplete disclosure or misstatement of material facts, or manipulative or deceptive practices shall also be grounds for denial, suspension or revocation of registration.

Appendix D

FORM ADV (Paper Version)
UNIFORM APPLICATION FOR INVESTMENT ADVISER REGISTRATION

PART 1A

WARNING: Complete this form truthfully. False statements or omissions may result in denial of your application, revocation of your registration, or criminal prosecution. You must keep this form updated by filing periodic amendments. See Form ADV General Instruction 3.

Check the box that indicates what you would like to do (check all that apply):

- ☐ Submit an initial application to register as an investment adviser with the SEC.
- ☐ Submit an initial application to register as an investment adviser with one or more states.
- ☐ Submit an *annual updating amendment* to your registration for your fiscal year ended _____.
- ☐ Submit an other-than-annual amendment to your registration.

Item 1   Identifying Information

Responses to this Item tell us who you are, where you are doing business, and how we can contact you.

A. Your full legal name (if you are a sole proprietor, your last, first, and middle names):

_____

B. Name under which you primarily conduct your advisory business, if different from Item 1.A.

_____

List on Section 1.B. of Schedule D any additional names under which you conduct your advisory business.

C. If this filing is reporting a change in your legal name (Item 1.A.) or primary business name (Item 1.B.), enter the new name and specify whether the name change is of ☐ your legal name or ☐ your primary business name:

_____

D. If you are registered with the SEC as an investment adviser, your SEC file number: 801-_____

E. If you have a number ("*CRD* Number") assigned by the *NASD's CRD* system or by the IARD system, your *CRD* number:

_____

If your firm does not have a CRD number, skip this Item 1.E. Do not provide the CRD number of one of your officers, employees, or affiliates.

FORM ADV	Your Name _____	*CRD* Number _____
Part 1A	Date _____	SEC 801-Number _____
Page 2 of 14		

F. *Principal Office and Place of Business*

(1) Address (do not use a P.O. Box):

_____

(number and street)

_____

(city)   (state/country)   (zip+4/postal code)

If this address is a private residence, check this box: ☐

List on Section 1.F. of Schedule D any office, other than your principal office and place of business, at which you conduct investment advisory business. If you are applying for registration, or are registered, with one or more state securities authorities, you must list all of your offices in the state or states to which you are applying for registration or with whom you are registered. If you are applying for registration, or are registered only, with the SEC, list the largest five offices in terms of numbers of employees.

(2) Days of week that you normally conduct business at your *principal office and place of business*:

☐ Monday - Friday   ☐ Other: _____

Normal business hours at this location: _____

(3) Telephone number at this location: _____

(area code)   (telephone number)

(4) Facsimile number at this location: _____

(area code)   (telephone number)

G. Mailing address, if different from your *principal office and place of business* address:

_____

(number and street)

_____

(city)   (state/country)   (zip+4/postal code)

If this address is a private residence, check this box: ☐

H. If you are a sole proprietor, state your full residence address, if different from your *principal office and place of business* address in Item 1.F:

_____

(number and street)

_____

(city)   (state/country)   (zip+4/postal code)

<table>
<tr><td>**FORM ADV**
Part 1A
Page 3 of 14</td><td>Your Name _____
Date _____</td><td>*CRD* Number _____
SEC 801-Number _____</td></tr>
</table>

I. Do you have World Wide Web site addresses?   Yes ☐   No ☐

If "yes," list these addresses on Section 1.I. of Schedule D. If a web address serves as a portal through which to access other information you have published on the World Wide Web, you may list the portal without listing addresses for all of the other information. Some advisers may need to list more than one portal address. Do not provide individual electronic mail addresses in response to this Item.

J. Contact *Employee:*

_____
(name)

_____
(title)

_____   _____
(area code) (telephone number)   (area code)   (facsimile number)

_____
(number and street)

_____
(city)   (state/country)   (zip+4/postal code)

_____
(electronic mail (e-mail) address, if contact *employee* has one)

The contact employee should be an employee whom you have authorized to receive information and respond to questions about this Form ADV.

K. Do you maintain some or all of the books and records you are required to keep under Section 204 of the Advisers Act, or similar state law, somewhere other than your *principal office and place of business*?

Yes ☐   No ☐

If "yes," complete Section 1.K. of Schedule D.

L. Are you registered with a *foreign financial regulatory authority*?   Yes ☐   No ☐

Answer "no" if you are not registered with a foreign financial regulatory authority, even if you have an affiliate that is registered with a foreign financial regulatory authority. If "yes," complete Section 1.L. of Schedule D.

| **FORM ADV** Part 1A Page 4 of 14 | Your Name _____ Date _____ | *CRD* Number _____ SEC 801-Number _____ |

Item 2   SEC Registration

Responses to this Item help us (and you) determine whether you are eligible to register with the SEC. Complete this Item 2 only if you are applying for SEC registration or submitting an *annual updating amendment* to your SEC registration.

  A. To register (or remain registered) with the SEC, you must check at least one of the Items 2.A(1) through 2.A(11), below. If you are submitting an *annual updating amendment* to your SEC registration and you are no longer eligible to register with the SEC, check Item 2.A(12). You:

☐ (1)   have *assets under management* of $25 million (in U.S. dollars) or more;

See Part 1A Instruction 2.a. to determine whether you should check this box.

☐ (2)   have your *principal office and place of business* in the U.S. Virgin Islands or Wyoming;

☐ (3)   have your *principal office and place of business* outside the United States;

☐ (4)   are an investment adviser (or sub-adviser) to an investment company registered under the Investment Company Act of 1940;

See Part 1A Instruction 2.b. to determine whether you should check this box.

☐ (5)   have been designated as a nationally recognized statistical rating organization;

See Part 1A Instruction 2.c. to determine whether you should check this box.

☐ (6)   are a pension consultant that qualifies for the exemption in rule 203A-2(b);

See Part 1A Instruction 2.d. to determine whether you should check this box.

☐ (7)   are relying on rule 203A-2(c) because you are an investment adviser that *controls,* is *controlled* by, or is under common *control* with, an investment adviser that is registered with the SEC, and your *principal office and place of business* is the same as the registered adviser;

See Part 1A Instruction 2.e. to determine whether you should check this box. If you check this box, complete Section 2.A(7) of Schedule D.

☐ (8)   are a newly formed adviser relying on rule 203A-2(d) because you expect to be eligible for SEC registration within 120 days;

See Part 1A Instruction 2.f. to determine whether you should check this box. If you check this box, complete Section 2.A(8) of Schedule D.

☐ (9)   are a multi-state adviser relying on rule 203A-2(e);

See Part 1A Instruction 2.g. to determine whether you should check this box. If you check this box, complete Section 2.A(9) of Schedule D.

☐ (10) are an Internet investment adviser relying on rule 203A-2(f);

See Part 1A Instructions 2.h. to determine whether you should check this box.

☐ (11) have received an SEC *order* exempting you from the prohibition against registration with the SEC;

If you checked this box, complete Section 2.A(11) of Schedule D.

☐ (12) are no longer eligible to remain registered with the SEC.

See Part 1A Instructions 2.i. to determine whether you should check this box.

FORM ADV	Your Name _____	CRD Number _____
Part 1A	Date _____	SEC 801-Number _____
Page 5 of 14		

B. Under state laws, SEC-registered advisers may be required to provide to *state securities authorities* a copy of the Form ADV and any amendments they file with the SEC. These are called *notice filings*. If this is an initial application, check the box(es) next to the state(s) that you would like to receive notice of this and all subsequent filings you submit to the SEC. If this is an amendment to direct your *notice filings* to additional state(s), check and circle the box(es) next to the state(s) that you would like to receive notice of this and all subsequent filings you submit to the SEC. If this is an amendment to your registration to stop your *notice filings* from going to state(s) that currently receive them, circle the unchecked box(es) next to those state(s).

☐ AL ☐ CT ☐ HI ☐ KY ☐ MN ☐ NH ☐ OH ☐ SC ☐ VA
☐ AK ☐ DE ☐ ID ☐ LA ☐ MS ☐ NJ ☐ OK ☐ SD ☐ WA
☐ AZ ☐ DC ☐ IL ☐ ME ☐ MO ☐ NM ☐ OR ☐ TN ☐ WV
☐ AR ☐ FL ☐ IN ☐ MD ☐ MT ☐ NY ☐ PA ☐ TX ☐ WI
☐ CA ☐ GA ☐ IA ☐ MA ☐ NE ☐ NC ☐ PR ☐ UT
☐ CO ☐ GU ☐ KS ☐ MI ☐ NV ☐ ND ☐ RI ☐ VT

If you are amending your registration to stop your notice filings from going to a state that currently receives them and you do not want to pay that state's notice filing fee for the coming year, your amendment must filed before the end of the year (December 31).

Item 3   Form of Organization

A. How are you organized?

☐ Corporation   ☐ Sole Proprietorship   ☐ Limited Liability Partnership (LLP)
☐ Partnership   ☐ Limited Liability Company (LLC)
☐ Other (specify): _____

If you are changing your response to this Item, see Part 1A Instruction 4.

B. In what month does your fiscal year end each year? _____

C. Under the laws of what state or country are you organized? _____

If you are a partnership, provide the name of the state or country under whose laws your partnership was formed. If you are a sole proprietor, provide the name of the state or country where you reside.

If you are changing your response to this Item, see Part 1A Instruction 4.

Item 4   Successions

A. Are you, at the time of this filing, succeeding to the business of a registered investment adviser?
☐ Yes   ☐ No

If "yes," complete Item 4.B. and Section 4 of Schedule D.

B. Date of Succession: _____
                                              (mm/dd/yyyy)

If you have already reported this succession on a previous Form ADV filing, do not report the succession again. Instead, check "No." See Part 1A Instruction 4.

<table>
<tr><td>**FORM ADV**
Part 1A
Page 6 of 14</td><td>Your Name _____

Date _____</td><td>*CRD* Number _____

SEC 801-Number _____</td></tr>
</table>

Item 5   Information About Your Advisory Business

Responses to this Item help us understand your business, assist us in preparing for on-site examinations, and provide us with data we use when making regulatory policy. Part 1A Instruction 5.a. provides additional guidance to newly-formed advisers for completing this Item 5.

Employees

A. Approximately how many *employees* do you have? Include full and part-time *employees* but do not include any clerical workers.

☐ 1- 5   ☐ 6 - 10   ☐ 11 – 50   ☐ 51-250   ☐ 251-500   ☐ 501-1,000   ☐ More than 1,000
If more than 1,000, how many? _____   (round to the nearest 1,000)

B.

(1) Approximately how many of these *employees* perform investment advisory functions (including research)?

☐ 0   ☐ 1-5   ☐ 6-10   ☐ 11 – 50   ☐ 51-250   ☐ 251-500   ☐ 501-1,000
☐ More than 1,000   If more than 1,000, how many? _____ (round to the nearest 1,000)

(2) Approximately how many of these *employees* are registered representatives of a broker-dealer?

☐ 0   ☐ 1-5   ☐ 6-10   ☐ 11 – 50   ☐ 51-250   ☐ 251-500   ☐ 501-1,000
☐ More than 1,000   If more than 1,000, how many? _____ (round to the nearest 1,000)

If you are organized as a sole proprietorship, include yourself as an employee in your responses to Items 5.A(1) and 5.B(2). If an employee performs more than one function, you should count that employee in each of your responses to Item 5.B(1) and 5.B(2).

(3) Approximately how many firms or other *persons* solicit advisory *clients* on your behalf?

☐ 0   ☐ 1-5   ☐ 6-10   ☐ 11 – 50   ☐ 51-250   ☐ 251-500   ☐ 501-1,000
☐ More than 1,000   If more than 1,000, how many? _____ (round to the nearest 1,000)

In your response to Item 5.B(3), do not count any of your employees and count a firm only once — do not count each of the firm's employees that solicit on your behalf.

Clients

C. To approximately how many *clients* did you provide investment advisory services during your most-recently completed fiscal year?

☐ 0   ☐ 1-10   ☐ 11-25   ☐ 26-100   ☐ 101-250   ☐ 251 – 500
☐ More than 500   If more than 500, how many? _____   (round to the nearest 500)

FORM ADV
Part 1A
Page 7 of 14

Your Name _____

Date _____

CRD Number _____

SEC 801-Number _____

D. What types of *clients* do you have? Indicate the approximate percentage that each type of *client* comprises of your total number of *clients*.

	None	Up to 10%	11-25%	26-50%	51-75%	More Than 75%
(1) Individuals (other than *high net worth individuals*)	☐	☐	☐	☐	☐	☐
(2) *High net worth individuals*	☐	☐	☐	☐	☐	☐
(3) Banking or thrift institutions	☐	☐	☐	☐	☐	☐
(4) Investment companies (including mutual funds)	☐	☐	☐	☐	☐	☐
(5) Pension and profit sharing plans (other than plan participants)	☐	☐	☐	☐	☐	☐
(6) Other pooled investment vehicles (e.g., hedge funds)	☐	☐	☐	☐	☐	☐
(7) Charitable organizations	☐	☐	☐	☐	☐	☐
(8) Corporations or other businesses not listed above	☐	☐	☐	☐	☐	☐
(9) State or municipal *government entities*	☐	☐	☐	☐	☐	☐
(10) Other: _____	☐	☐	☐	☐	☐	☐

The category "individuals" includes trusts, estates, 401(k) plans and IRAs of individuals and their family members, but does not include businesses organized as sole proprietorships.

Unless you provide advisory services pursuant to an investment advisory contract to an investment company registered under the Investment Company Act of 1940, check "None" in response to Item 5.D(4).

Compensation Arrangements

E. You are compensated for your investment advisory services by (check all that apply):

☐ (1) A percentage of assets under your management

☐ (2) Hourly charges

☐ (3) Subscription fees (for a newsletter or periodical)

☐ (4) Fixed fees (other than subscription fees)

☐ (5) Commissions

☐ (6) *Performance-based fees*

☐ (7) Other (specify): _____

Assets Under Management

F. (1) Do you provide continuous and regular supervisory or management services to securities portfolios? ☐ Yes   ☐ No

(2) If yes, what is the amount of your assets under management and total number of accounts?

		U.S. Dollar Amount		Total Number of Accounts
Discretionary:	(a)	$_____.00	(d)	_____
Non-Discretionary:	(b)	$_____.00	(e)	_____
Total:	(c)	$_____.00	(f)	_____

Part 1A Instruction 5.b. explains how to calculate your assets under management. You must follow these instructions carefully when completing this Item.

FORM ADV Part 1A Page 8 of 14	Your Name _____ Date _____	CRD Number _____ SEC 801-Number _____

Advisory Activities

G. What type(s) of advisory services do you provide? Check all that apply.

☐ (1)   Financial planning services

☐ (2)   Portfolio management for individuals and/or small businesses

☐ (3)   Portfolio management for investment companies

☐ (4)   Portfolio management for businesses or institutional *clients* (other than investment companies)

☐ (5)   Pension consulting services

☐ (6)   Selection of other advisers

☐ (7)   Publication of periodicals or newsletters

☐ (8)   Security ratings or pricing services

☐ (9)   Market timing services

☐ (10) Other (specify): _____

Do not check Item 5.G(3) unless you provide advisory services pursuant to an investment advisory contract to an investment company registered under the Investment Company Act of 1940.

H. If you provide financial planning services, to how many *clients* did you provide these services during your last fiscal year?

☐ 0   ☐ 1-10   ☐ 11-25   ☐ 26-50   ☐ 51-100   ☐ 101 – 250   ☐ 251-500

☐ More than 500   If more than 500, how many? _____   (round to the nearest 500)

I. If you participate in a *wrap fee program*, do you (check all that apply):

☐ (1)   *sponsor* the *wrap fee program*?

☐ (2)   act as a portfolio manager for the *wrap fee program*?

If you are a portfolio manager for a wrap fee program, list the names of the programs and their sponsors in Section 5.I(2) of Schedule D.

If your involvement in a wrap fee program is limited to recommending wrap fee programs to your clients, or you advise a mutual fund that is offered through a wrap fee program, do not check either Item 5.I(1) or 5.I(2).

Item 6   Other Business Activities

In this Item, we request information about your other business activities.

A. You are actively engaged in business as a (check all that apply):

☐ (1)   Broker-dealer

☐ (2)   Registered representative of a broker-dealer

☐ (3)   Futures commission merchant, commodity pool operator, or commodity trading advisor

☐ (4)   Real estate broker, dealer, or agent

☐ (5)   Insurance broker or agent

☐ (6)   Bank (including a separately identifiable department or division of a bank)

☐ (7)   Other financial product salesperson (specify): _____

B. (1)   Are you actively engaged in any other business not listed in Item 6.A. (other than giving investment advice)?   ☐ Yes   ☐ No

FORM ADV Part 1A Page 9 of 14	Your Name _____ Date _____	_CRD_ Number _____ SEC 801-Number _____

    (2) If yes, is this other business your primary business?   ☐ Yes ☐ No

        If "yes," describe this other business on Section 6.B. of Schedule D.

    (3) Do you sell products or provide services other than investment advice to your advisory *clients*?
        ☐ Yes ☐ No

Item 7   Financial Industry Affiliations

In this Item, we request information about your financial industry affiliations and activities. This information identifies areas in which conflicts of interest may occur between you and your *clients.*

Item 7 requires you to provide information about you and your *related persons.* Your *related persons* are all of your *advisory affiliates* and any *person* that is under common *control* with you.

    A. You have a *related person* that is a (check all that apply):

        ☐ (1) broker-dealer, municipal securities dealer, or government securities broker or dealer

        ☐ (2) investment company (including mutual funds)

        ☐ (3) other investment adviser (including financial planners)

        ☐ (4) futures commission merchant, commodity pool operator, or commodity trading advisor

        ☐ (5) banking or thrift institution

        ☐ (6) accountant or accounting firm

        ☐ (7) lawyer or law firm

        ☐ (8) insurance company or agency

        ☐ (9) pension consultant

        ☐ (10) real estate broker or dealer

        ☐ (11) sponsor or syndicator of limited partnerships

        If you checked Item 7A.(3), you must list on Section 7.A. of Schedule D all your related persons that are investment advisers. If you checked Item 7A.(1), you may elect to list on Section 7.A. of Schedule D all your related persons that are broker-dealers. If you choose to list a related broker-dealer, the IARD will accept a single Form U-4 to register an investment adviser representative who also is a broker-dealer agent ("registered rep") of that related broker-dealer.

    B. Are you or any *related person* a general partner in an *investment-related* limited partnership or manager of an *investment-related* limited liability company? ☐ Yes ☐ No

        If "yes," for each limited partnership or limited liability company, complete Section 7.B. of Schedule D. If, however, you are an SEC-registered adviser <u>and</u> you have related persons that are <u>SEC-registered</u> advisers who are the general partners of limited partnerships or the managers of limited liability companies, you do not have to complete Section 7.B. of Schedule D with respect to those related advisers' limited partnerships or limited liability companies.

        To use this alternative procedure, you must state in the Miscellaneous Section of Schedule D: (1) that you have related SEC-registered investment advisers that manage limited partnerships or limited liability companies that are not listed in Section 7.B. of your Schedule D; (2) that complete and accurate information about those limited partnerships or limited liability companies is available in Section 7.B. of Schedule D of the Form ADVs of your related SEC-registered advisers; and (3) whether your clients are solicited to invest in any of those limited partnerships or limited liability companies.

Item 8   Participation or Interest in *Client* Transactions

In this Item, we request information about your participation and interest in your *clients'* transactions. Like Item 7, this information identifies areas in which conflicts of interest may occur between you and your *clients.*

<table>
<tr><td>FORM ADV
Part 1A
Page 10 of 14</td><td>Your Name _____
Date _____</td><td>CRD Number _____
SEC 801-Number _____</td></tr>
</table>

Like Item 7, Item 8 requires you to provide information about you and your *related persons*.

Proprietary Interest in *Client* Transactions

A. Do you or any *related person*:   <u>Yes</u>   <u>No</u>

   (1) buy securities for yourself from advisory *clients*, or sell securities you own to
        advisory *clients* (principal transactions)?   ☐   ☐

   (2) buy or sell for yourself securities (other than shares of mutual funds) that you
        also recommend to advisory *clients*?   ☐   ☐

   (3) recommend securities (or other investment products) to advisory *clients* in
        which you or any *related person* has some other proprietary (ownership)
        interest (other than those mentioned in Items 8.A(1) or (2))?   ☐   ☐

Sales Interest in *Client* Transactions

B. Do you or any *related person*:   <u>Yes</u>   <u>No</u>

   (1) as a broker-dealer or registered representative of a broker-dealer, execute
        securities trades for brokerage customers in which advisory *client* securities
        are sold to or bought from the brokerage customer (agency cross transactions)?   ☐   ☐

   (2) recommend purchase of securities to advisory *clients* for which you or any *related
        person* serves as underwriter, general or managing partner, or purchaser
        representative?   ☐   ☐

   (3) recommend purchase or sale of securities to advisory *clients* for which you or any
        related person has any other sales interest (other than the receipt of sales
        commissions as a broker or registered representative of a broker-dealer)?   ☐   ☐

Investment or Brokerage Discretion

C. Do you or any *related person* have *discretionary authority* to determine the: <u>Yes</u>   <u>No</u>

   (1) securities to be bought or sold for a *client's* account?   ☐   ☐

   (2) amount of securities to be bought or sold for a *client's* account?   ☐   ☐

   (3) broker or dealer to be used for a purchase or sale of securities for a *client's* account?   ☐   ☐

   (4) commission rates to be paid to a broker or dealer for a *client's* securities transactions?   ☐   ☐

D. Do you or any *related person* recommend brokers or dealers to *clients*?   ☐   ☐

E. Do you or any *related person* receive research or other products or services
    other than execution from a broker-dealer or a third party in connection with
    client securities transactions?   ☐   ☐

F. Do you or any *related person*, directly or indirectly, compensate any *person* for
    client referrals?   ☐   ☐

   *In responding to this Item 8.F., consider in your response all cash and non-cash compensation that you or a related person
   gave any person in exchange for client referrals, including any bonus that is based, at least in part, on the number or
   amount of client referrals.*

<table>
<tr><td>

FORM ADV
Part 1A
Page 11 of 14

</td><td>

Your Name _____
Date _____

</td><td>

CRD Number _____
SEC 801-Number _____

</td></tr>
</table>

Item 9   *Custody*

In this Item, we ask you whether you or a *related person* has *custody* of *client* assets. If you are registering or registered with the SEC and you deduct your advisory fees directly from your *clients'* accounts but you do not otherwise have *custody* of your *clients'* funds or securities, you may answer "no" to Item 9A.(1) and 9A.(2).

A. Do you have *custody* of any advisory *clients'*:   <u>Yes</u>   <u>No</u>

   (1) cash or bank accounts?   ☐ ☐
   (2) securities?   ☐ ☐

B. Do any of your *related persons* have *custody* of any of your advisory *clients'*:

   (1) cash or bank accounts?   ☐ ☐
   (2) securities?   ☐ ☐

C. If you answered "yes" to either Item 9.B(1) or 9.B(2), is that *related person* a broker-dealer registered under Section 15 of the Securities Exchange Act of 1934?   ☐ ☐

Item 10   *Control Persons*

In this Item, we ask you to identify every *person* that, directly or indirectly, *controls* you.

If you are submitting an initial application, you must complete Schedule A and Schedule B. Schedule A asks for information about your direct owners and executive officers. Schedule B asks for information about your indirect owners. If this is an amendment and you are updating information you reported on either Schedule A or Schedule B (or both) that you filed with your initial application, you must complete Schedule C.

Does any *person* not named in Item 1.A. or Schedules A, B, or C, directly or indirectly, *control* your management or policies?

☐ Yes   ☐ No

If yes, complete Section 10 of Schedule D.

Item 11   Disclosure Information

In this Item, we ask for information about your disciplinary history and the disciplinary history of all your *advisory affiliates*. We use this information to determine whether to grant your application for registration, to decide whether to revoke your registration or to place limitations on your activities as an investment adviser, and to identify potential problem areas to focus on during our on-site examinations. One event may result in "yes" answers to more than one of the questions below.

Your *advisory affiliates* are: (1) all of your current *employees* (other than *employees* performing only clerical, administrative, support or similar functions); (2) all of your officers, partners, or directors (or any *person* performing similar functions); and (3) all *persons* directly or indirectly *controlling* you or *controlled* by you. If you are a "separately identifiable department or division" (SID) of a bank, see the Glossary of Terms to determine who your *advisory affiliates* are.

If you are registered or registering with the SEC, you may limit your disclosure of any event listed in Item 11 to ten years following the date of the event. If you are registered or registering with a state, you must respond to the questions as posed; you may, therefore, limit your disclosure to ten years following the date of an event only in responding to Items 11.A(1), 11.A(2), 11.B(1), 11.B(2), 11.D(4), and 11.H(1)(a). For purposes of calculating this ten-year period, the date of an event is the date the final order, judgment, or decree was entered, or the date any rights of appeal from preliminary orders, judgments, or decrees lapsed.

FORM ADV	Your Name _____	*CRD* Number _____
Part 1A	Date _____	SEC 801-Number _____
Page 12 of 14		

For "yes" answers to the following questions, complete a Criminal Action DRP:

Yes   No

A. In the past ten years, have you or any *advisory affiliate*:

   (1) been convicted of or pled guilty or nolo contendere ("no contest") in a domestic, foreign, or military court to any *felony*?   ☐   ☐

   (2) been *charged* with any *felony*?   ☐   ☐

If you are registered or registering with the SEC, you may limit your response to Item 11.A(2) to charges that are currently pending.

B. In the past ten years, have you or any *advisory affiliate*:

   (1) been convicted of or pled guilty or nolo contendere ("no contest") in a domestic, foreign, or military court to a *misdemeanor* involving: investments or an *investment-related* business, or any fraud, false statements, or omissions, wrongful taking of property, bribery, perjury, forgery, counterfeiting, extortion, or a conspiracy to commit any of these offenses?   ☐   ☐

   (2) been *charged* with a *misdemeanor* listed in Item 11.B(1)?   ☐   ☐

If you are registered or registering with the SEC, you may limit your response to Item 11.B(2) to charges that are currently pending.

For "yes" answers to the following questions, complete a Regulatory Action DRP:

Yes   No

C. Has the SEC or the Commodity Futures Trading Commission (CFTC) ever:

   (1) *found* you or any *advisory affiliate* to have made a false statement or omission?   ☐   ☐

   (2) *found* you or any *advisory affiliate* to have been *involved* in a violation of SEC or CFTC regulations or statutes?   ☐   ☐

   (3) *found* you or any *advisory affiliate* to have been a cause of an *investment-related* business having its authorization to do business denied, suspended, revoked, or restricted?   ☐   ☐

   (4) entered an *order* against you or any *advisory affiliate* in connection with *investment-related* activity?   ☐   ☐

   (5) imposed a civil money penalty on you or any *advisory affiliate*, or *ordered* you or any *advisory affiliate* to cease and desist from any activity?   ☐   ☐

D. Has any other federal regulatory agency, any state regulatory agency, or any *foreign financial regulatory authority*:

   (1) ever *found* you or any *advisory affiliate* to have made a false statement or omission, or been dishonest, unfair, or unethical?   ☐   ☐

<table>
<tr><td>FORM ADV
Part 1A
Page 13 of 14</td><td>Your Name _____
Date _____</td><td>CRD Number _____
SEC 801-Number _____</td></tr>
</table>

	Yes	No

(2) ever *found* you or any *advisory affiliate* to have been *involved* in a violation of *investment-related* regulations or statutes? ☐ ☐

(3) ever *found* you or any *advisory affiliate* to have been a cause of an *investment-related* business having its authorization to do business denied, suspended, revoked, or restricted? ☐ ☐

(4) in the past ten years, entered an *order* against you or any *advisory affiliate* in connection with an *investment-related* activity? ☐ ☐

(5) ever denied, suspended, or revoked your or any *advisory affiliate's* registration or license, or otherwise prevented you or any *advisory affiliate*, by *order*, from associating with an *investment-related* business or restricted your or any *advisory affiliate's* activity? ☐ ☐

E. Has any *self-regulatory organization* or commodities exchange ever:

(1) *found* you or any *advisory affiliate* to have made a false statement or omission? ☐ ☐

(2) *found* you or any *advisory affiliate* to have been *involved* in a violation of its rules (other than a violation designated as a "*minor rule violation*" under a plan approved by the SEC)? ☐ ☐

(3) *found* you or any *advisory affiliate* to have been the cause of an *investment-related* business having its authorization to do business denied, suspended, revoked, or restricted? ☐ ☐

(4) disciplined you or any *advisory affiliate* by expelling or suspending you or the *advisory affiliate* from membership, barring or suspending you or the *advisory affiliate* from association with other members, or otherwise restricting your or the *advisory affiliate's* activities? ☐ ☐

F. Has an authorization to act as an attorney, accountant, or federal contractor granted to you or any *advisory affiliate* ever been revoked or suspended? ☐ ☐

G. Are you or any *advisory affiliate* now the subject of any regulatory *proceeding* that could result in a "yes" answer to any part of Item 11.C., 11.D., or 11.E.? ☐ ☐

For "yes" answers to the following questions, complete a Civil Judicial Action DRP:

	Yes	No

H. (1) Has any domestic or foreign court:

(a) in the past ten years, *enjoined* you or any *advisory affiliate* in connection with any *investment-related* activity? ☐ ☐

(b) ever *found* that you or any *advisory affiliate* were *involved* in a violation of *investment-related* statutes or regulations? ☐ ☐

(c) ever dismissed, pursuant to a settlement agreement, an *investment-related* civil action brought against you or any *advisory affiliate* by a state or *foreign financial regulatory authority*? ☐ ☐

(2) Are you or any *advisory affiliate* now the subject of any civil *proceeding* that could result in a "yes" answer to any part of Item 11.H(1)? ☐ ☐

Your Name _____

Date _____

CRD Number _____

SEC 801-Number _____

Item 12   Small Businesses

The SEC is required by the Regulatory Flexibility Act to consider the effect of its regulations on small entities. In order to do this, we need to determine whether you meet the definition of "small business" or "small organization" under rule 0-7.

Answer this Item 12 only if you are registered or registering with the SEC <u>and</u> you indicated in response to Item 5.F(2)(c) that you have assets under management of less than $25 million. You are not required to answer this Item 12 if you are filing for initial registration as a state adviser, amending a current state registration, or switching from SEC to state registration.

For purposes of this Item 12 only:

- Total Assets refers to the total assets of a firm, rather than the assets managed on behalf of *clients*. In determining your or another *person's* total assets, you may use the total assets shown on a current balance sheet (but use total assets reported on a consolidated balance sheet with subsidiaries included, if that amount is larger).

- Control means the power to direct or cause the direction of the management or policies of a *person*, whether through ownership of securities, by contract, or otherwise. Any *person* that directly or indirectly has the right to vote 25 percent or more of the voting securities, or is entitled to 25 percent or more of the profits, of another *person* is presumed to control the other *person*.

	<u>Yes</u>	<u>No</u>
A. Did you have total assets of $5 million or more on the last day of your most recent fiscal year?	☐	☐

If "yes," you do not need to answer Items 12.B. and 12.C.

B. Do you:

	Yes	No
(1) *control* another investment adviser that had assets under management of $25 million or more on the last day of its most recent fiscal year?	☐	☐
(2) *control* another *person* (other than a natural person) that had total assets of $5 million or more on the last day of its most recent fiscal year?	☐	☐

C. Are you:

	Yes	No
(1) *controlled* by or under common *control* with another investment adviser that had assets under management of $25 million or more on the last day of its most recent fiscal year?	☐	☐
(2) *controlled* by or under common *control* with another *person* (other than a natural person) that had total assets of $5 million or more on the last day of its most recent fiscal year?	☐	☐

FORM ADV (Paper Version)
UNIFORM APPLICATION FOR INVESTMENT ADVISER REGISTRATION

PART 1B

You must complete this Part 1B only if you are applying for registration, or are registered, as an investment adviser with any of the *state securities authorities*.

Item 1   State Registration

Complete this Item 1 if you are submitting an initial application for state registration or requesting additional state registration(s). Check the boxes next to the states to which you are submitting this application. If you are already registered with at least one state and are applying for registration with an additional state or states, check the boxes next to the states in which you are applying for registration. Do not check the boxes next to the states in which you are currently registered or where you have an application for registration pending.

☐ AL	☐ CT	☐ HI	☐ KY	☐ MN	☐ NH	☐ OH	☐ SC	☐ VA
☐ AK	☐ DE	☐ ID	☐ LA	☐ MS	☐ NJ	☐ OK	☐ SD	☐ WA
☐ AZ	☐ DC	☐ IL	☐ ME	☐ MO	☐ NM	☐ OR	☐ TN	☐ WV
☐ AR	☐ FL	☐ IN	☐ MD	☐ MT	☐ NY	☐ PA	☐ TX	☐ WI
☐ CA	☐ GA	☐ IA	☐ MA	☐ NE	☐ NC	☐ PR	☐ UT	
☐ CO	☐ GU	☐ KS	☐ MI	☐ NV	☐ ND	☐ RI	☐ VT	

Item 2   Additional Information

    A. *Person* responsible for supervision and compliance:

_____
(name)

_____
(title)

_____   _____
(area code)   (telephone number)   (area code)   (facsimile number)

_____
(number and street)

_____
(city)   (state/country)   (zip+4/postal code)

_____
(electronic mail (e-mail) address, if the *person* has one)

If this address is a private residence, check this box: ☐

    B. Bond/Capital Information, if required by your *home state*.

       (1) Name of Issuing Insurance Company:

       _____

       (2) Amount of Bond: $_____.00

       (3) Bond Policy Number:_____

	Yes	No
(4) If required by your *home state*, are you in compliance with your *home state's* minimum capital requirements?	☐	☐

FORM ADV	
Part 1B	Your Name _____ *CRD* Number _____
Page 2 of 4	Date _____ SEC 801-Number _____

	<u>Yes</u>	<u>No</u>

For "yes" answers to the following question, complete a Bond DRP:

   C. Has a bonding company ever denied, paid out on, or revoked a bond for you? ☐ ☐

For "yes" answers to the following question, complete a Judgment/Lien DRP:

   D. Do you have any unsatisfied judgments or liens against you? ☐ ☐

For "yes" answers to the following questions, complete an Arbitration DRP:

   E. Are you, any *advisory affiliate*, or any *management person* currently the subject of, or have you , any *advisory affiliate*, or any *management person* been the subject of, an arbitration claim alleging damages in excess of $2,500, involving any of the following:

     (1) any investment or an *investment-related* business or activity? ☐ ☐

     (2) fraud, false statement, or omission? ☐ ☐

     (3) theft, embezzlement, or other wrongful taking of property? ☐ ☐

     (4) bribery, forgery, counterfeiting, or extortion? ☐ ☐

     (5) dishonest, unfair, or unethical practices? ☐ ☐

For "yes" answers to the following questions, complete a Civil Judicial Action DRP:

   F. Are you, any *advisory affiliate*, or any *management person* currently subject to, or have you, any *advisory affiliate*, or any *management person* been *found* liable in, a civil, *self-regulatory organization*, or administrative *proceeding* involving any of the following:

     (1) an investment or *investment-related* business or activity? ☐ ☐

     (2) fraud, false statement, or omission? ☐ ☐

     (3) theft, embezzlement, or other wrongful taking of property? ☐ ☐

     (4) bribery, forgery, counterfeiting, or extortion? ☐ ☐

     (5) dishonest, unfair, or unethical practices? ☐ ☐

   G. Other Business Activities

     (1) Are you actively engaged in business as a(n) (check all that apply):

        ☐ Attorney
        ☐ Certified public accountant
        ☐ Tax preparer

FORM ADV Part 1B Page 3 of 4	Your Name _____ Date _____	*CRD* Number _____ SEC 801-Number _____

(2) If you are actively engaged in any business other than those listed in Item 6.A. of Part 1A or Item 2.G(1) of Part 1B, describe the business and the approximate amount of time spent on that business:

_____

_____

_____

_____

_____

_____

_____

_____

H. If you provide financial planning services, the investments made based on those services at the end of your last fiscal year totaled:

	Securities Investments	Non-Securities Investments
Under $100,000	☐	☐
$100,001 to $500,000	☐	☐
$500,001 to $1,000,000	☐	☐
$1,000,001 to $2,500,000	☐	☐
$2,500,001 to $5,000,000	☐	☐
More than $5,000,000	☐	☐

If securities investments are over $5,000,000, how much?
$ _____ (round to the nearest $1,000,000)

If non-securities investments are over $5,000,000, how much?
$ _____ (round to the nearest $1,000,000)

I. *Custody*

	Yes	No
(1) Do you withdraw advisory fees directly from your *clients'* accounts?	☐	☐
(2) Do you act as a general partner for any partnership or trustee for any trust in which your advisory *clients* are either partners of the partnership or beneficiaries of the trust?	☐	☐

(3) If you answered "yes" to Item 2.I(1) or 2.I(2), respond to the following:

	Yes	No
(a) Do you send a copy of your invoice to the custodian or trustee at the same time that you send a copy to the *client*?	☐	☐
(b) Do you send quarterly statements to your *clients* showing all disbursements for the custodian account, including the amount of the advisory fees?	☐	☐
(c) Do your *clients* provide written authorization permitting you to be paid directly for their accounts held by the custodian or trustee?	☐	☐
(d) If you are the general partner of a partnership, have you engaged an attorney or an independent certified public accountant to provide authority permitting each direct payment or any transfer of funds or securities from the partnership account?	☐	☐
(4) Do you require prepayment of fees of more than $500 per *client* and for six months or more in advance?	☐	☐

FORM ADV Part 1B Page 4 of 4	Your Name _____ Date _____	*CRD* Number _____ SEC 801-Number _____

J.   If you are organized as a sole proprietorship, please answer the following:

Yes   No

  (1) (a)   Have you passed, on or after January 1, 2000, the Series 65 examination?   ☐   ☐

     (b)   Have you passed, on or after January 1, 2000, the Series 66 examination
         and also passed, at any time, the Series 7 examination?   ☐   ☐

  (2) (a)   Do you have any investment advisory professional designations?   ☐   ☐

        If "no," you do not need to answer Item 2.J(2)(b).

     (b)   I have earned and I am in good standing with the organization that issued the following credential:

       ☐   1.   Certified Financial Planner ("CFP")

       ☐   2.   Chartered Financial Analyst ("CFA")

       ☐   3.   Chartered Financial Consultant ("ChFC")

       ☐   4.   Chartered Investment Counselor ("CIC")

       ☐   5.   Personal Financial Specialist ("PFS")

       ☐   6.   None of the above

  (3)   Your social security number: _____

FORM ADV

Uniform Application for Investment Adviser Registration

Part II - Page 1

OMB APPROVAL	
OMB Number:	3235-0049
Expires:	July 31, 2008
Estimated average burden hours per response.	9.402

Name of Investment Adviser:

Address:	(Number and Street)	(City)	(State)	(Zip Code)	Area Code:	Telephone number:
					( )	

This part of Form ADV gives information about the investment adviser and its business for the use of clients.
The information has not been approved or verified by any governmental authority.

Table of Contents

Item Number	Item	Page
1	Advisory Services and Fees	2
2	Types of Clients	2
3	Types of Investments	3
4	Methods of Analysis, Sources of Information and Investment Strategies	3
5	Education and Business Standards	4
6	Education and Business Background	4
7	Other Business Activities	4
8	Other Financial Industry Activities or Affiliations	4
9	Participation or Interest in Client Transactions	5
10	Conditions for Managing Accounts	5
11	Review of Accounts	5
12	Investment or Brokerage Discretion	6
13	Additional Compensation	6
14	Balance Sheet	6
	Continuation Sheet	Schedule F
	Balance Sheet, if required	Schedule G

(Schedules A, B, C, D, and E are included with Part I of this Form, for the use of regulatory bodies, and are not distributed to clients.)

Potential persons who are to respond to the collection of information contained in this form
are not required to respond unless the form displays a currently valid OMB control number.

FORM ADV **Part II - Page 2**	Applicant:	SEC File Number: 801-	Date:

1. A.   Advisory Services and Fees. (check the applicable boxes)   For each type of service provided, state the approximate % of total advisory billings from that service. (See instruction below.)

Applicant:

☐ (1) Provides investment supervisory services .... _____ **%**
☐ (2) Manages investment advisory accounts not involving investment supervisory services .... _____ **%**
☐ (3) Furnishes investment advice through consultations not included in either service described above .... _____ **%**
☐ (4) Issues periodicals about securities by subscription .... _____ **%**
☐ (5) Issues special reports about securities not included in any service described above .... _____ **%**
☐ (6) Issues, not as part of any service described above, any charts, graphs, formulas, or other devices which clients may use to evaluate securities .... _____ **%**
☐ (7) On more than an occasional basis, furnishes advice to clients on matters not involving securities ...... _____ **%**
☐ (8) Provides a timing service .... _____ **%**
☐ (9) Furnishes advice about securities in any manner not described above .... _____ **%**

(Percentages should be based on applicant's last fiscal year. If applicant has not completed its first fiscal year, provide estimates of advisory billings for that year and state that the percentages are estimates.)

                                                                                                    Yes   No
B.   Does applicant call any of the services it checked above financial planning or some similar term? .... ☐ ☐

C.   Applicant offers investment advisory services for: (check all that apply)

☐ (1) A percentage of assets under management   ☐ (4) Subscription fees

☐ (2) Hourly charges   ☐ (5) Commissions

☐ (3) Fixed fees (not including subscription fees) ☐ (6) Other

D.   For each checked box in A above, describe on Schedule F:

• the services provided, including the name of any publication or report issued by the adviser on a subscription basis or for a fee

• applicant's basic fee schedule, how fees are charged and whether its fees are negotiable

• when compensation is payable, and if compensation is payable before service is provided, how a client may get a refund or may terminate an investment advisory contract before its expiration date

2.   Types of clients - Applicant generally provides investment advice to: (check those that apply)

☐ A. Individuals   ☐ E. Trusts, estates, or charitable organizations

☐ B. Banks or thrift institutions   ☐ F. Corporations or business entities other than those listed above

☐ C. Investment companies   ☐ G. Other (describe on Schedule F)

☐ D. Pension and profit sharing plans

Answer all items. Complete amended pages in full, circle amended items and file with execution page (page 1).

FORM ADV Part II - Page 3	Applicant:	SEC File Number: 801-	Date:

3.   Types of Investments. Applicant offers advice on the following: (check those that apply)

□   A.   Equity securities

□   (1) exchange-listed securities
□   (2) securities traded over-the-counter
□   (3) foreign issuers

□   B.   Warrants

□   C.   Corporate debt securities (other than commercial paper)

□   D.   Commercial paper

□   E.   Certificates of deposit

□   F.   Municipal securities

     G.   Investment company securities:
□   (1) variable life insurance
□   (2) variable annuities
□   (3) mutual fund shares

□   H.   United States government securities

     I.   Options contracts on:
□   (1) securities
□   (2) commodities

     J.   Futures contracts on:

□   (1) tangibles
□   (2) intangibles

     K.   Interests in partnerships investing in:
□   (1) real estate
□   (2) oil and gas interests
□   (3) other (explain on Schedule F)

□   L.   Other (explain on Schedule F)

4.   Methods of Analysis, Sources of Information, and Investment Strategies.

A.   Applicant's security analysis methods include: (check those that apply)

(1) □   Charting

(2) □   Fundamental

(3) □   Technical

(4) □   Cyclical

(5) □   Other (explain on Schedule F)

B.   The main sources of information applicant uses include: (check those that apply)

(1) □   Financial newspapers and magazines

(2) □   Inspections of corporate activities

(3) □   Research materials prepared by others

(4) □   Corporate rating services

(5) □   Timing services

(6) □   Annual reports, prospectuses, filings with the Securities and Exchange Commission

(7) □   Company press releases

(8) □   Other (explain on Schedule F)

C.   The investment strategies used to implement any investment advice given to clients include: (check those that apply)

(1) □   Long term purchases (securities held at least a year)

(2) □   Short term purchases (securities sold within a year)

(3) □   Trading (securities sold within 30 days)

(4) □   Short sales

(5) □   Margin transactions

(6) □   Option writing, including covered options, uncovered options or spreading strategies

(7) □   Other (explain on Schedule F)

Answer all items. Complete amended pages in full, circle amended items and file with execution page (page 1).

FORM ADV	Applicant:	SEC File Number:	Date:
Part II - Page 4		801-	

5.   Education and Business Standards.

Are there any general standards of education or business experience that applicant requires of those involved in determining or giving investment advice to clients? ....   Yes ☐   No ☐

(If yes, describe these standards on Schedule F.)

6.   Education and Business Background.

For:

- each member of the investment committee or group that determines general investment advice to be given to clients, or

- if the applicant has no investment committee or group, each individual who determines general investment advice given to clients (if more than five, respond only for their supervisors)

- each principal executive officer of applicant or each person with similar status or performing similar functions.

On Schedule F, give the:

- name
- year of birth
- formal education after high school
- business background for the preceding five years

7.   Other Business Activities. (check those that apply)

☐   A.   Applicant is actively engaged in a business other than giving investment advice.

☐   B.   Applicant sells products or services other than investment advice to clients.

☐   C.   The principal business of applicant or its principal executive officers involves something other than providing investment advice.

(For each checked box describe the other activities, including the time spent on them, on Schedule F.)

8.   Other Financial Industry Activities or Affiliations. (check those that apply)

☐   A.   Applicant is registered (or has an application pending) as a securities broker-dealer.

☐   B.   Applicant is registered (or has an application pending) as a futures commission merchant, commodity pool operator or commodity trading adviser.

     C.   Applicant has arrangements that are material to its advisory business or its clients with a related person who is a:

☐   (1)   broker-dealer   ☐   (7)   accounting firm

☐   (2)   investment company   ☐   (8)   law firm

☐   (3)   other investment adviser   ☐   (9)   insurance company or agency

☐   (4)   financial planning firm   ☐   (10) pension consultant

☐   (5)   commodity pool operator, commodity trading   ☐   (11) real estate broker or dealer
          adviser or futures commission merchant

☐   (6)   banking or thrift institution   ☐   (12) entity that creates or packages limited partnerships

(For each checked box in C, on Schedule F identify the related person and describe the relationship and the arrangements.)

                                                                                                        Yes   No
     D.   Is applicant or a related person a general partner in any partnership in which clients are solicited to invest?. .   ☐   ☐

(If yes, describe on Schedule F the partnerships and what they invest in.)

Answer all items. Complete amended pages in full, circle amended items and file with execution page (page 1).

| **FORM ADV**
Part II - Page 5 | Applicant: | SEC File Number:
801- | Date: |

9.   Participation or Interest in Client Transactions.

Applicant or a related person: (check those that apply)

☐   A.   As principal, buys securities for itself from or sells securities it owns to any client.

☐   B.   As broker or agent effects securities transactions for compensation for any client.

☐   C.   As broker or agent for any person other than a client effects transactions in which client securities are sold to or bought from a brokerage customer.

☐   D.   Recommends to clients that they buy or sell securities or investment products in which the applicant or a related person has some financial interest.

☐   E.   Buys or sells for itself securities that it also recommends to clients.

(For each box checked, describe on Schedule F when the applicant or a related person engages in these transactions and what restrictions, internal procedures, or disclosures are used for conflicts of interest in those transactions.)

Describe, on Schedule F, your code of ethics, and state that you will provide a copy of your code of ethics to any client or prospective client upon request.

10.   Conditions for Managing Accounts. Does the applicant provide investment supervisory services, manage investment advisory accounts or hold itself out as providing financial planning or some similarly termed services *and* impose a minimum dollar value of assets or other conditions for starting or maintaining an account?

Yes ☐   No ☐

(If yes, describe on Schedule F)

11.   Review of Accounts. If applicant provides investment supervisory services, manages investment advisory accounts, or holds itself out as providing financial planning or some similarly termed services:

A.   Describe below the reviews and reviewers of the accounts. **For reviews**, include their frequency, different levels, and triggering factors. **For reviewers**, include the number of reviewers, their titles and functions, instructions they receive from applicant on performing reviews, and number of accounts assigned each.

B.   Describe below the nature and frequency of regular reports to clients on their accounts.

Answer all items. Complete amended pages in full, circle amended items and file with execution page (page 1).

FORM ADV Part II - Page 6	Applicant:	SEC File Number: 801-	Date:

12.   Investment or Brokerage Discretion.

A.   Does applicant or any related person have authority to determine, without obtaining specific client consent, the:

(1)   securities to be bought or sold? ....   Yes ☐   No ☐

(2)   amount of the securities to be bought or sold? ....   Yes ☐   No ☐

(3)   broker or dealer to be used? ....   Yes ☐   No ☐

(4)   commission rates paid? ....   Yes ☐   No ☐

B.   Does applicant or a related person suggest brokers to clients? ....   Yes ☐   No ☐

For each yes answer to A describe on Schedule F any limitations on the authority. For each yes to A(3), A(4) or B, describe on Schedule F the factors considered in selecting brokers and determining the reasonableness of their commissions. If the value of products, research and services given to the applicant or a related person is a factor, describe:

- the products, research and services

- whether clients may pay commissions higher than those obtainable from other brokers in return for those products and services

- whether research is used to service all of applicant's accounts or just those accounts paying for it; and

- any procedures the applicant used during the last fiscal year to direct client transactions to a particular broker in return for product and research services received.

13.   Additional Compensation.

Does the applicant or a related person have any arrangements, oral or in writing, where it:

A.   is paid cash by or receives some economic benefit (including commissions, equipment or non-research services) from a non-client in connection with giving advice to clients? ....   Yes ☐   No ☐

B.   directly or indirectly compensates any person for client referrals?..................................   Yes ☐   No ☐

(For each yes, describe the arrangements on Schedule F.)

14.   Balance Sheet. Applicant must provide a balance sheet for the most recent fiscal year on Schedule G if applicant:

- has custody of client funds or securities (unless applicant is registered or registering only with the Securities and Exchange Commission); or

- requires prepayment of more than $500 in fees per client and 6 or more months in advance

    Has applicant provided a Schedule G balance sheet?..   Yes ☐   No ☐

Answer all items. Complete amended pages in full, circle amended items and file with execution page (page 1).

Schedule F of **Form ADV** **Continuation Sheet for Form ADV Part II**	Applicant:	SEC File Number: 801-	Date:

(Do not use this Schedule as a continuation sheet for Form ADV Part I or any other schedules.)

1. Full name of applicant exactly as stated in Item 1A of Part I of Form ADV:	IRS Empl. Ident. No.:

Item of Form (identify)	Answer

Complete amended pages in full, circle amended items and file with execution page (page 1).

Schedule G of Form ADV Balance Sheet	Applicant:		SEC File Number: 801-	Date:

(Answers in Response to Form ADV Part II Item 14.)

1. Full name of applicant exactly as stated in Item 1A of Part I of Form ADV:	IRS Empl. Ident. No.:

Instructions

1. The balance sheet must be:

    A. Prepared in accordance with generally accepted accounting principles

    B. Audited by an independent public accountant

    C. Accompanied by a note stating the principles used to prepare it, the basis of included securities, and any other explanations required for clarity.

2. Securities included at cost should show their market or fair value parenthetically.

3. Qualifications and any accompanying independent accountant's report must conform to Article 2 of Regulation S-X (17 CFR 210.2-01 et. seq.).

4. Sole proprietor investment advisers:

    A. Must show investment advisory business assets and liabilities separate from other business and personal assets and liabilities

    B. May aggregate other business and personal asset and liabilities unless there is an asset deficiency in the total financial position.

Complete amended pages in full, circle amended items and file with execution page (page 1).

Schedule H of Form ADV Page 1	Applicant:	SEC File Number: 801-	Date:

(for sponsors of wrap fee programs)

Name of wrap fee program or programs described in attached brochure:

1. *Applicability of Schedule.* This Schedule must be completed by applicants that are compensated under a wrap fee program for sponsoring, organizing, or administering the program, or for selecting, or providing advice to clients regarding the selection of, other investment advisers in the program ("sponsors"). A wrap fee program is any program under which a specified fee or fees not based directly upon transactions in a client's account is charged for investment advisory services (which may include portfolio management or advice concerning the selection of other investment advisers) and execution of client transactions.

2. *Use of Schedule.* This Schedule sets forth the information the sponsor must include in the wrap fee brochure it is required to deliver or offer to deliver to clients and prospective clients of its wrap fee programs under Rule 204-3 under the federal Advisers Act and similar rules of jurisdictions. The wrap fee brochure prepared in response to this Schedule must be filed with the Commission and the jurisdictions as part of Form ADV by completing the identifying information on this Schedule and attaching the brochure. Brochures should be prepared separately, not on copies of this Schedule. Any wrap fee brochure filed with the Commission as part of an amendment to Form ADV shall contain in the upper right corner of the cover page the sponsors' registration number (801-).

3. *General Contents of Brochure.* Unlike Parts I and II of this form, this Schedule is not organized in "check-the-box" format. These instructions, including the requests for information in Item 7 below, should not be repeated in the brochure. Rather, this Schedule describes minimum disclosures that must be made in the brochure to satisfy the sponsor's duty to disclose all material facts about the sponsor and its wrap fee programs. **Nothing in this Schedule relieves the sponsor from any obligation under any provision of the federal Advisers Act or rules thereunder, or other federal or state law to disclose information to its advisory clients or prospective advisory clients not specifically required by this Schedule.**

4. *Multiple Sponsors.* If two or more persons fall within the definition of "sponsor" in Item 1 above for a single wrap fee program, only one such sponsor need complete the Schedule. The sponsors may choose among themselves the sponsor that will complete the Schedule.

5. *Omission of Inapplicable Information.* Any information not specifically required by this Schedule that is included in the brochure should be applicable to clients and prospective clients of the sponsor's wrap fee programs. If the sponsor is required to complete this Schedule with respect to more than one wrap fee program, the sponsor may omit from the brochure furnished to clients and prospective clients of any wrap fee program or programs information required by this Schedule that is not applicable to clients or prospective clients of that wrap fee program or programs. If a sponsor of more than one wrap fee program prepares separate wrap fee brochures for clients of different programs, each brochure must be filed with the Commission and the jurisdictions attached to a separate copy of this Schedule. Each such brochure must state that the sponsor sponsors other wrap fee programs and state how brochures for those programs may be obtained.

6. *Updating.* Sponsors are required to file an amendment to the brochure promptly after any information in the brochure becomes materially inaccurate. Amendments may be made by use of a "sticker", *i.e.*, a supplement affixed to the brochure that indicates what information is being added or updated and states the new or revised information, as long as the resulting brochure is readable. Stickers should be dated and should be incorporated into the text of the brochure when the brochure itself is revised.

7. *Contents of Brochure.* Include in the brochure prepared in response to this Schedule:

    (a) on the cover page, the sponsor's name, address, telephone number, and the following legend in bold type or some other prominent fashion:

    This brochure provides clients with information about [name of sponsor] and the [name of program or programs] that should be considered before becoming a client of the [name of program or programs]. This information has not been approved or verified by any governmental authority.

    (b) a table of contents reflecting the subject headings in the sponsor's brochure.

    (c) the amount of the wrap fee charged for each program or, if fees vary according to a schedule established by the sponsor, a table setting forth the fee schedule, whether such fees are negotiable, the portion of the total fee (or the range of such amounts) paid to persons providing advice to clients regarding the purchase or sale of specific securities under the program ("portfolio managers"), and the services provided under each program (including the types of portfolio management services);

Schedule H of Form ADV Page 2	Applicant:	SEC File Number: 801-	Date:

(d) a statement that the program may cost the client more or less than purchasing such services separately and a statement of the factors that bear upon the relative cost of the program (*e.g.,* the cost of the services if provided separately and the trading activity in the client's account);

(e) if applicable, a statement that the person recommending the program to the client receives compensation as a result of the client's participation in the program, that the amount of this compensation may be more than what the person would receive if the client participated in other programs of the sponsor or paid separately for investment advice, brokerage, and other services, and that the person may therefore have a financial incentive to recommend the wrap fee program over other programs or services;

(f) a description of the nature of any fees that the client may pay in addition to the wrap fee and the circumstances under which these fees may be paid (including, if applicable, mutual fund expenses and mark-ups, mark-downs, or spreads paid to market makers from whom securities were obtained by the wrap fee broker);

(g) how the program's portfolio managers are selected and reviewed, the basis upon which portfolio managers are recommended or chosen for particular clients, and the circumstances under which the sponsor will replace or recommend the replacement of the portfolio manager;

(h) (1) if applicable, a statement to the effect that portfolio manager performance information is not reviewed by the sponsor or a third party and/or that performance information is not calculated on a uniform and consistent basis,

(2) if performance information is reviewed to determine its accuracy, the name of the party who reviews the information and a brief description of the nature of the review,

(3) a reference to any standards (*i.e.,* industry standards or standards usely solely by the sponsor) under which performance information may be calculated;

(i) a description of the information about the client that is communicated by the sponsor to the client's portfolio manager, and how often or under what circumstances the sponsor provides updated information about the client to the portfolio manager;

(j) any restrictions on the ability of clients to contact and consult with portfolio managers;

(k) in narrative text, the information required by Items 7 and 8 of Part II of this form and, as applicable to clients of the wrap fee program, the information required by Items 2, 5, 6, 9A and C, 10, 11, 13 and 14 of Part II;

(l) if any practice or relationship disclosed in response to Item 7, 8, 9A, 9C and 13 of Part II presents a conflict between the interests of the sponsor and those of its clients, explain the nature of any such conflict of interest; and

(m) if the sponsor or its divisions or employees covered under the same investment adviser registration as the sponsor act as portfolio managers for a wrap fee program described in the brochure, a brief, general description of the investments and investment strategies utilized by those portfolio managers.

8. *Organization and Cross References.* Except for the cover page requirements in Item 7(a) above, information contained in the brochure need not follow the order of the items listed in Item 7. However, the brochure should not be organized in such a manner that important information called by the form is obscured.

Set forth below the page(s) of the brochure on which the various disclosures required by Item 7 are provided.

		Page(s)			*Page(s)*			*Page(s)*
Item	7(a)	cover	Item	7(f)		Item	7(j)	
	#7(b)			#7(g)			#7(k)	
	#7(c)			#7(h)			#7(l)	
	#7(d)			#7(i)			#7(m)	
	#7(e)							

Form ADV (Paper Version)
UNIFORM APPLICATION FOR INVESTMENT ADVISER REGISTRATION

DOMESTIC INVESTMENT ADVISER EXECUTION PAGE

You must complete the following Execution Page to Form ADV. This execution page must be signed and attached to your initial application for SEC registration and all amendments to registration.

Appointment of Agent for Service of Process

By signing this Form ADV Execution Page, you, the undersigned adviser, irrevocably appoint the Secretary of State or other legally designated officer, of the state in which you maintain your *principal office and place of business* and any other state in which you are submitting a *notice filing*, as your agents to receive service, and agree that such *persons* may accept service on your behalf, of any notice, subpoena, summons, *order* instituting *proceedings*, demand for arbitration, or other process or papers, and you further agree that such service may be made by registered or certified mail, in any federal or state action, administrative *proceeding* or arbitration brought against you in any place subject to the jurisdiction of the United States, if the action, *proceeding* or arbitration (a) arises out of any activity in connection with your investment advisory business that is subject to the jurisdiction of the United States, and (b) is *founded,* directly or indirectly, upon the provisions of: (i) the Securities Act of 1933, the Securities Exchange Act of 1934, the Trust Indenture Act of 1939, the Investment Company Act of 1940, or the Investment Advisers Act of 1940, or any rule or regulation under any of these acts, or (ii) the laws of the state in which you maintain your *principal office and place of business* or of any state in which you are submitting a *notice filing.*

Signature

I, the undersigned, sign this Form ADV on behalf of, and with the authority of, the investment adviser. The investment adviser and I both certify, under penalty of perjury under the laws of the United States of America, that the information and statements made in this ADV, including exhibits and any other information submitted, are true and correct, and that I am signing this Form ADV Execution Page as a free and voluntary act.

I certify that the adviser's books and records will be preserved and available for inspection as required by law. Finally, I authorize any *person* having custody or possession of these books and records to make them available to federal and state regulatory representatives.

Signature: _____   Date: _____

Printed Name: _____   Title: _____

Adviser *CRD* Number: _____

Form ADV (Paper Version)
UNIFORM APPLICATION FOR INVESTMENT ADVISER REGISTRATION

STATE-REGISTERED INVESTMENT ADVISER EXECUTION PAGE

You must complete the following Execution Page to Form ADV. This execution page must be signed and attached to your initial application for state registration and all amendments to registration.

1. Appointment of Agent for Service of Process

By signing this Form ADV Execution Page, you, the undersigned adviser, irrevocably appoint the legally designated officers and their successors, of the state in which you maintain your *principal office and place of business* and any other state in which you are applying for registration or amending your registration, as your agents to receive service, and agree that such *persons* may accept service on your behalf, of any notice, subpoena, summons, *order* instituting *proceedings*, demand for arbitration, or other process or papers, and you further agree that such service may be made by registered or certified mail, in any federal or state action, administrative *proceeding* or arbitration brought against you in any place subject to the jurisdiction of the United States, if the action, *proceeding* or arbitration (a) arises out of any activity in connection with your investment advisory business that is subject to the jurisdiction of the United States, and (b) is *founded*, directly or indirectly, upon the provisions of: (i) the Securities Act of 1933, the Securities Exchange Act of 1934, the Trust Indenture Act of 1939, the Investment Company Act of 1940, or the Investment Advisers Act of 1940, or any rule or regulation under any of these acts, or (ii) the laws of the state in which you maintain your *principal office and place of business* or of any state in which you are applying for registration, or amending your registration.

2. State-Registered Investment Adviser Affidavit

If you are subject to state regulation, by signing this Form ADV, you represent that, you are in compliance with the registration requirements of the state in which you maintain your *principal place of business* and are in compliance with the bonding, capital, and recordkeeping requirements of that state.

Signature

I, the undersigned, sign this Form ADV on behalf of, and with the authority of, the investment adviser. The investment adviser and I both certify, under penalty of perjury under the laws of the United States of America, that the information and statements made in this ADV, including exhibits and any other information submitted, are true and correct, and that I am signing this Form ADV Execution Page as a free and voluntary act.

I certify that the adviser's books and records will be preserved and available for inspection as required by law. Finally, I authorize any *person* having custody or possession of these books and records to make them available to federal and state regulatory representatives.

Signature: _____ Date: _____

Printed Name: _____ Title: _____

Adviser *CRD* Number: _____

Form ADV (Paper Version)
UNIFORM APPLICATION FOR INVESTMENT ADVISER REGISTRATION

NON-RESIDENT INVESTMENT ADVISER EXECUTION	PAGE 1

You must complete the following Execution Page to Form ADV. This execution page must be signed and attached to your initial application for SEC registration and all amendments to registration.

1. Appointment of Agent for Service of Process

By signing this Form ADV Execution Page, you, the undersigned adviser, irrevocably appoint each of the Secretary of the SEC, and the Secretary of State or other legally designated officer, of any other state in which you are submitting a *notice filing*, as your agents to receive service, and agree that such *persons* may accept service on your behalf, of any notice, subpoena, summons, *order* instituting *proceedings*, demand for arbitration, or other process or papers, and you further agree that such service may be made by registered or certified mail, in any federal or state action, administrative *proceeding* or arbitration brought against you in any place subject to the jurisdiction of the United States, if the action, *proceeding* or arbitration (a) arises out of any activity in connection with your investment advisory business that is subject to the jurisdiction of the United States, and (b) is *founded,* directly or indirectly, upon the provisions of: (i) the Securities Act of 1933, the Securities Exchange Act of 1934, the Trust Indenture Act of 1939, the Investment Company Act of 1940, or the Investment Advisers Act of 1940, or any rule or regulation under any of these acts, or (ii) the laws of any state in which you are submitting a *notice filing*.

2. Appointment and Consent: Effect on Partnerships

If you are organized as a partnership, this irrevocable power of attorney and consent to service of process will continue in effect if any partner withdraws from or is admitted to the partnership, provided that the admission or withdrawal does not create a new partnership. If the partnership dissolves, this irrevocable power of attorney and consent shall be in effect for any action brought against you or any of your former partners.

3. *Non-Resident* Investment Adviser Undertaking Regarding Books and Records

By signing this Form ADV, you also agree to provide, at your own expense, to the U.S. Securities and Exchange Commission at its principal office in Washington D.C., at any Regional or District Office of the Commission, or at any one of its offices in the United States, as specified by the Commission, correct, current, and complete copies of any or all records that you are required to maintain under Rule 204-2 under the Investment Advisers Act of 1940. This undertaking shall be binding upon you, your heirs, successors and assigns, and any *person* subject to your written irrevocable consents or powers of attorney or any of your general partners and *managing agents*.

Signature

I, the undersigned, sign this Form ADV on behalf of, and with the authority of, the *non-resident* investment adviser. The investment adviser and I both certify, under penalty of perjury under the laws of the United States of America, that the information and statements made in this ADV, including exhibits and any other information submitted, are true and correct, and that I am signing this Form ADV Execution Page as a free and voluntary act.

I certify that the adviser's books and records will be preserved and available for inspection as required by law. Finally, I authorize any *person* having custody or possession of these books and records to make them available to federal and state regulatory representatives.

Signature: _____   Date: _____

Printed Name: _____   Title: _____

Adviser *CRD* Number: _____

Index

Numerics

401(k) plans, 313
403(b) plans, 304
  contribution limits, 306
  definition of employee, 306
  eligibility requirements, 305
  tax advantages, 304
70% corporate dividend exclusion, 370

A

access person, 146
account
  approval, 328
  fiduciary and custodial, 334
  opening cash and margin accounts, 329
accounts receivable, 397
accredited investor, 13
active
  and passive management, 366
administrative personnel
  exclusions from definition of agent, 56
ADRs, 199
ADSs, 199
after-tax return, 421
agency cross transactions, 165
agent, 56
  effective date of registration, 63
  fee and commission sharing, 59
  termination procedures, 61
aggressive investor, 358
alternative minimum tax. *See AMT*
American Depositary Receipt (ADR), 199
American Depositary Shares (ADSs), 199
AMT, 371
analysis
  fundamental, 395
  technical, 409
annualized returns from investment, 421
annuity
  advantages, 254
  disadvantages, 255
  payments, variables, 247
  plans, 242, 244
  receiving distributions from, 249
  taxation 252-253
appeals, 35, 103

arbitrage, 89
ask price, 231
assessable stock, 92-93
asset
  allocation, 364
  current asset, 398
  fixed, 398
  other, 398
assumed interest rate (AIR), 251
average
  cost basis, 373

B

back-end load, 234
balance
  sheet equation, 397
basic economics, 385
benchmark portfolios, 432
beneficial owner, 331
beneficiary, 303
beta coefficient, 394
bid price, 231
blue-sky law. *See also* registration
  requirements, state
bond
  callable, 218
  convertible, 218
  high-yield, 212
  pricing, 215
  ratings, 211
  secured debt, 205
  tax-equivalent yield, 215
  yield computations, 213, 418-420
  zero-coupon, 217
book value, 403
borrowing money or securities from
  clients, 87
breakout, 412
breakpoint, 33
brochure rule, 147, 148
broker/dealer
  Canadian, 59
  definition of, 51
  differences between, 281
  role of, 280
  registration requirements, 53
business cycle
  characteristics of contractions, 387

characteristics of expansions, 387
business risk, 429
buy and hold technique, 367

C

C corporation, 357
CCO, 171
call
  money rate, 390
callable, 198
cancellation of registration, 100
capital asset pricing model, 395
capital
  gains and losses, 191, 372
call protection, 218
Canadian broker/dealer and agent
  registration, 59
carryover basis, 375
cash and equivalents, 397
cash flow statement, 406
cash flow, 406
cash referral fees, 165
catch-up contributions
  for older IRA owners, 292
CDs, 359
cease and desist orders, 12, 97, 98
chief compliance officer, 171
churning, 23, 86
civil liabilities, 101
Class A shares, 234
Class B shares, 234
Class C shares, 234
client personal profile, 357
clients
  types of, 351
closed-end investment company, 28
COGS, 405
coincident indicator, 392
college savings plans, 301
commingling, 88
common stock, 191
  benefits of owning, 191
  limited liability, 193
  proxy voting, 193
  risks, 194
  voting rights, 192
comparison of IRAs and Keogh Plans, 303
completely diversified portfolio, 395

conduct investigations, 97

consent to service of process, 62

conservative investor, 358

conservator accounts, 335

consolidation, 410

control person
  investment advisor, 141
  investment company, 32
  stock, 14

conversion privilege, 237

convertible, 198

cooling off period, 10

coordination, registration by, 72

corporate
  account, 333
  resolution, 333

corporate financial statements, 396

corporate taxes, 370

correlation coefficient, 424

cost basis, 372
  inherited securities, 375
  gifted securities, 375
  purchased securities, 372

cost of goods sold, (COGS), 406

counter-cyclical industries, 396

Coverdell Education Savings Accounts
  (Coverdell ESAs), 294, 360, 363

covered call writing, 267

CPI, 422

credit agreement, 330

criminal penalties
  SEC, 34
  USA, 102

CTR, 35

cumulative preferred stock, 197

currency risk, 199

currency transaction reports, (CTR), 35

custodial account, 336

custody of funds and securities, 150, 151

customer
  account, 325
  complaints, 90

cyclical industry, 396

D

day order, 282

de minimis exemption, 132, 133

debenture, 206

decreased or no income, 194

deferred compensation plan, 317

defined benefit plan, 313

defined contribution plan, 313

denial of registration, 99

depreciation, 406

derivative, 260

developed markets, 200

disclosure and consent, 158

discount rate, 389

discretion, 19, 87

discretionary account, 339
  account, 339
  power, 329

distributable net income, 354

diversification modern portfolio theory
  and, 416

dividend exclusion rule, 370

dividend payout ratio, 408

DNI. *See Distributable net income*

dollar cost averaging, 368

donee, 375

donor, 338

Dow Jones Industrial Average, 414

DRIPs, 369

duration, 426

E

earnings multiplier, 395

earnings per share, 406, 407

EBIT, 405

economic activity: barometers of, 392

economic concepts
  efficient market hypothesis, 415
  future value, 416–417
  liquidity, 431
  opportunity cost, 431
  present value, 416
  random walk, theory, 416

Economic Growth and Tax Relief
  Reconciliation Act of 2001, 292

Education IRA, 294, 360

efficient market hypothesis, 415

EGTRRA, 292

emerging markets, 200

Employee Retirement Income Security
  Act of 1974, 307
  fiduciary responsibility, 307
  investment policy statement, 311

EPS, 407

Equipment trust certificate, 205

equity REITs, 202

ERISA, 307
  Section 404, 310

escrow, 80

estate and gift taxes, 376

eurobond, 395

exceptions to jurisdiction
  broadcast, 94
  publishing, 94

excess IRA contributions, 296

exchange market, 279

exchange privilege, 237

exempt securities, 57
  federal, 5
  state, 7, 74

exempt transactions, 57
  federal, 7
  state, 75

expected returns, 422

F

face-amount certificate companies, 229

federal covered investment adviser, 135

federal covered security, 69

Federal Reserve Board (FRB), 330, 388

fiduciary accounts, 334

fiduciary, 125, 157, 212, 335

FIFO, 373, 405

filing fees, 62

financial goals, 359

financial statements
  analysis tools, 396
  footnotes, 404

FinCEN Form 104, 35

first-in first-out method, 405

fixed assets, 397

fixed rate of return, 196

foreign investments, 199

foreign markets: investment risks, 200

Form ADV, 136

Form ADV-W, 138

fraudulent and prohibited practices, 101
  sale of securities, 81

FRB, 330

front-end load, 234

front-running, 89-91

fundamental investment analysis, 395

Future value, 416–417

G

general obligation bond, 207

gift tax exclusion, 376

gift tax, 376

GO bond, 207

grantor, 352

gross domestic product (GDP), 385, 391

gross national product (GNP), 391

growth, 191

guaranteed bond, 206

guardian
  account, 335

H

head and shoulders, 410
hedge clauses, 158
HR-10 plans. *See* Keogh (HR-10) plans
hypothecation
  agreement, 330

I

impersonal investment advice, 165
in arrears, 197
income reinvestment, 369
income statement, 405
  components of, 405
income taxes, 370
income, 192
incomplete information, 328
indicators
  coincident, 393
  lagging, 393
  leading, 393
individual account, 331
individual retirement account, 291
  characteristics of, 296
  contributions, 296
  excess contributions, 296
  ineligible investments, 297
  nondeductible capital withdrawals, 294
  participation, 296
  rollovers, 297
  transfers, 297
  withdrawal options, 293
individual retirement arrangements, 291
individual retirement plans, 293
  withdrawal options, 293
industries
  counter-cyclical, 396
inflation adjusted return, 422
inflation risk, 430
inflation
  causes of, 387
initial application, 61
initial public offerings. *See* IPO
initial public offerings (IPOs)
  registration of, 3–4
inside information, 85
insider, 21
institutional investor, 78
Interest rate risk, 430
interest rates, 388
  nominal and real, 389
internal rate of return, 423
intrastate offering, 7
inventory, 398

investment adviser advertising, 159
investment adviser code of ethics, 144, 146
investment adviser compensation, 128
investment adviser contracts, 162
investment adviser representative, 60, 126, 141
  termination procedures, 63
Investment Adviser Act of 1940, 123, 125
Investment Company Act of 1940, 27, 229
investment company securities, 229
investment company, 27, 229
  affiliated person, 33
  control person, 33
  contracts with advisers, 32
  diversified, 28, 228
  minimum size, 32
  nondiversified, 28, 228
  transactions of affiliated persons, 32
  types, 27, 225
investment counsel, 138
investment discretion, 19
investment policy statement, 311
investment style
  buy/hold, 367
  growth, 366
  indexing, 367
  value, 366
IPO, 3, 66
IRAs, 291
IRR, 423
irrevocable life insurance trust, 361
isolated nonissuer transaction, 76
issuer transaction, 67
issuer, 56

J

jagging indicator, 390
joint account, 332
joint account: agreement, 332
joint tenants with right of survivorship (JTWROS), 332
JTWROS, 332
Judicial Review of Orders, 103

K

keogh plan, 302
  eligibility, 302
  nontax-deductible contributions, 302

L

lagging indicator, 393
large cap stock, 367, 432
last-in first out, 405
leading indicator, 393
legal list, 335
legislative risk, 430
lending money to clients, 87
letter of intent, 235
leverage, financial, 403
liabilities, 397, 398
  long-term, 398
LIFO, 405
limit order, 283
limited liability, 255
  as a partner, 255
  as a stockbroker, 193-194
limited partners, 255
limited partnership (LP), 255
limited power of attorney, 340
limited trading authorization, 336
liquidity risk, 431
LLC, 356
loan
  consent, 330
LOI, 235
long stock and short calls, 267

M

maintenance of investment adviser
  records, 146
management investment company, 230
margin agreement, 330
margin on new issues, 22
margin
  account, 329, 330
market capitalization, 367
market maker, 14, 280
market manipulation, 88
market order, 282, 283
market risk, 424, 429
market theory
  odd lot, 415
  short interest, 415
  technical, 415
markets
  securities, 279
markup, 281
matched orders, 23, 89
material
  fact, 82
  inside information, 85
mid cap stock, 367, 432

minimum capital requirements, 54
ministerial personnel, 56
minus tick, 279
misleading statements
   material fact, 85
modern portfolio theory, 416
money laundering, 35
money supply, 386
Monte Carlo simulations techniques,
   427–428
mortgage REITs, 202
moving averages, 412
municipal securities, 370
mutual fund, 233
   advantages, 245
   characteristics, 233
   disadvantages, 245
   expense ratio, 241
   performance, 241
   portfolio turnover, 241
   suitability, 242
   taxation, 242

N

NASAA, 47
NASAA Statements of Policy
   Appendix B, C
National Conference of Commissioners on
   Uniform State Laws (NCCUSL), 47
National Securities Markets Improvement
   Act of 1996 (NSMIA), 68, 125, 132
net asset value (NAV), 231
net present value, 423
net worth requirements, 58
net worth, 397
new account form, 327
New York Stock Exchange (NYSE), 277
nominal rate of interest, 389
nominal yield, 422
nominal yield curve, 388
nonexempt security, 65
nonissuer transaction, 57, 66
nonqualified corporate retirement plans, 316
   types, 317
nonqualified deferred compensation plan,
   317
nonqualified plan, 316
normal yield curve, 390
North American Securities Administrators
   Association (NASAA), 47
notice filing, 71

notification, 70
NPV, 423
NYSE, 277, 279

O

odd-lot theory, 415
offer: to sell, 92
omitting prospectus, 9
open-end investment company, 28, 230
opportunity cost, 431
optimal portfolio, 432
options, 260
   at-the-money, 263
   contracts, 260
   hedging, 267
   in-the-money, 262
   long-term equity, 261
   out-of-the-money, 263
order tickets, 23
OTC, 277, 279
overbought, 409
oversold, 410
over-the-counter (OTC) market, 277

P

paid-in surplus, 400
par value, 196
partnership agreement, 257
partnership investments, 256
partnership
   account, 333
passive income, 296
passive management style, 366
payroll deduction plans, 317
penalties for early withdrawal from
   retirement plans, 293, 303
pension consultant, 127, 134
performance fees, 164
pegging, 23
person, definition
   federal, 4
   state, 48
persons
   Regulated by the Uniform Securities
      Act, 125
person associated with an investment
   adviser, 126
plus (up) tick, 279
portfolio income, 371
portfolio management

active and passive, 366
   styles and strategies, 364
positive yield curve, 390
power of attorney, 329, 334, 336
preferred stock
   callable preferred, 198
   cumulative preferred, 197
   features of, 196
   straight (noncumulative), 197
   adjustable-rate preferred, 197
pre-organization certificate, 77
prepaid expenses, 398
prepaid tuition plans, 301
present value, 417
price to earnings multiple, 432
price-to-earning (P/E) ratio, 395
primary market, 279
prior written authority, 86
private placement
   under federal law, 11
   under state law, 78
private rights of action, 24
private securities transaction, 90, 479
profit-sharing plan, 313
progressive cost, 370
progressive tax, 370
prohibited practices, 81, 89
prohibited transactions under ERISA, 311
property dividends, 192
proportionate sharing, 88
prospectus, 3–5, 9
prudent investor rule, 308
public educational 403(b), 305
public offering price (POP), 231
publicly traded fund, 231

Q

qualification, 73
qualified corporate retirement plans, 307
qualified custodian, 152
quantitative evaluation, 416
quote, 282

R

random walk theory, 416
rate
   broker call loan, 394
   call loan or money, 394
   discount, 393
   federal funds, 393

prime, 393

real estate investment trust (REIT), 202

real return, 422

realized gain, 192

realized losses, 374

red herring prospectus, 9

redeemable security, 231

redeemable, 198

registered owner, 199

registered representatives, 56

Registration of Securities under the USA

by coordination, 71

by notice filing, 71

by notification, 70

by qualification, 72

effective date, (coordination), 72

effective date, (qualification), 73

withdrawal of a registration, 81

registration requirements

federal

for securities and exchange, 15

prospectus, 3–4

regressive tax, 370

Regulation A, 6

Regulation D, 12

regulatory risk, 430

Release IA-1092. *See* SEC Release
IA-1092

required minimum distributions, 293, 315,
371

rescission, 102

resistance level, 412

restricted security, 13

revenue bond, 207

rights of accumulation, 235

rights, 203

of rescission, 101

of succession, 332

voting, 192

risk adjusted return, 422

risk

liquidity, 431

market, 194, 429

Monte Carlo simulation, as analytical
tools, 427–428

nonsystemic, 424–425

of Inflation, 430

of interest rates, 430

of owning stock, 194

regulatory, 430–431

Sharpe ratio, 426

systemic (systematic), 424, 429

unsystematic, 424

RMDs. *See* required minimum
distributions

rollovers, 297

Roth IRA, 291, 295, 363

Rule 12b-1, 30

Rule 147, 6

Rule 482, 9

Rule 72t, 293, 315

Rule of 72, 418

Russell 2000, 432

S

S corporation, 356

S&P 400, 432

S&P 500, 413, 432

safe harbor

401(k) plan, 311

ERISA Section 404(c), 308

Section 28(e) soft dollars, 168

sale, 4, 92

Schedule D, 21

Schedule G, 22

Schedule I, 136

SEC disclaimer, 11

SEC Release IA-1092, 126, 127

secondary market, 279

Section 13(f) filings, 21

Section 13(f) filings, 21

Section 16 filings, 22

Section 28(e), 169

Section 529 Plans, 301, 360, 363

sector fund, 232

Securities Act of 1933, 3, 229

Securities and Exchange Commission (SEC)

creation of, 15

regulatory power of, 14

Securities Exchange Act of 1934, 54, 55

Securities information processor, 16

securities

correlation coefficient between, 424

donated, 375

gifted, 375

inherited, 375

standard deviation of, 425

security, definition of

federal, 3

state, 63

self regulatory organization.. *See* SRO

sell, 92

selling away, 89

SEP IRA, 299

separate account, 247

SEPs, 299

settlor, 352

share identification, 373

shareholders' equity, 399

shares of beneficial interest, 230

sharing in client accounts, 88

Sharpe ratio, 426

short interest theory, 415

simplified employee pensions

funding, 299

participation, 299

vesting, 299

small cap stock, 367, 432

specialist, 279

soft dollar compensation, 169

sole proprietorship, 356

solicitors, 165

solo 401(k), 313

specialized funds, 232

SRO, 14, 17

stabilizing, 23

Standard deviation, 425

statistical concepts

correlation coefficient, 424

Monte Carlo simulation, 427–428

standard deviation, 425

statutory disqualification, 18

stock ahead, 283

stock dividends, 192

stock exchange, 17

stock market indexes and averages, 413

stock

benefits of owning, 191

common, 191

preferred, 191

stop order, 284

straight preferred stock, 197

strategic asset allocation, 365

street name, 330, 338

structured transactions, 35

subordinated debt, 207

suitability information, 328

suitability requirements, 86

support level, 412

surety bonds, 54

systematic risk, 395

T

tactical asset allocation, 365

tax reporting for partnerships, 258

taxation of foreign securities, 377

taxation, 313, 317, 370

tax-exempt 501(c)3, 305

Taxpayer Relief Act of 1997, 291

tax-sheltered annuities, 304

tenants in common (TIC), 332

third-party account, 334

TIC, 332

time horizon, 363
time value of money, 416
time, 341
Tippee, 24
Tipper, 24
TIPS, 209
TOD account, 332
top-heavy 401(k), 314
total returns from investment, 420
trading authorization, 86, 334, 340
traditional IRAs, 291
transfer agent, 16
transfer on death, 332
treasury bill, 208
treasury bond, 209
Treasury Inflation Protection Securities, 209
treasury note, 208
treble damages, 24
trendline, 410
trigger, 284
trust accounts, 334, 335
trustee, 335

trusts, 351–353
  complex, 352
  irrevocable, 354
  living, 353
  revocable, 353
  simple, 352
  testamentary, 353
TSA, 304

U

UGMA, 336, 338
underwriter, 4
Uniform Prudent Investor Act of 1994, 308
Uniform Transfers to Minors Act (UTMA), 336
Uni-k, 313
unit investment trust UIT, 230
unmanaged investment company, 230
unsolicited transaction, 76
unsuitable investment recommendations, 85
unsystematic risk, 395
untrue statements, 82
UTMA, 336

V

Violation of the Uniform Securities Act
  civil liabilities, 101
  criminal penalties, 102

W

warrant, 203
wash sale
  market manipulation, 23
  tax rule, 246
withdrawal of registration, 100
wrap account, 334
wrap fee programs, 149

Y

yield curve, 388
  inverted, 390
yield, 421

Z

zero-coupon bonds, 360

HotSheets

Securities Act of 1933

— Nonexempt issuers must file registration statements with the SEC

— Requires use of prospectus when selling new issues

— Requires full and fair disclosure of new issues

— Regulates primary market activity (issuing and underwriting)

— 20-day cooling-off period—no orders, sales, advertising, or sales literature

Regulation A

— $5 million or less in 12 months

— Offering circular for disclosure

Regulation D (Private Placements)

— No more than 35 nonaccredited investors

— Unlimited accredited investors

— Institutions, broker/dealers, individuals with net worth of $1 million or income of more than $200,000 single, $300,000 married, in last 2 years

— Sign investment letter; hold for 1 year

— Private placement memorandum (circular) for disclosure

Rule 144

— 1-year hold on restricted securities; insiders or noninsiders

— Insiders cannot sell short; short-swing profits must be disgorged

Rule 144A

— No holding period on unregistered securities sold to qualified institutional buyers (QIBs)

Rule 147

— Home office in state; 80% of business and assets in state

— Only state residents can buy; no resale to nonresidents for 9 months

Securities Exchange Act of 1934

— Regulates secondary market activity

— Requires registration of representatives and firms that trade securities for the public

— Oversees exchanges and OTC market

— Regulates extension of credit

— Prohibits fraudulent trading activities

— Regulates insider transactions, short sales, proxies, and client accounts

— Prohibits use of inside information

Investment Company Act of 1940

— Defines and regulates investment companies

— 3 types: FAC, unit investment trust, and management company

— Insurance company separate accounts are investment companies

Open-End Company

— Mutual fund

— Continuous primary offering; NAV calculated once per business day; no-load shares sold at NAV

Closed-End Company

— Trade in secondary market; sold with prospectus in IPO only

Management Companies

— SEC exemption required for someone guilty of crime in past 10 years or under court injunction to serve

— No more than 60% of directors can be interested

— Change in investment objective requires majority vote of outstanding shares

— Advisers and affiliates cannot buy property from fund (may invest in fund)

— Cannot sell property or securities to fund, borrow money or property

— Annual SEC reports filed; semiannual reports to shareholders with portfolio list

— Destruction, falsification of records, and guaranteeing performance are grounds for civil action and penalties

— No deceptive names for fund

— Records/accounts subject to SEC audit at any time

Contract Between Fund Company and Manager

— 2-year initial contract; approved by both majority of outstanding shares and board of directors

— Renewed annually by majority of outstanding shares or board of directors

— Terminate without penalty by majority vote of outstanding shares or board of directors with no more than 60 days' notice

— No assignment of responsibilities to third party

— Written contract; includes description of compensation

— Breach of fiduciary duty to receive excess compensation

— Manager must be registered under the Investment Advisers Act of 1940

Insider Trading and Securities Fraud Enforcement Act of 1988 (ITSFEA)

— Tippers and tippees can be liable

— Penalties up to the greater of $1 million or 3 times profits made/losses avoided

— Broker/dealers must have written supervisory procedures

— Chinese walls prohibit sensitive information from being passed between departments of firms

— Private rights of action against contemporaneous traders

HotSheets

Person

— Individual, company, association, or government

Broker/Dealer Registration

— Must register in state where business is done unless exempt
— Effective after Administrator notification; expires December 31

Exempt from State Registration as a Broker/Dealer

— Banks, savings institutions, other financial institutions, agents, issuers
— Broker/dealers with no office in state only doing business with institutions
— Broker/dealers registered in another state transacting business with a current client passing through a different state

Exemptions from Agent Registration

— Represents issuer in exempt transaction
— Represents issuer in exempt securities
— Represents issuer in sale of employee benefit plans
— Must not receive compensation that is sale related

Agent Registration

— Agents must be registered in state of residence of the client where securities are offered, and where securities are sold
— Agents who represent broker/dealers must be registered if they sell exempt or nonexempt securities
— Broker/dealers can only employ registered agents
— Agents who represent issuers generally must be registered if they sell nonexempt securities

— Effective after Administrator notification, no later than noon of the 30th day; expires December 31

— Notification by agent and old and new broker/dealer for employment change

— Notification by state-registered investment adviser or investment adviser representative of federal covered adviser for employment change

— Automatic registration of partners, officers, and directors when new broker/dealers and investment advisers register

Investment Adviser Registration

— File Form ADV and appropriate fees

— Effective after Administrator notification, no later than noon of the 30th day; expires December 31

Investment Adviser Recordkeeping

— All specific customer and investment adviser records kept for 5 years; must be kept in investment adviser's principal office for the first 2 years

Security (Howey Decision)

— Investment of money

— Common enterprise

— Expectation of profits

— Solely from efforts of others

Nonexempt Security

— Must register

Issuer

— Company, government, or government subdivision that offers or proposes to offer securities

Nonissuer

— Secondary market transaction

— Proceeds do not go to issuer

Primary Offering

— Initial public offering and any subsequent offering of new securities

Methods of Registration

— Coordination, qualification

Notice Filing

— Federal covered investment company securities—file documents with states, pay fees

Exempt Security

— No registration under USA required
— Look at who the issuer is
— Still subject to antifraud provisions

Exempt Transaction

— Transaction need not be registered under USA
— Look at who the purchaser is or how the trade is made

Practices Prohibited of All Securities Professionals

— Misleading or untrue statements
— Failure to state material facts
— Use of insider information
— Unsuitable transactions
— Market manipulation (pegging, front running, wash sales, matched purchases)

Other Prohibited Sales Practices

— Unauthorized third-party trading
— Borrowing money from customers who are not banks, broker/dealers, or lending institutions
— Commingling client funds with those of the agent or the firm
— Failing to follow client instructions

— Exercising discretion without written authority

— Effecting transactions not on the books (selling away)

— Failing to report written complaints

— Guaranteeing against loss

— Failing to inform clients of higher than normal charges

— Misrepresenting customer account status

— Creating misleading trading activity

— Promising undeliverable services

— Unauthorized sharing in customer accounts

— Solicitation of unregistered, nonexempt securities

— Misrepresenting Administrator approval

USA as Model Legislation

— USA is not actual but model legislation for each state's own legislation

NSMIA of 1996

— Eliminates state and federal registration duplication

Federal Covered Securities

— Covered by national, not state, regulation

— Includes securities listed on US exchanges, Nasdaq Stock Market, issued by investment companies, or sold under Regulation D (Private Placement)

— Includes government and municipal bonds (but not municipal bonds issued within that state)

Administrator

— State official responsible for the implementation of the USA

Powers of the Administrator

— Make rules and orders

— Conduct investigations and issue subpoenas

— Issue cease and desist orders and seek injunctions

— Deny, suspend, cancel, or revoke registrations

Fraud

— Willful misrepresentation for unlawful gain

Civil Liabilities

— Attorney's costs *plus* losses on investment *plus* interest *minus* any income received

Rescission

— Right to rescind a transaction in violation of the USA—30-day letter

Criminal Penalties

— Fines, imprisonment, or both

Statute of Limitations

— Time limits for bringing suit in a case
— Civil—3 years from date of sale or of rendering of advice or 2 years after discovering violation, whichever occurs first
— Criminal—5 years after date of the transaction

HotSheets

Purpose of the Investment Advisers Act of 1940

— Regulation of individuals and firms in the business of providing investment advice

— Creation of ethical rules of business conduct

1940 Act Definition of Investment Adviser

— Person who, for compensation and as part of a business, provides advice about securities

— Advice could be provided directly or via publications

Federal versus State Regulation

— Federally registered if adviser manages $30 million or more

— State registered if adviser manages less than $25 million

— Adviser has choice of federal or state registration if managing at least $25 but less than $30 million

— Investment company advisers register federally

Federal Exclusions from the Definition of Investment Adviser

— Banks and bank holding companies

— Lawyers, accountants, teachers, or engineers if advice is solely incidental to the professional practice

— Broker/dealers if advice is solely incidental to their business and no special compensation is received for advice

— Publishers of newspapers, magazines, or business and financial publication of general and regular circulation

— Persons who provide advice exclusively relating to US government securities

State Exclusions from the Definition of Investment Adviser

— Investment adviser representatives

— Banks, savings institutions, and trust companies

— Lawyers, accountants, teachers, or engineers if advice is solely incidental to the professional practice

— Broker/dealers or agents whose investment advice is solely incidental to their business and who receive no special compensation for the investment advisory service

— Publishers of bona fide newspapers of general circulation

— Investment advisers registered at the federal level, federal covered advisers

— Persons excluded from the definition under the Investment Advisers Act of 1940

— Any person the state Administrator excludes

Investment Advisers Exempt from Federal Registration

— Whose only clients are residents of the state and who do not provide advice on securities that are listed or trade on national exchanges

— Fewer than 15 clients, none of which is an investment company, during the preceding 12 months and do not hold themselves out as investment advisers

— Whose only clients are insurance companies

Investment Advisers Exempt from State Registration

— No office in state and communications directed to 5 or fewer clients in 12 months

— No office in state and clients are financial institutions

Federal Covered Adviser

— Required to be or is registered with the SEC

— Excluded from the definition of investment adviser by the 1940 act

— Manages an investment company

Investment Counsel

— Investment advice is principal business

— Provides continuous advice based on individual client needs

Investment Adviser Representatives

— Investment adviser associated persons

— Officers, directors, and partners of adviser

— Employees or persons controlled by adviser other than clerical staff

— Always natural persons

— Register with states when representing a state-registered investment adviser or when representing a federal covered adviser

— Individuals who give advice on behalf of investment adviser are subject to supervision and control

Unlawful or Unethical Investment Advisory Practices

— Unsuitable investments

— Unauthorized discretion

— Unauthorized third-party transactions

— Excessive trading

— Commingling funds

— Misrepresentation of material facts

— Nondisclosure of information sources

— Excessive fees

— Conflicts of interest

— Unauthorized custody of customer funds

— Operating without advisory contracts

— Performance-based compensation, when not legally permitted

— Failing to disclose material legal action in past 10 years at least 48 hours before contracting with client

— Failing to disclose principal or agent capacity

Books and Records

— All records for 5 years

— Most recent 2 years of records must be at adviser's office

— Records may be kept by photographic or computer formats provided means to access, read, and make copies

SEC RELEASE IA-1092

Investment Advisers Include

— Financial planners, pension consultants, and sports/entertainment representatives with financial roles

— Persons who provide advice/analyses regarding securities, in the business of, for compensation, need not be principal activity

— Compensation can be paid by someone other than client and can be for sales of securities or nonsecurities instruments

— Subject to definition of investment adviser if advice is about specific securities or general in nature or even about nonsecurities instruments

— Subject to definition of investment adviser if advertises or receives separate compensation such as fees or commissions

— Lawyers and accountants subject to investment adviser regulation if advertise availability of investment advice and charge separate fee

— Broker/dealers and agents considered adviser or IAR if charge separate fees for advice

HotSheets

Preemptive Rights

— Allow common stockholders to maintain proportionate interest

Voting Rights

— Directors, issuance of convertible bonds or preferred stock; not on dividend payment or amount

Preferred Stock

— Par value determines stated (fixed) dividend rate
— Priority over common in liquidation and dividend payment
— Typically no voting rights

Current Yield

— Annual dividends divided by current market price

Rights and Warrants

Rights	Warrants
30–45-day exercise period	Long-term (2–10 years)
Strike price is below market	Strike price above market
Trade as separate security	Trade as a separate security
Available to existing shareholders only	Offered as sweeteners
One right per share outstanding	Anyone can purchase

ADRs

— Foreign dividends converted to US dollars so they have currency risk

— Issued by US bank

Investment Grade

— Baa or BBB and above, based on default risk, ability to pay interest and principal when due

High-Yield (Junk)

— Ba or BB and below based on default risk, ability to pay interest and principal when due

— Highly speculative

Corporate Bonds

— Secured—mortgage, collateral trust (backed by securities), equipment trust certificates

— Unsecured—backed by full faith and credit, debentures and subordinated debentures

Convertibles

— Convertible into issuer's common stock at predetermined ratio

Governments

— Bills quoted at a discount, notes and bonds in increments of $\frac{1}{32}$; backed in full by the US government

Agencies

— Ginnie Maes are backed in full by US government

— FNMA, FHLMC, FICB not backed directly by US government

CMOs

— Corporate instrument with tranches; taxable monthly interest; and subject to interest rate risk and prepayment risk

Money Markets

— Commercial paper; corporate issue; usually issued at a discount, 270-day maximum maturity

— Negotiable CD—minimum face of $100,000, issued by banks

— Banker's acceptances—time draft, letter of credit for foreign trade; 180-day maximum maturity

HotSheets

OTHER SECURITIES PRODUCTS HOTSHEET

Investment Company Act of 1940

— Defines and regulates investment companies

— Three types—face-amount certificate, UIT, management company

Open-End Company

— Mutual fund; continuous primary offering, redemption in 7 days, price by formula in prospectus, fractional shares

Closed-End Company

— Trade in secondary market, issues debt and equity, fixed number of shares, sold with prospectus in IPO only

Diversified Status

— 75% invested in other companies so that maximum 5% in any one company and can own no more than 10% of a target company's voting stock

— No restrictions on the other 25%

— Status applies to open- and closed-end companies

Registration

— Minimum $100,000 capital, clearly defined investment objective requirements

Prohibited Investing

— No margin, no short sales, no short naked options

Shareholder Votes

— Change investment objective, change sales load policy, change fund classification

Shareholder Report

— Annual audited report, semiannual unaudited report (2 per year)

Sector Funds

— Minimum of 25% of assets in area of specialty; more aggressive

Money Market Funds

— No load, fixed NAV, check-writing privileges, daily interest
— Portfolio consists of short-term debt instruments

Letter of Intent

— Must be in writing, maximum 13 months, can be backdated 90 days

Objectives

— Growth = stock funds
— Income = bond funds
— Safety of principal = government bond funds
— Immediate liquidity = money market funds
— Aggressive growth = technology stock funds or stock funds invested in new companies, small caps
— Conservative growth = large-cap stock funds
— Highest possible income with little concern for risk = corporate bond fund
— High tax bracket seeking income = municipal bond fund
— Income-producing stock = large-cap stock fund, preferred stock fund, utility stock fund
— Mirror performance of the stock market overall = index fund

DPPs

— Not investment companies, provide flow-through of income, gains, losses, deductions, and credits to investors

Limited Partners	General Partners
No management	Active management
Limited liability	Unlimited liability
Passive investors only	Fiduciary responsibility
Can sue GP	Cannot borrow, compete, or commingle

Taxation

— Only passive loss can be used to shelter passive income

Reason to Invest

— Economic viability is first concern in DPP investments

Methods of Analysis

— Cash flow analysis and internal rate of return computations

Liquidation Priority

— Secured creditors, other creditors, limited partners, general partner(s)

Fixed Annuity

— Guaranteed rate of return

— Insurance company has investment risk

— Subject to purchasing power risk

— Fixed income guaranteed for life

— Not a security

Variable Annuity

— Rate of return dependent on separate account performance

— Investor has investment risk

— Sold with prospectus

— Can keep pace with inflation

— Variable income guaranteed for life; principal is not guaranteed

— Is a security

Accumulation Phase

— Investor pays premiums to insurer

— Units vary in number and in value

Annuity Phase

— Investor receives payments from insurer

— Fixed number of units, vary in value

Purchase Methods

— Periodic deferred—paid in installments, payouts taken later

— Single premium immediate—lump-sum payment, payouts begin immediately, no accumulation period

— Single premium deferred—lump-sum payment, payouts taken later

Distribution Options

— Lump-sum or random withdrawals

— Annuitization (monthly income guaranteed for life)

— Life income—no beneficiary, largest monthly payment

— Life with period certain—minimum guaranteed period

— Joint life with last survivor—annuity on two lives; smallest monthly payment

Taxation

— Life income (monthly)—part return of cost basis, part taxable, amount per exclusion ratio

— Lump-sum amounts exceeding basis taxable as ordinary income (59½ penalty may apply)

— Random withdrawals—LIFO applies; earnings withdrawn first, taxable as ordinary income; no tax on remainder because it is a return of cost basis

Options–Calls

— Option to buy

— Buyer pays premium, has right to buy stock at exercise price by expiration date

— Seller receives premium, has obligation to sell stock at exercise price if option is exercised by the buyer before expiration; keeps premium

Options–Puts

— Options to sell

— Buyer pays premium, has right to sell stock at exercise price by expiration date

— Seller gets premium, obligation to buy stock at exercise price if option exercised by the buyer before expiration; keep premium

	Maximum Gain	Maximum Loss
Long call	Unlimited	Premium
Short call	Premium	Unlimited
Long put	Strike price – premium	Premium
Short put	Premium	Strike price – premium

Strategies–Long Calls

— Speculate on upward price movement (bullish)

— Protect short stock position

Short Calls

— Speculate on downward price movement (bearish)

— Generate income through covered call writing

Long Puts

— Speculate on downward price movement (bearish)

— Protect long stock position

Short Puts

— Speculate on upward price movement (bullish)

— Buy stock at reduced price

HotSheets

Securities Markets

— Exchanges—listed securities, auction market

— OTC—unlisted securities, negotiated transactions

Specialist

— Maintains orderly market, acts as agent and principal, priority to customer orders

— Holds book of stop and limit orders, sets opening quote for exchange-traded stock

Market Makers

— Purchase and sell securities to others from inventory (like a car dealer); price of OTC stocks is established by competition between market makers

Broker/Dealers

— Broker—acts as agent between buyer and seller, receives commission

— Dealer—acts as principal and trades from inventory, receives markup/markdown

— A firm cannot act as both broker and dealer in one transaction

Market Orders

— Executed immediately at the best available price

Limit Orders

— Orders held for execution at the stated price or better

— Buy limits executed at or below the stated price

— Sell limits executed at or above the state price

Stop Orders

— Buy stop—triggered at or above order price, executed at next price; protect short positions

— Sell stop—triggered at or below order price, executed at next price; protect long positions

Short Sales

— Investor borrows stock anticipating market decline so that borrowed stock can be purchased for repayment at a lower price

— Short seller is bearish

Time Sensitive Orders

— Good till canceled—order is open until it is filled or canceled

— Fill or kill—execute all immediately or cancel entire order

— All or none—execute all, immediacy is not important; hold as GTC on book until filled

— Immediate or cancel—execute whatever is available now, remainder is canceled

HotSheets

IRAs

— Maximum contribution is $4,000, or 100% of earned income, whichever is less

— Spousal IRA allows $8,000 between two spouses filing joint returns, split between two accounts

— Age 50 or older has catch-up of additional $1,000

— No life insurance or collectibles

— 10% penalty, plus applicable ordinary income tax, on withdrawals before age 59½

— 6% excess contribution penalty

— 50% insufficient distribution penalty (after 70½)

— One rollover allowed each 12 months to be completed within 60 days

— Unlimited trustee to trustee transfers

SEPs

— Qualified plan allows employers to contribute to employee IRAs

— Contribution maximum = 25% of employee salary up to $45,000

— Contributions are immediately vested

Roth IRAs

— Nondeductible contributions only; generally tax-free distributions

— Maximum contribution of $4,000 per individual, $8,000 per couple

— Does not require distributions to begin at age 70½

Coverdell ESAs

— Allows after-tax contributions for children under age 18

— Maximum contribution is $2,000 per year

— Tax-free distributions if funds are used for higher education

Keoghs (HR-10)

— Available to self-employed persons, owners of unincorporated businesses, and professional practices

— All employees must participate if age 21 or older, employed more than one year, work more than 1,000 hours per year

— Life insurance permitted

403(b) Plans (TSAs)

— Available to employees of nonprofit organizations

— Typically funded by elective employee salary reductions, usually no cost basis

Pension Plans

— Require annual contribution

— Defined benefit—benefit based on formula factoring age, salary, years of service, calculated by actuary; favor older key employees

— Defined contribution—simpler to administer, contribution is typically a percentage of compensation

Profit-Sharing Plans

— Annual contribution not required; great investment and contribution flexibility

Withholding Rule

— 20% withholding applied to distributions from qualified plans made payable to participant

Fiduciary Responsibility

— Ethical and legal obligation to invest prudently on behalf of others; no margin accounts in retirement plans

— No short sales, no naked options; minimize risk

— Suitable investments only (prudent expert rule)

ERISA

— Protects participants in corporate (private sector) plans versus public plans

— Rules for participation, funding, vesting, communication, and nondiscrimination

Nonqualified Plans

— Nondeductible contributions, can be discriminatory

— Examples are payroll deduction, deferred compensation

— Risk of deferred compensation is employer failure

HotSheets

New Account Forms

— Required for all accounts

— Birth date required

— Customer signature not required for cash accounts; needed for margin accounts

— Signed by agent/investment adviser representative and approving principal

Unsolicited Transactions

— Must mark order ticket "Unsolicited"

— Do not need to be suitable

Account Approval

— By principal, before the first transaction

Trading Authorization

— Limited—third party can trade only

— Full—third party can trade and withdraw cash and securities

Margin Agreement

— Credit agreement—required; specifies loan terms

— Hypothecation agreement—required; pledges customer securities as collateral

— Loan consent form—optional; allows broker/dealer to loan customer margin securities for short sales

— Not allowed for UGMAs/UTMAs

Joint Accounts

— All signatures required to open

— Any party can trade

— Distributions payable to all

TIC

— Unequal interests OK

— Passes by will to heirs, probate

JTWROS

— Equal ownership interest

— Passes to survivor(s) at death; no probate

Fiduciary Accounts

— Subject to prudent investor rule or legal list

— All require written legal document, except UGMA/UTMA

— Margin accounts permitted only if authorized in document

— No short sales, naked options

UGMA/UTMA

— Cash accounts only

— Minor is beneficial owner

— Minor's Social Security number on account

— One minor, one custodian

— No short sales, no options, no margin

Discretionary Accounts

— Authority from customer must be in writing

— Account must be approved before the first trade

— Principal must review discretionary accounts frequently for churning

— Time and price not discretionary

HotSheets

Individual Accounts

— One beneficial owner; orders by others allowed only with power of attorney

Joint Accounts

— All signatures required to open; any signer can trade; distributions payable to all; each owns undivided interest

Trust Accounts

— Managed by trustee according to terms of trust agreement

Estate Accounts

— Managed by executor on behalf of a deceased person

Sole Proprietorship Accounts

— Business account in name of an individual businessowner

Partnership Accounts

— Subject to terms of partnership agreements
— Profits and losses flow-through to partners; taxation based on partners' tax status

Limited Liability Companies

— Limited liability like a corporation, but flow-through taxation like a partnership; unlimited number of members

C Corporations

— Require corporate resolution, limited investor liability, corporate resolution names persons who may trade on behalf of the account

S Corporations

— Operate like C corporation, but flow through taxation like a partnership; maximum of 100 shareholders

Life Insurance Death Benefit

— Coverage should pay off insured's mortgage and other debts

— Provide survivor income, pay college tuition, and cover estate taxes due

Disability

— Replacement income from workers' compensation, Social Security, personal disability insurance

Asset Allocation

— Balancing stock, bonds, and cash within investment portfolio asset allocation

— Strategic long-term portfolio mix

— Tactical short-term portfolio adjustments

Active Management

— Direct stock/bond selection and/or market timing

Passive Management

— Manages portfolio by mirroring index or buy/hold

— Little trading for low-cost, consistent returns

Growth Investing

— Select stock of companies with higher than average growth rates

Value Investing

— Select stock of undervalued companies evidenced by low stock prices relative to earnings or book value

Market Capitalization

— Micro cap—less than $300 million

— Small cap—between $300 and $2 billion

— Mid cap—between $2 billion and $10 billion

— Large cap—more than $10 billion

Dollar Cost Averaging

— Produces an average cost per share that is lower than average price per share with consistent amount of dollars invested at regular intervals

— Buy more shares in declining market, fewer shares in rising market

Income Reinvestment Plans

— For mutual funds, stocks; reinvested income distributions are currently taxable

Individual Taxes

— Regressive equal percentage regardless of income (sales, gas tax)

— Progressive tax rate increases as income increases (income, estate tax)

Alternative Minimum Tax

— Forces high income persons to pay income tax

— Certain excludable (preferenced) items are added back into tax computation

Cost Basis

— Compared to sales proceeds to determine capital gain or loss; high basis results in lower taxable gain

Capital Gains Taxation

— Net long-term capital gain taxed at maximum current rate of 15%; $3,000 of net loss deductible annually against earned income; remainder carried forward indefinitely

Foreign Stock

— Income taxed by country of investor's citizenship; 15% withholding on foreign distributions may be offset by tax credit

Wash Sales

— Loss disallowed if same or substantially identical security purchased within 30 days before or after sale for loss

Dividend Taxation

— 70% exclusion on corporate dividends; no dividend exclusion for individuals

Suitability

Investor Objective	Suitable Recommendation
Preservation of capital; safety	Government securities or Ginnie Maes
Growth — Balanced/moderate growth — Aggressive growth	Common stock or common stock mutual funds — Large-cap stocks, defensive stocks — Technology stocks, sector funds, or cyclical stocks
Income — Tax-free income — High-yield income — From a stock portfolio	Bonds (but not zero-coupons) — Municipal bonds or muni bond funds — Corporate bonds or corporate bond funds — Preferred stock and utility stocks
Liquidity	Money market funds — (DPPs, CDs, real estate, and annuities are not considered liquid)
Speculation	Volatile stocks, high-yield bonds, stock/index options

HotSheets

Business Cycle

— Expansion—low unemployment, increased business activity

— Peak

— Contraction—falling stock markets, rising inventories, decreasing GDP

— Trough—(recession = 2 quarters of declining GDP; depression = 6 quarters of declining GDP) accompanied by high unemployment

CPI

— Measures inflation through comparison of constant dollars

Economic Theories

— Keynesian—federal government intervention is encouraged for management of taxation and government spending

— Monetarist—supply of money determines price levels

Yield Curves

— Normal yield curve depicts long-term interest rates higher than short-term interest rates

— Inverted yield curve when short-term rates are higher than long-term rates, typically when interest rates have peaked

Economic Indicators

— Leading—money supply, building permits, number of initial unemployment claims, orders, stock prices

— Coincident—personal income, GDP, nonagricultural unemployment, sales

— Lagging—duration of unemployment, corporate profits, commercial loans outstanding

Technical Analysis

— Charting, market timing, price predictions based on price patterns

Fundamental Analysis

— Study of company prospects based on overall economy, industry, financial statements

Industry Analysis

— Defensive—food, tobacco, pharmaceuticals, energy
— Cyclical—heavy machinery
— Growth—technology (low dividend payouts)

Balance Sheet

— Assets – liabilities = net worth
— Assets = liabilities + net worth
— Used to compute capitalization and liquidity ratios

Income Statement

— Summarizes revenues, expenses to determine efficiency, profitability

Time Value of Money

— Future value—value of an investment made now at specific point in the future, if earning at a specified rate
— Present value—the amount that needs to be invested today to equal a state value in the future

Investment Risks

— Inflation risk—purchasing power risk (fixed returns lose buying power)
— Business risk—(unsystematic risk) that business will fail or become obsolete
— Market risk—(systematic risk) diversification does not reduce
— Regulatory risk—new laws may adversely impact performance of investments
— Interest rate risk—prices of fixed income securities respond inversely to interest rate changes
— Credit risk—risk of issuer's default causing loss of principal

— Liquidity risk—risk investor cannot convert to cash quickly at fair price

— Opportunity cost—return given up when alternative investment is chosen

Investment Returns

— Total return—includes interest and dividends and capital appreciation

— Holding period return—the total return over time an investor owns the security

— Annualized return—investor's return computed as if over a 1-year period

— After-tax return—investor return reduced for payment of taxes

— Inflation-adjusted return (real return)—investor return adjusted downward for inflation; **nominal return** is not inflation-adjusted

— Risk-adjusted return—investor return adjusted for market risk associated with it

— Expected return—an investment's probable return

Beta

— Measurement of a stock's volatility (price movement); market overall has beta of 1; beta more than 1 is more volatile than market overall; beta less than 1 is less volatile than market overall

— Higher beta stocks are considered more aggressive

Standard Deviation

— Measures how much a return differs from the expected performance of the security

Duration

— Estimates the change in price of a bond that would result from a change in interest rates

— The time it takes for a bond to pay for itself

Correlation

— Measures the movement of the price between 2 or more securities or portfolios

Systematic Risk

— Risk that cannot be diversified away—market risk

Sharpe Ratio

— Measures the amount of risk per unit of risk taken—the higher the better
— Risk-adjusted return using risk-free rate and standard deviation